ALL THESE PEOPLE

The Nation's Human Resources in the South

ALL THESE PEOPLE

The Nation's Human Resources in the South

BY

RUPERT B. VANCE

IN COLLABORATION WITH

NADIA DANILEVSKY

CHAPEL HILL
THE UNIVERSITY OF NORTH CAROLINA PRESS
1945

309.175
V24a

21693
May/46

PRINTED IN THE UNITED STATES OF AMERICA BY
THE SEEMAN PRINTERY, INC., DURHAM, N. C.

To

HOWARD W. ODUM

Teacher, Friend
Theorist of Regionalism
Academic Statesman of the South at Its Best

FOREWORD

THIS BOOK was begun in the period when the South's population increase seemed a danger to the Nation. "The central irony of the era," Gerald W. Johnson wrote then, "is the fact that if we have overproduced anything in this country, what we have overproduced is Americans." The volume was finished in a period of crisis in manpower when every atom of our human resources counted for national survival. It looks forward to the period when returning soldiers and war workers may again bring surplus manpower to fields and factories.

Against these changing conditions the book takes a long-time view, applying population and regional analysis in the manner made familiar by previous studies from the University of North Carolina. Care has been taken to make the statistical analysis and the graphic presentation as complete and clear as possible with the idea that, in addition to population students, specialists in agriculture, government, industry, health and education may be able to make use of our figures even when they disagree with our interpretations.

The problem of how far research can go in indicating choices of public policy is perennial, but nowhere is the treatment meant to be dogmatic. Since public policy is as much related to the values held by a society as to the social facts developed by research, the first chapter is devoted to the various aspects of the population interest. While the doctrine of human resources advanced is assumed to be based on values widely held in our society, they are given initial treatment so that the reader may thus relate the body of facts to the conclusions that emerge from the study. Throughout we should like to have the reader feel that this is a book about the nation in which we discuss the nation's human resources in the region we know best.

All These People has been more than seven years in the making. They told us in school that all the cells of the human body changed every seven years. I should like to believe that, for now it is finished I would feel a new man. All I know for the moment is that I feel a more chastened—I don't say a wiser—man. Seven years or no, this book could never have been done alone and I would be more tired of it than I am were it not for the pattern of cooperation developed in the Institute for Research in Social Science. My obligations to Howard W. Odum are but imperfectly conveyed in the dedication; I should be greatly pleased if this should come to be regarded as a companion volume to *Southern Regions of the United States*. Nadia Danilevsky has been more than collaborator. She assumed responsibility for the statistical calculations and evidences of her industry and ingenuity are sprinkled on almost every page. Minna Abernethy took up this analysis where she left off and helped in editing the work to completion. When our draftsmen Eric Laddey and Nat Welch joined the services, Mary Alice Eaton and Rheba Usher Vance completed the graphics. Special figures were done by A. E. Bevacqua and F. C. Erickson. Throughout, if she had been working in government, Katharine Jocher, I have the feeling, would have carried the title of coordinator. For the record be it said that we enjoyed working with Mr. E. D. Fowler of the Seeman Printery and we are still good friends.

Colleagues here and elsewhere who have read sections or influenced the treatment by discussion or otherwise are T. J. Woofter, S. H. Hobbs, Jr., Margaret Jarman Hagood, Katharine Jocher, Harriet L. Herring, Guy B. Johnson, Gordon W. Blackwell, Carter Goodrich, Glenn E. McLaughlin, Frank Lorimer, Frederick Osborn, William S. Davlin, Albert S. Keister, Erich W. Zimmermann, P. K. Whelpton, and Warren S. Thompson. Nadia Danilevsky has read manuscript and proof at least three times.

Among former graduate students whose researches have proved valuable are Ellen Hull Neff, Harold L. Geisert, Bernice Milburn Moore, Kenneth Evans, Robert Millikan, Ruth Crowell Leafer, Robin Williams, J. Herman Johnson, John M. Maclachlan, Mary Alice Eaton, and the late Floyd M. Cox. Treva Williams Bevacqua and the entire secretarial staff of the Institute have been both patient and efficient in the many retypings of the manuscript. Since I have no desire to minimize the fact that I was around while all this was going on, I had best assume responsibility for all the errors still left in the work.

Portions of various chapters have previously been published in different form. The author acknowledges the courtesy of the editors of *Social Forces, The Milbank Memorial Fund Quarterly, The Southern Economic Journal, The Journal of Farm Economics, The Southwest Review, The Southern Review, The Virginia Quarterly Review* and representatives of the Duke University Press, The University of North Carolina Press, the

Social Science Research Council, the Study of Population Redistribution, the Public Affairs Committee, the Tennessee Valley Authority, and the National Resources Planning Board in permitting use of this material. The University of Chicago Press has graciously given permission to use as a basis for the regional analyses the map of the United States adapted by the Institute for Research in Social Science from Goode's Base Map Series.

Most of the computations were done from final releases of the Bureau of the Census in advance of publication of the 1940 Census volumes. Footnotes to these releases have been retained as source notes, but those who wish to follow up references will find an outline table of contents of the 1940 Census in the bibliography.

In addition the author wishes to acknowledge the aid received from deliberations of Research Conferences on the Cotton Economy, Population, Income, and Health sponsored by the Southern Regional Committee of the Social Science Research Council. Perhaps more than routine acknowledgment should be made for the continued support of the General Education Board and for assistance in publication by the Julius Rosenwald Fund. A grant of $100 for graphic materials was made by the Graduate Board of the University of North Carolina from the Smith Fund.

R. B. V.

Chapel Hill
February, 1945.

TABLE OF CONTENTS

PART I

The Dynamics of Population

PART II

Population and the Agrarian Economy

[xi]

LIST OF TABLES

LIST OF FIGURES

ALL THESE PEOPLE

The Nation's Human Resources in the South

PART I
THE DYNAMICS OF POPULATION

CHAPTER I

HUMAN RESOURCES AND SOCIAL VALUES

WHETHER it's a mystery novel or a sociological excursion, finding a title for a book after it is written is likely to be an adventure. Our title, *All These People,* comes out of one of the main points of the book, namely, that Southerners are doing more to replace themselves in the next generation than any of the Nation's folks. The subtitle came out of another point and an attitude we took toward it. The fact is that Southerners have less on which to live.

Here we could have our choice of attitudes: we could view with alarm or we could take it in our stride. We believe that the Nation and the region need these people and we decided not to be horrified. Hence the subtitle, *The Nation's Human Resources in the South.* This attitude comes out of a philosophy about human resources and the future place of the South in the nation. Those interested in these values will read the first chapter and the last two. Those interested in the facts will find them in the chapters in between.

It is an assumption of this study that the value complexes of the great institutions of our society center in the population interest. Family and nation, church and school, community and industry often appear united in the feeling: "People—what else matters?" This unity of values, however, does not make for unity of policy. In many instances, class, economic, religious, and national interests are so divergent that agreement on population policy appears difficult if not impossible, even though general agreement may be secured as to the facts. It is the task of this chapter to introduce the significance of population trends with a discussion of the underlying assumptions and social values involved. These values are coextensive with society itself, but they may be discussed in terms of the nation, the family, and economic institutions.

NATIONAL SURVIVAL AND FAMILY REPLACEMENTS

A major interest in population clusters around the values of national survival. Given adequate numbers as in the United States, national safety demands the maintenance of these numbers at a high level of efficiency. Once this was identical with the family interest for it was held that every family was committed to the perpetuation of its name and stock. While this sentiment is by no means universally held among the families of the western world, we still hold that it is the first duty of a nation to survive. Interest in population replacement is thus coextensive with the sentiment of nationalism and patriotism itself. It is accordingly a characteristic of the perilous times in which we live that for the democratic nations the population problem has become part of the problem of survival.[1]

Along with the spread of industrialism and rising standards of living in the nations of the Western World has gone a falling birth rate. The spread of the practice of family limitation already has a long and respectable history behind it. Beginning with the upper classes it has spread with the diffusion of such modern characteristics as popular education, secular attitudes, urbanism, and industrialism. Before the war it was agreed that the spread of the family pattern of the middle classes to the peasants and industrial workers would so sharply reduce reproduction as to threaten national survival. The incidence of the world depression convinced the middle classes of their insecurity, increased the poverty of the poor, and brought the equalization of class fertility rates that much closer. Some believe that the populations of democracies will cease to replenish themselves unless the costs of child rearing are further socialized, while others feel that, as the burden of replenishing the population is lifted from the lower classes by the spread of birth control, there is no certainty that the upper classes will raise their net reproduction. If child rearing makes no contribution to the personal happiness of citizens in a democracy, they admit no duty to the society to replenish the population, and aside from the interest in national survival there exists no system of values which contradicts them.

Modern war brings added emphasis to the value of survival and renewed threats to population renewals. For the European democracies the second World War in a generation has hastened the downward spiral in population. The last war meant large losses among the males of reproductive ages and even greater losses in births to the war generation. Figure 1 shows how the declining fertility of western Europe was affected by the first World War. In almost every country involved, births declined from 20 to 40 percent and remained below normal from four to five years. The rise in births that came after the war soon subsided and the downward trend continued at a faster rate.

The further effect of war is made clear in Figure 2 which gives the

[1] Gunnar Myrdal, *Population: A Problem for Democracy* (Cambridge, Harvard University Press, 1940).

age distribution of the main combatant nations in the first post-war census. The sharp dips at the early age group of children represent births lost because of the catastrophe. In Germany in 1925 children of age 15, a prewar group, amounted to 650,000 as compared with 300,000 children aged 8, born in the midst of war. In France children of age 4 were no more numerous than men and women aged 65 when normally they would have exceeded the latter by two to one.

FIGURE 1. INCIDENCE OF WORLD WAR I ON THE DECLINING BIRTH RATES OF FIVE COUNTRIES OF NORTHWESTERN EUROPE, 1870-1934

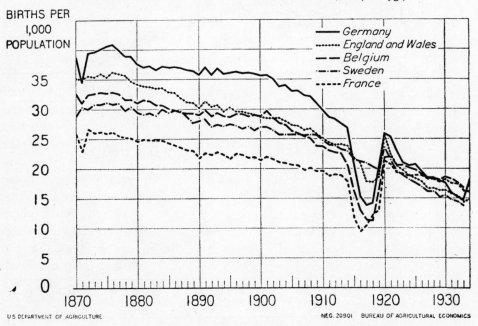

In addition there is loss of males of military age made evident by comparison with females in Figure 2. In France the loss among the youngest troops was especially noticeable. In Germany there were five one-year age groups in which women exceeded men by 100,000. It is this discrepancy in the sex ratios which condemned many women to celibacy and thus accelerated the downward trend in births. One of the tragedies of the second World War was that it bore heavily on the "hollow classes," those young men whose numbers were already depleted because they were born during the first world struggle. This further diminishes the chance of marriage for women after the war. It has been estimated that in all over 22 millions were lost to Europe exclusive of Russia in the first World War. About 6.5 millions were killed in the armed services, 5

FIGURE 2. THE INCIDENCE OF WORLD WAR I ON TOTAL BIRTHS AND MALE
DEATHS AS SHOWN IN THE AGE DISTRIBUTIONS OF POPULATION OF FRANCE,
ENGLAND, AND GERMANY AT FIRST POSTWAR CENSUS, 1921 AND 1925

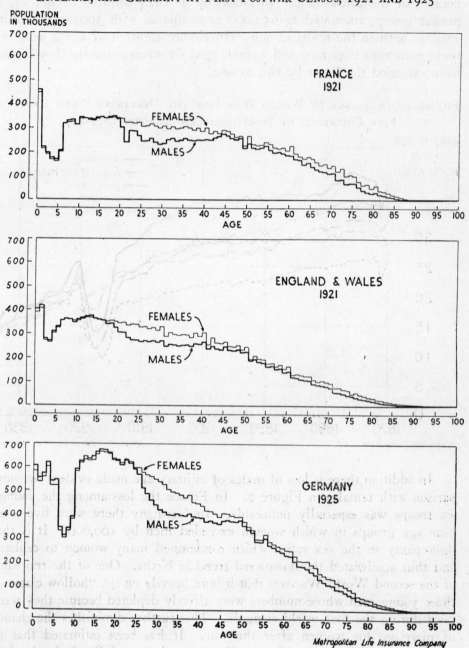

Source: *Statistical Bulletin*, Metropolitan Life Insurance Company, 21, No. 4 (April, 1940), 4.

million civilians died who otherwise would have lived and 11 millions were never born.[2]

In the United States the population trend was very little affected by the first World War. Figure 3, based on data of 1937 and projection of median fertility and mortality, shows one of the best predictions of our future population trends. At the balance of births and deaths attained in 1937 the net reproduction rate was below unity and, when the effects of a favorable age distribution wore off, by 1980 the population would begin to decline. Since 1937 the depression has lifted, marriages increased, and the birth rate has risen. Whether our population will fall below replacement depends among other things on the length and severity of the war. To Europe and America the present war brings greater dangers. Granted that peoples will be willing to fight for survival through air raids and threatening famines, there seems little doubt that futility and hopelessness will be expressed in the refusal of married couples to bring children into the world. A prolonged war with millions in service all over the world will reduce births and give the phenomena of "hollow classes," and result in a disturbed sex ratio that further depresses the downward trend of fertility.

FIGURE 3. THE TREND OF NATURAL INCREASE IN THE UNITED STATES: OBSERVED TO 1937, PROJECTED TO 2000

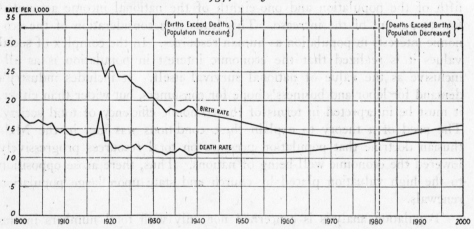

Source: *Statistical Bulletin*, Metropolitan Life Insurance Company (July, 1938), p. 12.

Thus while armies of men in all parts of the world are battling to destroy life, an army of approximately 2,250,000 women in the United States is in any given year bearing the burden of maternity to renew human life and maintain the stream of the generations. Actually, the

[2] Frank W. Notestein and others, *The Future Population of Europe and the Soviet Union* (Geneva, League of Nations, 1944), p. 75.

number of women who assume the hazards of childbirth is greater than this, for, in addition to the two and a quarter million births, there are annually about eighty thousand stillbirths in this country and a large number of miscarriages and abortions, estimated at well over half a million.

The crux of the population problem is found in change in natural increase. Stability is the goal. Thus while it appears that national survival would be threatened by an appreciable decline in population, economic theory has held that social well-being and economic efficiency would be threatened by large population increases.

THE ECONOMIC INTEREST

The strain toward higher standards of living has reduced fertility in urban areas and among upper economic classes until the burden of replacements is left largely to agrarian and folk groups. If they are too isolated from the stream of urban culture to be adept in the practice of family limitation, they are usually too poor in worldly goods to provide their children with an adequate start in life. Fifty-five percent of the total increase in the population from 1930-1934 came from three agrarian regions, the Northwest, Southwest, and Southeast that in 1930 had about one-third of the Nation's population. The Southeast with slightly over one-fifth of the population and one-eighth of the national income accounted for 35 percent of the increase. This leads to a consideration of the economic interests in population as human resources. In the complex of social values it is realized that the economic interest in population is as all-inclusive as the value of national survival itself. It includes industry's demand for labor and business's hope for consumers, but wider than either, it must be interpreted in terms of the economic efficiency of total society. The need of a theory to explain these conditions was met in the Malthusian doctrine that population pressure on total resources progressively lowered the economic well-being of nations. Thus, there arose opposition to the high valuation placed by church and state upon large population renewals.

Population analysis is concerned not only with total numbers in the nation as a whole but with the location of those numbers in specific regions and in specific occupations. The maldistribution of population is limited to certain regional areas and to certain overcrowded occupations. With approaching stabilization of numbers and with rising national standards of living, in the Western World there now exists no fear of general overpopulation. With increasing industrialization and increasing urbanization, however, there have emerged wide differences in regional economies, a complex occupational hierarchy, and differential birth rates. The fundamental fact is the great inequalities in regional wealth and income that exists within the nation. From the analysis to follow it can be concluded that population pressures may exist in certain regions and occupational groupings without lending support to any Malthusian dictum that the nation as a whole faces overpopulation.

Accordingly, density of population alone is no sufficient criterion of population pressure on the one hand or of ineffective use of resources on the other. T. N. Carver has said that the modern population problem may be regarded as one of occupational density.[3] Thus if certain occupational groups, or if the population living in certain areas, have a much higher rate of natural increase than those in other occupational groups or areas, it is felt that their wages will tend to be low and unemployment greater. This is true unless the educational system, labor exchanges, and interregional migration are able to shunt enough of the present and oncoming generation from points of overconcentration to points of relative underconcentration. In addition there is the question raised by economists as to whether barriers of skill and lack of opportunity do not operate to render certain occupational groups noncompeting with each other.

Population pressure is the resultant of dynamic and not of static conditions. Population itself is to be regarded as a flow not a store, and its unequalized pressures result from its unequal flow. Stated in another way, population trends rather than population status are to be considered. Into areas of unequal resource structures flow unequal streams of population increases. The attainment and maintenance of equalized population pressures in a country of unequal resource areas thus depends on the flow of two interacting factors: (1) differential reproduction and (2) the mobility of the population. This unequal flow of population replacements also holds true with reference to occupational groups. These increases tend to unloose a flow of mobility which alleviates but rarely completely equalizes the pressure of population on resources. Social mobility must be here interpreted as including both internal migration and occupational mobility. Internal migration often puts the migrant in a position to climb the occupational ladder, as when the rural migrant by going to the city changes his location and his occupation at the same time.

POPULATION AS HUMAN RESOURCES

This study of the Southern People follows Howard W. Odum's analysis of the resources of society in terms of natural "wealth," capital "wealth,"

[3] In *World Population Conference at Geneva* (London: Arnold, 1927), pp. 125-27.

technological "wealth," human "wealth," and institutional "wealth."[4] The idea has been well put by Lancelot T. Hogben in *Retreat from Reason*, where he points out that the wealth and the welfare of nations depends on (a) the material resources of man's environment, (b) the biological resources of social personnel, (c) and the social resources of organization and institutions for mobilizing the common will to make the fullest use of the first two.

Here it must be realized that natural resources and human resources are potential, not absolute. Natural resources, as Erich W. Zimmermann[5] has pointed out, are to be estimated in terms not only of their existence but of their availability. They may exist but they are not made available apart from the skills, the needs, and the demands of men organized for their utilization. Not simply the existence of minerals in the ground but the degree of technology, the efficiency of economic organization, the availability of capital and the existing social demands determine the availability of natural resources for any particular area.

In our economic scheme of things, human beings are both means and ends. It is the skill, the intelligence, and the labor of the population that give shape and form to all the useful aspects of our environment. Man as an agent of production is the greatest of all resources. "He contributes," writes Erich W. Zimmermann, "his labor, mental and physical; he directs the process of production; he discovers new ways of utilizing his environment; his aspirations furnish aim and purpose."[6] Among all resources, human resources rank the highest. In acquiring skills and scientific procedures, men have laid up technical resources that are registered in their very brain and brawn.

But man is also the end of the productive process. Mankind we rightly think is the ultimate beneficiary of all production from the radiation of solar energy to the last ear of grain garnered from the fields and the last film of cloth taken from the loom. All resources exist for man if he can but use them. Thus man, the paradox, is at one and the same time the end and goal beyond the productive process, and part and parcel of it, the chief resource and means toward its attainment.

Physical resources, unused and unneeded, lie inert. Coal left alone for a million years is still coal. Human resources left unutilized deteriorate. Untrained, unskilled, uneducated, modern man would grow up unable to make the adjustments demanded in modern industry. Unem-

[4] Howard W. Odum, *Southern Regions of the United States* (Chapel Hill: University of North Carolina Press, 1936).

[5] *World Resources and Industries* (New York: Harper and Brothers, 1933); "Resources of the South," *South Atlantic Quarterly*, 32 (July, 1933), 213-226.

[6] *World Resources and Industries*, p. 122.

ployed or delayed in the adjustment to the job, to marriage and family life, to community responsibilities, normal human beings develop traits of disorganization and deterioration.

In the modern temper we can readily admit that whether the South's population is finally to be regarded as resource or liability depends on more than the population itself. Yet we can never escape the realization that the motivation of any population group furnishes the greatest assurance that its potentialities will be developed and utilized. It is in accord with this view that we have come to accept as part of the democratic ideal in Amercia a belief in the greatest possible equality of opportunity, opportunity for every individual to develop the best that in him lies, hoping in turn to receive from each his highest contribution to the total ongoing of society. Consequently, we are coming to believe that the greatest investment any society can make is in its human resources, their conservation and development. Thus we justify expenditures in public education, public health, public welfare and, in times of stress and strain, public relief.[7]

With these considerations in mind we begin the study of the Southeast, rightly called the seedbed of the Nation.

[7] See. Alva Myrdal, *Nation and Family* (New York: Harper and Brothers, 1941), for Sweden's attempt to integrate social policies with population policy.

CHAPTER 2

HOW THE PEOPLE GREW

THE STUDY of population, fascinating as it is said to be by those who practice it, has some complicating factors that should be firmly dealt with at the outset. Space, time, mass, and movement are the essence as the philosopher might say of population study, and we can well begin by dealing with these ideas. For space we shall use the idea of regions, for time we shall refer to the economist's idea of economic cycles and the demographer's idea of population trends. For mass we shall find that the demographers talk simply enough about population numbers and density. As for population movements we shall later represent our regions by making use of the idea of a series of connected reservoirs.

REGIONS AND POPULATION

For the purpose of understanding a nation so large and so diverse as the United States, it is necessary to examine it piecemeal, using indices of physical, cultural and economic factors. Howard W. Odum has visualized the Nation as divided into a minimum number of six regions. In its geography, the Nation has a humid East, a semi-arid West, a cold North, and a warm South. Related to the historical development of the sections, our six regions represent one earlier North, the Northeast; one earlier South, the Southeast; and four later developing Wests, the Middle States, the Southwest, the Northwest, and the Far West. Figure 4 outlines these regions and suggests their historical emergence by showing the date at which each State was admitted to the Union.

The six great regional empires differ widely in area, population, and wealth. Table 1 shows that in 1940 the Northeast led in population and wealth, followed by the Middle States. The Northwest which led in area came last in population. The Southeast came third in population and total wealth. Figure 5, where the size of the States is determined by the 1930 population, indicates the importance of the Northeast, Middle States, and Southeast as compared with the sparsely settled western areas.

FIGURE 4. SIX MAJOR REGIONS OF THE UNITED STATES WITH DATES
OF ADMISSION BY STATES, 1776-1912

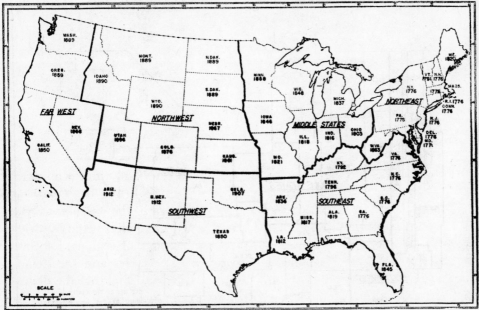

Source: Charles O. Paullin and J. K. Wright, *Historical Atlas of the United States* (Washington, D. C., 1932), Plates 61-66.

These are the regions, and if we want to know how the people grew we must consider population movements.

Population study, it can be said in literal terms, is a matter of life and death. It may help us somewhat to think, as some demographers have done, of our regions as great reservoirs of population. Into each region population flows by the entrance of births—"the immigration from heaven" —and out of every area population flows by the exit of deaths. The difference between these two rates of flow will give us the rate of natural in-

TABLE 1. POPULATION, AREA, AND WEALTH, UNITED STATES AND
THE SIX MAJOR REGIONS, 1940

Region	Population		Wealth*		Area	
	Number	Percent	Million dollars	Percent	Square miles	Percent
UNITED STATES.........	131,669,275	100.0	300,750	100.0	3,022,387	100.0
Northeast..............	39,966,500	30.4	117,908	39.2	206,168	6.8
Southeast..............	28,261,829	21.5	34,527	11.5	525,609	17.4
Southwest.............	9,782,337	7.4	15,749	5.2	572,833	18.9
Middle States..........	35,741,574	27.1	86,930	28.9	458,305	15.2
Northwest.............	7,410,435	5.6	18,501	6.1	824,997	27.3
Far West..............	9,843,509	7.5	24,230	8.1	434,406	14.4
District of Columbia.....	663,091	0.5	2,904	1.0	69	0.0

*Data for 1937.
Source: Population data: *Sixteenth Census of the United States, 1940*, Series PH-3; wealth data: National Industrial Conference Board, *The Economic Almanac, 1940*; area data: *Statistical Abstract of the United States*, 1941, Table 2.

FIGURE 5. THE RELATIVE VOLUME OF POPULATION, UNITED STATES
AND THE SIX MAJOR REGIONS, 1930

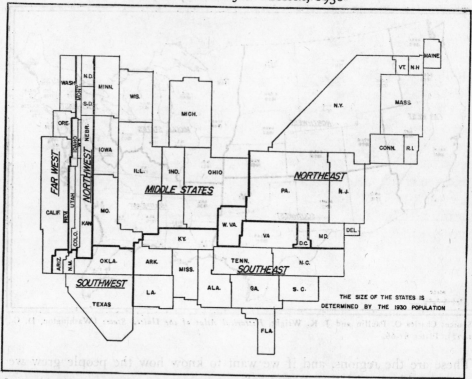

THE SIZE OF THE STATES IS
DETERMINED BY THE 1930 POPULATION

Source: Adapted from a map by W. P. A., Research Division, Urban Section (Washington, D. C., 1938).

crease—or of natural decrease if the level of the reservoir is falling. But these reservoirs, it must be remembered, are connected, and migration flows in and out of every region. These forces constitute the dynamics of population and the level attained by their flow and reflow gives us an ever changing regional balance of settlement. The units of population, however, are not homogeneous, for individuals differ in sex, age, and race. Once every ten years in our country the census is taken and the level of population is measured by States, urban, rural and farm areas in terms of sex, age, and race.

The census, it must be pointed out, measures the level of the reservoir without measuring the flows that contributed to its attainment. To do that a nation must record the vital statistics on births and deaths, annually. This is a gigantic undertaking attained only in the most civilized countries, but we shall find that the problem of birth and death registration has been brought nearer solution in the United States than the problem of securing figures on internal migration.

The level attained by these flows gives us an ever changing regional balance of population which, no doubt, bears some relation to the supporting capacity of the area when viewed in (1) terms of physical resources, (2) the state of economic organization and the technical arts, (3) the training and abilities of the population, and (4) the relation of the region to other areas. Such a view sees the region as a reservoir of population, the inflow of births as a dynamic force, and views migration into or out of the area as an index of important economic and social changes.

We have followed this figure of how the people grow because, by pointing out the way in which population facts are discovered, it foreshadows the sequence we shall follow in their analysis. In the chapters to follow a presentation of decennial census changes is followed by a discussion of the elemental population differences that enter into the sex ratio and the age composition. This leads in turn to a consideration of the trend of fertility, the natural increase of births over deaths, and the flow of interregional migration.

THE LONG-TIME TREND

As a new country the United States was characterized by large population increases based on high fertility, foreign immigration, and a high degree of internal migration. Figure 6 shows the growth curve of the Nation in the 15 decades since the First Census as a component of regional growth. The importance of the two earlier settled regions, the emergence

FIGURE 6. POPULATION GROWTH OF THE UNITED STATES AS COMPONENTS OF THE SIX MAJOR REGIONS, 1790-1940

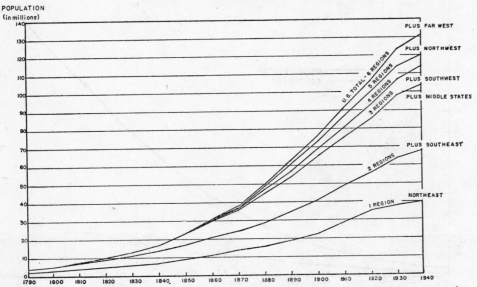

Source: Bureau of the Census, "Urban Population of the United States, 1790-1930," Release of October 31, 1939; *Sixteenth Census of the United States, 1940*, Series P-2, Nos. 1-49, Table 1.

of the Middle States, the late entrance of the western regions, and the large recent gains of the Far West stand out clearly in this graph. These are long-time trends and it must be remembered that population, like business cycles, has long-time trends and short-time fluctuations.

Figure 6 centers attention on the growth curve of the Nation and the regions in the 15 decades since the First Census—a growth that has only recently begun to slacken. The Nation has increased from less than 4 million people to almost 132 millions; the Southeast has grown from 1½ to over 28 million.

In his earlier work Malthus pointed to the United States as a country that doubled its population every generation. If the length of a generation could be regarded as the median of overlapping reproductive periods and be set at approximately thirty years, it can be seen that the Nation's population, with the help of immigration, continued to double each generation until the generation of 1870 reached 1900. The Southeast, receiving little foreign immigration after the colonial period and contributing greatly to migration to other areas, ceased to double in the generation 1840 to 1870. Only twice since 1840, the decades 1870 to 1880 and 1930 to 1940, has the region shown a higher rate of recorded increase than the Nation.

The rising line of Figure 7 does not, however, represent the curve of natural increase of the American people. Immigration of the foreign-

FIGURE 7. POPULATION INCREASE, UNITED STATES AND SOUTHEAST, 1790-1940

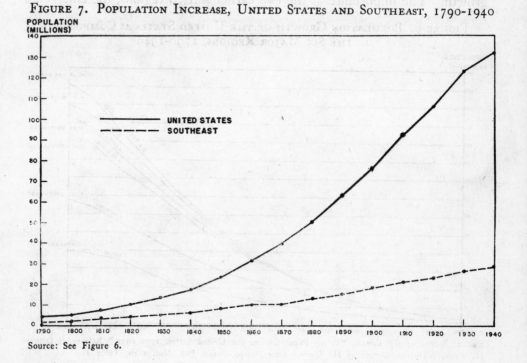

Source: See Figure 6.

born had reached about 14,000 per year in the 1820's and increased rapidly to over half a million in the 1880's. In the first decade of the twentieth century it reached the amazing average of approximately 900,000 persons per year. Since then it has fallen off until in the decade after 1930 it averaged around 50,000 a year and was sometimes exceeded by those leaving the country. The Southeast received but little of this immigration after the 1820's and thus its changes come nearer representing the forces of natural increase and internal migration.

Since the region's difficulties have sometimes been blamed on the quality of the original stock, we may well compare the regional-national distribution of ethnic stocks in the early formative period. For colonial and ante-bellum populations we can make use of three measures: (1) the allocation of family names in the 1790 Census by national and linguistic stocks, (2) the location of congregations of major religious bodies in 1775, (3) and the distribution of the foreign-born population by nationality in the Census of 1850.

TABLE 2. ESTIMATED NUMBER OF WHITE PERSONS BELONGING TO INDICATED NATIONAL OR LINGUISTIC STOCKS, UNITED STATES AND SOUTHEAST, 1790

Stock	Enumerated Area					Continental Area		
	Number		Percent			Percent		
	United States	Southeast	United States	Southeast	Difference	United States	Southeast	Difference
TOTAL	3,172,444	1,017,408	100.0	100.0	....	100.0	100.0	...
English	1,933,416	662,328	60.9	65.1	4.2	60.1	62.7	2.7
German	276,940	65,499	8.7	6.4	-2.3	8.6	6.3	-2.3
Scotch	260,322	126,564	8.2	12.4	4.2	8.1	12.0	3.9
Ulster-Scotch	190,075	69,666	6.0	6.9	0.9	5.9	6.6	0.7
Irish	115,886	52,948	3.6	5.2	1.9	3.6	5.0	1.4
Dutch	100,000	4,100	3.2	0.4	-2.8	3.1	0.4	-2.7
French	60,900	20,000	1.9	2.0	0.1	2.3	3.1	0.8
Swedish	21,100	4,425	0.6	0.4	-0.2	0.7	0.4	-0.3
Spanish	......	......	0.0	0.0	0.0	0.8	2.4	1.6
Unassigned	219,805	11,878	6.9	1.2	-5.7	6.8	1.1	5.7

Source: Mary Alice Eaton, The Provenience of the Southern People, 1500-1850 (unpublished paper, University of North Carolina, 1939). Computed from *Annual Report* of the American Historical Society, I, Tables 11, 13, pp. 124-125.

The preponderance of English stocks among the white population of the Southeast is of long standing. It existed, as early records show, at the First Census and increased as foreign immigration tended more and more to settle in the Northeast. *The Report of the Committee on Linguistic and National Stocks in the Population of the United States* estimated for the continental area that 60.1 percent of the family names in the census of 1790 were of English origin (Table 2). In the Southeast this proportion reaches 62.7 percent. When the Scotch and the Ulster-Scotch are added the proportion becomes 81.3 percent for the region as against 74.1 percent for the Nation. Data for the enumerated area gives the

region a higher proportion of Scotch and English stock, 84.4 to 75.1 percent for the Nation. The Nation exceeded the Southeast in the proportion of German, Dutch, and Swedish stock. The Southeast of 1790 exceeded in the proportion of Spanish, French, and Irish stock in the continental area.

The report underestimated, if anything, the importance of the Scotch
group for the future. They constituted 12 percent of the total, to which
can be added the 6.6 percent assigned to Ulster-Scotch. This gave the
Southeast 18.6 percent of their stock Scotch as against 14 percent for the
Nation. Next in the region came Germans with 6.3 percent and Irish with
5 percent. Only the French, among other groups, reached as high as 3.1
percent and the Spanish as high as 2.4 percent of the total.

TABLE 3. PERCENTAGE DISTRIBUTION OF CONGREGATIONS,
UNITED STATES AND SOUTHEAST, 1775

Denomination	Percent			Percent of United States total in Southeast	Denomination	Percent			Percent of United States total in Southeast
	United States	Southeast	Differ- ence			United States	Southeast	Differ- ence	
TOTAL..........	100.0	100.0	....	25.7	Dutch Reformed .	3.7	0.0	−3.7	0.0
					Methodist.......	2.0	1.3	−0.7	16.9
Congregational..	20.7	0.4	−20.3	0.4	Roman Catholic..	1.7	0.1	−1.6	1.8
Presbyterian....	18.2	24.6	6.4	33.0	Moravian........	1.0	0.6	−0.4	16.1
Episcopal.......	15.4	26.0	10.6	43.4	Dunker..........	0.8	0.4	−0.4	12.5
Baptist.........	15.3	30.1	14.8	52.4	Mennonite.......	0.5	0.2	−0.3	12.5
Friends.........	9.6	8.9	− 0.7	23.9	Jewish..........	0.2	0.4	0.2	60.0
GermanReformed	4.9	2.9	− 2.0	15.1	French Protestant	0.2	0.2	0.0	28.6
Lutheran.......	4.7	3.9	− 0.8	21.3	Other..........	1.1	0.0	−1.1	0.0

Source: Mary Alice Eaton, The Provenience of the Southern People, 1500-1850 (unpublished paper, University of North Carolina, 1939). Computed from J. K. Wright (ed.), *Atlas of the Historical Geography of the United States*, Plate 86.

Some corroboration of this ethnic distribution can be secured from an
analysis of the number of congregations established by 1775 (Table 3).
To some extent church membership may suggest class alignment and ethnic
groups in the population. One drawback in using this material for estimate is to be found in the unknown size of the congregations. From rural
to urban places this factor must have varied greatly. There is available,
however, no method by which allowance can be made for these variations.

By these criteria both the Nation and the region were overwhelmingly
Protestant and English in 1775. One-half of one percent of the congregations were Jewish and Catholic in the area as compared with 1.9 percent
for the Nation. Germanic and Dutch congregations reached 7.6 percent
of the total in the Southeast as compared with 14.8 percent in the Nation.
The South's most important groups were Baptist, Episcopal, and Presbyterian accounting respectively for 30.1, 26.0, and 24.6 percent of the
region's congregations. The region had 52.4 percent of all the Baptist
congregations in the country, 43.4 percent of the Episcopal, and 33 percent
of the Presbyterian churches. If we might accept the conclusion that from

the Episcopal churches were to come the upper-class groups, from the Presbyterian the middle class, and from the Baptist and Methodist the middle and lower classes we would have some idea of the emerging class structure. Actually it is doubtful that any such division of class groups is warranted by the facts. The major lack in the Southeast is in Congregational churches for the region has only 0.4 percent of the Nation's total. Methodist groups had shown little development as yet, less than 2 percent of the churches belonging to that denomination. Important in the social fabric were the Friends who had 8.9 percent of the region's congregations and 9.6 percent of the Nation's.

TABLE 4. NATIONALITY OF THE FOREIGN-BORN POPULATION, UNITED STATES AND SOUTHEAST, 1850

Nationality	Number		Percent		
	United States	Southeast	United States	Southeast	Difference
TOTAL	2,210,839	157,773	100.0	100.0	....
Ireland	961,719	62,794	43.5	39.6	−3.9
Germany	583,774	45,110	26.4	28.5	2.1
England	278,675	14,083	12.6	8.9	−3.7
British America	147,711	1,546	6.7	1.0	−5.7
Scotland	70,550	6,337	3.2	4.0	0.8
France	54,069	14,815	2.4	9.4	7.0
Wales	29,868	538	1.4	0.3	−1.1
Switzerland	13,358	1,583	0.6	1.0	0.4
Mexico	13,317	603	0.6	0.4	−0.2
Norway	12,678	129	0.6	0.1	−0.5
Holland	9,848	315	0.4	1.0	0.6
West Indies	5,772	2,438	0.3	1.6	1.3
Italy	3,679	1,556	0.2	1.0	0.8
Sweden	3,559	441	0.2	0.3	0.1
Spain	3,113	1,802	0.1	1.1	1.0
Denmark	1,838	442	0.1	0.3	0.2
Central and South America	1,684	65	0.1	0.05	−0.05
Russia	1,414	214	0.1	0.1	0.0
Belgium	1,313	208	0.05	0.1	0.05
Portugal	1,274	307	0.05	0.2	0.15
Asia	1,135	77	0.05	0.05	0.0
Turkey	1,106	50	0.0	0.0	0.0
Austria	946	276	0.0	0.2	0.2
Greece	86	35	0.0	0.0	0.0
Africa	551	174	0.0	0.1	0.1
Other	8,802	1,815	0.35	1.7	1.35

Source: Mary Alice Eaton, The Provenience of the Southern People, 1500-1850 (unpublished paper, University of North Carolina, 1939). Computed from Seventh Census of the United States, 1850, Table XV, p. xxxvii.

The extent to which these colonial stocks were to be reenforced can be gathered from an analysis of the foreign-born population reported in the Census of 1850 (Table 4). In that year 2,210,839 foreign-born lived in the United States. Only 7.1 percent of this number lived in the Southeast. Here much of the variety of ethnic stocks can be traced to one State, Louisiana. Predominant groups can be compared for the Nation and the region. Forty-three and a half percent of the Nation's foreign-born were Irish as compared with 39.6 percent for the region; 26.4 percent were German for the Nation and 28.5 percent for the region. In the Nation 12.6 percent were English as compared with 8.9 percent in the South. The South, however, had 9.4 percent French as compared with only 2.4

TABLE 5. DECENNIAL CHANGE IN POPULATION BY RACE,
SOUTHEAST, 1790-1940

Year	(Population in thousands)							
	Total population*	Percent change	White population	Percent change	Free colored population	Percent change	Slave population	Percent change
1790......	1,583**	....	1,017	....	20	....	546	....
1800......	2,201**	39.0	1,427	40.3	33	65.0	742	35.9
1810......	2,983**	35.5	1,885	32.1	58	75.8	1,040	40.2
1820......	3,906	30.9	2,437	29.3	77	32.8	1,391	33.8
1830......	5,144**	31.7	3,170	30.1	107	39.0	1,868	34.3
1840......	6,359**	23.6	3,901	23.1	127	18.7	2,331	24.8
1850......	8,044**	26.5	4,949	26.9	132	3.9	2,962	27.1
1860......	9,655	20.0	5,946	20.1	143	8.3	3,564	20.3
1870......	9,990	3.5	6,078	2.2	3,908	5.4	.....	....
1880......	13,047	30.6	7,803	28.4	5,238	34.0	.....	....
1890......	15,330	17.5	9,424	20.8	5,898	12.6	.....	....
1900......	18,074	17.9	11,212	19.0	6,851	16.2	.....	....
1910......	20,786	15.0	13,271	18.4	7,500	9.5	.....	....
1920......	22,860	10.0	15,291	15.2	7,550	0.7	.....	....
1930......	25,551	11.8	17,746	16.1	7,784	3.1	.....	....
1940......	28,261	10.6	20,059	13.0	8,169	5.0	.....	....

*Includes all other persons.
**Excludes all other persons.
†Percentage based on total number of Negroes in the population in 1860.
Source: H. L. Geisert, The Balance of Inter-State Migration in the Southeast, (unpublished doctoral dissertation, University of North Carolina, 1938), p. 82; Sixteenth Census of the United States, 1940, Population, Second Series, State Bulletins, Table 4.

percent in the Nation. Excepting the Scotch who reached 4 percent in the region, no other foreign group was of especial importance.

The region's substitute for the labor force afforded by immigration was of course the Negro slave. The slave trade was outlawed in 1808, and practically all of the growth of slave population after this date came from natural increase. Examination of Table 5 shows that the recorded slave population increased at a faster rate than the white population in every decade from 1790 to 1860 except the first. Throughout this period it made up more than one-third of the population of the Southeast, increasing slightly from 34.4 percent to 36.6 percent of the total. The decade 1820 to 1830 was the last in which free colored population showed a higher rate of increase than slaves. After that period the practice of manumission slackened, freedmen were forced to migrate from some States, and their rate of natural increase was likely lower than that of the slaves.

On the surface, the Census of 1870 indicated the demoralizing effect of the Civil War, for the increase of Negro population dropped from 16.9 percent to 5.4 percent, while white population increase dropped from 20.1 percent to 2.2 percent. Taken under the disturbed conditions of Reconstruction, the census undoubtedly represents an undercount of the total population of the South, even though the loss of West Virginia accounts for some of the decrease. This is indicated by the jump to a 28.4 percent increase in white and 34.0 percent increase in Negro population in the next decade. Negro increase has consistently declined, falling below

10 percent in every decade since 1900. The low point was reached in 1910-1920 when Negro migration gives the Southeast a recorded increase of only 0.7 percent. The white population increase of the region declined to 13 percent in 1930-40. Its rate of increase, however, has consistently been from two to five times greater than that of the Negro.

TREND OF RURAL AND URBAN GROWTH

The curve of rural and urban growth goes far to explain regional variation in population increase. Figure 8 shows that increases in rural

FIGURE 8. URBAN POPULATION AS PERCENTAGE OF THE TOTAL POPULATION, UNITED STATES AND SOUTHEAST, 1790-1940

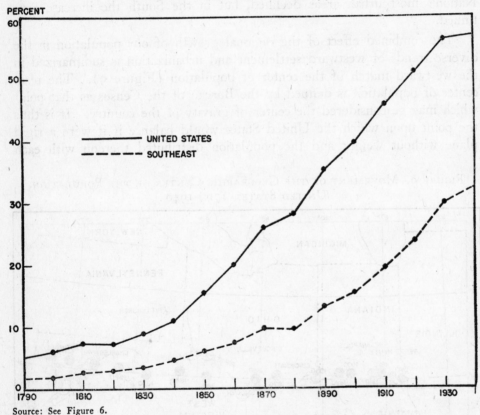

Source: See Figure 6.

population have tended to dominate southern regional development throughout its history. From the First Census in 1790 to the Fifth in 1830 population in urban areas in the United States grew from 201,655 to 1,127,247—from 5.1 to 8.8 percent of the total population. By that time the Southeast which began with 1.8 percent urban had only 3.4 percent of its people in cities as compared with 14.4 percent in the North-

east. Fifty years later, in 1880, the region still had less than ten percent of its people urban, and it had been passed by all the other regions
except the Southwest. Not until 1890 was the region to find more than
one-tenth, 13.2 percent, of its people in cities. By this decade the Nation
was over one-third (35.1 percent) urban. Forty years was to place over
56 percent of the Nation's inhabitants in cities, but 1930 served to bring
the Southeast to 29.8 percent urban, slightly past the point reached by the
Nation in 1880. In 1930, almost three-fourths in the Northeast, two-
thirds in the Far West, and three-fifths in the Middle States were urban
dwellers. By 1940 the Southeast had not yet placed one-third of its
people within the circle of urbanism. From 1930 to 1940 many of the
Nation's most urban areas declined, but in the South the increase continued.

The combined effect of the regional growth of our population in the
diverse trends of westward settlement and urbanization is summarized in
the westward march of the center of population (Figure 9). The term
center of population is defined by the Bureau of the Census as that point
which may be considered the center of gravity of the country. It is thus
the point upon which the United States would balance if it were a rigid
plane without weight and the population distributed thereon with each

FIGURE 9. MOVEMENT OF THE GEOGRAPHIC CENTER OF THE POPULATION,
UNITED STATES, 1790-1940

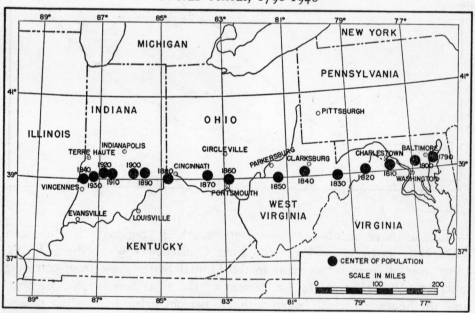

Source: *Sixteenth Census of the United States, 1940.* Map.

individual being assumed to have equal weight and to exert influence on a central point proportional to his distance from the point.

In 150 years the center of demographic gravity has moved westward 602 miles from a point 23 miles east of Baltimore, Maryland, to two miles southeast of Carlisle, Indiana. The greatest movement was in the decade 1850 to 1860 when the center advanced 80.6 miles. The least movement westward occurred from 1910 to 1920 when it advanced only 9.8 miles. The point farthest north was the 1790 location, and the point farthest south was the 1940 location, but the difference was only 22.5 miles.

The growth of our people finds another record in the density of settlement. Density of population is largely a function of urban concentration except for the agricultural population where it is a function of the intensity of utilization of land, which depends largely on fertility and rainfall. The Southeast, considering its rurality, ranks surprisingly high in density of population, coming after the Northeast and the Middle States. Here the 1940 Census came at a time to record the cumulative effect of the great drought on the Northwest.

Figure 10 shows that practically all of Rhode Island, Massachusetts, and Connecticut fall in the area of maximum density, as do most of New Jersey, half of Pennsylvania, and much of New York. Large groups of counties with high density are also located in the Southern Appalachian coal fields of Virginia, West Virginia, and Kentucky, the textile areas of

FIGURE 10. DENSITY OF POPULATION BY COUNTIES, UNITED STATES, 1940

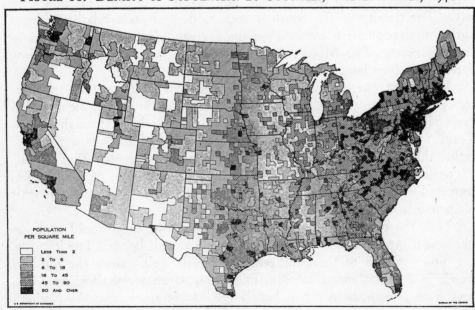

Source: *Sixteenth Census of the United States, 1940*, Series P-3, No. 20.

FIGURE 11. POPULATION DISTRIBUTION OF THE UNITED STATES, 1940

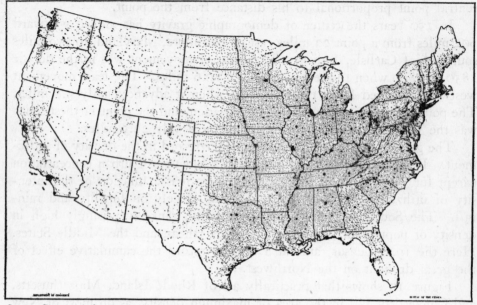

Source: Bureau of the Census, U. S. Department of Commerce.

the Virginia and Carolina Piedmont, industrial areas bordering Lake Erie, Michigan, and the San Francisco, Los Angeles, and Puget Sound districts. Figure 11, with each dot representing 2,000 population, indicates the extent to which urban concentrations are involved in areas of high density. The density of the South is seen to depend on a relatively dense agricultural population rather than upon great urban concentration as in the Northeast. The Middle States possess a balance of relatively dense agricultural population with large urban centers.

In contrast, the counties with an average density of less than two persons per square mile are all located west of the 98th meridian, the so-called "rainfall line" that runs from Valley City, North Dakota, through Austin, Texas. Here rainfall is adequate for grazing and extensive agriculture rather than for general agriculture. In this territory density that exceeds 18 persons per square mile is explained by the presence of large cities, increased rainfall, or irrigation projects. The dot map presents this phenomenon more accurately.

Thus the people grew and thus we could hope they would continue to grow, if growth meant survival and increased well-being. The immediate future growth of the Southern people will spring from the regional trends in fertility, mortality, and migration, which we shall shortly discuss. Such growth, however, is hardly predictable apart from the Nation's growth and development. Figure 12 furnishes one such projection. It

FIGURE 12. POPULATION OF THE SOUTH-
EAST BY DECADES WITH LOGISTIC CURVE
FITTED: ACTUAL 1830-1930, TRENDS,
1930-1960

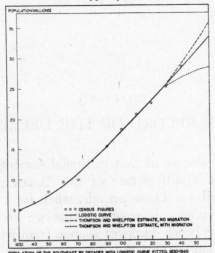

POPULATION OF THE SOUTHEAST BY DECADES WITH LOGISTIC CURVE FITTED, 1830-1940

Source: See Figure 6. Warren S. Thompson
and P. K. Whelpton, *Estimates of Future
Population by States* (Washington, D. C.:
National Resources Board, 1934). Mimeographed.

fits the logistic curve to a century of population growth in the Southeast, 1830-1930, and projects it to 1960 under three assumptions: (1) the trend of the curve, (2) no migration, and (3) migration assumed as of the decade 1929-1930. These assumptions were tested when the regional population for 1940, 28,262,000, was superimposed on the three projections. The point at which this dot fell (Figure 12) suggests that the population of the Southeast increased as though little or no migration had taken place in the depression decade.

It is to the record of the decade that we turn our attention before we discuss the trends of fertility and migration behind regional-national growth.

CHAPTER 3

THE RECORD OF THE DECADE

EVERY ten years the shutter of that decennial camera, the United States Census, clicks to take a still picture of the American people as of one instant, midnight April 1. These periods, when for a moment we feel—if we can accept the census as accurate—that we know who and where the people are, give us bench marks of change from which to calculate the progress of the Nation. It is the purpose of the present chapter to examine the record of the recent decades.

Here it would serve us well to keep in mind the significance of the particular moment at which the camera of the census makes its record. Our recent decades may be characterized somewhat as follows:

1910-1920—Decade of Economic Expansion. World War I
1920-1930—Decade of Post-War Prosperity
1930-1940—Decade of World Depression
1940-1950—Decade of World War II

Figure 13, which gives the trend of economic activity in terms of physical production and changing price levels enables us to relate the population census to the flow of time. Thus we shall be prepared to find that the 1920's was a period of great rural-urban migration, that the 1930's checked the process, that the 1940 Census recorded some of the results of the depression decade without forecasting many of the conditions of the coming war.

The United States is approaching its demographic maturity for its rate of growth is slowing down. The 1940 Census found 131,669,275 people in our country, hardly nine million more than were counted ten years before. This was an increase of 7.2 percent in ten years and represented the lowest rate of gain the country had seen since the census was first taken in 1790. It was less than half the rate of growth from 1920 to 1930, when our population increased by 16.1 percent. The Southeast increased by some 2,700,000 in 1940—a gain of 10.6 percent.

FIGURE 13. ECONOMIC CYCLES IN THE UNITED STATES, 1900-1943

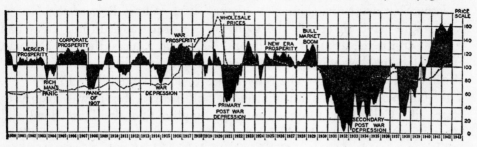

Source: Leonard P. Ayres, The Cleveland Trust Company, 1943.

The country undoubtedly is reaching its maturity when it will taper off and cease to grow. Population experts agree that two things are responsible: the United States birth rate has fallen sharply during the ten years, and there has been no large amount of foreign immigration. That it is a little too early, however, for anyone to worry about the effect of declining population on our national defense is shown by the fact that we have 16.8 million men of military age, 21 to 35.

The great urban and industrial areas, like the Northeast with New York and Pennsylvania, and the Middle States with Chicago and Detroit,

FIGURE 14. PERCENTAGE CHANGE IN TOTAL POPULATION,
UNITED STATES, 1930-1940

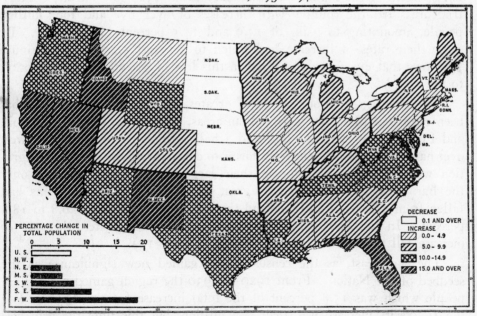

Source: *Sixteenth Census of the United States, 1940*, Series PH-3.

still lead in population but the regions of agriculture like the Southeast and the Southwest are gaining on them. The Wheat Belt of the Northwest might have shared in the gains of the other agricultural areas had it not been for the drought. As it was, Nebraska, Kansas, the two Dakotas, and Oklahoma lost more than 290,000 people, mainly from their farms. With Vermont they were the only States to lose population (Figure 14). The Far West gained a million and a half people, for it was mainly to States like California, Oregon, and Washington that the Dust Bowl and other migrants went. Americans have become climate conscious, and the resulting struggle between California and Florida has become a kind of census horse race. From 1920 to 1930, California's population increased 65.7 percent to Florida's 51.6 percent; from 1930 to 1940, Florida increased 29.2 percent and California 21.7 percent.

THE RURAL-URBAN CONTRAST

The important contrast in our population growth, however, is that between the urban and industrial areas which grow by migration and the rural areas which grow by natural increase, that is, by the surplus of births over deaths. When we look at the Nation's regions it would seem that the decade of the great depression was devoted to undoing much of the work accomplished by the period of prosperity, 1920 to 1930. The Northeast and Middle States respectively have 40 and 36 million people, 67.5 percent of the Nation's population. From 1920 to 1930 these industrial areas led the country with increases of over five and four million people, amounting to gains of 15.9 and 14.5 percent (Figure 15). By 1940 their rates of increase had fallen to 5.1 and 5.2 percent. Figure 15 shows that every region shared in this loss of growth from the 1920's to the 1930's.

The twenties were our period of greatest migration to cities and it has been estimated that four metropolitan areas, New York, Chicago, Detroit, and Los Angeles attracted four and a half million people—a figure well over half the net movement from farms to cities during the decade. Migration was the deciding factor in their large growth; but by 1940 only the Far West had continued its great increase and there the gains had fallen from 2.6 to 1.6 millions and the rate of increase from 46.8 to 18.8 percent. In the Northwest, Northeast, and Middle States, the rate of increase fell below the Nation's average (Figure 15).

The Southeast, as the census shows, gained new significance as the seedbed of the Nation. From 1920 to 1930 the region gained 2.7 million people which was 15.8 percent of the total increase for the Nation. For the 1930's its increase was again 2.7 million, but this time the gain was

FIGURE 15. PERCENTAGE INCREASE IN POPULATION, UNITED STATES AND
THE SIX MAJOR REGIONS, 1920-1930, 1930-1940

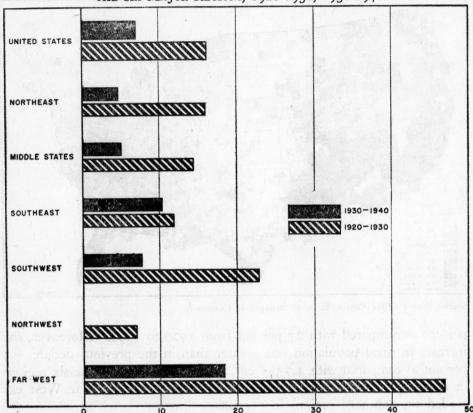

Source: See Figure 14. *Statistical Abstract of the United States, 1941*, Table 6.

over 30 percent of the Nation's growth. The Southwest including Oklahoma which lost population, accounted for 7.9 percent of the decade's
growth (Figure 15).

These population changes are shown by counties in Figure 16. Large
blocks of counties with increasing population are shown in the south
Appalachians, Florida, and along the Gulf of Mexico, and in most of the
West beyond the Great Plains. There the decrease ranged from the
Canadian border through Texas.

These considerations call for a closer comparison of population increases in the cities and in the countryside. There are now almost 74 1/2
million people in our urban areas as compared with almost 57 1/4 million
people in rural areas. Over the whole course of our history cities have
grown much faster than the whole population. As indicated, this trend
is slowing down. While the urban population increased during the thirties
from 56.2 to 56.5 percent of the whole, its rate of growth was only 7.9

FIGURE 16. POPULATION CHANGE BY COUNTIES, UNITED STATES, 1930-1940

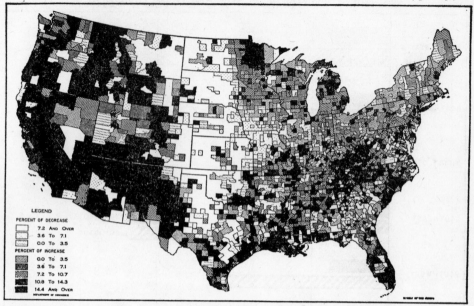

Source: Bureau of the Census, U. S. Department of Commerce.

percent as compared with 27 percent from 1920 to 1930. Moreover, the increase in rural population was greater than in the previous decade, 6.4 percent as compared with 4.7 percent. Figure 17 compares the six regions in the proportion of rural and urban growth. Only the Far West exceeded the southern regions in percentage increase.

The rural farm population remained practically stationary from 1930 to 1940, increasing only 0.2 percent. This, however, represents a reversal in trend, since this group declined 3.8 percent in the previous decade. Between 1930 and 1940 the number of farms declined by 3.1 percent, so that the average number of persons per farm increased from 4.8 to 5.0. The Far West was the only region to show large gains. The Northwest lost 13.5 of its rural farm population, the Southwest 7 percent, while the Southeast and the Middle States remained practically stationary with a 2.2 and 1.5 percent increase, respectively. By States the increase in rural farm people ranged from 19.2 percent in Connecticut and 18.7 percent in West Virginia to losses of over 20 percent in South Dakota (Figure 18).

The most disturbing fact shown by the census was this same growth of our rural people in certain special areas during the very time that the depression was undermining the agriculture on which they live. This occurred at a time when the government was struggling with the problem of lost export markets, agricultural surpluses, and reduced crop quotas for every farm. Many of the farm increases occurred on poor land, in

FIGURE 17. PERCENTAGE CHANGE IN TOTAL, URBAN AND RURAL POPULATION,
UNITED STATES AND THE SIX MAJOR REGIONS, 1930-1940

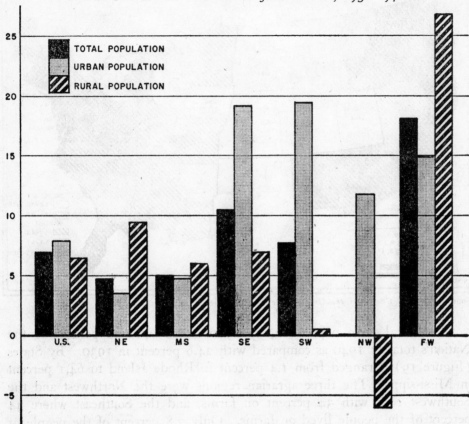

Source: *Sixteenth Census of the United States, 1940*, Series P-3, No. 7; P-10, No. 2.

rural problem areas, or in the suburban fringes around cities. In a few
cases there were new lands opened up to which people could go. The
greatest increases were in rural areas of southern Florida and California
where a large migrant-labor problem existed and labor camps were taxed
to the limit.

Other large increases came in new lands of the western Cotton and
Delta areas, rising to 30 percent in the southeastern Missouri bootheel
where tenant strikes and roadside camps showed the danger signs of too
many people on the land. Increases also occurred in mountainous sections, the Rockies, Appalachians, and Ozarks, where during the depression
many small subsistence farms have been taken up. The good commercial
farming areas of the old plantation South, the corn belt, and the dairy
regions remained practically stationary (Figure 16).

FIGURE 18. PERCENTAGE CHANGE IN RURAL FARM POPULATION, 1930-1940

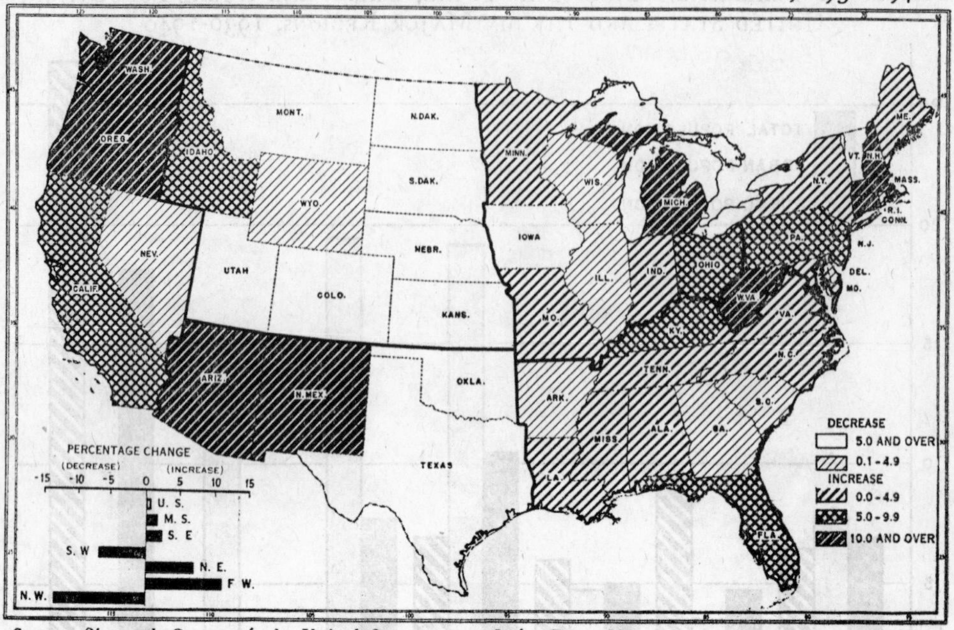

Source: *Sixteenth Census of the United States, 1940*, Series P-10, No. 2.

The rural farm population, by 1940, made up 23.0 percent of the Nation's total in 1940 as compared with 24.6 percent in 1930. By States (Figure 19) it ranged from 1.4 percent in Rhode Island to 64.1 percent in Mississippi. The three agrarian regions were the Northwest and the Southwest each with 34 percent on farms, and the Southeast where 44 percent of the people lived on farms. Only 7.8 percent of the people of the Northeast have rural farm residence.

The greatest gains of the decade were found in the rural nonfarm population which increased 14.2 percent, almost twice as fast as the urban population. This group amounted to slightly over 27 million or 20.5 percent of the 1940 population. Rural nonfarm population is more evenly distributed among the regions than any other residence group. They ranged from 26.3 percent in the Northwest to 17.7 percent in the Middle States.

Sometimes regarded as village population, this group presents extremely different characteristics the country over. It meets two negative criteria. It must live outside incorporated places of 2,500 or more but must not live on farms. In terms of density it ranges from population living on isolated nonfarm homes in the open country to the people living just outside the city limits of great metropolitan centers. The Bureau of the Census expresses the view that barely one-third of this group in 1940 lived in the

FIGURE 19. RURAL FARM POPULATION AS PERCENTAGE OF TOTAL POPULATION,
UNITED STATES, 1940

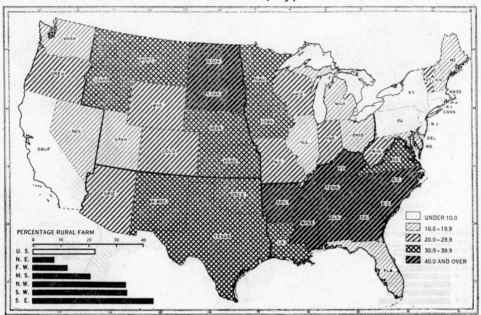

Source: See Figure 18.

13,000-odd rural incorporated places, and that probably not more than
another third lived in unincorporated villages and suburban areas.

In part, the growth of rural nonfarm population reflects the growth of
metropolitan districts from 1930 to 1940. While the central cities increased 6.1 percent, the areas outside the cities grew by 16.9 percent. Much
of this was rural nonfarm territory as defined by the census.

The West and Southeast regions led with about 25 percent of the population in rural nonfarm areas. By States, our Figure 20 shows this range
from 7 percent in Rhode Island to 46.6 percent in Nevada. Increases in
this category were greatest in western regions, least in the Northeast, and
medium in the Southeast.

In numbers and in wealth the Nation's cities have long been ahead
of the rural areas. Table 6 indicates that the Southeast has 654 cities as
compared with 3,464 for the Nation. The region contains no city larger
than 500,000 and only 32.1 percent of its population is urban as compared
with 56.5 percent in the Nation.

For the first time since the census was begun the figures indicated
that the big cities may be giving way to the suburbs and small cities.
Smaller cities grew much faster than large ones from 1930 to 1940. Four
hundred and twelve cities in the United States have a population of 25,000

FIGURE 20. RURAL NONFARM POPULATION AS PERCENTAGE OF TOTAL
POPULATION, UNITED STATES, 1940

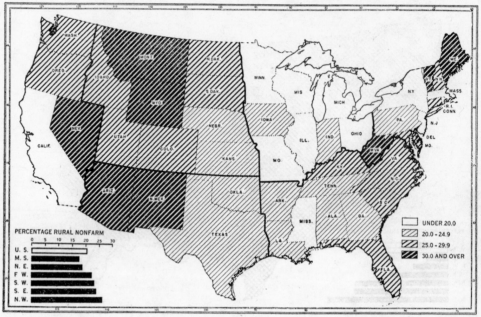

Source: See Figure 18.

TABLE 6. NUMBER OF CITIES BY SIZE AND POPULATION IN EACH SIZE GROUP AS
PERCENTAGE OF TOTAL POPULATION, UNITED STATES AND SOUTHEAST, 1940

City Size	United States		Southeast	
	Number cities	Percent of population	Number cities	Percent of population
TOTAL.....................	3,464	56.5	654	32.1
1,000,000 or more............	5	12.1	...	...
500,000 - 1,000,000........	9	4.9	...	...
250,000 - 500,000........	23	5.9	5	5.9
100,000 - 250,000........	55	5.9	9	4.6
50,000 - 100,000........	107	5.6	20	4.8
25,000 - 50,000........	213	5.6	30	3.5
10,000 - 25,000........	665	7.6	98	5.2
5,000 - 10,000........	965	5.1	170	4.1
2,500 - 5,000........	1,422	3.8	232	4.0

Source: *Sixteenth Census of the United States, 1940*, Population, First Series, United States Summary, Tables 10, 11, 13.

or more. They hold 52.7 millions of our people but their population
grew only 7.1 percent. In contrast, a gain of 30.4 percent, more than
four times as great, was recorded among this group of cities from 1920
to 1930 (Figure 21). The Southeast has 64 in this size class contain-
ing some 18.8 percent of its population.

There are now 92 cities with 100,000 population or more. They contain almost 38 million people and increased only 4.6 percent. Only 14
of this size are found in the Southeast but they contain 10.5 percent of the

FIGURE 21. PERCENTAGE CHANGE IN URBAN POPULATION BY SIZE OF CITY,
UNITED STATES, 1920-1930, 1930-1940

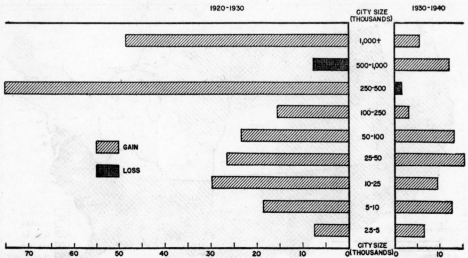

Source: *Sixteenth Census of the United States, 1940,* Population First Series, Tables 10 and 11.

region's population. Newcomers to this list of figures were Sacramento, California, and Charlotte, North Carolina, while El Paso, Texas, Lynn, Massachusetts, and Evansville, Indiana, dropped below 100,000. Twenty-seven of the cities of over a 100,000 lost people from 1930 to 1940. Of the ten largest cities, population actually declined in four—Philadelphia, Cleveland, St. Louis, and Boston—and in Pittsburgh and Chicago the increases were unimportant, 0.3 and 0.6 percent. New York City gained the largest numbers, almost 450,000, but Washington, the "Boom City on the Potomac," made the largest relative gain, 36.2 percent. The greatest gain in the country was a 331 percent increase for Miami Beach, Florida, while Miami itself grew 55.6 percent and jumped all the way from the 78th to the 48th city in the country. Among the moderate-sized cities Austin, Texas, with an increase of 65.5 percent, made the best gains.

In what parts of the country have our cities been growing and where have they had the hardest sledding? The rate of urban growth showed the widest variations between the main regions of the country. It was greatest in the southern regions which had the smallest proportion, 29.8 percent, of its population in cities in 1930; and it was the least, 3.6 percent, in the Northeast, which was 74.4 percent urban in 1930. The Far West, already two-thirds urban, continued its city growth by virtue of continued migration in the 1930's. By States, the rate of urban growth ranged from 65.1 percent in New Mexico to less than 1 percent in Pennsylvania and Massachusetts. Five Southeastern States showed gains in

FIGURE 22. PERCENTAGE CHANGE IN URBAN POPULATION,
UNITED STATES, 1930-1940

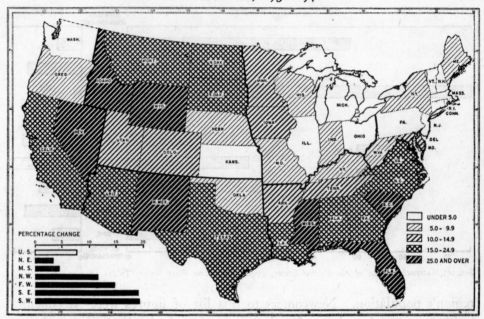

Source: *Sixteenth Census of the United States, 1940*, Series P-3, No. 7.

FIGURE 23. URBAN POPULATION AS PERCENTAGE OF TOTAL POPULATION,
UNITED STATES, 1940

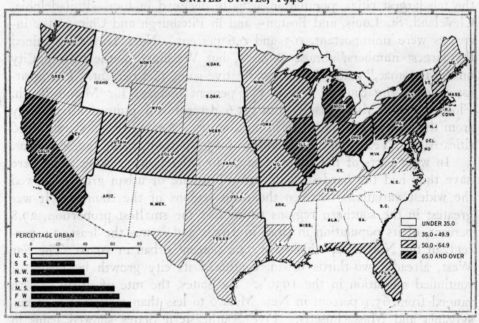

Source: See Figure 22.

excess of 20 percent (Figure 22). There was, however, no prospect of immediate equalization among the States and regions. The Southeast still remained the least urban and the Northeast the most urbanized. By States, Mississippi represented the essence of agrarianism, with only 19.8 percent urban; Rhode Island the quintessence of urbanism, 91.6 per cent (Figure 23).

It was thus the highly urbanized areas that failed to maintain gains in city population. Together the Northeast and Middle States contain 71.1 percent of our population found in cities of 10,000 or more (Table 7). From 1930 to 1940 their proportion in this size city grew 3.7 percent. On the other hand, other regions saw their similar populations make large gains. Thus, in the Southwest they increased by 21.4 percent; in the Southeast by 19.2 percent; in the Far West by 15.1 percent; and in the Northwest by 13.1 percent (Table 7). It is significant that while the total population in the drought States declined, their cities continued to grow. More significant is the growth in the South. While the Southeast increased its proportion of the Nation's population in cities of 10,000 and over from 9.8 to 10.8 percent, the Northeast saw its share decline from 43 to 41.5 percent. These figures suggest that in contrast with densely settled areas the southern regions continued its movement towards cities and industrialization throughout the depression.

TABLE 7. PERCENTAGE DISTRIBUTION AND PERCENTAGE CHANGE OF URBAN POPULATION IN CITIES OF 10,000 AND OVER, UNITED STATES AND THE SIX MAJOR REGIONS, 1930-1940

Region	1930	1940	Percent change	Region	1930	1940	Percent change
UNITED STATES	100.0	100.0	7.5	Middle States	30.7	29.6	3.6
Northeast	43.0	41.5	3.8	Northwest	3.2	3.4	13.1
Southeast	9.8	10.8	19.2	Far West	8.2	8.8	15.1
Southwest	4.3	4.8	21.4	D. C.	0.8	1.1	36.2

Source: *Sixteenth Census of the United States, 1940*, Population, First Series, United States Summary, Table 11.

METROPOLITAN DISTRICTS

Not all the population of great urban clusters are found within city limits. For this reason the Bureau of the Census has set up the category of metropolitan districts in connection with cities of 50,000 or more. In addition to a central city or cities, adjacent minor civil divisions having a population density of 150 or more per square mile are included. Such a district is not a political unit, but is a unified population concentration and possesses common economic, social, and administrative interests.

In 1940, about half, 47.8 percent, of the Nation's population lived within the 140 metropolitan districts. The greatest of these was the New York City-New Jersey concentration which contained in its central cities almost 8.5 million, with another 3¼ million in outlying districts. The Northeast showed (Figure 24) a concentration stretching, with few breaks, from Boston to Washington and including New York, Trenton, Philadelphia, Wilmington, and Baltimore. In contrast the South contained only 31 such areas with an aggregate population of 5,796,153.

FIGURE 24. METROPOLITAN DISTRICTS OF THE UNITED STATES, 1940

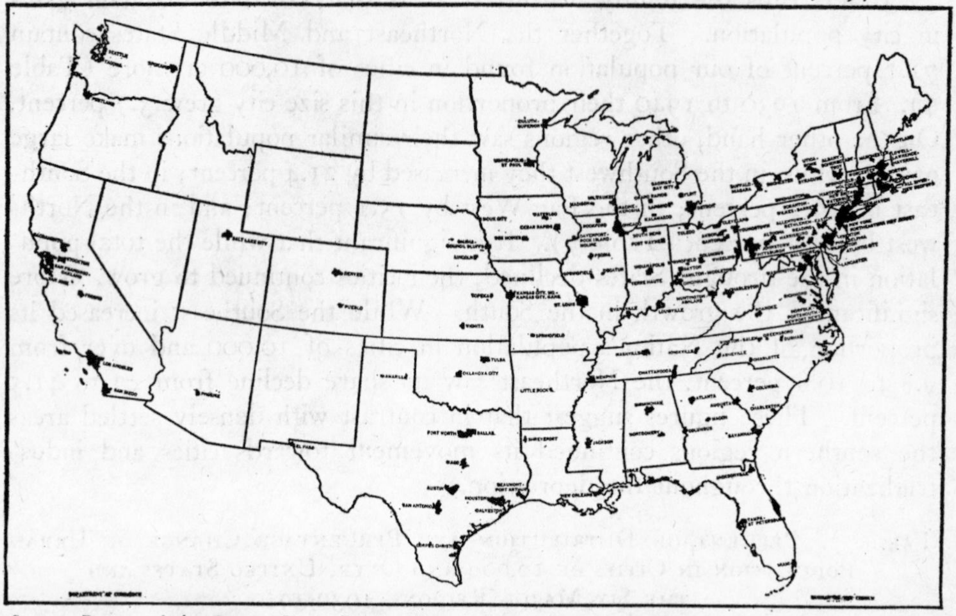

Source: Bureau of the Census, U. S. Department of Commerce.

The population in the Nation's central cities was 42,796,170, and that in the surrounding civil divisions was 20,169,603, or 32.0 percent of the total. In the Southeast the outlying districts contained a smaller proportion, 24.7 percent, of the total (Table 8). In the Nation the population of these areas grew at a rate of 9.3 percent from 1930 to 1940; for the region they showed an increase of 21.2 percent. Population of the central cities of the Nation increased only 6.1 percent, whereas in the district outside the city limits the population increased 16.9 percent. The Southeast showed a higher rate of growth with increases of 15.5 percent for the population in central cities and a 42.2 percent increase in surrounding townships (Table 8). Greater proportionate growth of metropolitan districts has been characteristic in regions of less development.

The Census of 1940 came in time to measure the results of a decade of depression and attempted recovery but too soon to register the effects of war on crowded industrial centers. The changes in the growth of our cities reflect the working of many factors in our economy and our society.

Some of these were national and some were regional in scope. Undoubtedly the greatest single factor affecting all changes, city and country alike, was the continued decline in births during the last decade. With foreign immigration virtually cut off and internal migration restricted, it is not surprising that the greatest urban growth should occur among the cities located in the midst of those rural areas whose birth rates remained the highest. The long depression has been most important, for few industries expanded and many contracted in the ten years. The belief has been expressed that relief rather than industrial jobs was the cause of migration to towns. Others have expressed the opinion that relief actually increased the birth rate among the very poor. This, however, seems a mistake. While several million children were born to families on relief, it better suits the facts to say that they had high birth rates before they came on relief and that these rates continued.

TABLE 8. POPULATION INCREASE IN METROPOLITAN DISTRICTS, UNITED STATES AND SOUTHEAST, 1930-1940

Metropolitan districts*	Population		Increase	
	1930	1940	Number	Percent
UNITED STATES				
Total....................	57,602,865	62,965,773	5,362,908	9.3
In central cities................	40,343,442	42,796,170	2,452,728	6.1
Outside central cities............	17,259,423	20,169,603	2,910,180	16.9
Percent outside central cities........	30.0	32.0		
SOUTHEAST				
Total....................	4,783,706	5,796,153	1,012,447	21.2
In central cities................	3,777,028	4,364,244	587,216	15.5
Outside central cities............	1,006,678	1,431,909	425,231	42.2
Percent outside central cities........	21.0	24.7		

*For the United States there were 140 metropolitan districts in 1940 and 133 in 1930; for the Southeast, 31 in 1940 and 29 in 1930.

Source: *Sixteenth Census of the United States, 1940*, Population, First Series, United States Summary, Table 18.

Changes in our industrial economy were also reflected by the census. Partial displacement of coal by oil and hydroelectric power meant declines in certain cities dependent on steel or coal mining and the rise of populations, particularly in the Southwest, where cities largely depend on a growing oil industry. There also was some relocation of industry from large to smaller cities. Here hydroelectric power played a part as in the textile industry of the Carolinas and the developing industrial zone of the TVA. In the main, however, the automobile before the war had done more to curb the growth of the city than any one thing. The greater numbers in use, their increased reliability in winter weather, and the accompanying development of hardsurfaced, all-weather roads enabled our working people to travel greater distances by auto and bus to and from work. All over the country the suburban areas grew and the crowded zones inside city limits shrank or showed but little gain.

Before war bestirred renewed activity we might have concluded that the great mushroom growth of American cities was drawing to an end. This might have meant many things for our society. While the metropolitan areas continued large because of suburban zones, this did the city governments little good unless the population could be brought inside the city limits for taxation. While there was less reason than ever for cities to plan great projects based on hopes of expanding population, they could begin to look to the crowded and insanitary housing in their slums. With less immigration it was felt that these areas would gradually be abandoned by all families who could leave the slums, land values would go down, and cities should be able, with the aid of the Federal Government, to take up the slack at the close of the war by greater development in housing, parks, and recreation. Less and less could the excuse of rapid growth and crowding be offered for the slums that disgrace America's otherwise modern cities.

War has changed all this. The thirties were the decade of depression, but the 1940's bid fair to repeat the twenties as a decade of concentration. Again heavy industry booms and to Detroit is added Norfolk. At the close of war the cycle may repeat itself and dispersion begin anew.

Then, with declining births and decreasing migration, our cities will probably need to build fewer schoolhouses in the future. Thus it may be that we can devote more of our funds and attention to the improvement of the process that goes on within these buildings. Along with this, cities should now take on a more attractive appearance and attempt the development of institutions devoted to the fine arts and intellectual interests of their mature and settled population. Even moderate-sized cities can hope to afford a municipal auditorium which will serve as the home of a local symphony orchestra, a little theater group, a museum, and many varied municipal exhibits and gatherings. Our cities are coming of age and there will be less excuse in the future for the low standards of taste and the low grade of municipal government which some of them have exhibited.[1]

[1] See "Growth of American Cities in the Last Decade," *Statistical Bulletin* (New York: Metropolitan Life Insurance Company, September, 1940).

CHAPTER 4

MALE AND FEMALE

COMPOSITION of the population is the scientific if prosaic term used to designate the interesting division of society into two sexes and many age groupings. Of all the distinctions between humankind, none exceeds this in importance to the individuals concerned. Demographers take an equal, if more scientific, interest. The individual is born into a sex group and from infancy grows through various age groupings. For the individual, these conditions of age and sex set up involuntary groupings to which under the rule of biology and culture are adjusted his routines and functions, habits and personality. Any imbalance or changes in age and sex ratios will affect both the reproductive and economic functions of a society.

The regional analysis of these ratios helps to estimate the effect of past events and point the trend of future ones. The sex ratio of a population for example is but little affected by normal changes in birth or death rates, so that any excess of females in a region usually measures the amount of emigration or the effect of war. While changes in age composition are also affected by war and migration, they can be traced to the effect of a falling birth rate and an increasing life expectancy. Future changes in age groups always grow out of the present distribution. In this way, the composition of the population throws important light on such diverse topics as the task of child welfare, the economic burden of education, the number of available workers, the emergence of problems of youth, and the extent of the problem of old age security.

SEX RATIOS

Sex has been called "the most fundamental cleavage in society,"[1] creating "involuntary groups"[2] into which individuals are born, willy-nilly. This cleavage decrees for women, along with the biologically determined function of childbearing, many associated functions which are culturally

[1] C. H. Cooley, R. C. Angell, and L. J. Carr, *Introductory Sociology* (New York: Scribner's, 1933), p. 219.
[2] H. P. Fairchild, *General Sociology* (New York: Wiley, 1934), p. 4.

determined. Here exists what might be called a distinctly feminine culture, predominantly of a primary group nature,[3] centered on mating, child care, and homemaking. These functions afford occupations and patterns of life more nearly similar for womankind than are the varied means of gainful employment for the corresponding age groups of men.

We may begin our study by the analysis of regional variations in the ratio between the sexes, leaving the discussion of age composition for a later chapter. How evenly are the sexes distributed throughout the country? Thirty-two States mainly western and agrarian, as Figure 25 shows, had more males than females in their population in 1940. This condition, represented in the sex ratio by a percentage higher than unity, reached 125.4 in Nevada. Fifteen States, mainly southern but including five urban States had an excess of females, reaching a sex ratio of 95 in Massachusetts. An equal sex ratio, one male for every female, represented in statistics by 100, was attained in 1940 by only one State, Pennsylvania.

FIGURE 25. THE SEX RATIO IN THE TOTAL POPULATION, UNITED STATES, 1940

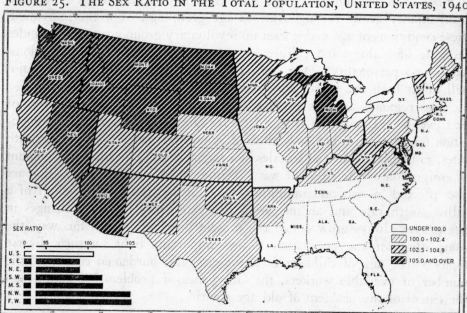

Source: *Sixteenth Census of the United States, 1940*, Preliminary Release, Series P-10, No. 14.

The simplest explanation of extreme dislocation in the sex ratio is migration. Foreign immigration to the United States has always selected more males than females. As Figure 25 indicates, this pattern has predominated in the westward migration of our own population. Urban migration on the contrary (Figure 26) has selected females so that in our

[3] Cooley, Angell, and Carr, *op. cit.*, p. 220.

FIGURE 26. THE SEX RATIO IN THE URBAN POPULATION, UNITED STATES, 1940

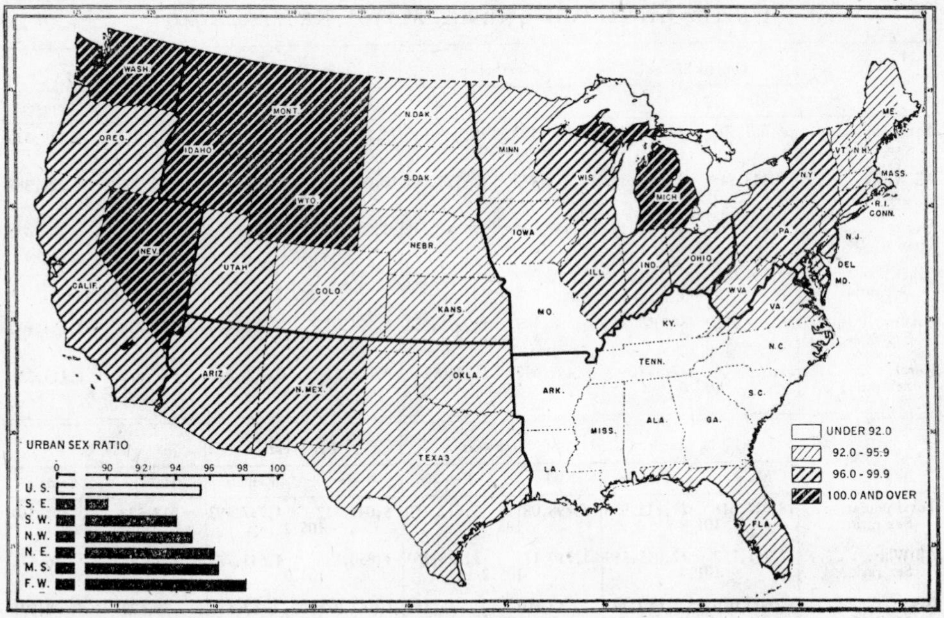

Source: *The Sixteenth Census of the United States,* Preliminary Release, Series P-6.

urban population only six States, all western except Michigan, have a sex ratio of over 100. Lowest of all in the number of males are the urban areas of the Southeast where five States had a sex ratio below 90.

A glance at the sex ratio by regions (Table 9) and by rural-urban groups indicates that in 1940 the most urban region, the Northeast, and the most rural, the Southeast, had the lowest sex ratios, 99. The regions of the West show the greatest male predominance, exceeding 105 in the Northwest and Far West. A low sex ratio, it may be pointed out, is found in older settled regions and in cities. The familiar excess of women over men in the urban environment is found for all regions, with the Southeast showing the lowest sex ratio, 90.1, and the Far West the highest, 98.2. For every region the rural population shows an excess of males. This is highest in the western areas and lowest again in the two eastern regions. The village and suburban population classified as rural non-farm shows, except for the Far West, the most evenly balanced sex ratios of any community, bettering in several regions the balance attained by the total sex ratio. The Negro has the lowest sex ratio in all regions. All other colored races show the familiar predominance of males among their recent migrants.

Differences in sex ratio, as Table 9 indicates, are racial as well as regional. For the foreign-born the masculine sex ratio is explained by the

TABLE 9. SEX COMPOSITION OF POPULATION, BY RACE AND RESIDENCE, UNITED STATES AND THE SIX MAJOR REGIONS, 1940

	United States		Northeast		Southeast		Southwest	
	Male	Female	Male	Female	Male	Female	Male	Female
Total population .	66,061,592	65,607,683	19,883,405	20,083,095	14,056,436	14,205,393	4,933,011	4,849,326
Sex ratio......	100.7		99.0		99.0		101.7	
All White........	59,448,548	58,766,322	18,971,272	19,128,607	10,060,711	9,998,657	4,305,992	4,204,885
Sex ratio......	101.2		99.2		100.6		102.4	
Negro...........	6,269,038	6,596,480	882,104	943,332	3,977,757	4,190,795	545,284	567,621
Sex ratio......	95.0		93.5		94.9		96.1	
Other Races......	344,006	244,881	30,029	11,156	17,968	15,941	81,735	76,820
Sex ratio.....	140.5		269.2		112.7		106.4	
Urban...........	36,363,706	38,059,996	14,385,308	14,936,852	4,304,919	4,777,346	2,007,334	2,134,100
Sex ratio......	95.5		96.3		90.1		94.1	
Rural...........	29,697,886	27,547,687	5,498,097	5,146,243	9,751,517	9,428,047	2,925,677	2,715,226
Sex ratio......	107.8		106.8		103.4		107.8	

	Middle States		Northwest		Far West		D. C.	
	Male	Female	Male	Female	Male	Female	Male	Female
Total poulation...	18,027,616	17,713,958	3,798,085	3,612,350	5,045,517	4,797,992	317,522	395,569
Sex ratio......	101.8		105.1		105.2			
All White........	17,341,752	17,015,559	3,710,175	3,528,263	4,830,898	4,643,773	227,748	246,578
Sex ratio......	101.9		105.2		104.0			
Negro...........	660,036	680,298	47,907	48,159	67,278	67,681	88,672	98,594
Sex ratio......	97.0		99.5		99.4			
Other Races......	25,828	18,101	70,003	35,928	147,341	86,538	1,102	397
Sex ratio.....	142.7		111.3		170.3			
Urban...........	10,747,969	11,131,415	1,430,165	1,506,003	3,170,489	3,228,711	317,522	345,569
Sex ratio......	96.6		95.0		98.2			
Rural...........	7,279,647	6,582,543	2,367,920	2,106,347	1,875,028	1,569,281		
Sex ratio......	110.6		112.4		119.5			

Source: *Sixteenth Census of the United States, 1940,* Series P-10, No. 14; P-6, State Summaries.

selective factor in migration. The Negro in the United States has had an excess of females, a factor which helps to account for the position of the Southeast. For the region the white sex ratio is 100.6; the colored, 94.9. This phenomenon deserves further analysis for it helps to shed light on the whole phenomena of an unbalanced sex ratio.

FACTORS DETERMINING SEX COMPOSITION

The most important factors causing differences in the sex ratio of populations are (1) the sex ratio at birth which, although not constant, is consistently in favor of males; (2) age-specific differences in mortality by sex, which, while showing considerable fluctuations for different periods and areas, remain on the whole in favor of females; (3) sex differences in net migration, which so far have always been in favor of males for the United States as a whole, although cities attract more females than males; (4) composition of population by age, due to the fact that a "young" population or one with a rising birth rate will tend to increase its sex ratio, while an "aging" population will suffer a decrease in the sex ratio, since, barring migration, the combined effect of the birth ratio in favor of males and mortality rates in favor of females will always mean more males than females among the young and more females than males among the aged; (5) the stillbirth rate of the population. Since the latter is much higher for males than for females, a high stillbirth rate will mean more males than females dead before they are born and therefore will depress the sex ratio at birth. Thus five factors are listed, the last one influencing the sex ratio indirectly by affecting the sex ratio at birth.

The first two lines of Table 10 show the sex ratio of the populations of the Nation and the Southeast for 1930 and 1940. Here it is obvious in both periods that the ratio for "all white" is much higher than for the Negroes. Moreover, the sex ratio for both areas and races decreased from 1930 to 1940. How shall we explain these differences? Let us begin with the difference between the races. The first factor listed as contributing to differences in sex ratio was the sex ratio at birth. Comparing these ratios in 1930 for both areas (Table 10, line 5), we notice a very considerable difference: the sex ratio at birth for whites is about 106, while it is only 103 for Negroes. This difference is evidently one of the causes of a lower sex ratio for the Negro population.

TABLE 10. SEX RATIOS FOR SELECTED VITAL STATISTICS, UNITED STATES AND SOUTHEAST, 1930 AND 1940

Sex ratio and year	United States			Southeast		
	All	White	Negro	All	White	Negro
1940						
Population......................	100.7	101.2	95.0	99.0	100.6	94.9
1930						
Population......................	102.5	102.9	97.0	99.6	101.3	95.2
1929-31						
Life-Table Population (Equal number of births for each sex)........	.....	94.3	96.1	.....	95.1	95.8
Life-Table Population (Actual number of births for each sex)........	.....	99.9	99.1	.....	101.0	98.8
1930						
Births...........................	105.6	105.9	103.2	105.2	106.2	103.1
Stillbirths.......................	133.3	133.1	134.1	136.2	137.9	134.6
Births and stillbirths..............	106.5	106.7	105.2	106.5	107.1	105.3

Note: The white population in the United States as a whole in 1930 has been corrected to include Mexicans, since such definition was adopted in 1940; the number of whites in the Southeast has been left as reported in 1930 because the negligible number of Mexicans residing in the Southeast could not affect the sex ratio. The Bureau of Vital Statistics tabulated Mexicans with colored in 1930.

Source: *Sixteenth Census of the United States, 1940*, preliminary releases Series P-10, Nos. 6, 14; Series P-6; *Fifteenth Census of the United States, 1930*, Population, II, Chap. 10, Table 24; *Birth, Stillbirth and Infant Mortality Statistics, 1930*, Tables 2, 11; Bureau of the Census, *United States Life Tables, 1930;* all sources used for the computation of Life Tables for the Southeast, 1929-1931.

The question naturally arises: Is this variation in the sex ratio at birth due to biological differences? While this problem is outside the scope of our study, still we can be reasonably sure of a negative answer, since the reported stillbirth rate accounts for most of the difference. Table 10, line 6, shows that the sex ratio in stillbirths is about 134 for both races, that is, that many more males than females are lost between the fetal age of 7 months and birth. Since the stillbirth rate for Negroes is at least double that for whites,[4] the loss of males during prenatal life influences the sex ratio at birth for Negroes much more than for whites. This is evident from our computation on line 7 of Table 10. When we add stillbirths to births and compute their ratio by sex, we see that the new ratio (based on the assumption of all stillborn babies being born alive) rises less than one point for whites but at least two points for Negroes (compare ratios on lines 7 and 5). If we could evaluate the loss of males through abortions and miscarriages and through all the unregistered stillbirths, it is very likely that all the difference between the birth rate ratios by race could be accounted for. Thus, we have found that the high stillbirth rate of the Negroes lowers their sex ratio at birth and therefore is one of the causes of the excess of females in their population.

Next, let us consider the influence that sex difference in mortality has on the sex ratio by race. To isolate the influence of this factor from the disturbing effect of all others, we take the sex ratio for the life table population computed on the basis of an equal number of births for males and females (Table 10, line 3). The sex ratios for the populations thus obtained depend only on sex differences in mortality rates existing for the period covered by the life table (1929-31). It is evident that the sex ratio should be below 100, since the life expectation for males is consistently lower than for females; we generally find it to be near 95. However, the sex ratio for the Negro life table is a little higher than for the white; this means that there is less difference in mortality (and consequently, in life expectation) by sex for Negroes than for whites. Table 11, giving age-specific death rates and their ratios by sex, shows that, while the mortality of white males is consistently higher for all age-groups than that for white women, this is not true for the colored population. For males the infant death rate is about 30 percent higher than for females in both groups. But for the colored age-group from 15 to 24, the death rates for both sexes become equal, due partly to the heavy loss of Negro women through maternal mortality. Comparing ratios among the older age groups, we see that the mortality of white men of working age is nearly 50 percent higher than that of white women. The difference is much less between the colored sexes, since in our culture Negro women work harder and are less protected than white women. Our first conclusion, then, is that the difference in infant death rates by sex is the chief factor in mortality that serves to lower the sex ratio of the Negro population, while, for whites, the difference in mortality between sexes depends on differences for all ages and is,

[4] In 1940, it was 27.6 for whites and 58.1 for Negroes in the United States (*Vital Statistics—Special Reports*, Vol. 15, No. 3).

TABLE 11. AGE-SPECIFIC DEATH RATES BY SEX WITH RATIO OF
MALE TO FEMALE RATES, UNITED STATES, 1940

	White age-specific death rates			Non-white age-specific death rates		
	Male	Female	Ratio	Male	Female	Ratio
All ages..............	11.6	9.2	126.1	15.1	12.6	119.8
Under 1..............	56.7	43.6	130.0	101.2	77.4	130.7
1 - 4.................	2.8	2.4	116.7	5.3	4.4	120.4
5 - 14................	1.1	0.8	137.5	1.6	1.4	114.3
15 - 24...............	2.0	1.4	142.9	5.0	5.0	100.0
25 - 34...............	2.8	2.2	127.3	8.5	7.4	114.9
35 - 44...............	5.1	3.7	137.8	13.2	11.7	112.8
45 - 54...............	11.4	7.5	152.0	24.5	21.1	116.1
55 - 64...............	25.2	16.8	150.0	39.5	35.7	110.6
65 - 74...............	54.0	41.5	130.1	56.5	46.3	122.0
75 - 84...............	122.2	105.6	115.7	109.7	84.7	129.5
85 and over...........	249.3	224.7	110.9	193.2	156.2	123.7

Source: *Vital Statistics—Special Reports*, 14, No. 55.

therefore, an even more potent factor in decreasing the sex ratio than it is for Negroes.

Now let us see whether the two factors analyzed so far are sufficient to explain the actual sex ratio of the population. In order to combine the effect of the two factors (sex ratio at birth and sex differences in mortality) and to eliminate the effect of all others, we can weight the number of males and females in the life table population by the proportion of births by sex in the actual population. This is the procedure used when combining the life tables for the two sexes into one table for the total population. The result is a sex ratio which is still too low for the white population and too high for the Negro (Table 10, line 4). This means that for the white population there must be another important factor which tends to increase the sex ratio. This is certainly our third factor—the sex ratio of immigrants to the United States. One could trace the influence of this factor for the Nation as a whole by studying the net migration to the United States by sex. It is simpler, however, to isolate the effect of this factor by computing sex ratios for the native white and the foreign-born whites as was done in Table 12. We find that sex ratios for the foreign-born are very high for the Nation and especially for the Southeast, while sex ratios of native whites are much lower and very similar for both areas. Since the percentage foreign-born are of all whites is much lower for the Southeast, their high sex ratio fails to increase the total sex ratio for all whites in the Southeast as it does for the Nation, thus explaining the difference in sex ratio for all whites in both areas (Table 10, line 1).

For Negroes, the migration factor is negligible. The fact that the sex ratio of the actual Negro population is lower than can be expected on the basis of present birth rates and mortality rates alone is due to the fact that the sex ratio reflects not only the present conditions but experience during the whole life-span of the population. This would mean, then, that the

TABLE 12. SEX COMPOSITION OF THE POPULATION BY RESIDENCE AND
NATIVITY, UNITED STATES AND SOUTHEAST, 1930 AND 1940

Characteristic and year	United States			Southeast		
	Male	Female	Ratio	Male	Female	Ratio
1940						
Urban...............	36,363,706	38,059,996	95.5	4,304,919	4,777,346	90.1
Rural...............	29,697,886	27,547,687	107.8	9,751,517	9,428,047	103.4
1930						
Urban...............	34,154,760	34,800,063	98.1	3,638,826	3,978,005	91.5
Rural...............	27,982,320	25,837,903	108.3	9,112,956	8,821,111	103.3
1940						
Native white........	53,437,533	53,358,199	100.1	9,950,327	9,910,456	100.4
Foreign-born white....	6,011,015	5,408,123	111.1	110,384	88,201	125.2
1930						
Native white..........	48,420,037	47,883,298	101.1	8,818,199	8,707,457	101.3
Foreign-born white....	7,502,491	6,480,914	115.8	121,978	91,618	133.2

Note: The population by nativity for the United States as a whole in 1930 has been corrected to include Mexicans as whites, since such definition was adopted in 1940. The number of whites in the Southeast has been left as reported in the Census; however, the number of Mexicans residing in the Southeast is too small to affect computed sex ratios.
Source: *Sixteenth Census of the United States, 1940*, Preliminary release, Series P-10, Nos. 6, 14; Series P-6, State Summaries; *Fifteenth Census of the United States, 1930*, Population, II, Chap. 10, Tables 24, 31.

two most important factors which contribute to the lowering of the Negro sex ratio, the stillbirth rate and infant mortality, must have had even larger effect in past decades. This is in perfect agreement with the known facts, since both the stillbirth and infant mortality rates for Negroes were higher in 1930 than in 1940 and higher again in 1920 than in 1930.

To sum up, we have shown that the low sex ratio of the Negroes can be explained by (1) the effect of a high stillbirth rate which serves to lower the sex ratio at birth, and (2) by higher mortality rates among males as compared with females, especially for infants. Moreover, these two factors have been even more effective in the past decades. The higher sex ratio for whites is due to a higher sex ratio at birth and especially to the preponderance of males among immigrants to the United States. Since this factor loses its importance at the present time with the sharp decline of foreign-born population, we may expect a rapid drop in the sex ratio of all the white population of the Nation.

Finally, we have to explain the fact that for all classes the sex ratio was lower in 1940 than in 1930. We have already seen that for the whites, one of the contributing factors is the rapid decline in immigration and, consequently, in the foreign-born population. Another important factor effective for Negroes as well as whites is the change in the age composition of the population (our fourth factor listed above). The decrease in birth rates together with a general increase in life expectation causes the rapid "aging" of the American population; this lowers the number of males by reducing the population of younger ages where they are predominant, and increases the number of females who are predominant among older people.

Thus, we see that an aging population tends to become more feminine, while a younger population tends to be more masculine. We also see that the higher life expectation of the female is not entirely due to the fact that she is better protected in her home against the strain and competition of the outside world and spared from some of the particularly dangerous occupations of males. Since the wastage of male life by stillbirth and infant death is especially high, it seems probable that the really frail sex is the male, while nature protects the future child-bearer by endowing her with greater vitality and resistance to disease.

The causes of disproportionate sex ratios are mainly economic and are brought about by different rates of international and internal migration. The one exception is found in the differential effect of mortality on males and females at various ages. Here the greatest difference is found in the incidence of male stillbirths among Negroes. The major effect of abnormal sex ratios are found in marriage and reproduction. To understand these effects we must carry further our discussion of age composition and the factors affecting fertility.

CHAPTER 5

THE YOUNG, THE OLD, AND THE MATURE

THE BASIC importance of sex and age differences may be sought in their relation to economics and fertility, production and reproduction—the major economic and biological functions performed by individuals in society. Military service is a third function definitely circumscribed by sex and age qualifications, as is citizenship and the privilege of voting.

The most important age grouping in any society is that delimited by the period of maturity and vigor. Reproduction by the very nature of biological structure falls most heavily on women aged 15-49, an age range that is further restricted by cultural considerations as in the age of marriage. In nation and family the task of economic support, partially, because of cultural considerations, falls most heavily on males, and here the age range is very elastic indeed.

Certain age groups, the very young and the very old, are to be regarded as society's natural dependents. The definition of youth and age in terms of natural dependents must vary with the degree of economic and cultural complexity of the society. Normally in the United States we are coming to consider the natural dependents as those below ages 15 to 20 and those above age 65. In our society these groups are supported, in the main, either in the family by those in the productive ages, 20 to 65, or by the State in terms of social insurance or relief. The main exception is offered by those of older ages who have investments and savings and are thus able to provide for themselves.

It is difficult to set up age limits for a maturity group that will include both the functions of production and reproduction in modern society. In his population groupings Sundbärg, the Swedish demographer, delimited maturity by the ages 15 to 49, a grouping that comes nearer to fitting the biological conditions of reproduction than the economic and cultural functions of mature populations in modern society. Sundbärg concluded that in populations unaffected by migration this mature group made up approxi-

[48]

mately 50 percent of the total. With some allowance for the effects of
varying life expectancy and differing age of marriage, we may use his
classifications of populations into three types: progressive, stationary, and
retrogressive, on the basis of varying proportions in the pre-maturity and
post-maturity groups. Table 13, showing the estimated limits of his classification, has suggestive value for our culture.

TABLE 13. POPULATION TYPES ACCORDING TO SUNDBÄRG'S
CLASSIFICATION OF AGE GROUPS

Age group year	Progressive type	Stationary type	Retrogressive type	Age group year	Progressive type	Stationary type	Retrogressive type
TOTAL...........	100.0	100.0	100.0	15 - 49.........	50.0	50.0	50.0
				50 - up..........	10.0	17.0	30.0
0 - 14..........	40.0	33.0	20.0				

Table 14 shows that in the Nation well over half of the population,
54.6 percent, is in the mature group, one-fourth in the pre-maturity group
and one-fifth in the post-maturity group. America's large proportions in
the productive ages indicate that the effect of foreign immigration is still
felt on our age composition. This effect is reenforced by both rural-urban
and westward migration, giving our industrial and Western States the
largest proportions of mature people. Thus the Northeast leads with 55.9
percent followed by the Far West with 55.5 percent. Every State with
more than 55.0 percent in the mature group, as Figure 27 shows, is either
western or highly industrial with the exception of Florida. New York,
appropriately enough, has the highest percentage, 57.5, in this group, while
only Maine and Vermont have less than 50 percent. All States that lose
migration fall in the lower groups but the Northwest with its Dust-Bowl
exodus showed the smallest proportion of mature people, 52.2.

Among the regions the contrast is between the Far West as nearer a
regressive population and the Southeast as furthest from a stationary popu-

TABLE 14. NUMBER AND PERCENTAGE DISTRIBUTION OF POPULATION BY
MATURITY, PRE-MATURITY AND POST-MATURITY AGE GROUPS,
UNITED STATES AND THE SIX MAJOR REGIONS, 1940

	All ages		0-14		15-49		50 and over	
	Number	Percent	Number	Percent	Number	Percent	Number	Percent
UNITED STATES...........	131,669,275	100.0	32,972,081	25.0	71,848,829	54.6	26,848,365	20.4
Northeast................	40,629,591	100.0	9,144,212	22.5	22,723,155	55.9	8,762,224	21.6
Southeast................	28,261,829	100.0	8,656,747	30.6	15,072,079	53.3	4,533,003	16.0
Southwest................	9,782,337	100.0	2,816,976	28.8	5,328,953	54.5	1,636,408	16.7
Middle States............	35,741,574	100.0	8,404,441	23.5	19,392,209	54.3	7,944,924	22.2
Northwest................	7,410,435	100.0	1,959,731	26.5	3,870,715	52.2	1,579,989	21.3
Far West.................	9,843,509	100.0	1,989,974	20.2	5,461,718	55.5	2,391,817	24.3

Source: *Sixteenth Census of the United States, 1940*, Series P-6, State Summaries.

FIGURE 27. PERCENTAGE OF THE POPULATION IN THE MATURE AGE
GROUP, 15-49, UNITED STATES, 1940

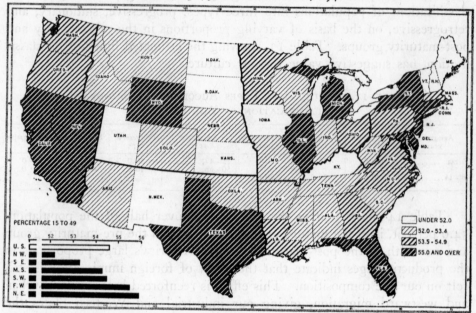

Source: *Sixteenth Census of the United States, 1940,* State Summaries, Series P-6.

FIGURE 28. PERCENTAGE OF THE POPULATION IN THE PRE-MATURITY AGE
GROUP, 0-14, UNITED STATES, 1940

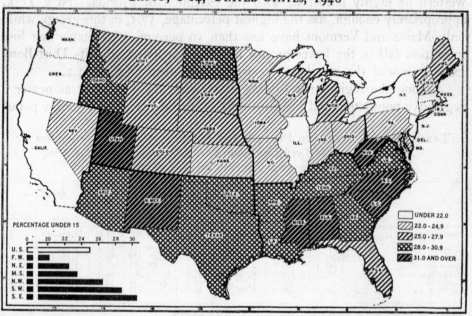

Source: See Figure 27.

FIGURE 29. PERCENTAGE OF THE POPULATION IN THE POST-MATURITY AGE
GROUP, 50 AND OVER, UNITED STATES, 1940

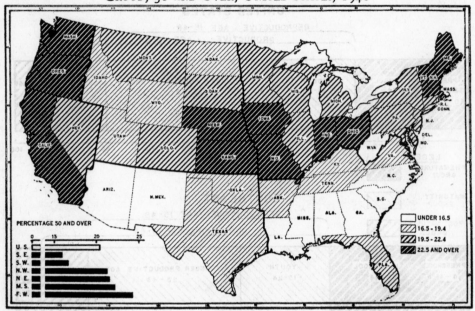

Source: See Figure 27.

lation. Judged by the proportion of children 0-14 in Figure 28, New
Mexico with 34.5 percent is the youngest State and California with only
19.8 percent is the oldest. Judged by the proportion 50 and over in
Figure 29, New Mexico with 13.4 percent is again one of the youngest
and New Hampshire with 25.3 percent the oldest.

If we are to relate age composition to the actual tasks of our society
this division of the people must be further broken down. Here we are
concerned, as Figure 30 shows, with certain transitional groups, especially
those entering and leaving the mature phase. Youth, older workers, and
children present special problems.

The task of child care and welfare is concerned with those natural
dependents aged 0-14, but we can distinguish between a childhood which
lasts until 5 and older children aged 5-14 who normally spend almost
three-fourths of each year in the care of the schools. The number of
children under 5 are discussed in the chapter on fertility, where they are
related to the regional proportions of women of childbearing age.

The distribution of children age 5-14 gives some measure of the "educational load" of our States and regions. In the Southeast (Figure 30)
children of this age make up 20.7 percent of the total population as compared with 17 percent in the Nation. The States of the Union show wide
differences in the prominence of this group (Figure 31), varying from
California with 13.2 percent to South Carolina with 22.7 percent, aged

FIGURE 30. PERCENTAGE OF THE POPULATION IN THE MAIN AGE GROUPS,
UNITED STATES AND SOUTHEAST, 1940

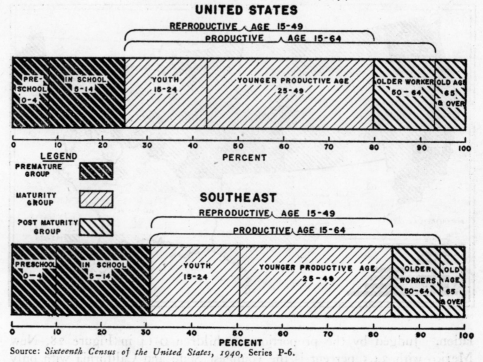

Source: *Sixteenth Census of the United States, 1940*, Series P-6.

FIGURE 31. PERCENTAGE OF THE POPULATION OF ELEMENTARY
SCHOOL AGE, 5-14, UNITED STATES, 1940

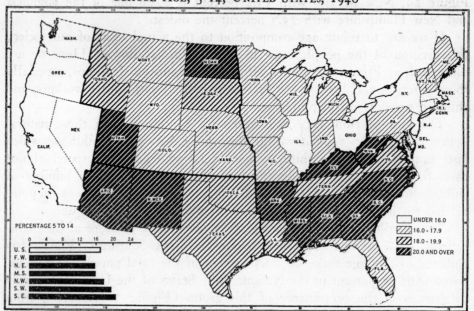

Source: See Figure 27.

5-14. The map demonstrates the familiar truth that regions of greatest economic ability, the Far West, Northeast, and Middle States, have the smallest proportions of children of school age to total population. Regions with least resources from which to support education, the Southwest, Northwest, and Southeast, have the largest proportions of school children. This condition will be discussed in succeeding chapters on the education of the people.

THE YOUTH GROUP, 15-24

In the age period 15-24 children make the transition from natural dependents to potential and actual human resources. For most people in our culture formal education in the school ceases in the transitional period of youth, self-support begins, migration from the paternal roof and the home community takes place, marriages are consummated, and separate homes and families set up. The State recognizes the new status of this population group, for it is here that legal responsibility for personal acts must be accepted, the function of citizenship is exercised, and in time of crisis military service may be exacted of the newly maturing male.

The 1940 Census showed that youth aged 15-19, with over 12.3 millions, comprised the most numerous 5-year age group in the population. The group 20-24, numbering over 11.5 millions, were the third most numerous. Together they constituted 18.2 percent of our population. In the Southeast, however, youth made up 19.9 percent of the population, reaching 22 percent in South Carolina. Figure 32 shows that the lowest proportion of youth is found in the Far West with 16.4 percent. California, land of glamorous youth, ranked the lowest of all the States with 16.2 percent. Almost 80 percent of all youth, Table 15, were found in the three eastern regions, leaving only 20.1 percent in the western areas.

TABLE 15. NUMBER AND PERCENTAGE DISTRIBUTION OF YOUTH, 15-24 YEARS OF AGE, UNITED STATES AND THE SIX MAJOR REGIONS, 1940

Area	Number	Percent	Area	Number	Percent
UNITED STATES	23,921,358	100.0	Southwest	1,838,076	7.7
			Middle States	6,253,848	26.1
Northeast	7,255,188	30.3	Northwest	1,345,689	5.6
Southeast	5,612,641	23.5	Far West	1,615,916	6.8

Source: *Sixteenth Census of the United States, 1940*, Series P-6, State Summaries.

Whether youth ends at 20 or at 25 depends largely on distinctions of class, education, and occupation. For those in the upper economic brackets and those aspiring to the professions, dependency and education continue beyond the teens. Farmers and less-skilled industrial groups leave school earlier, marry at earlier ages, and thus take on the responsibilities of maturity. This represents the situation in the South where the pre-

FIGURE 32. PERCENTAGE OF THE POPULATION IN THE YOUTH GROUP,
15-24, UNITED STATES, 1940

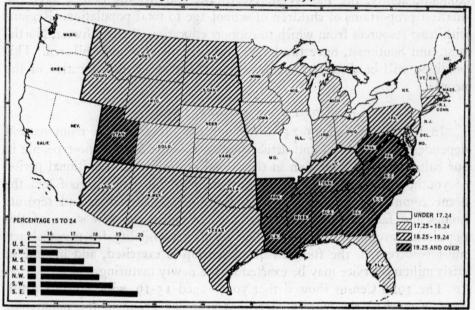

Source: See Figure 27.

ponderant youth group leaves school to go into occupations requiring less
training. It is not easy, however, for youth, trained or untrained, to gain a
foothold in the labor market, and unemployment, as Chapter 21 demonstrates, is greatest among this group. In times of war young men 18-24
make the hardiest soldiers and it is on that group that the casualties of war
fall the heaviest. It is noteworthy that the South in the 1940's led all
areas in voluntary enlistment in the armed services, reflecting to some extent
the lack of economic adjustment.

THE AGED

The aged, too, have their transitional group which in our analysis may
serve to span the period between maturity ending at 50 and the legal age
for old age security at 65. In relation to economic function this period
serves to delimit the problem of the older workers, although some have
pointed out the special hazards to workers after 40, especially women
workers. In biological functions, this general period which closes the
chapter on fertility for females and finds males with failing powers is not
less transitional than adolescence. Here, however, peculiar problems of
the aging had best be left to the columns for the lovelorn and the medical
textbooks. We can, however, determine the location and economic significance of this group.

FIGURE 33. PERCENTAGE OF THE POPULATION IN THE OLDER PRODUCTIVE
AGES, 50-64, UNITED STATES, 1940

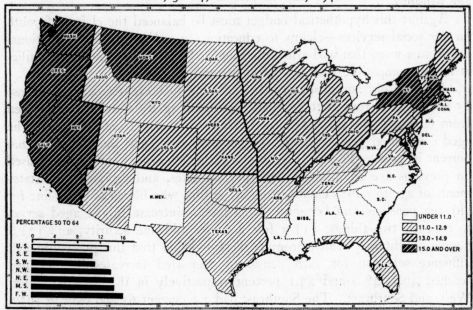

Source: See Figure 27.

Over 17.8 million or 13.5 percent of the Nation's population were reported in this category of older workers in 1940 (Figure 33). Largest proportions were found in the Far West where 16.2 percent of the population was reported aged 50-64, followed by the Middle States and the Northeast with 14.6 and 14.5 percent respectively. The extremely low rates of the Southeast and Southwest, with 10.7 and 11.2 percent, would be accounted for by migration and the lower life expectations of Negroes were it not for the exaggerated reporting of ages over 65 to be discussed presently. Less than half of this transitional group are males but the economic problem is not insistent. Of the 17.8 millions aged 50-64, 6 millions are found in the Northeast, 5.2 millions in the Middle States, and 3 millions in the Southeast.

Changes in age composition grow out of two fundamental population trends—the falling birth rate and the increase in life expectancy. Both of these tendencies in our time are leading to a progressive aging of the population. In terms of our analysis of maturity they tend to set the problems of old age and of youth in juxtaposition. By 1980 it is estimated that those 65 years and over will have increased from 9.0 millions in 1940 to 22 millions. In the same period those aged 20-64 will have increased from 73 to over 91.6 millions. If all those over 65 received cash benefits raised by direct taxation, the average tax on each man and woman in the productive ages would be $24 for every $100 paid in old age pensions.

Against this hypothetical budget must be balanced the claims of youth on our social services—claims to education, to a place in the occupational order, to a wage that will allow marriage and the establishment of families at an age compatible with biological maturity.

The real old age problem is thus coming to be centered around those 65 and over. From 1930 to 1940 population aged 65 and over increased from 6,642,053 to 9,019,314, an increase of 35.8 percent. Whereas the aged constituted 5.4 percent of the population in 1930 they made up 6.9 percent in 1940. This increase was in excess of normal expectations based on previous age composition and survival rates, and represents misstatements of age to census enumerators by persons who hoped to be in line for old age pensions and benefits. This pseudo-increase in the aged serves to measure two things: (1) a felt need for old age security, and (2) a degree of illiteracy which prompts the conviction that this procedure will influence selection for such pensions. Reported increases in the aged reached 49.1, 48.0 and 43.1 percent respectively in the Southwest, Far West, and Southeast. The Southeast had 4.2 percent 65 and over in 1930. It was expected on the best estimates to have 4.8 percent in 1940 but reported 5.4 percent over 65. Figure 34 shows the range of increase in

FIGURE 34. PERCENTAGE CHANGE IN THE POPULATION 65 AND OVER, UNITED STATES, 1930-1940

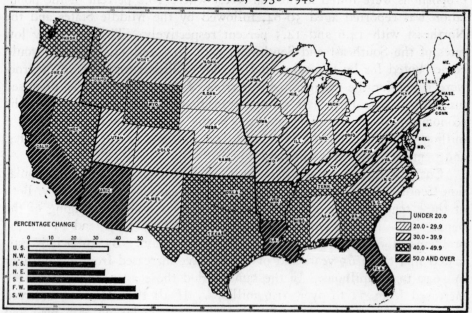

Source: See Figure 27.

those reported 65 and over by States. In Florida the aged increased 84.3 percent but migration statistics would lead us to believe that a majority of this increase was genuine. The number over 65 in Vermont declined by 12.6 percent, although the proportion increased from 8.7 to 9.6.

Figure 35 indicates that the reported incidence of old age ranged from 4.2 percent in South Carolina to 9.9 percent in New Hampshire. The oldest States in this respect are found in New England where some reported 9.5 to 9.9 percent of their people over 65. The authentic home of those who looked for "Ham and Eggs" and "Thirty Dollars Every Thursday" was the Far West with 8.1 percent. Next came the Middle States with 7.7. The southern regions, least able to shoulder the public burden of aged dependents, fortunately have the smallest proportions of their population aged 65 and over. In the Southwest 5.5 percent of the people reported themselves as over 65; in the Southeast, 5.4 percent.

FIGURE 35. PERCENTAGE OF THE POPULATION IN OLD AGE GROUP,
65 AND OVER, UNITED STATES, 1940

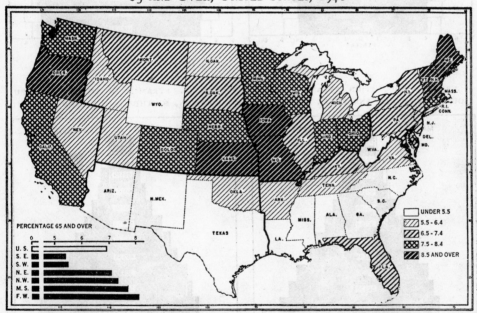

Source: See Figure 27.

THE POPULATION PYRAMID: THE TOTAL PICTURE

We have been discussing the age composition in its most important segments. In the population pyramid, however, we have a graphic device that shows the significance of sex and age composition at a glance. A study of regional trends over a forty-year period, 1890-1930, by Bernice Milburn Moore, made it plain that the divergent regions are approaching

FIGURE 36. POPULATION PYRAMIDS, UNITED STATES AND SOUTHEAST, 1940

FIGURE 37. PYRAMIDS OF THE TOTAL POPULATION OF THE SOUTHEAST, 1930 AND 1940

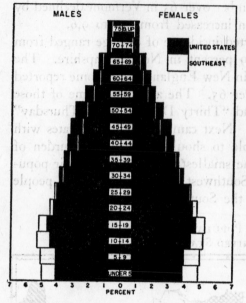

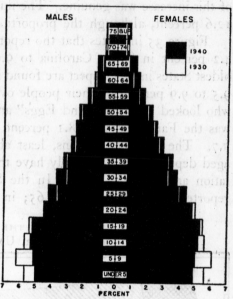

FIGURE 38. POPULATION PYRAMIDS OF THE SOUTHEAST, URBAN AND RURAL FARM, 1940

FIGURE 39. PYRAMIDS OF THE URBAN POPULATION, SOUTHEAST, 1930 AND 1940

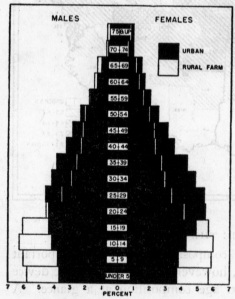

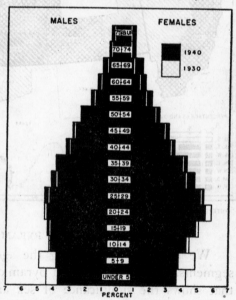

Source: See Figure 27.

a sex and age distribution nearer the national average. In western regions, the pioneer characteristics of excess males in the mature ages with deficiencies among the old and the young have given way to more balanced age and sex ratios. By the same comparison, it can be seen that the Southeast now lags some forty years behind the Nation in its age distribution. By 1930 the region had attained the pattern held by the Nation in 1890. In 1890 the Nation had 35.5 percent of its population under 15 as compared with 60.3 percent aged 15-64. By 1930 the Southeast had attained a comparable ratio of youth to age of 34.9 to 60.3, while the Nation had passed on to a ratio of 29.3 percent under 15 to 65.2 percent aged 15-64.

For our most fertile region we can observe the evolved patterns in comparison with the Nation as they existed in 1940 (Figure 36). The predominance of the South in the proportions of youth ceases at 30; thereafter, the Nation leads in the mature age-sex groupings. In Figure 37, which compares the Southeast of 1930 and 1940, we can see how the cohorts move up with the census period, decreasing the base and strengthening the body of the pyramid. The base is undercut as the decline in fertility makes itself evident by each five-year period to age 20-24.

Figure 38 makes it clear that the farms are the homes of children and youth until migration begins to drain off the girls at age 20 and boys at age 25. In Southeastern cities, as in cities everywhere, those of vigorous ages predominate. In older ages, however, more men tend to remain on farms as compared with women who seek the shelter of urban comforts. A final comparison of the urban Southeast, 1930 and 1940, (Figure 39) shows continued decline in children under 15 and some slight failure of cities to retain the proportion of youth held in 1930. In 1940 proportionately more females than males aged 30 and over were evident in cities. Implicit in these figures is the suggestion of significant changes in reproduction and migration to be discussed in later chapters.

THE BALANCE OF PRODUCERS AND CONSUMERS

The region's relation to the total national economy is made clearer when these pyramids are related to the balance of producers and consumers. In the Southeast this balance differs greatly from that obtaining in the Nation. The Southeast is a young population and the ratio of its workers to its natural dependents can be explained in terms of the relation of producing to consuming units. By assigning weights to sex and age groups based on needs of consumers and the employment ratios and comparative efficiency of producers, Ernst Gunther has designed a scale for relating the productive powers of a population to its consuming needs. Thus males aged 25-30 represent 100 in both production and consumption while females of the same age represent 50 in production. Adapting

these methods, Thompson and Whelpton have worked out the ratio of producing to consuming units in the United States from 1870 to 1980.[1]

Calculation of similar data for the Southeast in Table 16 brings out
interesting comparisons. In both the Nation and the region the decline
in births has meant that the ratio of producers to consumers has been slowly

TABLE 16. NUMBER AND RATIO OF PRODUCING TO CONSUMING UNITS IN THE
POPULATION, UNITED STATES AND SOUTHEAST, BY DECADES, 1890-1930

Year and population group	UNITED STATES			SOUTHEAST		
	Producing units (thousands)	Consuming units (thousands)	Ratio of Producing to consuming	Producing units (thousands)	Consuming units (thousands)	Ratio of Producing to consuming
1890..................	25,104	43,721	1:1.74	5,385	10,257	1:1.90
1900..................	30,754	53,058	1:1.72	6,503	12,060	1:1.85
1910..................	39,118	65,464	1:1.67	7,904	14,270	1:1.81
1920..................	44,751	75,219	1:1.68	8,834	15,727	1:1.78
1930..................	52,958	88,441	1:1.67	10,064	17,833	1:1.77
" Rural.............	21,383	37,665	1:1.76	6,669	12,277	1:1.84
Rural—Farm....	11,552	20,904	1:1.81	4,353	8,260	1:1.90
Rural—Nonfarm.	9,831	16,761	1:1.70	2,316	4,017	1:1.73
" Urban............	31,575	50,776	1:1.61	3,395	5,556	1:1.64

Source: Warren S. Thompson and P. K. Whelpton, *Population Trends in the United States*, (New York: McGraw-Hill, 1933),
Table, 45, p. 169; National Resources Committee, *Population Statistics, Urban Data*, October 1937, Table 16, p. 17; Bernice
M. Moore, Age and Sex Distribution of the People as Conditioning Factors in Cultural Participation (unpublished doctoral
dissertation, University of North Carolina, 1936).

FIGURE 40. THE ESTIMATED FUTURE
DISTRIBUTION OF MAJOR AGE GROUPS
BY RESIDENCE WITH MIGRATION AS OF
1920-1930, SOUTHEAST, 1920-1960

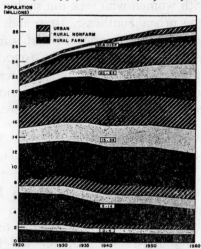

Source: Warren S. Thompson and P. K.
Whelpton, *Estimates of Future Population
by States*, National Resources Board,
December, 1934.

[1] W. S. Thompson and P. K. Whelpton, *Population Trends in the United States* (New York: Mc-
Graw-Hill, 1933), p. 169.

increasing.   In no classification, however, does the ratio of consumer to producer units on the Gunther scale fall below 1.60. Where, in 1930, the Nation had 167 consuming units for every 100 producing units in the population, the Southeast had 177.   In this slow increase in the proportion of producers to consumers, the Southeast has lagged behind the Nation failing to reach in 1930 the ratio passed by the Nation in 1890. In 1890 the Nation had 174 consuming units to every 100 producing units; by 1930 this had fallen to a ratio of 167 to 100.   In the Southeast the ratio fell from 1.90 in 1890 to 1.77 in 1930. Rural urban comparisons show the excess of young consumers in the rural Southeast.   On the Nation's farms consuming units exceeded producing units by 81 percent, on Southeastern farms by 90 percent.   The excess of consumers is lowest in cities where people in the productive phase of life congregate—61 for the Nation and 64 for the Southeast's urban population.

The Southeast thus remains the region where the potentialities and problems of youth prevail above the problems of age.   Figure 40 which shows the changes in age over two generations indicates that here as elsewhere the youth group is decreasing and old age is increasing.   The projection of 1920-1940 trends to 1960 in Figure 40 suggests that by 1960 the younger age classes 10-15 will decline while those 40-64 will increase their proportion from 22 to 28 percent.   Those over 65 should not exceed the children under five.   Youth of elementary school age will have declined from 20 to 16.5 percent.   If migration continues at the rate established in the decade, 1920-1930, greater numbers of those in the productive ages, 15-64, will be living in urban areas. Farm population will show a steady decline except for the aged.

CHAPTER 6

THE TREND OF FERTILITY

Russia being mentioned as likely to become a great empire, by the rapid increase of population: Johnson, "Why, Sir, I see no prospect of their propagating more. They can have no more children than they can get. I know of no way to make them breed more than they do. It is not from reason and providence that people marry, but from inclination. A man is poor; he thinks, 'I cannot be worse, and so I'll even take Peggy.' " Boswell, "But have not nations been more populous at one period than another?" Johnson, "Yes, Sir; but that has been owing to the people being less thinned at one period than another, whether by emigrations, war or pestilence, not by their being more or less prolific. *Births at all times bear the same proportion to the same number of people.*"—Boswell's *Life of Johnson*.

IN SPITE of Doctor Johnson, fertility in the Western World is now the variable factor while mortality, except for war, has tended to become the constant. Today only a few like Johnson's mythical Peggy and her husband have as many children as they can get. Within the sphere affected by modern medicine and sanitation, variations in births have an effect on the replacement rates of population groups five to twenty times greater than usual variations in death rates. Now that life expectancy for females at birth is over sixty years, well beyond the end of the reproductive period, births are greatly affected by mortality only for those groups in the population like the American Negro whose life expectancy in 1930 was almost thirteen years below that of the whites.

FERTILITY—THE PROBLEM IN ITS SETTING

Contrary to Doctor Johnson, this leaves birth rates influenced by more factors than deaths. The number of births in any country is affected by (1) the size of the base population, (2) the age and sex distribution of the population, and (3) the rates at which women of various ages give birth to children. This last figure, usually called the age-specific fertility rate, is calculated on the basis of births per 1,000 women of various ages grouped

[62]

at five year intervals of 15 to 19, 20 to 24, etc. When we come to consider what conditions affect the rates at which women of the different age groups bear children we have an almost unlimited choice of factors. For any population we should like to know (4) the proportions married and (5) the ages at which they marry. Next in our ideal scheme we should like to know (6) what proportions of married couples are sterile and what proportions are fecund. Here we enter an area of guesswork for no one knows the answer to this question of involuntary sterility.

Given this account of the biology of reproduction, we need some measure of the amount of conscious effort made to escape the hazards of fertility. Here we need to know (7) the extent to which women in each age group and social class resort to methods of birth control and (8) the degree to which these methods are successful. These facts will, no doubt, never be known for any great mass of the population. Birth control clinics have studied their clients, and Raymond Pearl, using the best technique yet developed, studied a large group of confinement cases in city hospitals.[1] To secure comparable knowledge of a cross section of the population that includes rural groups and is unselected either by visits to hospital delivery rooms or attendance at contraceptive clinics we may have to wait a long time.

There yet remains one link. The products of conception may be lost before full-term delivery, either by miscarriage or abortion. Accordingly (9) the degree to which pregnancy wastage reduces the birth rate should be determined in any study of fertility. Good research has been done in this field by Pearl and by the staff of the Milbank Memorial Fund. Ratios of reproductive wastage as high as 30 to 38 percent have been found among urban groups which practice contraception.[2] Here again no mass figures covering the whole population are likely to be secured.

So much for the total aspects of fertility. In its social and class aspects the biological processes leading to births give rise to all types of class differences. Clear-cut differences in reproductive behavior are found, in every Western country, in inverse relation to practically every test of social, economic, and class status that can be devised. This simply means that the higher the income, the occupational level, the social prestige of the classes, the lower their fertility rates are likely to be. In order to be prepared for the analyses which follow it may be well to list some of these variations. In the United States, where figures are admittedly incomplete, it is possible to demonstrate differences in fertility by social groups: (1) on the basis of occupation, (2) on the basis of income per family,

[1] See Raymond Pearl, *The Natural History of Population* (New York: Oxford University Press, 1939), pp. 169-248 for results, and pp. 341-355 for methods of study.
[2] *Ibid.*, pp. 68-73.

(3) by size of community from the great metropolis to the isolated farmstead, (4) on the basis of race and nativity, (5) by geographic location of major regional groups, (6) on the basis of broad educational classifications such as illiterate, primary school, high school, and college training, and (7) on the basis of religious affiliation such as Protestant, Catholic, and Jewish.

This is a country of wide contrasts in economic conditions and resources, in health and standards of living. The same studies which demonstrate class differences in fertility show that regional differences in reproductive tendency in this country are now greater than the differences between social classes and racial groups within the same community.

The Southeastern States lead the Nation in large families and high birth rates. The region's preponderance of young population, except as changed by migration, and its large numbers now entering the employable ages bear witness to the fertility of the generation just closing. Long among the highest in the Nation, fertility rates in the South now show a sharp decline. These trends can best be understood by examining regional changes against the background of national changes.

THE HISTORICAL DECLINE IN BIRTHS

In the early days of our Republic it seems clear in spite of meager statistics that the average family must have consisted of about seven or eight. Today the average size of family is between three and four. Counting the women who do not marry, those who have no children, and those who are widowed or divorced before the end of the childbearing period, it is estimated that approximately an average of 3 1/3 children per fertile family is required to keep the population stationary, neither increasing nor declining. Manifestly this is related to the birth rate, which according to our best estimates for the white population has fallen from about 55 per 1,000 in 1800 to below 20 in the 1930's (Figure 41).

In 1800 the proportion of women in the childbearing age, 20-49, was much smaller than today—33 percent according to one calculation as compared with 46 percent in 1930. This relation is shown graphically in Figure 42 where the trends are projected forward on the basis of reasonable estimates to show that some 39 percent of American women will be in that group by the year 2,000. Thus, in view of the slow-moving but inevitable decline in the proportion of the population in the reproductive ages, it is possible to show that without any decrease in the average size of families our national birth rate would greatly decline. When these age-specific fertility rates are also falling, the effect is cumulative, and the decline will occur at a more rapid rate.

FIGURE 41. ESTIMATED TREND OF WHITE BIRTH RATE, PER 1,000
POPULATION, UNITED STATES, 1800-1940

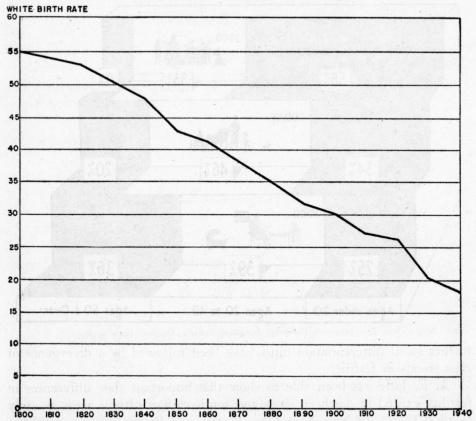

Source: Warren S. Thompson and P. K. Whelpton, *Population Trends in the United States* (New York:
McGraw-Hill, 1933), Table 74.

Historically and logically the emergence of differential fertility among
the social classes coincides with the general fall of the birth rate, as has
been demonstrated by the work of J. W. Innes, Frank W. Notestein, and
D. V. Glass for England and Wales.[3] Beginning in 1851 and fully apparent by 1880, upper, middle, and intermediate economic classes showed
the greatest decline while miners, agricultural workers, and unskilled
laborers showed the least.

Little comparable information is available for the American population
before the Milbank Memorial Fund studied fertility as of the period 1890-
1910. In an undifferentiated frontier the fertility of many families must
have been close to the biological limits. With the growth of colonial cities,
the emergence of upper classes, and the coming of slaves and immigrants,

[3] J. W. Innes, *Class Fertility Trends in England and Wales* (Princeton University Press, 1938).
Frank W. Notestein "Class Differences in Fertility," *The Annals*, American Academy of Political
and Social Science, 188 (November, 1936), pp. 26-36.

FIGURE 42. PROPORTION OF WOMEN IN CHILDBEARING AGE AND AVERAGE
SIZE OF FAMILY, UNITED STATES, 1800, 1940, AND 2000

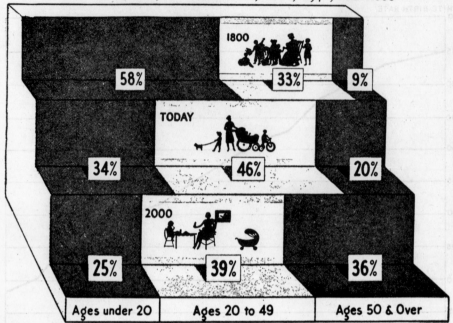

Source: Metropolitan Life Insurance Company, *Statistical Bulletin*, October, 1940, p. 6.

further social differentiation must have been followed by a divergence of class trends in fertility.

A. F. Jaffe has been able to show that important class differences in fertility existed in northern cities and southern agricultural areas as early as 1800-1820. In New York City, Boston, and Providence, wards of the largest property owners averaged gross reproductive rates only 80 to 57 percent of those having the least property. In North Carolina, Georgia, and South Carolina the white population in counties with the highest proportion of slave-ownership had fertility rates ranging from only 79 to 66 percent of the rate for counties with the lowest proportion of slaves.[4]

REGIONAL TRENDS

What of the population in the Southeast during the century long decline in fertility? This trend is indicated by maps giving the ratio of white children under 5 to 1,000 white women 15-49 from 1800 to 1930 (Figure 43). The decline in fertility which was begun in New England had accounted for a 50 percent decline in that area by 1860. The decline spread South and West with the development of urbanization and industry. The advancing frontier up to 1880 is shown to possess the highest fertility ratios.

[4] A. F. Jaffe, "Differential Fertility in the White Population in Early America," *Journal of Heredity,* XXXI (September, 1940), 407-411.

FIGURE 43. TREND IN THE NUMBER OF WHITE CHILDREN UNDER 5 PER 1000
WHITE WOMEN, 15-49, UNITED STATES, 1800-1930

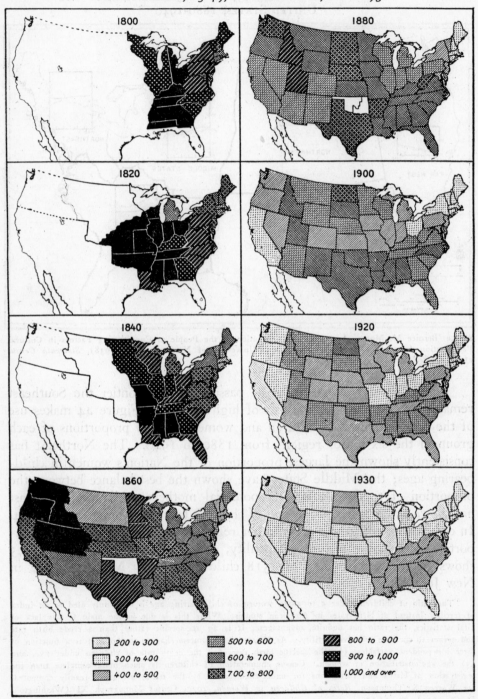

FIGURE 44. PERCENTAGE DISTRIBUTION OF CHILDREN UNDER 5 AND WOMEN
OF CHILDBEARING AGE, 15-45, SIX MAJOR REGIONS OF THE
UNITED STATES, 1880-1940

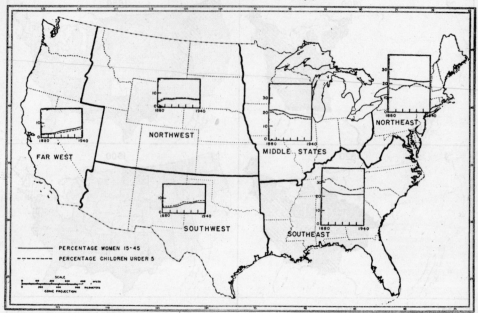

Source: Bernice M. Moore, Age and Sex Distribution of the People as Conditioning Factors in Cultural
Participation (unpublished doctoral dissertation, University of North Carolina, 1938), *Sixteenth Census
of the United States, 1940*, Series P-6, Nos. 1-49.

Figure 43 shows that with the passing of the frontier the Southeast
remained as the outstanding area of high fertility. Figure 44 makes use
of the familiar index of children and women to show proportions of each
group in the six major regions from 1880 to 1940. The Northeast has
consistently shown the largest proportion of the Nation's women in childbearing ages; the Middle States have shown the best balance between the
proportion of total children and potential mothers, while the Southeast
has shown the greatest proportion of children to 1,000 women aged 15-44.
In comparison with these areas, other regions are shown to play a less important part in the picture of fertility, actual and potential. Figure 45
shows that States ranged from 518 children in New Mexico to 242 in
New Jersey.[5]

[5] The ratio of children under 5 to 1,000 women of child-bearing age is commonly used as an index
of fertility instead of birth rates in American studies. While this is due in the main to our lack of
vital statistics, the ratio has definite advantages. It is an age-specific rather than a crude birth rate
and serves to measure effective fertility. As Warren S. Thompson has pointed out, it is a function of
three independent variables: (1) the specific birth rate, (2) the death rate of children under five, and
(3) the age distribution of women. Census enumeration of children is much more complete than the
registration of births and corrections for under-enumeration by the census are more readily computed.
See Warren S. Thompson, *Ratio of Children to Women, 1920*, Census Monograph XI (Washington,
D. C., 1931), pp. 15-17.

FIGURE 45. FERTILITY RATIO (CHILDREN UNDER 5 PER 1,000 WOMEN 15-44),
UNITED STATES, 1940

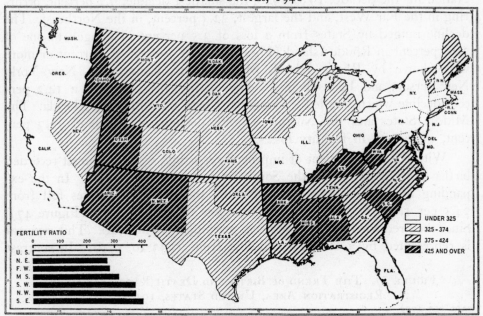

Source: *Sixteenth Census of the United States, 1940*, Series P-6, Nos. 1-49.

FIGURE 46. PERCENTAGE DECLINE IN FERTILITY RATIO,
UNITED STATES, 1930-1940

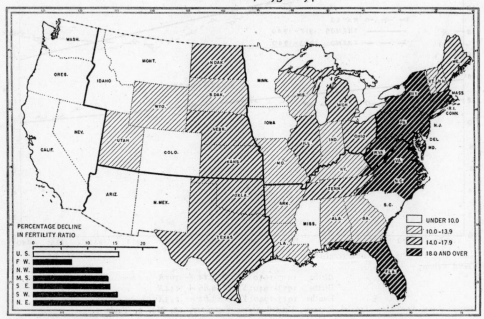

Source: See Figure 45.

In terms of this measure, total fertility declined 15.9 percent in the Nation for the decade, 1930-1940, the smallest decline, 7.2 percent, occurring in the Far West, and the largest, 22.3 percent, in the Northeast. The decline ranged by States from a loss of 3.5 percent in Oregon to one of 26.9 percent in Rhode Island (Figure 46). Losses of 20 percent or more were shown by Rhode Island, Massachusetts, Connecticut, New York, New Jersey, and Pennsylvania. The Southeast experienced a 14.2 percent decline which was led by Virginia, North Carolina, and Florida. The Middle States and the Northwest, with declines of 13.8 and 12.7 percent, come next in fertility losses.

With the development of improved reporting, we can contrast recorded births in the Nation and the Southeast from 1917 to 1940. In the expanding registration area of the Nation, the crude birth rates fell from 24.5 per 1,000 in 1917 to an all-time low of 16.6 in 1933 (Figure 47). Since then recorded births have risen, reaching 17.9 in 1940. This reversal is represented by a second trend line from 1933 to 1940. In contrast

FIGURE 47. THE TREND OF BIRTH AND DEATH RATES, EXPANDING REGISTRATION AREA, UNITED STATES, 1917-1940

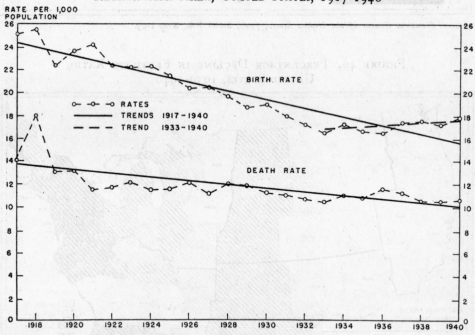

Note: Not corrected for underregistration.
Trend values:

$$\text{Births} \quad 1917\text{-}1940: Y_c = 24.15 - .367X$$
$$\text{Births} \quad 1933\text{-}1940: Y_c = 16.66 + .144X$$
$$\text{Deaths} \quad 1917\text{-}1940: Y_c = 13.62 - .153X$$

Source: *Vital Statistics—Special Reports*, United States Summary, 15, No. 2, Table 1.

FIGURE 48. THE TREND OF BIRTH AND DEATH RATES, SOUTHEAST, EXPANDING REGISTRATION AREA, 1917-1940

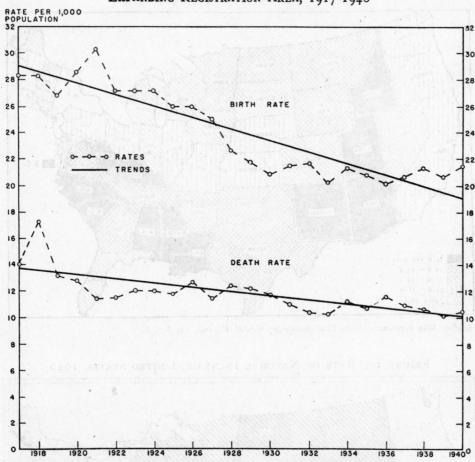

Note: Trend Values for Births: $Y_c = 29.006 - .434X$
Trend Values for Deaths: $Y_c = 13.66 - .161X$

Source: *Birth, Stillbirth, and Infant Mortality Statistics*, United States, 1917-1936; *Vital Statistics—Special Reports*, Vol. 14. State summaries, *Statistical Abstract of the United States*, 1937, Tables 6, 11.

the Southeast (Figure 48) began with a much higher birth rate, one that reaching a high point of 30.3 in 1921 fell to 20.2 in 1936, lower than the depression point in 1933. Accordingly the Southeast's second trend line 1933-1940 shows no such rise as is found in the Nation's.

In 1940 birth rates ranged all the way from 14.1 in New Jersey to as high as 27.7 in New Mexico (Figure 49). The Southeast attained the highest rates, 21.3 per 1,000 as compared with 17.9 for the Nation. Only three Southeastern States, Florida, Tennessee, and Arkansas, fell below the rate of 20.5 while only seven States outside the Southeast reached that high. Rates of natural increase ranged from 3.3 for New Jersey to

FIGURE 49. CRUDE BIRTH RATE PER 1,000 ENUMERATED POPULATION,
UNITED STATES, 1940

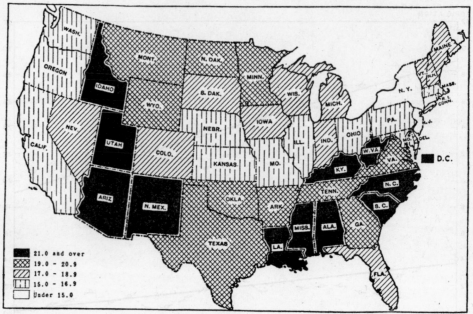

Source: Map reproduced from *Vital Statistics—Special Reports*, 14, No. 2.

FIGURE 50. RATE OF NATURAL INCREASE, UNITED STATES, 1940

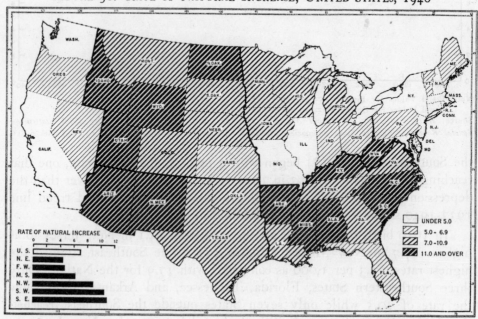

Source: *Vital Statistics—Special Reports*, 14, No. 2, Table 2.

17.2 for New Mexico. For the Southeast the rate was 11, for the Nation, 7.1. Again Florida fell the lowest in the Southeast with 5.7, no other State going below 8 per 1,000. And again the Southeast is approached by only a few Western States like Utah and New Mexico (Figure 50).

Figures 47 and 48 include the death rate and are thus designed to show the greater rate of natural increase in the Southeast. In the Nation the trend line of births and deaths gradually carried the rate of natural increase down from 10.5 to 5.9 per 1,000 in 1933 when it was reversed and rose to 7.1 in 1940. The Southeast, however, showed a trend of natural increase that began at 14.2, narrowed to 8.7 in 1936, and then rose to 11 per 1,000 in 1940. Since the downward trend of deaths is similar in the two areas, the figures show the extent of the South's high natural increase due to excess fertility.

Adjustments for underregistration of births show even greater regional differences in fertility than those presented. Such adjustments can be made by matching birth certificates in a precensus year with census counts of infants one year old and under in the census year. There is one difficulty, however. Where complete, birth registration figures show that census enumerators themselves fail to account for all infants under one.

FIGURE 51. REGISTERED BIRTHS PER 100 ESTIMATED BIRTHS,
UNITED STATES, 1940

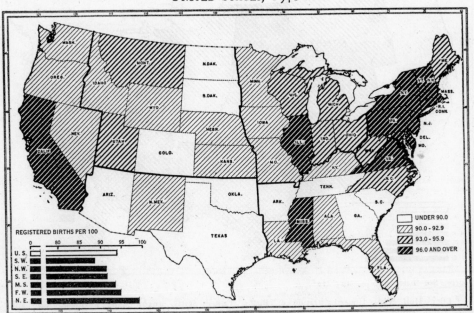

Source: Ellen Hull Neff, Underregistration of Births, United States, 1940: State, Regional, Race, and Rural-Urban Differences (unpublished master's thesis, University of North Carolina, 1943).

Figure 51 shows Ellen Hull Neff's estimates of proportion of under-registration of births in 1939.[6] It will be noticed that in the States admitted latest to the registration area, Southern States with large Negro population and in rural areas, registered births were only 80 to 90 percent of total births as estimated. The States ranged from 81 percent for Arkansas to 101.1 percent for Massachusetts. In eastern and urban States the degree of registration on this estimate ranked around 96 to 101 percent. The overregistration of births in Massachusetts was no doubt due to the fact that hospitals draw from surrounding rural areas outside the State. Ellen Neff's studies indicated that all the southern States, with the exception of Mississippi and Virginia, had high rates of unrecorded births.[7]

Estimates of the underregistered births enable us to make use of census changes in determining the change in population from 1930 to 1940 due to natural increase. By States this varied from 3 percent in California to 18 percent in New Mexico (Figure 52). The Nation gained 7.28 percent by natural increase. The Southeast and Southwest had 12.3

FIGURE 52. PERCENTAGE CHANGE IN TOTAL POPULATION DUE TO NATURAL INCREASE, UNITED STATES, 1930-1940

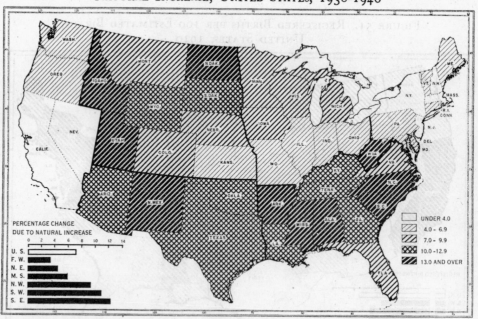

Source: See Table 30, pp. 125, 126.

[6] Ellen Hull Neff, Underregistration of Births, United States, 1940; State, Regional, Race and Rural-Urban Differences (unpublished master's thesis, University of North Carolina, 1943).

[7] Compare these figures with the results of birth-test survey in 1940. See *Vital Statistics Rates in the United States, 1900-1940*, Gov't Print. Office, Washington, D. C., 1943, p. 99.

FIGURE 53. PERCENTAGE CHANGE IN THE COLORED POPULATION DUE TO
NATURAL INCREASE, UNITED STATES, 1930-1940

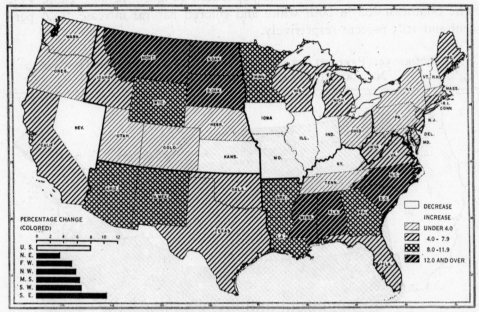

Source: See Tables 30 and 31, pp. 125, 126.

TABLE 17. WHITE POPULATION CHANGE DUE TO NATURAL INCREASE AND
MIGRATION, UNITED STATES AND THE SIX MAJOR REGIONS, 1930-1940

Area	Amount Change, 1930-1940			Percent Change, 1930-1940		
	Net	Due to natural increase	Due to migration	Net	Due to natural increase	Due to migration
UNITED STATES.........	7,928,130	7,942,382	− 14,252	7.2	7.2	...
Northeast..............	1,681,663	1,682,840	− 1,177	4.6	4.6	...
Southeast..............	2,313,465	2,314,333	− 868	13.0	13.0	...
Southwest.............	643,281	921,746	− 278,465	8.2	11.7	− 3.5
Middle States..........	1,622,179	2,051,521	− 429,342	5.0	6.3	− 1.3
Northwest.............	25,559	688,429	− 662,870	0.4	9.6	− 9.2
Far West..............	1,521,638	261,174	1,260,464	19.1	3.3	15.8

Source: *Statistical Abstract, 1930, 1934, 1937*, Tables 17, 18; United States Birth Schedules and Infant Mortality, 1930-1936; Mortality Statistics, 1930-1936; Vital Statistics, 1937-1939; *Fifteenth Census of the United States, 1930*, Population IV, United States Summary, Tables 13, 23; *Sixteenth Census of the United States, 1940*, Population, Series P-6, P-10; *Report of the Committee on Population Problems of the National Resources Committee, 1938*, "The Problems of a Changing Population," pp. 75-76; National Resources Committee, *Population Statistics, National Data*, Tables 28, 32.

and 11 percent gains in natural increase; the Far West only 3.4 percent.
Colored populations showed a natural decrease in nine States and their
rates ranged from a loss of 3.6 percent in Kentucky to a gain of 22.7
percent in North Dakota (Figure 53). While the total gain was 8 percent, greater than that of the white population, the colored population
showed a smaller rate of natural increase than the white in both southern
regions. By States, the white population ranged from a 2.9 percent gain

in California to 18.6 percent natural increase in New Mexico where Mexicans are classified with the white population (Figure 54 and Table 17). The Southeast led in both white and colored natural increase, 13.0 percent and 10.5 percent respectively.

FIGURE 54. PERCENTAGE CHANGE IN WHITE POPULATION DUE TO NATURAL INCREASE, UNITED STATES, 1930-1940

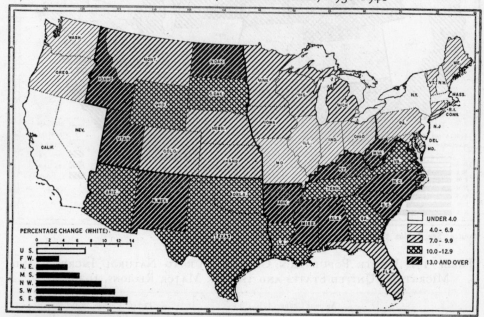

Source: See Tables 30 and 31, pp. 125, 126.

DECLINE IN FERTILITY BY AGE GROUPS

The picture of total fertility is incomplete until we know what has happened to the birth rate among women of different ages. Figure 55 from P. K. Whelpton does more than document the fact that the most fertile period for the human female is found in early maturity, and the least fertile in the later periods. It indicates year by year that from 1920 to 1940 native white women of the two groups have shown different fertility trends. Among females of age 35-39 and 40-44 there has been a large decline in fertility, practically uninterrupted since 1920. Here rates have been cut almost in half. In contrast, birth rates for women aged 20-24 and 25-29 declined until 1933 and then turned upward. The two most fertile age groups have reversed position. Before 1927 women 25-29 had the highest reproductive rate of all groups, in 1927 they were passed by the group aged 20-24. While births have not increased among women aged 30-34, their fertility has been fairly stable since 1933.

FIGURE 55. ANNUAL TREND OF AGE SPECIFIC BIRTH RATES PER 1,000 NATIVE WHITE WOMEN 15-44, BY 5-YEAR AGE GROUPS, UNITED STATES, 1920-1939

FIGURE 56. ANNUAL TREND OF BIRTHS PER 1,000 NATIVE WHITE WOMEN, 15-49, BY ORDER OF BIRTH, UNITED STATES, 1920-1939

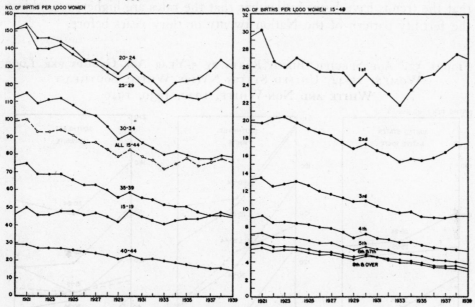

Source: P. K. Whelpton, "Recent Fertility Trends," *Human Fertility*, VI, No. 6 (December, 1941), p. 163.

Figure 57, based on three decades, brings the fertility differential home to the Southeast. Fertility at all ages, as is expected, is highest among the Southeast's white women, and next highest among its Negroes. Most striking, however, is the regional decline in the fertility of white women above 25. Among those 25-29, births fell (1920-1940) from 204 to 130. Total fertility for ages 15-44 fell from 142 to 92. Only younger women 15-19 and 20-24 show stable rates after 1930. Negroes showed the expected decline in older ages but their total fertility rose after 1930 due to increased births among younger women, 15-19 and 20-24.

Fertility among younger women is of course directly related to births of first-born and second-born children. P. K. Whelpton (Figure 56) has shown the extent to which the higher order of births have declined while lower orders have remained stable. Thus from 1920 to 1939 first births per 1,000 native white women remained fairly stable around 27 per 1,000 except for the depression decline, and second births declined but slightly from 19.8 to 17.4. On the other hand all births of the fourth order and over declined from 27.4 to 15.1 per 1,000. Births of the third order have declined from 13.4 to 9.2 per 1,000. Probably this may be taken to mean that while families still want two children, those mothers with two or three do not want additional children sufficiently to maintain previous rates of reproduction. Comparisons with the Southeast, in Chapter 8, suggest that the trends have been similar but that the rates are higher, resembling the fertility pattern of the Nation twenty or thiry years before.

FIGURE 57. AGE SPECIFIC BIRTH RATES BY 5-YEAR AGE GROUPS PER 1,000 WOMEN, 15-44, UNITED STATES NATIVE WHITE, SOUTHEAST WHITE AND NON-WHITE, 1920, 1930, 1940

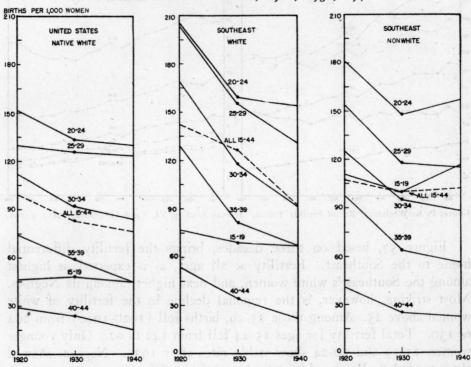

Source: See Figure 55. Also *Population Statistics, State Data,* National Resources Committee (October, 1937), pp. 3, 7; *Fourteenth Census of the United States, 1920,* Population II, Ch. 3, Table 13; *Fifteenth Census of the United States, 1930,* Population II, Ch. 10, Table 24; *Sixteenth Census of the United States, 1940,* Series P-10, No. 6; *Vital Statistics—Special Reports,* 14, United States and State Summaries, 1940; Department of Commerce, Bureau of the Census, "Live Female Births by Place of Residence, Race, Age of Mother, United States and Selected States, 1940."

CHAPTER 7

FAMILY SIZE AND REPLACEMENTS

So FAR we have discussed fertility in the impersonal terms of population composition and age specific birth rates. Children, however, are had by families and marriage is the entrance requirement of the family institution. Our discussion of regional differences in fertility is continued in terms of the degree of marriage in the population, the number and size of families, and the extent to which under present conditions of family life we are replacing the population.

Excepting illegitimacy, the factors producing what we understand as the effective fertility of a region have been classified into two categories: (1) all the biological and cultural factors which operate to cause married women to produce children at a certain rate; (2) the percentage of women of childbearing ages who are married and are thus subject to the action of the first group of factors.

In the proportion of its native white women 20-44 married in 1930, the Southwest ranked first with 79.1 percent, the Southeast next with 75.8, and the Northeast last with 66.5 percent. The ratio for the Nation was 71.9 percent. Tabulation by five-year age groups, of females married, showed a relatively high percentage of those aged 20-29 married in the southern areas. These differences were especially important in the younger groups where specific fertility rates for married women are highest. Figure 58 shows that the southern regions led in the proportion of native white women, aged 20-44, who were married. This predominance was especially marked for the earlier age groups, 15-19, 20-24, and 25-29.

For all native white women over 15, however, the predominance was shared with the Northwest which had 62.8 of its native white women married as compared with 62.7 for the Southeast. Figure 59 presents the marital condition for this group by regions. Especially noticeable was the higher proportion widowed in the Far West and Southeast and the lower proportion divorced in the urban and Catholic Northeast and the

FIGURE 58. PERCENTAGE MARRIED OF NATIVE WHITE WOMEN, BY AGE,
UNITED STATES AND THE SIX MAJOR REGIONS, 1930

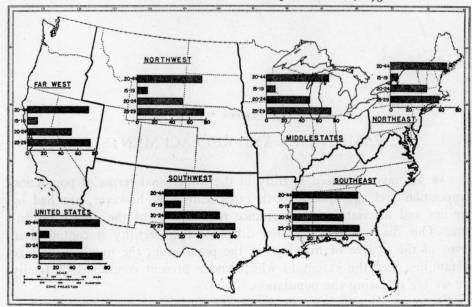

Source: Margaret Jarman Hagood, Mothers of the South: A Population Study of Native White Women
of Childbearing Age of the Southeast (unpublished doctoral dissertation, University of North Carolina,
1937), Tables 15, 17.

rural and Protestant Southeast. Lowest in the proportion married was
the urban Northeast, and highest in the population divorced was the Far
West.

When a predominantly young population accepts the custom of early
marriage usual in rural society, we may expect to find a high fertility associated with a higher percentage of young mothers. Calculations of the
percentage of children born to mothers under twenty shows the Southeast
fulfilling these conditions of high fertility. Of those reported, it was
found that 13 percent of all cases of births in the Nation in 1940 occurred
to mothers under twenty. As Figure 60 indicates, no southern State
fell lower than 17 percent and three exceeded 20 percent. Lowest, as
expected, were the Northeastern States and, less expected, the Dakotas,
Minnesota, and Wisconsin.

Figure 61 confirms the above trend for it shows that the estimated marriage rate was highest in the southern regions and lowest in the Northeast
in 1940. The range was from an estimate of 3.7 marriages per 1,000
persons in North Carolina to 35.4 in Nevada. Western and southern States
had a consistently high rank. For comparison, Figure 62 gives the estimated divorce rates for the same period. Here the Far West and the

FIGURE 59. MARITAL CONDITION OF NATIVE WHITE WOMEN OVER 15, UNITED STATES AND SIX MAJOR REGIONS, 1930

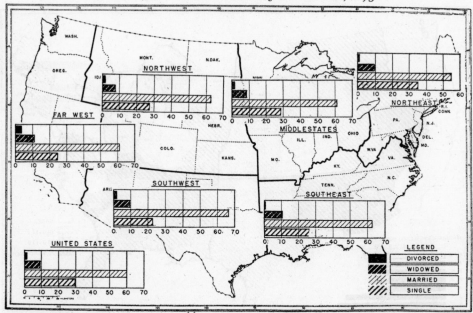

Source: Margaret Jarman Hagood, Mothers of the South: A Population Study of Native White Women of Child Bearing Age of the Southeast (unpublished doctoral dissertation, University of North Carolina, 1937), Table 17.

FIGURE 60. BIRTHS TO MOTHERS UNDER 20 AS PERCENTAGE OF ALL CASES OF BIRTHS* TO MOTHERS OF KNOWN AGES, UNITED STATES, 1940

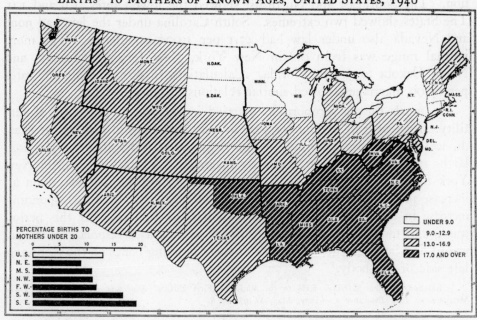

* A multiple birth in which at least one child is born alive is considered one case of birth.
Source: Vital Statistics—Special Reports, 14, Table F.

FIGURE 61. ESTIMATED NUMBER OF MARRIAGES PER 1,000
POPULATION, UNITED STATES, 1940

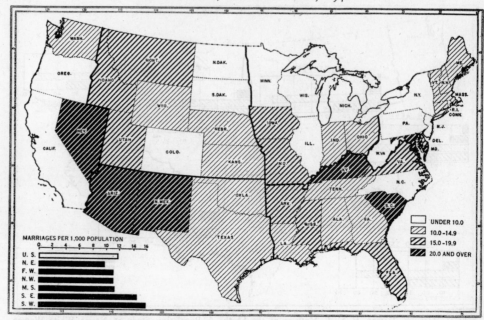

Source: *Vital Statistics—Special Reports*, 15, No. 13. *Sixteenth Census of the United States, 1940,*
Series P-10, No. 2.

Southwest led with estimates of 4 to 4.1 divorces per 1,000 population. The Southeast and Northeast showed the lowest rates, 1.9 and 1.0.
The States showed two extremes. South Carolina under the law had none
and Nevada also under law had 47.1 per 1,000 population. The more
normal range was from 0.8 in New York, New Jersey, Delaware, and
North Dakota to 5.9 in Florida. Calculations in terms of divorce rates
per 1,000 marriages showed similar relations (Figure 63).

So much for the proportions married in relation to the level of fertility. If we wish to account for year by year variations in fertility we shall
do well to investigate trends in marriage rates. Despite contraception,
births still tend to occur soon after marriage. A study of rates in New
York State from 1919 to 1937 showed that almost without exception an
increase in the marriage rate is followed the next year by a corresponding
increase in the birth rate. The coefficient of correlation over this period
was found to be very high, .874—almost as close a correspondence as one
would find between the dimensions of corresponding bones on the right and
left side of the body.[1]

---

[1] "Relations of the Marriage Rate to the Ratio of First Births," *Statistical Bulletin* (New York:
Metropolitan Life Insurance Company, May, 1939), p. 6.

FIGURE 62. NUMBER OF DIVORCES* PER 1,000 POPULATION,
UNITED STATES, 1940

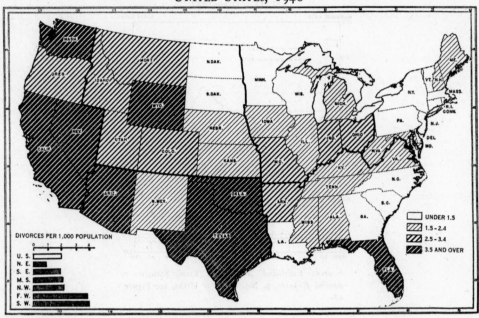

* No divorces are granted in South Carolina.

Source: *Vital Statistics—Special Reports*, 15, No. 18.

FIGURE 63. ESTIMATED NUMBER OF DIVORCES PER 1,000 MARRIAGES,
UNITED STATES, 1940

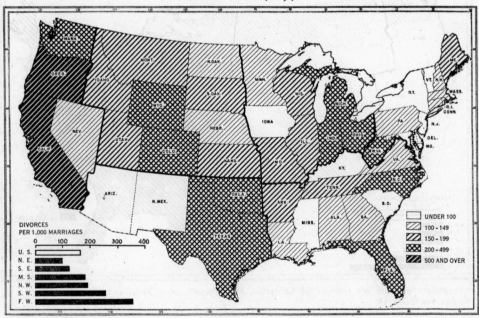

Source: See Figures 61 and 62.

FIGURE 64. THE TREND OF MARRIAGE AND BIRTH RATES PER 1,000 POPULATION, UNITED STATES, 1929-1941

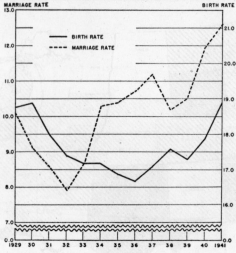

Source: Estimated Marriages, *Vital Statistics— Special Reports*, 9, No. 60. For births, see Figure 47.

FIGURE 65. REGISTERED ILLEGITIMATE BIRTHS* AS PERCENTAGE OF ALL LIVE BIRTHS, UNITED STATES, 1938

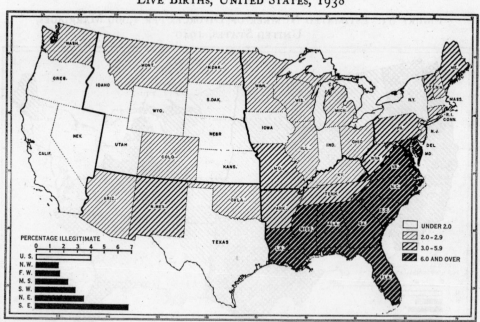

* Legitimacy data are not recorded in California, Massachusetts, New York, and Texas.
Source: See Table 18.

TABLE 18. REGISTERED ILLEGITIMATE BIRTHS AS PERCENTAGE OF ALL LIVE BIRTHS, BY RACE, UNITED STATES AND SELECTED STATES,* 1938

Area	Negro Births			White Births		
	Total	Illegitimate		Total	Illegitimate	
		Percent	Rank		Percent	Rank
UNITED STATES.........	241,224	17.20		1,562,344	2.05	
Delaware...............	748	31.02	1	3,683	3.72	2
Maryland...............	6,287	26.75	2	22,713	2.40	10
Virginia...............	14,997	19.50	3	38,462	2.79	3
South Carolina.........	20,754	19.37	4	20,352	2.48	8
Alabama...............	23,207	19.27	5	38,812	1.81	20
Florida...............	9,302	18.56	6	21,756	1.80	21
North Carolina.........	24,665	18.35	7	54,459	2.65	4
Tennessee.............	8,047	17.81	8	45,602	2.03	13
Louisiana.............	20,070	17.53	9	28,684	1.84	18
Pennsylvania..........	8,782	17.39	10	157,159	2.60	5
Georgia...............	25,723	16.65	11	38,899	1.57	27
Missouri..............	3,690	16.64	12	54,855	2.44	9
Illinois...............	6,203	16.52	13	116,263	1.93	14
Kentucky..............	3,193	16.19	14	58,685	1.92	15
Oklahoma.............	2,324	16.09	15	39,972	1.63	24
Mississippi............	29,505	14.00	16	24,098	1.09	30
New Jersey............	4,345	13.42	17	51,680	1.62	25
Ohio.................	5,931	12.63	18	106,695	1.76	23
West Virginia..........	2,301	12.52	19	40,129	3.99	1
Arkansas.............	8,691	11.82	20	28,477	1.58	26
Michigan.............	3,410	11.73	21	93,388	2.04	12
Kansas...............	886	11.40	22	28,638	1.31	29
Indiana.............	1,884	10.93	23	58,307	1.48	28
Rhode Island..........	238	10.92	24	10,287	2.59	6
Wisconsin............	191	10.47	25	54,402	1.88	17
Iowa.................	263	9.51	26	42,935	1.79	22
Connecticut...........	610	9.02	27	23,164	1.83	19
Colorado.............	194	8.76	28	20,299	2.53	7
Minnesota............	106	8.49	29	49,408	2.16	11
Arizona..............	200	6.00	30	9,574	1.91	16
Nebraska.............	189	4.23	31	22,082	0.91	31

*Births not registered by legitimacy in California, Massachusetts, New York, and Texas. States with less than 100 Negro births also omitted.

Source: *Vital Statistics—Special Reports*, 9, No. 20.

These variations in first births account for a large share of the variations in total fertility from year to year. The depression accumulated a large backlog of delayed marriages which were consummated in the upswing and showed in the Nation's rise in births from 1933 to 1942. As the curve of marriages shows (Figure 64), the selective service act and the declaration of war increased the marriage rate which rose from 10.3 in 1939 to 11.9 in 1940. The 1941 marriage rate of 12.6 per 1,000 population was the highest ever reached in the United States. The second highest rate reached, 12.0, was reached in 1920 after the close of the first World War. The extent to which these marriages served to increase births is shown in Figure 64. The phenomenon is normal at the outbreak of war and is usually followed by sharply declining fertility contingent upon the breaking up of many young families.

The preceding discussion is not to suggest that the unmarried never have any children but the difference between the legitimate and the illegitimate fertility rate is very large indeed. Registered illegitimate births were 4.1 percent of all live births in the Nation in 1938, ranging from 1.7

percent for the Northwest and 1.8 for the Far West to 6.9 percent in the Southeast (Figure 65). By States the range was from 0.9 percent in Nebraska to 11 percent in South Carolina. Only Delaware and Maryland joined the Southeastern States in exceeding 6.8 percent. The high rate of illegitimate births in the region is explained by the Negro, whose national rate was 17.2 percent, ranging from 4.2 percent in Nebraska to 31 percent in Delaware (Table 18). This can be compared with 2 percent for the white population (Figure 66).

FIGURE 66. PERCENTAGE OF TOTAL WHITE BIRTHS REGISTERED AS ILLEGITIMATE, UNITED STATES, 1938

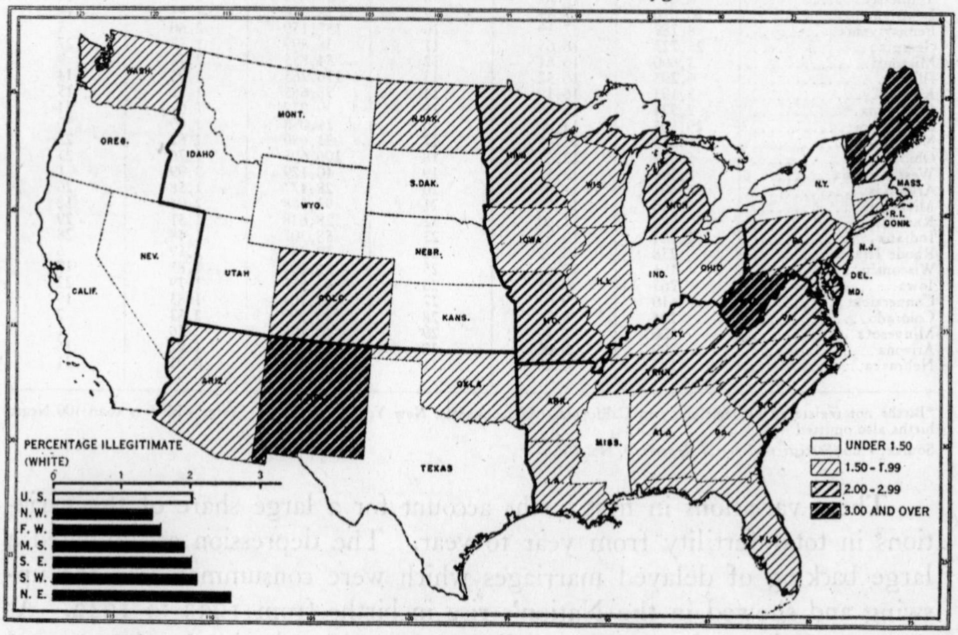

Source: See Table 18.

THE NUMBER AND SIZE OF FAMILIES

The First Census showed more families consisting of five persons than any other number. A century later the most frequent size of family consisted of four persons. By 1900, as Paul C. Glick has pointed out, there were more three-person families, and by 1930 the two-person family was the most prevalent type.[2] This modal or typical family is smaller than the average sized family which from 1790 to 1940 decreased from 5.7 to 3.8, a loss of one-third in 150 years.

Decrease in fertility serves to explain much of the decline in family size. The constant in family size except for broken homes is the couple,

[2] Paul C. Glick, "Family Trends in the United States 1890 to 1940," American Sociological Review, IV (August, 1942), 505-516.

but family size it must be remembered is not equivalent to two plus the number of children that live. Children grow up, leave home, and begin families of their own. Accordingly, increased life expectancy has served to decrease the average size of the family for it has increased the number of couples living together after their children have departed the parental roof. Under the pattern of lowered fertility the wife completes her brief period of childbearing by thirty and the family which began as two may again be two by age fifty. Thus not only decreased childbearing but longer life has increased the number of two-person families enumerated by the census.[3]

Roughly speaking, our early period of high fertility was characterized by larger size of family but a smaller number of families in proportion to the total population. Since 1890 the decrease in average size of household has amounted to two-tenths of a person per decade, but from 1930 to 1940 the decrease was three-tenths of a person. Population per dwelling unit returned in 1940 is not strictly comparable to numbers per family since households contain a small number of persons who are not members of private families. In this same decade, while the total population increased only 7.2 percent, the number of households increased 16.6 percent, or nearly 5 million. The increase in number of families is as significant as increases in the population, for it measures the demand for new houses and for all types of household goods and conveniences. Over a long period it represents rising levels of living as more young couples are able to move from under the parental roof to start housekeeping on their own. The trend is explained partly by age make-up, for we are now in the period where large proportions of the population are in the youthful ages at which family attachments are formed. If these couples had families as large as their parents had, population would be increasing instead of tending toward a declining phase.

Regional trends in the number and size of families follow the familiar fertility differentials except that the setting up of new households is closely related to the supply of new housing. Regional rates of increase in the number of family units are due to many factors: the age composition of the population, the rate of marriage, the level of well-being, and inter-regional migration. This rate was greater in urban than in rural areas, being 18.6 and 13.8 percent. Figure 67 shows that by States the rate at which the number of households increased ranged from 2.7 percent in South Dakota to 38.2 percent in Florida. The Far West with in-migration and the economic ability to build houses ranked the highest; New England and the Great Plain States with their out-migration, the lowest.

[3] *Ibid.*

FIGURE 67. PERCENTAGE INCREASE IN THE NUMBER OF FAMILIES,
UNITED STATES, 1930-1940

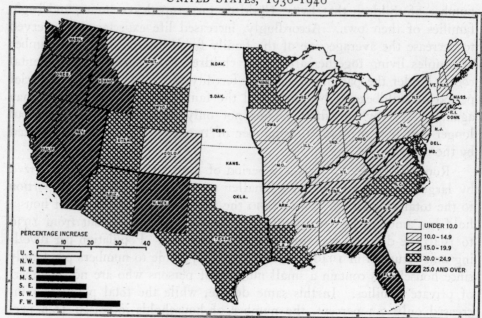

Source: *Sixteenth Census of the United States, 1940,* Series PH-3, No. 2.

FIGURE 68. PERCENTAGE DECREASE IN SIZE OF FAMILY UNIT,
UNITED STATES, 1930-1940

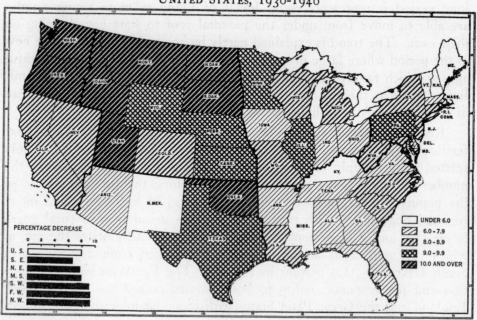

Source: See Figure 67.

The Southeast with its large population increases failed to establish a comparable number of new households, partly because of inability to build houses.

The decline in average size of family unit, like the other figures discussed, may have been somewhat affected by the census change from the enumeration of private families in 1930 to that of occupied dwelling units in 1940. In urban areas the decline in average size of family was 9 percent as compared with 7 percent in rural areas. Figure 68 shows that the decline was greatest in the Northwest and Far West and least in the Southeast. By States it ranged from 13 percent in Washington to 4 percent in Maine, Vermont, Mississippi, and New Mexico. Surprisingly enough it was smallest in the District of Columbia, 2 percent. This rate of change is related to present family size, for, as it approaches the ultimate limit of two persons per household, the rate of decline will stabilize.

In 1940 the average population per occupied dwelling unit was 3.8, a decline of 8 percent from the average size of family, 4.1 in 1930. The size of household was greatest, 4.1, in the Southeast and smallest, 3.2, in the Far West. Figure 69 shows that size of household in 1940 ranged from 4.5 in North Carolina to 3.2 in Washington, Oregon, and California. Average size of the household was largest among the farm population, 4.25 for the Nation, over 4.5 in the Southeast, and highest

FIGURE 69. AVERAGE POPULATION PER OCCUPIED DWELLING UNIT, UNITED STATES, 1940

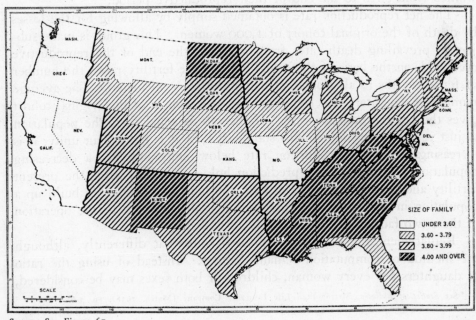

Source: See Figure 67.

of all, 4.99 in North Carolina. Nonwhite families were larger the country over but largest in the rural Southeast, reaching 5.66 in North Carolina. Nearly 95 percent of all the nonwhite farm families are located in the census South. In the South's urban areas white and colored households are the same size, 3.7 persons.

REPLACEMENT RATIOS

The discussion in the preceding chapter indicates what happens to the trend of total fertility as age-specific birth rates change among women of various ages. The value of the next measures to be discussed, the replacement ratios, is that they indicate the trend of total fertility if age-specific rates are held constant while the age make-up itself is changing. There are two such rates, gross and net reproduction.

The gross reproduction rate is the figure obtained by computing the number of children that would be born to 1,000 women (1) passing, without losses by death, through the reproductive period, and (2) subject to the prevailing rates of reproduction at the several age periods. For the population to maintain its number on this basis, it would be necessary for 1,000 mothers to have 1,000 daughters. If both sexes are considered, as they might well be, the figure would be 2,057 per 2,000 parents. (The sex ratio at birth is normally 1,057 boys for every 1,000 girls.) This represents the absolute minimum compatible with a self-sustaining population. The gross reproduction rate leaves no place for improvement in mortality, for it assumes the ideal of no deaths for these women from birth to the end of their reproductive period.[4]

The net reproduction rate is obtained simply by allowing for the losses by death of the original cohort of 1,000 women. This group is made subject to prevailing death rates from age 0 to the end of the reproductive cycle and, on the basis of the actual age-specific fertility rates, the number of female births to all women remaining alive is calculated. The average number of daughters thus computed for each woman of the original cohort gives the net reproduction rate. If the rate is equal to 1, the population is just replacing itself (remains stationary); if it is more than unity, it is increasing. A net reproduction rate below unity indicates a decreasing population. However, this prediction holds good only after the present fertility and mortality have been held constant long enough to build up a population in which the age composition is due entirely to the operation of these two factors.

Replacement ratios can be expressed somewhat differently, although the method of computation remains similar. Instead of using the ratio of daughters per every woman, children of both sexes may be considered,

---

[4] See *Statistical Bulletin*, Metropolitan Life Insurance Company (March, 1938), pp. 3-6.

and their number may be computed per married woman, or per fertile married woman only. This may be illustrated by current data.

With birth rates at each age of life as they were during 1930-34, 1,000 native white women living through the child-bearing period would bear 2,158 children. In 1928 A. J. Lotka calculated that out of every 100 females born, 21.8 die single, 78.2 marry eventually, and 64.8 become mothers. For white American wives he calculated net infertility for all causes, sterility, premature death of husband or wife, divorce, etc., at 13.1 percent.[5] Counting then only women who marry before age 50, there were about 2,410 births per 1,000 married women. Decreasing the number of women still further by excluding those who bear no children (about one-sixth of the group) raises the expected number of births to approximately 2,900 per 1,000 fertile women. This fertility of approximately 3 children per fertile married woman was just sufficient with the mortality current as of 1930-34 to replace the population, that is, to keep it stationary. Actually, the white population of the United States continued to show a high rate of natural increase during the period 1930-34. This was due to the fact that the number of women in the reproductive ages was higher than could be expected on the basis of fertility rates of 1930-34, since these women were born at a time when higher birth rates prevailed. With fertility and mortality rates held constant, the rate of natural increase would continue to decline, simply because lower births have already left fewer young females to move up in the next decade into the fertile age groups. Thus, with no decline in age-specific fertility, the population will on the average be too old to keep up its present high rate of increase. Finally, if persons of all age groups are replaced by those subject through their lives to fertility and mortality rates as of 1930-34, the population would become stationary, as predicted by the replacement ratio of 3 children per fertile married woman, and the natural increase would then remain zero.

In 1930 the Nation's net reproduction rate stood at 108, by 1933 it was 100, and by 1936 it had fallen to 95. Under these conditions 100 newborn girls would eventually have 95 daughters. This figure expressed here on the basis of 100 represents net reproductivity. On this basis the daughters eventually would give birth to 90 granddaughters. But in the Southeast in 1930, 100 newborn girls would live to have 125 daughters and 156 granddaughters (Figure 70). White rates were much higher than colored. Whereas 100 newborn white girls would have 134 daughters and 180 granddaughters, 100 colored girls would have 107 daughters and 114 granddaughters.

[5] A. J. Lotka, "Sterility in American Marriages," *National Academy of Science Proceedings*, XIV (January, 1928), 99-109.

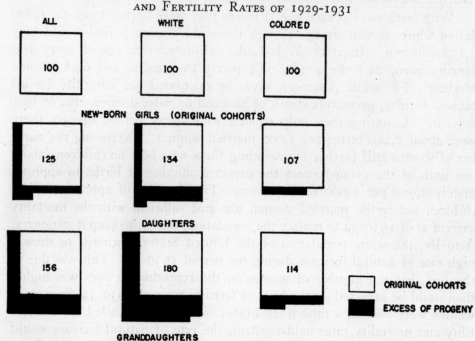

FIGURE 70. EVENTUAL DAUGHTERS AND GRANDDAUGHTERS OF 100 NEW-BORN
GIRLS BY COLOR, SOUTHEAST, ACCORDING TO MORTALITY
AND FERTILITY RATES OF 1929-1931

Source: *Fifteenth Census of the United States*, 1930, Population, II, Chap. 10, Tables 24 and 28; *Birth, Stillbirth, and Infant Mortality Statistics*, 1929-31, Tables 1 and 4; *Mortality Statistics*, 1929-31, Table 4.

TABLE 19. NET REPRODUCTION INDEX NATIVE WHITE POPULATION,
UNITED STATES AND THE SIX MAJOR REGIONS, 1930

Area	Ratio of children to women*	Permanent replacement quota†	Index of net reproduction per generation	Area	Ratio of children to women*	Permanent replacement quota†	Index of net reproduction per generation
UNITED STATES...	503	444	1.13	Southwest.......	572	456	1.25
				Middle States....	476	442	1.08
Northeast........	442	442	1.00	Northwest.......	561	441	1.27
Southeast........	668	447	1.49	Far West........	349	443	0.79

*Ratio of children under 5 per 1,000 native white women aged 20 to 44 years inclusive, in the actual population, 1930, corrected for under-enumeration.

†Ratio of children under 5 per 1,000 women aged 20 to 44 years inclusive, in the stationary population, computed for native whites in 1929-31.

Source: National Resources Committee, *Population Statistics, National Data*, Table 12, pp. 31-40 and Table 14, p. 50; Margaret Jarman Hagood, Mothers of the South: A Population Study of Native White Women of Child-bearing Age of the Southeast (doctoral dissertation, University of North Carolina, 1937), p. 67.

The index of net reproduction is computed by relating the ratio of children under five per 1,000 women aged 20-44 in the actual population to the same ratio in the stationary population. For the native white population of the Southeast in 1930 it was 1.49 as compared with .79 for the Far West and 1.00 for the Northeast. The Middle States showed a

FIGURE 71. INDEX OF NET REPRODUCTION FOR NATIVE WHITE
POPULATION, UNITED STATES, 1930

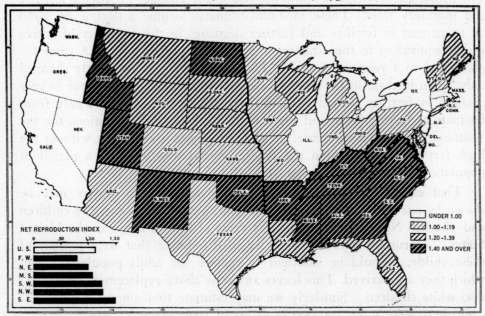

Source: *Population Statistics, National Data,* National Resources Committee (1937), Tables 12 and 14.

replacement ratio of 1.08 while both Northwest and Southwest were replacing themselves by 127 and 125 percent respectively (Table 19).
Variations by States are indicated in Figure 71. Ten States were below
replacements, ranging from .99 for Nevada to .72 for California. They
included all the highly industrialized States except Michigan and Pennsylvania. Fourteen States had replacements ranging from unity to 1.20,
and nine ranged from 1.20 to 1.40. The highest group consisted of
southern and western States with the exception of West Virginia which
had the highest replacement rate of all, 1.67. In the Southeast, only
Louisiana and Florida fell below the highest grouping.

CONCLUSION

We are now better able to appreciate the significance of Figure 3 in
Chapter 1. Thus we can show that this chart brings much of the previous
discussion to bear on the future of population in the United States: (1)
From 1915 to 1937 the birth and death rates in Figure 3 are those reported
in the expanding registration area adjusted for underregistration. (2) Net
reproduction rates calculated as of the mid-thirties allow for the effects
of changing age distribution if no further changes occur in age-specific
fertility and mortality. (3) Finally, calculations based on "medium"

population estimates made for the National Resources Committee by Thompson and Whelpton allow for reasonable changes in specific fertility and mortality rates. These medium estimates assume a decline by 1980 of 13 percent in fertility and further decreases in the mortality of native whites equivalent to the attainment of a life expectancy of 68.8 years for males and 71.2 years for females. These figures would be greatly changed only by an increase in the average size of American families. Year to year changes in fertility do not reverse the trend if they result largely from fluctuations in marriages and first births. Comparable calculations for the Southeast have not been made. Figure 70 makes it clear that without the high fertility of the region the Nation would have entered a period of population decline much sooner.

That excess replacements were largely an agrarian matter may be shown by one calculation. There were in 1930, 2,665,000 white children and 589,000 Negro children under 5 years of age on farms in the United States. At current survival rates we may estimate that 61.7 percent of these children would be sufficient to replace the adult population from which they are derived. This leaves an excess above replacement of 1,000,-000 white children. Similarly we may estimate that among Negro children there were some 200,000 in excess of replacement.

Southern fertility, like national fertility, is an average of the differential fertility of the constituent groups of the population. Such an analysis of the Southeast cannot be made at present for the knowledge required is lacking. No studies comparable, for example, to the Milbank analysis of fertility by social-occupational classes have been made south of the Potomac. Clues to class differences can be found in analyses of fertility by race, by size of community and by geographic location. This last can be related to economic standing by ranking the counties on some such scale of per capita wealth as that developed by the Study of Population Redistribution. All three classifications are related to economic differentials but none have the merit possessed by the Milbank studies of arranging the population in a hierarchy of socio-economic classes, to be discussed in Chapter 11.

All of these differences indicated the familiar differential. Rural dwellers in the Southeast are much more prolific than city dwellers, younger populations than older ones, those in poor areas than those in well-to-do areas, and whites than Negroes because the effect of excess fertility among Negro females was largely offset in 1930 by a life expectancy of 13 years less than that among white females. These differentials raise questions as to the content of the high fertility complex in the Southeast and it is to this regional pattern that we turn our attention in the next chapter.

CHAPTER 8

THE PATTERN OF HIGH FERTILITY

To WHAT conditions shall we attribute the high birth rates of the population of the Southeast? Speaking in historical terms we know that high fertility existed in most of the areas of early United States, that it declined more rapidly in other regions, leaving the Southeast outstanding for its high replacement rates. It is the task of this chapter to explore the factors connected with high fertility and to see what explanation can be offered in terms of economic and social conditions.

To understand the pattern that fertility assumes in the region we shall begin with the determination of the rate at which women may expect to be married and the number of children married women have. We shall be interested in the extent to which the Southeast's high birth rate can be related to special conditions of the area, the extent to which the decline in fertility from 1920 to 1930 is due to changes in certain social conditions, and the effect that mortality has on potential births. After discussing the above conditions, all of which are open to some degree of statistical measurement, we shall be concerned with the type of culture associated with the high fertility of the Southeast.

MARRIAGE EXPECTATION AND PROLIFICACY RATES

High fertility of a population, as often pointed out, is accompanied by a greater frequency of marriage and younger age of marriage. We have already seen that higher proportions are married in the Southeast and that marriage comes at an earlier age. Our calculations (Figure 72) indicate that women in the Southeast have a high rate of expectation of marriage, to speak in terms of the life table.[1] On the basis of survival rates and

---

[1] Rates of "marriage expectation" or probability to marry were computed on the assumption of marital status and mortality rates of 1930 remaining constant for the period from birth to the end of marriageable age. Marriage rates at various ages by States were not available at the time of writing. For method see the authors' "School Life Expectation and Marriage Expectation" *Proceedings of the Conference on Analysis and Interpretation of Social and Economic Data* (N. C. State College, Raleigh, Mimeographed, 1941), pp. 72-78.

[95]

FIGURE 72. MARRIAGE EXPECTATION FOR WHITE AND COLORED
WOMEN OF THE SOUTHEAST, 1929-1931

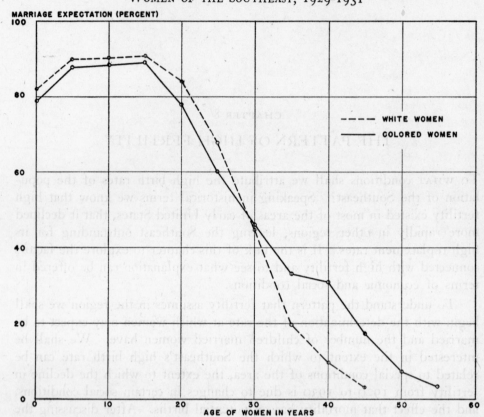

Source: *Fifteenth Census of the United States, 1930*, Population, II, Ch. 11, Tables 9, 17, 18, 19; Ch. 10, Table 28. All sources necessary for the computation of life tables for the Southeast.

TABLE 20. SPECIFIED INDICES OF FERTILITY AND MARITAL STATUS,
UNITED STATES AND SOUTHEAST, 1930

Index	UNITED STATES		SOUTHEAST	
	White	Negro	White	Negro
Probability at birth of future marriage*	82.0	80.1	83.3	77.9
Median age of bride at marriage (years)	21.8	19.6	21.2	19.7
Median age of mother at first birth (years)	....	....	22.6	20.0
Median number of legitimate children ever borne per wife	1.86	....	2.24	1.30†

*Chances out of 100.
†Including illegitimate for Negro mothers.

Note: The first two measures computed on the assumption of marital status and mortality rates as of 1930 remaining constant to the end of the marriageable age; the next measures (median age of mother and median number of children) derived from computation of prolificacy rates. The median number of children of both sexes ever borne per wife for the United States in 1930 and for southeastern Negroes for 1920 and 1930 is below 2.00; however, this does not indicate that these populations reached the fertility level below replacement. The distribution of wives by number of children ever borne is so heavily skewed to the right that we should expect the mean of the distribution to exceed considerably the median, and therefore the mean number of children ever borne per wife may be higher than 2.00 (or net reproduction rate exceed 1.00), as is actually true for the given populations.

marital status prevailing in the region in 1930 we estimate that at birth 83.3 percent of white females will live to be married. Similar calculations for Negroes give a percentage of 77.9. These ratios are low partly because of the toll that mortality takes before these females reach nuptial age. At its highest point, age 15 for white and colored, the rate is 90.8 percent first marriage expectancy for whites and 89.2 percent for colored. After this age the rate diminishes until few of the women left single at age 45 can look forward to marriage. In the older age Negro women have a much better chance of marrying than white women. According to our calculations, 21.2 percent of the single colored women of 45 and 4.2 percent of the white women will marry. Marriage expectancy rates are slightly higher at early ages than for the Nation, although the chances of white women's marrying after the age of 35 drop more rapidly in the Southeast.

We would expect the region's greater addiction to marriage to eventuate in higher birth rates. The median age of white brides at marriage is 21.2

FIGURE 73. THE PROLIFICACY DISTRIBUTION OF WHITE WIVES, UNITED STATES AND SOUTHEAST, 1929-1931

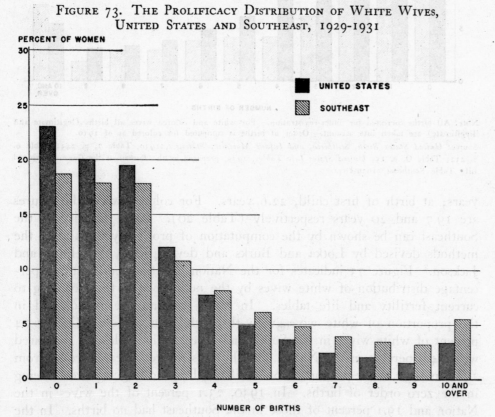

Source: United States data computed by P. K. Whelpton and N. E. Jackson, "Prolificacy Distribution of White Wives for Registration Area," *Human Biology*, XII (February, 1940), 54. Sources for the Southeast given in Figure 74.

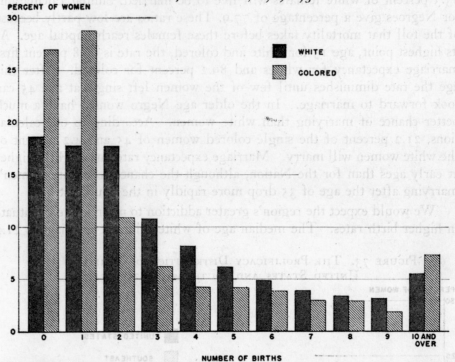

FIGURE 74. THE PROLIFICACY DISTRIBUTION OF WHITE AND COLORED WIVES, SOUTHEAST, 1929-1931

Note: All births corrected for under-registration. For white and colored wives all births (legitimate and illegitimate) are taken into account. Order of births is computed for colored as of 1930.

Source: *United States Birth, Stillbirth, and Infant Mortality Statistics, 1930,* Table 7, p. 243; Table 6, p. 232; Table Q, p. 15; *United States Life Tables, 1930,* prepared by the Bureau of the Census, abridged Life Table Southeast, 1929-1931.

years; at birth of first child, 22.6 years. For colored wives the figures are 19.7 and 20 years respectively (Table 20). Extra fertility of the Southeast can be shown by the computation of prolificacy rates after the methods devised by Lotka and Burks and developed by Whelpton and Jackson.[2] Figure 73 indicates for the Nation and the Southeast the percentage distribution of white wives by the number of births according to current fertility and life tables. In 1930 we find the Nation led in the proportion of white wives with three children or less. Only 65.4 percent of white wives in the South had three births or less as compared with 74.6 percent in the Nation. Both areas showed great increase from 1920 to 1930 in the proportion of small families, the largest increase being in the zero order of births. In 1930, 23.1 percent of the wives in the Nation and 19.1 percent of those in the Southeast had no births. In the

[2] P. K. Whelpton and Nelle E. Jackson, "Prolificacy Distribution of White Wives according to Fertility Tables for the Registration Area," *Human Biology,* XII (February, 1940), 54.

proportion with six or more births, the region has 20.6 percent of its white wives as compared with 12.8 for the Nation.

Comparison of prolificacy distribution as between white and colored women in the Southeast (Figure 74) is made difficult by the high percentage of Negro illegitimacy, reaching about 13 percent of all births in 1930. Illegitimate births are largest among first-order births, but with these included, a much larger proportion of Negro wives are found to have one or no children. Childlessness is much more common among Negroes. Figure 74 shows that 27 percent of Negro women have no births as compared with 19.1 percent of white women, while 28.8 percent Negroes have one birth as compared with 17.8 percent of white women. Up to the ninth child white women are more fertile than Negroes; but 7.3 percent of Negro wives have 10 children or more as compared with 5.5 percent of white wives.

THE DECLINE IN BIRTHS, 1920-1930

Certain of the important factors influencing recent changes in the birth rate can be stated in terms that are open to statistical measurement from figures that are available or can be estimated. Of these changes, four are of the greatest importance; namely, changes (1) in age-specific birth rates, (2) in the rural-urban distribution of the population, (3) in the age of the population, and (4) in the nativity and race distribution of the population. Following the method developed by Thompson and Whelpton,[3] we have attempted to measure the influence of these factors on the decline in births in the Southeast from 1920 to 1930 (Figure 75). The decline in age-specific fertility was found to be of much greater importance than all other changes in population composition. The 641,689 births occurring in 1929-1931 amounted to 88.1 percent of the births in 1918-1921. Twelve percent of the births, however, were due to the increase in the numbers of the population of 1930 over 1920. Changes in age-sex composition were actually favorable to a slight increase of 2.2 percent in births while changes in rural-urban distribution accounted for a loss of only 1.6 percent. Thus for the total population of the Southeast, the decline in specific fertility accounted for a loss of 180,733 births, a decline of 28.8 percent from the 1918-1921 level.

For the total population, changes in race composition accounted for practically no differences. For the white population considered separately it meant a gain of 4.3 percent in births, for the colored a loss of 8.6 percent. Change in rural-urban distribution meant slight losses in births—1.5

[3] Procedure described by Warren S. Thompson and P. K. Whelpton, *Population Trends in the United States* (New York: McGraw-Hill, 1933), p. 273, had to be somewhat modified because of the absence of some data required.

FIGURE 75. DIFFERENCE IN NUMBER OF BIRTHS BY RACE AS ATTRIBUTED
TO CHANGE IN FIVE FACTORS, SOUTHEAST, 1920-1930

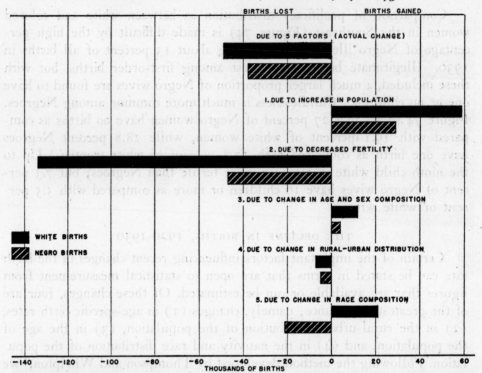

Source: *Population Statistics, State Data*, National Resources Committee, 1937, pp. 3 and 7; *Fourteenth Census of the United States, 1920*, Population, Vol. II, Ch. 3, Table 13; Vol. III, Table 10; *Fifteenth Census of the United States, 1930*, Population, Vol. II, Ch. 10, Table 24; Vol. III, Table 12; *United States Birth, Stillbirth, and Infant Mortality Statistics*, 1918-21 and 1929-31.

percent for the white and 2 percent for the colored. The change in age-sex distribution favored increased births for both races, 2.4 percent among the white and 1.8 percent among the colored population. For the whites the decline in age-specific fertility accounted for the greater loss in births, a decline of 27.4 percent as compared with a loss of 19.4 percent of the Negro births as of 1920. A much greater loss of potential Negro births since 1920 can be laid to the race's losses from interregional migration. Here they lost 8.6 percent of 1920 births as compared with a 4.3 percent gain among the white group.

FACTORS IN THE SOUTH'S EXTRA FERTILITY

These trends raise the question: What is responsible for the Southeast's extra fertility? Do the people of the region have a higher birth rate because they are more rural, because they are younger, or because of their racial composition? To the extent that southern fertility is found

FIGURE 76. CALCULATED LOSS OF BIRTHS IN THE SOUTHEAST UNDER THE
ASSUMPTION OF DEMOGRAPHIC CONDITIONS AS IN THE
UNITED STATES, 1930

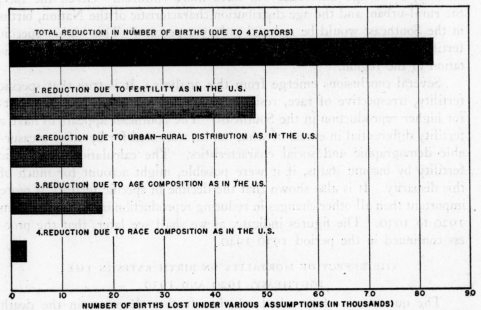

TOTAL REDUCTION IN NUMBER OF BIRTHS (DUE TO 4 FACTORS)

1. REDUCTION DUE TO FERTILITY AS IN THE U.S.

2. REDUCTION DUE TO URBAN—RURAL DISTRIBUTION AS IN THE U.S.

3. REDUCTION DUE TO AGE COMPOSITION AS IN THE U.S.

4. REDUCTION DUE TO RACE COMPOSITION AS IN THE U.S.

NUMBER OF BIRTHS LOST UNDER VARIOUS ASSUMPTIONS (IN THOUSANDS)

Source: *United States Birth, Stillbirth, and Infant Mortality Statistics,* 1930; Tables I and IV. Statistical
Abstract of the United States, 1937, Table 11.

not to depend on these factors, it must be due simply to the tendency of
women of given ages to have more children; that is, to higher age-
specific fertility.

There is available a technique for measuring the comparative importance of these four various factors on southern fertility. It consists of
assuming that all factors affecting fertility are held at the same rate as
in the Nation. This simply means that we must assume that the population of the Nation has shrunk to the size of that of the Southeast, keeping unchanged its ratios of (1) racial, (2) rural-urban, and (3) age distributions as well as all its specific birth rates.[4] When all factors affecting
fertility in the Southeast are held as in the Nation, it is found that births
in the Southeast in 1930 (Figure 76) would have been reduced by 82,760—
a decrease of 14.6 percent. National ratios in the distribution of races
would reduce total southern births by only .5 percent; in rural-urban residence,[5] by 2.5 percent; in age, 3.2 percent. Age-specific fertility is thus
responsible for a reduction of 47,691 births or 8.4 percent of the former

[4] Procedure used in these computations was an adaptation of method by Thompson and Whelpton
mentioned above.

[5] Urban population is here defined as in the *Vital Statistics Reports* as population in cities of 10.000
and over.

number. Thus it can be seen that over half of the area's extra fertility is simply due to the tendency of women in the region—irrespective of race, rurality, or of age difference—to have more children. Given the race, the rural-urban, and the age distribution characteristic of the Nation, births in the Southeast would be reduced only 6.2 percent. This higher specific fertility may be taken as an index of the lag in the practice of family limitation in the region.

Several conclusions emerge from this analysis. It is true that specific fertility, irrespective of race, residence, and age-sex composition, accounts for higher reproduction in the Southeast. The Southeast appears to have a fertility differential in excess of what can be accounted for by other measurable demographic and social characteristics. The calculation of specific fertility by income status, if it were possible, might account for much of this disparity. It is also shown that the decline in specific fertility is more important than all other changes in reducing reproduction in the region from 1920 to 1930. The figures indicate, as we shall see later, that the process continued in the period 1930-1940.

THE EFFECT OF MORTALITY ON BIRTH RATES IN THE SOUTHEAST, 1920 AND 1930

The question is often asked whether further decreases in the death rate will not serve to compensate for expected declines in births. The answer to this question is suggested for the Southeast in the following analysis. The death of women before they have passed through the child-bearing period has undoubtedly reduced births in the past; and with knowledge of death and birth rates by specific ages we can calculate the loss of births due to such deaths. The life of women, it was suggested, may be thought of as divided into three periods: the reproductive period, roughly 15-50; and the periods before and after. For purposes of our analysis the post-reproductive period can be disregarded. For, while increase in length of life of women after age 50 adds to the total population, such increase adds nothing to the number of births.

What, then, is the effect of deaths of mothers, actual and potential, on births in the Southeast? The actual annual loss in births because of mortality among women in the child-bearing ages, 15 to 50, is very small, falling under 1 percent of all births for the period 1929-31. However, this computation may be misleading because it only accounts for the actual loss of births—not the potential births that could have occurred if women could have been saved from death until the end of the reproductive period. It also disregards the very important loss of prospective mothers due to deaths of girls under 15, especially infant mortality. The importance of mortality among women in the reduction of births can be fully appraised only when the cumulative effect of all female deaths from age 0 to 50 is taken into account. Thus, using life table procedure and assuming age-specific fertility and mortality as of 1929-31, it can be shown that 13.9 percent of all white births and 28.1 percent of colored births could be saved in the Southeast, if no female deaths occurred from age 0 to the end of the child-bearing age (Figure 77). For 1918-21, the potential loss of births was much greater—22 percent for white mothers and 41.4 percent for colored. Obviously, deaths of colored women exact a much higher toll than those of white; however, both white and colored reproduction rates would have been considerably higher if a drastic reduction in female deaths could be accomplished.

These calculations lead us to several conclusions. As the South becomes more like the Nation, its births will decline; but as health conditions improve, births would presumably rise. Contraception for the masses thus would still remain an important issue in southern population.

FIGURE 77. ACTUAL NUMBER OF BIRTHS AND COMPUTED NUMBER OF BIRTHS LOST ANNUALLY BECAUSE OF MORTALITY OF WOMEN FROM BIRTH TO END OF THE REPRODUCTIVE PERIOD, SOUTHEAST BY RACE, 1929-1931

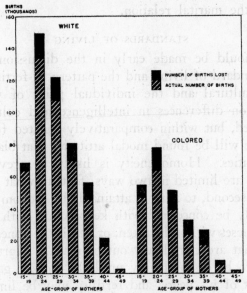

Source: *Population Statistics, State Data,* National Resources Committee, pp. 3 and 7; *Fifteenth Census of the United States, 1930,* Population, Vol. II, Chapter 10, Table 24; *United States Mortality Statistics, 1929, 1930, 1931;* Mary Gover, "Mortality Among Southern Negroes Since 1920," *Public Health Bulletin, No. 235,* p. 8; Frank Lorimer and Frederick Osborn, *Dynamics of Population* (New York, 1934), Appendix B, p. 356.

CULTURAL CONDITIONS

This is about as far as we can go in the attempt to explain reproductive behavior on the basis of statistical data gathered from the population *en masse*. Many students feel that we can not explain fertility patterns except in terms of the culture of the people and their personal attitudes, much as the anthropologist studies a new folk group. Cultural studies of the high fertility complex in folk-regional areas, however, are few and far between.[6] It is safe to say that none of the attempts yet made satisfy the criteria established by anthropology for cultural studies or those set up by social psychology for studies of motivation and attitudes.

Admitting the obvious difficulties faced by such studies, we may well discuss two unsolved problems in this field. The first has to do with the involved relation of that culture complex known as the standard of living to the actual level of living as affected by the size of the family. Here we may well inquire as to what extent groups with excess fertility possess standards higher than their actual levels of living. The second unsolved problem is reached when we ask why standards do not go over into family limitation practices. This question should also be attacked as a problem in the culture complex. It leads to a consideration of folk attitudes toward sex behavior in the marital relation.

STANDARDS OF LIVING

The point should be made early in the discussion that phenomena related to the standard of living and the pattern of fertility can be viewed from both the cultural and the individual point of view. Individual variations based on differences in intelligence and cultural participation should be expected, but within comparatively isolated folk, regional, and class groups there will be found modal attitudes that blanket these homogeneous communities. Homogeneity is likely to prevail in such areas because standards are limited in two ways: first, to what is known by communication; and, second, to what is attainable by economic status. A tenant family will hardly be concerned with keeping up with the Joneses, (1) if there are no Joneses within their ken, or (2) if the Joneses they encounter have standards that are completely out of reach. Marriage in such folk groups is likely to be delayed only until the worker gains a competence equivalent to that of his peers, and fertility may be limited little or not at all.

[6] A cooperative study of social and psychological factors affecting fertility among a selected native white group in Indianapolis is now being made under the auspices of the Milbank Memorial Fund, with grants from the Carnegie Corporation of New York. A progress report was presented by P. K. Whelpton, field director of the investigation, at the Nineteenth Annual Conference of the Milbank Memorial Fund. For a summary of the report, see: Lowell J. Reed, "Research in Factors Influencing Fertility," *American Journal of Public Health*, XXXI (September, 1941), 984-985.

The implications of the cultural point of view may be further explored. We have been told by practically every study in the field that contraceptives, including widely known folk methods, are only the means or mechanics of family limitation. The motivation to their use must come largely from the family's desire to attain or maintain a certain standard of living. Here we are concerned with groups on whom the ordinary prudential controls weigh so lightly that such means are but little used. Stix and Notestein rightly point out that "the situation will not be rapidly altered merely by making modern contraception available to populations that have not utilized the folkway methods at their disposal. There must also be the will to reduce fertility."[7]

So far our analysis has shown the association of low levels of living with high fertility but it has not explained that association in terms of values and attitudes; that is, of the culture content of the standard of living of these groups. Thus the introduction of contraceptive practices involves the invasion of new values and the adoption of new attitudes—not merely the acceptance of an efficient technique.

The structure of prevailing attitudes is to be found in the cultural content of the standard of living. If there exists the validity assumed in the distinction between the standard of living and the level of living, this distinction should be of value in determining why folk and other methods of family limitation are not more widely used.

The question involved may be posed in such fashion as to bring out the distinction between standards and actual levels of living. Is it possible, for example, that a people can be led to raise their standard of what they expect from life without having first experienced an increase in their actual levels of living? We so often see this accomplished by highly motivated individuals that we may feel it is unnecessary to ask the question about groups. Such a question intimates that a group may glean a cultural definition of the situation from something other than cultural experience. The experiencing which conditions the motivation to raise standards would thus be vicarious and symbolic, deriving from verbal conditioning.

Concretely, the calculation of a standard versus a level of living is best carried on in a money economy by an informal process of balancing the books of a family budget. The subsistence areas of the Appalachians and the credit and "furnish" system of southern tenancy areas, it must be recalled, have largely remained outside the cash nexus of our money economy. This is especially true in relation to the economics of large families. Initial costs of child birth and prenatal care are met by the minimum services of midwives and neighborhood help. The system of

[7] R. K. Stix and F. W. Notestein, *Controlled Fertility* (Baltimore: The Williams and Wilkins Company, 1940), p. 152.

cost accounting and anticipation forced on the urban dweller is largely evaded and only gradually makes its appearance as the number of children increases in the rural household. Deferred payments and do-without enter largely into the lower level of living which creeps with less evident calculation upon the growing family in agrarian areas. Less is done for children in such culture areas, and more is expected from them in co-operative farm work and family labor—an evasion which the city dweller cannot make.

We may ask what, for example, does high-school education, slowly making its way among some of these groups, do for those in the lower levels? It is usually assumed that such acculturation operates to raise standards and lower fertility, and that these trends then go over into increased incomes and improved levels of living. We have many campaigns to raise the levels of living of groups. What would happen to a campaign which, making no attempt to increase incomes, attempted to raise a people's standards?

One of the techniques of revolution, it is pointed out, has been found in the attempt to raise a people's expectations and standards above any reasonable hope of immediate attainment. The resulting tension is then assumed to offer the motivation for revolt. In the economic field this would involve changes in the cultural definition of the situation based not on experienced reality but on vicarious and symbolic experience, founded on propaganda or education.

Negatively, a lowering of actual levels of living should operate to restrict fertility in a way that the attempts to effect a rising standard have not yet achieved among folk groups. That this is no idle theory is indicated by the one example of Ireland. A dire famine that threatened, in fact destroyed, subsistence for many has given that country the lowest marriage rate in the world. Ireland is the one country which followed Malthus' advice, namely, limitation of population increase by practice of "delayed marriage with moral restraint." Carr-Saunders has shown that from 1841 to 1926 the proportion of females aged 25 to 35 who were unmarried rose from 28 to 53 percent.[8] For those who marry, age-specific fertility has fallen but little. What Ireland accomplished by following Malthus and the Catholic Church, other peoples do by family limitation when their standards are threatened. Yet the socially isolated mountain people, rural Negroes, and farm tenants who have not been led to adopt contraceptive practices by an urge to raise standards in a subsistence or a credit economy do accept family limitation when they migrate to cities. Any serious threat to their present low levels of living might also reduce fertility.

[8] A. M. Carr-Saunders, *World Population* (Oxford: Clarendon Press, 1936), pp. 90-92.

In the expansive period of cotton culture, farm youth lacking capital and experience were able to enter marriage and agriculture at the same time on the low level of cropper tenancy. Pre-war conditions in cotton culture, discussed in Chapter 16, suggest that these openings are being closed, and the displacement of farm tenants and the threatened disintegration of the system bring up certain comparisons with the situation of the Irish peasantry. Such drastic changes may operate to delay marriage and depress fertility at a faster rate than anticipated after the war.

SEX ATTITUDES

Sex behavior has its motivations no less than economic behavior. Sex attitudes of the folk in the marital relation deserve more discussion in this connection than they have yet received. One of the contributions of Margaret Jarman Hagood's study of farm tenant mothers was to show that among the folk this relation is not often discussed between husband and wife, and that, moreover, there exists no scientific or objective terminology in which it can be discussed.[9]

Dr. Hagood found that the general attitude of not wanting more children was unaccompanied by any general practices designed to prevent their conception. Of 69 tenant farm mothers questioned only 8 used contraceptives. Nevertheless 37 out of 42 expressed opinions favoring birth control. She found a common complaint that "doctors tell you not to have any more children but won't tell you nothing to do about it." Fourteen asked directly what to do.

This attitude on the part of farm mothers is one of hopeless resignation rather than one of either revolt or prudential control. Revolt would involve negative attitudes toward customary morality, toward religion, and toward their husbands to whom they acknowledge affection and duties. Prudential behavior would involve more control over marital relations than can be assumed of wives in the folk group.

Here we may be confronted by a masculine-feminine dichotomy which is not resolved by interaction in the marriage relation. In patriarchal cultures the consideration of these questions of family limitation may go by default, largely because of the unseen factors of masculine aggression and dominance in the sex relation. Folk methods of family limitation are not used and technical methods which depend upon the initiative of the wife are not introduced. Here we need a knowledge of the sex and fertility attitudes of husbands comparable to that of the mothers studied by Dr. Hagood.

[9] Margaret Jarman Hagood, *Mothers of the South* (Chapel Hill: University of North Carolina Press, 1939), pp. 122-125.

Masculine domination, however, is but a partial approach if we admit validity to the previous discussion of economic status and standards of living. One would find, no doubt, that among husbands the conflict between prudential and hedonistic motives had given rise to a feeling of resignation involving rationalizations similar to those of the wives. The uncovering of such attitudes, however, would be much more difficult.

It is now realized that the most optimistic assumption of the early birth-control movement was that of an ideal contraceptive which would place little or no restraint on the pleasure principle. We now realize that the libido will be subject to prudential restraint and that the motivation of this behavior among folk groups must come from economic pressures that represent the resolution of forces and motives engendered by desires for an improved level of living. Much has been said of the place of contraceptive clinics in the public health program. It can be added that public health programs devoted to the diffusion of better prenatal and obstetric care, if at all implemented in economic terms, would do much to raise standards and thus lower fertility among folk groups. The more care that is devoted to each child under the influence of rising standards, the fewer children the family in any cultural group is likely to have. It is in this field that individual attitudes meet with public policy—a topic that must be reserved for discussion in later chapters on population policy and planning.

CHAPTER 9

MOVING ACROSS THE MAP

If all the [farm] laborers in a village bring up several Sons in the same work there will be too many Laborers to cultivate the land belonging to this village and the superfluous adults will have to seek their living somewhere else, ordinarily in the Cities: if some stay with their Fathers, since they will not find enough work they will live in great poverty, and will not marry or if they marry the children born will soon die of misery along with the Father and the Mother, as we see every day in France.—Richard Cantillon, "Essai Sur La Nature Du Commerce en Général," 1755, in A. E. Monroe, *Early Economic Thought*, p. 247.

PRECEDING chapters have indicated the high rate of natural increase in the Southeast. The population resulting could have been retained in the region only by a greatly expanding economy. Economic expansion in agriculture and industry, once the area was fully settled, has not been large enough to take care of all natural increase. The Southeast was among the first areas to be settled and its states have contributed a large share to the streams of internal migration which have flowed across our country. There are, for example, certain Coastal and Piedmont counties in Virginia which had less population in 1930 than at the time of the first Census in 1790.

As an important part of population study the trend of migration since 1850 will be reviewed in this chapter. It may help somewhat, as we have suggested, to think of our regions as great reservoirs of population connected with each other by streams of migration. Into each region, population flows by the entrances of birth and immigration. Out of each region population flows by the exits of death and emigration. The level attained by these flows gives us an ever changing regional balance of population which, no doubt, bears some relation to the supporting capacity of the area viewed in terms of (1) physical resources, (2) the state of economic organization and the technical arts, (3) the training and abilities of the population, and (4) the relationship of the region to other areas. Such a view sees the region as a reservoir of population and views migration into or out of the area as an index of important economic and social changes.

When the inflow of natural increase is great, the outflow of migration is also likely to be large. The only alternative, Cantillion believed in 1755, is likely to be death of part of the population. We realize today that within certain undefined limits the reservoir itself can increase in size—that is to say there may be an expansion of the basis of economic support of the people. This has happened in the Southeast and one object of our study is to show something of the trend of migration as it relates to economic development in the region and the Nation.

THE TREND OF MIGRATION

The Southern population has taken part in three great migrations: one agricultural and two industrial. These are (1) the expansion westward of the Cotton Kingdom, (2) the great interstate migration to the Northeast and Middle States, and (3) the movement to the region's own cities.

The first, the expansion of the Cotton Kingdom, is a familiar theme of historians of the Old South and lies largely outside our consideration. The pull of new resources and the push of population increase and soil exhaustion prompted it, and the movement carried the Cotton Kingdom from the Sea Islands to the Panhandle. We will never know how many sons of farm owners moved West to become tenants, but we do know that as the Cotton Belt approached the limits of its geographic and market expansion, the proportion of tenants and croppers increased. This population increase is a fact of importance for the region's later migrations.

The early agricultural migration was characterized by the continued position of the East as a reservoir of population. Thornthwaite uses State of birth data to show that by 1850 Virginia, the Carolinas, Kentucky, Georgia, and Tennessee were losing native white population by migration.[1] By 1870 Alabama had become a State of net outward migration to be joined by Mississippi in 1880, Louisiana in 1890, and Arkansas in 1920. In the Southeast only Louisiana and Florida have consistently gained more population than they have lost by migration since 1880. Between 1890 and 1900 the principal movements were into Texas from the old South

---

[1] C. Warren Thornthwaite, *Internal Migration in the United States* (Philadelphia: University of Pennsylvania Press, 1934), Plate II and pp. 9-11. Estimates of the amount of the population movements have to be calculated from the very inadequate data we have on interstate migration and rural-urban migration. All figures on internal migration, it must be emphasized, are estimates and vary according to types of data and methods used in their calculation. Until the 1940 Census there were four main sources: (1) Census materials on State of birth and of residence of the white and Negro population born in continental United States furnish partial evidence on the nature and course of migrations. (2) Age-group data from the Census can be manipulated with life tables to show net migration by States. (3) Vital statistics can be used in connection with the Census to show net migration for units as small as counties. (4) Estimates made by the Department of Agriculture since 1920 show rural urban migration, but by Census Divisions only. In the interpretation of migration figures based on any of these sources, two qualifications must be kept in mind: that the figures are estimates rather than direct measures of migration, and that all except the rural-urban estimates are of net movement rather than of total magnitudes.

(102,000) and into Oklahoma from the Middle West (152,000). In addition there was a small movement from the Middle West into California (10,000). Between 1900 and 1910 the movement into Oklahoma assumed large proportions (445,000 without including 111,000 from Texas), as did also a movement from the more northernly of the middle western states into Washington and Oregon (295,000).[2]

The second movement has been the great interstate migration to industrial areas, mainly in the Northeast and Middle States. Thornthwaite feels that the migration history of all agricultural areas follows a uniform pattern. About three decades after the first settlement, the immigration surplus reaches a maximum and after about three more decades of decreasing surplus, emigration sets in. This pattern is made clear by mapping States of surplus and deficit migration from State of birth data offered in the Census. This transition is further shown by the decline in the East-West migration and the increase in the South-North movement. In 1890, 10.1 percent of the people born east of the Mississippi River were living west of it while only 2.9 percent of those born west were living east of the River. By 1930 these percentages had changed to 6.6 and 5.4 respectively. From 1890 to 1930 the percentage born South and living in the North increased from 5.8 to 8.6. Similarly the proportions born in the North and living in the South have grown slowly from 2.0 percent in 1890 to only 3.2 in 1930.[3]

THE RECORD OF THE SOUTHEAST

Calculations for the Southeast on the basis of age-group data show that by decades the net loss by migration of native whites grew from a mere trickle of 21,200 in the 1870's to over a million in the 1920's. Table 21 shows that over six decades this net loss increased from —0.4 percent to —7.5 percent of the region's native white population. Over the sixty year period following 1870 the Southeast experienced a net loss of three and a third million native white people. In each decade before 1930 the numerical loss has increased and in every decade, except 1890-1900, the percentage loss has increased. For 1920 *Southern Regions* computed for the region a net migration loss since birth of over 2,375,000; by 1930 this had grown to 3,412,000 indicating a net outward movement of over a million in the 1920-1930 decade. From 1930 to 1940, however, this outflow decreased to a mere trickle of less than 1,000.

More males than females migrated outside the area in every period except the decade 1910 to 1920 (Table 22). Just what is indicated by the

---

[2] *Ibid.*, pp. 16-18.

[3] Warren S. Thompson. *Research Memorandum on Internal Migration in the Depression* (New York: Social Science Research Council, 1937), p. 15.

TABLE 21. DECENNIAL NET LOSS BY MIGRATION OF NATIVE WHITE
POPULATION, SOUTHEAST, 1870-1940

Decennial period	Population at beginning of decennial period	Expected population at end of decennial period	Actual population at end of period	Loss	
				Number	Percent
	(in 1000's)				
1870-1880..................	5,889.9	7,662.7	7,601.5	− 21.2	−0.4
1880-1890..................	7,601.5	9,596.5	9,184.2	− 421.3	−5.4
1890-1900..................	9,184.2	10,963.8	10,504.7	− 459.1	−5.2
1900-1910..................	10,504.7	13,108.5	12,528.8	− 579.8	−5.5
1910-1920..................	12,528.8	15,322.5	14,522.3	− 800.2	−6.4
1920-1930..................	14,522.3	18,042.9	16,958.3	−1,084.6	−7.5
1930-1940..................	16,598.3	19,272.6	19,271.7	− 0.9	−0.0

Source: H. L. Geisert, The Balance of Inter-State Migration in the Southeast (unpublished doctoral dissertation, University of North Carolina, 1938), p. 125. Based on age-group data from the Census with special adjustment for the population under ten years of age.

TABLE 22. DECENNIAL CHANGE BY NET MIGRATION IN NATIVE WHITE
POPULATION, BY SEX, SOUTHEAST, 1870-1930

Decennial period and sex	Net change by migration		Decennial period and sex	Net change by migration	
	Number	Percent		Number	Percent
1870-1880			1900-1910		
Male............	− 42,468	−1.5	Male............	−298,793	−5.6
Female..........	21,244	0.7	Female..........	−280,971	−5.4
1880-1890			1910-1920		
Male............	−211,821	−5.6	Male............	−399,402	−6.3
Female..........	−200,515	−5.3	Female..........	−400,783	−6.5
1890-1900			1920-1930		
Male............	−240,741	−5.5	Male............	−569,708	−7.7
Female..........	−218,370	−5.0	Female..........	−514,917	−7.2

Source: H. L. Geisert, The Balance of Inter-State Migration in the Southeast (unpublished doctoral dissertation, University of North Carolina, 1938), p. 125.

predominance of male migrants is difficult to say because of the paucity of data. It may suggest that while men were drawn to heavy industries outside the region the women of the South were not taking advantage of clerical and other opportunities open to women. On the other hand there is the suggestion drawn from 1920-1930 data that women move in greater number to the towns and cities within the region. The differences in any case are not great.

The year 1930 offers a point of vantage for balancing the migration accounts of our total native-born population. The regional picture of migration since birth can be presented from the State birth-residence data. In 1930, 86.4 percent of all native population were still living in the State where they were born. Table 23 shows that the Far West and the Northeast have held the largest proportion of their people, 93.2 and 91.8 percent respectively; the Northwest even in 1930 had lost the most—holding only 73.5 percent of its native born. Next come the Southeast, Southwest, and Middle States, each retaining about 85 percent of their native born. Inspection of the table will also serve to indicate where the natives of each

TABLE 23. NATIVE POPULATION BY REGION OF BIRTH WITH NUMBER AND PERCENTAGE OF INHABITANTS RESIDING WITHIN OR OUTSIDE THE REGION OF THEIR BIRTH, UNITED STATES AND THE SIX MAJOR REGIONS, 1930

Region of birth		Region of Residence								
		All regions	Northeast	Southeast	Southwest	Middle States	Northwest	Far West	D. C.	Total living in other regions
UNITED STATES	Number	108,065,719	30,475,611	25,283,743	8,567,855	29,875,047	6,705,322	6,706,480	451,661	14,679,375
	Percent	100.0	28.2	23.4	7.9	27.6	6.2	6.2	0.5	13.6
Northeast	Number	31,108,045	28,543,905	316,461	105,025	1,312,064	182,461	535,633	112,496	2,564,140
	Percent	100.0	91.8	1.0	0.3	4.2	0.6	1.7	0.4	8.2
Southeast	Number	28,695,893	1,102,954	24,220,863	1,132,742	1,635,508	176,092	308,140	119,594	4,475,030
	Percent	100.0	3.8	84.4	3.9	5.7	0.6	1.1	0.5	15.6
Southwest	Number	7,286,848	37,253	170,191	6,448,379	149,045	177,365	301,412	3,203	838,469
	Percent	100.0	0.5	2.3	88.5	2.0	2.4	4.1	0.1	11.5
Middle States	Number	30,947,423	619,379	494,223	601,651	26,144,216	1,455,394	1,604,157	28,403	4,803,207
	Percent	100.0	2.0	1.6	1.9	84.5	4.7	5.2	0.1	11.5
Northwest	Number	6,310,780	71,103	49,207	240,427	564,923	4,638,248	741,819	5,053	1,672,532
	Percent	100.0	1.1	0.8	3.8	9.0	73.5	11.8	0.1	26.5
Far West	Number	3,442,614	44,203	13,750	38,069	60,415	74,260	3,209,869	2,048	232,745
	Percent	100.0	1.3	0.4	1.1	1.8	2.1	93.2	0.1	6.8
D. C.	Number	274,116	56,814	19,048	1,562	8,876	1,502	5,450	180,864	93,252

Note: The small number of persons for whom State of birth was not reported are omitted from this table. The total number of persons in the United States living in their State of birth are 93,386,344, or 86.4 percent of all native population.
Source: *Abstract of the Fifteenth Census of the United States, 1930*, Population (General), Table 56.

region lived in 1930. Thus we can pick out the favorite areas of migration by showing that 4.2 percent of those born in the Northeast lived in the Middle States while 5.2 percent of the natives of the Middle States live in the Far West. From the Southeast 5.7 percent have gone to the Middle States, 3.9 percent to the Southwest, and 3.8 percent to the Northeast.

Figure 78 gives the ranking by States in percentage of natives lost. Only 8.3 percent of those born in California live elsewhere, as compared with more than 35 percent from such diverse States as Montana, Iowa, Vermont, Kansas, and Nevada. While native-born Southerners have moved in smaller proportions than natives of the Northwest, 15.6 percent as compared with 26.5 percent, the States of the Southeast rank higher in their contribution of numbers.

FIGURE 78. PERCENTAGE OF NATIVE-BORN POPULATION LIVING IN
OTHER STATES, UNITED STATES, 1930

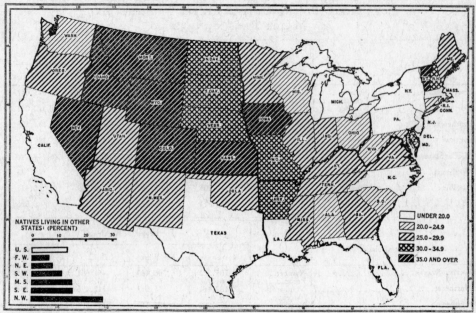

Source: *Abstract of the Fifteenth Census of the United States, 1930*, Population, General, Table 53.

Table 24 and Figure 79 indicate the areas of birth of the resident populations. Thus Table 24 shows that 52.1 percent of the residents in the Far West were born elsewhere, as compared with only 30.8 percent for the Northwest and 24.7 percent for the Southwest. The Southeast has received the smallest proportion from other regions, 4.2 percent. Further examination of the table shows the regions of origin. Thus 13.2 percent of the native resident population of the Southwest was from the Southeast. The Middle States have drawn more of their residents from the Southeast, 5.5 percent, than elsewhere. The Southeast, drawing but lightly, drew most from the Middle States and the Northeast, 1.9 percent and 1.3 percent respectively.

Figure 79, which shows similar data for States, admits only Oklahoma and Florida to that western group of states which drew more than 45 percent of their resident population from other States. Among the States drawing less than 15 percent of their residents from other areas will be found 8 States of the Southeast and 3 of the Northeast.

The differences that we have recounted are so great that we may attempt from Figure 80 to balance accounts in the ledger of migration. The Far West has received a net immigration of 3,263,866, amounting to 48.7 percent of its resident native population. The absolute loss of the

TABLE 24. NATIVE POPULATION BY REGION OF RESIDENCE WITH NUMBER AND PERCENTAGE OF INHABITANTS BORN WITHIN OR OUTSIDE THE REGION OF THEIR RESIDENCE, UNITED STATES AND THE SIX MAJOR REGIONS, 1930

Region of Residence		Region of Birth				
		All regions	Northeast	Southeast	Southwest	Middle States
UNITED STATES.........	Number......	108,065,719	31,108,045	28,695,893	7,286,848	30,947,423
	Percent......	100.0	28.8	26.6	6.7	28.6
Northeast..............	Number......	30,475,611	28,543,905	1,102,954	37,253	619,379
	Percent......	100.0	93.7	3.6	0.1	2.0
Southeast.............	Number......	25,283,743	316,461	24,220,863	170,191	494,223
	Percent......	100.0	1.3	95.8	0.7	1.9
Southwest.............	Number......	8,567,855	105,025	1,132,742	6,448,379	601,651
	Percent......	100.0	1.2	13.2	75.3	7.0
Middle States...........	Number......	29,875,047	1,312,064	1,635,508	149,045	26,144,216
	Percent......	100.0	4.4	5.5	0.5	87.5
Northwest..............	Number......	6,705,322	182,461	176,092	177,365	1,455,394
	Percent......	100.0	2.7	2.6	2.6	21.7
Far West..............	Number......	6,706,480	535,633	308,140	301,412	1,604,157
	Percent......	100.0	8.0	4.6	4.5	23.9
D. C.................	Number......	451,661	112,496	119,594	3,203	28,403

Region of residence		Region of Birth				
		Northwest	Far West	D. C.	All other than region of residence	Total Movement†
UNITED STATES.........	Number......	6,310,780	3,442,614	274,116	14,679,375	29,358,750÷2= =14,679,375
	Percent......	5.8	3.2	0.3	13.6	
Northeast..............	Number......	71,103	44,203	56,814	1,931,706	4,495,846
	Percent......	0.2	0.1	0.2	6.3	14.8
Southeast..............	Number......	49,207	13,750	19,048	1,062,880	5,537,910
	Percent......	0.2	*	0.1	4.2	21.9
Southwest..............	Number......	240,427	38,069	1,562	2,119,476	2,957,945
	Percent......	2.8	0.5	*	24.7	34.5
Middle States...........	Number......	564,923	60,415	8,876	3,730,831	8,534,038
	Percent......	1.9	0.2	*	12.5	28.6
Northwest..............	Number......	4,638,248	74,260	1,502	2,067,074	3,739,606
	Percent......	69.2	1.1	*	30.8	55.8
Far West..............	Number......	741,819	3,209,869	5,450	3,496,611	3,729,356
	Percent......	11.1	47.9	0.1	52.1	55.6
D. C.................	Number......	5,053	2,048	180,864	270,797	364,049

*Less than 0.1 percent.

†Total movement from and to region, i. e., arithmetic sum of inhabitants born outside of the region where they reside (Table 24) and those born in a given region but residing outside of it (Table 23). For the United States as a whole the total sum (29,358,750) of migrants should be divided by 2 to get total number of migrants without duplication, since every movement affects two regions at one time, and should be counted as one movement, and not as two when we consider the United States total. For instance, in this table, we see that 316,461 persons were born in the Northeast and moved to the Southeast; they would therefore be included among the 1,062,880 migrants for the Southeast (total born in other regions). But in Table 23 these same 316,461 persons appear in the row for the Northeast as residing outside the region where they were born and are therefore included among the 2,564,140 migrants from the Northeast. Since we obtain the total volume of movement by adding the two last columns in Tables 23 and 24, we see that our 316,461 migrants would be counted twice in the total for the Nation. The net interregional gain or loss through migration (algebraic sum of the same last columns of Tables 23 and 24) is given in Table 25 (last column, net balance).

Note: The small number of persons for whom State of birth was not reported are omitted from this table.

Source: *Abstract of the Fifteenth Census of the United States, 1930*, Population, General, Table 56.

Southeast, 3,412,150, was larger but it amounted to only 13.5 percent of the resident population. Table 25 also shows the region to or from which the interregional migration took place. Thus we can find that of the net loss of over 3,400,000 in the Southeast, 1,141,000 went to the Middle States, 962,000 to the Southwest, and so on. Interestingly enough the Southeast sent to the District of Columbia almost twice as many net migrants, 100,546, as did any other region.

Figure 81 which shows data by States serves to emphasize the losses

FIGURE 79. PERCENTAGE OF STATE RESIDENTS BORN IN OTHER STATES, UNITED STATES, 1930

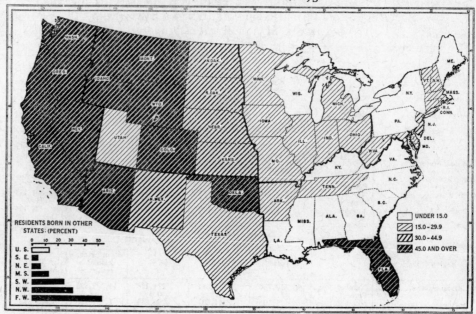

Source: See Figure 78.

FIGURE 80. THE BALANCE OF INTERREGIONAL MIGRATION AMONG THE NATIVE POPULATION SINCE BIRTH, THE SIX MAJOR REGIONS, 1930

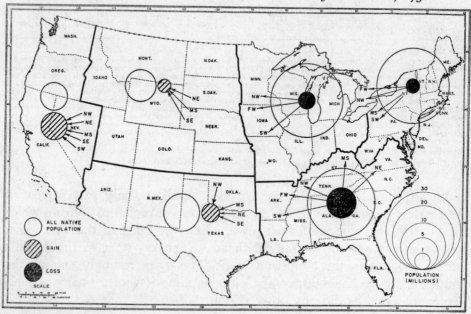

Source: See Figure 78.

of the Southeast and the gains of Far Western States. Vermont lost 32.1 percent of its population. California gained 53.2 percent by net migration.

TABLE 25. BALANCE OF INTERREGIONAL MIGRATION AMONG ALL NATIVE POPULATION, UNITED STATES AND THE SIX MAJOR REGIONS, 1930

Region for which net gain (+) or loss (−) is indicated	Region to or from which interregional migration took place							Total net gain	Total net loss	Net balance
	North-east	South-east	South-west	Middle States	North-west	Far West	D. C.			
UNITED STATES..	+632,434	+3,412,150	−1,281,007	+1,072,376	−394,542	−3,263,866	−177,545	+8,739,981	−8,739,981	0
Northeast..	....	+ 786,493	− 67,772	− 692,685	−111,358	− 491,430	− 55,682	+ 786,493	−1,418,927	− 632,434
Southeast..	−786,493	....	− 962,551	−1,141,285	−126,885	− 294,390	−100,546	0	−3,412,150	−3,412,150
Southwest..	+ 67,772	+ 962,551	....	+ 452,606	+ 63,062	− 263,343	− 1,641	+1,545,991	− 264,984	+1,281,007
Middle States...	+692,685	+1,141,285	− 452,606	....	−890,471	−1,543,742	− 19,527	+1,833,970	−2,906,346	−1,072,376
Northwest..	+111,358	+ 126,885	− 63,062	+ 890,471	....	− 667,559	− 3,551	+1,128,714	− 734,172	+ 394,542
Far West..	+491,430	+ 294,390	+ 263,343	+1,543,742	+667,559	....	+ 3,402	+3,263,866	0	+3,263,866
D. C......	+ 55,862	+ 100,546	+ 1,641	+ 19,527	+ 3,551	− 3,402	....	+ 180,947	− 3,402	+ 177,545

Source: *Abstract of the Fifteenth Census of the United States, 1930*, Population (General), Table 56.

FIGURE 81. NET CHANGE IN THE NATIVE POPULATION THROUGH INTERSTATE MIGRATION, UNITED STATES, 1930

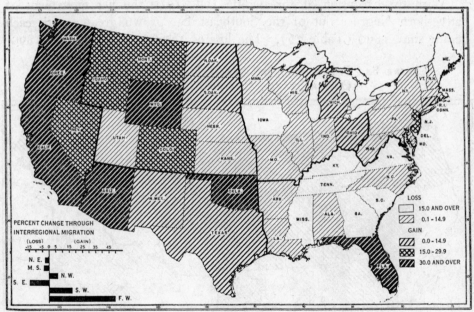

Source: See Figure 78.

NEGRO MIGRATION

Negro migration deserves separate treatment. By 1930, 26.3 percent of the Negroes born in the Southeast were living outside, making a net loss of over 1,840,000 population. This figure may be compared with the 15.6 percent of all southern born population who were living outside the region in 1930. Figure 82 shows that the proportion of Negroes living outside their States of birth in 1930 ranged from only 12.6 percent for Texas to 75.1 percent for North Dakota. Of the Southern States, Florida, Louisiana, and North Carolina had lost the smallest proportion of their Negro population. Kentucky, Virginia, and Tennessee had lost the largest proportions. In the West where Negroes are numerically unimportant they appear the least firmly settled. These States have lost from 40 to 75 percent of the Negroes born within their borders. Conversely Figure 83 shows that from 60 to 90 percent of the resident Negroes in these States were born outside. It is the southern States of densest Negro population that have drawn the smallest proportion from outside their borders. Thus only 2.2 percent of the Negroes in South Carolina came from elsewhere, and less than 10 percent of their resident Negroes were born outside the States of Louisiana, Georgia, Mississippi, and Alabama. Florida, with 38.1 percent, and Arkansas, with 28.6 percent, have drawn the largest proportion from outside. In Texas, surprisingly enough, only 11.4 percent of the resident Negroes were born in other states.

With the exception of the decade 1900-1910 the net movement of native-born Negroes out of the Southeast has grown greater with each decade since 1890 (Table 26). The loss of 129,000 in the decade 1890-

FIGURE 82. PERCENTAGE OF NATIVE-BORN NEGROES LIVING IN
OTHER STATES, UNITED STATES, 1930

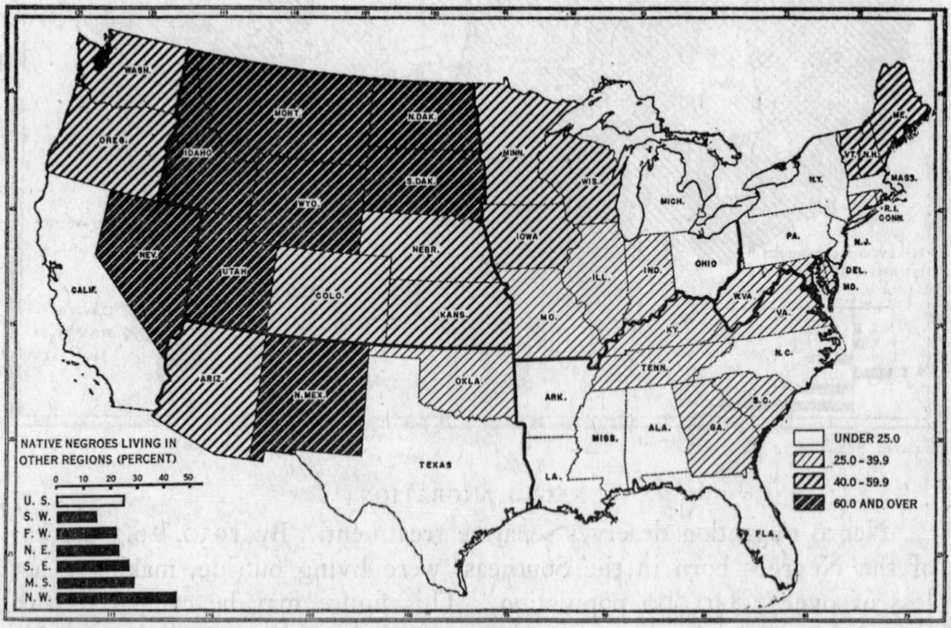

Source: *Abstract of the Fifteenth Census of the United States, 1930*, Population, General, Table 55.

FIGURE 83. PERCENTAGE OF NEGRO RESIDENTS BORN IN OTHER
STATES, UNITED STATES, 1930

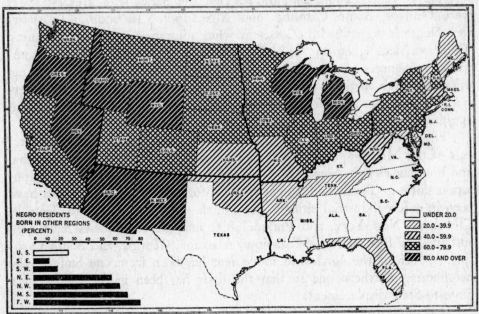

Source: See Figure 82.

TABLE 26. NET LOSS BY MIGRATION OF NATIVE NEGRO
POPULATION, SOUTHEAST, 1890-1930

Decade	Native Negro population*	Loss by migration	Percent loss	Decade	Native Negro population*	Loss by migration	Percent loss
1890 - 1900....	5,899,000	−129,000	2.2	1910 - 1920...	6,591,000	−323,000	4.9
1900 - 1910....	6,845,000	− 99,000	1.4	1920 - 1930...	7,536,000	−615,000	8.2

*At beginning of decennial period. All figures rounded to the nearest thousand.

Source: C. Warren Thornthwaite, *Internal Migration in the United States* (Philadelphia: University of Pennsylvania Press, 1934); *Eleventh Census of the United States, 1890; Twelfth Census of the United States, 1900; Abstract of the Fifteenth Census of the United States, 1930*, Population, General, Table 55.

TABLE 27. NET CHANGE BY MIGRATION OF NEGRO AND NATIVE WHITE
POPULATION FROM THE SOUTHEAST, 1920-1930

State	State of birth data		Age-group data		State	State of birth data		Age-group data	
	Negro	White	Negro	White		Negro	White	Negro	White
SOUTHEAST.......	−615,000	−478,000	−796,000	−582,000	Georgia.........	−212,000	−117,000	−261,000	−156,000
					Florida.........	+ 79,000	+202,000	+ 54,000	+267,000
Virginia.........	− 64,000	− 51,000	−117,000	−111,000	Alabama.......	− 56,000	− 45,000	− 81,000	− 70,000
North Carolina...	+ 3,000	+ 43,000	− 16,000	+ 4,000	Mississippi.....	− 81,000	− 14,000	− 69,000	− 34,000
South Carolina...	−149,000	− 26,000	−205,000	− 53,000	Arkansas.......	− 80,000	−192,000	− 47,000	−139,000
Kentucky........	+ 1,000	−124,000	− 15,000	−188,000	Louisiana........	− 55,000	− 23,000	− 25,000	+ 1,000
Tennessee........	− 1,000	− 31,000	− 14,000	−101,000					

Note: One reason for the higher figures in the age-group data is that they include all Negroes whereas the State of birth data embrace only native-born Negroes.

Source: C. Warren Thornthwaite, *Internal Migration in the United States* (Philadelphia: University of Pennsylvania Press, 1934), Column 1, Plate III, D, p. 8; Column 2, Plate II, H, p. 8, Columns 3, 4, Plate VII, A and B.

1900 grew to a loss of 615,000 by 1920-1930. In the 1920's the region lost 8.2 percent. Table 27 indicates that the States with greatest losses were Georgia, South Carolina, and Mississippi. In addition it shows that Negro losses exceed the losses by white migration except for Arkansas, Tennessee, and Kentucky. Finally the table affords an interesting comparison of sources, showing that age-group data give larger estimates of net migration than State of birth figures. For whites the excess is 21.8 percent, for Negroes it is higher, 29.4. This is due in part to the fact that age-group calculations were not limited to native Negroes.

The movement of Negro population has been concentrated in States east of the Mississippi and has been from South to North across the Ohio and Potomac rivers. Some Negro migration has paralleled the great population shifts to Texas, Oklahoma, and California, but the great gains have been in a few industrial cities in the North—St. Louis, Chicago, Detroit, Cleveland, New York, and Philadelphia; and the chief losses have been sustained by four States—Mississippi, Alabama, Georgia, and South Carolina. Much of the northward movement has been from one State to the neighboring northern one so that the drift has been in the nature of a State-to-State displacement.

It is interesting to note, from maps by Thornthwaite giving the source of Negro population in the 12 cities of over 70,000 Negro population, that this northward movement was roughly along meridians of longitude. That is, the Negroes in New York City, Philadelphia, Baltimore, and Washington have come as though by direct lines from the Atlantic Coastal States. Those in Chicago and St. Louis have come largely from Mississippi, Tennessee, Alabama, Arkansas, and Louisiana. While New York and Philadelphia have not drawn large numbers from the interior states, Chicago and St. Louis did not attract many Negroes from the Atlantic Coastal States. Detroit and Cleveland followed the pattern less closely. The southern cities, New Orleans, Birmingham, and Atlanta, received few Negroes from outside the States in which they are situated.[4] Memphis, however, drew heavily upon Mississippi.

RURAL-URBAN MIGRATION, 1920-1930

The third great migration of the southern people has been to the rapidly growing towns and cities within the region. Internal migration must also be considered from the point of view of rural-urban mobility. Southern migrants, by and large, originate on farms and they move in large numbers to towns and cities in the Southeast.

In the following analysis it is estimated that the regional movement to cities of the population since birth was about 76 percent of the move-

[4] Thornthwaite, *op. cit.*, Plate IV, pp. 14-15.

TABLE 28. NET FARM-URBAN MIGRATION BY AGE GROUPS,
SOUTHEAST, 1920-1930

(Population in Thousands)

Residence and Age Groups	Alabama	Arkansas	Florida	Georgia	Kentucky	Louisiana	Mississippi	North Carolina	South Carolina	Tennessee	Virginia	Total for the Southeast
TOTAL												
0-9	− 38.6	− 18.1	17.8	− 43.1	−34.2	.8	− 7.7	− 6.2	− 25.9	− 28.8	− 24.0	− 209.6
10-19	− 30.8	− 31.7	66.5	− 63.2	− 45.2	16.2	4.6	14.6	− 23.8	− 16.6	− 43.3	− 152.7
20-29	− 65.6	− 71.1	77.2	−130.5	− 85.4	− 4.0	− 46.6	− 17.7	− 98.7	− 53.0	− 94.5	− 589.9
30-39	− 36.9	− 34.5	65.1	− 93.7	− 38.4	− 3.4	− 23.4	− 4.7	− 57.4	− 24.5	− 53.4	− 305.2
40-49	− 1.5	− 3.2	47.2	− 43.9	− 15.4	3.1	− 8.0	15.4	− 14.5	− 14.0	− 15.5	50.3
50-59	− 6.6	− 16.7	24.8	− 8.1	− 7.6	− 10.6	− 6.1	5.8	− 16.7	11.2	− 10.9	41.5
60-69	− 2.9	− 10.2	17.4	− 18.0	− 5.4	1.6	− 3.7	4.4	.9	− 7.8	− 3.9	41.4
70-up	− 3.1	− 6.5	9.1	− 9.9	− 2.2	.8	− 5.5	2.3	− 5.4	− 5.1	− 4.1	35.8
All	−186.0	−192.0	325.1	−410.4	−233.8	− 1.9	− 96.4	.5	−243.3	−138.6	−249.6	−1426.4
RURAL FARM												
0-9	− 35.0	− 23.3	− 5.4	− 56.3	− 42.3	− 13.8	− 15.1	− 26.7	− 36.3	− 34.6	− 17.5	− 306.3
10-19	− 49.5	− 41.6	5.0	−113.4	− 72.6	− 12.7	− 5.7	− 36.0	− 65.4	− 49.4	− 47.3	− 498.6
20-29	−134.5	−100.4	− 29.4	−208.6	−139.4	− 67.4	− 85.4	−124.0	−140.3	−122.2	−128.5	−1280.1
30-39	− 40.7	− 37.7	− 5.2	− 87.1	− 53.3	− 19.4	− 30.0	− 34.7	− 55.5	− 43.9	− 37.5	− 445.0
40-49	− 4.8	− 15.5	.6	− 45.4	− 24.8	− 4.5	− 11.0	− 4.1	− 21.3	− 20.0	− 10.4	− 161.2
50-59	− 6.6	− 17.6	− 1.9	− 18.6	− 14.2	− 9.7	− 7.8	− 5.0	− 20.6	.2	− 8.8	− 111.0
60-69	− 5.2	− 12.6	− 1.8	− 21.7	− 9.7	− 5.7	− 7.1	− 8.3	− 6.2	− 9.6	− 5.8	− 93.7
70-up	− 5.5	− 9.2	− 2.9	− 13.4	− 6.8	− 5.5	− 8.3	− 5.6	− 7.3	− 6.8	− 6.7	− 78.0
All	−281.8	−257.9	− 51.0	−564.5	−363.1	−138.7	−170.4	−244.4	−352.9	−286.7	−262.5	−2973.9
RURAL NON-FARM AND URBAN												
0-9	− 3.6	5.2	23.2	13.2	8.1	13.0	7.4	20.5	10.4	5.8	− 6.5	96.7
10-19	18.7	9.9	71.5	50.2	27.4	28.9	10.3	50.6	41.6	32.8	4.0	345.9
20-29	68.9	29.3	106.6	78.1	54.0	63.4	38.8	106.3	41.6	69.2	34.0	690.2
30-39	3.8	3.2	70.3	− 6.6	14.9	16.0	6.6	30.0	− 1.9	19.4	− 15.9	139.8
40-49	3.3	12.3	46.6	1.5	9.4	7.6	3.0	19.5	6.8	6.0	− 5.1	110.9
50-59	0.0	.9	26.7	10.5	6.6	− .9	1.7	10.8	3.9	11.4	− 2.1	69.5
60-69	2.3	2.4	19.2	3.7	4.3	4.1	3.4	3.9	5.3	1.8	1.9	52.3
70-up	2.4	2.7	12.0	3.5	4.6	4.7	2.8	3.3	1.9	1.7	2.6	42.2
All	95.8	65.9	376.1	154.1	129.3	136.8	74.0	244.9	109.6	148.1	12.9	1547.5

Source: Robin M. Williams, Rural-Urban Migration in the Southeastern Region, 1920-1930 (unpublished paper with estimates based on figures supplied by Warren S. Thompson and C. Horace Hamilton).

ment outside the area. Of the native born population of the United States in 1930, 28,700,000 were born in the Southeast, 24,100,000 born in the rural districts, and 4,600,000 in cities. Since only about 17,500,000 of these southeastern rural-born live in the area of their birth, it is evident that over 6,600,000 have moved elsewhere. Of these, 3,800,000 have left the section entirely, while 2,900,000 have moved to southern cities. On the other hand 400,000 have come into the region leaving a net loss of 3,400,000. The rural districts of the Southeast have thus exported 2,900,000 of their natural increase to the region's cities, have sent 3,400,000 to other regions, and have continued to grow.[5]

Table 28, on the basis of calculations from age-group data made by Robin Williams, enables us to show these movements in some detail for 1920-1930. The farms of the Southeast lost by net migration some 2,973,-900 persons and the villages and cities (rural-nonfarm and urban areas) gained 1,547,500 population. This left a net migration out of the region of some 1,426,400 people. No State was exempt but the greatest losses were experienced by the farms of Georgia, South Carolina, and Kentucky

[5] Howard W. Odum, *Southern Regions of the United States,* p. 463.

TABLE 29. POPULATION CHANGES BY COLOR, SEX, AND RESIDENCE, SHOWING
CHANGE ATTRIBUTABLE TO NATURAL INCREASE AND MIGRATION,
FIVE TENNESSEE VALLEY STATES,* 1920-1930

Population group	Total change		Change attributable to Natural increases		Net migration	
	Number (1000's)	Percentage of 1920 population	Number (1000's)	Percentage of 1920 population	Number (1000's)	Percentage of 1920 population
TOTAL AREA............	1,462.5	12.2	2,295.8	19.2	− 833.3	− 7.0
White Male.............	619.9	13.7	926.4	20.5	− 306.5	− 6.8
White Female..........	666.3	15.1	931.3	21.2	− 265.1	− 6.2
Colored Male..........	74.6	5.0	198.1	13.2	− 123.5	− 8.2
Colored Female........	101.8	6.6	240.0	15.5	− 138.2	− 8.9
TOTAL URBAN..........	940.0	32.2	401.3	13.8	538.6	18.5
White Male.............	341.7	33.4	174.4	17.1	167.2	16.4
White Female..........	385.3	36.4	162.3	15.3	223.0	21.2
Colored Male..........	89.2	22.4	34.5	8.7	54.8	13.8
Colored Female........	123.7	28.1	30.1	6.9	93.6	21.2
TOTAL RURAL NON-FARM	714.0	27.6	633.3	24.5	80.8	3.1
White Male.............	332.9	32.8	269.5	27.3	53.4	5.4
White Female..........	343.2	35.7	267.3	27.8	76.0	7.9
Colored Male..........	22.6	7.1	44.3	13.9	− 21.7	− 6.8
Colored Female........	25.4	7.9	52.2	16.3	− 26.8	− 8.4
TOTAL RURAL FARM.....	− 191.5	− 3.0	1,261.2	19.5	−1,452.7	−22.5
White Male.............	− 44.7	− 1.8	482.4	19.2	− 527.1	−21.0
White Female..........	− 62.3	− 2.6	501.8	21.1	− 564.1	−23.7
Colored Male..........	− 37.2	− 4.7	119.4	15.2	− 156.6	−19.9
Colored Female........	− 47.3	− 6.1	157.6	19.9	− 205.0	−25.9

*Alabama, Kentucky, North Carolina, Tennessee, Virginia.
Source: C. Horace Hamilton, "Rural-Urban Migration in the Tennessee Valley between 1920 and 1930, *Social Forces*, XIII (October 1934), 57-64.

which lost from 33.5 to 27.8 percent of their 1920 farm population. Mississippi had the smallest losses, 13.4 percent.

Low farm incomes, boll weevil invasions in Georgia and South Carolina, submarginal farming conditions in mountain areas of Kentucky and Tennessee, and the high rate of rural births everywhere help to explain these losses. Nonfarm areas showed gains in every southern State.

Detailed figures (Table 28) indicate that the great bulk of the migration in each category was in the young ages. Of the 2,973,900 net migrants from farms, 1,280,000 were aged 20 to 29. Migrants 10 to 30 years of age composed 67 percent of the net movement to the region's cities, 59.8 percent of the movement from the region's farms and 52.7 percent of the net movement out of the region.

A detailed analysis, by C. Horace Hamilton, of the Tennessee Valley area (Table 29) gave migration by sex and race and distinguished changes by natural increase and migration in farm, rural-nonfarm, and urban areas. Thus the farms lost 22.5 percent of their 1920 population by migration but, since they gained 19.5 percent by natural increase, the net loss was only 3 percent. To a migration gain of 18.5 percent the cities added 13.8 percent in natural increase to gain 32.3 percent. A net migration out of the region of 7 percent was offset by a natural increase of 19.2 percent to give the area a 12.2 percent gain.

For both races the migration of females from farms to cities within the area was greater than the migration of males. In migration out of the area males led among whites and females among colored groups. Whites led in the proportion migrating to cities in the area while Negroes led in the proportions migrating outside the area. The rural nonfarm areas, small towns for the most part, gained white migrants but lost colored migrants.

The decade of the 1920's resembled nothing so much as the opening of a great safety valve whereby the pent-up pressure of the South's population could seek economic release from a crowded agriculture. In the next chapter we raise the question of the future of migration. What did the decade of the 1930's mean? What will the decade of World War II mean for future migration from the South?

CHAPTER 10

THE TREND OF SOUTHERN MIGRATION

THE SOUTH's contribution to future migration in this country is likely to be very large indeed. It is not difficult to show that the region's need is great and that the Southern people are accustomed to moving in search of opportunity. It is evident that the decade from 1920 to 1930, when agricultural depression and industrial prosperity coincided, was the greatest period of rural-urban migration yet known. The decade did not relieve rural areas of their poverty; in fact it did not prove that migration alone could perform this service. It did, however, set a mark at which all future rural-urban migration might aim.

Many considerations must be taken into account in estimating the future trend of southern migration. It depends upon the back log of delayed migration accumulated during the depression and upon changing economic conditions in both agriculture and industry. Separate sections are devoted to the relation of population to the agrarian and industrial economies but throughout our discussion the contrast between the periods of the depression decade, of World War II, and of the post-war period must be held in mind.

INTERSTATE MIGRATION, 1930-1940

The decade 1930 to 1940 served to reverse the trends of internal migration for all regions except the Far West which continued to gain. The reduction of regional changes in population to their constituent elements of natural increase and migration (Table 30) indicates that the Far West was the only region to show an appreciable gain by migration, 15.4 percent. Over 1,279,500 went to the Far West in this decade. As Table 30 shows, the gains of all other regions were due to excess of births over deaths.

The Southeast's census gain of 2,710,931 was the Nation's largest, making up over 30 percent of the total increase in population. The region led the Nation in the rate of natural increase, 12.3 percent. Unlike the

TABLE 30. TOTAL POPULATION CHANGE DUE TO NATURAL INCREASE AND MIGRATION, UNITED STATES AND THE SIX MAJOR REGIONS, 1930-1940

Area	Amount Change, 1930-1940			Percent Change, 1930-1940		
	Net	Due to natural increase	Due to migration	Net	Due to natural increase	Due to migration
UNITED STATES.........	8,894,229	8,940,747	− 46,518	7.24	7.28	−0.04
Northeast..............	1,940,298	1,739,797	200,501	5.1	4.6	0.5
Southeast..............	2,710,931	3,136,723	−425,792	10.6	12.3	−1.7
Southwest..............	702,692	1,002,556	−299,864	7.7	11.0	−3.3
Middle States...........	1,780,130	2,057,843	−277,713	5.2	6.0	−0.8
Northwest..............	25,938	698,594	−672,656	0.4	9.5	−9.1
Far West..............	1,558,018	278,438	1,279,580	18.8	3.4	15.4

Source: *Statistical Abstract, 1930, 1934, 1937,* Tables 17, 18; U. S. Birth Schedules and Infant Mortality 1930-1936; Mortality Statistics 1930-1936; Vital Statistics, 1937-1939; *Fifteenth Census of the United States, 1930,* Population IV, U. S. Summary, Tables 13, 23; *Sixteenth Census of the United States, 1940,* Population, Preliminary Release, Series P-6, P-10; *Report of the Committee on Population Problems to the National Resources Committee,* 1938, "The Problems of a Changing Population," pp. 75-76; National Resources Committee, *Population Statistics, National Data,* Tables 28, 32; Ellen Hull Neff, Under-registration of Births, United States, 1939; State, Regional, Race and Rural-Urban Differences (unpublished master's thesis, University of North Carolina, 1943).

FIGURE 84. PERCENTAGE CHANGE IN TOTAL POPULATION DUE TO MIGRATION, UNITED STATES, 1930-1940

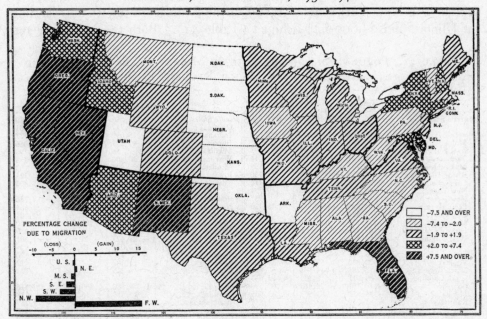

Source: See Table 30.

previous decade, however, there was little migration from the Southeast, only 1.7 percent. With natural increase estimated at 3,136,723 for the decade most of the population was confined at home by the depression. With due allowance for underregistration of births we estimate less than 426,000 left the area during the depression decade.

Figure 84 shows the net balance of interstate migration as calculated by the vital statistics method.[1] In all, 19 States gained migrants and 29 States lost. The Dakotas lost the largest proportions, over 18 percent of their population; Florida gained the largest by migration, 22.2 percent. Seventeen States, however, showed changes of less than 2 percent by migration.

An examination of the Southeast brings to light an important contrast in racial migration. The net migration out of the Southeast was due to the continued movement of the Negroes; the white population remained at home. By net migration the region lost 868 white and 424,924 colored population (Table 31). The Southeast lost 5.4 percent of its Negroes by migration ranging from South Carolina's loss of 11.7 percent to Louisiana's loss of 1.4 percent (Figure 85). Only Tennessee, 3.5 percent, and Florida, 14.3 percent, gained Negro population by migration. In round numbers Georgia lost over 100,700, South Carolina over 92,500, Alabama over 75,000, Mississippi over 71,600, and North Carolina 67,800.

Of this migration 201,678 Negroes went to the Northeast, almost 150,000 to New York; and 151,629 to the Middle States, 59,000 landing in Illinois, and 28,000 in Michigan (Table 31). Both the Northeast and

TABLE 31. POPULATION CHANGE DUE TO MIGRATION, BY RACE, UNITED STATES AND THE SIX MAJOR REGIONS, 1930-1940

Area	Total	White	Colored	Area	Total	White	Colored
UNITED STATES	− 46,518	− 14,252	− 32,266	*Middle States*	−277,713	−429,342	151,629
				Ohio	− 68,717	− 96,698	27,981
Northeast	200,501	− 1,177	201,678	Indiana	15,050	4,623	10,427
Maine	801	510	291	Illinois	− 49,297	−108,363	59,066
New Hampshire	9,496	9,891	− 395	Michigan	− 36	− 28,234	28,198
Vermont	− 18,152	− 17,938	− 214	Wisconsin	− 40,800	− 41,198	398
Massachusetts	− 70,791	− 72,389	1,598	Minnesota	404	− 486	82
Rhode Island	− 2,059	− 2,809	750	Iowa	−109,250	−108,925	− 325
Connecticut	37,783	35,667	2,116	Missouri	− 24,259	− 50,061	25,802
New York	469,902	320,108	149,794				
New Jersey	− 16,178	− 24,135	7,957	*Northwest*	−672,656	−662,870	− 9,786
Pennsylvania	−286,521	−311,941	25,420	North Dakota	−128,598	−128,034	− 564
Delaware	17,826	15,113	2,713	South Dakota	−125,998	−123,817	− 2,181
Maryland	121,244	106,089	15,155	Nebraska	−182,787	−182,537	− 250
Dist. of Columbia	(149,426)	(98,006)	(51,420)	Kansas	−205,945	−203,776	− 2,169
West Virginia	− 62,850	− 59,343	− 3,507	Montana	− 25,473	− 23,672	− 1,801
				Idaho	20,053	20,978	− 925
Southeast	−425,792	− 868	−424,924	Wyoming	− 170	450	− 620
Virginia	22,820	57,204	− 34,384	Colorado	14,487	14,984	− 497
North Carolina	− 82,785	− 14,965	− 67,820	Utah	− 38,225	− 37,446	− 779
South Carolina	− 83,012	9,531	− 92,543				
Georgia	−129,151	− 28,461	−100,690	*Far West*	1,279,580	1,260,464	19,116
Florida	325,977	263,972	62,005	Nevada	16,273	16,391	− 118
Kentucky	− 81,719	− 77,884	− 3,835	Washington	105,461	110,720	− 5,259
Tennessee	12,164	− 4,433	16,597	Oregon	97,893	99,340	− 1,447
Alabama	−181,282	−106,248	− 75,034	California	1,059,953	1,034,013	25,940
Mississippi	− 99,785	− 28,171	− 71,614				
Arkansas	−155,096	−108,364	− 46,732				
Louisiana	26,077	36,951	− 10,874				
Southwest	−299,864	−278,465	− 21,399				
Oklahoma	−329,690	−280,302	− 49,388				
Texas	− 22,180	− 37,150	14,970				
New Mexico	32,111	28,469	3,642				
Arizona	19,895	10,518	9,377				

Source: See Table 30.

[1] Net migration computed as difference between total change of population and change due to balance of births and deaths during decade.

FIGURE 85. PERCENTAGE CHANGE IN COLORED POPULATION DUE TO
MIGRATION, UNITED STATES, 1930-1940

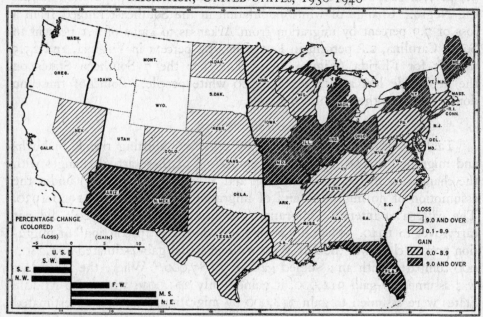

Source: See Table 30.

FIGURE 86. PERCENTAGE CHANGE IN WHITE POPULATION DUE TO
MIGRATION, UNITED STATES, 1930-1940

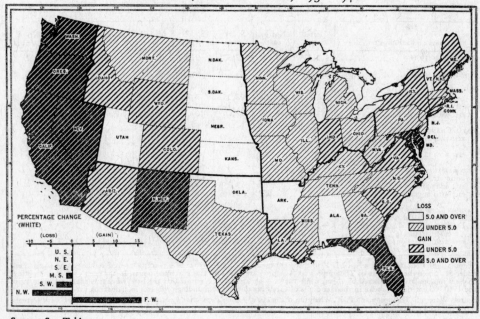

Source: See Table 30.

the Middle States increased their colored population over 12 percent. The 5.7 percent gain of the Far West included other colored population besides the Negro. Change of white population in the Southeast ranged from a loss of 7.9 percent by migration from Arkansas to gains of 1.1 percent in South Carolina, 2.8 percent in Louisiana, 3.2 percent in Virginia, and 25.5 percent for Florida (Figure 86). Together the 7 Southern States on the debit side lost a total of 368,500 white people. Some of these no doubt went to other Southern States.

RECENT TRENDS

Table 30 shows actual changes by regions. Shifting trends in births and migration can be shown by a comparison of these actual changes with the changes estimated by Thompson and Whelpton (Table 32) under the assumption of no migration and of migration continued as of 1920-1930. The pattern of interstate migration prevailing during the 1920's did not carry over to 1940. The only region for which the "prediction" of migration proved close was the Far West with an actual gain estimated at 1,280,-000 compared with an assumed gain of 1,087,000. Where the Northeast was assumed to gain 912,000, it gained only 201,000; where the Middle States were assumed to gain 318,000 by migration, they lost an estimated 278,000. The Southeast, which could have expected to lose 1,706,000,

TABLE 32. ACTUAL CHANGE IN POPULATION AND ESTIMATED CHANGE UNDER TWO ASSUMPTIONS, UNITED STATES AND THE SIX MAJOR REGIONS, 1930-1940

(Population in Thousands)

Item and assumption	United States	North-east	South-east	South-west	Middle States	North-west	Far West	Dist. of Columbia
POPULATION 1930.................	122,775	38,026	25,551	9,080	33,961	7,385	8,285	487
POPULATION 1930*................	123,233	38,153	25,670	9,118	34,077	7,412	8,312	488
POPULATION 1940								
actual........................	131,669	39,966	28,262	9,782	35,742	7,410	9,844	663
est: no migration.............	132,098	39,853	28,908	10,278	35,940	8,137	8,500	488
est: with migration............	131,865	40,754	27,069	10,068	36,215	7,656	9,586	513
TOTAL CHANGE (1930-1940)								
actual........................	8,894	1,940	2,711	703	1,780	26	1,558	174
est: no migration.............	8,865	1,700	3,238	1,160	1,863	725	188	0
est: with migration............	8,632	2,601	1,399	950	2,138	244	1,274	25
NATURAL INCREASE (1930-1940)								
Estimate of actual..............	8,941	1,740	3,137	1,003	2,058	699	278	27
est: no migration.............	8,865	1,700	3,238	1,160	1,863	725	188	0
est: with migration............	8,632	1,689	3,105	1,139	1,820	692	187	0
GAIN OR LOSS THROUGH MIGRATION (1930-1940)								
Estimate of actual..............	− 47	201	− 426	− 300	− 278	− 673	1,280	149
est: no migration.............	0	0	0	0	0	0	0	0
est: with migration............	0	912	−1,706	− 189	318	− 448	1,087	25

*Population as enumerated on April 1, 1930 corrected by adding an allowance of 4 percent for underenumeration of children under 5. Since the forecasts of Thompson and Whelpton are based on this corrected figure, it has been used in computing changes in population predicted by them, while "actual" changes were computed on the basis of census enumeration in 1930 and 1940. Some discrepancies in the last digits of totals are due to the rounding of figures in thousands.

Source: Warren S. Thompson and P. K. Whelpton, *Estimates of Future Population by States*, (National Resources Board, December, 1934, mimeographed).

lost only 426,000. The drought increased the migration losses of the Northwest from an estimated 448,000 to 673,000.

Equally significant were the regional contrasts shown in estimated natural increase (Table 32). The reversal of declining fertility that set in with returning prosperity and the threat of war gave greater gains in natural increase than were assumed. The high fertility areas, the Northwest, Southwest, and Southeast, showed a somewhat greater decline in natural increase than assumed in the Thompson-Whelpton estimates. Without migration the Southeast was expected to show a natural increase of 3,238,000. While but little migration occurred, actual natural increase was only 3,137,000. In the Southwest the actual natural increase of 1,003,000 fell below assumed increase. In the Far West the change from assumed to actual natural increase was from 188,000 to 278,000.

We may help to account for these changes by examining the assumptions underlying the Thompson-Whelpton estimates. Thompson and Whelpton assumed that in the Nation as a whole the birth rate by five-year age periods would drop about 30 percent from 1930 to 1960 and that by 1960 "the difference between the United States birth rate and that for the urban and rural population of each State would be only one-half as great as in 1930." Two trends seem evident from the 1940 figures: (1) in States of low fertility the birth rate did not drop at the rate assumed; (2) in States of high fertility births fell at a higher rate. In the field of migration, our especial interest, the assumption of no migration, came nearest fitting conditions in the Southeast, 1930-1940.

RURAL-URBAN MIGRATIONS

In order to compare depression migration from southern farms to towns and cities[2] with that prevailing during the 1920's we can make use of the Department of Agriculture's annual estimates for the census South, an area that includes Texas, Oklahoma, and certain border States. Figures 87 and 88 contrasting the Nation and the South indicate the greater number of births on southern farms and the great amount of urbanward migration necessary to hold the South's farm population at a stable level in a period of declining agriculture. From 1920 to 1941 annual births in southern farm areas have fallen from around 500,000 to 431,000. For the rest of the Nation farm births which never went above 333,000 have fallen to 271,000. On southern farms deaths have not climbed beyond 190,000, giving the farm population an annual natural increase that gradually fell from around 350,000 to 280,000. For the rest of the Nation, natural increase on the farm has fallen from around 190,000 to about 150,000.

[2] The 1940 age sex composition of the rural farm, rural nonfarm, and urban population was not available at time of writing. Accordingly, no use has been made of the age group data in calculating 1940 migration.

FIGURE 87. ANNUAL CHANGE IN THE FARM POPULATION AS AFFECTED BY
BIRTHS, DEATHS, AND MIGRATION, CENSUS SOUTH, 1920-1941

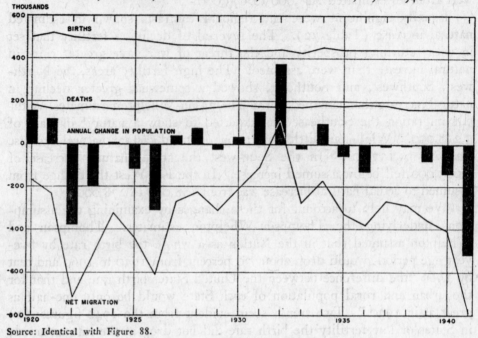

Source: Identical with Figure 88.

FIGURE 88. ANNUAL CHANGE IN THE FARM POPULATION AS AFFECTED BY
BIRTHS, DEATHS, AND MIGRATION, UNITED STATES WITHOUT
THE CENSUS SOUTH, 1920-1941

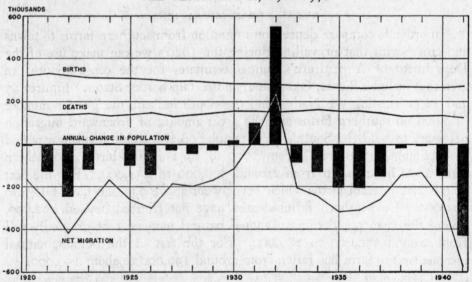

Source: United States Department of Agriculture, Bureau of Agricultural Economics, Annual Estimates
of the Farm Population, Births, Deaths . . . and Number of Persons Moving to and from Farms (By
Census Division), January 1, 1937; January 1, 1938; Revised September, 1942.

In the function that migration serves, the contrast between the 1920's and the 1930's is startling. In the period 1920-1930 a net movement of over 3 3/4 millions from southern farms meant a net loss of only 637,000 farm population. In the 1930's southern farms lost 2 1/4 millions by migration but gained over 1/3 million population. For only one year in these two decades, and that only in the depth of the depression, 1932, did the tide of net migration flow back to the southern farms. Yet so great was natural increase that the farms actually lost population only when out-migration exceeded 250,000, during 13 of the 22 years, 1920-1941. Farms elsewhere lost population for 18 out of the 22 years, an outward movement of 137,000 accounting for net loss in one of the years. These estimates can be related to net farm migration by States from 1930 to 1940.

Later estimates of the Department of Agriculture based on survival rates showed that the Nation's rural farm population had a net loss during the decade 1930-40 of 3.5 million persons by migration.[3] This loss of 12.7 percent of the 1930 population on farms just about offsets their excess of births over deaths so that the group increased only 0.2 percent during the decade. The greater tendency of women and non-whites to migrate is demonstrated in the farm's net loss of 22.4 percent non-white females, and 17 percent non-white males as compared to losses of 14 percent white females and 9 percent white males. For all classes the greatest migration occurred among those aged 15-20 in 1930, the least among those aged 30-45. By States farm migration ranged from a net gain of 30 percent in Connecticut to a 31.8 percent loss in South Dakota (Figure 89). In regional terms only the Far West gained farm population while all other regions lost. Because of the movement to New England farms the losses of the Northeast were comparatively low. With a loss of 650 thousand the Northwest showed the highest proportionate losses but was second in total losses to the Southeast which was over 1,624 thousands.

Other figures can be carried through from the 1940 Census to the close of 1943 to show the effect of war on population movements. Census estimates, based on registration for War Ration Book Four November 1943, indicate that induction into the armed forces so exceeded natural increase that the total civilian population lost 4 millions or 3.1 percent.[4] These estimates are valuable for they suggest the trend of future migration. On the one hand they show (Figure 90) the extent to which rural areas have been drained. On the other they indicate the war centers which have attracted civilian population. In all there were 2,620 counties which lost

[3] Eleanor H. Bernert, Volume and Composition of Net Migration from the Rural Farm Population. (Washington, D. C.: U. S. Department of Agriculture, January, 1944, mimeographed), pp. 6-7 for Method, pp. 8-37 for Tabulations.

[4] Bureau of the Census, Special Reports, Series P-44, No. 3, February 15, 1944.

FIGURE 89. NET MIGRATION FROM THE RURAL FARM POPULATION,
UNITED STATES, 1930-1940

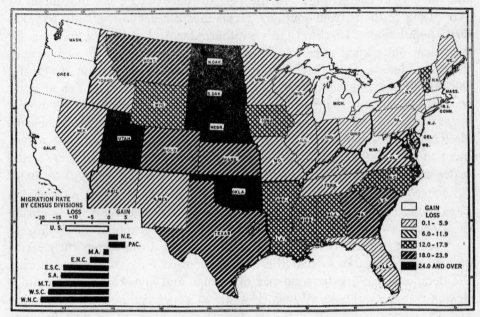

Source: See footnote 3, this chapter.

FIGURE 90. ESTIMATED PERCENTAGE CHANGE IN THE CIVILIAN POPULATION
BY COUNTIES, UNITED STATES, APRIL 1, 1940 TO NOVEMBER 1, 1943

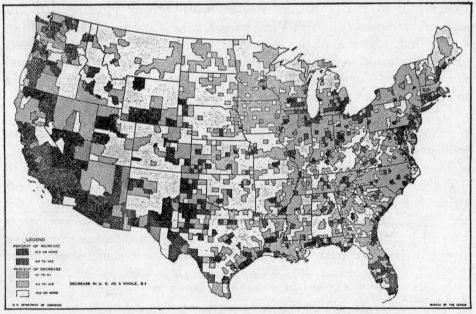

Source: Bureau of the Census, United States Department of Commerce, Release P-44, No. 3 and No. 6,
February 15 and March 23, 1944.

civilian population, amounting to more than 8,879,000. While these counties were largely rural they included 92 metropolitan counties in 50 out of the 137 metropolitan areas. Together all metropolitan areas gained 2.2 percent. Among regions only the Far West gained in civilian population while the Northwest continued the losses of the 1930 decade. By States California gained over a million population while New York lost over a million. Of the 12 States to show gains the Southeast had 2, Florida and Virginia. In all, 469 counties gained civilian population, amounting to almost 4,858,000. Because of the location of camps and industries in the region only 7 of the 29 metropolitan areas in the Southeast lost population. The greatest gains were experienced in seaport and shipbuilding areas. Savannah grew 29 percent, Charleston 37 percent, Norfolk 57 percent and Mobile 61 percent. Thus the immediate post-war problem is the back flow of migration from boom towns to rural areas but once this is accomplished the long pull will witness the resumption of rural urban migration.

INCREASES IN THE FARM POPULATION OF WORKING AGE, 18 TO 65

The conditions of 1930-1940 came nearer to stopping internal migration than any recent decade. The rise of war industries in the 1940's tended to repeat the migration experience of 1920-1930. On the basis of current trends in births and deaths it can be shown that without migration the farm population in the Southeast would grow from 12,236,000 in 1930 to 19,960,000 by 1960, an increase of over 7,700,000 people. With migration continued as in the period 1920 to 1930 the farms of the Southeast would find their population declining from 12 millions to 11.6 millions.[5] Figure 91, which shows the change from 1920 to 1960 under this assumption, indicates that urban population would grow from 7.6 million in 1930 to 9.6 million in 1960 while rural nonfarm would increase from 5.8 to almost 8 millions.

In order to avoid assumptions about what will happen to the birth rate, T. J. Woofter, Jr. has calculated the additions that would be made to our labor force, those aged 18-65 to 1950.[6] This potential working population 18-65 was increasing at the rate of over a million a year. Seven-tenths of these new workers came from rural families. Allowing for deaths, and for those reaching the retirement age of 65, the United States would have by 1950, 5.6 million more urban, 7.3 million more rural farm, and 4.1 million more rural nonfarm people of working age than in 1930.

[5] These figures are based on W. S. Thompson and P. K. Whelpton, *Estimates of Future Population by States* (Washington, D. C.: Government Printing Office, 1934).

[6] "The Future Working Population," *Rural Sociology*, IV (September, 1939), 275-282.

FIGURE 91. PROJECTED TREND OF
POPULATION BY RESIDENCE WITH
MIGRATION AS OF 1920-1930,
SOUTHEAST, 1920-1960

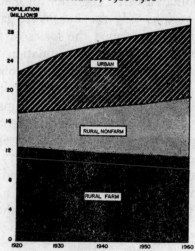

Source: Warren S. Thompson and P.
K. Whelpton, *Estimates of Future Population by States*, National Resources
Board, 1934.

The pressure that replacements in the farm population exercise on migration is shown by Woofter's analysis of 1930 data. The annual rate of replacement of males in the farm population was 2.4 for the United States. This replacement rate is the relation between the number of males becoming 18 each year and those 18-64 years of age inclusive. From the 1930 farm population figures the rate is calculated as follows: From the number of farm males 18 years old—363,793—is subtracted those becoming 65 years of age and the number dying that year aged 19-64 years old—162,390 in all. The result—an excess maturity of 201,403—is then computed as a percentage of the farm males 18-64—8,263,405—to secure the annual replacement rate—2.4 percent.

The replacement rate is thus a measure of pressure on economic opportunity, the pressure of farm youth on the land. Figure 92 ranks the states in this respect and shows that 6 states of the Southern Regions had over 300 farm youths for every 10,000 farm males 18-64. Even in the Dakotas before the droughts there were more than twice as many farm youths becoming 18 as could possibly be absorbed by the economic opportunities open through death and old age on farms.[7] Of the Nation's additional 7 1/3 million rural farm population 18-65 it was found that

[7] Bruce L. Melvin and Elna N. Smith, *Rural Youth: Their Situation and Prospects* (W. P. A., Division of Social Research, Washington, D. C., 1938), pp. 12-13.

FIGURE 92. MALE REPLACEMENT RATE PER 10,000 IN THE RURAL FARM
POPULATION, 18-64 YEARS OF AGE, UNITED STATES, 1930

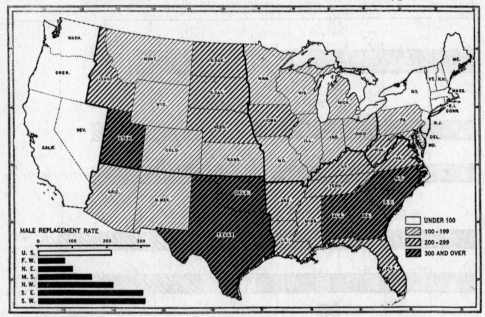

Source: T. J. Woofter, Jr., "The Future Working Population," *Rural Sociology*, IV (September, 1939),
275-282; T. J. Woofter, Jr., "Replacement Rates in the Productive Ages," *Milbank Memorial Fund
Quarterly*, XV (October, 1937), pp. 348-354.

over 3,200,000 would be found in the Southeast unless migration draws
them away. These people, it must be realized, were already born and
the only thing that would keep them from maturing into productive
population, working or seeking work, was an increase in the death rate.
They furnish the oncoming manpower for agriculture, for war industry,
and for the armed forces.

In the Nation, total population aged 18-65 would grow from 73 million to almost 91 million by 1950. The extent to which they migrate
will depend on the total amount of unemployment in the Nation in the
post-war decade. If 1930 conditions of employment should prevail, appoxi-
mately only 2.9 percent of that group will thus be unemployed. But if
conditions uncovered by the Special Unemployment Census of 1937 prevail, 12.2 percent will be unemployed and looking for work. (Figure
93). The difference amounts to 8 1/2 million more unemployed. By
now we know that one effect of loss of jobs is to force other members
of the family to look for work, thus increasing the unemployed. If 1930
conditions should prevail in 1950, 35.6 million of those 18-65 will not
seek gainful employment. Should the conditions of 1937 prevail, how-

FIGURE 93. EMPLOYMENT STATUS OF POPULATION, 18-64 YEARS OF AGE UNDER
CONDITIONS OF 1930 AND 1937, UNITED STATES, 1940,
WITH ESTIMATE FOR 1950

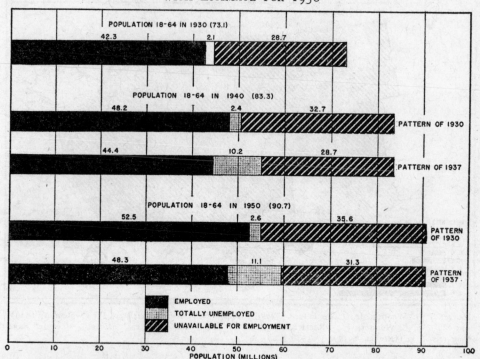

Source: *Fifteenth Census of the United States, 1930,* Vol. II, Chap. 10, Tables 9, 21, 24, 27. *Census of Unemployment, 1930,* Vol. I; *Census of Unemployment, 1937,* Vol. IV, Enumerative Check Census; Warren Thompson and P. K. Whelpton, *Estimates of Future Population by States,* National Resources Board, 1934.

TABLE 33. REASONS FOR LEAVING SETTLED RESIDENCE GIVEN BY MIGRANT
FAMILIES, UNITED STATES AND THE SIX MAJOR REGIONS, 1935

Region of former settled residence	All families inquired		Economic distress			Personal distress		Not in distress (Percent)
	Number	Percent	Unemployment (Percent)	Inadequate earnings (Percent)	Farm failure (Percent)	Ill health (Percent)	Domestic and other trouble (Percent)	
UNITED STATES....	4,195	100	40	20	8	11	15	6
Northeast.........	695	100	*44*	20	2	12	15	7
Southeast.........	922	100	42	*25*	6	7	15	5
Southwest.........	594	100	40	20	9	*14*	12	5
Middle States......	1,000	100	42	20	6	10	16	6
Northwest.........	629	100	32	18	*22*	12	10	6
Far West..........	355	100	40	17	1	11	*24*	7

Note: Percentages in *Italics* are those higher for a given region than for all other regions. The Middle States follow very closely the United States pattern and do not rank first for any factor of emigration. Factor headed "Inadequate earnings" is mostly low wages, part-time work, but includes also insufficient relief, pressing debts, eviction from homes, etc. "Domestic and other trouble" includes divorce, family quarrels, dislike of community, and other personal maladjustments. The group "not in distress" did not suffer from any economic hardship or any pressing personal distress

Source: *Migrant Families,* Works Progress Administration, Division of Social Research, 1938, Appendix, Table 2.

ever, only 31.3 million will not be seeking employment. Thus 4.3 million more will be added to the labor market because of unemployment.

The bearing of these trends on future migration should be evident when we examine the reasons given for migration. Table 33 indicates that for all regions unemployment is the major reason migrants give for leaving their homes. Interestingly enough the people from the Southeast ranked highest among those giving inadequate income as the reason for migration, the Northwest leads in farm failure, while 24 percent of those from California and the Far West had no more serious reason for leaving home than domestic troubles.

MIGRATION AND THE ECONOMIC FUTURE

What influence is the economic future likely to exert on migration? No one knows but we may gain some idea by describing the condition that prevailed during the depression in contrast with the conditions of World War II. For some time to come, the source of southern migrants will be the farms; the only question is whether they will move to industrial areas within or outside the region. We know that the Southeast has two great problem areas in the old Cotton Belt and its Appalachian Mountains. The South can grow cotton and lots of it for a price and a market. The market in the 1930's was vanishing before our eyes, and cotton prices were held up only by the support of governmental operations. In 1937 the Nation grew 18 1/4 million bales, sold 5 2/3 million abroad, consumed 5 3/4 million, and had a carry over of 11 1/2 million bales. In 1939 by heroic efforts we reduced production to 11 2/3 million bales, sold only 3 1/3 million, used 6 4/5 million, and carried over 13 million bales. The region seemed fated to reduce production to an annual take of 9 million bales, or worse, to the domestic consumption of less than 7 million bales. It had reduced cotton production to 9 2/3 million bales in 1934-1935 and in spite of government subsidies, it nearly killed the southern farmer. Those who would estimate future migration out of the Cotton Belt will have to tell us what policies the government will adopt toward the cotton problem, what chance cotton will have in the world market, what other paying crops the South can grow, and what other methods of using the land the region could employ besides cotton tenancy and sharecropping.

The war and its probable outcome have already made the question loom larger and more complex than the old familiar problem of recovering foreign markets. The region is faced with the long-time problem of reconstructing an outmoded cotton economy. Unless we make some progress toward agricultural reconstruction, the post-war pressure toward migration will be great indeed. Drastic reduction of cotton production would, no doubt, force new displacements of population but the government's program of carrying the crop on loans could hardly be justified without further reduction in quotas.

The problem of the Southern Appalachians resulted from the pressure of the Nation's fastest growing population upon diminishing resources of timber lands, coal mining, and limited farm lands. The areas at current birth and death rates will double their population every thirty years without migration. Migration was greatly needed, for there was no additional land supply that would not quickly erode if put to the plow. Regrowing timber was a long time job not likely to offer early returns for the present generation except in government employment for conservation. Only the bituminous coal mines of Kentucky could produce more than they were then producing. Here is a problem of markets which war activity bade fair to increase. Such were the forces back of migration previous to December 7, 1941.

THE FORCES BEHIND SOUTHERN MIGRATION

The preceding discussion indicates the strength of forces behind normal outward migration from the Southeast. They show what serious effects the reversal or stoppage of the rural-urban flow would have in an area where farms are already too small and too much given over to erosion and tenancy. The total force of migration has not been interregional, for our figures have presented migration to towns and cities in the region as well as outside. They are valuable in indicating how impossible it will be to stop the rural-urban drift in the Southeast as long as its high birth rate continues. There is not sufficient demand for farm products nor sufficient land, good, poor, and indifferent, to provide for the farm surplus if migration were cut off. Certainly our regional figures cast doubt on the ability of southern cities to absorb all the population increase on southern farms.

Migration is not only a constitutional right of every American citizen recently reaffirmed by the decision of the Supreme Court in the Edwards Case; it is an economic necessity in the American system. The country is an economic unit with a predominantly national market. Industries, investments, goods, and labor respond to this economic and legal fact by crossing State lines at will. Such movements are necessary to develop, maintain, and stabilize the national economy. The economic order is a continually adjusting and readjusting equilibrium which presupposes a flow of industries to resources, a flow of goods to markets, and a flow of workers to industries. The causes of migration are, therefore, so fundamental and pervasive as to leave little expectation that the population may be immobilized.

As new areas develop and old ones decline, workers must migrate in order to develop the new resources and to relieve the older communities of surplus workers. The "push" of stranded communities resulting from shifting work opportunities are accentuated by the "pull" of new developments in industry. After employment has shifted from one area or one type of industry to another, migration gives rise to fewer problems than would the continuance of stranded communities as the result of insufficient migration.

Population increase is slowing down, but migration retains its importance. Without great migratory movements we cannot equalize our unequal flow of population increase, redress our regional inequalities, balance the demand for labor between changing employment capacities, nor "use our human and material resources to the best advantage." It was by large migrations that the frontier was settled; by foreign immigration that the American labor supply was recruited; and it is mainly by spontaneous internal migrations that the future needs of population redistribution in the United States must be served. Migration is no cure-all but, vagrancy laws to the contrary, the fact that a man has little or no money in his pocket is no valid reason for depriving him of his right to take up settlement across State lines. The right to move may seem a poor substitute for real security, but it must not be forgotten that for many of our citizens it has proved the road to increased well-being.

CHAPTER II

THE CHANGING OCCUPATIONAL DISTRIBUTION

OCCUPATIONAL distribution is one of the main phases of population study, bearing as it does a major relationship to class differences in fertility, to rural-urban residence, and to migration. Furthermore, population pressure, wherever it exists, is likely to be evident in an unbalanced occupational distribution accompanied by low incomes for the crowded trades and callings.

OCCUPATIONAL STATUS

The occupational distribution of our regional populations may well be considered against the background of our dominant economies. For convenience we shall begin with the simple division of our economies into two: the agrarian and industrial, preliminary to a discussion of those auxiliary groups concerned with distribution and the services and finally to the classification of occupations by socio-economic status. Figure 94 makes use of two comparisons, (1) the comparison of the region's share of the Nation's wage earners in manufacturing with its share of farm operators, and (2) the comparison of its proportion of the total population with its share of the Nation's land area. The chart thus indicates that three regions, Northeast, Middle States, and Far West, are characteristically industrial, while the Southeast, Southwest, and Northwest are agrarian. Three regions, Northeast, Middle States, and significantly enough the Southeast, have a density pattern more characteristic of urbanism, namely the excess of population over land area, while the three western areas show characteristic sparsity of total settlement.

Outstanding is the concentration in the three eastern areas. The Northeast emerges as the predominant industrial area with 43.6 percent of the Nation's wage earners to only 10.4 percent of the country's farm operators and 6.8 percent of the land area. It is followed by the Middle States, well balanced with 32 percent of the nation's wage earners and 27.4 percent of its farmers. Thus the Northwest with 1.5 percent wage earners to 9.9

FIGURE 94. THE PERCENTAGE DISTRIBUTION OF THE NATION'S POPULATION AND
LAND AREA, WAGE EARNERS IN MANUFACTURING AND FARM OPERATORS,
THE SIX MAJOR REGIONS OF THE UNITED STATES, 1940

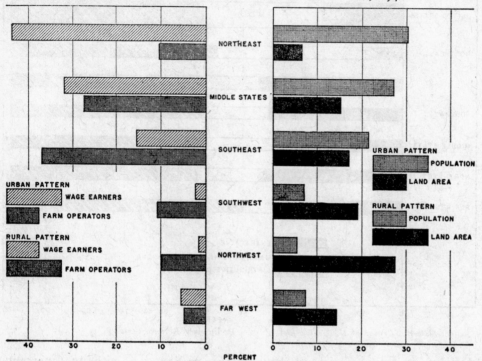

Source: *Statistical Abstract of the United States, 1941*, Tables 2, 6, 630 and 868.

percent farm operators emerges as more agrarian than the Southeast, which
has 15.3 percent of all wage earners and 37 percent of the farmers. Actually the Southeast, partly because of the density of its agricultural population, has the third highest proportion of population to land area.

From this basic relation of agricultural and industrial workers we proceed to consideration of the occupational range. While some work has been
done on the topic it has proved extremely difficult to estimate the ratio of
workers needed in distributive, service and auxiliary occupations to supply
and serve the major sectors of our economy. It is agreed, however, that
larger numbers of service workers are needed by 1,000 workers in industry
than by 1,000 in agriculture, due partly to the higher returns received by
workers in manufacturing. This conclusion receives some support from
the occupational statistics of regions. Thus in 1940 the Northeast with
the highest proportions in manufacturing and mechanical occupations, 38.9
percent, was second only to the Far West in the proportion in distribution
and services, 52.9 to 59.5 percent (Figure 95). The Southeast, however,

FIGURE 95. THE PERCENTAGE DISTRIBUTION OF GAINFUL WORKERS BY THREE
MAJOR GROUPS, UNITED STATES AND THE SIX MAJOR REGIONS, 1940

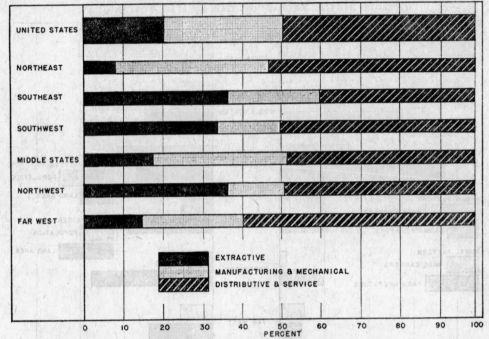

Source: *Sixteenth Census of the United States, 1940*, Preliminary Release, Series P-11.

fell below its proportionate share of the services for, with 23.4 percent in the industrial sector, it had only 40.1 percent in the service group, falling below two regions that it outranked in industry, the Northwest and the Southwest. Here we have a definite suggestion of a regional maladjustment in occupational distribution.

Occupational distribution can well be examined in terms of Alba M. Edwards' arrangement of census occupations into socio-economic classes in terms of the income status and social prestige.[1] Figure 96, which gives total occupied population for all regions in 1940, clearly shows the predominance of farm workers including unpaid family labor in the Southeast as compared with the Nation and the more industrialized regions. Especially notable is the region's shortage of professional, clerical, and skilled classes as compared with the Northeast, Middle States, and the Far West. The Southeast's 789,937 domestic servants account for the region's only predominance in the nonfarm occupations. Figure 97 shows, by comparison with the Nation, that female workers in the Southeast exhibit the same occupational maldistribution shown by males. More females are found

[1] "A Social-Economic Grouping of the Gainful Workers in the United States" (Washington, D. C.: Government Printing Office, 1938).

FIGURE 96. THE PERCENTAGE DISTRIBUTION OF GAINFUL WORKERS BY SOCIAL-ECONOMIC GROUPS, UNITED STATES AND THE SIX MAJOR REGIONS, 1940

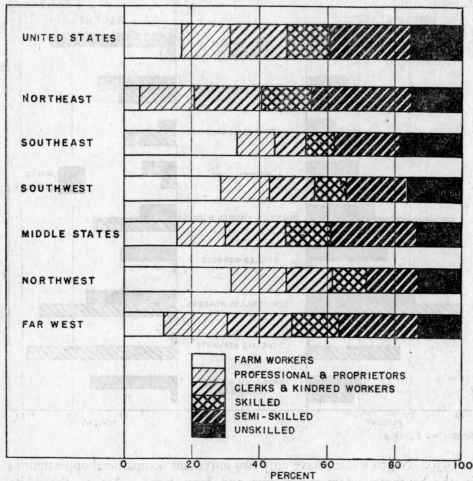

Source: See Figure 93.

in agriculture in the region as compared with those in the Nation and fewer in professional, proprietor, and clerical positions.

Figure 98 compares the Southeast and the Nation in terms of race in 1930. For the white group the Nation has a clear predominance over the Southeast in the proportion in all classes except farm owners, tenants, and laborers. Figure 98 also serves to show the extent to which the Southeast's low ranking is due to the large proportion of its Negroes in the servant, unskilled, farm labor, and tenant groups. In professional, clerical, skilled, and semiskilled ranks the Nation's Negroes had a clear lead over those of the Southeast.

Figure 99 compares the occupational distribution of the sexes by race

FIGURE 97. THE PERCENTAGE DISTRIBUTION OF GAINFUL WORKERS BY SOCIAL·
ECONOMIC GROUPS, BY SEX, UNITED STATES AND SOUTHEAST, 1940

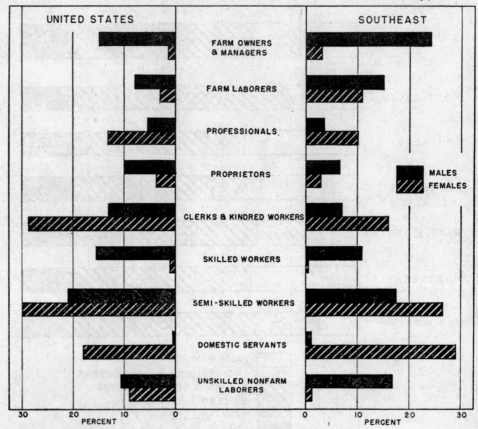

Source: See Figure 93.

in 1930. Negro women have only two important occupational opportunities in the Southeast—domestic service and farm labor. Among the white group, women are coming to take proportionately more important places in professional, clerical, and service ranks where they are represented largely by teachers, sales clerks, and beauty shop operatives.

The occupational distribution of the southern population remains one of imbalance—an imbalance that is alleviated but never quite corrected by a continuous flow of migration and social mobility. That this condition is appreciably changed by industrialization and its related development can be shown by a comparison of the fringe State of Virginia with agrarian Mississippi, representative of the Deep South (Figure 100). Virginia's class structure shows a clear predominance in industrial labor, skilled, unskilled, and semiskilled that carries on into the upper reaches of clerical,

FIGURE 98. THE PERCENTAGE DISTRIBUTION OF GAINFUL WORKERS BY SOCIAL-ECONOMIC GROUPS, BY RACE, UNITED STATES AND SOUTHEAST, 1930

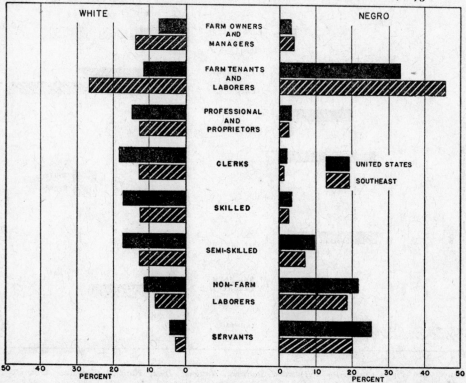

Source: "The Problems of a Changing Population," National Resources Committee, May, 1938, pp. 75-76. *Population Statistics, National Data,* National Resources Committee, Table 27.   Alba M. Edwards, "A Social-Economic Grouping of the Gainful Workers in the United States," *Journal of the American Statistical Association,* December, 1933, pp. 377-387. *Fifteenth Census of the United States, 1930,* Population, IV, *United States Summary,* Table 13.

professional, and proprietor groups. Outside the farm workers in which she leads, Mississippi's class structure approaches Virginia's only in the proportion of unskilled labor. Over 75 percent of Virginia's workers were non-farm in 1940 as compared to 45 percent in Mississippi.

DIFFERENTIAL REPLACEMENTS BY OCCUPATIONAL CLASSES

Occupational status and occupational trends thus occupy a key position in the explanation of population dynamics because they are closely related to fertility differentials, rural-urban residence, and migration. Differential reproduction has simply come to mean that in the sphere of western civilization those occupational groups with the lowest incomes usually have the highest replacement rates. Differential reproduction in inverse relation to income has been shown by many studies to exist in terms of economic regions, social classes, and by size of community—all related to the average

FIGURE 99. THE PERCENTAGE DISTRIBUTION OF GAINFUL WORKERS BY SOCIAL-ECONOMIC GROUPS, BY RACE AND SEX, SOUTHEAST, 1930

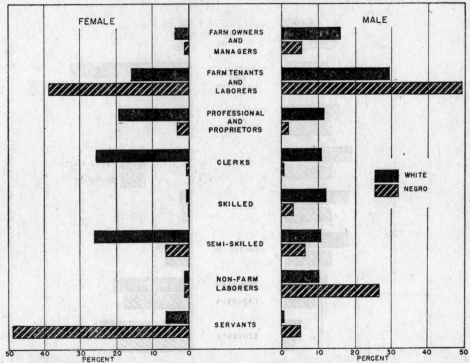

Source: See Figure 96. Also *Population Statistics, National Data,* National Resources Committee, Table 28.

fertility of occupational classes. A fundamental distinction exists between urban and farm classes, for the lowest urban occupational group rarely has average fertility as high as the highest farming class. Thus the Milbank study of almost 100,000 families returned in the Census of 1910 found that the number of children per 100 wives progressively increased down the occupational scale as follows: professional, 129; business, 140; skilled workers, 179; unskilled workers, 223; farm owners, 247; farm renters, 275; farm laborers, 299.[2] No comparable study has been made of the occupational classes in the South, but the analysis of the region's pattern of high fertility in Chapter 8 indicates similar conditions.

The influence that differential fertility exerts on the occupational distribution has been neatly demonstrated for one class—the farmers. We have seen that the rate of replacements of males 18-64 in the farm population in 1930 would give 240 young farmers to replace every 100 farmers who died or became 65. In both southern regions, there were over 300

[2] Frank Notestein in G. H. L. Pitt-Rivers, *Problems of Population* (London: Allen and Unwin, 1931), p. 9.

FIGURE 100. THE PERCENTAGE DISTRIBUTION OF GAINFUL WORKERS BY SOCIAL-
ECONOMIC GROUPS, VIRGINIA AND MISSISSIPPI, 1940

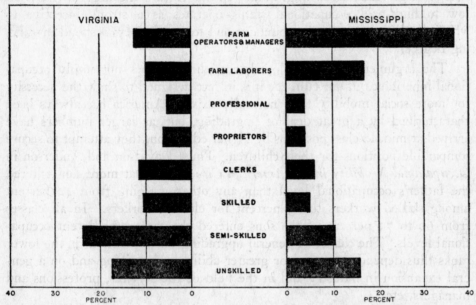

Source: *Sixteenth Census of the United States, 1940*, Series P-10, No. 9; Series P-11, Nos. 20 and 43.

replacements for every 10,000 farmers; in the Southern Appalachians, approximately 350.   These annual replacement rates ranged from zero or below in New York, New Hampshire, and Rhode Island to 405 in South Carolina (Figure 92).   It should be pointed out here that if it were possible to segregate other occupational groups from the census, the unskilled and semiskilled classes would show replacement trends nearest to those found in the farm groups.

With a replacement rate far in excess of the normal need for farmers, the obvious question arises: To what extent is farming an inherited occupational status?   Certainly there exists the tendency toward the social inheritance of class and occupational status, a tendency that for many reasons proves especially strong in an agrarian society like that of the Southeast. For one thing farmers comprise a distinctive locality group and the change to alternative employments, so common in the urban environment, involves an initial move of the farmer's son to town or city. Equally important in a period characterized by almost complete abandonment of the family apprenticeship system is the fact that the farmer's son still learns his "trade" on the home farm. On the other side of the ledger is the fact that poorer schooling in rural areas leaves the farmer's children with less knowledge of alternative opportunities and less capable of competing for them.   In opposition to this view, it may be pointed out that our society has been characterized by a high rate of mobility, especially apparent in our discussion of large rural-urban migration. In our culture the urge to rise from low to high-paid occupational status operates as a strong incentive to which dwellers in southern mountains and tenant farmers respond in varying degrees.

The argument here developed, accordingly, does not imply occupational inheritance in our culture; it is in fact designed to show the necessity for more social mobility than normally exists. America has always been characterized by a great deal of upgrading, but, as larger numbers have arrived at middle-class positions by higher education, they attempt to secure comparable positions for their children. Thus, Davidson and Anderson in *Occupational Mobility in An American City* found that more sons entered the father's occupational level than any other, ranging from 42 percent among skilled workers to 23 percent for clerical workers. In all classes from 60 to 73 percent of the sons entered the same or adjacent occupational levels.[3] The chance of general upgrading for populations in the lower ranks thus depends on equal or greater ability and training and on a general expansion in industry and in the field of the services, professions and managers, etc.

For many the initial chance of better well-being may depend on the opportunity of moving out of the sector of farm labor into that of industrial labor. Thus Paul Douglas in *Real Wages in the United States, 1890-1926*[4] showed that a 6 percent national increase in real earnings in the United States was due to rural-urban migration. In a refined statistical analysis of the rise in real wages he showed that there was a total rise of 16.5 percent in the real buying power of all workers between 1920-1926. Of this total, 2.5 percent was attributed to the transfer of labor from farms to cities. This figure offers some measure of economic pressure on agricultural classes to make an occupational shift.

PRESSURES IN THE SHIFTING OCCUPATIONAL DISTRIBUTION

Against the varying replacement rates of class groups must be set the changing employment capacity of the various sectors of our economy. For convenience three major groups will again be considered: (1) agricultural and extractive, (2) manufacturing and mechanical, and (3) distributive and service occupations. Here we should undertake an explanation of the pressures behind our changing patterns of occupations. The capacity of any major sector of our economy to employ people depends upon a moving ratio—the relation between (1) increasing output per worker and (2) the

[3] Percy E. Davidson and H. Dewey Anderson, *Occupational Mobility in an American City* (Stanford, California: Stanford University Press, 1937), pp. 17-38, 162-167.

[4] (Boston: Houghton Mifflin, 1930), Table 146 and p. 395.

changing rate of total physical production in that field. This last is dependent on the amount of demand, that is, the extent of the market for
such products. Output per worker has increased constantly in farming,
mining, and manufacturing for the 60 years previous to the depression of
1930. If the demand for products at the prices prevailing in an industry
expands as fast as the increasing output per worker, the proportions in that
industry may expect to remain constant; if the proportionate demand declines, however, increased efficiency will operate to push workers into other
sectors of the economy, if not into unemployment.

Figure 101 presents the changing trend of employment in the three
major sectors of the American economy for 120 years. During the whole
period the employment capacity of agriculture has been steadily downward, for increasing output per worker has met no appreciable increase in
the per capita consumption of agricultural products, while exports of food
and fibers have shown a steady decline. Agriculture offers still the main
source of employment in the Southeast but in the Nation the proportions
so employed have declined from 72.3 percent in 1820 to less than half in
1880, less than one-third in 1910, to hardly more than one-fifth in 1940.

FIGURE 101. THE TREND IN THE NUMBER OF GAINFUL WORKERS BY THREE
MAJOR OCCUPATIONAL GROUPS, UNITED STATES, 1820-1940

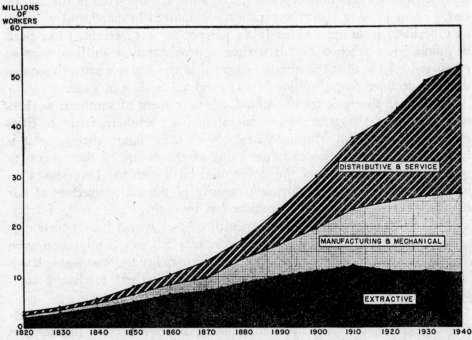

Source: Leon E. Truesdell, "Growth of Urban Population in the United States," United States Bureau
of the Census Release, 1937, p. 6, Table 2; *Sixteenth Census of the United States, 1940*, Series P-11.

Not only have relative proportions declined but recently the Nation has seen a decline in absolute numbers from a peak of 11.9 millions in 1910 to 10.5 millions in 1940.

In the same period those employed in manufacturing and construction have increased from 358,000, 12.4 percent of those employed in 1820, to almost 16 million, 30.4 percent in 1940, passing agriculture shortly after 1910. Here an increasing output per worker has met an increasing per capita demand for industrial products. If, following Mordecai Ezekiel's analysis in the *Annals* for November 1936,[5] we take the 1900 average as representing 100 in the total volume of physical production, we find that the physical volume of production in agriculture from 1880 to 1930 changed from 33.6 to 33.3 per capita of the total population. For industrial products in the same period the index rose from 37.1 to 121.5 per capita of the consuming public. Thus, while per capita demand barely remained constant for agricultural products, it increased over threefold for industrial products. Already, however, due to increased efficiency, the proportions employed in industry had begun to slacken, declining in the period 1920-1940 from 33.2 to 30.9 percent of the total gainfully employed.

Figure 102 shows the extent to which this process, forcing population from agriculture into industry and the services, has operated in the Southeast. From 1870 to 1940 the percentage employed in the extractive economy declined from approximately 84 percent to 36.5 percent. The peak in number was reached in 1910 when approximately 5 million were so employed. Since then the number engaged in the region's extractive economy has declined to 4.4 million in 1930 and 3.8 million in 1940.

These are the basic trends behind the movement of southern workers to industry and the great Negro migration from southern farms to cities of the Northeast and Middle States. With these figures before us it is hardly necessary to leave the description of the nature of the process to speculation. The trend of the differential birth rate has long shown an inverse relation to the employment capacity of the various sectors of our economy. Here southern agriculture has been the focal point of crisis. The piling up of population in agriculture has lowered its proportionate returns. Thus the search for economic security has forced migration upon those displaced and has offered upward social mobility to those whose training and knowledge of other opportunities enabled them to change occupations.

Here a main oportunity has offered itself in the fields of transportation and trade, attendant upon distributing the products of industry, as

[5] "Population and Unemployment," *Annals* of the American Academy of Political and Social Science, 188 (November, 1936), pp. 230-242.

FIGURE 102. THE TREND IN THE NUMBER OF GAINFUL WORKERS BY THREE MAJOR OCCUPATIONAL GROUPS, SOUTHEAST, 1870-1940

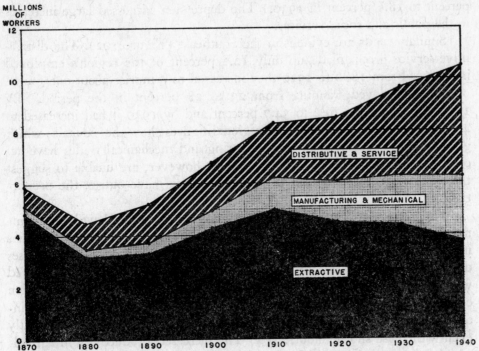

Source: Occupational data by States from the *United States Census* from 1870 to 1940.

well as in the increasing number of occupations that purvey services rather than goods. In this field extreme regional concentration is not feasible for, unlike those who extract or fabricate goods, most workers who furnish services, professional, clerical, or domestic, must be located close to the populations they serve.

An examination of Figure 101 adds support to the view that the trend of employment in the clerical and service groups has been uniformly upward in most fields, for growing demand has more often been met by improvement in the quality of services rather than by large increases in the output per worker. While the combined volume of such services is difficult to measure in terms comparable to the physical volume of goods, Figure 101 suggests the increased output of services in terms of their increased share of the working force. From 1820 to 1930 the population engaged in transportation, and trade increased from 2.5 to 28.6 percent of all gainful workers. This multiplication by 11 furnished an increase far in excess of that experienced by any other group in our economy. Whether distribution and trade is overexpanded in our economy, and the middleman is a social parasite may be most questionable; but in terms of demand and income the shift has pragmatic justification. In addition, the services, domestic, professional, public, etc., have increased from 12.8 percent to 18.6 percent in 1930. The depression witnessed large increases in the public and social services.

Similar trends are evident in the Southeast (Figure 102). The distributive-service group made up only 12.2 percent of the region's employed in 1870. From 1880 to 1920 they increased to comprise about one-fourth of those employed, ranging from 23 to 28 percent in the period. By 1930 the proportion rose to 34.7 percent and by 1940 it had increased to 40.1 percent. Both national and regional figures show the extent to which gains in those employed in manufacturing and mechanical trades have accompanied these increases. These graphs, however, are unable to suggest the extent to which increases in physical volume have outrun the proportions employed in industry.

The trends in occupational distribution up to 1930 have been summarized by Mordecai Ezekiel as follows: "(1) Output per worker has increased constantly in farming, mining, and manufacturing. The increases during the recent decade of 1920-1930 were not extraordinary, compared with previous rates of increase. (2) The proportion of the population occupied has increased rather than decreased. (3) Hours per week [in industry] have decreased gradually, but output per worker has risen rapidly even with these shorter hours. (4) The increased productivity in agriculture has been accompanied by [no decrease in hours but by] a corresponding reduction in the proportion of the workers engaged in agriculture, leaving a substantially constant output of farm products per capita of population. (5) The increased productivity in industry has been accompanied by a doubling in the proportion of workers engaged in industry, resulting in a great expansion in the volume of industrial products per capita of population. (6) Commerce, trade, and administration absorbed half of the workers displaced from agriculture from 1820 to 1900, while half went to manufacturing and mining. Since 1900 the proportion in industry has remained constant, with virtually all the reduction in the proportion in agriculture being represented by increases in transportation, trade, and administration, or in the professional and other service industries."[6]

In conclusion we are faced with the fact that the differential trends in income returned and in the employment capacity of agriculture, industry, and the services still remain in inverse relation to the differential reproduction of the class groups they employ. For farmers and less skilled wage earners this means pressure upon them and their children to climb into higher occupational ranks. In the middle classes, however, it means that the failure of white collar and service groups to replace themselves in the

[6] *Ibid.*, pp. 241-242.

population leave an "occupational vacuum" into which the more able children of the lower classes can climb, provided they have knowledge of the situation, adequate motivation, and educational opportunity.   To make this shift many southern youth will continue to migrate to large cities where rates of replacement are already below unity.

Obviously migration in itself is not the complete and perfect answer. Some balancing of the differential birth rate is to be expected as the pattern of family limitation continues to percolate downward through the social strata.   In a final chapter on population policy we shall consider the question whether this trend should not be hastened for the poorer classes by the inclusion of birth control as a part of public health programs.   At the same time the Southeast will continue to shift part of its resources and manpower from agriculture to industry, thus balancing its agrarian economy with needed goods and services.   Here the invitation to industry, so persistently extended by all chambers of commerce in peace times and war, raises the question of the limits of regional dispersion of manufacturing consistent with sound national policy.   It will be the purpose of the two succeeding sections to discuss the relation of the region's human resources to the agrarian and the industrial economies.

PART II

POPULATION AND THE AGRARIAN ECONOMY

CHAPTER 12

FARM POPULATION AND THE LAND USE PATTERN

THE POPULATION problem of the Southeast is basically agrarian in setting and in origin. Current discussion has emphasized the fact that the farm population is predominant, that farms are small and the region's farm incomes are among the lowest in the Nation. These conditions pose basic questions for the developing science of land utilization which, we assume, is the connecting link between the physical and the human factors in agriculture.

It is a fallacy to think of either farming or land-use analysis as simple procedures. Many factors that must be considered from an individual point of view in farm management studies are considered from the viewpoint of social welfare and public policy in land utilization studies. Thus the amount and type of land available to the population is related to the average size of farms and the distribution of farm land as between the various cropping systems. In conjunction with available markets, these physical factors help determine the type of farm as measured by its chief sources of income. These factors lead to a study of the productivity of the farm in terms of the support of the farm family by products sold on the market and those used at home. Basic to all farming, however, is access to the land. Attention therefore will be paid in following chapters to the conditions of land ownership and tenancy.

In the changing equation of agricultural production, the quantity and quality of land available afford one set of limiting factors, the extent of markets and the trend of prices offer another. Into this hypothetical equation comes as an intrusive, dynamic factor, the increasing farm population, pressing against the land supply, pressing against available markets, pressing against the limits of subsistence farming. Perfectly willing, often anxious to be drained off to cities and industries, these oncoming youth also assert their rights under private property and individual freedom to enter agriculture.

[154]

This is the challenge of population to land utilization, a challenge that finds its core in the Southeast, area of greatest importance and greatest increase in the farm population. Calculations discussed in Chapter 10, Figure 90, showed there were three times as many youth in the region's farm population in 1930 as were needed for replacements in southern agriculture.

If it were conceivable to think of caring for a sizeable proportion of this increase in the region, what potential land resources would we find? The great leeway for land expansion in the region was indicated by Howard W. Odum's estimate that the Southeast might easily add 40 million acres, the commonly cited post-war surplus of harvested cropland in the Nation; or take out of cultivation that amount and, through better utilization and management, enrich its agricultural capacity and output. There is available for replanning and future use no less than 100,000,000 acres within the former area of the South's piney woods alone. Of the nation's nearly 100,-000,000 acres of drainable land suitable for cultivation after reclamation, the South has nearly two-thirds.[1] Large stretches of the South's Coastal Plains are said to hold the best undeveloped land left in the United States.

We shall realize, of course, that the poor quality of land, the cost of development, and the trend of prices will operate against putting any such amounts of land into cultivation. As for the level of farm prices in relation to quality of land, however, we need to examine this in relation to the price of land itself.

It is here that we come to the core of the sub-marginal land problem. It is not only that farmers with little capital but large families furnishing unpaid family labor cannot secure access to good land; actually they get a higher return on their meager financial resources from cheap land. As much as any one index, the ratio of gross value of farm products to the value of farm property serves to explain this situation. Strangely enough, it reaches its highest in the Southeast (Figure 103). The gross value of farm production per $1,000 of investment was lowest—under $150—in the Nation's blue ribbon land areas, the richest lands of the Corn Belt, Dairying Regions, and Fruit Growing Districts of California and Florida. It was highest—$250-500—in the Eastern and Central Cotton Belts. Here, of course, fertilizer and labor constitute a higher share of total production costs. Close behind these areas come the poor and cheap lands of the Appalachians and the Ozarks. Thus, as O. E. Baker points out, it would seem that persons having little capital and much unpaid family labor can obtain a larger return by investing in cheap lands. Persons seeking investment only are likely to buy high quality land and thus keep its value in close alignment with productivity.

[1] Howard W. Odum, *Southern Regions of the United States*, p. 31.

FIGURE 103. VALUE OF FARM PRODUCTS PER $1,000 INVESTMENT IN FARM
PROPERTY, UNITED STATES BY COUNTIES, 1930

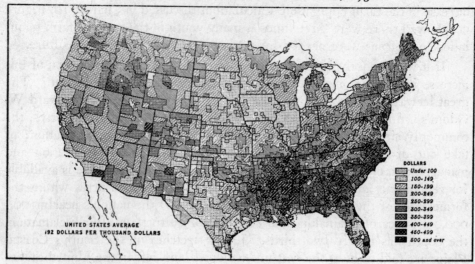

Note: Gross value of farm products is that reported for 1929; the value of farms and farm property
is reported as of April 1, 1930.
Source: Bureau of Agricultural Economics, U. S. Department of Agriculture, Negative 28476.

We should begin, of course, by saying that competent studies indicate
that, under efficient practices, half the farm people of the South, working
the better part of our present area of tilled lands, could meet all the normal domestic and export needs for the products of southern agriculture
and could thereby double their present individual family incomes. Thus,
for example, the National Resources Committee asked the question: Suppose new opportunities attracted workers from the rural Southeast until
the average value productivity per male worker became as high for those
remaining in agriculture in this area as for farm workers in other parts of
the country, how many agricultural workers would be needed in the Southeast? The average gross productivity in 1924-1928 was $768 for the
Southeast as compared with $1726 per year for all sections outside the
Southeast. At this rate of value productivity, the products of 1½ million
male workers would equal that of the total value of all farm commodities
produced in the Southeast. This would release nearly 2 million male workers, who with their families comprising some 9 million people, would be
sufficient to overrun the labor market of the rest of the country.[2]

THE AVAILABLE LAND SUPPLY

These conflicting points of view set the stage for an examination of the
facts of land resources, the cropping system, available markets, and possible shifts in land use in the region.

[2] National Resources Committee, *Problems of a Changing Population* (Washington, D. C.: United
States Government Printing Office, 1938), p. 66.

As compared with other countries, the ratio of land resources to total population in the United States is still very large. Normally we harvest nearly three acres of cropland per person as compared with one acre in Germany, one-half acre in China, and one-fourth acre in Japan. In addition, the Nation has large resources of range and forest lands. The United States has slowly changed from a nation exporting agricultural products until, before World War II, nearly all our production was normally consumed within our borders. The per capita requirements are now about 2.5 acres; of this figure 0.4 of an acre per person are required to feed horses and mules used in the process of production.[3]

Of the major types of land, cropland offers more adequate support for population, plowable pasture next, and woodland comes last. The Middle States, with one-third of the Nation's cropland harvested in 1939 and 28.7 percent of its plowable pasture, ranks highest in this respect followed by the Northwest and the Southeast (Table 34). The Southeast has 39.2 percent of its farm acreage in cropland as compared with 54.1 percent for the Middle States, and 14.3 percent in plowable pasture as compared with 17.5 percent for the Middle States (Table 35). The Southeast, however, has almost half, 47.7 percent, of the farm woodland in the Nation, 35.7 percent of its farm acreage being in woodland.

TABLE 34. PERCENTAGE DISTRIBUTION OF THE NATION'S LAND ACREAGE IN FARMS CLASSIFIED ACCORDING TO USE, UNITED STATES AND THE SIX MAJOR REGIONS, 1939

Area	Total	Cropland harvested	Crop failures	Cropland idle or fallow	Plowable pasture	All woodland	All other†
UNITED STATES.........	100.00	100.00	100.00	100.00	100.00	100.00	100.00
Northeast..............	5.75	6.37	1.97	5.09	6.95	11.59	3.13
Southeast.............	17.31	18.93	7.82	16.39	20.08	47.74	5.01
Southwest.............	22.35	12.86	17.72	12.69	14.70	14.42	37.06
Middle States..........	20.28	33.16	7.24	14.32	28.68	18.00	9.29
Northwest.............	27.95	24.53	62.88	41.72	24.39	3.92	36.50
Far West..............	6.36	4.15	2.36	9.77	5.17	4.30	8.99
District of Columbia....	*	*	*	*	*	*	*

†This classification includes pasture land other than plowable and woodland pasture, all wasteland, house yards, barnyards, feed lots, lanes, roads, etc.
*Less than 0.01 percent.
Source: *Sixteenth Census of the United States, 1940*, Agriculture, Preliminary U. S.-1, Table 2, p. 2.

While no measures of land resources in the United States are completely satisfactory, three maps serve to indicate high economic density in the Southeast. Figure 104 shows the size of farm population in proportion to amount of farm land in crops in 1930. The proportionate size of the State rectangles indicates the proportion of total land in farms, while the cross hatching indicates that only Kentucky and Louisiana, for example,

[3] O. E. Baker, *Graphic Summary of Physical Features and Land Utilization*, U. S. D. A., Miscellaneous Publication 260 (1936), pp. 1-2.

TABLE 35. PERCENTAGE DISTRIBUTION OF THE REGIONAL LAND ACREAGE IN FARMS CLASSIFIED ACCORDING TO USE, UNITED STATES AND THE SIX MAJOR REGIONS, 1939

Area	All farm land	Cropland harvested	Crop failure	Cropland idle or fallow	Plowable pasture	All woodland	All other
UNITED STATES.........	100.00	30.3	1.9	5.4	12.3	13.0	37.1
Northeast..............	100.00	33.5	0.7	4.8	14.9	26.0	20.1
Southeast..............	100.00	33.2	0.9	5.1	14.3	35.7	10.8
Southwest	100.00	17.5	1.5	3.0	8.1	8.3	61.6
Middle States..........	100.00	49.6	0.7	3.8	17.5	11.5	16.9
Northwest.............	100.00	26.6	4.4	8.0	10.8	1.8	48.4
Far West..............	100.00	19.8	0.7	8.2	10.0	8.8	52.5
District of Columbia....	100.00	43.4	3.2	5.2	9.1	16.5	22.6

Source: *Sixteenth Census of the United States, 1940*, Agriculture, Preliminary U. S.-1, Table 2, p. 2.

FIGURE 104. THE RELATIVE SIZE OF THE FARM POPULATION IN RELATION TO AMOUNT OF LAND IN FARMS AND PROPORTION CLASSIFIED AS ARABLE, UNITED STATES, 1930

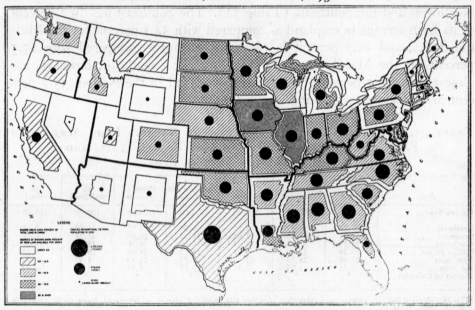

Source: *Problems of a Changing Population*, National Resources Planning Board, 1938, p. 54.

had as much as 60 percent of their farm land in crops. Figures 105 and 106 show the size of farm population as related (1) to arable or improved land, (2) to value of farm land per capita of the farm population. Note the large number of counties in the Southeast with less than 10 acres of arable land per farm person in 1930, and worth less than $500 per farm person. These maps, which suggest the real effect of over-population pressing on the land supply should be compared with Figure 107 which shows the degree of productivity of farm land.

FIGURE 105. ACRES OF ARABLE LAND PER CAPITA OF THE FARM POPULATION
BY COUNTIES, UNITED STATES, 1935

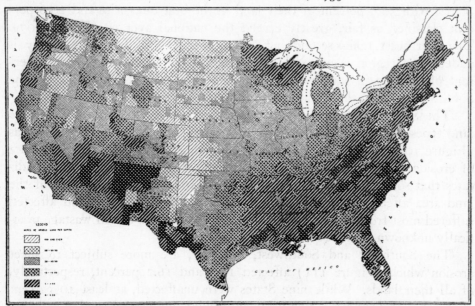

Source: *Problems of a Changing Population*, National Resources Committee, 1938, p. 56.

FIGURE 106. VALUE OF FARM LAND PER CAPITA OF THE FARM POPULATION
BY COUNTIES, UNITED STATES, 1930

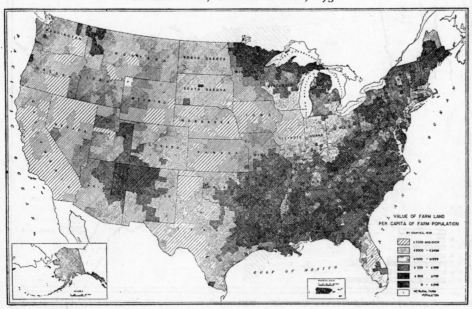

Source: *Problems of a Changing Population*, National Resources Committee, 1938, p. 57.

In terms of productivity some 16 percent of our farm land has been classified as excellent and good and 18 percent as fair. Only the Middle States, with 52.6 percent of their land in the best categories and 20.6 percent classified as fair, greatly exceed the national average (Figure 107). The Northeast ranks second but, when the land of fair productivity is added, that region is passed by the Southeast, each having over 43 percent of its land in the first three grades as compared with 29.4 for the Southwest, 23.8 in the Northwest, and only 6.6 in the Far West.

The Southeast is shown to fall midway between the more productive land types as in Iowa and the least productive as in the western range areas (Figure 108). These conditions can be explained in part by the prevalence of erosion. Figure 109 which gives the effect of man-made erosion indicates that southern and western states have from 60 to 98 percent of the land area affected. The Northwest, with 76 percent of its land affected suffered most from wind erosion (Figure 110), a form of soil wastage practically unknown in the Southeast.

The Southeast and Southwest, however, are more subject to sheet erosion which (Figure 111) affected 14.5 and 16.2 percent, respectively, of all their lands. While nine States were unaffected, at least 40 percent of the area of Tennessee, Kentucky, and Oklahoma was affected.

FIGURE 107. LAND OF FIRST THREE GRADES (EXCELLENT, GOOD AND FAIR) AS PERCENTAGE OF ALL LAND, UNITED STATES, 1934

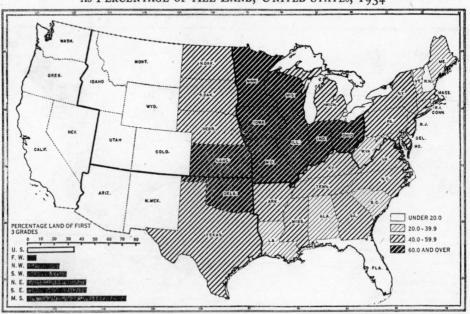

Source: *Report of the Land Planning Committee*, National Resources Board, November 15, 1934. Table 7, p. 127.

FIGURE 108. PERCENTAGE DISTRIBUTION OF FARM LAND CLASSIFIED AS
EXCELLENT, GOOD AND FAIR, UNITED STATES AND THE
SIX MAJOR REGIONS, 1934

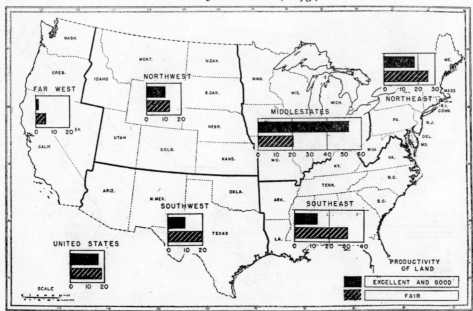

Source: See Figure 107.

FIGURE 109. PERCENTAGE OF AREA AFFECTED BY EROSION,*
UNITED STATES, 1934

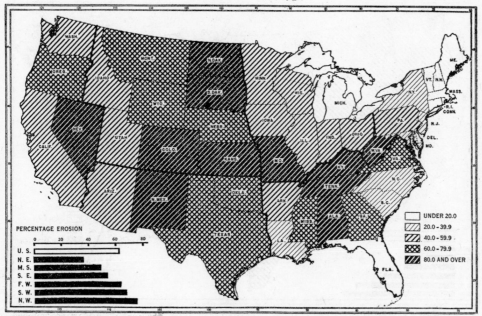

* Erosion is here defined as man-induced erosion with a loss of 25 percent or more topsoil caused by
sheet erosion, wind erosion, gullying, or a combination of these conditions.

Source: *Soil Erosion, A Critical Problem in American Agriculture*, Part V, Supplementary Report of the
Land Planning Committee to the National Resources Board (Washington, D. C., 1935).

FIGURE 110. PERCENTAGE OF AREA AFFECTED BY WIND EROSION, UNITED STATES, 1934

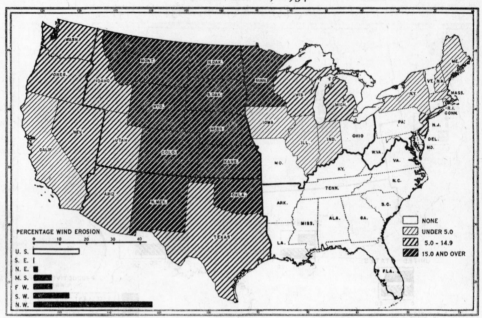

Source: See Figure 109.

FIGURE 111. PERCENTAGE OF AREA AFFECTED BY SEVERE SHEET EROSION,* UNITED STATES, 1934

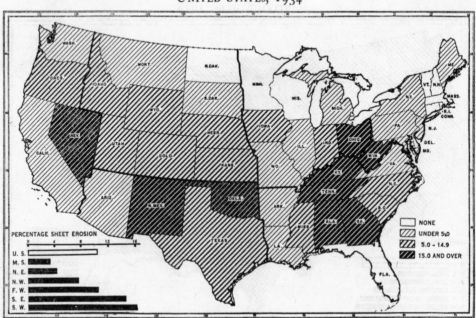

* Area affected by severe sheet erosion is that which has lost three-fourths or more of its topsoil and possibly some of its subsoil.

Source: See Figure 109.

THE SIZE OF HOLDINGS

The Southeast is commonly regarded as the stronghold of the small farm in American agriculture. Only if we follow the practice of the census which considers the plantation's tenant farms as separate holdings is this view justified. Considered in terms of tillage units, however, the area has 76.7 percent of its farms under a hundred acres—with average size around 81 acres and average cropland less than 45. This small acreage is associated with crops which demand a great deal of labor and possess relatively high value per acre, cotton, tobacco, and truck crops.

What has been the region's trend of land use in terms of size of farm and the amount of land available to farm operators? Here it must be pointed out we run into that transition from plantations to farm operator units first encountered in the Census of 1870. The Southeast of 1850-1860 (Table 36) was expansive in its land holdings and extensive in cultivation. In 1860 only 597,032 farms were listed in the 11 plantation States of the Southeast but they held over 194¼ million acres of farm land—a total that has been exceeded only in the prosperous decades of 1900 and 1910. The 600,000 odd ownership units of 1860 comprised both small

TABLE 36. FARMS, FARM LAND, AND FARM VALUES, UNITED STATES AND SOUTHEAST, 1850-1940

Area and census year	Farms		All land in farms		Improved land in farms*		Value of land and buildings	
	Number	Percent change	Thousands of acres	Percent change	Thousands of acres	Percent change	Thousands of dollars	Percent change
UNITED STATES								
1850.........	1,449,073	....	293,561	....	113,033	....	$ 3,271,575	.....
1860.........	2,044,077	41.1	407,213	38.7	163,111	44.3	6,645,045	103.1
1870.........	2,659,985	30.1	407,735	0.1	188,921	15.8	7,444,054	12.0
1880.........	4,008,907	50.7	536,082	31.5	284,771	50.7	10,197,097	37.0
1890.........	4,564,641	13.9	623,219	16.3	357,617	25.6	13,279,253	30.2
1900.........	5,737,372	25.7	838,592	34.6	414,498	15.9	16,614,647	25.1
1910.........	6,361,502	10.9	878,798	4.8	478,452	15.4	34,801,126	109.5
1920.........	6,448,343	1.4	955,884	8.8	503,073	5.1	66,316,003	90.6
1925.........	6,371,640	− 1.2	924,319	− 3.3	505,027	0.4	49,467,647	− 25.4
1930.........	6,288,648	− 1.3	986,771	6.8	522,396	3.4	47,879,838	− 3.2
1935.........	6,812,350	8.3	1,054,515	6.9	513,514	− 1.7	32,858,844	− 31.4
1940.........	6,096,799	−10.5	1,060,852	0.6	530,131	3.2	33,641,739	2.4
SOUTHEAST								
1850.........	474,622	....	153,933	....	48,009	....	931,815	....
1860.........	597,032	25.8	194,296	26.2	61,826	28.8	2,054,104	120.4
1870.........	749,373	25.5	157,055	−19.2	52,126	−15.7	982,585	− 52.2
1880.........	1,244,518	66.1	182,206	16.0	65,432	16.0	1,363,789	38.8
1890.........	1,476,086	18.6	187,251	2.8	77,917	19.1	1,793,794	31.5
1900.........	2,011,359	36.3	196,342	4.8	88,183	13.2	2,027,259	13.0
1910.........	2,332,924	16.0	197,030	0.4	96,184	9.1	4,204,030	107.4
1920.........	2,433,102	4.3	188,871	− 4.1	98,412	2.3	9,224,903	119.4
1925.........	2,318,777	− 4.7	169,329	−10.4	87,997	−10.6	6,683,193	− 27.6
1930.........	2,388,806	3.0	170,508	0.7	90,794	3.2	6,731,231	0.7
1935.........	2,547,952	6.7	188,543	10.6	94,018	3.6	4,839,744	− 28.1
1940.........	2,259,030	−11.3	183,677	− 2.6	98,162	4.4	5,690,359	17.6

*Data refer to year preceding the census year. Beginning with 1925, the census discontinued the classification "improved land." Therefore, for the period 1925-40 the sum of all crop land (crop land harvested, crop failure, and crop land idle or fallow) and plowable pasture is substituted as the nearest equivalent.

Source: Bureau of the Census, *Plantation Farming in the United States* (Washington: Govt. Printing Office, 1916); *Thirteenth Census of the United States, 1910*, V, Agriculture; *Abstract of the Fourteenth Census of the United States, 1920; United States Census of Agriculture, 1935*, V. III; *Sixteenth Census of the United States, 1940*, Agriculture, First Series, Table 5.

farms and plantations and cannot be related either to units of tillage or to the farm population.

The number of farms increased by decades. With 11 million less acres in farms in 1940, the Southeast had over 2¼ million farm units. Not all of the increase in number of farm operators shown in Table 36 represents growth of farm population. The break-up of the plantations into small farms and tenant holdings is represented by the steady decline in average size of farm unit from 325 acres in 1860 to 98 acres in 1900 (Table 37). The year 1910 represents the high water mark of agricultural expansion in the region, when 197 million acres in farms were divided among 2.3 million farm operators, owners, and tenants (Table 36). Great changes were concentrated in the period from 1900 to 1940. With the decline in total farm land, it is worth remarking that the average amount of improved land per farm (cropland plus plowable pasture) remained fairly stable around 40 acres. In this period the amount of unimproved land declined by 22 million acres, improved land increased by 10 million acres, and the number of farms increased by some 248,000. The average size of farm, for whatever the figures are worth, decreased from 97.6 acres in 1900 to 71.4 acres in 1930 and then rose to 81.3 in 1940 (Table 37). In 1900 improved land suitable for crops and plowed pasture averaged about 44 acres per operator; this figure was 43.5 in 1940. With large decreases in the size of farms the average amount of improved land per farm has remained fairly constant. Together with the development of commercial fertilizer for staple crops, this one fact helps to explain how the region has managed to retain so many of its people on the land.

Size of farm may be accepted as a most important measure of population pressure on land, often operating as a limiting factor to adequate land utili-

TABLE 37. AVERAGE ACREAGE PER FARM AND AVERAGE VALUE PER FARM AND PER ACRE, UNITED STATES AND SOUTHEAST, 1850-1940

Area and census year	Average total acreage (Acres)	Average improved acreage Acres	Percent of total	Value of land and buildings Per farm Dollars	Per acre of land Dollars	Area and census year	Average total acreage (Acres)	Average improved acreage Acres	Percent of total	Value of land and buildings Per farm Dollars	Per acre of land Dollars
UNITED STATES						**SOUTHEAST**					
1850	202.6	78.0	38.5	$2,258	$11	1850	324.3	101.2	31.2	$1,963	$6
1860	199.2	79.8	40.1	3,251	16	1860	325.4	103.6	31.8	3,440	11
1870	153.3	71.0	46.3	2,799	18	1870	209.6	69.6	33.2	1,311	6
1880	133.7	71.0	53.1	2,544	19	1880	146.4	52.6	35.9	1,096	7
1890	136.5	78.3	57.4	2,909	21	1890	126.9	52.8	41.6	1,215	10
1900	146.2	72.2	49.4	2,896	20	1900	97.6	43.8	44.9	1,008	10
1910	138.1	75.2	54.4	5,471	40	1910	84.5	41.2	48.8	1,802	21
1920	148.2	78.0	52.6	10,284	69	1920	77.6	40.4	52.1	3,791	49
1925	145.1	79.3	54.6	7,764	54	1925	73.0	37.9	51.9	2,882	39
1930	156.9	83.1	53.0	7,614	49	1930	71.4	38.0	53.2	2,818	39
1935	154.8	75.4	48.7	4,823	31	1935	74.0	36.9	49.9	1,899	26
1940	174.0	87.0	50.0	5,518	32	1940	81.3	43.5	53.4	2,519	31

Source: See Table 36.

zation. That a distinction must be made in this connection between crop-land and range land is shown by the fact that in a State like Wyoming the average farm unit has over 1400 acres in pasture.

Figure 112 compares the regional trends in farms of various sizes from 1900 to 1940. The Southeast and Far West and Northeast over a 40 year period have attained the largest proportion of small farms while the North-west has gained an increasing proportion of farms over 500 acres. The movement has been toward larger farms in regions of large farms: the Northwest, Middle States and Southwest; and toward smaller farms in the Far West and Southeast (Figure 112). From 1930 to 1940 all regions showed increases in the proportion of farms under 100 acres except the southern regions where the average size of farm increased.

Many farm management people feel that farms are too small in the Southeast to be efficient business units, making the best use of their labor, land, and necessary overhead investment. Not only have southern farmers been forced to crop small acreages too intensively, but the recent emphasis on their lack of livestock and forest products would suggest that they need additional acreage for the extensive utilization implied in the building up of permanent pastures and wood lots.

Such criticisms of prevailing practices are not to be silenced by refer-ence to the family-sized farm. It is precisely the family-sized farm that should be large enough to give scope to the labor of growing sons and to allow for normal overlapping of the generations in handing down the patri-mony. Usually the farmer's son will want to marry and settle down be-fore the farmer is willing or able to retire. Unless the farm enterprise is large enough to absorb his labor, he will seek to become established in another occupation and will not return to the farm when it becomes vacant. For continuity of the generations, the size of the family farm should thus be much larger than is generally assumed.

In many areas of the Nation farms are large enough to satisfy these conditions. The average farm operator in 1940 had 174 acres at his dis-posal with 87 acres for crops and pasture. The Southeast and Northeast have the smallest farms, the Northwest the largest, the Middle States the medium-sized farms (Figure 112). By States, the average size of farm ranged in 1940 from 60 and 65 acres in Massachusetts and Mississippi, respectively, to 1,866 acres in Wyoming (Figure 113). Florida's average size of 134 acres per farm was the largest in the Southeast. Over half, 53.7 percent, of the farms in the region were under 50 acres, and over three-fourths, 76.7 percent, were under 100 acres. In contrast with the Far West which has 60 and 73 percent of its farms in the same size groups, the Northwest has 77 percent of its farms over 100 acres and 21 percent over 500 acres. Figure 112 shows other regional contrasts.

FIGURE 112. THE PERCENTAGE DISTRIBUTION OF FARMS BY SIZE,
THE SIX MAJOR REGIONS, 1900-1940

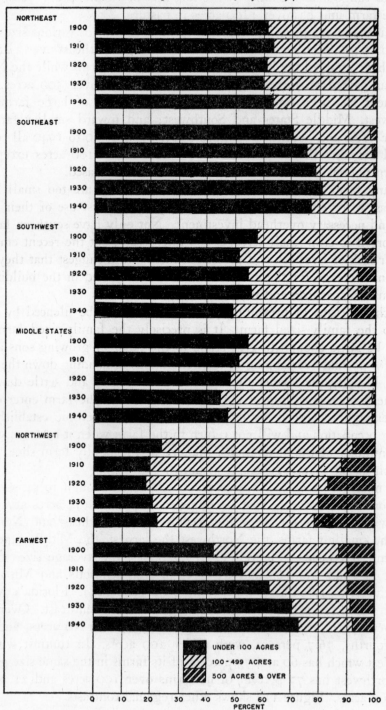

Source: Howard W. Odum, *Southern Regions of the United States*, p. 378 and our Figure 113.

FIGURE 113. AVERAGE SIZE OF FARM, UNITED STATES, 1940

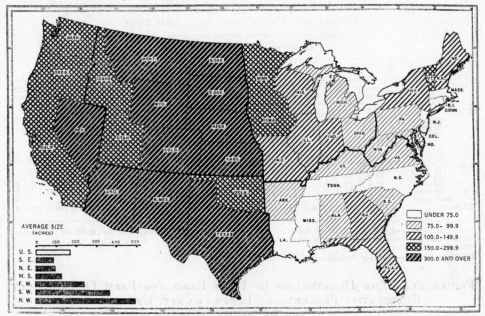

AVERAGE SIZE
(ACRES)

0   100   200   300   400   500

U. S.
S. E.
N. E.
M. S.
F. W.
S. W.
N. W.

UNDER 75.0
75.0- 99.9
100.0-149.9
150.0-299.9
300.0 AND OVER

Source: *Sixteenth Census of the United States, 1940*, Agriculture, First Series, United States Summary,. Tables 5 and 7.

In spite of the preponderance of small farms, the figures would seem to indicate a more equitable division of farm land among farm operators in the Southeast than in the Nation. Table 38 relates the number of farm operators by the size of their farms in 1935 to the amount of land in farms and available for crops. Thus, while 39.5 percent of all farm operators in the Nation held farms of less than 50 acres, they controlled only 5.6 of the Nation's farm land and 8.4 percent of the cropland. Comparably, in the Southeast, 56.8 percent of all operators had tracts of less than 50 acres and controlled 17.3 percent of the land in farms and 26.3 percent of all cropland. On the Lorenz curves, Figure 114, we can read by interpolation the following comparisons: In the Nation the 50 percent of the farmers with the smaller farms operated 10 percent of the farm lands; in the Southeast they operated 13 percent of the land. Directing our attention to the large farms, we find that 50 percent of the farm land in the Nation was in blocks of 250 acres and more and was operated by about 7 percent of the farmers. In the Southeast, 50 percent of the land was in tracts of over 140 acres, and was tilled by 12½ percent of the operators. By comparing the Nation and the Southeast at their greatest point of divergence, we find that 10 percent of the farmers in the United States operated 55 percent of the farm land while the same proportion of farmers in the Southeast oper-

TABLE 38. CUMULATIVE PERCENTAGES OF FARM OPERATORS, ALL LAND IN FARMS, AND LAND AVAILABLE FOR CROPS,* BY SIZE OF FARM, UNITED STATES AND SOUTHEAST, 1930 AND 1935

| Size of farm | UNITED STATES | | | | | | SOUTHEAST | | | | | |
| | 1930 | | | 1935 | | | 1930 | | | 1935 | | |
	Oper-ators	All land	Crop land	Oper-ators	All land	Crop land	Oper-ators	All land	Crop land	Oper-ators	All land	Crop land
Under 3 acres.....	0.7	**	....	0.5	**	**	0.3	**	....	0.4	**	**
" 10 acres.....	5.7	0.2	....	8.4	0.3	0.4	6.0	0.5	....	9.3	0.7	1.1
" 20 acres.....	14.6	1.0	....	18.4	1.2	1.9	20.8	3.5	....	25.3	3.8	6.4
" 30 acres.....	....	....	....	26.6	2.4	3.9	....	....	....	38.7	8.0	....
" 50 acres.....	37.5	5.7	....	39.5	5.6	8.4	57.4	19.4	....	56.8	17.3	26.3
" 70 acres.....	....	....	....	48.0	8.8	12.5	....	....	....	67.7	25.7	....
" 100 acres.....	59.4	15.7	....	60.7	15.5	21.0	79.8	40.9	....	78.7	37.8	49.4
" 140 acres.....	....	....	....	71.8	23.7	31.2	....	....	....	87.5	51.4	....
" 175 acres.....	80.8	34.0	....	81.3	33.4	43.8	92.7	63.7	....	91.8	60.4	70.5
" 260 acres.....	89.1	45.2	....	89.2	44.2	57.4	96.8	75.6	....	96.1	72.6	80.8
" 500 acres.....	96.3	61.1	....	96.1	59.8	77.0	99.2	87.3	....	98.8	85.0	90.5
" 1000 acres.....	98.8	72.1	....	98.6	70.6	88.6	99.9	93.4	....	99.6	92.0	95.6
All Sizes...........	100.0	100.0	100.0	100.0	100.0	100.0	100.0	100.0	....	100.0	100.0	100.0

*Crop land harvested, crop failure, idle or fallow crop land, and plowable pasture; comparable data could not be computed for 1930 since crop failure by size of farm is not available.
**Less than 0.1 percent.
Source: *United States Census of Agriculture, 1935*, III, Chap. II, Table 6.

FIGURE 114. THE DISTRIBUTION OF FARM LAND AND FARM OPERATORS BY CUMULATIVE PERCENTAGES, LORENZ CURVE, UNITED STATES AND SOUTHEAST, 1935

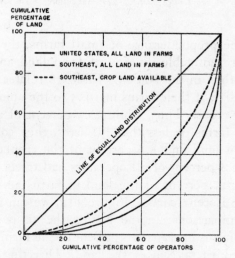

Source: See Table 38.

ated 43 percent of all the land. This condition holds for operation, not for the ownership of land.

The conclusion that, on the basis of present statistics, land is more equitably distributed in the Southeast than in the Nation is more apparent than real. It requires a much larger farm in the sub-humid West to equal net returns from farms of the humid East. The large holdings represented by stock ranches in the Great Plain and large scale farms worked by hired labor in the Far West are adequately represented in the census figures. Not so for the plantations of the Southeast. All tenant and cropper holdings are returned as operators' tracts, although many such tenants have no higher status than hired agricultural labor elsewhere.

THE TYPE OF FARM

The size of farm is so intimately related to the type of farming that it is unrealistic to discuss them separately. The analysis by type of farm, first introduced in the Census of 1930, was based on value of products sold. When the value of a commodity sold from a farm such as grain, cotton, poultry, livestock or dairy products exceeded 40 percent of all products the farm was classified under that category. A farm was classified as a general farm when it had several products, none exceeding 40 percent total value; as a self-sufficing farm when the value of products consumed by the family exceeded the value of those sold; as a part-time farm when the operator worked elsewhere for pay more than 150 days and the value of products was less than $750.

Figure 115, which compares the main type of farms in the region with those in the Nation in 1930, shows the region's predominance of cotton and tobacco (crop specialty) farms. Figure 116 shows the type of farm by counties. In relation to type of farming, the size of farm is associated with the labor requirements per acre and that is dependent in large part on the use of power machinery. Cotton and tobacco make heavy requirements on hand labor and these farms, most of which are tenant and cropper holdings, average less than 75 acres in size. In the Southeastern States, the cotton farms, the predominant type, averaged 45 to 75 acres. Only part-time farms which have from 33 to 52 acres were smaller. Both cash grain and general farms averaged well over 100 acres in the Southeast but were exceeded by dairy farms. Largest of all were the small number of ranches which in the Southeast range from an average of 250 acres in Tennessee to over 1,000 acres in Alabama, Georgia, and South Carolina.

The type of farm analysis used in the 1940 Census offers less enlightenment because of the use of the blanket classification, "field crops." In the Southeast, Figure 117, this included almost half the farms, 49.1 percent. An additional 41.2 percent were included under the classification "farm products used by farm households." While it is more than improbable that subsistence farms increased to this extent in the depression period, comparison with the national distribution, Figure 117, shows the predominance of these two types in southern agriculture along with the under representation of livestock, dairy farms, and other specialties. Analysis of the crop system in the succeeding chapter will bring out further distinctions.

FIGURE 115. THE PERCENTAGE DISTRIBUTION OF FARMS BY TYPE, UNITED STATES AND SOUTHEAST, 1929

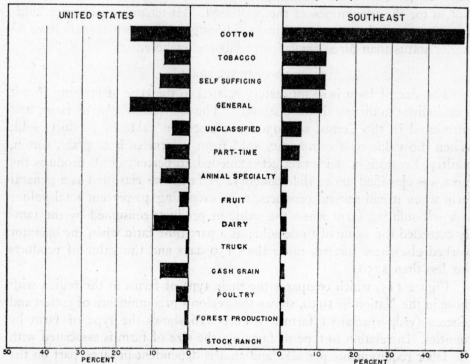

Source: *Fifteenth Census of the United States, 1930*, Agriculture, III, *Type of Farm*, United States and State Summaries.

FIGURE 116. THE MOST IMPORTANT TYPE OF FARM BY VALUE OF PRODUCTS BY COUNTIES, UNITED STATES, 1929

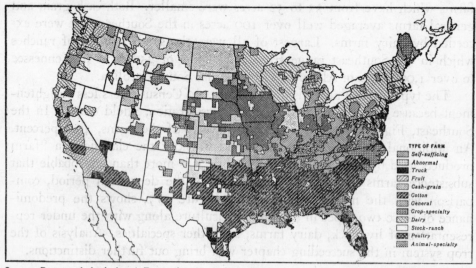

Source: Bureau of Agricultural Economics, U. S. Department of Agriculture, Negative 27204.

FIGURE 117. THE PERCENTAGE DISTRIBUTION OF FARMS CLASSIFIED BY TYPE
OF PRODUCTS SERVING AS MAJOR SOURCE OF INCOME, UNITED STATES
AND SOUTHEAST, 1939

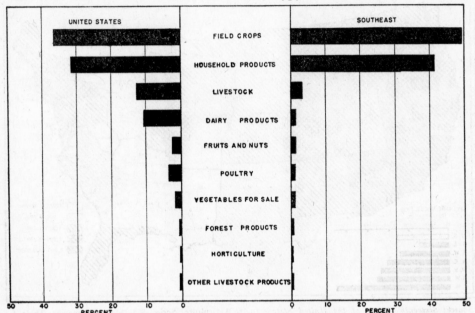

Source: *Sixteenth Census of the United States, 1940,* Agriculture, Third Series, United States and State
Summaries.

THE VALUE OF PRODUCTS PER FARM

The results of our varying size of farms, cropping systems, and available markets are to be seen in the different values of products provided by farms the country over. In his attempt to make adequate use of physical resources and to supply the demand for food and fiber, it is also the task of the farmer as manager to support the farm family. A good measure of the results attained is found in the value of products sold, traded, and consumed per farm. In 1939 this figure averaged $1,309 per farm and ranged from $747 in the Southeast, $1,220 in the Southwest, and $1,552 in the Northeast to $1,621 in the Middle States, $1,794 in the Northwest, and $2,659 in the Far West (Figure 118). Alabama had the lowest average, $522 per farm, and California the highest, $3,658. Florida with $1,517 per farm was the highest in the Southeast.

In 1939 almost two-thirds of the farms in the Nation produced less than $1,000 gross value of products. Over half of these farms were in the Southeast, and over 82 percent of all the farms in the region produced less than $1,000 worth of products. Table 39 and Figures 119 and 120 show that over two-fifths of the region's farms produced below $400 worth of products and almost two-thirds below $600.

FIGURE 118. AVERAGE VALUE OF FARM PRODUCTS SOLD, TRADED AND USED BY FARM HOUSEHOLDS, UNITED STATES, 1939

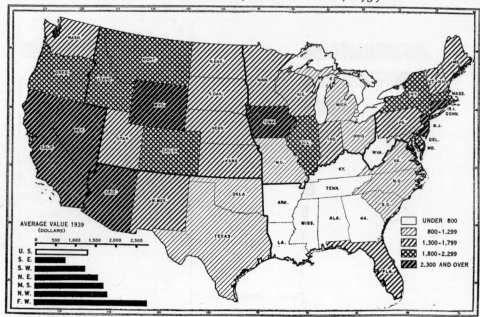

Source: *Sixteenth Census of the United States, 1940*, Agriculture, Series S-3, State Summaries, Table I.

TABLE 39. CUMULATIVE PERCENTAGE DISTRIBUTION OF FARMS BY VALUE OF PRODUCTS SOLD, TRADED OR USED BY FARM HOUSEHOLDS, UNITED STATES AND SOUTHEAST, 1929 AND 1939

Value of products	1929		1939		Value of products	1929		1939	
	United States	South-east	United States	South-east		United States	South-east	United States	South-east
Under $ 250.........	6.6	8.5	19.2	22.7	Under $ 2,500......	80.8	95.3	88.6	96.7
Under 400.........	15.3	20.9	33.0	42.4	Under 3,500......	91.2	98.2	94.9	98.6
Under 600.........	28.0	39.8	47.6	62.8	Under 6,000......	96.1	99.1	97.7	99.3
Under 1,000.........	48.0	68.8	65.3	82.8	Under 10,000......	98.5	99.6	99.2	99.7
Under 1,500.........	64.4	85.5	77.2	91.6	All values	100.0	100.0	100.0	100.0

Source: *Sixteenth Census of the United States, 1940*, Agricultural Series S-3.

Comparison of relative values for 1929 and 1939 shows the extent to which the depression has increased the number of farms in the lower income brackets (Figs. 119, 120). Thus, whereas some 40 percent of Southeastern farms had total products valued at less than $600 in 1929, over 62 percent fell below that value in 1939. The proportion of farms with gross values below $250 increased from 8.5 to 22.7 percent. Increases in subsistence farms and decreases in staple crops offer partial explanation. Comparison with the Nation shows that, while the trends were similar, the Nation did not suffer as great a decline. Analysis of the southern states (Table 40) indicates that North Carolina had the most equitable distribution of values among its farms, Kentucky and Alabama the least equitable divisions.

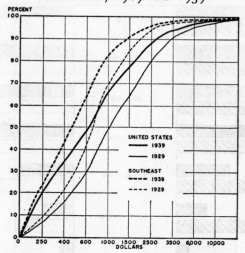

Source: See Table 39.

Comparison of the 1939 farm incomes with the comparatively prosperous year of 1929 shows how total value productivity was affected by depression. Average value of products declined from $1,835 to $1,309 per farm in the United States. Figures 118 and 121 serve to compare these periods by States. Whereas less than one-half, 48 percent, of the Nation's farms produced crops worth less than $1,000 in 1929, almost two-thirds, 65.3 percent, were so classified in 1939. In 1929, about two-thirds of the Southeastern farms were in this low group; in 1939 there were 83 percent. These serious losses represented both the effects of the fall in price levels and the reduction of staple crops set up under the quota systems. Small farms suffered greatly because their crop acreages devoted to staples were already near the margin. These figures, however, do not include crop benefits, ranging from $20 to $126 per farm from 1933 to 1940.

Several considerations serve to shed light on these figures. It will be realized that these gross values do not represent what the farmer has left after paying his bills. Out of these figures all operators must meet their costs of production and in addition all tenants must pay their rents either in cash or in a share of the product. The amount of additional income received by farmers from non-agricultural sources such as gifts, pensions, investments, etc., while variously estimated, is not large. The extent of part-time farming is better known. We know from the 1930 Census that there were 339,207 farms producing less than $750 whose operators supplemented their income by working 150 days or more off the farm. This

FIGURE 120. THE PERCENTAGE DISTRIBUTION OF FARMS BY VALUE OF ALL
PRODUCTS SOLD, TRADED AND USED, UNITED STATES, 1939,
SOUTHEAST, 1929 AND 1939

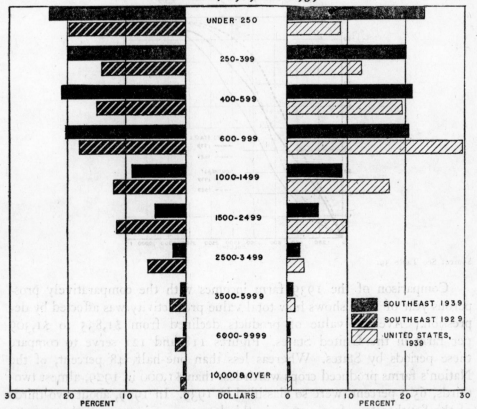

Source: See Tables 39 and 40.

group represented 5.7 percent of all farms or 20 percent of all the farms
producing less than $600 worth of products. In the 1940 enumeration,
when no upper limit was placed on the value of products, over 760,000
farms were returned as part-time. In the South, 27 percent of operators
worked off farms, spending an average of 50 days' work on other farms
and 165 days in nonfarm work. This fell below the proportions in New
England and the Far West. In the Southeast such part-time farms were
most numerous in coal areas of the Southern Appalachians and around
cities. They undoubtedly serve to raise the income level of the lower
bracket of farmers. In addition, some of these part-time operators no doubt
are full-time industrial workers who may enjoy higher standards because
of farm residence.

In the Southeast, as elsewhere, the value of products per farm varied
according to the type of farming practiced. The mode is set by the predominant types of cotton and tobacco farms, but in 1929 values were even

TABLE 40. PERCENTAGE DISTRIBUTION OF FARMS BY VALUE OF PRODUCTS SOLD, TRADED OR USED BY FARM HOUSEHOLDS, UNITED STATES AND SOUTHEAST, 1939

Value of products	United States	Southeast	Virginia	North Carolina	South Carolina	Georgia	Florida	Kentucky	Tennessee	Alabama	Mississippi	Arkansas	Louisiana
All values.............	100.0	100.0	100.0	100.0	100.0	100.0	100.0	100.0	100.0	100.0	100.0	100.0	100.0
Under $ 250.........	19.2	22.7	25.0	14.2	17.5	15.1	30.0	31.7	25.8	30.6	24.2	18.5	19.6
$ 250 - 399.........	13.8	19.7	17.9	12.9	15.8	19.1	16.6	19.0	20.5	23.8	24.6	20.8	22.5
400 - 599.........	14.6	20.4	17.4	15.9	20.9	23.4	14.6	16.0	20.2	21.5	24.0	22.9	25.1
600 - 999.........	17.7	20.0	18.2	23.6	24.6	24.2	14.8	15.6	19.2	16.2	19.0	22.3	19.8
1,000 - 1,499.........	11.9	8.8	9.5	16.6	11.5	10.0	8.2	8.0	7.7	4.7	5.2	8.3	6.2
1,500 - 2,499.........	11.4	5.1	6.5	11.8	6.1	5.0	6.6	5.6	4.1	1.9	1.8	4.0	3.2
2,500 - 3,999.........	6.3	1.9	2.7	3.6	2.0	1.7	3.5	2.4	1.5	0.6	0.6	1.6	1.6
4,000 - 5,999.........	2.8	0.7	1.2	0.9	0.8	0.7	2.0	0.9	0.6	0.3	0.3	0.7	0.9
6,000 - 9,999.........	1.5	0.4	0.8	0.3	0.3	0.4	1.6	0.5	0.3	0.2	0.2	0.5	0.7
10,000 and over.........	1.0	0.3	0.6	0.2	0.3	0.3	2.2	0.2	0.2	0.2	0.2	0.4	0.5

*Excludes unclassified farms as well as farms with no farm products sold, traded, or used by farm households.
Source: *Sixteenth Census of the United States, 1940*, Agricultural Series S-3, State Summaries.

FIGURE 121. AVERAGE VALUE OF FARM PRODUCTS SOLD, TRADED AND USED BY FARM HOUSEHOLDS, UNITED STATES, 1929

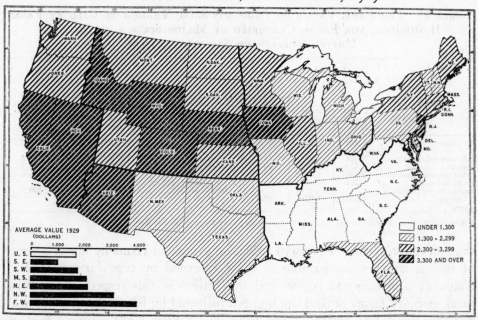

Source: See Table 40.

lower in part-time and subsistence farms. Highest gross returns were made by the few stock ranches in the region, and by the more numerous dairy farms. Figure 122, which points out these distinctions for 1929, shows that average production values on general farms and truck farms were no higher

FIGURE 122. THE AVERAGE VALUE OF ALL FARM PRODUCTS PER FARM
BY TYPE OF FARM, 1929

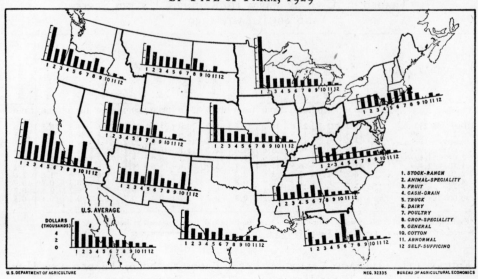

TABLE 41. PER FARM VALUE OF PRODUCTS SOLD, TRADED OR USED BY FARM
HOUSEHOLD, FOR FARMS CLASSIFIED BY MAJOR SOURCE OF INCOME,
UNITED STATES AND SOUTHEAST, 1939

Major source of income	Per farm value of products			Major source of income	Per farm value of products		
	United States *Dollars*	South-east *Dollars*	Ratio Southeast to United States *Percent*		United States *Dollars*	South-east *Dollars*	Ratio Southeast to United States *Percent*
All sources reported......	1,309	747	57.1	Dairy products.........	1,962	2,786	142.0
				Poultry and poultry			
Horticultural specialties..	6,924	5,064	73.1	products...........	1,650	1,407	85.3
Livestock..............	2,529	1,679	66.4	Field crops...........	1,379	871	63.2
Other livestock products .	2,488	1,425	57.3	Forest products........	1,113	1,296	116.4
Fruits and nuts.........	2,251	1,912	84.9	Farm products used by			
Vegetables harvested				farm household......	360	363	100.8
for sale..............	2,241	1,981	88.4				

Source: *Sixteenth Census of the United States, 1940*, Agriculture, Third Series, U. S. Summary.

than on cotton farms. The 1939 values on groups of farms by major source
of income are not comparable to those returned by type farm in 1929.
Table 41 compares the region and the Nation in this respect. Horticul-
tural specialty farms ranked the highest, followed by livestock, truck farms,
and orchards. The region's dairy farms and timber lands return a higher
income than the national average. In all other categories excepting subsistence farms values are much less than for the Nation.

Our next step, accordingly, will be to examine the supporting capacity
of the prevailing cropping system and to show how the crop control program affected land use in the Southeast.

CHAPTER 13

THE SUPPORTING CAPACITY OF THE CROP SYSTEM

THE PERIOD from 1930 to 1940 marks the most drastic changes the Southeast has undergone in its major crop systems since the abolition of slavery and the breaking up of the plantation. In view of the low returns from cotton and tobacco, the suggestion has often been made that the region make a transfer to livestock, general farming, and specialty crops. The depression offered a test of this advice in the initiation of control of staple crops and the diversion of land to forage and cover crops.

A review of the evidence indicates that cotton, even at the low prices prevailing from 1930-1939, had comparative advantage over any commercial crop or combination of crops that can be substituted for it. The Bureau of Agricultural Economics over a ten-year period has estimated the average gross returns to labor on the five principal crops in the Cotton Belt. From 1923 to 1932 the average return to labor from cotton was $13.45 per acre as compared with $2.00 from corn, $0.70 from wheat, $0.65 from oats, and $69.54 from tobacco. The high gross returns from tobacco as compared with those from cotton are largely offset by the large amount of labor required—approximately 400 man hours per acre as compared with 85 in cotton. While the returns per hour of man labor were estimated at about 16 cents in cotton and 17 cents in tobacco, they were only 3 to 5 cents in corn, wheat, and oats.[1]

Grain prices, it should be realized, are relatively higher in deficit areas such as the South than in the main grain producing areas. Accordingly, increases in grain production in the South will lower prices nearer to the level found in other regions and thus may serve to increase the relative advantage of cotton as a commercial crop.

Under prevailing conditions this disadvantage also extends to livestock production. In eight cotton States of the Southeast over the ten-year period, it required from 2 to 9 times as many acres in cropland and improved

[1] United States Department of Agriculture, Bureau of Agricultural Economics, *The World Cotton Situation: Part II, Cotton Production in the United States* (Washington, D. C.: 1936), p. 58.

pastures to produce $100 worth of dairy, beef cattle, and hog products as were required to produce $100 worth of cotton. The acreage requirements for poultry were 50 percent greater than those for cotton. The low returns from livestock can be attributed largely to low feed yields and to the low carrying capacity of pastures in many Cotton Belt areas. Correction of these shortcomings will be required to develop an adequate livestock industry. At present an average of 125 acres in crops and improved pasture is required to produce a gross income from beef cattle equal to that obtained from 15 acres in cotton—the average cotton acreage per family in many areas of the region.[2] In some areas such as the Black Prairies of Alabama feed yields are now high enough to allow stock raising to supplant cotton.

In the main, however, livestock production in the Cotton Belt is incidental to the production of cash crops. It is thus that farm by-products and feeds with no other outlet are utilized in producing livestock. In turn this enterprise has contributed toward higher returns, a better adjusted cropping system, and increased yields. Further expansion in this direction is feasible, but at present price levels only few areas in the Cotton Belt can be found where the commercial production of livestock can compete with cotton for the use of farm land, labor, and capital.[3]

In terms of employment the production of cotton in the region has provided for almost 3 times as much employment as the principal grains combined, 3½ times as much as corn, 9 times as much as tobacco, and 20 times as much as wheat.

GROSS FARM INCOME BY SOURCES

It has been pointed out that gross agricultural income per farm is lowest in the Southeast (Figure 123). In 1940 it was $919 per farm as compared with $1,698 for the United States and $3,508 for the Far West. Table 42 shows that more than in any other region, Southeastern and Far Western farmers placed their reliance on crop production to the exclusion of livestock. In 1940 crops furnished 55.6 percent of the average gross income per farm in the Southeast. Amounting to only $511 per farm, this was the second highest proportion in the Nation and can be compared with 38.3 percent income from crops for the Nation and 26.8 percent for the Middle States. In contrast, the Middle States received incomes of $567 per farm from crops and $1,418 from livestock. The region had crop values of more than $1,155,000,000, or 29.1 percent of the Nation's total gross income from crops; and was approached by the Middle States with some 23.9 percent. Conversely, Table 43 shows that the Southeast accounted for only 12.8 percent of the Nation's gross value from livestock

[2] *Ibid.,* pp. 64-65.
[3] *Ibid.,* p. 65.

FIGURE 123. GROSS INCOME PER FARM FROM CROPS, LIVESTOCK, LIVESTOCK
PRODUCTS AND BENEFIT PAYMENTS, UNITED STATES, 1940

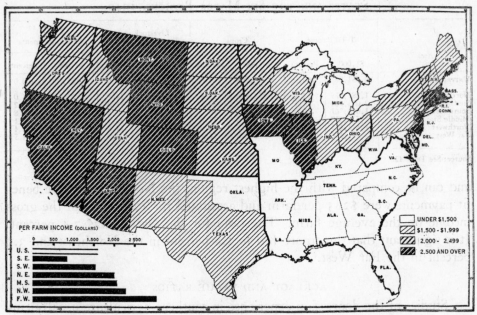

Source: Bureau of Agricultural Economics: *Gross Farm Income and Government Payments*, Table 5
(May 26, 1941).

TABLE 42. AMOUNT AND PERCENTAGE DISTRIBUTION OF GROSS INCOME PER
FARM, FROM FARM PRODUCTION BY ORIGIN OF INCOME, UNITED STATES
AND THE SIX MAJOR REGIONS, 1940

Origin of income	United States		Northeast		Southeast		Southwest		Middle States		Northwest		Far West	
	Dollars	Percent	Dollars	Percent	Dollars	Percent	Dollars	Percent	Dollars	Percent	Dollars	Percent	Dollars	Percent
TOTAL............	1,698	100.0	2,032	100.0	919	100.0	1,597	100.0	2,114	100.0	2,384	100.0	3,508	100.0
Crops.............	650	38.3	712	35.0	511	55.6	651	40.8	567	26.8	711	29.8	2,004	59.1
Livestock and live- stock products...	922	54.3	1,283	63.2	319	34.7	760	47.6	1,418	67.1	1,388	58.2	1,382	39.4
Benefit payments...	126	7.4	37	1.8	89	9.7	186	11.6	129	6.1	285	12.0	122	3.5

Source: *Sixteenth Census of the United States, 1940*, Agriculture, First Series, United States Summary, Table V; United States
Department of Agriculture, Bureau of Agricultural Economics, *Gross Farm Income and Government Payments*, (May 26,
1941), Table 5.

products, and its average farm received $319, or only 34.7 percent of its
income from this source. In contrast over 54 percent of the Nation's agricultural income came from livestock and its products. Besides the Southeast, only the Far West fell as low as 39.4 percent in this respect.

Benefit payments accounted for the remainder of the farmer's income.
For the Southeast they amounted to $89 per farm or 9.7 percent of all
income (Table 42). This is below the national average of $126 per farm

TABLE 43. GROSS INCOME FROM FARM PRODUCTION BY ORIGIN OF INCOME AND PERCENTAGE DISTRIBUTION OF EACH SOURCE OF INCOME, UNITED STATES AND THE SIX MAJOR REGIONS, 1940

Area	Total income		Crops		Livestock and livestock products		Benefit payments	
	$1,000	Percent	$1,000	Percent	$1,000	Percent	$1,000	Percent
UNITED STATES........	10,351,987	100.0	3,966,008	100.0	5,620,180	100.0	765,799	100.0
Northeast.............	1,287,925	12.4	451,126	11.4	813,472	14.5	23,327	3.0
Southeast.............	2,075,204	20.1	1,155,188	29.1	719,457	12.8	200,559	26.2
Southwest.............	1,038,367	10.0	423,241	10.7	494,361	8.8	120,765	15.8
Middle States..........	3,535,610	34.2	948,486	23.9	2,371,822	42.2	215,302	28.1
Northwest.............	1,433,445	13.8	427,277	10.8	834,530	14.8	171,638	22.4
Far West.............	981,436	9.5	560,690	14.1	386,538	6.9	34,208	4.5

Source: See Table 42.

and can be compared with the highest region, the Northwest, where benefit payments were $285 per farm and accounted for 12 percent of the gross income on the average farm. The ratio for the Nation was 7.4 percent. It is significant that this figure fell to 1.8 percent in the Northeast and 3.5 percent in the Far West.

ACREAGE AND VALUE RATIOS

Studies of the depression experience in southern agriculture usually emphasize it as an experiment in acreage and price control. To show its relation to basic conditions of farm population and support it can be viewed as a change from an intensive to a more extensive use of the land. In terms of various cropping systems, the region's capacity to hold population on the land may be suggested by comparing the proportion of gross values to proportion of total acreage harvested.

The Agricultural Census of 1935 (Table 44, Figure 124) served to show the new relation between the acreage and the gross value of crops produced in the Southeast.[4] In 1934 under the Bankhead Act cotton acreage reached its lowest point of importance. With 21.8 percent of the region's acreage it accounted for 32 percent of total gross crop value. Next came corn. Occupying the largest share of cropland, 44.3 percent, it accounted for only 20.6 percent of the region's crop values. Cotton and corn thus represent the high and low value crops in southern agriculture. Tobacco, fruits, vegetables, and sugarcane furnish crops of high gross value in relation to acreage while grains, hay, legumes, and sorghum occupy an acreage in excess of their proportionate value in the region.

Highest in value per acre was tobacco, a crop which occupied only 1.8 percent of the acreage but accounted for 13 percent of crop values. The important vegetable crop is difficult of analysis. All vegetables grown for

[4] However unorthodox this procedure may have been considered under a regime of fluctuating prices, it may be an allowable device in a regime of stabilized prices.

TABLE 44. ACREAGE HARVESTED AND VALUE OF CROPS, SOUTHEAST, 1929 AND 1934

Crops	Acreage harvested				Value of crops			
	1929		1934		1929		1934	
	1,000 acres	Percent of total	1,000 acres	Percent of total	1,000 dollars	Percent of total	1,000 dollars	Percent of total
ALL CROPS...............	59,888		61,821		2,072,954		....	
Miscellaneous crops*.....	342		704		46,187		....	
TOTAL COMPARABLE CROPS..	59,546	100.0	61,117	100.0	2,026,767	100.0	1,524,568	100.0
All corn................	22,260	37.4	27,084	44.3	358,829	17.7	313,022	20.6
Cotton..................	21,260	35.7	13,346	21.8	887,046	43.8	487,568	32.0
Hay and sorghums.......	4,600	7.7	5,824	9.5	78,203	3.9	72,907	4.8
All cereals (except corn) ..	3,858	6.5	4,746	7.8	32,491	1.6	50,787	3.3
Annual legumes**........	2,483	4.2	4,731	7.8	61,830	3.1	92,721	6.1
Vegetables †(incl. potatoes)	1,543	2.6	2,210	3.6	262,332	13.0	202,694	13.3
Fruit and strawberries......	1,580	2.6	1,654	2.7	105,403	5.2	87,477	5.7
Tobacco.................	1,667	2.8	1,119	1.8	218,200	10.6	198,633	13.0
Sugar cane..............	295	0.5	403	0.7	22,433	1.1	18,759	1.2

*Miscellaneous crops include minor crops such as sorghum grown for sirup, broomcorn, other berries, etc., the value of which is not given for 1934; for this reason, and also because these minor crops are not strictly comparable for both years, they were excluded from totals to make values and acreages comparable for 1929 and 1934.
**Acreage of annual legumes grown alone (acreage grown with companion crops excluded to avoid duplication when computing totals); value comprises all annual legumes—grown alone and with other crops, both harvested for grain and for hay.
†Acreage of vegetables for both years includes vegetables grown for sale only, while value includes all vegetables for sale and home use, the latter value being 70,799 in 1934 and 98, 465 thousand dollars in 1929.
Source: U. S. Census of Agriculture, 1935, III, Chap. VI: Agricultural Statistics; 1937, Table 124, p. 104, and 1938, Table 333, p. 242. *Abstract of the Fifteenth Census of the United States, 1930*, Agriculture, Tables 85-144.

sale occupied 3.6 of the acreage and accounted for 9.2 percent of values. In addition, the value of vegetables grown for home use amounted to almost $70,800,000, bringing vegetables to 13.3 percent of total values. Since no acreage was returned for vegetables grown for home use, the ratio cannot be computed. Legumes came near an even balance, for with 7.8 percent of crop acreage they accounted for 6.1 percent of gross values. Here again the figures furnish difficulty, for acreage is returned for annual legumes grown alone, while values include legumes grown with companion crops. All other hay and sorghums occupied 9.5 percent of the acreage and returned 4.8 percent of the gross value, in contrast with fruits and strawberries whose share of 2.7 percent acreage returned 5.7 percent of values.

In relating these figures to the amount of livestock on southern farms, we have followed the device of reducing all types to comparable units in terms of the amount of feed consumed. In 1935 it can be computed that there were something over 83.5 million livestock units on United States farms. Of these 34 percent were in the Middle States and 19.8 percent in the Northwest (Table 45). The Southeast had the next highest proportion, 17.4 percent. When the figures are reduced to units per farm the region falls in the lowest rank with only 5.7 livestock units per farm as compared with 12.3 for the Nation, 24.2 for the Northwest, 16 for the Far West, and 15.9 for the Middle States. Table 46 shows the division of livestock among the regions and indicates how they are reduced to com-

FIGURE 124. ACREAGE AND VALUE OF INDIVIDUAL CROPS AS PERCENTAGE OF ACREAGE AND VALUE OF ALL CROPS, SOUTHEAST, 1929 AND 1934

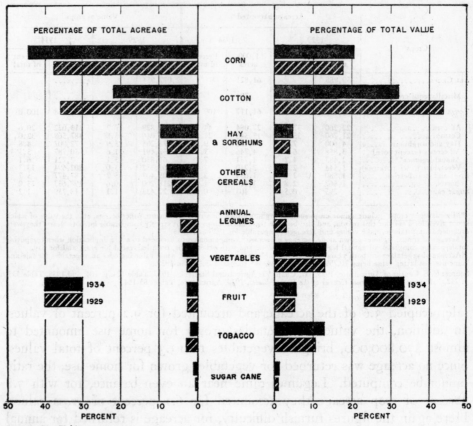

Source: See Table 44.

TABLE 45. SUMMARY OF LIVESTOCK UNITS ON FARMS, UNITED STATES AND THE SIX MAJOR REGIONS, 1935

Area	All livestock units	Percent distribution	Livestock units per farm	Area	All livestock units	Percent distribution	Livestock units per farm
UNITED STATES...	83,550,499	100.0	12.3	Southwest.......	12,075,639	14.4	15.6
				Middle States....	28,434,415	34.0	15.9
Northeast........	7,062,678	8.6	9.9	Northwest.......	16,565,084	19.8	24.2
Southeast........	14,561,499	17.4	5.7	Far West........	4,849,800	5.8	16.0

Note: For method see footnote to Table 46.
Source: *United States Census of Agriculture, 1935*, III, Chap. I, Table 3; Chap. V, Tables 5,8, 9, 10, 13, 16, 21, 23, 24.

parable units. The table shows that much of the Southeast's strength must be attributed to its 3,680,000 horses and mules rather than to dairy and beef cattle. The area is notably lacking in sheep, and should produce more swine and poultry than at present.

TABLE 46. LIVESTOCK ON FARMS, UNITED STATES AND THE
SIX MAJOR REGIONS, 1935

Livestock Number and units	United States	Northeast	Southeast	Southwest	Middle States	Northwest	Far West	D. C.
Horses and Mules....	16,676,010	1,126,671	3,683,904	2,497,983	5,266,213	3,466,732	634,348	159
Livestock units (x 1)...	16,676,010	1,126,671	3,683,904	2,497,983	5,266,213	3,466,732	634,348	159
Dairy Cows (number) .	24,581,669	3,503,151	4,099,686	2,092,731	10,195,517	3,512,946	1,177,173	465
Livestock units (x 1.1)..	27,039,836	3,853,466	4,509,655	2,302,004	11,215,069	3,864,241	1,294,890	511
Calves (number)......	16,116,819	825,903	2,532,016	2,966,718	4,725,251	4,213,682	853,077	172
Livestock units (x 0.25).	4,029,205	206,476	633,004	741,680	1,181,313	1,053,420	213,269	43
OtherCattle*(number)	27,585,921	1,381,824	4,360,808	6,636,757	6,178,952	6,914,813	2,112,551	216
Livestock units (x 0.52).	14,344,679	718,548	2,267,620	3,451,114	3,213,055	3,595,703	1,098,527	112
Hogs (number)........	37,212,967	1,461,297	9,236,268	2,245,975	19,011,655	4,423,049	832,912	1,811
Livestock units (x 0.23).	8,558,982	336,098	2,124,342	516,574	4,372,681	1,017,301	191,570	416
Sheep (number).......	48,357,506	1,675,208	2,498,101	10,067,081	9,729,769	17,871,199	6,516,132	16
Livestock units (x 0.17).	8,220,776	284,785	424,677	1,711,404	1,654,061	3,038,104	1,107,742	3
Goats (number).......	4,093,441	34,601	650,853	2,833,296	263,003	103,544	208,143	1
Livestock units (x 0.17).	695,885	5,882	110,645	481,660	44,711	17,602	35,385	—
Turkeys (number).....	5,381,912	413,236	847,232	1,112,799	1,072,235	1,097,427	838,978	5
Livestock units (x 0.05).	269,096	20,662	42,362	55,640	53,612	54,871	41,949	—
Chickens (Thousands).	371,603	51,009	76,529	31,758	143,370	45,711	23,212	14
Livestock units (x 0.01).	3,716,030	510,090	765,290	317,580	1,433,700	457,110	232,120	140
Total Units....	83,550,499	7,062,678	14,561,499	12,075,639	28,434,415	16,565,084	4,849,800	1,384

*Heifers 1 year old and under 2, steers and bulls 1 year old and over, and beef cows.
Note: Animals converted to livestock units on the basis of their feed requirements as follows: One horse or mule—1 unit; one dairy cow—1.1 units; one calf under 1 year—0.25 units; other cattle—0.52 units; one hog—0.23 units; one sheep or goat—0.17 units; one turkey—0.05 units; one chicken—0.01 units (method adapted from O. E. Baker, *Graphic Summary of Farm Animals and Animal Products*, U. S. Dept. of Agriculture, Miscellaneous Publication, No. 269, 1939, p. 4).
Source: *United States Census of Agriculture, 1935*, III, Chap. V, Tables 5, 8, 9, 10, 13, 16, 21, 23, 24.

From 1929 to 1934 Table 44 shows the region saw decreases in the acreage of all crops where gross values were in excess of proportionate acreage requirements except vegetables and fruits. Cotton's share of total acreage decreased from 36 to 22 percent, its contribution to total value from 44 to 32 percent. Tobacco's share declined from 2.8 to 1.8 percent of total acreage but price changes were such that tobacco increased its proportion of total value from 10.6 to 13 percent. In the higher value crops, vegetables (including potatoes) increased their share of the total acreage from 2.6 to 3.6 percent but maintained 13.3 percent of gross values, while fruits including strawberries, increased from 2.6 to 2.7 percent of acreage. Sugarcane also increased from 0.5 to 0.7 percent. Among the crops of lower values, corn increased its acreage from 37.4 to 44.3 percent of the total, and its value from 17.7 to 20.6 percent. Hay and sorghum acreage increased from 7.7 to 9.5 percent, all cereals except corn from 6.5 to 7.8 percent, and annual legumes from 4.2 to 7.8 percent. Proportionate value increases from these crops did not compensate for the loss of cotton values. During this period cultivated acreage increased slightly from 59.5 million to over 61 million, but gross crop values declined from 2 billion to 1.5 billion dollars. This represents the changes from high to low value crops as well as the decline in the price level. The trend to legumes and feed cover

TABLE 47. CHANGE IN ACREAGE OF ALL CROPS HARVESTED FOR
FEED, HUMAN FOOD, AND OTHER HUMAN NEEDS, SOUTHEAST,
1929-1934, 1934-1939, 1929-1939

Crops	(Estimated) Acreage in crops			Percentage change in acreage		
	1929 1,000 Acres	1934 1,000 Acres	1939 1,000 Acres	1929-1934	1934-1939	1929-1939
ALL CROPS...........................	59,546	61,117	61,015	2.6	− 0.2	2.5
Feed Crops..........................	*31,037*	*39,568*	*41,064*	*27.5*	*3.8*	*32.3*
Corn, all purposes...................	22,260	27,084	25,880	21.7	− 4.4	16.3
Oats, barley, rye, mixed grains.......	1,694	1,929	2,346	13.9	21.6	38.5
Sorghums, all except for syrup........	203	518	291	155.2	−43.8	43.3
Hay (excl. annual legumes and sorghums).......	4,397	5,306	6,700	20.7	26.3	52.7
Legumes...........................	2,483	4,731	5,847	92.6	23.6	135.5
Food Crops..........................	*5,582*	*7,084*	*6,212*	*26.9*	*−12.3*	*11.3*
Wheat.............................	1,612	2,317	1,933	43.7	−16.6	19.9
Rice...............................	552	500	560	− 9.4	12.0	1.4
Potatoes, Irish and sweet............	900	1,289	1,020	43.2	−20.9	13.3
Vegetables harvested for sale.........	643	921	744	43.2	−19.2	15.7
Fruits, berries, nuts.................	1,580	1,654	1,586	4.7	− 4.1	0.4
Sugar cane.........................	295	403	369	36.6	− 8.3	25.1
Other Crops.........................	*22,927*	*14,465*	*13,739*	*−36.9*	*− 5.0*	*−40.1*
Cotton.............................	21,260	13,346	12,050	−37.2	− 9.7	−43.3
Tobacco............................	1,667	1,119	1,689	−32.9	50.9	1.3

Note: In addition to the total for all crops given here there was an acreage (amounting to about 1 percent of the total) planted in miscellaneous minor crops which is not comparable for the two years and therefore had to be omitted. Acreage of crops harvested is generally somewhat larger than "crop land harvested" since two or more crops may be harvested from the same land in a given year.

Source: *Fifteenth Census of the United States, 1930*, Agriculture, Vol. IV, Chapter 11; *United States Census of Agriculture, 1935*, Vol. III, Chapter VI; *Sixteenth Census of the United States, 1940*, Agriculture, First and Second Series, State Summaries.

crops went over into increased values of livestock products—a figure not yet represented in our crop analysis.

The new balance between food, feed, and staple cash crops has been largely brought about by the program of the A.A.A. Table 47 represents an attempt to compare the changes in (1) staple, (2) food and (3) feed crops in the Southeast from 1929-1934. It shows that although the absolute increase in feed crops was greater, the relative increases for food and feed crops were practically equal. Acreage in all crops increased one and a half million from 1929 to 1934. A retraction of almost 8.5 million acres in the staple cash crops of tobacco and cotton was offset by an increase of over 8.5 million acres in feed crops including corn for all purposes. In addition there was an increase of 1.5 million acres in food crops, mainly in land devoted to wheat, potatoes, and vegetables. Among foods, only rice showed a decline. The greatest total increases were found in corn (4.8 million acres) and legumes (2.2 million acres). Percentage increases were greatest in sorghum, 155; annual legumes, 93; wheat, 44; potatoes and vegetables, 43; sugarcane, 37; and corn, 22 percent. The acreage released by cotton and tobacco was about equal to that gained by feed crops.

Table 48 shows how the extent to which the region's decline in acreage devoted to staple crops from 1929 to 1934 can be accounted for by the

TABLE 48. ESTIMATED NUMBER OF ACRES RETIRED UNDER THE PROVISIONS OF THE AGRICULTURAL ADJUSTMENT ACT, UNITED STATES AND SOUTHEAST, 1934

Area	TOTAL		CORN		WHEAT		COTTON		TOBACCO	
	Acres	Per-cent of total	Acres	Per-cent of total	Acres	Per-cent of total	Acres	Per-cent of total	Acres	Per-cent of total
UNITED STATES......	35,767,899	100.0	12,655,986	100.0	7,829,986	100.0	14,585,181	100.0	696,746	100.0
SOUTHEAST..........	8,831,685	24.7	516,020	4.1	67,717	0.9	7,669,531	52.6	578,417	83.0
Virginia............	138,826	....	45,000	....	32,114	....	23,440	....	38,272	....
North Carolina....	719,765	....	32,000	....	3,297	....	499,697	....	184,771	....
South Carolina....	761,838	....	20,000	....	—	....	712,998	....	28,840	....
Georgia............	1,230,929	....	9,500	....	627	....	1,198,657	....	22,145	....
Florida............	62,058	....	17,000	....	—	....	43,280	....	1,778	....
Kentucky..........	425,868	....	140,000	....	20,958	....	5,248	....	259,662	....
Tennessee..........	617,769	....	172,900	....	10,449	....	391,591	....	42,829	....
Alabama...........	1,318,171	....	30,800	....	—	....	1,287,280	....	91	....
Mississippi........	1,471,064	....	3,700	....	—	....	1,467,364	....	—	....
Arkansas..........	1,352,098	....	39,500	....	272	....	1,312,297	....	29	....
Louisiana..........	733,299	....	5,620	....	—	....	727,679	....	—	....

Source: U. S. Dept. of Agriculture, *Agricultural Adjustment, 1933-35*, a Report of Administration of the Agricultural Adjustment Act, p. 46.

acreage retirement program of the A.A.A. Thus for the more than 7.9 million acres dropped out of cotton from 1929 to 1934, the records show that the A.A.A. retired 7.7 million cotton acres in 1934. For the 548,000 acres dropped from tobacco production, the A.A.A. in 1934 retired 578,000 tobacco acres, mainly in Kentucky and North Carolina. In food and feed crops great gains were made in spite of some retirement of corn and wheat acreage. Wheat increased by 705,000 acres although the A.A.A. retired 67,000 acres from wheat production in the Southeast in 1935. Similarly, corn increased by 4.8 million acres although the A.A.A. retired half a million corn acres. In all, the Southeast had 8.8 million acres on which subsidies were paid for retirement from commercial production. This represented 83 percent of the tobacco acreage, 53 percent of the cotton acreage, and only 5 percent of the corn and wheat acreage retired. The Southeast had one-fourth (24.7 percent) of the total farm land retired by the A.A.A. in the Nation.

The increases in food and feed crops are not fully explained until we show how they carried over into increased livestock production. From 1930 to 1935 Table 49 shows that livestock units on Southeastern farms increased by 10 percent. The only losses of the period were shown by sheep, turkeys, and workstock. Horses and mules continued their downward trend with an 8.6 percent decrease, turkeys showed a loss of 5.9 percent, while sheep decreased by one-third. The greatest livestock unit gains were registered by dairy cows whose numbers increased by almost a million, 25.9 percent. Calves increased by 34.1 percent, and beef cattle increased 35.5 percent. Poultry production showed important gains, 20.9 per-

TABLE 49. NUMBER AND PERCENTAGE CHANGE IN LIVESTOCK AND ESTIMATED LIVESTOCK UNITS ON FARMS, SOUTHEAST, 1930-1935

Livestock	Number of animals		Change (1930-35)		Number livestock units		Change (1930-35)	
	1930	1935	Number	Percent	1930	1935	Number	Percent
Horses and mules........	4,033,128	3,683,904	− 349,224	− 8.6	4,033,128	3,683,904	− 349,224	− 8.6
Swine, all ages...........	9,070,964	9,236,268	165,304	1.8	2,086,322	2,124,342	38,020	1.8
Dairy cows..............	3,255,285	4,099,686	844,401	25.9	3,580,814	4,509,655	928,841	25.9
Calves (under 1 yr.)......	1,887,610	2,532,016	644,406	34.1	471,902	633,004	161,102	34.1
Other cattle.............	3,218,047	4,360,808	1,142,761	35.5	1,673,384	2,267,620	594,236	35.5
Sheep (all ages).........	3,750,172	2,498,101	−1,252,071	−33.4	637,529	424,677	− 212,852	−33.4
Goats (all ages)..........	477,661	650,853	173,192	36.2	81,202	110,645	29,443	36.2
Turkeys*(over 3 mo. old).	900,032	847,232	− 52,800	− 5.9	45,002	42,362	− 2,640	− 5.9
Chickens (over 3 mo. old) in thousands.........	63,282	76,529	13,247	20.9	632,820	765,290	132,470	20.9
TOTAL............	.....	.....	.....	.....	13,242,103	14,561,499	1,319,396	10.0

*In 1935, the number of turkeys over 3 months was listed, while in 1929, the census enumerated the number of turkeys "raised," which is 1,818,247. In order to arrive at an estimate of turkeys over 3 months old in 1930, the ratio of chickens raised in 1929 to those over 3 months old in 1930 was computed and this ratio (0.495) was assumed to be the same as the ratio for turkeys. This estimate is very rough and can only be accepted because the difference both in number of turkeys and in corresponding livestock units is very small for the 2 years and does not influence the results.

Note: Animal units [computed here] are based on feed requirements, on the following basis: a horse or mule equals 1 unit; dairy cow—1.1 unit; steer—0.52 units; calf—0.25 units; hog—0.23 units; sheep or goat—0.17 units; chicken—0.01 unit; turkey—0.05 units (Source: O. E. Baker, *Graphic Summary of Farm Animals and Animal Products*, p. 4).

Source: *United States Census of Agriculture, 1935*, III, Chap. 5.

TABLE 50. ESTIMATE OF FEED RATIONS IN TERMS OF CORN AND HAY WITH CORRESPONDING LIVESTOCK UNITS

Livestock	Daily Ration		Yearly Amount			Livestock units
	Corn (pounds)	Hay (pounds)	Corn (bushels)	Hay (tons)	Corn equiv. (bushels)	
Horse or mule......................	11.0	12.0	71.7	2.20	99.0	1.00
Dairy cow.........................	10.0	20.0	65.2	3.6	110.0	1.10
Calf (under 1 yr.)..................	1.8	6.0	11.7	1.1	25.5	0.25
Other cattle.......................	4.0	11.0	26.0	2.0	51.0	0.52
Hog (all ages).....................	3.6	—	23.4	—	23.4	0.23
Sheep (goat)......................	1.0	4.4	6.5	0.8	17.0	0.17
Chicken (3 mo. and older)..........	0.15	—	1.0	—	1.0	0.01
Turkey (3 mo. and older)...........	0.75	—	5.0	—	5.0	0.05

Note: Livestock units for all animals except turkeys estimated by O. E. Baker, *Graphic Summary of Farm Animals and Animal Products*, 1931, p. 98, and 1939, p. 4, on the basis of feed requirements.

Standard horse ration estimated by Z. R. Pettet, *The Farm Horse*, p. 60.

Rations for other animals computed on the basis of data given in "Food and Life," *Yearbook of Agriculture, 1939*; rations readjusted to take care of animals of ages given above and to comply with Baker's livestock units estimated on the basis of feed requirements.

Conversion factors used: 1 bushel of corn equals 56 lbs; 1 ton equals 2,000 lbs. 1 lb. of hay equivalent in feed value to 0.35 lbs. of corn, or 1 ton of hay equivalent to 12.5 bushels of corn.—"Food and Life," p. 558.

cent, reaching the total of 76 million. There were more than 9 million swine on southern farms, but this number remained practically stationary during the period. Although the number of goats increased 36.2 percent, they remained comparatively unimportant except in special areas. Columns 5 to 8 of Table 49 reduce farm animals to equivalent units based on the amount of feed required. This process, based on corn and hay rations, is explained in Tables 46 and 50.

CHANGES SINCE 1934

The year 1934 marked a high point in the acreage devoted to food and feed production. The 1940 figures indicate that this level has been held. Table 51 shows that during the 1930's, while the Nation was decreasing

TABLE 51. ACREAGE AND PRODUCTION OF SPECIFIED CROPS HARVESTED, AND PERCENTAGE CHANGE, UNITED STATES AND SOUTHEAST, 1929-1939

Specified crop	UNITED STATES				SOUTHEAST			
	Number			Percentage change 1929-39	Number			Percentage change 1929-39
	1929	1934	1939		1929	1934	1939	
All corn harvested acreage (acres)........	97,740,740	87,476,444	86,989,626	−11.0	22,259,959	27,084,243	25,879,784	16.3
Cotton harvested acreage (acres)........	43,227,488	26,753,697	22,811,004	−47.2	21,260,796	13,346,971	12,049,801	−43.3
Cotton production (running square bales)......	14,574,405	9,472,022	11,481,300	−21.2	8,929,792	6,142,086	7,064,066	−20.9
Tobacco (acres harvested)............	1,888,365	1,237,117	1,853,230	− 1.9	1,667,597	1,119,888	1,689,023	1.3
Tobacco production (thousands of pounds).	1,456,510	1,021,449	1,699,728	16.7	1,234,387	907,884	1,520,774	23.2
Wheat threshed (acres harvested)......	61,999,908	41,943,387	50,490,296	−18.6	1,612,223	2,316,996	1,919,468	19.1
Oats threshed (acres harvested)......	33,466,025	24,588,766	29,933,108	−10.6	396,478	440,007	1,013,176	155.5
All hay (acres harvested)*.....	67,827,899	68,624,510	65,979,445	− 2.7	6,240,142	9,572,355	10,249,907	64.3

*All hay excluding sorghums but including annual legumes harvested for hay.
Source: United States Census of Agriculture, 1935, III, Chap. 6, Tables 6, 10, 13, 30, 40, 43; Sixteenth Census of the United States, 1940, Agriculture, preliminary press release of April 7, 1941.

its food and feed acreages, the Southeast made notable increases. Thus while the Nation decreased acreage devoted to corn by 11 percent, to wheat by 18.6 percent, to hay by 2.7 percent, to oats by 10.6 percent, the Southeast showed acreage increases in these crops of 16, 19, 64, and 155 percent respectively. According to the figures, from 1934 to 1939 corn and wheat showed the only declines in production in the region.

The percentage distribution of total values and total acreage are shown in Figure 125. In spite of discrepancies due to changes in the census, the distribution can be compared with those of 1929 and 1934 (Figure 124). Corn and cotton lost in proportionate acreage and value while hay, forage, and legumes showed proportionately greater increases in acreage than in values. The wonder crop was again tobacco which on 2.7 percent of total crop acreage accounted for 15.3 percent of total gross values.

Table 47 presents acreage changes during the period in terms of livestock feed, human food, and the staple money crops, cotton and tobacco. In this analysis the acreage devoted to the main money crops declined 40.1 percent from 1929 to 1939 with cotton bearing all the brunt since tobacco showed a slight increase. Crops for human consumption increased 11.3 percent, large gains from 1929 to 1934 being reduced by some losses in the 1934-1939 period. The interesting question here has to do with the proportion of the southern corn crop used for human food. It increased from 22 to almost 26 million acres. If all corn grown could be counted among livestock feed crops, the total acreage gained in this division would amount to 32.3 percent. Gains made in the first half of the decade were held for all crops except corn and sorghum. Legumes increased 135.5 percent.

FIGURE 125. THE ACREAGE AND VALUE OF INDIVIDUAL CROPS AS PERCENTAGE
OF ACREAGE AND VALUE OF ALL CROPS, SOUTHEAST, 1939

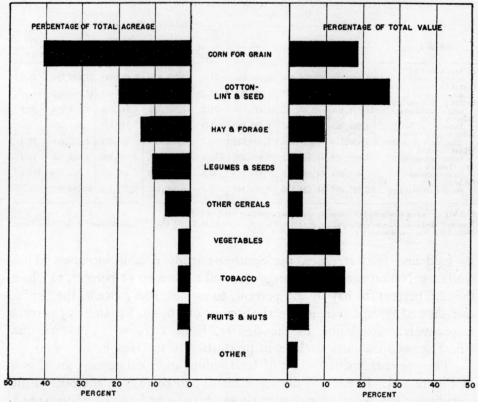

Source: See Table 51 and *Sixteenth Census of the United States, 1940*, Agriculture, First, Second, and Third Series, United States and State Summaries.

TABLE 52. PERCENTAGE CHANGE IN POPULATION AND NUMBER OF LIVESTOCK,
UNITED STATES AND THE SIX MAJOR REGIONS, 1930-1940

Item	United States	Northeast	Southeast	Southwest	Middle States	Northwest	Far West
Population............	7.2	5.1	10.6	7.7	5.2	.4	14.5
Horses and colts........	−24.6	−18.3	− 0.4	−19.3	−21.2	−40.3	−25.1
Mules and colts........	−28.2	−16.1	−11.5	−50.0	−36.5	−60.6	−54.3
Cattle and calves.......	11.8	4.2	33.1	11.9	16.7	− 5.4	16.7
Hogs and pigs..........	3.8	18.5	45.1	33.1	6.6	−51.9	36.9
Sheep and lambs........	− 4.0	−29.2	1.2	28.3	6.6	−11.8	−34.6
Cows milked..........	3.8	1.6	12.2	12.5	4.9	−11.5	6.8
Chickens..............	−10.8	1.7	1.6	− 6.5	−13.7	−25.4	−20.8

Note: Chickens and pigs over 3 months old in 1930 and over 4 months old in 1940; all other livestock over 3 months old at each enumeration.

For sources and specification of ages of animals classified see Table No. 53.

Source: *United States Census of Agriculture, 1935*, III, Chap. V, Tables 5, 8, 10, 12, 13, 16, 24; *Sixteenth Census of the United States, 1940*, Agriculture, press releases March 29, April 2, 1941.

The changes in hay, forage, and legumes went over into livestock production where the Southeast made notable gains in every field except workstock. Table 52 shows that the region led the Nation in proportionate gains

FIGURE 126. PERCENTAGE OF FARMS WITHOUT MILK COWS,
UNITED STATES, 1939

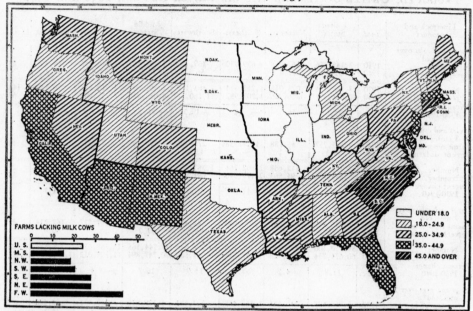

Source: *Sixteenth Census of the United States, 1940*, Agriculture First Series, United States Summary,
Tables V, VIII.

FIGURE 127. PERCENTAGE OF FARMS WITHOUT HOGS AND PIGS,
UNITED STATES, 1939

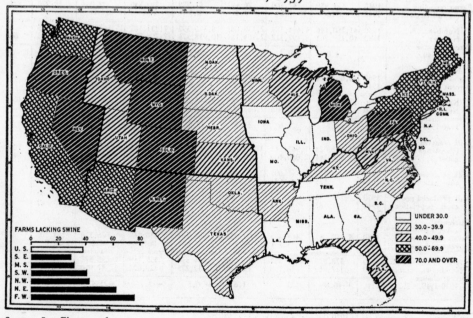

Source: See Figure 126.

TABLE 53. SPECIFIED CLASSES OF LIVESTOCK ON FARMS AND RANCHES AND MILK PRODUCED, UNITED STATES AND THE SIX MAJOR REGIONS, 1930 AND 1940

Livestock and product	Year	United States	Northeast	Southeast	Southwest	Middle States	Northwest	Far West	D. C.
Horses and colts over 3 mos. old									
Farms reporting......	1940	3,148,656	362,918	629,930	369,508	1,224,463	446,977	114,837	23
Percent all farms.....	1940	51.6	57.3	27.9	56.8	73.2	74.4	41.1	
Number..........	1930	13,383,574	1,073,048	1,212,374	1,463,118	5,104,602	3,910,148	620,140	144
Number..........	1940	10,086,971	876,926	1,207,982	1,180,271	4,022,436	2,335,104	464,185	67
Percent change 1930-1940........			−24.6	−18.3	− .4	−19.3	−21.2	−40.3	−25.1	
Mules and colts over 3 mos. old:									
Farms reporting......	1940	1,845,217	45,188	1,277,384	276,995	179,285	51,337	15,017	11
Percent all farms.....	1940	30.3	7.1	56.5	42.6	10.7	8.5	5.4	
Number..........	1930	5,353,950	112,688	2,802,264	1,382,765	652,001	325,069	79,134	29
Number..........	1940	3,844,560	94,567	2,479,940	691,521	414,188	128,175	36,135	34
Percent change 1930-1940........			−28.2	−16.1	−11.5	−50.0	−36.5	−60.6	−54.3	
Cattle and calves over 3 mos. old:									
Farms reporting......	1940	4,843,917	465,647	1,690,668	548,493	1,458,833	512,527	167,734	15
Percent all farms.....	1940	79.5	73.5	74.8	84.3	87.2	85.3	60.0	
Number..........	1930	54,250,300	5,197,846	7,103,708	8,898,598	17,344,165	12,368,630	3,336,573	780
Number..........	1940	60,674,734	5,416,928	9,457,226	9,957,580	20,247,894	11,702,012	3,892,257	837
Percent change 1930-1940........			11.8	4.2	33.1	11.9	16.7	− 5.4	16.7	
Hogs and pigs over 3 mos. old[*]:									
Farms reporting......	1940	3,766,675	239,824	1,587,448	384,483	1,139,070	347,433	68,408	9
Percent all farms.....	1940	61.8	37.8	70.3	59.1	68.1	57.8	24.5	
Number..........	1930	32,793,628	1,125,304	5,830,683	1,783,007	16,610,821	6,776,815	665,981	1,017
Number..........	1940	34,037,253	1,333,422	8,460,994	2,372,512	17,701,041	3,256,584	911,700	1,000
Percent change 1930-1940........			3.8	18.5	45.1	33.1	6.6	−51.9	36.9	
Sheep and lambs over 6 mos. old:									
Farms reporting......	1940	584,935	47,560	76,491	52,989	299,840	89,084	18,970	1
Percent all farms.....	1940	9.6	7.5	3.4	8.1	17.9	14.8	6.8	
Number..........	1930	41,780,146	1,694,189	2,138,081	8,526,392	7,231,182	15,868,941	6,321,355	6
Number..........	1940	40,129,261	1,199,312	2,164,181	10,938,375	7,706,794	13,989,345	4,131,188	66
Percent change 1930-1940........			−4.0	−29.2	1.2	28.3	6.6	−11.8	−34.6	
Cows milked:									
Farms reporting......	1940	4,663,701	455,525	1,623,780	516,617	1,418,734	490,490	158,537	18
Percent all farms.....	1940	76.0	71.9	71.9	79.4	84.8	81.6	56.7	
Number..........	1930	21,124,221	3,265,356	3,255,285	1,695,022	8,745,491	3,059,827	1,102,776	464
Number..........	1940	21,936,556	3,316,536	3,653,800	1,906,947	9,174,404	2,706,630	1,177,677	562
Percent change 1930 1940........			3.8	1.6	12.2	12.5	4.9	−11.5	6.8	
Milk produced: (thousands of gallons)..........	1930	11,052,023	1,963,942	1,291,434	707,455	4,825,566	1,490,005	773,119	504
	1940	11,508,244	2,060,409	1,428,698	798,794	5,069,218	1,296,688	853,890	547
Milk produced per cow (gallons)......	1930	523	601	397	417	552	487	701	
	1940	525	621	391	419	553	479	725	
Milk produced per capita population..	1930	90	52	51	78	142	202	93	
	1940	87	52	51	82	142	175	87	
Chickens: (over 3 mos. old)[**]									
Farms reporting......	1940	5,150,055	463,891	1,991,921	566,181	1,440,349	506,378	181,308	27
Percent all farms.....	1940	84.5	73.2	88.2	87.1	86.1	84.2	64.8	
Number (thousands)	1930	378,878	47,381	63,282	34,534	150,159	56,377	27,132	13
Number (thousands)	1940	337,949	48,190	64,289	32,275	129,622	42,060	21,495	18
Percent change 1930-1940........			−10.8	1.7	1.6	− 6.5	−13.7	−25.4	−20.8	

[*]Pigs over 3 months old in 1930 and pigs over 4 months old in 1940.
[**]Chickens over 3 months old in 1930 and over 4 months old in 1940.

Source: *Sixteenth Census of the United States, 1940*, Agriculture, press release of March 29 and April 2, 1941. *United States Census of Agriculture, 1935*, III, Chap. V, Tables 5, 8, 13, 10, 12, 16, 24.

in cattle, hogs, chickens, and, next to the Southwest, in cows milked. The Southwest led in sheep and lambs. The greatest losses of any region were experienced in the Northwest.

Questions of the adequacy of home-grown supplies on southern farms are more pertinent than ever because of the decreased cotton acreage and income since 1930. The census figures for 1939 (Table 53) indicate that cattle were found on 75 percent of the region's farms, milk cows on 72 percent, hogs and pigs on 70 percent, and chickens on 88 percent. These figures, which indicate that from 12 to 30 percent of our farms are still lacking in needed farm animals, are worthy of examination in greater detail.

The presence of milk cows is possibly the farm's greatest contribution to adequate nutrition in the family living. The proportion of farms without milk cows in 1939 was less than a fourth (24 percent) the country over, ranging from 10 percent in Iowa to 62.8 percent in Arizona (Figure 126). The Middle States, where 84.8 percent, and the Northwest, where 81.6 percent of the farms had cows, led the procession. The Far West with only 56.7 percent lagged. In both the Southeast and Northeast cows were reported on 71.9 percent of the farms. In the Southeast, the range was from Kentucky where only 19 out of 100 farms lacked milk cows to Florida where 57 out of each 100 farms lacked cows.

The extent to which farmers try to provide their own meat supply may be indicated by the proportion of farms having hogs, pigs, and chickens. In the Nation, 38.2 percent of all farms are without pigs, ranging from 14.9 percent in Iowa to 91 percent lacking pigs in Connecticut (Figure 127). Less than 25 percent of the farms in the Far West and 38 percent of the farms in the Northeast grow any pork. Other regions had pork on from 58 to 59 percent of the farms, but the Middle States with 68 percent was exceeded by the Southeast with 70.3 percent. The range in the region was from Georgia, where only 23.7 percent of the farms lacked pigs, to Florida, where 48.4 percent were lacking. The region leads but it should do better. Pork is a favorite food, easily raised and needed on the small tenant farms. Chickens, however, are more popular and rightly so. Only 15.2 percent of the country's farms are without them, ranging from a lack of only 7.1 percent in Iowa to a 55.7 percent deficiency in Arizona (Figure 128). Again the Far West where only 64.8 percent of the farms have poultry and the Northeast with 73.2 percent made the poorest showing. The Southeast with chickens on 88.2 percent of all farms made the best showing. Given the region's climate and diet needs, its rate should be 100 percent. Again Florida, with 31.4 percent of its farms without poultry, made the lowest showing in the region.

The vegetable garden, most popular support of the living of the farm

FIGURE 128. PERCENTAGE OF FARMS WITHOUT POULTRY,
UNITED STATES, 1939

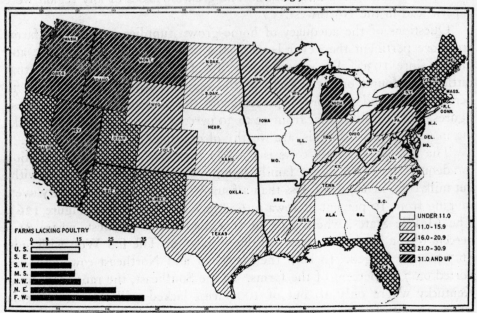

Source: See Figure 126.

family, was reported by 79 percent of all United States farms and contributed an average of $44 worth of vegetables to the family larder (Fig-
ure 129). The poorest States were those in dry and subhumid areas, and
the best States were in the Southeast and Northeast. The States ranged
from Utah, where only 25 percent of all farms had gardens, to Virginia
and West Virginia, with gardens on over 90 percent of the farms. Least
values were returned in Nebraska, Kansas, and South Dakota; the highest
in Rhode Island and the Virginias.

These figures probably record the pre-war high-water mark attained by
the region in pursuit of the doctrine that abundance like charity should begin
at home. They clearly show the need for further development. One-
fourth to one-third of our farms lack essential animals, nor is there any
reason to assume that family needs are actually met on all farms reporting
poultry, pork, milk cows, and gardens. Moreover, population increased
by 10 percent in the Southeast from 1930 to 1940, and since the region has
never supplied its own markets, it seems doubtful that we have experienced
any per capita advances in food and feed production. This can be verified
for milk production by reference to the figures from 1930 to 1940 (Table
53). While the number of milk cows increased by 12.2 percent, and the
amount of milk produced increased from 1,291 million gallons to 1,429

FIGURE 129. PERCENTAGE OF FARMS REPORTING GARDEN VEGETABLES
GROWN FOR HOUSEHOLD USE,* UNITED STATES, 1939

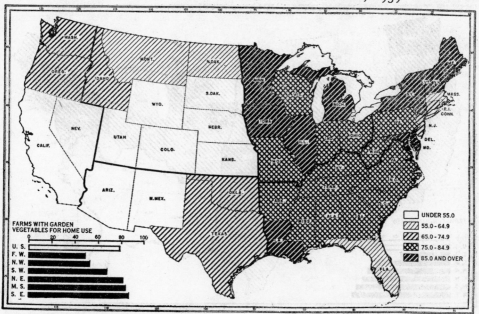

* Not including Irish and sweet potatoes.

Source: Tabulations from the Census in *The Land and the People on the Land*, U. S. Department of
Agriculture, Bureau of Agricultural Economics, October, 1941.

million, the per capita production remained constant at the low level of 51
gallons, and the production per cow actually declined from 397 to 391
gallons a year. The region's figures were the lowest in the Nation. Figure
130 shows that in southern States few farmers purchased stock feed, ranging from 16.9 percent of all farms in South Carolina to 54.9 percent in
Virginia. In the United States in 1939, 54.8 percent of the farms bought
feed averaging $219 per farm. In the Southeast only 37 percent were re-
turned as purchasing stock feed. As the Southeast increases its livestock,
however, it must plan for increased feed production if the enterprise is to
show a profit.

Commercial fertilizer has long been regarded as an inadequate substitute for the manure and cover crops that accompany livestock production.
With the South's long history of clean cultivation and soil erosion, we
should not expect our slight increases in livestock to have made much
change by 1939. Figure 131 shows that, as compared with the 38.3 percent
of the Nation's farms which purchased commercial fertilizer, well over 60
percent of the Southeastern farms made such purchases. Purchases ranged
from one-fourth of the farms in Arkansas to 92 percent in South Carolina,
where the cost of fertilizer averaged $120 per farm as compared with $84
for the Nation. The fertilizer bill of the Southeast still exceeds that of the
rest of the nation.

FIGURE 130. PERCENTAGE OF FARMS REPORTING FEED PURCHASED, UNITED STATES, 1939

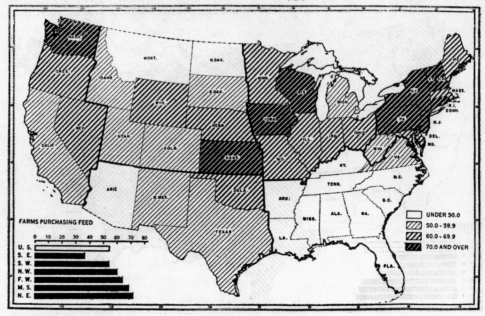

Source: See Figure 129.

FIGURE 131. PERCENTAGE OF FARMS REPORTING PURCHASE OF COMMERCIAL FERTILIZER, UNITED STATES, 1939

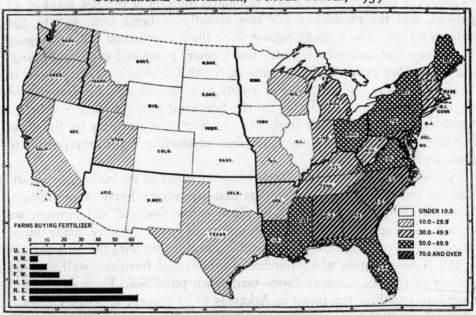

Source: *Sixteenth Census of the United States, 1940*, Agriculture, Second Series, U. S. Summary, Table 26.

There have been large increases in the production of hay, forage, and other stock feed, but the amount produced is still low in the Southeast. If all the legume hay grown in the Southeast should be fed to cattle and work-stock, it would amount to only 0.3 tons per animal unit. Moreover, the increases in legume hay have been more than offset by the decline in cotton-seed products once available for stock feed. The average decline in cotton-seed meal and hulls for the period 1933-1938 has been equivalent to an annual loss of 276 million bushels of corn, a 9.5 percent decline in feed content over the 1928-1932 average. It may be concluded, therefore, that the Southeast is not yet taking full advantage of its opportunity to grow feed.[5]

An adequate livestock program for the Southeast remains a thing of the future. Production has not yet met the needs of the people on the farm, and the increases from 1930 to 1940 hardly did more than keep pace with the actual increase in population. Counting the loss of cottonseed products, the region will have far to go. Chickens still average 35 per farm, 30 per-cent of the farms lack milk cows, and the total per capita production of pork, butter, and milk had shown little or no increase by 1940.

UTILIZATION OF PASTURE AND WOODLAND

In line with these trends, it is worth while to estimate what increased utilization of pasture and forest land may mean for better support of the farm population.

With its small farms and small crop acreage, the Southeast has surpris-ing resources in its forest and grazing land. In 1940 six out of every ten acres in the Southeast were in forested land, public or private. In its south-ern area, the United States Forest survey found 202 of the 461 million acres of the Nation's commercial forest land in 1938. In its 31 units in 9 States the Southern Forest Survey found 59 percent of all land in forests, 35 percent agricultural, and 6 percent waste and subject to other uses. Only half (52.3 percent) of the Southeast's nearly 325,000,000 acres were in farm land.[6]

A great handicap in the South has been and remains the lack of im-proved pastures essential to the economical production of livestock. The discovery of an all-purpose grass for the South, such as timothy in the Northeast, that will produce both hay and permanent pasture would be a real boon.

Many types of improved pastures in the South are subject to climatic injuries and require frequent artificial reseeding, planting or other cultural encouragement. Their chief limitation is that they require better than

[5] J. B. Hutson, Changes in the Production of Feed Crops in the Cotton Belt. Talk before American Farm Bureau Federation, New Orleans, December 12, 1938.

[6] Data from the Southern Forest Survey.

average soils and occasional applications of fertilizer. Their grazing capacity, however, is more than five times as great as that of the native range and the rate of gain in live weight almost twice as rapid. The region still has vast areas where an expansion in livestock is possible and desirable. The Piedmont-Appalachian country is capable of producing ample stocks of dairy products for southern markets, while the Coastal Plain offers opportunity for the production of beef and other meat animals.

The forest range itself offers another resource for livestock: "At least 95 percent of the forest land in the South is privately owned. Much of it is in the hands of large owners who are not especially interested in live-stock production. In accordance with custom they tolerate grazing on their forest lands by the livestock of numerous small farmers. The typical forest range is open, no permits are required, no fees are charged and often no attempt is made to control fires set by the stock owners to benefit the forage."[7]

In the few steps that have been taken, definite progress has been made in improving conditions for southern cattle. Most outstanding has been the elimination of the cattle-fever tick from most of the region. This work has removed one discouraging obstacle to the wider use of improved strains in breeding. Another worthwhile accomplishment has been the development of the dairy industry, particularly in the upper Coastal Plains region. In relatively limited local areas it has brought about the fencing and improvement of pasture lands for controlled and intensive use. Superior forage and feed plants have been introduced into the region through the experiment stations.

The number of packing plants, creameries, milk processing and cheese factories in the South is slowly increasing and, given encouragement and opportunity, the region may some day become self-sufficient in the production of livestock and livestock products.

FOREST LANDS[8]

Most of the South's development in scientific forestry, multiple use, and sustained yield will come in the large holdings of those interests best able to provide the necessary capital and scientific management. From high grade timber to naval stores, to thinning for pole and pulp wood, to grazing, the Southeast with its cheap land and fast growing species offers the greatest opportunities. Of major importance is the trend toward wood utilization plants. In fact these are now increasing so rapidly that over-

[7] See *The Western Range*, Section on Southern Forest Ranges, United States Congress, Senate Document 199 (1936), pp. 567-80.

[8] See E. L. Demon, *Place of Forests in a Land Use Program for the South, Economics for Our Southern Forests*, Occasional papers 62, 59, Southern Forest Experiment Station (New Orleans, 1937).

cutting may result unless accompanied by (1) better forestry, (2) better methods of cutting timber and sawing lumber to prevent waste of a large proportion of the tree, (3) utilization of waste for pulp to replace use of good timber trees for other purposes.

For the small farm-owner, woodlands offer a great and increasing resource. Many southern farmers have from 20 to 40 acres of woodland adjacent to their crop acres. Each year farmers derive from this resource several million dollars worth of forest products, some sold and others used at home or in the interfarm trade.

The farmer's utilization of his woodlands is far from ideal. "Although farmers cannot carry on work in the woods the entire year, they can add considerably to their present and future incomes by taking a few simple forestry measures, such as protecting their woods against fire and over-grazing, by cutting their fuelwood from over-mature, suppressed, and defective trees, by thinning growing stands to promote more rapid growth of desirable trees, and by 'shopping around' to get the best prices for their stumpage or for forest products they cut themselves. Many farmers do not know the value of their timber and have put distress timber on the market simply because a small 'peckerwood' mill happened to be operating in the vicinity."[9]

[9] E. L. Demon, *Occasional Paper No. 59*, Southern Forest Experiment Station (1937), p. 7.

CHAPTER 14

MEN, MULES, AND MACHINES

The discussion of livestock in the preceding chapter leads logically to a treatment of work stock, still the basic power resource on southern farms. In the feeding of work stock the problem of energy resources on the farm is intimately related to the crops grown. Basic as it is to agriculture, the question of farm power is no longer the simple alternative of manpower versus animal power. In its wider aspects, this topic ranges from increased use of gasoline-powered machinery to decreased use of human labor. Moreover the problem exceeds that of the comparable cost and efficiency of horsedrawn and gasoline-powered equipment, for the acres released from feed production go into the "surplus" production of staple crops and thus operate to change price ratios. This fact in addition to mechanization decreases the demand for labor on the farm. Accordingly, the social and economic changes connected with the decrease in farm horses are important enough to warrant special analysis.

REPLACEMENT RATES OF WORK ANIMALS IN THE SOUTHEAST

The chief source of energy, next to human labor in the Southeast, has long been the much abused mule. The region still shows the highest ratios of work stock per 1,000 acres in crops, but the numbers of horses and mules have been declining rapidly. Farm horses and mules increased steadily in this country from 1850 until about 1920.[1] Since then they have shown a sharp decrease, first evident in the statistics from 1920 to 1930 and continued in the agricultural Census of 1935 and 1940.

Much importance attaches to these decreases in farm animals. Since the explanation is to be found in the use of automotive power, these changes serve as a rough index of increased mechanization in agriculture. The disappearance of horses served to release acreage previously devoted to the growing of feed and forage in a period when the effort was being made to

[1] Z. R. Pettet, *The Farm Horse*, Bureau of the Census, 1933.

reduce the production of staple crops in favor of forage and cover crops. With these trends in mind we shall review the changes in farm draft animals in the Southeast.

From 1920 to 1930, Table 54 indicates that over 6,250,000 horses were lost from the Nation's farms, a decline of 31.7 percent. In the Southeast the proportionate decrease was greater, 43.7 percent. These decreases continued from 1930 to 1935. During this period the Nation's farm horses decreased 12.2 percent, the region's declined by 17.2 percent. The decrease in mules according to Table 55, was slight during the twenties when the Southeast actually gained some 32,600 mules. By the next period the decline in mules was evident, for the Nation lost 536,000, 10 percent of its supply and the Southeast lost 4.9 percent. In round figures this meant a total decrease in the Southeast of over 918,000 draft animals during the 1920's and another decrease of 349,224 from 1930-1935.

TABLE 54. NUMBER OF HORSES ON FARMS AND RANCHES WITH PERCENTAGE DECREASE, UNITED STATES AND SOUTHEAST, 1920-1940

| Area | Number of Horses | | | | Decrease In Number of Horses | | | | | |
| | | | | | 1920–1930 | | 1930–1935 | | 1935–1940 | |
	1920	1930	1935	1940	Number	Percent	Number	Percent	Number	Percent
UNITED STATES	19,767,161	13,510,839	11,857,850	10,909,745	6,256,322	31.7	1,652,989	12.2	948,105	8.0
SOUTHEAST	2,176,850	1,226,046	1,015,173	1,221,798	950,804	43.7	210,873	17.2	+206,625	+20.4
Virginia	312,465	203,174	162,633	165,461	109,291	35.0	40,541	20.0	+ 2,828	+ 1.7
North Carolina	171,436	86,716	66,716	75,565	84,720	49.4	20,000	23.1	+ 8,849	+13.3
South Carolina	77,517	30,497	20,420	21,139	47,020	60.7	10,077	33.0	+ 719	+ 3.5
Georgia	100,503	37,325	25,180	35,696	63,178	62.9	12,145	32.5	+ 10,516	+41.8
Florida	38,570	21,300	17,976	20,432	17,270	44.8	3,324	15.6	+ 2,456	+13.7
Kentucky	382,442	247,955	209,641	242,310	134,487	35.2	38,314	15.5	+ 32,669	+15.6
Tennessee	317,921	175,375	140,621	176,739	142,546	44.8	34,754	19.8	+ 36,118	+25.7
Alabama	130,462	64,840	49,593	62,341	65,622	50.3	15,247	23.5	+ 12,748	+25.7
Mississippi	214,852	102,677	76,508	109,205	112,175	52.2	26,169	25.5	+ 32,697	+42.7
Arkansas	251,926	137,747	124,527	168,096	114,179	45.3	13,220	9.6	+ 43,569	+35.0
Louisiana	178,756	118,440	121,358	144,814	60,316	33.7	+ 2,918	+2.5	+ 23,456	+19.3

Note: Number of horses includes horses of all ages as given by the census of January 1, 1920, on April 1, 1930, on January 1, 1935, and an estimate of all on April 1, 1940. Omission of sign means decrease; plus means increase.
Source: *United States Census of Agriculture, 1935,* III, Chap. 5, Table 5; *Fifteenth Census of the United States, 1930,* Census of Agriculture, *The Farm Horse* (1933); *Sixteenth Census of the United States, 1940,* Agriculture, First Series, U. S. Summary

By 1940, 1,907,000 more draft animals had disappeared from the Nation's farms—a loss of some 11.4 percent. This figure represented losses in both horses and mules. The Southeast reversed its trends slightly, gaining 22,000 draft animals. This increase of only 0.6 percent was due to the fact that the region gained some 207,000 horses while it was losing 185,000 mules (Tables 54 and 55).

The question is often asked whether the decline in farm work stock will continue. The situation may aptly be compared with that obtaining in any population whose numbers are being reduced. Inherent in the present death and breeding rates of horses and mules are trends significantly

TABLE 55. NUMBER OF MULES ON FARMS WITH PERCENTAGE DECREASE, UNITED STATES AND SOUTHEAST, 1920-1940

| Area | NUMBER OF MULES | | | | DECREASE IN NUMBER OF MULES | | | | | |
| | | | | | 1920-1930 | | 1930-1935 | | 1935-1940 | |
	1920	1930	1935	1940	Number	Percent	Number	Percent	Number	Percent
UNITED STATES...	5,432,391	5,375,017	4,818,160	3,859,669	57,374	1.1	535,790	10.0	958,491	19.9
SOUTHEAST.......	2,774,473	2,807,082	2,668,731	2,484,108	+ 32,609	+ 1.2	138,351	4.9	184,623	6.9
Virginia.........	96,830	94,573	93,198	89,748	2,257	2.3	1,375	1.5	3,450	3.7
North Carolina...	256,569	294,308	295,388	299,336	+ 37,739	+14.7	+ 1,080	+ 0.4	+ 3,948	+ 1.3
South Carolina...	220,164	188,895	182,645	179,824	31,269	14.2	6,250	3.3	2,821	1.5
Georgia..........	406,351	353,633	333,529	316,057	52,718	13.0	20,104	5.7	17,472	5.2
Florida..........	42,046	40,916	40,946	36,311	1,130	2.7	+ 30	+ 0.1	4,635	11.3
Kentucky........	292,857	252,250	240,196	218,623	40,607	13.9	12,054	4.8	21,573	9.0
Tennessee........	352,510	318,567	304,827	277,488	33,943	9.6	13,740	4.3	27,339	9.0
Alabama.........	296,138	332,133	321,613	292,547	+ 35,995	+12.2	10,520	3.2	29,066	9.0
Mississippi.......	308,216	369,345	350,481	338,180	+ 61,129	+19.8	18,864	5.1	12,301	3.5
Arkansas.........	322,677	361,508	307,160	260,895	+ 38,831	+12.0	54,348	15.0	46,265	15.1
Louisiana........	180,115	200,954	198,748	175,099	+ 20,839	+11.6	2,206	1.1	23,649	11.9

Note: Number of mules includes mules and mule colts of all ages as given by the census on January 1, 1920, on April 1, 1930, on January 1, 1935 and an estimate of these on April 1, 1940; omission of sign means decrease; plus sign means increase.
Source: See Table 54.

below replacement. Z. R. Pettet writing in 1933 estimated that the birth rate of horses and mules was only about three-sevenths replacements. Table 56 makes use of similar methods to indicate the situation in the Southeast. The ratio of horse and mule colts under one year to animals of all ages multiplied by 100 gives an effective "breeding rate." This rough measure of the birth rate of animals is very important for forecasts of the work stock that can be expected in the future. For horses the drop in this ratio from 1920 to 1930 was from 6.06 to 3.70 for the United States and from 4.55 to 2.41 for the Southeast. Slightly higher breeding rates for horses in 1935 indicated that the drop in the number of horses might level off in the near future. While this indication was borne out in the 1940 figures showing an increase in the number of horses in the Southeast in spite of the continued decline in the Nation, breeding fell in both areas. In relation to mules this index probably fails to represent the actual breeding situation. Nevertheless the sharp decline in the ratio of year-old colts to all mules, from 7.17 to 1.15, gives an accurate picture of the oncoming mule supply. In the Southeast this ratio declined from 3.59 in 1920 to .62 in 1935. By 1940 mules had suffered a further decline of 6.9 percent in the region, but breeding rates had increased slightly.

Birth rates alone cannot give a complete picture of replacements. Roughly speaking, replacement is achieved when the birth rate equals the death rate of animals. It is necessary, therefore, to measure death rates of draft animals as well as birth rates. In the case of animals, we have already arrived at a measure of birth rate, but the death rate is unknown for the obvious reason that deaths of work animals are not registered. We

TABLE 56. NUMBER OF HORSES AND MULE COLTS UNDER ONE YEAR OF AGE
WITH RATIO TO HORSES AND MULES OF ALL AGES, UNITED STATES
AND SOUTHEAST, 1920-1940

Item	UNITED STATES				SOUTHEAST			
	January 1, 1920	January 1, 1930	January 1, 1935	January 1, 1940	January 1, 1920	January 1, 1930	January 1, 1935	January 1, 1940
Horses:								
All ages............	19,767,161	13,383,574	11,857,850	10,086,971	2,176,850	1,212,374	1,015,173	1,207,982
Colts under 1 yr.....	1,198,236	494,762	548,972	401,495	99,124	29,198	35,489	34,509
Ratio (percent)......	6.06	3.70	4.63	3.98	4.55	2.41	3.50	2.86
Mules:								
All ages............	5,432,391	5,353,950	4,818,160	3,844,560	2,774,473	2,802,264	2,668,731	2,479,940
Colts under 1 yr.....	389,279	81,376	55,483	49,840	99,487	16,334	16,510	18,254
Ratio (percent)......	7.17	1.52	1.15	1.30	3.59	0.58	0.62	0.74

Note: Number of horses of all ages on January 1, 1930 estimated by subtracting number of colts under 3 months on April 1, 1930 from the total number of horses and colts on April 1, 1930; same procedure applied to estimate number of mules of all ages on January 1, 1930. Number of colts under one year in 1930 estimated by taking the number of colts from 3 to 15 months as enumerated on April 1, 1930. Number of colts under 1 in 1935 and 1940 obtained by dividing by two the total number of colts (1 and 2 years old).

Source: Z. R. Pettet, *The Farm Horse; United States Census of Agriculture, 1935*, III, Chap. 5, Table 5; *Sixteenth Census of the United States, 1940*, Agriculture, First Series, U. S. Summary.

have, therefore, to compute a value similar to the natural increase of the population. For the United States as a whole, we can arrive at a fairly satisfactory estimate of the rate of change in the number of animals for a given period. Thus, subtracting the total number of horses on January 1, 1930, from the number in 1920 (see Table 56) and dividing the difference by ten, we get an average annual decrease of 638,359 horses for the United States. Relating this yearly decrease to the number of horses in 1920, we get a rate of decrease of 3.23 percent (arithmetic method). Now, if we add this rate of decrease to the average breeding rate for the period,[2] we get 4.88 plus 3.23, or 8.11 as the death rate of horses in the United States (see Table 57). For the period 1930-1935 the average annual death rate is lower, 6.55 per hundred. The export and import of horses and mules since 1920 may be disregarded in our computation since they have not been considerable enough to affect the rate of decrease of these animals.

In the case of regions and States, we must take into account the influence of interstate movement and sales of animals, the net balance of which may be considerable and will tend to distort the computation of the correct death rate. According to *The Farm Horse*, the United States death rates rather than the computed State death rates may be used in conjunction with State breeding rates to estimate whether the contribution of the given State is above or below replacement rates (*The Farm Horse*, p. 24).

This would mean, accordingly, that the difference between breeding rates in the Southeast and the death rate in the Nation is a rough measure

[2] Following the procedure used in *The Farm Horse*, we assume that the birth ratio has been following a straight-line trend, and simply average birth rates in 1920 and 1930. See *The Farm Horse*, pp. 23, 28.

TABLE 57. AVERAGE BREEDING RATE, DEATH RATE, AND RATE OF CHANGE
PER 100 ANIMALS, HORSES AND MULES, UNITED STATES
AND SOUTHEAST, 1920-1940

Horses and Mules for Period	UNITED STATES			SOUTHEAST		
	Breeding Rate	Rate of Change	Death Rate	Breeding Rate	Rate of Change	Rate of Natural Increase
	(1)	(2)	(3)	(4)	(5)	(6)
			(1) — (2)			(4) — (3)
Horses:						
1920-1930	4.88	−3.23	8.11	3.48	−4.43	−4.63
1930-1935	4.16	−2.39	6.55	2.95	−3.48	−3.60
1935-1940	4.30	−2.99	7.29	3.18	3.80	−4.11
Mules:						
1920-1930	4.34	−0.15	4.49	2.09	0.10	−2.40
1930-1935	1.34	−2.00	3.34	0.60	−0.95	−2.74
1935-1940	1.22	−4.04	5.26	0.68	−1.41	−4.56

Source: Based on data given in Table 56.

of "natural increase" for animals (see last column of Table 57). The difference between the actual rate of change and the rate of natural increase indicates then the net balance of interstate movement of animals.

In the case of mules, the loss due to the balance of births and deaths is consistently much higher for all three periods than the actual loss. This is because the Southeast, which raises very few mules, imports large numbers raised in other regions. During the first two periods the total rate of change in the number of horses differs very little from the computed rate of natural increase, an indication that the net balance of the interstate movement of horses to and from the Southeast was very small. However, during the period from 1935 to 1940, the actual rate of change became positive, while the rate of natural increase continued to be negative, thus showing that the breeding rate of horses remained below replacement. Hence, to compensate for this loss, there must have been considerable imports of horses to the region between 1935 and 1940.

Table 58 shows the decrease in the number of work animals (horses and mules over 2 years of age) which occurred from 1930 to 1935. The two last columns of the table give an indirect measure of increased mechanization of farms in 1935, obtained by dividing the total acreage in crops by the number of work animals for both periods. Every State in the Southeast (with the exception of Louisiana) shows a marked increase in acreage per work animal since 1930. The extent to which this increased acreage is being worked by mechanized equipment is our next problem.

Table 59 is intended to compare the degree of mechanization in 1930 for the Nation, the Southeast, and the eleven Southeastern States. Tractors and motor trucks have been converted into work animal units, using the theoretical equivalents given by the census of agriculture (5.5 work stock

TABLE 58. WORK ANIMALS ON FARMS AND AVERAGE ACREAGE IN CROPS PER WORK ANIMAL, UNITED STATES AND SOUTHEAST, 1930-1935

Area	Number work animals Jan. 1, 1930	Number work animals Jan. 1, 1935	Decrease in work animals		Acreage in crops per work animal	
			Number	Percent	1929	1934
UNITED STATES	17,611,905	15,467,099	2,144,806	12.2	21.1	23.2
SOUTHEAST	3,927,432	3,579,905	347,527	8.8	15.5	17.2
Virginia	281,678	241,587	40,091	14.2	14.4	16.2
North Carolina	378,336	358,604	19,732	5.2	15.7	16.9
South Carolina	218,614	202,512	16,102	7.4	19.4	21.1
Georgia	389,506	357,657	31,849	8.2	21.8	24.6
Florida	60,780	57,829	2,951	4.9	24.7	28.2
Kentucky	473,162	425,423	47,739	10.1	11.6	13.0
Tennessee	471,623	424,328	47,295	10.0	13.2	15.1
Alabama	392,559	367,601	24,958	6.4	18.5	19.9
Mississippi	463,455	418,680	44,775	9.7	14.6	16.3
Arkansas	488,297	416,435	71,862	14.7	14.0	16.3
Louisiana	309,422	309,249	173	0.05	13.6	13.3

Note: Work animals on January 1, 1935 are horses and mules 2 years of age and over on this date; work animals on January 1, 1930 are horses and mules 27 months and over on April 1, 1930. Acreage in crops includes acres of crops harvested and of crop failure.

Source: *United States Census of Agriculture, 1935*, III, Chap. 5, Table 5.

TABLE 59. TOTAL WORK ANIMAL UNITS ON FARMS, UNITED STATES AND SOUTHEAST, 1930

Area	Number work animals	Mechanical Units			Work animal units		Percentage ratio mechanical to live work animal units
		Number tractors	Number motor trucks	Work animal equivalent	Total	Per farm	
	(1)			(2)	(1)+(2)		(2):(1) x 100
UNITED STATES	17,611,905	920,021	900,385	6,860,885	24,472,790	3.9	39.0
SOUTHEAST	3,927,432	70,852	139,002	667,690	4,595,122	1.9	17.0
Virginia	241,587	9,757	19,459	73,123	374,259	2.2	30.3
North Carolina	378,336	11,426	18,558	99,959	478,295	1.7	26.4
South Carolina	218,614	3,462	6,966	32,973	251,587	1.6	15.1
Georgia	389,506	5,870	15,967	64,219	453,725	1.8	16.5
Florida	60,780	5,244	12,203	53,248	114,028	1.9	87.6
Kentucky	473,162	7,322	7,188	54,647	527,809	2.1	11.5
Tennessee	471,623	6,865	9,039	55,836	527,459	2.1	11.8
Alabama	392,559	4,664	12,838	51,328	443,887	1.8	13.1
Mississippi	463,455	5,542	16,503	63,487	526,942	1.7	13.7
Arkansas	488,297	5,684	11,000	53,262	541,559	2.2	10.9
Louisiana	309,422	5,016	9,281	46,150	355,572	2.2	14.9

Note: The term "work animals" applies to horses and mules estimated to be 2 years old or over on January 1, 1930. The theoretical work animal equivalent of one tractor is 5.5 animals; that of one truck 2.0 animals.

Source: *The Farm Horse*, p. 40; *Statistical Abstract of the United States*, 1937, Table 577; *United States Census of Agriculture, 1935*, III, Chap. 5, Table 5.

units for each tractor and 2 units per truck). The total number of work stock units per farm shows the help obtained by human labor from its live and mechanical assistants. The United States' rate is about twice that for the Southeast (3.9 against 1.9 units). The last column of Table 59, which gives the percentage ratio of mechanical units to work stock units, may serve as a rough measure of the degree of mechanization of agriculture in the various States. Florida is the only southern State to exceed the average index of mechanization for the Nation. Of the other States, only Virginia and North Carolina come within striking distance of the national average. Among the low-ranking States, it should be pointed out that the indices for Kentucky and Tennessee are probably misleading because the large numbers of horses under two years of age on horse farms tend to inflate the number of work animals enumerated for these States.

TABLE 60. DECREASE IN HORSES AND MULES ON FARMS AND HYPOTHETICAL RELEASE OF ACREAGE OF SELECTED FEED CROPS, SOUTHEAST, 1920-1935

Area	1920-1930		1930-1935	
	Decrease in horses and mules	Estimated release of acreage	Decrease in horses and mules	Estimated release of acreage
SOUTHEAST...................	918,195	3,552,772	349,224	1,430,997
Virginia....................	111,548	451,550	41,916	175,209
North Carolina..............	46,981	196,564	18,920	79,464
South Carolina..............	78,289	329,114	16,327	66,288
Georgia.....................	115,896	470,639	32,249	130,931
Florida.....................	18,400	81,620	3,294	14,592
Kentucky....................	175,094	773,740	50,368	222,627
Tennessee...................	176,489	397,289	48,494	109,112
Alabama.....................	29,627	180,733	25,767	157,179
Mississippi.................	51,046	218,990	45,033	193,192
Arkansas....................	75,348	326,848	67,568	292,569
Louisiana...................	39,477	125,685	+ 712	+ 10,166

Note: Decrease in horses and mules given here is computed for the periods: January 1, 1920-April 1, 1930; April 1, 1930-January 1, 1935, and covers animals of all ages.

Source: *The Farm Horse*, pp. 56-64; *United States Census of Agriculture, 1935*, III, Chaps. 5 and 6, Tables 11 and 12; *Statistical Abstract of the United States*, 1926 and 1937.

The Nation's reduction of work stock has released for direct sale or for the feeding of other livestock the products of some 30 million acres of cropland and 15 million acres of pasture. Table 60 shows the decrease in the number of horses and mules of all ages from 1920 to 1930, and from 1930 to 1935, with an estimate of the release of acreage in feed crops that might be traceable to the decrease in draft animals. To assume, however, that these animals were fed on forage produced within the region is not warranted by what we know of the facts. Much of the feed consumed in the Southeast is imported. This release of acreage was computed on the following basis worked out by the census: the yearly "maintenance" ration of a horse or a mule was estimated to be equal to 62.8 bushels of oats and 2.2 tons of hay, or to 35.8 bushels of corn and 2.2 tons of hay, according to the kind of grain used. The maintenance ration, accordingly, is a "theoretical allowance necessary to keep animals that are not working in a good, thrifty condition," computed per thousand pounds of body weight. Since the ration for light work, or the so-called "standard" ration requires a double amount of grain, and the ration for heavy work or for heavier animals would be still greater, the assumption of "maintenance" ration is very conservative. Next, it was assumed that since oats are primarily a horse feed, the decrease in the acreage of oats from 1920 to 1930 should be attributed to the decrease in draft animals. Thus, the number of animals that could be fed on oats produced on this acreage of land according to the average decennial yield in each State has been computed. This figure was deducted from the total decrease in draft animals. The remaining animals were assumed to be kept on corn as a grain ration, and the necessary acreage was estimated on the average decennial yield of corn for each State. Likewise, the necessary hay acreage for the 918,195 animals representing the total decrease for the Southeast was estimated on the basis of 2.2 tons requirement per animal and the average yield per acre of hay by States. The total estimated release of acreage is the sum of the oats, corn, and hay acreage thus computed. For the period 1930-1935 we simply assumed that the necessary acreage to feed one animal was the same for each State as in the period from 1920 to 1930.

The total released acreage amounted to 3.5 million acres from 1920 to 1930. Its effect can be partly accounted for by the tremendous increase of 2 million acres planted in cotton as well as a small increase in tobacco acreage in the Southeast within this period (Table 61). But the released acreage of 1.5 million acres from 1930 to 1935 cannot be traced to the same change in crops, since there was a drastic reduction of 7.9 million acres in cotton and a half million acres in tobacco during these five years, in spite of the fact that total cropland planted in the Southeast remained almost constant from 1930 to 1935. We must, therefore, assume that acreage released by the decrease of draft animals has resulted in the increase of some other crops. From the discussion in Chapter 13 it seems that the striking increase in the acreage of soybeans, peanuts, potatoes, and other vegetables in the Southeast, as well as a surplus of corn and hay to take care of the increased number of cows and hogs, has absorbed the acreage

TABLE 61. CHANGE IN COTTON AND TOBACCO ACREAGE, UNITED STATES AND SOUTHEAST, 1919-1934

Area	1919-1929		1929-1934	
	Change in cotton acreage	Change in Tobacco acreage	Change in cotton acreage	Change in tobacco acreage
UNITED STATES	+9,487,382	+ 26,885	−16,473,791	−651,248
SOUTHEAST	+2,090,473	+ 74,013	− 7,913,827	−547,709
Virginia	+ 41,414	− 53,370	− 31,628	− 69,864
North Carolina	+ 266,697	+226,063	− 670,688	−202,582
South Carolina	− 658,491	+ 9,356	− 691,402	− 41,190
Georgia	−1,314,055	+ 65,103	− 1,249,344	− 39,397
Florida	+ 12,899	+ 6,011	− 31,832	− 4,188
Kentucky	+ 10,543	−165,320	+ 7,506	−169,452
Tennessee	+ 237,281	− 8,588	− 286,462	− 21,066
Alabama	+ 938,344	− 2,888	− 1,436,436	− 104
Mississippi	+1,061,147	− 1,637	− 1,481,102	+ 114
Arkansas	+ 892,674	− 390	− 1,283,571	+ 34
Louisiana	+ 602,020	− 327	− 758,868	− 14

Source: *The Farm Horse*, Tables 11 and 12; *United States Census of Agriculture*, 1935, III, Chap. 6, Tables 40 and 44.

ceded by cotton and tobacco together with that released by the decrease in draft animals.

MECHANIZATION ON THE FARM

Driven from the city streets by the automobile and the delivery truck, the horse has been threatened on his farm home by the tractor and the truck. Between 1915 and 1940 motorized equipment displaced nearly 10 million horses and mules on farms. One study has estimated that each tractor has taken the place of 2½ horses. Too few colts were being raised in 1940 to provide for sufficient replacement in work stock even if 500,000 additional tractors should be bought within the next ten years to replace 1,500,000 work animals. From these figures we may conclude that higher prices for work stock may serve to increase the purchase of tractors, if and when they are made available.

The improvement in the type and performance of tractors has been followed by their adoption on the farms of the Nation. Figure 132 from the Department of Agriculture shows that, although domestic sales of tractors have fluctuated with economic conditions, their number on farms has steadily increased. From an estimated 10,000 in 1910, tractors on

FIGURE 132. HORSES AND MULES, AND TRACTORS ON FARMS, JANUARY 1, UNITED STATES, 1910-1943

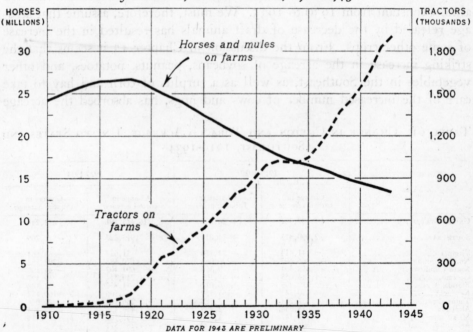

DATA FOR 1943 ARE PRELIMINARY

U. S. DEPARTMENT OF AGRICULTURE   NEG. 38745   BUREAU OF AGRICULTURAL ECONOMICS

farms rose to almost a quarter of a million in 1920, reached over 900,000 in 1930, and totaled over a million and a half in 1940. The adoption of tractors in the last twenty years has been rapid in all areas except the Eastern Cotton Belt. In the Delta, the Southeast has joined in with the trend toward mechanization, and in the Southwest the rates of adoption have been among the highest in the country.

Figure 133 which gives the percentage of farms having tractors in 1940 shows the familiar lag of the region. The States range from North Dakota with tractors on 59.2 percent of its farms to Mississippi with 2.7 percent. The highest rates of mechanization are found in the Northwest, while the Southeast has the lowest with 4.2 percent.

FIGURE 133. PERCENTAGE OF ALL FARMS REPORTING TRACTORS, UNITED STATES, 1940

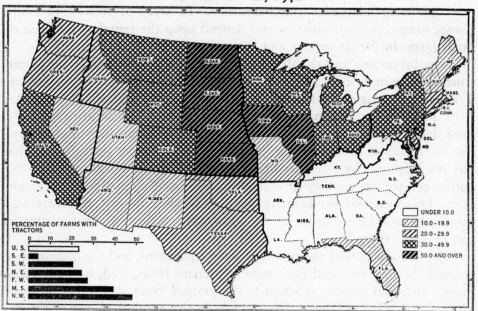

Source: *Sixteenth Census of the United States, 1940*, Agriculture, Series 2, No. 2.

Figures on the number of tractors should be related to the size of farm. It is doubtful if tractors are to be found on many farms smaller than 100 acres. The National Research Project estimated that, if fruit and vegetable farms and smaller-sized farms be omitted, there was in 1930 one tractor for every fourth farm over 50 acres or one for every third farm over 100 acres. By 1940 tractors had increased by 70.4 percent and the number of farms reporting tractors had increased 65.6 percent. Thus on the basis of the method set up by the National Research Project there must be in 1940

5 tractors for every 12 farms over 50 acres or 5 for every 9 farms over 100 acres. Thus the smaller size of farms in the Southeast would seem to explain the region's lag in mechanization. In eight States over 50 percent of the farms are less than 50 acres. Insofar as this applies to small owners with holdings of 100 acres or less the conclusion appears sound.

In the plantation areas, however, we encounter the fact that many of these small farms represent tenant operations on the plantation. Although tractors may operate on tenants' holdings, only the plantation owner's farm would be credited in the census with owning tractors. As the plantation with its centralized management introduces tractor-driven equipment, tenant holdings may be consolidated within the plantation and thus disappear from the census rolls. Later we shall investigate the changes in tenants and farm laborers to see the extent to which this trend is evident in the plantation areas. In the Southwest large-scale farming already existed, perfectly adapted to mechanization. In areas of small ownership, change toward mechanization would depend upon the rental or purchase of small farms by larger owners and business men.

New inventions and the development of new products have long been a major force in pushing people from one sector of employment to another. Tractors and tractor-driven equipment which have displaced farm horses have also displaced farm labor. Mechanization in agriculture rates as a most decisive factor in determining the amount of population that can expect to remain on farms and be supported by income from agriculture. This fact can be shown by estimates of recent trends. "From 1909 to 1929 the output per person working in agriculture increased approximately 37 percent. This increased productivity made it possible for 7.5 percent fewer persons to produce an agricultural output which was 27 percent greater in 1929 than in 1909."[3]

The introduction of the tractor, tractor equipment, and the combine has reduced the time required for a man to prepare lands, seed, harvest, stack, thresh, and haul an acre of wheat to the granary from about 12.7 hours in 1910 to 6.1 hours in 1935. The changes in the number of man hours required per acre for different crops under increasing mechanization in the United States are indicated in Table 62. Although mechanization elsewhere has been unable to duplicate its achievements in wheat, all crops have seen their labor requirements curtailed. Most laggard in these respects have been cotton, tobacco, and corn, main crops in the South.

Mechanization increases the size of farms by decreasing their number, it increases greatly the amount of capital needed to own and operate a farm enterprise, and it reduces the need for labor at the same time that it serves

---

[3] E. A. Shaw and J. A. Hopkins, *Trends in Employment in Agriculture 1909-1936*, National Research Project (Washington, D. C.: United States Government Printing Office, 1938).

TABLE 62. ESTIMATED MAN HOURS REQUIRED PER ACRE TO PRODUCE CROPS AT DIFFERENT PERIODS IN THE UNITED STATES, 1909-1936

Period	Estimated man hours to produce:					
	Wheat	Oats	Corn	Cotton	Potatoes	Beets
1909-1913.............	12.7	12.5	28.7	105	89	113
1917-1921.............	10.3	10.8	27.6	95	—	112
1927-1931.............	6.7	8.6	23.3	85	—	99
1934-1936.............	6.1	7.9	22.5	88	76	94

Source: Report of WPA National Research Project on Changes in Technology and Labor Requirement in Crop Production. Separate monographs on wheat and oats, pp. 95, 98; corn, p. 120; cotton, p. 103; potatoes, p. 67; sugar beets, p. 67.

to reduce the number of farms. This process operates on the different tenure classes in agriculture by producing different rates of change. Large operators increase, and small owners, tenants, and laborers show various rates of decrease. These rates of change may be expected to vary by subregions. In the Southeast smaller farms may be expected to give way to the larger farms already existing. Thus in the Delta area, plantations are already large and farm tenants would be displaced or changed to the status of wage hands. In the Eastern Cotton Belt small farm owners might be able to resist mechanization because of the influence that rough topography exerts in upland areas. Such farmers would suffer, however, in competition with the lower costs of production developed in mechanized areas. In the more level coastal plains of the Eastern Belt small farms could be assembled into larger holdings if the demand for products steadily increased.

The Cotton Belt has lagged behind other regions in the adoption of machinery. Until recently this has been true in the main plantation areas in spite of the fact that the plantation was already in possession of the large holdings, the integrated management, and the access to capital necessary for mechanization. For this reason some students of the problem have thought that mechanization in cotton would be forced to wait upon the development of a mechanical picker. It is now evident that tractor equipment by itself is sufficient to reduce the demand for farm workers in several types of areas.

In a southwestern study, Bonnen and Magee calculated that the use of two-row tractor equipment on all farm lands in the Texas High Plains would so increase the efficiency of operations as to make possible a reduction in the number of farms to 58 percent of the 1935 count. The use of four-row tractor equipment would reduce the number to 33 percent. In a Delta study Langsford and Thibodeaux have shown that the mechanization of plantations would reduce the labor for one plantation of 750 crop acres from 40 families under the one-row plow-mule system to 24 families under a four-row tractor system—a decrease of 40 percent. This is a conservative figure and is based on the assumption that some of the 24 families would be retained mainly for hoeing and picking cotton.[4]

H. G. Porter's unpublished study in Louisiana, reported by R. J. Saville, indicates a loss of 1.6 farm families for every tractor added on Louisiana plantations. By tenure groups this means an average decrease of 1.8 cropper families, 0.4 renter families, and an increase of 0.6 wage hands per tractor added on each plantation. To calculate the loss of farms Saville and Porter made use of the data and methods developed in the WPA studies. They found a decrease of 5.1 farms for every tractor adopted in the Eastern Cotton Belt, a decrease of 2 farms in the Delta, and a decrease of 1.1 farms for every tractor adopted in the Western Belt.[5] This would indicate that, in the Eastern Belt, the decrease in acreage devoted to staples such as cotton and tobacco has been the predominant influence. While at present it may be reasonable to conclude from these figures that one tractor takes the place of one farm family, the rate of displacement may be accelerated as the rationalization proceeds. Langsford and Thibodeaux found that with the increase in power machinery in the Yazoo Delta the proportion of cropland worked with share croppers dropped from 55 to 42 percent, while the proportion worked by wage hands increased from 31 to 53 percent from 1933 to 1936. The Department of Agriculture in its survey, *Technology on the Farm*, concluded in 1940 that the traditional plantation and share cropper system of farm organization in parts of the South was passing without the aid of a mechanical cotton picker.

FARMS LACKING POWER RESOURCES

There exists in the United States a sizeable number of farms which appear to have no power resources whatever—neither horse power nor mechanized power. Instead of tractors pushing horses off the farms in the Southeast, the 1940 Census indicates that horses and mules had left some farms before tractors made their appearance. Thus Figure 134 which gives the proportion of farms lacking horses and mules indicates a range from only 13.4 percent lacking work stock in Iowa to 66.8 percent in Massachusetts. A comparison of this Figure with Figure 133, showing the percentage of farms with tractors, serves to indicate the distribution of energy resources. It is evident that many farms in the Corn Belt possess power resources from both work stock and tractors. In New England and the Far West, however, many specialty farms have no source of power, either animal or mechanical. In West Virginia, Kentucky, Tennessee, Mississippi over 30 percent of all farms report no horses or mules while less

---

[4] See references and discussion in C. Horace Hamilton, "The Social Effects of Recent Trends in the Mechanization of Agriculture," *Rural Sociology*, VI (March, 1939), pp. 3-19.

[5] R. J. Saville, "Trends in Mechanization and Tenure Changes in the Southeast," *The People, the Land and the Church in the Rural South* (Chicago, Farm Foundation, 1941), pp. 81-82.

FIGURE 134. PERCENTAGE OF ALL FARMS NOT REPORTING HORSES OR MULES, UNITED STATES, 1940

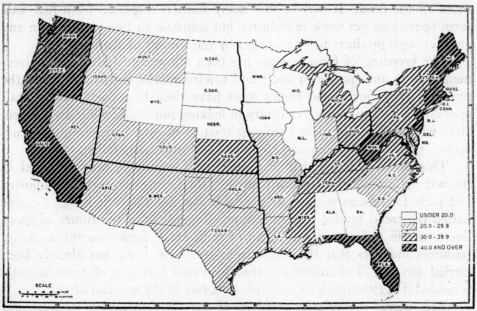

Source: Tabulations from the Census in *Farm Population and Rural Life Activities*, U. S. Department of Agriculture, Bureau of Agricultural Economics, XVI, p. 6, January, 1942.

than 4.4 percent of the farms have tractors. If we could assume that all farms lacking horses and mules possessed tractors, over one-fourth of the farms still would lack any source of power stronger than human muscle. A similar situation prevails in New England and Far Western States.

In areas where the plantation form of organization is prevalent, several farm units may use horse or tractor power supplied from a central headquarters. It is impossible to ascertain from the census figures how many tenant farms in the Mississippi Delta may have access to tractors and mules at central barns. Hamilton reported in 1939 that in some areas the mechanization of cotton farms had increased the number of what has been called "patch croppers" or "hoe croppers." The patch cropper receives a cash wage, working on the plantation when needed, and in addition cultivates on shares a small patch of some four or five acres of cotton. The power for breaking land, etc., may be furnished by the planter who charges the cropper a regular rate for the service.[6]

In other areas like Tennessee and Kentucky we know that many farmers must be undertaking the difficult task of operating without any power. In such cases the income can hardly be large enough to sustain a decent level of living. In other areas the answer is to be found in part-time work.

[6] C. Horace Hamilton, *op. cit.*, p. 13.

Thus in West Virginia, where 40 percent of all farmers have neither tractors nor work animals, one-third of all farm operators work 100 days or more off the farm. It may be that many farmers displaced from full-scale farm operations get work in industry but continue to live on the farm and grow enough products to be reported by the Census of Agriculture.

The breeding of farm animals has been allowed to fall below replacement rate in anticipation of the trend toward mechanization. Already the prices of farm horses and mules must have risen to a point where small operators have experienced difficulty in making purchases, while large operators were too interested in acquiring tractors to give breeders the encouragement needed for increasing the horse and mule population.

This is the situation that presented itself when the need for steel in the war industries cut off needed supplies for farm machinery. Equipment and parts for repairs were made available but, for the time being, the war halted the trend toward mechanization. Regardless of the future of gasoline power in agriculture, the plight of these small farmers without energy resources indicates that the flight from the farm horse has already been carried too far. Indications are that increased breeding of farm animals is needed if agriculture is to accomplish its task in the war and after.

This leaves the related problem of the displacement of tenants and farm laborers for treatment in a succeeding chapter.

CHAPTER 15

TENANCY—A FOOTHOLD ON THE LAND

THE BROAD relationships between population and land may be divided into two main types: land utilization and land tenure. The first is based on the physical aspects of land, the second on legal rights to occupy and make use of land as property. Both help to determine the distribution of farm income among the farm population. The first phase we have discussed as the connecting link between physical and human factors in the agriculture of the Southeast. Land tenure, the second phase, is basic to agriculture for it deals with the access to the land of both the propertied and the unpropertied as sanctioned in accepted legal codes. Land tenure is thus a deeply imbedded phase of culture for it deals with rights of private ownership that go back to the dim past. In its economic aspects this distribution of rights determines who shall occupy land and what share of its income they shall receive.

LAND TENURE

This chapter accordingly deals with tenure on the land as a basis of support for various classes of the population of the Southeast. People are seen as competing for a place on the land, rising and falling in the ranks of owners and tenants, and leaving the land for other opportunities. This chapter is neither a study in migration nor in the returns from agriculture, for both these topics have received attention elsewhere. It is rather a study of how people secure footholds on the land, how they lose them, and how they climb or fall from foothold to foothold. Tenure status in its broad aspects can be arrayed in a continuing series of stages, leading from farm labor at one end to large landed proprietor at the other.

In an agrarian society where land serves as the chief source of wealth, ownership and tenure relations offer a basis whereby the population is divided into social and economic classes with rights to income and even to social "standing." In its legal aspects this situation grows out of the fact that under the system of private property, rights in land are divided. Public rights are those exercised by government such as rights of eminent domain, taxation, conservation, etc. Private rights themselves are guarded and protected by government, as witness the laws of trespass, but they can be assigned among several persons. The chief form of this division occurs when the owner grants some of his rights to the use of land to a tenant for a fixed period in return for specified payments in money or kind. In range these rights vary from the limited ones granted a farm laborer working on land to those of a cash tenant operating over a long period. Since the tenant pays for the privilege of using these rights, questions of land tenure are also concerned with rent.[1]

Farms of the size and type suitable for family operation with some hired labor are still characteristic of the United States as a whole. Only the plantations of the South, western ranches, and some large farms elsewhere are too large for family operation. Owner-operated farms and owner-operated farm acreage still exceed tenant operated. The general trend until 1930, however, had been towards tenancy with farmers gradually losing ownership of the land they till. This can also be demonstrated for owners who, because of increased mortgage debt, hold less equity in the land they till.[2]

Tenancy is more prevalent in the South than in any other region. The link between tenancy and cotton production seems just as close today as ever. Once we leave the cotton farms, tenancy does not show up much worse in the South than in other parts of the Nation. In 1930 the rate of tenancy for non-cotton farms was just 32 percent for the entire country. In the 16 States of the census South, tenancy averaged 38 percent for non-cotton farms, but 73 percent of all cotton farms were tenant operated—a ratio almost double that of non-cotton farms.

More than in any other region of the country, tenure status in the Southeast tends to coincide with social rank and economic status of the people on the land. In the Midwest many tenants are better off than landowners, and their decision to rent rather than buy land represents a business man's decision as the best use to make of his funds. Cash rent is not prevalent in the Southeast and share renting has a different meaning. In the Southeast, where the cropper is nearest in lineal descent to the antebellum slave and the landowner has the prestige of position and independence, the various tenure levels come near to representing fixed social levels. With these considerations in mind we shall examine the various tenure stages and the changes that have occurred in farm tenancy.

[1] Adapted from George S. Wehrwein in *Research in Agricultural Land Tenure*, John D. Black, editor (New York: Social Science Research Council, 1933), pp. 1-3.

[2] H. A. Turner, *Graphic Survey of Farm Tenure*, United States Department of Agriculture, Miscellaneous Publication 261 (Washington, D. C., 1936), p. 1.

THE TENURE STAGES

Land tenure studies in the United States have given attention to the various tenure stages because in many sections farmers have expected to rise from laborer stage to ownership. If this movement were entirely lacking, tenure status would still be worthy of study as an index of class structure. Each class, beginning with the farm laborer, has rights in the use of land more extensive than those enjoyed by the common public. In securing access to the land, men may begin as laborers or inherit a farm; they may rise from the position of renter to one of landowner; they may be displaced by a contracting agriculture; or they may move to more remunerative jobs in factories and cities. In this changing panorama, various elements in the population may gain and lose footholds on the land and climb up and down the "agricultural ladder," whose rungs from low to high lead from farm laborer to farm owner.

In the Southeast this picture is variegated and complex. It is possible, for example, to name thirteen separate "rungs" on the "agricultural ladder" in the South, all the way from the unpaid family labor of a son working on his father's cropper farm to the status of casual wage hand, regular wage hand, cropper, share tenant, standing renter, cash renter, manager, part owner, mortgaged owner, full owner of a small farm, landlord, and large planter.

In the region's network of tenure relations, there are places where one status shades easily into the next. If a day laborer on a plantation is given a special tract of land to till and his wage for the year is established at one-half of the cotton and other cash crops which he grows on the tract, he has made the transition to share cropper. If he can finance a down payment on a mule and simple implements, he may become a share renter paying only one-third of the product in rent. If the mortgage on the mule is foreclosed, he reverts to cropper status and the landlord feeds the animal the next season. The step to landowner, however, is much more difficult, while the status of cash renter is definitely nearer that of the entrepreneur.

While each tenure status is capable of statistical definition, only a minimum number can be studied from the census. Usually returned are croppers, share tenants, managers, part owners, and owners. In addition the number of farm laborers can usually be ascertained from the occupational statistics. For several reasons, managers and part owners are often counted with full owners. It is impossible, however, in the regular figures to separate small owners from those who own large holdings and plantations.

There exists, moreover, not only mobility between each of these agricultural ranks but also mobility out of each status on the land. As an instrument for the study of population mobility the tenure ladder accordingly

TABLE 63. CHANGE IN NUMBER AND ACREAGE OF FARMS AND IN NUMBER AND DISTRIBUTION OF FARM WORKERS, UNITED STATES AND SOUTHEAST, 1930-1940

Area and Selected Agricultural Statistics	1930	1935	1940	Percent Change		
				1930-35	1935-40	1930-40
UNITED STATES						
1. Number of Farms...............	6,288,648	6,812,350	6,096,799	8.3	−10.5	− 3.1
2. Farm Acreage (Thousands of acres).	986,771	1,054,515	1,060,852	6.9	0.6	7.5
3. Total Farm Workers (14 years old and over), number..	10,266,435	12,407,614*	8,941,496	20.9	−27.9	−12.9
percent....	100	100	100			
3A. Operators and Managers, number...	6,079,234	6,488,246	5,241,589	23.8	−19.2	−13.8
percent....	59	52	59			
3B. Wage Workers, number...	2,714,588	1,645,602	2,490,603	−39.4	51.3	− 8.3
percent....	26	13	28			
3C. Unpaid Family Workers, number...	1,472,613	4,273,166	1,209,304	190.2	−71.7	−17.9
percent....	15	35	13			
4. Laborers per 100 Farms, all........	66	87	61			
Wage Workers..................	43	24	41			
Unpaid Family Workers...........	23	63	20			
SOUTHEAST						
1. Number of Farms...............	2,388,806	2,547,952	2,259,030	6.7	−11.3	− 5.4
2. Farm Acreage (Thousands of acres).	170,508	188,543	183,677	10.6	− 2.6	7.7
3. Total Farm Workers (14 years old and over), number...	4,041,631	5,199,849*	3,482,231	28.7	−33.0	−13.8
percent....	100	100	100			
3A. Operators and Managers, number...	2,316,047	2,425,531	2,005,785	4.7	−17.3	−13.4
percent....	57	47	58			
3B. Wage Workers, number...	826,716	573,271	842,525	−30.7	47.0	1.9
percent....	21	11	24			
3C. Unpaid Family Workers, number...	898,868	2,201,047	633,921	144.9	−71.2	−29.5
percent....	22	42	18			
4. Laborers per 100 Farms, all........	73	108	65			
Wage Workers..................	35	22	37			
Unpaid Family Workers......	38	86	28			

*Workers of all ages for 1935.
Note: Number of farm operators in 1930 and in 1940 (line 3A of the table) is derived from the occupational statistics of the Census of Population for 1930 and 1940 and therefore is smaller than the number of farms reported by the Census of Agriculture (line 1). This difference is due to the fact that farm operators may give other work outside of farming as their major occupation. The number of farm operators in 1935 is also smaller than the number of farms, although both figures are reported by the Census of Agriculture in 1935. This is explained by the fact that the 1935 Census was taken on January 1, when some farms were reported "vacant" due to absence of operators at this season. This change of date is also responsible for the low number of hired workers. The surprisingly high number of unpaid family workers may be partly explained by the depression but should also be attributed to the difference in definition of farm laborer in 1935 as compared with the other periods. The 1940 Census includes only workers 14 years old and over, and children under 14 have been excluded from the workers enumerated in 1930 to make the data comparable. No such correction could be applied to the data of the Census of Agriculture in 1935, and therefore the number of farm laborers in 1935, especially the number of unpaid family workers, must include some children under 14, which certainly exaggerates the total number. To make data comparable with figures for other years the number of farm workers in 1940 was corrected to include emergency workers in agriculture and a proportional share of workers with "occupations not reported".

Source: *Fifteenth Census of the United States, 1930*, Population, IV, Tables 4 and 23. *United States Census of Agriculture, 1935*, III, Chap. 4. *Sixteenth Census of the United States, 1940*: Population, Series P-11; Agriculture, First Series, Tables V and VI.

presents an added complication in that there are exits on every level to the non-agricultural occupations. One who watches, as from a bird's eye view, the population in its competitive struggle, on the one side for a foothold on the land, on the other for a chance to leave the land for better opportunities, would see varying degrees of mobility for each class and race. In our present state of knowledge, we know too little about these changes.

The total working force on the land consists of farm operators and farm laborers returned in the occupational statistics. The national total of all farm workers (operators and laborers) in 1940 was 8.9 millions of which the Southeastern States furnished 3½ millions. As Table 63 shows, 2 millions of this group were farm operators—owners, tenants, and croppers.

Table 64 classifies the Nation's farm operators by tenure status. Of the operators in the Southeast, 21.9 percent were croppers who paid one-half or more of the money cash for rent of land, workstock, and equipment; 18.5 percent were share tenants who owned and fed their workstock but paid one-fourth to one-third of their cash crops for rent; 8.8 percent were cash tenants who paid money rent.

TABLE 64. NUMBER AND PERCENT OF FARM OPERATORS BY COLOR AND TENURE, UNITED STATES AND THE SIX MAJOR REGIONS, 1930-1940

Region	Year	All farm operators		Full and part owners		Farm managers		All tenants		Croppers		Colored operators	
		Number	Percent	Number	Percent	Number	Percent	Number	Percent	Number	Percent	Number	Percent
UNITED STATES.....	1930	6,288,648	100.0	3,568,394	56.7	55,889	0.9	2,664,365	42.4	776,278	12.3	916,070	14.6
	1935	6,812,350	100.0	3,899,091	57.2	48,104	0.7	2,865,155	42.1	716,256	10.5	855,555	12.6
	1940	6,096,799	100.0	3,699,177	60.7	36,351	0.6	2,361,271	38.7	541,291	8.9	719,071	11.8
Northeast....	1930	618,079	100.0	516,855	83.6	10,814	1.8	90,410	14.6	3,705	0.6	7,931	1.3
	1935	715,465	100.0	587,007	82.0	9,256	1.3	119,202	16.7	4,979	0.7	8,297	1.2
	1940	633,676	100.0	529,898	83.6	6,592	1.0	97,186	15.3	2,992	0.5	7,247	1.1
Southeast....	1930	2,388,806	100.0	1,043,731	43.7	11,375	0.5	1,333,700	55.8	646,396	27.1	766,111	32.1
	1935	2,547,952	100.0	1,166,063	45.8	9,920	0.4	1,371,969	53.8	621,169	24.4	719,712	28.2
	1940	2,259,030	100.0	1,140,260	50.5	8,274	0.4	1,110,496	49.2	493,526	21.9	608,590	26.9
Southwest....	1930	744,932	100.0	304,263	40.8	5,019	0.7	435,650	58.5	126,177	16.9	116,298	15.6
	1935	774,535	100.0	341,369	44.1	5,201	0.7	427,965	55.2	90,108	11.6	99,310	12.8
	1940	650,262	100.0	335,133	51.5	4,895	0.8	310,234	47.7	44,773	6.9	80,118	12.3
Middle States.....	1930	1,622,625	100.0	1,097,113	67.6	13,206	0.8	512,306	31.6	—	—	9,743	0.6
	1935	1,787,429	100.0	1,171,410	65.5	10,679	0.5	605,340	33.9	—	—	9,876	0.6
	1940	1,672,864	100.0	1,127,187	67.4	8,879	0.5	536,798	32.1	—	—	7,440	0.4
Northwest....	1930	648,927	100.0	397,988	61.3	5,379	0.8	245,560	37.9	—	—	8,161	1.3
	1935	683,617	100.0	402,861	58.9	4,227	0.6	276,529	40.5	—	—	8,751	1.3
	1940	601,156	100.0	343,197	57.1	3,068	0.5	254,891	42.4	—	—	6,386	1.1
Far West.....	1930	265,175	100.0	208,385	78.6	10,075	3.8	46,715	17.6	—	—	7,815	2.9
	1935	303,263	100.0	230,330	76.0	8,804	2.9	64,129	21.1	—	—	9,597	3.2
	1940	279,746	100.0	223,472	79.9	4,620	1.7	51,654	18.5	—	—	9,286	3.3
District of Columbia..	1930	104	.....	59	.....	21	.....	24	.....	.....	.....	.....	.....
	1935	89	.....	51	.....	17	.....	21	.....	.....	.....	.....	.....
	1940	65	.....	30	.....	23	.....	12	.....	.....	.....	.....	.....

Source: *United States Census of Agriculture, 1935*, III, Chap. 3, Table 6; *Sixteenth Census of the United States, 1940*, Agriculture, First Series, press release of March 18, 1941.

In addition, in 1940 the Occupational Statistics show 842,525 white and Negro farm laborers in the Southeast classified as "wage hands over 14 not employed on the home farm," equal to 24 percent of all in agriculture (Table 63). Their major source of livelihood came from agriculture though we cannot be sure that all had permanent habitation on the land or that their employment was continuous except for periods of cultivation and harvest.

We know less about the upper range of the hierarchy than the lower. There is a group consisting of 6.2 percent of the operators who own part of the land they till and 44.2 percent who are full owners in the Southeast. This is not a completely significant figure, for about 30 percent of the full owners report mortgages covering 36.6 percent of the value of their properties, on which indebtedness they pay interest and other charges in addition to taxes and normal costs of production. Among these owners are to be found many of the landlords and large planters who own the tenant farms. We know little about the distribution of these holdings but, on the basis of 1900 and 1910 figures, it can be estimated that 7.3 percent of all operators were landlords who owned two to four tenant farms while another 2.5 percent owned five or more rented farms. This last group may be classified as planters. Around 1900-1910 they owned an average of 9.9 farms and held 22.4 percent of all farms listed in the area.[3]

FARM LABOR

Lowest in the tenure ladder are the farm laborers. In 1940, over 2,490,000 paid farm laborers and over 1,209,000 unpaid family laborers were to be found on American farms. Some of these, notably the "hired men" employed by the month on "family farms," have more security than many tenants. More than any other form of agriculture in our economy, cotton and tobacco, the dominant crops in the Southeast, are still labor oriented. This fact is evident in all discussions of the small size of farms in regions, but is made clearer when the amount of hired and unpaid family labor is added to farm operators.

In 1930 the Nation's farms supported a larger working force than ten years later. The United States' total of all farm workers (operators and laborers) 14 or more years of age in 1930 was 10,266,000, of which the Southeastern States furnished 4,042,000 (Table 63). For 170.5 million acres in farms, the Southeast in 1930 had 4 million agricultural workers. For 986.78 million acres, the nation had 10.3 million workers. Over 1.4 million of these—23 for every 100 farms—were unpaid family workers—wives and children of owners and tenants who worked part time on the home farm. Another 2,715,000—43 per 100 farms—were hired laborers. In the Southeast there were approximately 38 unpaid family workers and 35 hired laborers per 100 farms in 1930. Out of every 100 farm workers in the United States on April 1, 1930, approximately 59 were farm operators, 26 were wage hands and 15 were unpaid members of the family

[3] "Concentration of Landownership," U. S. Census of Agriculture, 1900. Special Census of Plantations, "Plantation Farms in the United States," Washington: Government Printing Office, 1916.

working on the home crops. In the Southeast there were 57 operators, 21 wage hands and 22 family workers.

While the acreage in farms increased both in the Nation and in the Southeast in 1940, the number of farms and of farm workers 14 years or older decreased. The Nation's farm acreage rose to 1,061 million acres, for which there were now 8,941,000 farm workers, a loss of more than a million during the decade. In the Southeast, the 170.5 million acres devoted to farms in 1930 was increased to 183.7 million acres in 1940, but the number of farm workers declined by more than half a million to 3,482,000. Among every 100 farm workers in the United States in 1940, there were still 59 operators, as in 1930. However, hired workers increased from 26 to 28, and unpaid family workers decreased correspondingly from 15 to 13 per 100 workers. By 1940 the number of hired laborers exceeded the number of unpaid family workers on the farms of the Southeast. Wage workers numbered about 842,500 in 1940, an increase of some 16,000 in number. Unpaid family workers declined by more than 250,000 from 1930 to 1940, when they numbered about 633,900. Of every 100 farm workers in the region in 1940, 58 were operators, 24 were hired laborers, and 18 were unpaid family workers (Table 63).

FIGURE 135. HIRED FARM LABORERS PER 100 FARMS,* UNITED STATES, 1940

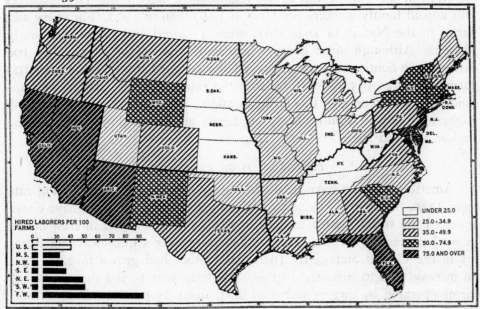

* Note: Emergency workers and workers with occupations unreported distributed *pro rata* by region but not by states.

Source: *Sixteenth Census of the United States, 1940*, Series P-11, State Summaries, Tables 1, 2.

FIGURE 136. UNPAID FAMILY WORKERS PER 100 FARMS, UNITED STATES, 1940

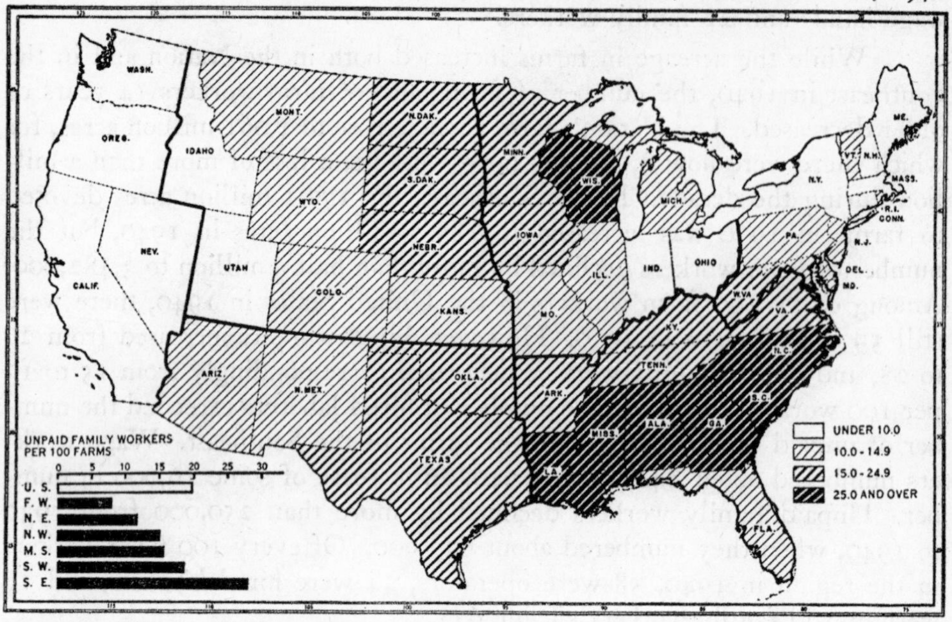

Source: See Table 63 and Figure 135.

Both in the Nation and in the region there were fewer farm laborers and unpaid family workers per farm in 1940 than in 1930. For every 100 farms in the Nation in 1940 there were 41 hired and 20 unpaid family workers. Although hired laborers increased from 35 to 37 for every 100 farms in the Southeast, unpaid family labor declined from 38 to 28 per 100 farms. Figures 135 and 136 indicate the ratios of hired laborers and unpaid family workers per 100 farms in 1940. The Southeastern States rank highest in unpaid family labor on farms and third lowest among the regions in hired labor.

THE GROWTH OF TENANCY

American farmers have been drifting into tenancy at an increasing rate since 1880. During this same period many European countries have either reversed the trend toward tenancy or made reforms in the interest of the general welfare. In 1880, there were slightly over a million tenant farmers in the United States. By 1940 the number had grown to 2,361,271, an increase of 130 percent. In this same sixty year period the number of farms operated by owners increased only about 25 percent. Each decade, except the last, showed an increasing proportion of tenancy; from 26 percent in 1880 to 35 percent in 1900; from 38 percent in 1920 to 42 percent in 1930 and 1935; with a drop to 39 percent in 1940 (Figure 137).

FIGURE 137. THE TRENDS IN THE EXPANSION OF MAJOR AREAS OF FARM TENANCY BY COUNTIES, UNITED STATES, 1880-1935

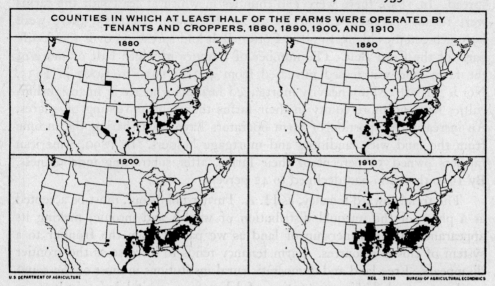

COUNTIES IN WHICH AT LEAST HALF OF THE FARMS WERE OPERATED BY TENANTS AND CROPPERS, 1880, 1890, 1900, AND 1910

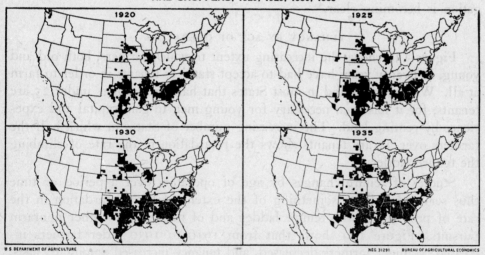

COUNTIES IN WHICH AT LEAST HALF OF THE FARMS WERE OPERATED BY TENANTS AND CROPPERS, 1920, 1925, 1930, 1935

There was not a decade between 1890 and 1930 in which the number of tenant farmers did not increase more rapidly than that of owners. The largest increase came between 1890 and 1900. From 1920 to 1930, this country had a new experience in seeing its total number of farms decline, but even then tenant farms increased.

During this period tenancy (Figure 137) has also shown a tendency to spread. In 1880, there were 180 counties in which at least half the farms were tenant-operated—practically all in the South. In 1935, there were 890 such counties blanketing the Cotton Belt and spreading over the fertile parts of the Corn Belt. The number of counties in which half or more of the farm land was leased increased from 403 in 1910 to 1,007 in 1935. Nor is this all. Many heavily mortgaged farmers who are in financial difficulties have no more equity in their farms than tenants renting on shares. An increasing proportion of farm operators have been sharing the income from the land with landlords and mortgage holders. In 1890, American farmers owned 59 percent of their farms, after subtracting indebtedness. By 1930 this ratio had declined to 42 percent.

The trend toward tenancy, as H. A. Turner points out, must be accepted as a phase of the unequal distribution of wealth and income, making its appearance in the ownership of land as we passed from the frontier to a system of closed resources. Farm tenancy tends to increase as the frontier disappears. Free land and democratic rural institutions in most of the country have retarded this segregation of labor from capital in agriculture as contrasted with the situation in industry, but the trend toward such segregation is becoming clear.[4]

TENANCY BY AGE OF OPERATORS

Figure 138 shows the increasing extent to which farmers, both old and young, in twenty years have had to accept status as tenants in order to farm at all. We expect to find in most States that half the farmers under 25 are tenants, for it has been necessary for young men to gain capital and experience by renting land. The increasing number of States in which half the farmers over 35 are tenants shows the retardation in the rate of climbing the tenure ladder.

Studies of tenure changes by age of operators over a period of time thus serve to indicate something of the extent of both retardation in the rate of progress up the tenure ladder and of migration to other nonfarm pursuits. Figure 139 shows that from 1910 to 1930 older farmers increased, younger farmers decreased, and tenancy increased among all ages. In these twenty years the number of farmers under 35 decreased by 412,000 while those aged 55 and over increased 238,000. In 16 southern States in which they are reported by color, white tenants and croppers under 35 increased by 23,000, colored tenants and croppers by 21,000. White owner farmers decreased by 129,000, colored owners decreased by 20,000. Apparently more young white farmers in the South than formerly are failing

[4] Turner, *op. cit.*, pp. 1-2.

FIGURE 138. THE INCREASE IN FARM TENANCY BY AGE OF FARMERS,
UNITED STATES, 1910-1930

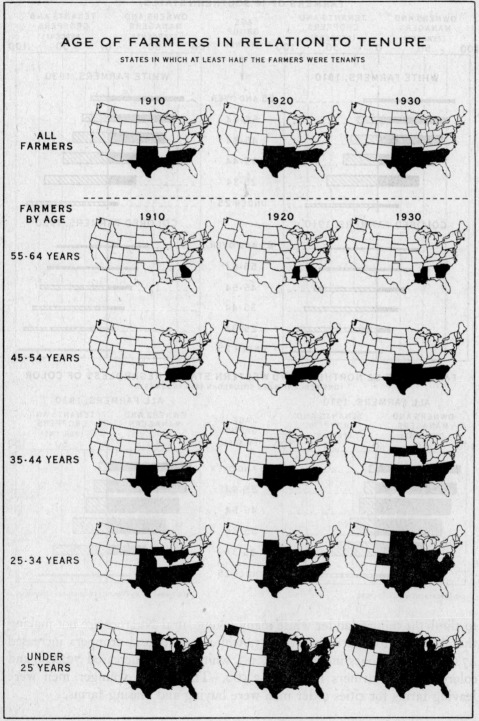

AGE OF FARMERS IN RELATION TO TENURE

STATES IN WHICH AT LEAST HALF THE FARMERS WERE TENANTS

FIGURE 139. AGE AND COLOR OF FARMERS IN RELATION TO
TENURE, 1910 AND 1930

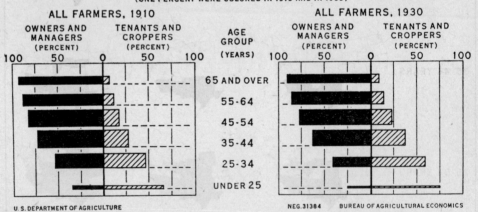

to climb the tenure ladder while many young rural Negroes are not making
the attempt. For farmers over 55, white tenants and croppers increased
47,000, colored ones increased 19,000, white owners increased 72,000, and
colored owner farmers increased 2,500. Thus while younger men were
leaving farms for cities older men were buying and leasing farms.

CHANGES 1930-1940

Tenancy, like poverty and unemployment, has come to be regarded as a major social ill. Accordingly, it offers something of a puzzle to find that the agricultural depression of the period 1930-1940 brought the first distinct reversal in the drift toward tenancy in this country since 1880. In the depression decade tenancy declined from 42.4 to 38.7 percent in the Nation and from 55.8 to 49.2 percent in the Southeast.

These figures need some degree of explanation. In spite of depression, the total number of farms in the United States declined less than 3.5 percent from 1930 to 1940. This would appear to indicate extraordinary stability in the face of the economic reverses of the period. When examined on a regional basis (Figure 140), it is found that this stability is due to the averaging of diverse trends. Some New England and Pacific Coast States increased the number of their farms as much as 15 to 20 percent. Farms in the Northwest, Southwest, and Southeast declined, losing as many as 14 percent of their number in Colorado, Texas, and Georgia. In the Southeast slight increases were found in only four States, Florida, Kentucky, Virginia, and Tennessee.

Thus, while the total number of farm operators in the Nation showed

FIGURE 140. PERCENTAGE CHANGE IN THE NUMBER OF FARMS, UNITED STATES, 1930-1940

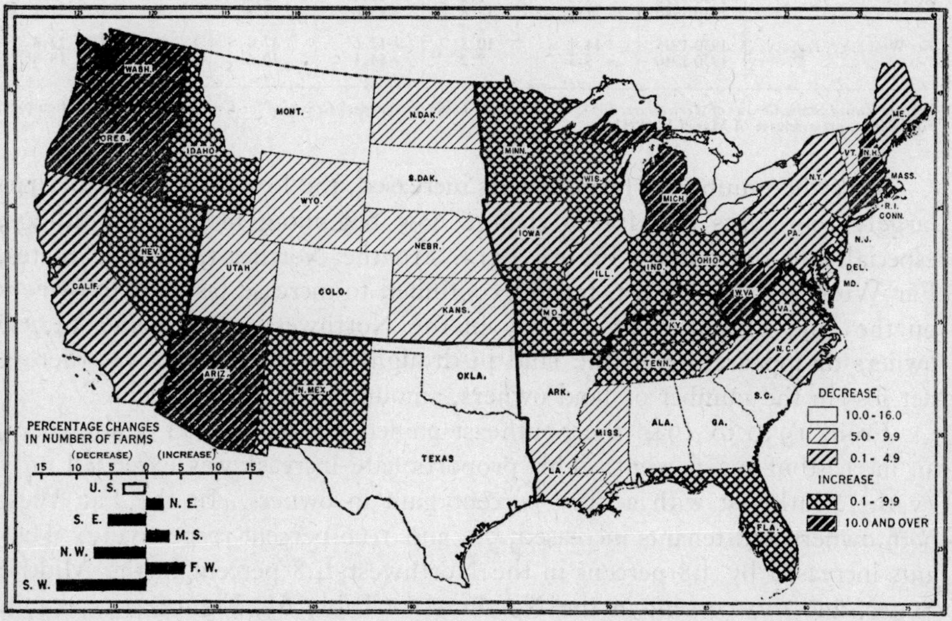

Source: *Sixteenth Census of the United States, 1940*, Agriculture, First Series, United States Summary, Table V.

surprising stability, their decrease of only 3.1 percent concealed several diverse trends (Table 65). Three regions gained in number of farm operators—the Northeast by 2.5 percent, the Middle States by 3.1 percent, and the Far West by 5.5 percent; three regions lost—the Southeast by 5.4 percent, the Northwest by 7.4 percent and the Southwest by 12.7 percent (Table 65). Figure 140 shows the changes in number of farms associated with this movement. Arizona and Massachusetts led with 30.3 and 24.6 percent increases respectively; Georgia and Texas on the other hand lost over 15 percent of their 1930 farms by 1940.

TABLE 65. PERCENTAGE CHANGE IN NUMBER OF FARM OPERATORS BY COLOR AND TENURE, UNITED STATES AND THE SIX MAJOR REGIONS, 1930-1940

Region	Period	All farm operators	Owners	Managers	All tenants	Croppers	Colored operators
		Percent change	Percent change	Percent change	Percent change	Percent change	Percent change
UNITED STATES.........	1930-1935	8.3	9.3	−13.9	7.5	− 7.7	− 6.6
	1930-1940	− 3.1	3.7	−35.0	−11.4	−30.3	−21.5
Northeast.............	1930-1935	15.8	13.6	−14.4	31.8	34.4	4.6
	1930-1940	2.5	2.5	−39.0	7.9	−19.2	− 8.6
Southeast.............	1930-1935	6.7	11.7	−12.8	2.9	− 3.9	− 6.1
	1930-1940	− 5.4	9.2	−27.3	−16.7	−23.6	−20.6
Southwest............	1930-1935	4.0	12.2	3.6	− 1.8	−28.6	−14.6
	1930-1940	−12.7	10.1	− 2.5	−28.8	−64.5	−31.1
Middle States..........	1930-1935	10.2	6.8	−19.1	18.2	−	1.4
	1930-1940	3.1	2.7	−32.8	4.8	−	−23.6
Northwest.............	1930-1935	5.3	1.2	−21.4	12.6	−	7.2
	1930-1940	− 7.4	−13.8	−43.0	3.8	−	−21.7
Far West.............	1930-1935	14.4	10.5	−12.6	37.3	−	22.8
	1930-1940	5.5	7.2	−54.1	10.6	−	18.8

Source: *United States Census of Agriculture, 1935*, III, Chap. 3, Table 6; *Sixteenth Census of the United States, 1940*, Agriculture, First Series, press release of March 18, 1941.

Since the number of farm owners increased, the loss from 1930 to 1940 largely represents the drastic change now beginning in tenant holdings, especially in the South (Figure 141). In the Northeast, Middle States, Far West, and Northwest, tenants continued to increase faster than owners on the land (Figure 142). Only in the Northwest where some 54,700 owners disappeared from the land in drought and depression, was there a net loss in the number of land owners, amounting to 13.8 percent.

From 1930 to 1940 the Southeast gained almost 97,000 new owners, an increase of 9.2 percent. This proportionate increase was exceeded only by the Southwest with a 10.1 percent gain in owners. In the Far West both owners and tenants increased, 7.2 and 10.6 percent respectively. Tenants increased by 3.8 percent in the Northwest, 4.8 percent in the Middle States, and 7.9 percent in the Northeast. (Table 65, Figures 141, 142).

The figures thus indicate that practically all the Nation's losses in farm

FIGURE 141. PERCENTAGE CHANGE IN NUMBER OF TENANTS, UNITED STATES, 1930-1940

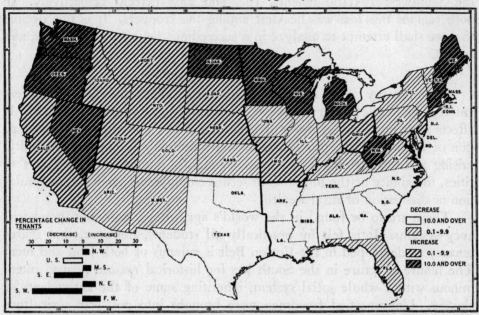

Source: *Sixteenth Census of the United States, 1940*, Agriculutre, First Series, Press Release of March 18, 1941.

FIGURE 142. PERCENTAGE CHANGE IN THE NUMBER OF FARM OWNERS, UNITED STATES, 1930-1940

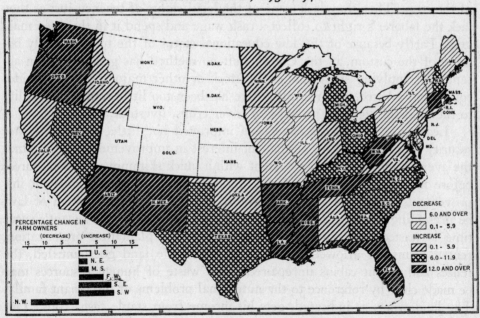

Source: *Statistical Abstracts of the United States*, 1940, p. 645; 1941, p. 682.

tenants occurred in the southern regions. The Southeast lost 223,200 and the Southwest 125,400 tenants, 16.7 and 28.8 percent respectively. In both regions this loss was heaviest among the croppers. It is this decline that we shall attempt to analyze in a succeeding chapter on race, class, and tenure.

TENANCY AS A SOCIAL PROBLEM

Farm tenancy carries many implications that are so diverse in the different regions of the country that we can hardly do more than list them. It affects such problems as those of balancing production with the consumption of farm products, providing for soil conservation, interfarm mobility, raising and maintaining educational standards, migration from farms to cities, the ability of the migrants to secure employment, and the accumulation or dissipation of rural wealth.

There are to be found in the world's agriculture, no doubt, good tenancy systems. It is felt by practically all students, however, that share-tenancy as developed in the Cotton Belt is ruinous of both land and men. The tenure structure in the South has for historical reasons proved coterminous with a whole social system, inheriting some of the antecedents of slavery. Unpropertied freedmen were brought into post-war agriculture on the cropper level and white farmers in competition with them soon acquired similar economic, legal, and even social status.

In law and actual practice then, both share-tenants and croppers in the region stand halfway between real tenants and laborers paid with a share of the crop. Thus they lack some of the legal rights of tenancy just as they lack the laborer's right to collect a cash wage and spend it in the open markets. Partly because of the low educational status of the tenant, partly because of the custom, in the Cotton Belt no method has generally been accepted of applying share-rent to livestock or other major products besides cotton and tobacco. Accordingly, there has been too little return of fertility to the land through the growing of cover crops, livestock, etc.

Leasing arrangements have been improved but little, and, with little security of tenure and no permanent interest in improvements in the land, the average tenant has been content with a quick skimming of its resources before he moves to another farm. Indeed, to incorporate permanent improvements in land or buildings would, under the present system of law, be presenting a free gift to the landlord. Thus much of the tenant's spare time is wasted and outside of the really stable plantation organization, rented farms are allowed to run down while the land goes untilled, the fences and tenant cabins unrepaired. The waste of human resources may be made clear by reference to the nutritional problems of the tenant family. The landowner, as indicated, gets his income from staple cash crops. Unless exceptional, he does not devote much of his supervision and financing to seeing that the tenant produces the fruits, meats, milk, and vegetables needed to feed his family. If any of these crops produced a marketable surplus they would offer a problem in share rent as well as interfere with the main business of producing staples. Moreover the tenants, caught in the staple routine and steeped in the need for cash in an economy of book credit, rarely acquire the means, the training, or possibly the inclination, to produce an adequate supply of food or feed crops. Considered in connection with the price level, these conditions help explain why the reduction in staples during the depression was followed by the dismissal of tenants rather than their transfer to other crops.

Measured by the returns to laborers, croppers, and share tenants, the South's agrarian economy represents the most uneconomic utilization of a large labor force to be found in our country. The tenant families on the southern plantations, studied by T. J. Woofter, Jr., in 1934, had an average net income of $309, or $73 per person, for a year's work. Share croppers received $312, or $71 per person, but wage hands had a net income of only $180 per family. The average for croppers ranged from $38 to $87 per person. An annual income of $38 per person was equal to slightly more than ten cents a day![5]

In a study of Negro croppers in Alabama, Harold Hoffsommer found that three-fourths of those who started as croppers never rose above that status and that only one-tenth rose to be owners.[6] Low income and the failure to accumulate wealth is of course the crux of the matter. Here Hoffsommer, in a study of 700 cropper families, found that they "broke even" during 45 percent of the total years, lost money during 30 percent, and cleared some profit above all expenses in 25 percent. Of 3,000 current cropper families studied, he found 40 percent indebted to their present landlords with a debt of more than one year's standing averaging more than $80. He estimated that this was the condition of one-third of the croppers in the State and concluded that the share cropper cannot expect from his labor more than a bare living in his characteristic situation of dependence on the landlord and time merchant for credit for family living, tools, work stock, and access to the land.

The labor force found in all tenure groups has been accumulated and retained on the land by a combination of high fertility and lack of alternative opportunities. It is both a population problem and an economic prob-

---

[5] T. J. Woofter, *Landlord and Tenant on the Cotton Plantation*, W.P.A. Division of Social Research, Washington, 1936, pp. xxvi-xxvii, ch. VI.

[6] H. C. Hoffsommer, *Landlord-Tenant Relations and Relief in Alabama.* Research Bulletin, Series II, No. 9, FERA (Washington, D. C., 1935, mimeographed).

lem. In the beginning it is likely that crops in the South demanded more labor per unit of cultivation than those elsewhere. Certainly as mechanization progressed in other areas, the concentration of labor on southern farms became more apparent. In terms of efficient practices and market adjustments, it seems likely that the Southeast faces a rationalization of its labor system that is long overdue. Increased mechanization, shifts from row crops to forage, livestock, and other forms of agriculture may serve to increase the acreage tended per operator and thus increase the farmer's income, but it will displace tenant operators from southern farms. In the next chapter we shall consider how such movements have affected race, class, and tenure groups.

CHAPTER 16

RACE, CLASS AND TENURE

THE PRECEDING chapter on the tenure status of the farm population of the Southeast serves here to introduce a discussion of the changing structure of race and class on the land. As an important population element in the South the Negro began on the land. This chapter involves a discussion of the economic mobility of the Negro. The present pattern of settlement on the land, developed during the 80 years since abolition, is a function of both racial competition and over-all economic factors.

RACE AND STATUS ON THE LAND

Race is an important element affecting land tenure throughout the South, the only area in which Negro farmers are found in appreciable numbers. The proportion of tenancy is still much less among the white farmers of the census South than among the colored farmers, although white tenancy is increasing. Thus in 1940, 41 percent of the census South's white farmers were tenants as against 75 percent of the Negro farmers. On the other hand, the rate of tenancy among Negroes has increased very little. It was 75 percent in 1900, 77 percent in 1930, and again 75 percent in 1940. From 1900 to 1930 tenancy for white farmers had increased from 36 to 46 percent and then declined to 41 percent in 1940 in the census South. In total numbers, white tenants exceeded colored by 942,655 to 506,638 in 1940. Thus about two-thirds of all tenants in the census South were white in 1940.

In the Southeast proper, Negroes constituted in 1940 but a little more than one-fourth, 26.9 percent, of the total number of farm operators (Table 66). White owners and managers, amounting to more than one million, made up the largest single group in agriculture, 44.5 percent of all farm operators. The white share and cash tenants constituted the next largest group, 19.3 percent. The largest group of colored operators were croppers, 12.5 percent of the total, followed by share and cash tenants, con-

[231]

TABLE 66. NUMBER AND PERCENTAGE DISTRIBUTION OF ALL FARM OPERATORS BY RACE AND TENURE GROUPS, SOUTHEAST, 1940

Race and tenure groups	Southeast Number	Percentage distribution	Virginia Number	Percentage distribution	North Carolina Number	Percentage distribution	South Carolina Number	Percentage distribution	Georgia Number	Percentage distribution	Florida Number	Percentage distribution
All farm operators	2,259,030	100.0	174,885	100.0	278,276	100.0	137,558	100.0	216,033	100.0	62,248	100.0
Owners and managers	1,148,534	50.9	127,778	73.1	154,800	55.6	60,374	43.9	86,183	39.9	46,580	74.8
Share and cash tenants	616,970	27.3	30,869	17.6	63,176	22.7	43,710	31.8	68,916	31.9	12,261	19.7
Croppers	493,526	21.8	16,238	9.3	60,300	21.7	33,474	24.3	60,934	28.2	3,407	5.5
All white operators	1,650,440	73.1	139,795	79.9	218,008	78.2	76,251	55.4	156,901	72.6	52,490	84.3
Owners and managers	1,004,226	44.5	105,492	60.3	136,526	49.0	43,261	31.4	76,129	35.2	41,025	65.9
Share and cash tenants	435,306	19.3	23,962	13.7	47,985	17.2	21,577	15.7	49,141	22.8	9,120	14.6
Croppers	210,908	9.3	10,341	5.9	33,497	12.0	11,413	8.3	31,631	14.6	2,345	3.8
All nonwhite operators	608,590	26.9	35,090	20.1	60,268	21.8	61,307	44.6	59,132	27.4	9,758	15.7
Owners and managers	144,308	6.4	22,286	12.8	18,274	6.6	17,113	12.5	10,054	4.7	5,555	8.9
Share and cash tenants	181,664	8.0	6,907	3.9	15,191	5.5	22,133	16.1	19,775	9.1	3,141	5.1
Croppers	282,618	12.5	5,897	3.4	26,803	9.7	22,061	16.0	29,303	13.6	1,062	1.7

Race and tenure groups	Kentucky Number	Percentage distribution	Tennessee Number	Percentage distribution	Alabama Number	Percentage distribution	Mississippi Number	Percentage distribution	Arkansas Number	Percentage distribution	Louisiana Number	Percentage distribution
All farm operators	252,894	100.0	247,617	100.0	231,746	100.0	291,092	100.0	216,674	100.0	150,007	100.0
Owners and managers	169,070	66.9	147,882	59.7	95,522	41.2	98,273	33.8	101,232	46.7	60,840	40.6
Share and cash tenants	60,291	23.8	58,245	23.5	94,854	40.9	67,336	23.1	67,776	31.3	49,536	33.0
Croppers	23,533	9.3	41,490	16.8	41,370	17.9	125,483	43.1	47,666	22.0	39,631	26.4
All white operators	247,347	97.8	219,642	88.7	158,382	68.3	131,552	45.2	159,649	73.7	90,423	60.3
Owners and managers	165,900	65.6	140,986	56.9	79,809	34.4	74,802	25.7	90,660	41.8	49,636	33.1
Share and cash tenants	59,421	23.5	51,036	20.6	56,537	24.4	33,377	11.5	54,445	25.2	28,705	19.1
Croppers	22,026	8.7	27,620	11.2	22,036	9.5	23,373	8.0	14,544	6.7	12,082	8.1
All nonwhite operators	5,547	2.2	27,975	11.3	73,364	31.7	159,340	54.8	57,025	26.3	59,584	39.7
Owners and managers	3,170	1.3	6,896	2.8	15,713	6.8	23,471	8.1	10,572	4.9	11,204	7.5
Share and cash tenants	870	0.3	7,209	2.9	38,317	16.5	33,959	11.6	13,331	6.1	20,831	13.9
Croppers	1,507	0.6	13,870	5.6	19,334	8.4	102,110	35.1	33,122	15.3	27,549	18.3

Source: *Sixteenth Census of the United States, 1940*, Agriculture, First Series, United States Summary, Table VI, Supplement for Southern States.

stituting 8 percent, and colored owners constituting 6.4 percent of all operators. Even here the white croppers, 9.3 percent of the total, exceeded each of the last two colored groups. Table 66 shows the distribution by States for the Southeast.

The significance of the share that Negroes now hold in southern agriculture cannot be understood apart from the historical trends. The whites have been increasing their representation on the land by moving into the lower levels of tenure. The Negroes in the period from emancipation to around 1930 were engaged in improving their status on the land and in leaving agriculture for other economic opportunity. The resulting urban migration of the Negro was considered in Chapters 9 and 10, but Table 67 serves to show the trend by regions. After 1910 the Negro rural popu-

TABLE 67. NEGRO RURAL AND URBAN POPULATION BY CENSUS
REGIONS, 1900-1940

Areas	(In thousands)				
	1900	1910	1920	1930	1940
Census South*					
Rural.....................	6,558	6,895	6,661	6,395	6,289
Urban......................	1,356	1,854	2,251	2,966	3,616
Northern and Western States					
Rural.....................	274	248	242	302	323
Urban......................	637	830	1,309	2,228	2,637

*Includes the census divisions, South Atlantic, East South Central, and West South Central.
Source: T. J. Woofter, Jr., "The Status of Racial and Ethnic Groups" in *Recent Social Trends in the United States* (New York: McGraw-Hill, 1933), p. 567; *Sixteenth Census of the United States, 1940*, Series P-6.

TABLE 68. NUMBER AND PERCENTAGE DISTRIBUTION OF FARM OPERATORS BY
RACE AND TENURE, AND NUMBER AND PERCENTAGE CHANGE,
CENSUS SOUTH, 1920-1940

Race and tenure groups	1920		1940		Change 1920-1940	
	Number	Percent distribution	Number	Percent distribution	Number	Percent
All farm operators..................	3,206,664	100.0	3,007,170	100.0	−199,494	− 6.2
Owners and managers.............	1,615,543	50.4	1,557,877	51.8	− 57,666	− 3.6
Tenants........................	1,591,121	49.6	1,449,293	48.2	−141,828	− 8.9
All white operators.................	2,283,750	71.2	2,326,904	77.4	43,154	1.9
Owners and managers.............	1,396,184	43.5	1,384,249	46.0	− 11,935	− 0.9
Tenants........................	887,566	27.7	942,655	31.4	55,089	6.2
All nonwhite operators..............	922,914	28.8	680,266	22.6	−242,648	−26.3
Owners and managers.............	219,359	6.9	173,628	5.8	− 45,731	−20.9
Tenants........................	703,555	21.9	506,638	16.8	−196,917	−28.0

Source: *Fourteenth Census of the United States, 1920*, Agriculture, V, Table 16; *Sixteenth Census of the United States, 1940*, Agriculture, First Series, Table VI.

lation of the South, in spite of high rural birth rates, showed a decline of more than half a million. At the same time Negroes in both northern and southern cities have grown by some 400 to 900 thousands each decade after 1910.

While Negro rural population reached its high point in 1910, Negro population on the land in the census South was greatest in 1920 when nonwhites owned or managed, in round figures, 219,000 farms and operated 704,000 others as tenants. By 1940 nonwhite owners and managers declined to 174,000 and tenants to 507,000 (Table 68). The South's white owners in this same period (1920-1940) declined from 1,396,000 to 1,384,000 while white tenants increased from 888,000 to 943,000. Thus, while colored tenants were decreasing by 197,000, white tenants were increasing by 55,000. In this period of increasing difficulty in agriculture, total nonwhite farm operators in the area decreased some 243,000; total white farm operators increased by 43,000 (Table 68).

In seven southeastern cotton States,[1] T. J. Woofter, Jr., has traced these changes by race and tenure since emancipation (Table 69). Here, total males engaged in agriculture increased from about 1,100,000 in 1860 to 2,100,000 in 1930, or 91 percent. This was for the most part a white increase since the Negroes in farming increased only about 28,000 or 3 percent, as against a white increment of 940,000 or nearly 300 percent. In 1860 Negroes made up 71.3 percent of those on the land; in 1930 they constituted only 39.7 percent.[2]

TABLE 69. COLOR AND TENURE STATUS OF MALES ENGAGED IN AGRICULTURE* IN SEVEN SOUTHEASTERN COTTON STATES,** 1860, 1910, 1930

| Color and tenure status | Males engaged in agriculture (in thousands) | | | | | |
| | 1860† (Estimated) | | 1910 | | 1930 | |
	Number	Percent	Number	Percent	Number	Percent
Total in agriculture......	1,132	100.0	2,105	100.0	2,102	100.0
White..................	325	28.7	1,180	56.0	1,267	60.3
Owners..............	325	....	527	25.1	484	23.0
Tenants.............	...	....	418	19.8	581	27.7
Laborers............	...	....	235	11.1	202	9.6
Negro.................	807	71.3	925	44.0	835	39.7
Owners..............	...	....	124	5.9	107	5.1
Tenants.............	...	....	477	22.7	486	23.1
Laborers............	807	....	324	15.4	242	11.5

*Exclusive of laborers on home farm.
**Alabama, Arkansas, Georgia, Louisiana, Mississippi, North Carolina, and South Carolina.
†In 1860 there was a very small number of free Negro and white tenants.
Source: T. J. Woofter, Jr., *Landlord and Tenant on the Cotton Plantation* (Washington, D. C.: WPA, Rural Research Division 1936), p. 11; *United States Census of Agriculture*.

In this time two entirely new classes came into being in southern agriculture—the white tenants and white hired laborers. Together these numbered in 1930 in the seven States 783,000 white agricultural workers who were competing with some 728,000 Negro tenants and laborers for a place on the land.

Negro farmers lost their proportional representation on the land during this period but markedly improved their agricultural position. Though their status upon emancipation was purely that of laborers, by 1930 only 29 percent of the Negro males in Agriculture were laborers. Fifty-eight percent had become tenants and 13 percent were owners. But among the white farm operators the rise of a tenantry has meant a great decrease in the proportion of ownership. After 1910 white owners declined from 527,000 to 484,000 in 1930.[3]

Thus until 1930 the result of competition for the land presents a pic-

[1] North Carolina, South Carolina, Georgia, Alabama, Mississippi, Louisiana, Arkansas.
[2] T. J. Woofter, Jr., *Landlord and Tenant on the Cotton Plantation* (Washington, D. C.: WPA, Social Research Division, 1936), pp. 11-12.
[3] *Ibid.*, pp. 12-13.

ture not altogether unfavorable to the Negro farmer. Present Negro owners and tenants are all the descendants of slave laborers, while the white tenants and laborers are children and grandchildren, in the main, of landowners. For the Negro, tenancy, as Woofter points out, was a step in advance of the previous generation; for the whites, it was a step backward.

Only about one-third of those gainfully employed among the Negroes remained in agriculture in 1930. The changing racial distribution of population in the South not only shows this cityward movement, it also indicates that among those remaining on the land there has been a filtering out from the main black belts into the white areas. The shrinkage of the black belts is perfectly obvious, for their migrants have contributed to both movements. Of 53 counties, all rural, having over 75 percent Negro population in 1910, only 18 remained in that category in 1930.

Monroe N. Work, in a careful analysis, showed a shrinkage of the black belts from 167,046 square miles in 1860 to 166,083 square miles in 1900 to 106,581 square miles in 1930. This was a decrease of 36 percent in seventy years. These black counties once held less than one-fifth of the South's white population and more than one-half (55.8 percent) of the total Negro population. By 1930 the black counties had dropped to 6.6 percent of the total white population and less than one-third (31.4 percent) of the total Negro population.[4]

In the black counties in the last 70 years the density per square mile of rural population changed as follows:

	1860	1900	1930
White	6.9	10.7	11.6
Negro	12.6	21.9	22.9

The density per square mile of the rural population in the white counties showed the following change:

	1860	1900	1930
White	10.9	16.7	22.5
Negro	2.4	2.8	3.7

Work concluded that while there had been a definite piling up of rural Negro population in black belt counties, there had been a movement into white county areas. There are 444 white counties in the South which showed an increase in their Negro population from 1920 to 1930. From this movement there resulted a more even distribution of the Negro population over the rural South. On the basis of suitability of the land for cotton production this seems a movement from richer to poorer soils.[5]

[4] Monroe N. Work, "Racial Factors and Economic Forces in Land Tenure in the South," *Social Forces*, XV (December, 1936), 206.

[5] *Ibid.*, pp. 207-208.

Negroes have not taken a large part in the westward movement of cotton production. Of the 600,000 farms in Texas and Oklahoma in 1940, a little over 66,000 were operated by Negroes—some 11 percent. Practically all of these are found in the eastern parts of the States. Slaves were introduced in east Texas before the State gained its independence, while it is well known that in Oklahoma the five civilized tribes held slaves and for that reason cast their lot with the Confederacy. The Eastern Coastal Plains of Texas and the small Alluvial Area of Oklahoma showed 25 percent of their farm operators colored, Texas Black Prairies and Oklahoma Eastern Prairies had 15 percent colored in 1930. No other cotton areas in the two States ranked as high as five percent. In South Texas, for example, the development of Mexican casual labor has left little place for the entrance of the Negro cropper.

LARGE LANDHOLDINGS AND THE PLANTATION

The obverse side of tenancy is the concentration of land in large holdings by the planters. Some studies have been made of large holdings in the plantation area. The 1900 Census returned landlords according to the number of rented farms owned and a special tabulation of plantations was made from the 1910 Census. Figure 143 shows the plantation areas and Table 70 gives the figures for resident landlords owning five or more tenant farms in seven main plantation States. In 1900 some 28,465 landlords owned 304,156 tenant farms or an average of 10.7 apiece. In 1910 there were 35,621 landlords who owned 370,728 rented farms, or an average of 10.4 apiece. The table indicates a close correspondence between the two periods in the concentration of ownership in blocks of 5 to 9 farms, 10 to 19 farms, and 20 farms and over. Thus those owning 5 to 9 farms made up two-thirds of the landlord group and owned two-fifths of the rented farms. On the other hand those owning 20 or more farms made up less than 10 percent of the landlords but held approximately 30 percent of the tenant farms.

A trend toward increased concentration of holdings is difficult to show because of the tendency to change plantation laborers to the cropper status. Table 70 indicates a 25 percent increase from 1900 to 1910 in the number of landlords and a 21.8 percent increase in the number of tenant farms owned in blocks of five or more. The table shows comparable increases in all ranges, but there is no method of showing whether additional landlords came from cash renters of large tracts or consisted of new purchasers of plantations. Nor can we tell from census data whether landlords from 1900 to 1910 purchased additional tenant farms or saw their laborers climb from the status of farm hands to that of croppers.

FIGURE 143. THE PLANTATION AREAS OF THE UNITED STATES BY MAJOR CROP SYSTEMS BY COUNTIES

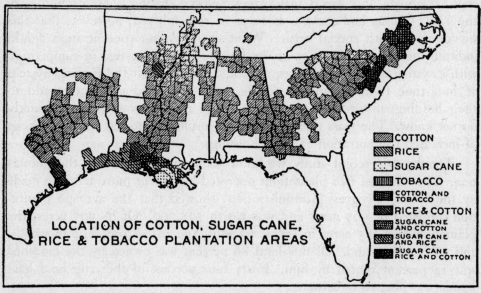

COTTON
RICE
SUGAR CANE
TOBACCO
COTTON AND TOBACCO
RICE & COTTON
SUGAR CANE AND COTTON
SUGAR CANE AND RICE
SUGAR CANE RICE AND COTTON

LOCATION OF COTTON, SUGAR CANE, RICE & TOBACCO PLANTATION AREAS

Source: From a map prepared by the U. S. Department of Agriculture, based largely on the Special Census of Plantations, 1910.

TABLE 70. CONCENTRATION OF OWNERSHIP OF TENANT FARMS IN SEVEN COTTON STATES,* 1900-1910

	All classes	5-9 Farms	10-19 Farms	20 Farms and over
Tenant Farms, 1900—Numerical Groups of:				
Number of:				
Landlords	28,465	18,974	6,811	2,680
Tenant farms	304,156	124,169	87,931	92,056
Percentage of:				
Landlords	100	66.6	23.9	9.5
Tenant farms	100	40.8	28.9	30.3
Tenant Farms, 1910				
Number of:				
Landlords	35,621	23,831	8,525	3,265
Tenant farms	370,728	151,153	110,705	108,870
Percentage of:				
Landlords	100	66.9	23.9	9.2
Tenant farms	100	40.7	29.8	29.5
Increases, 1900-1910				
Number of:				
Landlords	7,156	4,857	1,714	585
Tenant farms	66,571	26,984	22,774	16,814
Percentage of:				
Landlords	25.1	25.6	23.7	21.8
Tenant farms	21.8	23.3	25.9	18.2

*South Carolina, Georgia, Alabama, Mississippi, Arkansas, Louisiana, Texas.
Source: "Concentration of Landownership," *United States Census of Agriculture, 1900:* "Special Census of Plantations, 1910," *Plantation Farming in the United States* (Washington, D. C.: Government Printing Office, 1916).

In 1920 the Bureau of Agricultural Economics reported on landlord's holdings of five or more rented farms in special areas.[6] In every State except Oklahoma and Texas this survey showed greater concentration than the 1900 Census had shown. It must be remembered, however, that this survey dealt with special areas. Whether increasing concentration would indicate the greater efficiency of the landlord-tenant system in competition with a system of small holdings, or would indicate that the Federal system of long-time farm credits enacted in 1916 has aided planters to add to their holdings instead of assisting tenants to rise to ownership, we frankly do not know. The mass data at hand are insufficient to test this hypothesis of increased concentration of large holdings.[7]

Thanks to a recent study we know somewhat more about the plantation. The study of 646 plantations operated by five or more families made by the Works Progress Administration[8] showed that the average plantation consisted of 907 acres and was worth $28,700. Of its 907 acres, the plantation had 385 acres in crops, 63 idle, 162 in pasture, 214 in woods, and 83 in waste land. Of this land 86 percent was owned by the landlord and 14 percent rented by him. Forty-four percent of the crop land harvested was planted to cotton.

The typical plantation was occupied by the landlord and 14 additional families divided as follows: 3 wage hands, 8 croppers, 2 share tenants, and 1 renter. Two of these were white and 12 colored. The average age of family heads was 41 years; the average size of the family was 4, of whom 2 were employed on the farm.

The average gross income from the plantation was $9,500. Seven thousand came from the sale of crops and livestock products, $900 from AAA payments, $200 from land rented, and $1,400 from home-grown food. The net income amounted to $6,000, of which $2,600 went to the landlord and $3,400 to the tenants. Allowing the landlord 6 percent on his investment, this meant $850 for the landlord's labor or a capital return of two dollars per acre.

Credit and interest charges loom large for both landlord and tenant. Nearly one-half the landlords had long time debts averaging over 40 percent of the appraised value of their land, buildings, animals, and machinery. This trend is everywhere on the increase. From 1910 to 1928, the mortgage debt in seven Southeastern States almost quadrupled. Furthermore, 52 percent of the owners had short-term debts to meet current expenses on

[6] "Farm Ownership and Farm Tenancy," *Agricultural Yearbook* (Washington, D. C.: Department of Agriculture, 1923), pp. 529-532.

[7] See Rupert B. Vance, "Cotton and Tenancy," in *Problems of the Cotton Economy* (Dallas, Texas: The Arnold Foundation, 1936), especially pp. 30-31.

[8] T. J. Woofter, Jr., *op. cit.*, p. xxxi.

the crop. The average amount borrowed was $2,300, just half the sum necessary to meet annual expenses. On these accounts, the interest rate ran high; 10 percent on government loans, 15 percent on bank loans, and 16 percent on merchants' accounts. Most of the credit was furnished by banks, government loans amounting to only 22 percent of the short-term credit. All government loans went to landlords since they held the only acceptable security—the crop lien. For the landlord, the combined interest on loans and mortgage debt amounted to almost as much as his net labor income, approximately $850 a year.

On a different level, the credit problems of the tenants are equally serious. The high interest charges that tenants pay on the advances that are given them depress their standard of living and prevent them from rising in the tenure ladder. The amount advanced tenants averaged $12.80 per month and ran over a period of seven months. A study of 112 croppers in North Carolina, outside the main plantation areas, showed that advances, mostly in cash, amounted to over 63 percent of the croppers' cash farm income, while the interest paid amounted to more than 10 percent of their total cash income.

RISE OF NEGRO OWNERS

Out of this situation an important class of Negro landowners has arisen in the South. In the rise of the first Negroes to ownership interracial cooperation as well as competition must have played its part. Emancipation saw different classes of slaves in different positions to come into ownership. Besides the free Negro who had been practically exiled from many regions of the Deep South, there were the sub-overseers, the domestics, the skilled and semiskilled artisans, with the crude field hands bringing up the rear. In areas like Virginia these more favored groups were encouraged to buy lands.

Whatever assistance Negroes encountered in a cotton system heavily weighted against peasant proprietorship, it seems safe to assume that economic factors offered barriers to an unpropertied group as great as those offered by racial attitudes. The rise of a Negro peasantry out of slavery to the ownership of 173,000 farms in the census South valued at 250 million dollars in 1940 remains, on all accounts, an outstanding fact in the history of race relations. As racial attitudes have tended to relax, economic conditions appear to have increased the difficulties facing cotton producers.

Land purchase by Negroes, Arthur F. Raper[9] has pointed out, is as much social ritual as economic transaction. It may follow several patterns. Often an old-style white landlord encourages a favorite tenant to buy a small portion on his holdings. Sometimes he makes such a provision in his will. A debt-ridden owner may sell to a tenant he trusts, or an absentee owner may grow tired of long-distance contacts and arrange a sale. In all such transactions competitive relations are absent. Agents of loan companies, banks, stores, etc., sell lands they have foreclosed but to the Negro buyer they lack one important quality: they cannot afford him the protecting wing of a strong white friend in the community. Newer patterns are more competitive and the new Negro more often makes the first overtures. In many communities he would still be regarded as foolhardy to bid in open competition at an auction or sheriff's sale, but if tactful he might find a white friend to bid for him.

Many things, accordingly, suggest that the rise of Negroes to landownership is determined partly by local considerations. In its economic aspects this movement is related to land values, which can best be studied on a regional basis. The matter of interracial attitudes, it is felt, can best be viewed on a community basis. The first is self-explanatory. In areas of concentrated ownership of productive cotton lands the dense Negro population is largely excluded from climbing into ownership by the higher prices prevailing. Areas of lower land prices offer economic opportunity; interracial cooperation of a kind begins the process; and a community of Negro owners is formed which may slowly add to itself.

There were in 1930, 187 counties in the South in which Negro ownercommunities were sufficiently dense to give the county 400 or more Negro owners. Virginia with 38 and Mississippi with 35 possessed the greatest number of clustered areas as measured in terms of counties. In the competitive situation Negroes rise to ownership mainly in the poorer land areas that skirt the main plantation zones. Here the proportion of Negro owners in 1930 was more than double that in the more specialized cotton zones. Thus in the Southeast in 1930 48.7 percent of farmers in the 30 main cotton zones were colored but only 11.2 percent owned their farms. In the other areas where only 32.4 percent of operators were colored as high as 22.6 percent owned their farms.[10]

Usually the Negro owner acquires land that is agriculturally less desirable than the average of his county. The type of land Negroes secure in competition was examined by racial comparison of average per acre values in the 62 counties, covering the main areas of Negro landownership. In only 9 of the 62 counties in 1930 did the Negroes' land values exceed the county average for farm lands. This condition was found in a group of long settled Virginia counties and in areas where the whites had largely left the

[9] Arthur F. Raper, *Preface to Peasantry* (Chapel Hill: University of North Carolina Press, 1936), p. 121.

[10] Rupert B. Vance, *The Negro Agricultural Worker*. Prepared for the Committee on Negroes and Economic Reconstruction (Nashville: Tennessee, 1935, mimeographed), Chap. III, p. 126, Table 1.

TABLE 71. COMPARISON OF WHITE TENANTS WITH NONWHITE FARM OWNERS AND TENANTS IN FARM ACREAGE, VALUES PER FARM AND PER ACRE, SOUTHEAST, 1940

Area	Acreage per farm			Per farm value of land and buildings			Per farm value of land			Per acre value of land			
	White tenants	Nonwhite operators		White tenants	Nonwhite operators		White tenants	Nonwhite operators		White tenants	Nonwhite operators		Ratio nonwhite tenants to owners per acre value of land
		All owners	Tenants		All owners	Tenants		All owners	Tenants		All owners	Tenants	
SOUTHEAST	72	58	38	$2,108	$1,393	$1,108	$1,524	$938	$833	$21	$16	$22	137.5
Virginia	90	46	59	3,005	1,368	1,476	1,901	730	974	21	16	17	106.2
North Carolina	62	48	47	2,449	1,667	1,946	1,733	1,107	1,457	28	23	31	134.8
South Carolina	71	47	45	2,174	1,202	1,270	1,507	794	930	21	17	21	123.5
Georgia	93	84	73	1,853	1,424	1,230	1,285	945	898	14	11	12	109.1
Florida	102	46	42	2,299	1,098	869	1,747	750	641	17	16	15	93.8
Kentucky	67	45	41	2,480	1,626	1,912	1,757	1,057	1,353	26	23	33	143.5
Tennessee	66	53	33	2,232	1,581	1,208	1,635	1,100	945	25	21	28	133.3
Alabama	73	70	42	1,652	1,208	764	1,234	851	574	17	12	14	116.7
Mississippi	59	74	27	1,346	1,341	897	1,005	977	677	17	13	25	192.3
Arkansas	80	63	26	2,080	1,561	1,013	1,631	1,179	794	20	19	31	163.2
Louisiana	56	51	28	2,081	1,435	1,042	1,635	1,060	823	29	21	29	138.1

Source: *Sixteenth Census of the United States, 1940*, Agriculture, First Series, Table VI, Supplement for Southern States.

land as in Beaufort, South Carolina, and Liberty, Georgia. In 35 of the 62, total average land values fell below $22.50 per acre; in 42 counties Negro land values fell below this margin.[11]

It is possible from census figures of 1940 (Table 71) to suggest how much Negro owners have advanced in economic status beyond their tenant colleagues. This comparison showed that colored owners uniformly exceeded the proverbial 40 acres by 18 acres while the tenants fell under it by 2 acres. Yet tenants uniformly exceeded owners in value of land by $22 to $16 per acre. The Negro owner usually has a better house, more equipment, and a larger farm that consisted, however, of poorer land, valued at less per acre.

Similar contrasts between tenants by race serve to bring out some of the possible effects of competition. This comparison shows that on the average Negro tenants tilled the more valuable land but white tenants operated the more valuable farms. This again was due to the larger acreage worked by white tenants. For the whole Southeast in 1940 the value of tenant land and buildings per acre averaged $29 for both whites and Negroes. In Virginia, Georgia, Florida, and Alabama, however, white tenants worked land of greater value per acre. The average value of land and buildings per farm in the Southeast was $2,108 for white tenants to $1,108 for Negro tenants. Table 71 shows variations by States for the Southeast.

Although the differences were not great, it seems the white tenants emerged with the better of the comparison. True, their farms seemed less

[11] *Ibid.*, pp. 166-176.

fertile on an acreage basis but they were larger, permitting more efficient operation. Their farm buildings, including residences, were of greater value, and they possessed more farm implements and machinery.

THE PATTERN OF INTERRACIAL AND CLASS SETTLEMENT

How integration alternates with but never completely gives way to segregation of the races on the land can be seen by reference to the accompanying maps. It was the historic fate of the Negro to be settled in the South's most fertile areas, those best suited to cotton production. White farmers on their side had no racial competition in their occupancy of the Appalachian Highlands and some upland areas. Outside these areas, farmers, white and black, owners, tenants, and croppers occupy the land with varying degrees of concentration.

White owners are thus much more numerous in the less productive area of hilly land and subsistence farming than in the Cotton Belt. Colored owners are not so numerous anywhere but stretch clear across the South wherever Negro farmers are found. White tenants owning working stock are more evenly distributed over the South than the tenure class of any race. Where colored tenants are numerous white tenants are generally few. Colored croppers are the most highly concentrated of all groups, being found mainly in the Yazoo Delta of the Mississippi and adjacent alluvial lands in Arkansas. Outside the Cotton Belt colored croppers hardly find employment but white tenants are widespread, being found even in areas of subsistence agriculture (Figures 144-149).

Many areas are still to be found in which Negroes occupy the land in overwhelming majority. Nine counties in the Mississippi Delta and ten in the Alabama Black Belt furnish areas in which 84 percent or more of all farm operators were colored in 1930. The Mississippi Site Bluffs and Uplands (11 counties), South Carolina Upper Coastal Plains (7 counties), and the Louisiana Bottoms (17 counties) furnish the other areas with a majority of Negro farm operators.[12]

Many of the main cotton areas in the Southwest have few Negro farmers. In the Southeast, the areas most largely given over to white operators are Flatwoods, Wiregrass, Limestone Valleys, and Piedmont areas which because of relative infertility or recent development were not settled with slaves. The Alabama Limestone Valleys (7 counties) and Wiregrass (8 counties) each had 76 percent white farmers. The Georgia Piedmont and Upper Coastal Plains (21 counties) and the Tennessee Bluff and Uplands (17 counties) show 65 percent or more white farmers. For the main cotton growing subregions in the Southeast, white farmers in 1930 made up 61.5 percent of all farm operators.

[12] For these areas with discussion of changes by migration see the author's chapter on The Old Cotton Belt, in Carter Goodrich, et al., *Migration and Economic Opportunity*, pp. 139-147.

FIGURES 144-149. FARM OPERATORS BY COLOR AND TENURE,
THE CENSUS, SOUTH, 1935

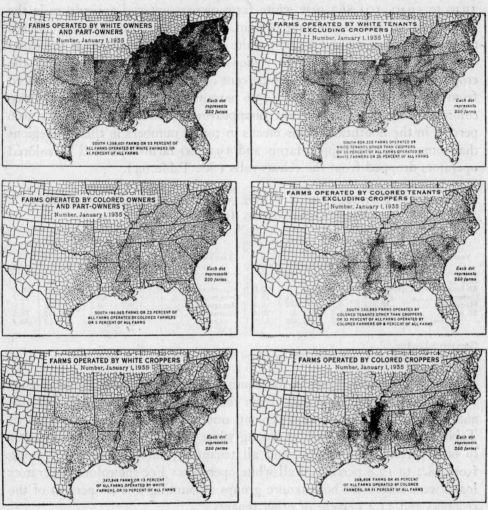

Source: Bureau of Agricultural Economics, U. S. Department of Agriculture, Negatives 31332-31337.

On the other hand, many agricultural areas of main Negro settlement are now entirely outside the cotton zones. Sea islands and coastal strips along South Carolina and Georgia furnish areas of unique Negro peasantry, small Negro yeomanry surviving in an area once given over to large rice and sea island cotton estates.

THE DEPRESSION TREND, 1930-1940

The decade of the great depression, as we have seen, reversed the trend toward tenancy. The impact of these changes, concentrated in the Southern regions, showed important racial differences. For the Nation farm owners increased by 3.7 percent; in the Southeast white owners and managers increased 10.9 percent but colored owners decreased by 3.7 percent. From 1930 to 1940, 101,862 new white farm owners entered agriculture in the Southeast—an increase of 11.4 percent. At the same time 151,925 colored tenants and croppers and 84,079 white croppers dropped out of the ranks (Table 72). In both southern regions the loss was heaviest among the croppers. In the Southwest 64.5 percent of the cropper farms disappeared from the rolls; in the Southeast, 23.6 percent. Losses were heaviest among colored operators, 31.1 percent disappearing in the Southwest and 20.6 percent in the Southeast. This means in round numbers in the two regions that some 234,300 cropper farms and 193,700 farms operated by colored operators dropped from the census rolls (See Table 64).

TABLE 72. DISTRIBUTION OF WHITE AND COLORED FARM OPERATORS BY TENURE, SOUTHEAST, 1930 AND 1940

Year and tenure	White		Colored		Year and tenure	White		Colored	
	Number	Percent	Number	Percent		Number	Percent	Number	Percent
1930					*1940*				
All farm operators .	1,622,695	100.0	766,111	100.0	All farm operators..	1,650,440	100.0	608,590	100.0
Owners............	894,377	55.1	149,354	19.5	Owners............	996,239	60.4	144,021	23.7
Managers.........	10,825	0.7	550	0.1	Managers.........	7,987	0.5	287	*
All tenants........	717,493	44.2	616,207	80.4	All tenants........	646,214	39.1	464,282	76.3
Croppers......	*294,987*	*18.2*	*351,409*	*45.9*	*Croppers......*	*210,908*	*12.8*	*282,618*	*46.4*

*Less than 0.1 percent.

Source: *Sixteenth Census of the United States, 1940*, Agriculture, First Series, press release of March 18, 1941.

The white tenant losses in the Southeast were concentrated among croppers, 28.5 percent disappearing from the lists. White share and cash tenants showed slight gains of 3 percent, numbering some 12,800. Thus as Table 72 shows, white owners among white operators increased from 55.1 to 60.4 percent of the total, and all tenants declined, croppers declining from 18.2 to 12.8 percent of all white operators. For the colored operators losses were severe for both tenure groups amounting to 19.6 percent of the croppers and 31.4 percent of other tenants.

In every Southeastern State white owners made the greatest gains, ranging from an increase of 6.4 percent in Alabama to one of 16.3 percent in Mississippi (Table 73). Negro owners lost 3.7 percent, gaining in only three states—South Carolina, Mississippi, and Louisiana. The greatest losses were those of the Negro share and cash tenants, losses that ranged from 17.3 percent in Virginia to over 40 percent in Mississippi, Arkansas, and Kentucky. White croppers also lost in every State, least in Virginia and North Carolina, but over 35 percent in South Carolina, Georgia, Alabama, and Arkansas. Negro croppers lost farms in every State—least in Mississippi and most in Georgia (41 percent), and Kentucky (52 percent).

TABLE 73. CHANGES IN LAND TENURE BY RACE, SOUTHEAST, 1930-1940

	White farm operators								
	Owners and managers			Share and cash tenants			Croppers		
State	1930	Change 1930-1940		1930	Change 1930-1940		1930	Change 1930-1940	
	Number	Number	Percent	Number	Number	Percent	Number	Number	Percent
SOUTHEAST.....	905,202	99,024	10.9	422,506	12,800	3.0	294,987	− 84,079	−28.5
Virginia........	98,115	7,377	7.5	22,366	1,596	7.1	10,456	− 115	− 1.1
North Carolina..	122,359	14,167	11.6	46,190	1,795	3.9	34,286	− 789	− 2.3
South Carolina..	39,100	4,161	10.6	23,513	− 1,936	− 8.2	17,893	− 6,480	−36.2
Georgia........	70,055	6,074	8.7	47,350	1,791	3.8	51,404	− 19,773	−38.5
Florida.........	36,564	4,461	12.2	7,936	1,184	14.9	3,423	− 1,078	−31.5
Kentucky......	153,888	12,012	7.8	56,373	3,048	5.4	27,134	− 5,108	−18.8
Tennessee......	124,271	16,715	13.4	52,503	− 1,467	− 2.8	33,745	− 6,125	−18.2
Alabama.......	75,021	4,788	6.4	50,983	5,554	10.9	37,562	− 15,526	−41.3
Mississippi......	64,327	10,475	16.3	33,147	230	0.7	32,301	− 8,928	−27.6
Arkansas.......	78,165	12,495	16.0	55,021	− 576	− 1.0	29,569	− 15,025	−50.8
Louisiana.......	43,337	6,299	14.5	27,124	1,581	5.8	17,214	− 5,132	−29.8

	Nonwhite farm operators								
	Owners and managers			Share and cash tenants			Croppers		
State	1930	Change 1930-1940		1930	Change 1930-1940		1930	Change 1930-1940	
	Number	Number	Percent	Number	Number	Percent	Number	Number	Percent
SOUTHEAST.....	149,904	− 5,596	− 3.7	264,798	− 83,134	−31.4	351,409	− 68,791	−19.6
Virginia........	24,525	− 2,239	− 9.1	8,351	− 1,444	−17.3	6,797	− 900	−13.2
North Carolina..	19,734	− 1,460	− 7.4	22,334	− 7,143	−32.0	34,805	− 8,002	−23.0
South Carolina..	16,063	1,050	6.5	30,316	− 8,183	−27.0	31,046	− 8,985	−28.9
Georgia........	11,153	− 1,099	− 9.9	26,186	− 6,411	−24.5	49,450	− 20,147	−40.7
Florida.........	5,665	− 110	− 1.9	3,985	− 844	−21.2	1,393	− 331	−23.8
Kentucky......	4,190	− 1,020	−24.3	1,798	− 928	−51.6	3,116	− 1,609	−51.6
Tennessee......	7,866	− 970	−12.3	10,713	− 3,504	−32.7	16,559	− 2,689	−16.2
Alabama.......	15,954	− 241	− 1.5	50,303	− 11,986	−23.8	27,572	− 8.238	−29.9
Mississippi......	22,719	752	3.3	57,177	− 23,218	−40.6	102,992	− 882	− 0.8
Arkansas.......	11,478	− 906	− 7.9	22,636	− 9,305	−41.1	45,465	− 12,343	−27.1
Louisiana.......	11,557	647	6.1	30,999	− 10,168	−32.8	32,214	− 4,665	−14.5

Source: *Sixteenth Census of the United States, 1940.* Agriculture First Series United States Summary, Table VI (Supplemental); *United States Census of Agriculture 1935*, Ch. III, Table 7 (Supplemental).

What do these changes mean? Large numbers of tenants undoubtedly were displaced by agricultural failures, increased mechanization, and the farm program of the depression. Have these tenants left the farm areas? Some students hold that in plantation areas large numbers of croppers have not left agriculture but have simply been transferred to day labor status. In such cases these families, would occupy the same houses but now work as gang labor on the plantations rather than tend a cropper strip. Census enumerations for 1930 and 1940 are not comparable in this field leaving changes in doubt. Calculated on the 1930 basis, changes in the numbers of farm wage hands and foremen show that this group decreased in every State in the Southeast except Arkansas and Florida. For the Southeast the number of farm laborers decreased 7 percent. In three States the proportionate decline exceeded that of all farm operators amounting to as much as 17 percent in Virginia and Kentucky. Instead of suggesting that croppers have become farm laborers these figures lead us to conclude that to the displacement of some 70,000 share tenants and 153,000 croppers is to be added that of 56,000 farm laborers. With the unemployed and unknown included, farm laborers increased 2 percent in the region. Even so, the flight from the land among the lower level tenants was thus a real phenomenon, concentrated mainly among the Negroes (Table 74).

Much has been written to explain the displacement of tenants and farm laborers during this period. Mechanization has played a part, as we have seen, but reductions also can be laid to the great decrease in cotton production forced by the depression and stabilized under the quota regulations of the AAA. Tenants and laborers forced out of agriculture by the failures of landowners in 1930 were prevented from returning to staple production by regulations which in the Bankhead Act for 1934 reduced average cotton acreage 40 percent. In previous depressions these displaced workers lacked many alternatives, but in the 1930's they found relief and made-work available with various alphabetical agencies, CWA, PWA, WPA, etc. Thus the pressure on the land was drained off into nonfarm employments and village and urban residence.

TABLE 74. FARMERS AND FARM LABORERS, 14 YEARS OF AGE AND OVER, SOUTHEAST, 1930-1940*

Area	Farmers, managers, and foremen 1930	Farmers and managers 1940	Percent change 1930-1940	Wage workers 1930	Wage workers and foremen 1940	Percent change 1930-1940	Unpaid family labor		Percent change 1930-1940
							1930	1940	
SOUTHEAST	2,316,047	2,005,785	−13	826,716	842,525	2	898,868	633,921	−30
Virginia	152,350	129,192	−15	81,569	68,103	−17	33,537	29,122	−13
North Carolina	271,777	248,388	− 9	92,726	80,902	−13	116,905	81,435	−30
South Carolina	153,161	123,795	−19	79,990	72,595	− 9	92,660	66,481	−28
Georgia	251,762	200,049	−21	112,277	106,350	− 5	112,477	71,129	−37
Florida	54,923	42,442	−23	61,676	66,096	7	13,641	9,082	−33
Kentucky	235,390	207,641	−12	67,950	56,709	−17	49,273	55,267	12
Tennessee	235,428	207,550	−12	68,095	60,610	−11	63,081	50,910	−19
Alabama	253,526	213,212	−16	78,558	71,852	− 9	130,098	74,121	−43
Mississippi	306,905	275,659	−10	53,965	49,379	− 8	161,511	97,175	−40
Arkansas	240,234	192,802	−20	59,107	69,948	18	70,617	44,503	−37
Louisiana	160,591	140,832	−12	70,803	68,122	− 4	55,068	42,882	−22

*Gainful workers 10-13 years of age have been subtracted in each occupational classification from 1930 Census data to make figures comparable with 1940 Census returns which list gainful workers 14 and over. Note that in 1930 farm foremen were included with managers, in 1940 with wage workers. Number of workers in the Southeast in 1940 is corrected to include emergency workers in agriculture and a proportional share of workers with "occupations not reported" and therefore slightly exceeds the sum of workers in individual States where this correction was not applied.
Source: *Fifteenth Census of the United States, 1930*, Population, IV, State Tables 4, 23; *Sixteenth Census of the United States, 1940*, Series P-11, State Summaries, Tables 1, 2.

Before 1930 we could have said that with all the unfavorable economic conditions visited upon southern agriculture the Negro had continued the twofold movement of improving his status on the land and leaving it for other opportunities. Increasing population pressure still served to force white increases on the land. The problem of racial attitudes, however serious, is equalled by the common problems of tenancy in which both races share increasing disabilities. In the 40 years since 1900 white owners and tenants have shown large increases. Negro landowners, probably the most tenacious of all tenure groups, were no greater in number in 1940 than in 1900; Negro tenants however declined in the period.

The Negro, many now feel, is bound to continue this process of gradually leaving the land. In spite of his agrarian background, the ideal of the Negro as a satisfied peasant farmer is not being realized. It is hardly accurate to say that racial competition has pushed him off the land, for the white farmer has migrated in almost equal numbers though smaller proportions. Both have been subjected to the "push" of a failing agriculture; and both alike have responded to the "pull" of industrial employment.

Deficient in capital and in training, with his deficiencies often accounted for in terms of antagonistic attitudes, the Negro's position has been well described by Charles S. Johnson in the following terms: "The Negro is the marginal man in industry, since industry came to power; he is the marginal man in agriculture, as agriculture's power declines."

Displaced in greater proportions during the depression, larger percentages of Negro tenants and farm laborers went on the relief rolls. Thus the depression may have initiated a trend toward the liquidation of the cropper system. The Negro, long accepted as basically rural in background and agricultural in occupation, was gradually making the transition to unskilled labor in urban and industrial life. The loss of their position on the lowest rungs of the agricultural ladder will prove an unmitigated misfortune to the members of this group only if they are unable to gain a foothold in the ranks of industry. Here the outlook, pessimistic enough before the war for the mass of white southern workers, is known to be darker for the Negro. Much of this is due to his own lack of training for which the community bears a deep responsibility, and much is due to deep-seated color prejudices which, instead of being confined to the South, is sanctioned by many labor unions that in their public programs and statements draw no color line. Many feel, however, that the key is still to be found in personnel policies and offices of major corporations. Changes in employment practices initiated under the pressure of war may prove important in developing new attitudes toward the Negro in industry. In the meantime, southern agriculture, which had benefited somewhat from the mass exodus of World War II, offered slight prospects to the unpropertied of either race who returned from the services. For those who can bring capital, skill, and science to the task, southern agriculture will offer challenge and opportunity after the War.

PART III
POPULATION AND THE INDUSTRIAL ECONOMY

CHAPTER 17
INCOME AND INDUSTRY

ALTHOUGH the question of social objectives is highly controversial, subject largely to individual and class interpretation, one conclusion can be generally accepted. This is simply that society should survive. Among the objectives that will enhance the survival-value of any economy there are two that stand out clearly: (1) The full utilization of human and material resources; and (2) the logical and fairly equitable distribution of incomes. By "fairly equitable distribution" we do not mean equal distribution of wealth and incomes but a range which in addition to reflecting individual contributions to the total welfare allows for a continuation of the economy at a level high enough to secure the objectives of full utilization of resources and thus of survival.[1]

That such objectives are far from being realized in the United States is evident from preceding discussions. The weight and seriousness of this problem is no longer evaded. Writing in 1936, John Maynard Keynes said: "The outstanding faults of the economic society in which we live are its failure to provide for full employment and its arbitrary and inequitable distribution of wealth and income." "It is certain," he added, "that the world will not much longer tolerate the unemployment which, apart from brief intervals of excitement, is associated—and in my opinion inevitably associated—with present day capitalistic individualism."[2]

It is the purpose of this section to examine the regional distribution of income, industry, and employment with a view to ascertaining what would be involved in a fuller use of material and human resources for the regions and the Nation. In succeeding chapters the effects of industrialization are examined in case studies of rural areas in the Southern Piedmont.

[1] I am indebted to Langston T. Hawley for the phrasing of the above statement.
[2] John Maynard Keynes, *The General Theory of Employment, Interest and Money*, pp. 372, 381.

[248]

THE REGIONAL DISTRIBUTION OF INCOME

We have discussed at length the preponderant agricultural economy, source of many of the ills that trouble the Southeast. No region can reasonably object to a geographic division of labor that adjusts production to resources, meets the needs of the Nation, and returns an equitable flow of income to the regional and occupational groups involved. It is this last criterion that our regional and occupational hierarchy fails to meet. The Southeast's per capita income is usually about 60 percent of the Nation's. Realized income in 1940 ranged from $198 per person in Mississippi to $818 in Connecticut, a spread that hardly seems justifiable unless one part of the country is devoting itself to the accomplishment of unneeded tasks in an unskilled manner. The Far West and the Northeast attained an average income of $692 and $685 per person but with a national average of $546, the Southeast fell to $317 per capita, below both the Southwest and Northwest. Figure 150 shows that every State with an average income below $350 was southern except North Dakota. Florida and Virginia were highest in the region with per capita incomes of $457 and $408 respectively.

Regional wealth is much more difficult to estimate for in addition to property owned by citizens it includes the value of all physical properties and capital equipment lying within each State. Unmined mineral resources are not included except as they have affected the estimated value of real

FIGURE 150. REALIZED INCOME PER CAPITA, UNITED STATES, 1940

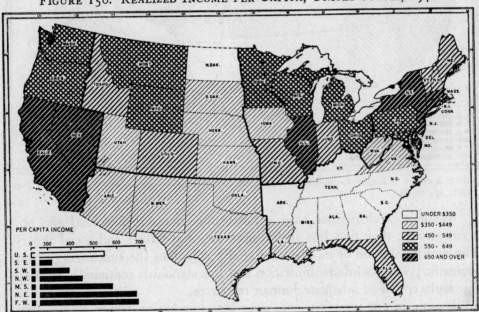

Source: National Industrial Conference Board; *Economic Record* (III, 6, March, 1941). *Sixteenth Census of the United States, 1940*, Series P-3, No. 3.

estate. The values of the United States Navy and all coinage and bullion are included for the national total but not distributed by states. Wealth thus estimated (Figure 151) shows similar regional disparities, ranging in 1936 from $6,511 per capita in Nevada to $736 in Mississippi. The Southeast possessed a per capita wealth of $1,189, hardly more than one-half of the Nation's average. Virginia with $2,017 was the only southern State to rise above $1,300 in the measure. Inequalities in wealth are characteristic of the capitalistic system, a gap which some feel need not be so great in regard to income. Wealth, however, represents physical equipment necessary for the production of future income as well as the accumulation from past incomes. Thus, while migration and the movement to new occupations should operate to redistribute income on a more adequate basis, it would take a long time for this process to equalize per capita wealth.

FIGURE 151. ESTIMATED NATIONAL WEALTH PER CAPITA, UNITED STATES, 1936

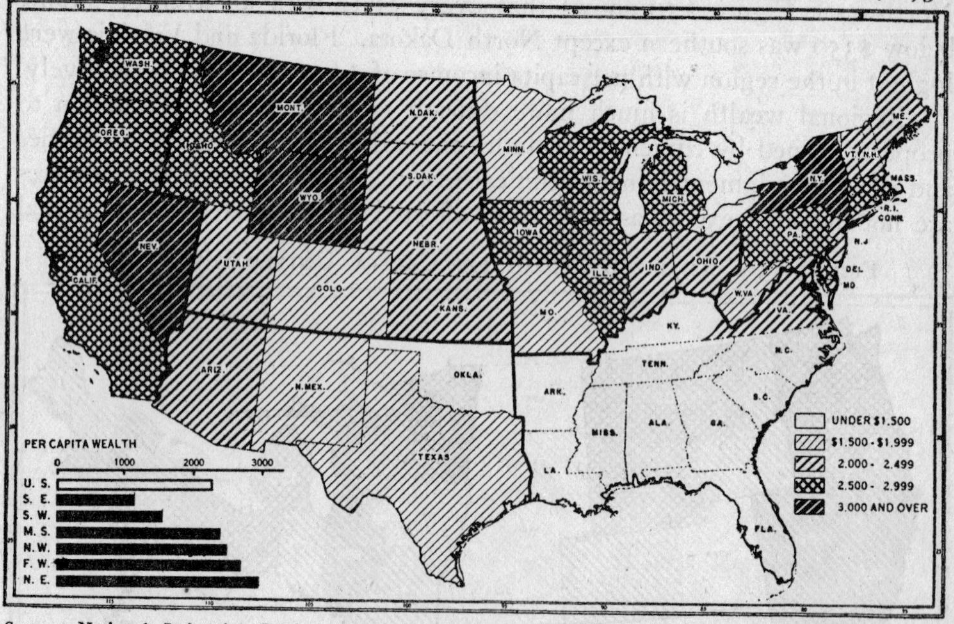

Source: National Industrial Conference Board; *Studies in Enterprise and Social Progress* (New York, 1939), pp. 62-64.

While such disparities have natural antecedents in historical and economic causes, they find less justification in social values and social theory. The maldistribution of income continually threatens the functioning of our economic system, while malnutrition and low standards continually threaten the replacement of adequate human resources.

Income in our economy goes over into purchasing power whose circulation in the medium of money performs a twofold function: (1) It helps

FIGURE 152. RETAIL SALES PER CAPITA, UNITED STATES, 1939

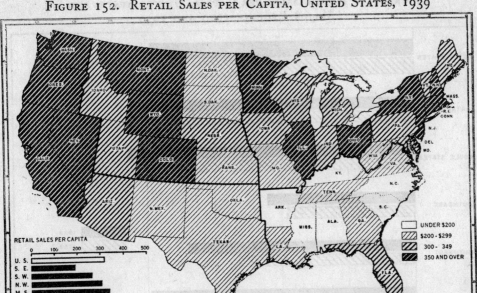

Source: *Sixteenth Census of the United States, 1940*, Census of Business, Preliminary Summary, December 17, 1940.

to keep the economic mechanism going by continually calling forth supplies of goods and services, and (2) it replenishes human resources whose biological efficiency and cultural adequacy result from the degree of wise consumption of such goods and services. With certain qualifications, therefore, Figure 152 on per capita retail sales in 1939 is offered as a measure of underconsumption in areas suffering from low income. The states ranged from an average of $129 per person spent in retail trade in Mississippi to $561 in Nevada. By regions (Figure 153), this measure of consumption varied from $193 per capita in the Southeast to $443 in the Far West.

With other qualifications as to changes in the price level, Figure 153 serves to estimate the extent of recorded damage done our economic system by the long depression 1929-1939. Retail sales declined from $394 to $319, or 19 percent in the Nation as compared with 22.3 percent in the Northwest. In the Southeast they fell from $222 to $193 per person. These inequalities should not be considered exclusively in terms of regional grievances although there probably exists no economic theory competent to silence such attitudes. More important, they should be considered as injuries to our ongoing economic system. Leon Henderson, before World War II, said that for the South to attain the national level of living would give the national economy an additional market worth $10 billions an-

FIGURE 153. RETAIL SALES PER CAPITA, UNITED STATES AND SIX MAJOR REGIONS, 1929 AND 1939

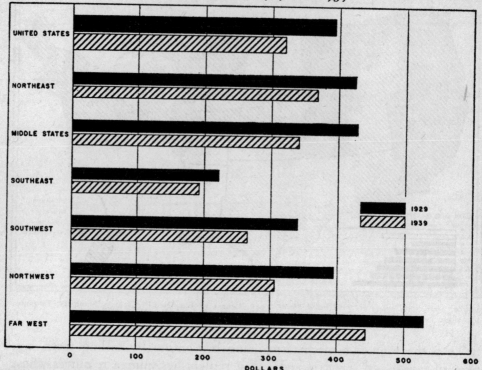

Source: See Figure 152 and *Fifteenth Census of the United States, 1930,* Retail Trade.

nually. In this connection we can consider the billions that were spent, loaned, and lost from 1918-1932 in the fruitless search for foreign markets.

THE COMPONENTS OF REGIONAL INCOME

An interesting comparison has been made between the normal curve of distribution of abilities and attainments among human beings and the distribution of income in our economic system.[3] The normal curve shows that the highest proportions of our population fall in the middle or average range, neither exceptionally superior nor inferior but average. The curve of income distribution in 1935-36 shows that the highest proportion of the families fell not in the middle but in the lowest range of income. Thus 35 percent of all nonrelief families had an average of less than $1,000 annual income, 60 percent less than $1,500, and 76 percent less than $2,000 (Figure 154).

Figure 155 shows the regional distribution of income found by the Consumer Research Project in 1935-36. New England and the Pacific show

[3] William F. Ogburn and Meyer F. Nimkoff, *Sociology* (Boston: Houghton Mifflin, 1940), p. 597.

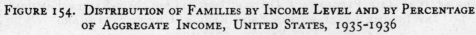

FIGURE 154. DISTRIBUTION OF FAMILIES BY INCOME LEVEL AND BY PERCENTAGE OF AGGREGATE INCOME, UNITED STATES, 1935-1936

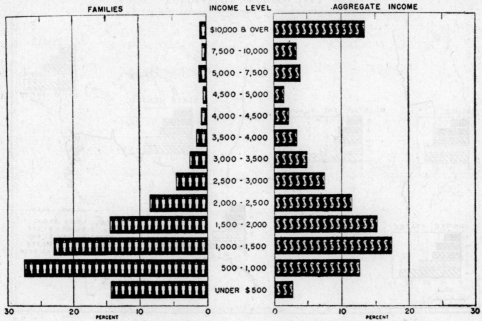

Source: *Consumer Incomes in the United States*, National Resources Board (August, 1938), p. 3.

the most equitable distribution of family incomes with those under $1,000 making up one-fourth of the total. In the southern regions, exclusive of those on relief, families with less than $1,000 annual income made up over fifty percent of the total.

The basic dichotomy in income as in fertility is that between the farm and urban populations. Table 75 shows this trend of farm and nonfarm income from 1910 to 1940. Per capita farm income in this period ranged from 45 to 17 percent of average nonfarm income. Since 1933 farm income has been augmented by government payments but the low income of many regions is still due to the preponderance of farm people in the population. This differential is increased in the Southeast where farmers have the lowest incomes of all. Figure 156 indicates a range in the 1940 per capita gross income for the farm population from $126 in Alabama to $1,004 in California. The Southeast had $166 per capita as compared with $764 in the Far West.

The regional aspect of this dualism in our economy is shown in Figures 157 and 158 which compare the income distribution among farm families with that of families living in cities of over 100,000, by regions. Incomes in cities in the North Central and Pacific States approach the normal curve

FIGURE 155. THE PERCENTAGE DISTRIBUTION OF ALL NON-RELIEF FAMILIES
BY INCOME LEVEL WITHIN EACH REGION, UNITED STATES AND
FIVE REGIONS, 1935-1936

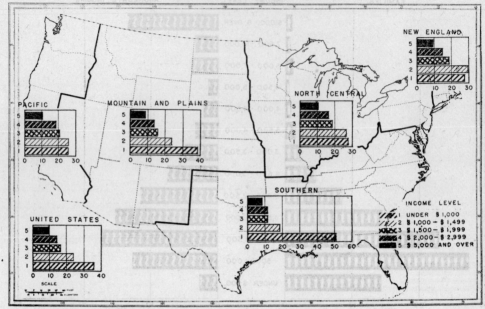

Source: *Consumer Incomes in the United States, 1935-1936*, National Resources Committee (August, 1938), Table 8, p. 25 and Tables 13B, 17B, and 18B, pp. 98-99.

of distribution suggesting that economic returns in these areas are more nearly commensurate with the normal incidence of human industry and abilities. While the South's cities show a larger proportion in the higher income brackets than the region's farms, 33 percent of the urban families have incomes below $1,000.

The contrast is with the farm incomes where over 52 percent of the families receive incomes of less than $1,000 as compared with only 25 percent in large cities in the Nation. Not only does the South have the largest proportions in agriculture, but the region has the lowest farm incomes, over 65 percent of farm families receiving less than $1,000 per year. This may be compared with the distribution in the Pacific, New England, and North Central States where about 35 percent of farm families fall in this low group.

The analysis of income by States developed by John A. Slaughter of the National Industrial Conference Board for 1935 enables us to calculate the proportion of regional income derived from various sources. Figure 159 shows that 56 percent of the Nation's estimated income of $390 per capita came in 1935 from the broad distributive and social group (including finance and government), 30 percent from manufacturing and mechani-

FIGURE 156. PER CAPITA GROSS INCOME (INCLUDING BENEFIT PAYMENTS),
FARM POPULATION, UNITED STATES, 1940

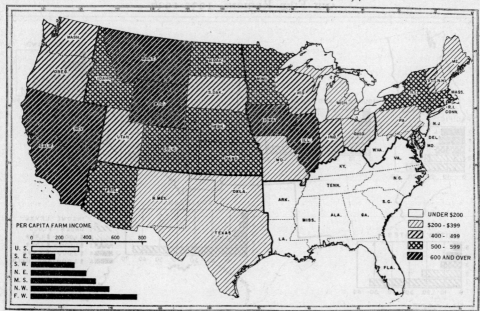

Source: Department of Agriculture, Bureau of Agricultural Economics, "Gross Farm Income and
Government Payments" (May 26, 1941), Table 5; *Sixteenth Census of the United States, 1940,*
Series P-10, No. 2.

TABLE 75. INCOME PER FARM AND INCOME PER PERSON ON FARMS AND NOT
ON FARMS, UNITED STATES, 1910-1940

Year	Net income from agriculture per farm (1) (Dollars)	Net income from agriculture per person on farms (2) (Dollars)	Income per person not on farms (3) (Dollars)	Year	Net income from agriculture per farm (1) (Dollars)	Net income from agriculture per person on farms (2) (Dollars)	Income per person not on farms (3) (Dollars)
				1930......	823	172	760
	Excluding government payments			1931......	551	115	605
1910......	703	139	482	1932......	355	75	442
1911......	617	123	468	1933......	431	91	417
1912......	679	135	483	1934......	466	99	487
1913......	686	137	521	1935......	672	144	540
1914......	701	141	482	1936......	781	165	626
1915......	679	137	502	1937......	915	192	670
1916......	777	157	579	1938......	741	154	625
1917......	1,282	259	638	1939......	751	154	657
1918......	1,487	305	670	1940......	792	161	700
1919......	1,536	321	762				
1920......	1,306	266	875				
1921......	587	120	718		Including government payments		
1922......	749	154	715	1933......	448	95	417
1923......	882	181	812	1934......	525	112	487
1924......	883	182	788	1935......	745	160	540
1925......	1,085	224	810	1936......	819	173	626
1926......	1,048	217	856	1937......	963	202	670
1927......	1,016	211	818	1938......	807	167	625
1928......	1,073	223	828	1939......	865	177	657
1929......	1,077	224	870	1940......	902	183	700

Source: *The Farm Income Situation,* Bureau of Agricultural Economics, U. S. Department of Agriculture (August 1941), p. 20.

FIGURE 157. THE PERCENTAGE DISTRIBUTION OF RURAL FARM FAMILIES (NON-RELIEF) BY INCOME LEVELS, WITHIN EACH REGION, UNITED STATES AND FIVE REGIONS, 1935-1936

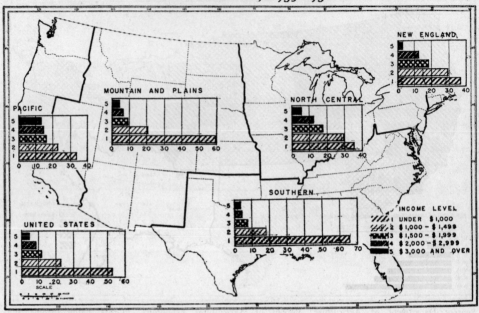

Source: See Figure 155.

FIGURE 158. THE PERCENTAGE DISTRIBUTION OF LARGE CITY FAMILIES (NON-RELIEF) BY INCOME LEVELS WITHIN EACH REGION, UNITED STATES AND FIVE REGIONS, 1935-1936

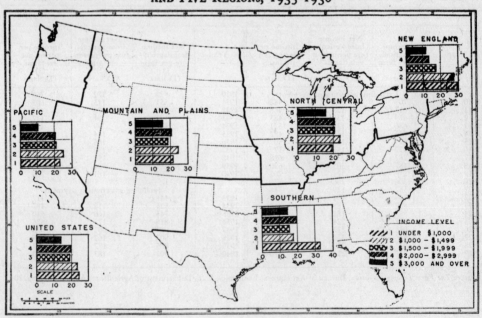

Source: See Figure 155.

FIGURE 159. PERCENTAGE DISTRIBUTION OF PRODUCTIVE INCOME BY ORIGIN,
UNITED STATES AND SIX MAJOR REGIONS, 1935

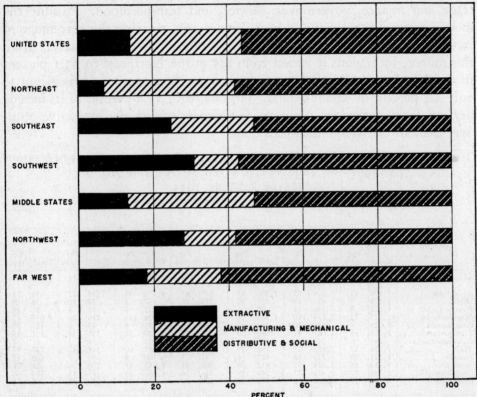

Source: John A. Slaughter, *Income Received in the Various States, 1929-1935*, National Industrial
Conference Board (New York: 1937), Table 23; *Statistical Abstract of the United States, 1937*, Table 11.

cal, and approximately 14 percent from extractive occupations. The estimated per capita income of the Southeast, $222 in that year, was the lowest
in the Nation. Fifty-three percent of the region's income came from the
distributive and social economy, 22 percent from manufacturing and mechanical, and 25 percent from extractive occupations.

The master table (Table 76), can be considered with the maps (Figures 160 to 167), to explore the sources of regional income by various
branches of industry. The Northeast, which ranked first in total per capita
income, ranked first in per capita income from manufacturing, finance, and
four other branches, second in income from five other sources. It came
last only in income received from agriculture. The Far West, which ranked
second in total per capita income, ranked first in five branches and second
in four. The Southeast, which ranked sixth, ranked fourth only in agriculture and manufacturing, fifth in construction, and last in other counts.

Figures 160 to 167 compare the States in the proportion of income derived from seven principal sources: agriculture, mining, manufacturing, trade and finance, government, service, and transportation. Possibly the most significant map in the series is Figure 160, showing the percentage of income received from agriculture. The Nation received 11.1 percent from this source; by regions it varied from 4.5 in the Northeast to 23.1 percent in the Northwest. By States it ranged from 34 percent in Mississippi to only 3.4 percent in Rhode Island. Virginia, with 15.8 percent of its income derived from agriculture, appears less dependent on the extractive economy than any other Southeastern State.

TABLE 76. TOTAL AND PER CAPITA PRODUCTION INCOME RECEIVED IN VARIOUS BRANCHES OF INDUSTRY, UNITED STATES AND THE SIX MAJOR REGIONS, 1935

(Total Income in Millions of Dollars, per Capita Income in Dollars)

Industry	UNITED STATES		Northeast		Southeast		Southwest		Middle States		Northwest		Far West	
	Total	Per capita	Total	Per capita	Total	Per capita	Total	Per capita	Total	Per capita	Total	Per capita	Total	Per capita
ALL.............	49,755	390	19,918	504	6,044	222	2,578	274	14,020	405	2,315	311	4,353	498
Agriculture........	5,498	43	894	23	1,266	47	589	63	1,564	45	534	72	638	73
Mining............	1,074	9	473	12	139	5	154	16	157	5	74	10	74	9
Electric Light......	1,002	8	548	14	70	2	31	3	231	7	32	4	83	10
Manufacturing.....	11,727	92	5,534	140	1,039	38	239	25	4,024	116	216	29	632	72
Construction.......	1,028	8	410	10	130	5	40	4	273	8	45	6	117	13
Transportation.....	4,253	33	1,667	42	539	20	253	27	1,120	32	256	34	391	45
Communications...	748	6	347	9	55	2	34	4	207	6	34	5	63	7
Trade.............	7,314	57	2,882	73	796	29	380	40	2,083	60	348	47	757	87
Finance...........	1,321	10	722	18	112	4	41	4	300	8	40	5	102	12
Service...........	5,913	46	2,271	57	812	30	306	33	1,552	45	270	36	624	71
Government.......	6,745	53	2,871	73	748	28	336	36	1,657	48	319	43	579	66
Miscellaneous......	3,134	25	1,300	33	336	12	176	19	854	25	150	20	292	33

Note: Data for United States include District of Columbia. Since total incomes by separate industries are given here in round numbers of millions, while totals for all industries by regions (top line) were computed from more complete data, there is a slight difference (generally, one or two units) between our totals and those obtained by straight addition of values as given here for each industry. Electric Light Industry includes manufacturing of electric power and gas industry; mining includes quarrying.

Source: John A. Slaughter, *Income Received in the Various States, 1929-1935* (New York: National Industrial Conference Board, 1937), Table 23. *Statistical Abstract of the United States, 1937*, Table 11.

Mining as a source of income shows great regional variations (Figure 161). It contributed less than 1 percent of the income of 21 States but as high as 10 percent or more in Nevada and New Mexico, and in West Virginia, 19.4 percent. The Southwest and the Northeast received the highest per capita incomes from mining; the Southeast and the Middle States, the lowest. Figure 162 which shows the value of mineral output per worker engaged in mining in 1929 furnishes the basic figure from which mining wages are paid. It ranged all the way from less than $1,700 in Alabama to over $11,000 in Minnesota, with its Mesabi iron range. This figure is a composite index which includes among other things the value of different minerals, the richness of ores, their availability as resources, the amount of machinery used per worker, as well as the degree of economic organization.

FIGURE 160. INCOME RECEIVED FROM AGRICULTURE AS PERCENTAGE OF
TOTAL PRODUCTIVE INCOME, UNITED STATES, 1935

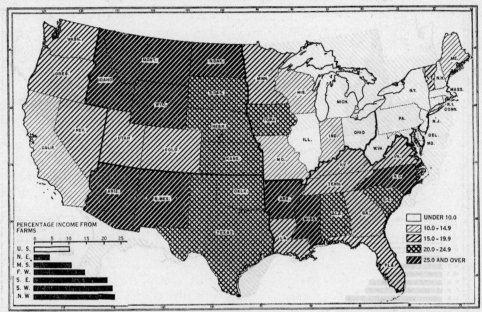

Source: See Table 76 and Figure 159.

FIGURE 161. INCOME RECEIVED FROM MINING AND QUARRYING AS PERCENTAGE
OF TOTAL PRODUCTIVE INCOME, UNITED STATES, 1935

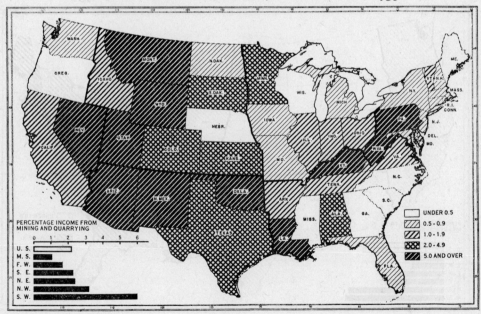

Source: See Table 76.

FIGURE 162. VALUE OF MINERAL PRODUCTS PER WORKER ENGAGED IN
MINING INDUSTRIES, UNITED STATES, 1929

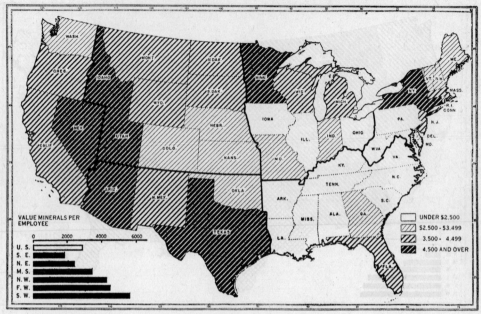

Source: *Statistical Abstract of the United States, 1941,* Table 790.

FIGURE 163. INCOME RECEIVED FROM MANUFACTURING AS PERCENTAGE
OF TOTAL PRODUCTIVE INCOME, UNITED STATES, 1935

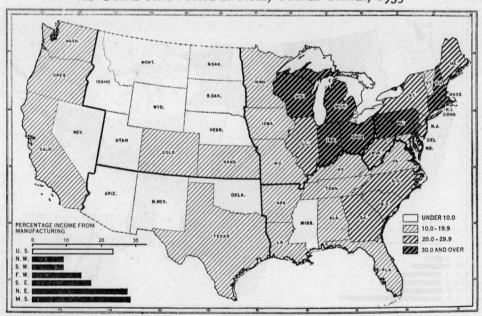

Source: See Table 76.

The Nation drew 23.6 percent of its income from manufacturing, ranging from 28.7 percent in the Middle States to 9.3 percent in the Southwest and the Northwest. The States ranged from 40.3 percent so derived in Rhode Island to 2.2 percent in New Mexico. In the Southeastern States, proportions ranged from 26.5 percent in North Carolina to 9.8 percent in Mississippi (Figure 163). As Figure 164 indicates, trade and finance were the source of 17.4 percent of the United States' income, ranging from more than 20 percent in Missouri and New York to 10.9 percent in Wyoming. In the Southeast it ranged from over 18 percent in Florida and Tennessee to 12.1 percent for North Carolina.

The proportion of income received from governmental occupations in the Nation (Figure 165) amounted to 13.6 percent and ranged from 17.7 percent in North Dakota to 8.9 percent in Indiana. In the Southeast it varied from 14.5 percent in Virginia to 9.5 percent in North Carolina. The services (Figure 166) contributed 11.9 percent of the Nation's income with a range from 15.2 percent for Georgia to 7.3 percent in Wyoming. North Carolina with 11.6 percent was lowest in the region. Transportation (Figure 167) which contributed 8.5 percent of the Nation's income contributes most in the sparsely populated States, leading in Nevada with 15.9 percent. In the Southeast it ranged from 12.2 percent in Louisiana to 5 percent for North Carolina, lowest in the Nation in this respect.

FIGURE 164. INCOME RECEIVED FROM TRADE AND FINANCE AS PERCENTAGE OF TOTAL PRODUCTIVE INCOME, UNITED STATES, 1935

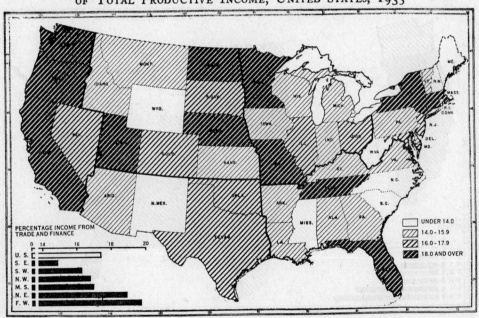

Source: See Table 76.

FIGURE 165. INCOME RECEIVED FROM GOVERNMENT AS PERCENTAGE OF
TOTAL PRODUCTIVE INCOME, UNITED STATES, 1935

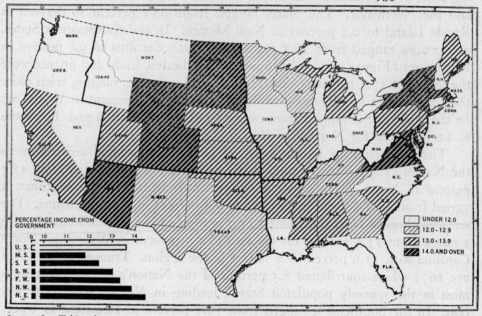

Source: See Table 76.

FIGURE 166. INCOME RECEIVED FROM THE SERVICE INDUSTRIES AS PERCENTAGE
OF TOTAL PRODUCTIVE INCOME, UNITED STATES, 1940

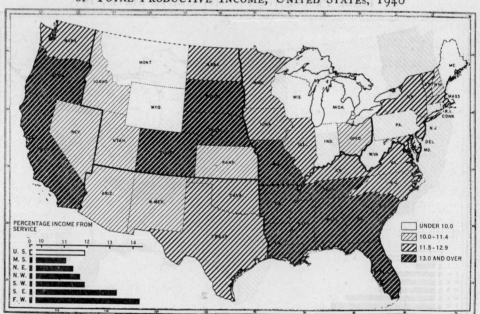

Source: See Table 76.

FIGURE 167. INCOME RECEIVED FROM TRANSPORTATION AS PERCENTAGE OF TOTAL PRODUCTIVE INCOME, UNITED STATES, 1935

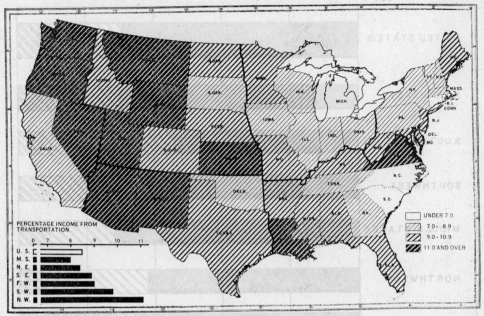

Source: See Table 76.

Not only does the Southeast secure smaller proportions of its total income from the better paying sources, but its per capita income in each case is below the Nation's. In 1935 the Nation drew an income of $219 per capita from distributive and social occupations compared with $119 for the Southeast. In manufacturing and mechanical occupations the national per capita was $116 to $48 for the Southeast; only in the extractive economy was the region's per capita equal to the Nation's at $55 (Figure 159). With this figure can be compared Figure 168 giving the regional distribution of income by type: (1) wages, (2) entrepreneurs' incomes, and (3) investments. Some 69 percent of the Nation's productive income in 1935 was drawn in the form of salaries and wages, 18.6 percent in entrepreneurs' income and 12.6 percent was drawn as dividends, rent, and interest. The farmer's income is classified as entrepreneurs' income, a fact which explains its predominance as a source of income in the Northwest, Southwest, and Southeast as contrasted with other regions. The Southeast, with 21 percent of the population and the lowest per capita income, received 11.3 percent of the Nation's wage income, 19 percent of its entrepreneurs' income, and only 7 percent of the income from investments. The dominant Northeast, with 30 percent of the population, received 41 percent of the Nation's wage and salary income, 26 percent of the entrepreneurs' income, and 56 per-

FIGURE 168. THE PERCENTAGE DISTRIBUTION OF PRODUCTIVE INCOME BY
THREE TYPES, UNITED STATES AND SIX MAJOR REGIONS, 1935

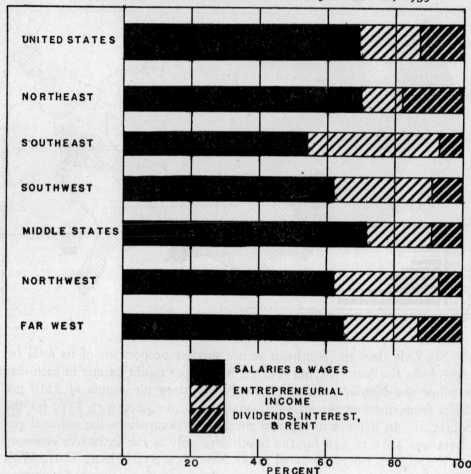

Source: See Figure 159.

cent of the interest, rent, and dividends. In contrast with other regions, more of its income came from investments, salaries, and wages, least from entrepreneurs' income.

Figure 154 serves to explain this relationship. It shows that while incomes of less than $1,000 were received by 42 percent of all the Nation's families in 1935-36, they accounted for only 16 percent of all income. At the other end of the scale the 1 percent of our families receiving $10,000 and over accounted for 13.5 percent of the total income in 1935-36. From the savings of this and similar groups come the investments which constitute a claim on future income in terms of interests, rents, and dividends. Here is the relation of income distribution to the colonial economy char-

FIGURE 169. THE MAJOR INDUSTRIAL AREAS OF THE UNITED STATES, 1939

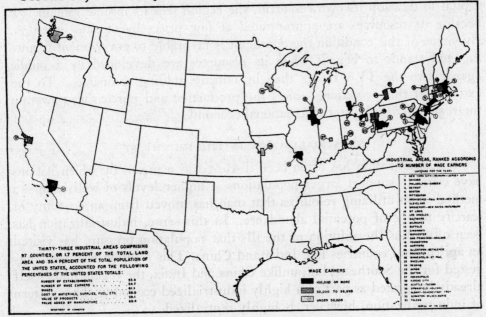

Source: United States Bureau of the Census, *Census of Manufactures, 1939.*

FIGURE 170. PRINCIPAL INDUSTRIAL COUNTIES ACCORDING TO THE NUMBER OF WAGE EARNERS IN MANUFACTURING, UNITED STATES, 1939

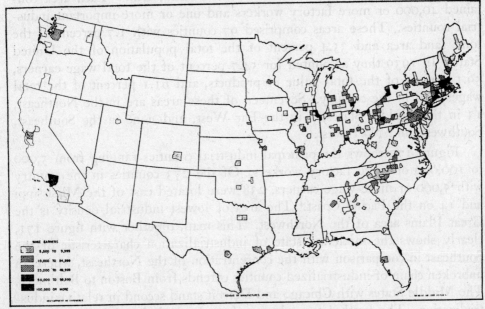

Source: United States Bureau of the Census, *Census of Manufactures, 1939.*

acteristic of the Southeast. Lacking the large incomes necessary to furnish capital to develop its own resources, the region sees its income remain low because its resources are appropriated at low prices by outside investors. By virtue of this condition the Southeast is favorable to government financing and stands to benefit when its resources are developed by a public agency like the TVA rather than by outside holding companies. To the extent that this procedure raises the productive and purchasing power in the region, it also bolsters the national economy.

INDUSTRIALIZATION IN THE SOUTHEAST

Industrialization has often been discussed as a means by which nations have come to support larger populations at higher levels of well-being—a method of so utilizing resources that man has moved from an economy of scarcity to one of potential abundance. In this sense, industrialization has been offered as the solution of the ills that population pressure has visited on agricultural countries like India and China. This solution has been suggested for the Southeast, but, unlike China and India, the region finds itself already integrated as part of a highly industrialized economy. This pattern of industrialization, however, is highly centralized.

Industry in the United States is characterized by extreme concentration of geographic location. Figure 169 shows that the 33 major industrial areas delimited by the census in 1939 ranged from the New York City-Newark-Jersey City concentration to Toledo, Ohio. Each area contained 40,000 or more factory workers and one or more important industrial counties. These areas comprised 97 counties with 1.7 percent of the total land area and 35.4 percent of the total population of the United States. In 1939 they accounted for 54.7 percent of the total wage earners, 59.1 percent of the total value of products, and 61.1 percent of the total wages paid in the country. Seventeen of these areas are in the Northeast, 13 in the Middle States, 3 in the Far West, and none in the Southeast, Southwest, and Northwest.

Figure 170 shows the principal industrial counties ranging from 5,000 to 100,000 or more factory workers. Of the 273 counties in the country with 5,000 or more wage earners, 238 were located east of the Mississippi and 14 on the Pacific Coast. The area of lowest industrial density is the Great Plains area of the Northwest. This map, together with figure 171, clearly shows the moderate state of industrialization characteristic of the Southeast in comparison with the concentration of the Northeast, where an unbroken chain of industrialized counties extends from Boston to Baltimore. The Middle States with Chicago and Detroit stand second in relative industrialization. The southeastern cluster of moderate industrial areas extends down the Appalachians from Virginia to central Alabama. In succeeding chapters certain zones of this industrial belt will be selected for special study.

Manufacturing was insignificant in the Southeast in 1880, employing only 7 percent of the region's working force. Since 1900, however, industrial development has been comparatively rapid. Between 1900 and 1930 the region's workers in manufacturing and mechanical industries more than doubled, increasing from 764,860 to 1,895,656.

In the four decades, 1900-1940, proportionate gains in population were greater in the Nation than in the Southeast, but the region showed greater percentage increases in urban population and gainful workers. From 1930 to 1940 all three of the rates of increase were greater in the Southeast.

Figure 172 compares the rate of gain in industrial workers in the Nation and the Southeast from 1900 to 1940. Since we have used the two sets of figures in comparing the Southeast and the Nation, the figure also serves the purpose of relating the biennial changes in industrial wage earners reported by the Census of Manufactures to the changes in gainful workers in manufacturing and mechanical industries enumerated by the Decennial Census, 1900-1940.[4]

The total increase in the number of gainful workers in manufacturing and mechanical industries during the three decades (1900-1930) was 99.1 percent for the United States and 147.8 percent for the Southeast, while the increase during the three decades (1899-1929) for the wage earners was somewhat less, 87.5 percent for the United States, and 113.4 percent for the Southeast. From 1930 to 1940 the rate of change for the Southeast was a 29.4 percent increase for the gainfully employed and a three percent gain in the number of wage earners, as compared with the Nation's 12 percent increase among the gainfully employed and a 10.8 percent loss in the number of wage earners. The comparable figures of the biennial census ran from 1929 to 1939.

[4] The two differ considerably in that the classification of gainful workers in the regular census greatly outnumbers the wage earners of the *Census of Manufactures*. Although the two categories are not strictly comparable, the change in their number reflects the same trend in the development of manufacturing industries, and the fact that data for wage earners are available by short intervals makes it possible to study fluctuations in the number of workers which are smoothed out by the decennial census. Gainful workers include both employed and unemployed, while wage earners are those actually at work in factories. Moreover, gainful workers include all workers in manufacturing and mechanical industries, whether working at home or in small or large establishments. The *Census of Manufactures* includes only those wage earners working in establishments reporting products valued at $5,000 or more. Prior to 1921, however, this figure was $500. Wage earners reported to the *Census of Manufactures* usually constituted from 62 to 70 percent of the gainful workers enumerated in the regular census. In 1900 the ratio of wage earners to gainful workers in the Nation was approximately 66.5 percent. In successive decades it has been 62, 71, and 62 percent. In the Southeast from 1900 to 1930 the range has been 72, 67, and 61 percent. In 1940 the ratio was only 50 for the Nation, 49 for the Southeast.

ALL THESE PEOPLE

FIGURE 171. THE NUMBER OF WAGE EARNERS ENGAGED IN MANUFACTURING, UNITED STATES BY COUNTIES, 1939

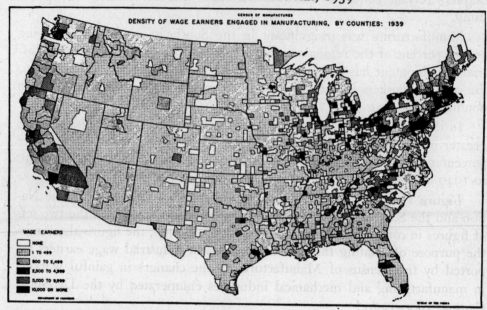

Source: *United States Census of Manufactures, 1939.*

FIGURE 172. NUMBER OF GAINFUL WORKERS IN MANUFACTURING AND MECHANICAL INDUSTRIES, DECENNIAL CENSUS, AND WAGE EARNERS IN MANUFACTURING, BIENNIAL CENSUS, UNITED STATES AND SOUTHEAST, 1900-1940

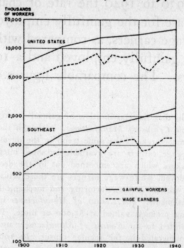

Source: See footnote 4 this chapter for explanation of sources and variations in the two enumerations.

While the Southeast did not loom large as a site for war industries, Figure 173 shows in the period June 1940 to November 1941 that the greatest increase in industrial wage earners came in California, New England, and seven Southeastern States. In this period the region secured 15.5 percent of industrial defense contracts allotted as compared with 20.8 percent for New York, New Jersey and Pennsylvania, and 25.6 percent for Ohio, Indiana, Illinois, and Michigan.[5]

FIGURE 173. PERCENTAGE CHANGE IN EMPLOYMENT IN NON-AGRICULTURAL ESTABLISHMENTS, UNITED STATES, JUNE, 1940 TO NOVEMBER, 1941

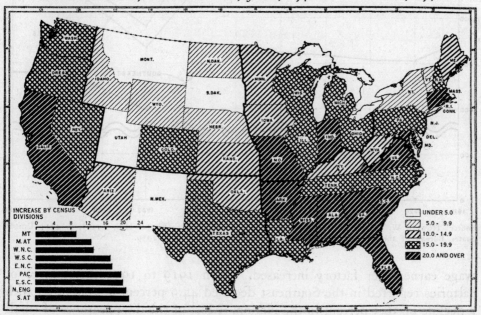

Source: United States Department of Labor, Bureau of Labor Statistics.

Before our entry in World War II the high point reached in the number of wage earners in manufacturing by the Nation and by the major industrial areas was in 1919. By 1939 when the Nation's wage earners had fallen to 86.7 percent of the 1919 level, the Southeast exceeded its 1919 level by 17 percent. Moreover in the depression years, 1935, 1937, and 1939, the Southeast was the only region which reported more industrial wage earners than in 1919.

In this period since 1919 the region took part in the national trend toward concentration, the number of establishments declining from 41,186 to 22,685. As the number of factories decreased, the output and number of

[5] See also Ralph C. Hon, "The South in a War Economy," *Southern Economic Journal*, VIII (January, 1942), 291-308.

FIGURE 174. THE TREND OF WAGES PER WAGE EARNER IN MANUFACTURING, UNITED STATES, FAR WEST AND SOUTHEAST, 1919-1939

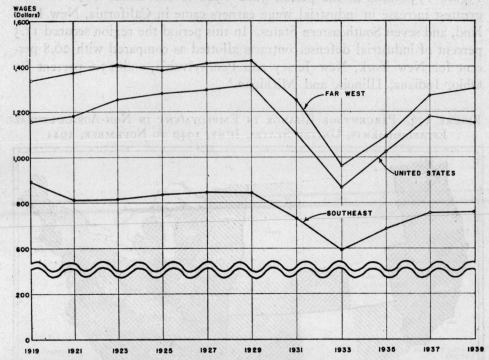

Source: Howard W. Odum, *Southern Regions of the United States* (Chapel Hill, 1936), p. 434; United States Bureau of the Census, *Biennial Census of Manufactures, 1933-1939.*

wage earners per factory increased. From 1919 to 1939 the number of factories reported in the Southeast declined 44.9 percent as compared with a decline of 36.5 percent in the Nation. Most of the disappearance of small factories came at the end of the first World War, but later gains in the number of establishments were cancelled out in the drastic years from 1929 to 1933. In this same period, from 1919 to 1939, the Southeast saw the average number of wage earners per establishment double, increasing from 25.1 to 53.2. In the Nation as a whole average workers increased from 31.4 to 42.8 per establishment. In the same period the average value of products per factory in the Southeast increased from $131 thousands to $283 thousands; in the United States it increased from $215 to $308 thousands, giving the region an increase of 116 percent as compared with a gain of 43 percent for the Nation. Whether these figures indicate greater gains for the region depends to some extent on the changed system of reporting inaugurated in 1921 (see footnote 4).

FIGURE 175. WAGES PER WAGE EARNER ENGAGED IN MANUFACTURING
INDUSTRIES, UNITED STATES, 1939

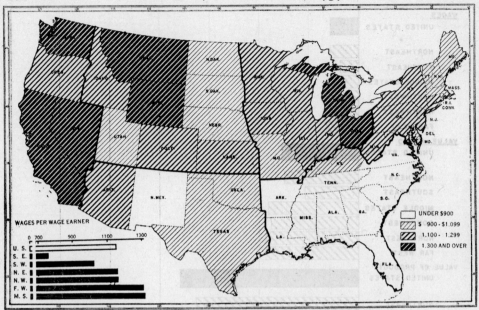

Source: United States Bureau of the Census, *Biennial Census of Manufactures, 1939.*

THE LEVEL OF WAGES

The rise in the level of wages in the Southeast has not kept pace with the region's increased value of output and number of workers. Great regional differences exist in average wages in manufacturing and industry throughout the United States. These variations are due to many things: (1) differences in variety and type of industry, (2) differences in productivity and skills among workers, (3) differences in the bargaining power of workers, (4) differences in efficiency and mechanization as among industries, and (5) as among plants in the same industry in different parts of the country, as well as (6) differences in the price policies prevailing in highly competitive industries as compared with those of a semi-monopolistic nature, and (7) invested capital per worker.

Whatever the causes, Figure 174 shows that the Southeast remains the region of the differential wage. In 1939 the region's average wage in manufacturing was $760, less than two-thirds of the Nation's average and only 58 percent of the average wage in the Middle States and Far West. Figure 175 shows that the average industrial wage ranged from $1,512 in Michigan, land of the great automotive industry, to $592 in Mississippi, home of the plan to balance agriculture with industry. The highest average wage paid in the Southeast, $986 in Kentucky, ranked only thirty-fourth in the

FIGURE 176. WAGES, VALUE ADDED BY MANUFACTURING AND VALUE OF PRODUCT PER WAGE EARNER, UNITED STATES AND SIX MAJOR REGIONS, 1939

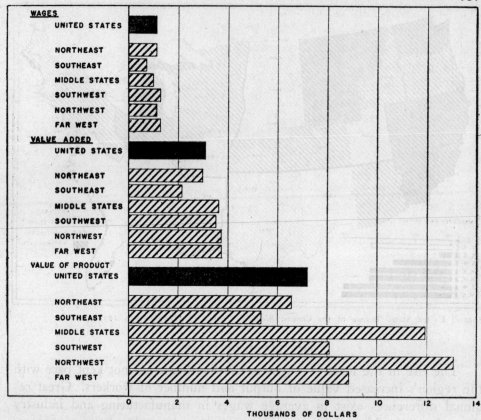

Source: United States Bureau of the Census, *Biennial Census of Manufactures, 1939.*

Nation. In the lowest group New Mexico was the only stranger to the Southeast.

Figure 176 enables us to relate wages to regional variations in two important measures reported by the Census of Manufactures, (1) value of product per wage earner and (2) the value added by manufacture per wage earner. In 1939 it is clear that in the Southeast the average wage earner drew the lowest wage, added least to the value of raw materials per wage earner by fabricating them, and turned out the cheapest product. Highest in all these measures came the western regions and the Middle States.

Figure 177 serves to compare trends in the Southeast and the Nation in these values from 1919 to 1939, showing that differentials have remained fairly constant. When available, data from 1941-45 may show decrease in major differentials due to the effect of the War (Table 79). Figure 178 depicts the trend in wages 1919-39 as percentages of value added in manufacturing industries. Wages are seen normally to take 40 percent of the value that manufacturing adds to the costs of raw materials, fuel, power, etc. On this basis the Southeast, although drawing the lower wage, receives a higher percentage of value added than the Southwest but fluctuates slightly below the Nation's average.

Both in total value of products and in total wage bill the Southeast showed increases from 1919-1939 as compared with the Nation. If we use the 1919 level as our base year, we find in Table 77 that by 1939 the total value of production reached an index of 118.8 in the Southeast as compared with 91 in the United States. Similarly total wages paid after fluctuations reached 100 in the Southeast as compared with 86.3 in the Nation (Table 78). An examination of the trends shows that the Southeast reacted more severely to the aftermath of World War I in 1919-1921, but that the Nation lost more in the depression both in production and wages. War has again changed the picture and later Censuses of Manufactures will no doubt show a greater proportion of war industries located outside the Southeast.

Table 79, designed to analyze these figures in further detail, serves to exhibit the Southeast's familiar two-thirds differential in industry by arranging three regional-national ratios per wage earner: (1) value of product, (2) value added, and (3) wages in parallel columns. Over a period of twenty years the average wage earner in the Southeast has turned out a product valued at two-thirds to three-fourths the national average, has added somewhat less to the value of the materials added by manufacturing them, and has received less still in average wages. Table 79 shows that the Southeast approached nearest national averages in the period of World War I when all three ratios exceeded 75 percent. Its ratio of wages fell lowest not in the depression but in the War's aftermath of the 1920's. As war industries invade the Southeast they will again raise the average wage level, a gain that will be preserved only if skills are increased, technology developed, capital invested, and the range of industry diversified.

THE INDUSTRIAL AND OCCUPATIONAL PATTERN

In the most careful analysis of the region's industry made to date, Harriet L. Herring shows the limitation of the Southeast in the type and variety of its industry. For a time it appeared that the Southeast was to develop a one-crop industry based on its agricultural specialty, cotton. Table 80, compiled from Herring's *Southern Industry and Regional Development*,[6] shows the share of the Southeast in 55 important industries. In the main the area leads in low-wage industries, turning out a product of low average value. This phenomenon is related to the South's surplus

[6] Chapel Hill: University of North Carolina Press, 1940.

FIGURE 177. WAGES, VALUE ADDED BY MANUFACTURE, AND VALUE OF PRODUCT PER WAGE EARNER, UNITED STATES AND SOUTHEAST, 1919-1939

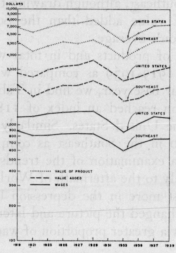

Source: Howard W. Odum, *op. cit.*, pp. 434, 436. United States Bureau of the Census, *Biennial Census of Manufactures*, 1931, 1933, 1935, 1937, and 1939.

FIGURE 178. WAGES AS PERCENTAGE OF VALUE ADDED IN MANUFACTURING SOUTHEAST AND SOUTHWEST, 1919-1939

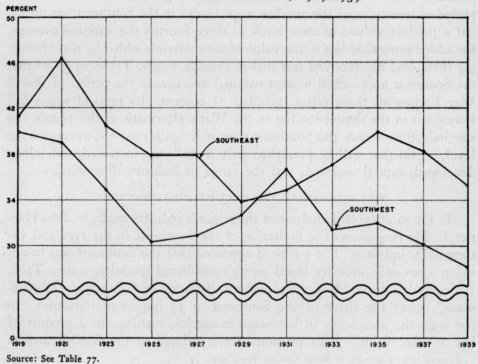

Source: See Table 77.

TABLE 77. INDEX OF CHANGE IN TOTAL VALUE OF PRODUCTION IN MANUFACTURING, UNITED STATES AND SOUTHEAST, 1919-1939
(1919 = 100.0)

Year	UNITED STATES		SOUTHEAST		Year	UNITED STATES		SOUTHEAST	
	Thousands of dollars	Index	Thousands of dollars	Index		Thousands of dollars	Index	Thousands of dollars	Index
1919......	$62,418	100.0	$5,395	100.0	1931......	41,350	66.2	4,115	76.3
1921......	43,653	69.9	3,575	66.3	1933......	31,359	50.2	3,521	65.3
1923......	60,556	97.0	5,153	95.5	1935......	45,760	73.3	4,866	90.2
1925......	62,714	100.5	5,643	104.6	1937......	60,713	97.3	6,351	117.7
1927......	62,718	100.5	5,643	104.6	1939......	56,829	91.0	6,409	118.8
1929......	70,435	112.8	6,309	116.9					

Source: Howard W. Odum, *Southern Regions of the United States*, pp. 435-436; *Fifteenth Census of the United States, 1930*, Manufactures, 1929, II, pp. 16-17; *Biennial Census of Manufactures, 1931*, pp. 21-22; *1933*, p. 20; *1935*, pp. 20-21; *1937*, part I, pp. 20-21; *1939*, preliminary summary, press release of January 9, 1941.

TABLE 78. INDEX OF CHANGE IN TOTAL AMOUNT OF WAGES, UNITED STATES AND SOUTHEAST, 1919-1939
(1919 = 100.0)

Year	UNITED STATES		SOUTHEAST		Year	UNITED STATES		SOUTHEAST	
	Thousands of dollars	Index	Thousands of dollars	Index		Thousands of dollars	Index	Thousands of dollars	Index
1919......	$10,533	100.0	$918	100.0	1931......	$ 7,186	68.2	$645	70.3
1921......	8,202	77.9	673	73.3	1933......	5,262	50.0	547	59.6
1923......	11,010	104.5	873	95.0	1935......	7,545	71.6	735	80.0
1925......	10,730	101.9	912	99.3	1937......	10,113	96.0	924	100.6
1927......	10,849	103.0	954	103.9	1939......	9,090	86.3	918	100.0
1929......	11,621	110.3	989	107.7					

Source: See Table 77.

TABLE 79. RATIO OF AVERAGE VALUES IN SOUTHEAST TO NATIONAL AVERAGE IN THREE INDICES OF MANUFACTURING, 1919-1939

Year	Average value of product per wage earner	Average value added by manufacture per wage earner	Average wage	Year	Average value of product per wage earner	Average value added by manufacture per wage earner	Average wage
1919......	0.762	0.782	0.769	1931......	0.735	0.695	0.662
1921......	0.685	0.664	0.687	1933......	0.738	0.668	0.684
1923......	0.697	0.685	0.650	1935......	0.734	0.652	0.672
1925......	0.692	0.691	0.654	1937......	0.737	0.676	0.643
1927......	0.667	0.677	0.653	1939......	0.737	0.688	0.660
1929......	0.675	0.693	0.642				

Source: See Table 77.

of human resources. Because of a labor supply greater than any demand of southern agriculture, industry finds cheap wage rates. It is, however, the highly competitive industries and those of low productivity that are forced to seek areas of low wage costs. Such industries have not greatly increased the skills of the population and are not likely to raise the general wage level until they find greater competition for the labor supply. The Southeast thus not only needs to increase its industrialization; it needs to broaden and diversify the pattern.

TABLE 80. THE SHARE OF THE SOUTHEAST IN FIFTY-FIVE INDUSTRIES

Industry	Percent in Southeast of National total					
	Wage earners	Wages	Value of product	Value added by manufacture	Salaried persons	Salaries
Turpentine and rosin......................	100.0	100.0	100.0	100.0	100.0	100.0
Cane sugar and manufacture................	100.0	100.0	100.0	100.0	100.0	100.0
Cigarettes................................	94.7	94.4	95.5	96.5	92.4	92.2
Cotton yarn and thread....................	78.5	72.6	74.4	71.1	55.0	54.8
Cotton woven goods (over 12 inches)........	74.0	70.9	74.1	72.0	64.1	64.9
Cottonseed oil, cake and meal.............	68.0	67.9	68.7	61.3	59.7	60.7
Rice cleaning and polishing................	67.0	52.0	55.8	47.4	64.3	58.8
Fertilizers...............................	62.3	45.7	57.2	52.7	60.5	55.4
Lumber and timber products................	44.5	27.9	33.1	32.2	40.9	38.5
Hosiery..................................	44.2	34.8	39.3	36.6	33.1	34.3
Boxes, wooden (not cigar).................	39.6	26.3	25.4	26.6	23.6	24.3
Rayon broad woven goods..................	36.0	33.8	34.6	33.1	24.3	22.4
Men's and boys' work clothing.............	35.3	28.6	31.8	27.0	24.0	22.4
Distilled liquors..........................	34.1	28.0	36.0	32.0	35.6	35.7
Knitted underwear........................	33.3	30.1	30.0	28.8	20.7	21.7
Beverages, nonalcoholic....................	30.4	27.1	32.2	31.7	27.5	31.5
Planing mill products.....................	28.2	19.5	23.2	20.7	20.9	19.1
Wood, turned and shaped.................	27.4	23.0	24.2	22.0	20.7	20.5
Ice, manufactured........................	26.4	19.9	22.8	22.4	30.0	25.4
Canned and cured fish, etc................	26.0	15.3	13.0	14.4	16.9	12.3
Furniture (household and office)............	22.7	17.0	18.0	16.6	14.0	14.7
Marble, etc., cut and shaped..............	22.5	16.9	16.4	17.5	17.5	16.0
Bone black, carbon black..................	19.3	16.5	14.1	12.8	8.7	10.3
Clay products (other than pottery).........	18.9	13.3	14.9	14.1	15.1	16.4
Brooms..................................	18.4	13.5	13.6	14.0	16.8	13.4
Mattress and bedsprings...................	14.6	11.0	12.0	11.8	12.3	14.4
Flour, other grain mill products............	14.5	9.7	9.0	9.6	12.7	11.5
Coffins, caskets, etc......................	13.7	9.9	10.2	8.5	11.0	10.6
Concrete products........................	13.5	9.9	9.7	9.4	12.4	11.9
Ice cream...............................	12.8	10.0	9.5	9.1	15.5	14.9
Feeds, prepared, for animals...............	12.5	8.1	8.7	9.2	13.3	12.8
Canned and dried fruits, pickles, etc.......	11.3	6.0	5.7	5.6	7.6	5.8
Heating and cooking apparatus (not electric) .	9.7	6.7	5.4	5.2	4.1	4.4
Chemicals not elsewhere classified..........	9.7	7.7	9.7	10.3	7.3	6.5
Structural and ornamental steel............	9.6	7.7	8.1	8.1	10.1	9.9
Bread and other bakery products...........	9.2	7.2	8.2	8.0	9.9	8.9
Newspaper and periodical publishing........	8.9	7.3	6.4	6.8	8.9	7.2
Miscellaneous food preparations............	8.6	5.5	6.0	5.7	6.8	6.7
Confectionery............................	8.4	6.4	7.7	7.6	10.2	9.3
Awnings, tents, sails, etc..................	8.0	7.5	6.9	7.7	8.9	8.7
Book and job printing.....................	6.2	5.1	4.9	4.7	5.4	4.7
Cheese..................................	5.8	4.9	4.2	5.2	10.4	7.5
Malt liquors.............................	5.8	4.6	3.9	4.0	5.9	4.9
Meat packing............................	5.6	3.9	3.8	4.4	5.0	4.8
Sheet metal work.........................	5.6	4.2	5.5	4.9	5.5	4.7
Drugs and medicines......................	5.5	3.7	4.8	4.5	7.2	6.2
Butter...................................	4.8	3.9	3.8	4.9	5.4	5.6
Paints, pigment, and varnish..............	4.7	3.7	4.0	4.1	5.1	5.7
Photoengraving...........................	4.5	3.7	4.0	3.9	4.6	4.3
Textile machinery and parts...............	4.5	3.3	4.1	3.6	3.7	3.6
Liquors, rectified and blended.............	4.1	3.5	3.8	4.0	4.8	4.6
Machinery not elsewhere classified..........	4.1	2.9	3.3	3.1	3.3	3.0
Foundry products.........................	4.0	2.9	3.7	3.5	5.9	4.9
Machine shop products....................	3.3	2.6	2.5	2.8	3.0	2.6
Electrical machinery......................	0.5	0.4	0.6	0.4	0.4	0.4

Source: Harriet L. Herring, *Southern Industry and Regional Development* (Chapel Hill: University of North Carolina Press. 1940), p. 72.

In a country characterized by free enterprise, great natural resources, and one of the highest rates of mobility of capital and labor yet known, it might be assumed that regional pockets of poverty, wherever developed, would be cleared out within a generation by migration of workers to points of opportunity or by the migration of industrial capital to areas of low cost resources and low wage levels.

The effect of the above recital of income differentials is to cast doubt on the assumption that such progressive equalization is in process. Southern incomes have risen along with national averages but the Southeast's level of well-being is not rising at the higher rate necessary to equalize conditions within any attainable future. Many millions of southern youth have migrated to seek their chances in the cities and to add to our industrial congestion. Differential fertility continues to replace them faster than southern agriculture and industry absorb them at present levels of development. For the Southeast to solve its problem by migration to the extent suggested by the Report of the Study of Population Redistribution would add to the congestion of more populated areas.[7] To migration must be added the development of a more complex economy than that now afforded by the Southeast.

It is not that the less complex economies are concerned simply with the employment and wage payments afforded by manufacturing. The proportions employed in manufacturing in a complex economy are not especially large nor are industrial wages always the highest. It is the complexity and diversity of a rich economy that the more backward States desire, and the development of manufacturing appears the first logical step to the development of such an economy. No one has determined the precise ratio of auxiliary services needed by manufacturing, but they include many in the higher level of professional and technical services as well as in clerical, trade, transportation, and others in the distributive groups. Compared with the range of specialized occupations and skills found in New York, the occupational structure of a State like Mississippi borders on the primitive. This condition has been offered to explain why a proportionately larger number of the South's able men are found serving in the higher rank of America's armed forces during peacetime. The occupational hierarchy at home does not offer sufficient richness and complexity, and not all can hope through migration and competition to climb to positions of trust and competence abroad.

The South's demand for a larger share in the industrialization of this country has been put on the defensive, as something contaminated with the evil companionship of Chambers of Commerce, municipal subsidies, and low wages. Actually it is no more sectional nor subversive in the competitive American pattern for an undeveloped area to try to secure more industry than for a highly concentrated area to try to increase its large supply. It has become orthodox to regard the South's industrial development as an

[7] Carter Goodrich and Others, *Migration and Economic Opportunity*, pp. 144-157, 495, 518.

attack on union organization and to feel that the region's problems can best be served by population redistribution, continuous migration, and continuous social mobility. While recent Federal legislation has offered a partial answer to this view, the persistence of great inequalities is still the strongest argument for further industrialization.

In regard to migration, the truth of the matter is that the South is not competent under its present economy and culture to continue to rear and educate and send out the Nation's population reserves. Not only is the region too poor, but such a process means a constant drain on its resources. Whatever may be the net worth of the region's human exports, it is safe to estimate that to rear and educate a child to adulthood costs family, community, and State some $2,000 to $5,000. Further development of the South's economy by increasing the variety and range of occupational opportunities will raise the level of living and of training, will reduce the differential birth rate, and will keep more of the South's human and material capital at home to participate in its own development.

Low wages and a one-crop system of industry are characteristic of the opening phases of industrialization. This condition should be accepted only as a transitional phase to whose passing both the region and the Nation are committed. When the region has increased its purchasing power through increasing its productive powers, the Nation too will benefit by its passing.

CHAPTER 18

INDUSTRIALIZATION OF RURAL AREAS

ONE OF the weak points in our understanding of modern society is to be found in our inadequate knowledge of the process of industrialization. The growth of manufacturing in areas formerly given over to agriculture indicates that the processes involved in the changing location of industry have both their positive and their negative aspects.

THE AREA

The Southeastern Piedmont offers a favorable area in which we may trace the effects of manufacturing developments that have occurred in textiles, tobacco, power, furniture, hosiery, rayon, and allied fields within the last generation. Stretching from Lynchburg, Virginia, to Birmingham, Alabama, the Piedmont Industrial area curves around the Southern Appalachians which set its upper boundary, for a distance of some 730 miles. Its southeastern boundary is set by the fall line where the rivers break on their last rapids and level out for a slow and steady flow to the Atlantic and the Gulf.[1] In order to limit the scope of the study, it has been focused on the consideration of the first hydroelectric power zone to emerge in the region, the Catawba Valley power province. This delimitation of the area was also dictated by the fact that water power was one of the main integrating forces in the region's industrial development. In this respect the Catawba Valley can be regarded as a forerunner of the later development visualized in the Tennessee Valley.

In all its ramifications hydroelectric power as a resource has helped to lay down the territorial organization and to integrate industrial development in the Piedmont. It has allowed the use of power at practically any point where the convergence of labor, raw materials, and markets made the construction of a factory advantageous.

[1] See Rupert B. Vance, *Human Geography of the South* (Chapel Hill: University of North Carolina Press, 1932), pp. 275-315.

[279]

As early as 1921 this point of view was stated by C. G. Gilbert and J. E. Pogue.[2]

> Coming into action late the industrialism of the South, unhampered by tradition and unencumbered by obsolescent power establishments, took over the practices best suited to its needs. Thus while the Northeastern states form an illustration of centralized industry . . . the South displays a regional development of industry nowhere intensely focused but spread, on the contrary in diluted form over a large area. The contrast is suggestive; for permanance, for national well-being, for the common good, it would appear that a balanced economic life in which each section manufactures, in a large measure, its own products, is preferable to a highly intensified manufacturing area setting up its own interests in opposition to the more extensive producing areas. The South presents an example of a power supply dispersed to create a normal development from within, with minimum detraction from the opportunities peculiar to other sections.

It is the purpose of this chapter to study the growth of industry in a specific regional area that a generation ago was overwhelmingly rural. In carrying forward this analysis we shall observe the area as it delimits itself in terms of natural resources, of developing technology and of emerging economic forces.

For such an area we chose a river basin as it developed into a power producing and a power distributing province. There is first the Valley Proper, the drainage basin of the Catawba River. Since it contains most of the installations, it can be regarded as the area of power production. Part of the drainage basin is in the Appalachian Highlands and thus the Valley Proper can be divided into the Upper and Lower Valley. In addition there is the surrounding area, 15 industrial counties, over which the power is largely distributed (Figure 179). This larger area will serve as the frame of reference which can be narrowed from time to time to focus on smaller areas for more intensive study. For a field study of a moderate-sized industrial city in relation to its hinterland and surrounding towns, High Point, North Carolina was selected.

Within this framework it should prove possible to show the changing location of industry from the point of view of the factors involved in the various community areas affected, the sequence in which industries appeared, and the changes involved in agriculture, population, and the economic and social conditions of the area. This section, in short, is a case study in the effects of industrialization upon a rural area.

[2] C. G. Gilbert and J. E. Pogue, *America's Power Resources* (New York: Century, 1921), pp. 136-137.

FIGURE 179. THE CATAWBA VALLEY, NORTH CAROLINA AND SOUTH CAROLINA

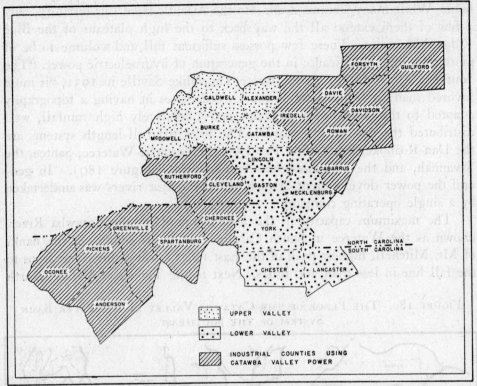

UPPER VALLEY

LOWER VALLEY

INDUSTRIAL COUNTIES USING
CATAWBA VALLEY POWER

Source: Study of the Catawba Valley (Unpublished manuscript, Institute for Research in Social Science, University of North Carolina, 1938).

FACTORS IN THE RISE OF INDUSTRY[3]

In the course of its development the Catawba Valley area has repeated much of the history of industrialization elsewhere. The same factors of resources, transportation, labor supply, low wages, community promotion, and lenient tax policies have prevailed at various times and places. Some special considerations bearing on the area's development, however, may be noted.

WATER POWER

From the Potomac River to the Savannah the topographical belts and the soil regions stretch from northeast to southwest, the slope being to the southeast. The rivers draining the Atlantic Coastal area thus cut across the

[3] This area has been studied by the author for the Industrial Location Section of the National Resources Planning Board to whom the writer is indebted for aid and advice. Much of Chapters 18 and 20 is based on T. J. Woofter, Jr., Harriet L. Herring, Rupert B. Vance, and J. Herman Johnson, The Survey of the Catawba Valley, 1935, an unpublished study made by the Institute for Research in Social Science, University of North Carolina, for the Research and Planning Section of the Tennessee Valley Authority. Acknowledgments are made to the Authority, the Institute, and the Planning Board for permission to make use of these unpublished reports.

grain, flowing eastward and southward across the soil and topographical belts. While many streams drain into the Atlantic from this territory, only a few of them extend all the way back to the high plateaus of the Blue Ridge Mountains. These few possess sufficient fall and volume to be of more than local significance in the generation of hydroelectric power. "The Southern Appalachian region," wrote Thorndike Saville in 1931, "is more favored than any other part of the United States in having a topography adapted to the construction of dams and a relatively high rainfall, well distributed throughout the year."[4] The principal full-length systems are the Dan-Roanoke, the Yadkin-Pee-Dee, the Catawba-Wateree, Santee, the Savannah, and the Chattahoochee-Appalachicola (Figure 180). In general the power development of each of these major rivers was undertaken by a single operating company.

The maximum capacity in the area is found on the Catawba River, known as the Wateree in South Carolina. With its source on the flanks of Mt. Mitchell, highest peak in the East (6,711 feet), this river drops to the fall line in less than 200 miles. Next to the Tennessee Valley, North

FIGURE 180. THE PLACE OF THE CATAWBA VALLEY IN THE RIVER BASIN SYSTEM OF THE SOUTHEAST

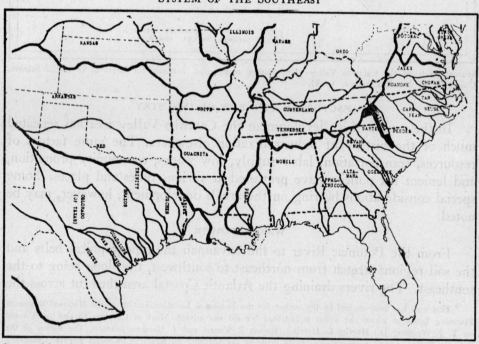

Source: Adapted from a map prepared by the United States Geological Survey.

[4] "The Power Situation in the Southern Power Province," *The Annals* of the American Academy of Political and Social Science, 153 (January, 1931), 99.

FIGURE 181. HYDRO-ELECTRIC DEVELOPMENT IN THE CATAWBA VALLEY
POWER PROVINCE, NORTH AND SOUTH CAROLINA, 1940

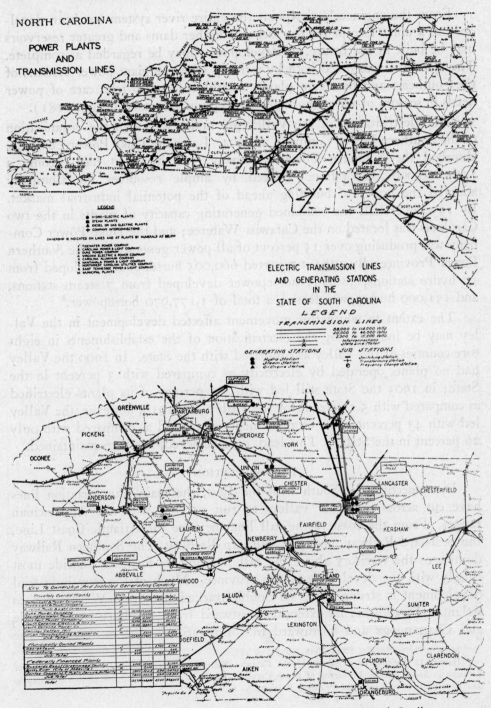

Source: Maps prepared by the State Public Utilities Commissions of North and South Carolina, 1940.

Carolina ranks the highest in the Southeast in both actual and potential water power.

From the engineer's viewpoint the entire river system has been developed as a unit. Except for the fact that higher dams and greater reservoirs may be built in the future, its development may be regarded as complete. The system is reinforced both by a tie-up with the giant power systems of the Southeast and by steam plants, suitably placed to take care of power needs in seasons of water shortage or exceptional demand (Figure 181).

The electrification of the Valley got under way with the organization of the Southern Power Company in 1904. Later the Duke Power Company absorbed the Southern Power Company, and by 1927 had become a $165,000,000 corporation. Backed by ample resources the Company adopted the policy of building ahead of the potential industrial market. By 1930 over half the combined generating capacity of plants in the two Carolinas was located on the Catawba-Wateree; and the Duke Power Company was producing over 15 percent of all power generated in the Southern Power Province. By 1934 it reported 660,005 horsepower developed from 17 hydro stations, 380,965 horsepower developed from 7 steam stations, and 131,000 horsepower leased, a total of 1,177,970 horsepower.[5]

The extent to which this movement affected development in the Valley may be indicated by the electrification of the establishments in eight core counties of the Valley as compared with the State. In 1900 the Valley had no plants operated by electricity as compared with 3 percent in the State; in 1905 the State still led with 7.3 percent of its plants electrified as compared with 5.1 percent for the Valley. By 1910, however, the Valley led with 43 percent of its establishments electrified as compared with only 26 percent in the State.[6] This lead, once achieved, has been maintained.

TRANSPORTATION

In connecting the South with the East, the main transportation lines have cut across the river valleys to run parallel with the Appalachian ranges. From the coast to the fall line they are the Atlantic Coast Line, the Seaboard Railway, and the Southern Railway. The Southern Railway dominates the territory above the fall line and its facilities coincide most closely with the developing power province. Much of the new industrial development is strung along its double-tracked line from Washington to Atlanta. In addition its extension westward from Salisbury to Knoxville and Chattanooga and northward to Cincinnati taps the resources of the

[5] Moody, *Public Utilities* (New York, 1934), p. 161.

[6] Harriet L. Herring in A Survey of the Catawba Valley, I (unpublished manuscript, Institute for Research in Social Science, University of North Carolina, 1935), p. 87. From Reports of the North Carolina Commissioner of Labor and Printing, Raleigh, N. C.

mountain area through the Asheville Basin. In 1921 North and South Carolina inaugurated their intensive program of highway construction, much of which was concentrated in the Piedmont area.

The importance of this factor is indicated by recent estimates which assign 13 percent of the total costs of producing and distributing commodities to costs of transportation. The costs of transporting commodities are estimated at almost one third of the costs of physically producing them.[7] Transportation costs have favored textiles more than furniture. During 1936 according to the Interstate Commerce Commission,[8] freight costs amounted to only 1.8 percent of the value of cotton cloth and cotton fabrics at destination. As a result no elaborate system of zone pricing or freight equalization prevails in the textile market. Cotton yarn, gray goods, finished cloth in general, and even the great bulk of finished apparel are sold on the basis of a simple f.o.b. system. The necessity of absorbing the cost of freight in his gross margin of profit has imposed no particular burden on the retailer, simply because freight ratios are so low. Moreover, transportation costs have been further reduced by the increasing use of truck delivery. It is common practice, for example, for manufacturers to allow free delivery by truck anywhere within the metropolitan area in which textiles and apparel are manufactured.

On the other hand, the ratio of freight costs to the value of household furniture at destination is relatively high, being 10.6 percent in 1936. In spite of this cost, household furniture is sold almost altogether on f.o.b. factory basis with virtually no freight allowance. Prices for furniture, however, are usually "crated" prices. Manufacturers often absorb costs of transportation by truck up to 50 or 100 miles if they are allowed to deliver furniture "uncrated."

THE LABOR FORCE

The labor force has played a most important part in the rise of industry in the Piedmont. More emphasis than necessary has been placed on its Anglo-Saxon inheritance; less emphasis than deserved has been given to the industrial heritage of the common man of the Piedmont and its valleys. As a matter of history the population of this area has been in the process of adjustment to industrialization for a period of some 150 years. The settlers in the back country of the Carolinas, most of whom came down the Shenandoah Valley from Pennsylvania, had little in common with the agrarian aristocracy of the lowlands. Living on the frontier they became jacks of all trades and tried their hands at all means of wresting a living

---

[7] *Does Distribution Cost Too Much?* (New York: Twentieth Century Fund, 1939), p. 118.

[8] *Price Behavior and Business Policy.* Temporary National Economic Committee, Monograph 1 (Washington, D. C.: U. S. Government Printing Office, 1940), p. 300.

from nature. Not only did the inhabitants of this area remain largely outside the early cotton economy, but they carried along with their general farming a healthy tradition of industry.

This heritage can hardly be understood apart from the history of this upland area. The seeds of industrial activity in this general area were first planted in the early frontier period. Domestic manufactures accompanied the spread of settlement in the back counties of Virginia, North and South Carolina. Travellers in the area remarked on the universality of home-made cloth; and Hamilton in his *Report of Manufactures* in 1799 estimated that in some districts of the South from two-thirds to four-fifths of all clothing was made at home. Pioneer skills flourished in a wide range of household and farm handicrafts.

The beginnings of local specializations and divisions of labor were found, writes Harriet L. Herring, in the presence of men and women who wove cloth for their neighbors, wool carders and fullers who took over the processes most inconvenient to perform without special equipment, millers, distillers, hatters, shoemakers, harness makers, saddlers, cabinet makers, and blacksmiths.

From 1790 to the close of the Napoleonic wars, it appeared as though the South might embark upon a manufacturing career. Already the household industries as in New England had received the complement of smuggled and imported machinery in wool carding, fulling, and cotton spinning mills. Power spinning was carried on in South Carolina as early as 1789 at Charleston, in 1798 in the Williamsburg district, and by 1790 at Statesburg. In 1816 Michael Bean made a set of cording, "roping," and spinning machinery for Michael Schencks' famous first cotton factory in North Carolina. There is evidence that there were workmen in the vicinity of Lincolnton two decades previous who knew how to make and operate water-driven cotton processing machinery. Immigrants from Rhode Island textile centers settled in the Piedmont about 1815 and built cotton mills on little streams in nearby South Carolina at Fingerville, Batesville, and Bivingsville.[9]

Obviously important in this development was the presence of a large working force, able and willing to enter new industries. Undoubtedly most of the early workers in the industry came from nearby farms. In a study of 500 textile workers families in Gaston County in 1925-26, Rhyne found that over three-fifths (62.6 percent) of the parents of male family heads had been farmers, and less than one-fifth (18.1 percent) had been mill operatives. Of the present heads, fully half (51.2 percent) had farmed

[9] Harriet L. Herring, History of the Southern Textile Industry (unpublished manuscript, Chapel Hill Institute for Research in Social Science, University of North Carolina), chaps. II, III, IV. Summarized in *The Annals* of the American Academy of Political and Social Science, 153 (January, 1931), 5.

before going into industry. The vast majority of persons (91 percent) were born in North Carolina or South Carolina. Only 13 persons, 0.7 percent, were born outside the Southeast.[10]

In a comparable analysis of the neighboring Leaksville-Spray-Draper development in 1937, Harriet Herring found that 23 percent of the workers were born in the towns, 18 percent in the county, and 38 percent in contiguous counties. Less than five percent were born outside the States of North Carolina and Virginia.[11]

While less than a fifth (18.1 percent) of the chief breadwinners were born in textile centers, Rhyne found that almost a third (30.9 percent) of the unmarried workers and over three-fifths (63 percent) of the children, 6-14 years of age, were born in cotton mill towns. For this group the percentage of those occupied permanently in the textile industry had increased from 18 to 70 percent within three generations. On the basis of the rate of increase he spoke of cotton mill workers as a possible hereditary occupational group and predicted that the industry would soon become independent of the agricultural reserve as a source of labor supply. Since then, however, southern agriculture has encountered a long period of depression while the industrialization of the area has continued partly as a result of the presence of this labor supply.

In the textile industry women serve as a complementary labor force making up some two-fifths of those employed. In the textile industry of the world women make up 52 percent of the workers; in the United States they constitute 41.6 percent; in the Leaksville-Spray-Draper area, 38.9 percent.[12]

WAGE AND HOUR STRUCTURE

Although wages are low in the area, labor costs take comparatively high rank among the costs of production in those industries in which the Southeast has shown a large development. Some indication of the regional wage structure in textiles is given below on page 290. Wages in furniture offer another example of lower costs in the South. Available data on wages and hours in the furniture industry, however, do not show the changes brought about by the wage and hour law, effective in 1938. While it appears that the extreme differential between northern and southern wages was reduced by the Fair Labor Standards Act, it is possible that little increase in the average wages of skilled and semi-skilled labor occurred before the rise in connection with war industries. It has been necessary to use data for the

[10] J. J. Rhyne, *Some Cotton Mill Workers and Their Villages* (Chapel Hill: University of North Carolina Press, 1930), chap. VIII.

[11] Harriet L. Herring, "The Outside Employer in the Southern Industrial Pattern," *Social Forces*, XVIII (October, 1939), 115-126.

[12] *Ibid.*

South since detailed statistics were not available for the North Carolina area. North Carolina wages on the whole are somewhat higher than the southern average and wages in High Point may be somewhat higher than the average for all furniture in North Carolina.[13]

The region's chief furniture product is wooden household furniture, including case goods (dining room and bedroom suites), upholstery, novelty, and kitchen furniture. The average hourly wage in the wooden household furniture industry in the United States in 1937 was 48 cents; in the North, 53 cents; in the South, 35 cents; and in North Carolina, 36 cents. Earnings in the High Point-Thomasville furniture area for this type of furniture were somewhat higher than the State average, being approximately 39 cents an hour.

TABLE 81.   AVERAGE HOURLY EARNINGS IN THE FURNITURE INDUSTRY, UNITED STATES AND REGIONS, 1937

Group	Case Goods			Upholstery		
	United States	North	South	United States	North	South
Skilled	51.8	57.8	41.9	68.1	74.2	47.8
Semi-skilled	42.2	49.4	33.0	50.5	55.6	37.1
Unskilled	33.9	40.2	28.0	33.9	40.2	28.0
Average	44.1	51.3	34.7	56.5	62.7	37.8

Group	Novelty Furniture			Kitchen Furniture		
	United States	North	South	United States	North	South
Skilled	55.0	56.4	39.2	48.8	50.2	41.3
Semi-skilled	49.1	50.5	32.6	42.7	44.2	36.5
Unskilled	39.2	40.5	27.2	35.1	36.6	30.0
Average	48.9	50.3	33.4	43.1	44.7	36.1

Source: *Wage and Hour Structure of the Furniture Industry*, U. S. Bureau of Labor Statistics, Bulletin 669 (October, 1937).

As indicated in Table 81, the regional differential in wages varied in some degree according to the type of wooden household furniture produced and the skills of those working in each type. As Figure 182 indicates, upholstery workers are the highest paid, while workers in kitchen furniture were the lowest paid. Comparison of wages paid skilled, semi-skilled, and unskilled workers gives significant content to the social-economic classification of occupations.

The actual weekly hours worked by all workers in the wooden household furniture industry in the United States averaged 42.5 in October, 1937. The South's work week averaged from 3 to 5 hours longer in the various types of product. The southern industry, at present, adheres to the 40 hour week as established by the wage-hour law. In October, 1937, southern wages were 73 percent of the national and 66 percent of the northern rates.

[13] *Wage and Hour Structure of the Furniture Industry*, U. S. Bureau of Labor Statistics, Bulletin 669 (Washington, D. C.: U. S. Government Printing Office, October, 1937).

FIGURE 182. AVERAGE HOURLY EARNINGS IN FOUR BRANCHES OF THE FURNI-
TURE INDUSTRY FOR SKILLED, SEMI-SKILLED, AND UNSKILLED
WORKERS, NORTH AND SOUTH, 1937

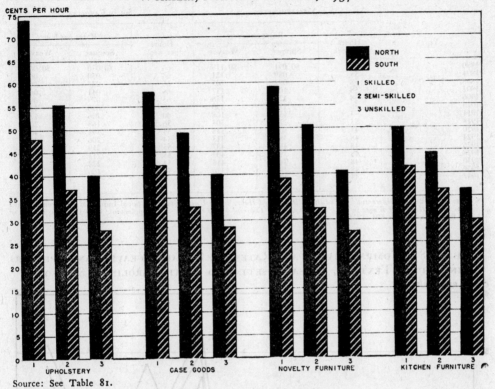

Source: See Table 81.

Highly competitive industries, such as cotton textiles, have sought the plentiful labor supply in the low wage areas of the Southeast. This very development, however, has been accompanied by a decrease in the initial wage differential. Table 82 shows that from 1890 to 1920 hourly rates for female spinners in South Carolina increased from 33 to 77 percent of Massachusetts rates; for female weavers from 52 to 85 percent. After the recession of 1920 the southern differential became greater. By 1937 hours were equalized and the South Carolina wage was 81 percent of that paid by Massachusetts for spinners and 93 percent for weavers (Figure 183).

An analysis of types shows the predominance in the Southeast of those industries which have comparatively low value of product and low value added by manufacturing. Included are furniture, cast iron pipe, shirts, cotton yarns, knitted underwear, work clothing, cotton goods, clay products, lumber, and hosiery.[14] Cigarette manufacturing, one of the South's most profitable industries, simply pays the going wage in the area.

[14] Harriet L. Herring, *Southern Industry and Regional Development* (Chapel Hill: University of North Carolina Press, 1940), pp. 8-9 and charts pp. 66-67.

TABLE 82. WAGE RATES AND HOURS FOR FEMALE SPINNERS AND WEAVERS IN THE COTTON INDUSTRY OF MASSACHUSETTS AND SOUTH CAROLINA, 1890-1937

| Year | MASSACHUSETTS | | | SOUTH CAROLINA | | |
| | Hours per week | Rates per hour | | Hours per week | Rates per hour | |
		Spinner	Weaver		Spinner	Weaver
1890	60	$0.091	$0.119	66	$0.030	$0.062
1894	55	.089	.121	66	.030	.067
1898	58	.092	.125	66	.033	.060
1902	58	.103	.137	66	.041	.068
1906	58	.122	.156	65.7	.079	.099
1910	56	.131	.150	60	.090	.122
1914	53.9	.150	.168	60	.106	.130
1918	53.7	.277	.303	56.5	.168	.200
1920	47.9	.506	.548	54	.391	.468
1924	48	.386	.415	54	.206	.260
1926	48	.437	.487	55	.219	.291
1928	48	.350	.405	55	.215	.277
1930	48	.342	.415	54.8	.222	.312
1932	48	.289	.336	55	.166	.262
1937	35.1	.454	.523	33.7	.350	.486

Source: M. A. Beney, *Differentials in Industrial Wages and Hours in the United States*, National Industrial Conference Board Studies, 1938; *History of Wages in the United States from Colonial Times to 1928*, with Supplement, 1929-32, U. S. Bureau of Labor Statistics, Bulletin 604 (1934).

FIGURE 183. COMPARATIVE WAGE RATES FOR FEMALE WEAVERS AND SPINNERS IN COTTON TEXTILES, MASSACHUSETTS AND SOUTH CAROLINA, 1890-1937

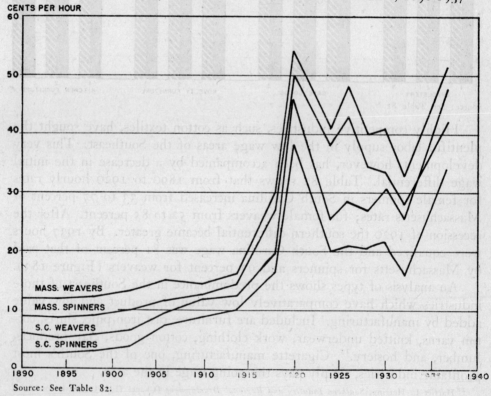

Source: See Table 82.

Variations in types of industry, in processes of manufacturing, and the degree of competition to which the industry and its workers are exposed may be as important as different skills, the composition of labor, lack of unionization, and industrial location. The value added by manufacturing (1937) per wage earner is much lower in the Southeast than in the Nation as a whole—$1,987 as compared with $2,938. South Carolina with a much lower average wage than New York ($707 as compared with $1,241), paid 52.3 percent of its value added by manufacture out in wages as compared with only 37.3 percent for New York. Nor is it necessarily true that all South Carolina industries have lower capital costs. Thus, as Harriet L. Herring points out, New York has nearly 300,000 wage earners (some 30 percent of its total) in clothing industries which require only from $400 to $1,000 per wage earner, while South Carolina has some 88,000 of its total wage earners in cotton mills which require around $3,000 capital investment per worker.[15]

THE RANGE AND SEQUENCE OF INDUSTRIAL DEVELOPMENT

Industries tend to assemble in typical cluster and to feed, as it were, at each others' tables on the goods and services they pass from hand to hand. One way of studying industrialization, accordingly, is to note the range and sequence of industrial development. The emergence of a textile complex, surrounded by a large degree of diversified small industry was evident in the Catawba Valley before the Civil War.

By 1860 nearly every county in the area had one or more factories to report to the census takers. Six of these counties reported 7 cotton mills with 114 workers and 2 woolen mills with 102 workers. In addition the Valley reported establishments engaged in making agricultural implements, boots and shoes, cabinet work and furniture, carriages, wagons and carts, clothing, cooperage, flour and meal, harness and saddles, hats, iron and brass castings, linseed oil, liquors, lumber, waste paper, tobacco, manufacturers tin, copper, and sheet iron works. Lincoln County reported 72 establishments with 21 different kinds of manufacturing, a greater variety than contained in the county today.[16] Many of the area's industries served the Confederacy during the War and then shared the fate of all industry during the period that followed.

After Reconstruction, the resurgence of cotton textiles initiated the new sequence of development and the Valley took its place as an entering wedge of industrialization in the Southeast. The shift of cotton manufacturing to

[15] *Ibid.*, pp. 8-9. See also Julius Hochman, *Industry Planning Through Collective Bargaining* (New York: I. L. G. W. Union, 1941), p. 10.

[16] Harriet L. Herring, "Early Industrial Development in the South," *The Annals* of the American Academy of Political and Social Science, 153 (January, 1931), 1-10.

the Southeast took three forms: the growth of southern enterprises, the outright removal of northern companies, and the building of branch plants in the South. The initial building of southern mills, financed largely by southern capital, undoubtedly began the southern migration.

In their various stages followed lumbering, tobacco, hydroelectric power, furniture, hosiery (knit goods), etc. For a long time textiles were synonymous with manufacturing in the South, bidding fair to become as much a field of concentration as the one-crop system. The first stage was in semifinished textiles and for a long time the area produced little beyond the basic yarns and gray goods.

By 1900 with one-fifth of the population, the whole Valley area had approximately 39 percent of the manufactures of the two States in terms of such measures as number of wage earners, wages paid, value of product, etc. The Valley has maintained the early lead it took in the industrialization of the two Carolinas. By 1920 the Valley with 24.5 percent of total population accounted for from 43 to 48 percent of the manufacturing; and by 1930 it had 27.8 percent of the population and from 52 to 54 percent of the wage earners and wages paid in the two Carolinas. Its proportion of establishments has been notably smaller, indicating the predominance of large-sized units in the area. From 1900 to 1930 the number of wage earners in the Carolinas increased over one and a half times (66 percent); whereas in the 23 counties the number increased almost two and one-half times (146.4 percent). Values of manufactured products in the Valley multiplied by 10 and more in the period. Physical quantities, on the other

TABLE 83. INDUSTRIES WITH FIVE OR MORE ESTABLISHMENTS, CATAWBA VALLEY, 1929

Industry	Number of Establishments	Industry	Number of Establishments
Cotton goods	326	Marble, granite, slate, etc.	18
Lumber and timber products	215	Silk and rayon manufacturing	15
Furniture, including store and office fixtures	92	Mattresses and bed springs	15
Planing mill products, not made in mills connected with saw mills	86	Concrete products	14
		Gas manufacturing, illuminating and heating	12
Knit goods	86	Clay products (other than pottery) and nonclay refractories	12
Flour and grain-mill products	74		
Ice, manufacturing	67	Cigars and cigarettes	10
Printing and publishing (news and periodicals)	66	Cordage and twine	10
Beverages	63	Copper, tin and iron sheet works	10
Printing and publishing (book and job)	56	Leather belting	8
Bakery products	55	Men's work clothing, not including shirts	8
Foundry and machine shop products; not elsewhere classified	50	Motor vehicle bodies and body parts	8
		Cotton small wares	6
Textile machinery and parts	30	Mirrors	6
Fertilizers	25	Women's clothing, n.e.c.	5
Oil, cake and meal, cotton seed	25	Men's furnishing goods	5
Ice cream	21	Shirts	5
Dyeing and finishing textiles	19	Signs and advertising novelties	5

Source: Harriet L. Herring in A Survey of the Catawba Valley, I (unpublished manuscript, Institute for Research in Social Science, University of North Carolina, 1935).

hand, probably increased no more than six or seven times, owing in part to the trend toward a more finished product.

Compared with its States, the Valley had a more varied group of manufactures, possessing according to the classification of the Census of Manufactures, 105 different kinds of industry as against 134 for North Carolina and 89 for South Carolina. Most of the variety, however, is contributed by a few counties, notably Mecklenburg and Guilford Counties in North Carolina. Lincoln County with 12 types has less variety than it possessed in 1860.

Table 83 gives the important manufacturing industries in the area in 1929 and indicates the industries that cluster around textiles, furniture, knit goods, etc. Recent data indicate a further shift from cotton textiles to hosiery and rayon.

CHAPTER 19

THE RISE OF AN INDUSTRIAL COMMUNITY

THE RELATION of rural, village, and urban areas in the industrial pattern of the Piedmont can be shown by a study of an industrial city of moderate size in relation to its hinterland. High Point, North Carolina, the area's pioneer furniture manufacturing center offers a case study in community development in this industrial area. It is surrounded by large and small industrial centers, many of which are still dominated by their agricultural hinterlands.[1]

High Point has a population of over 38,000 and the area within a 40 mile radius thereof contains over 500,000 people, with some 60 percent classified as rural. Seven miles from High Point is located Thomasville, another furniture manufacturing center with a population of 11,073. In the open country in nearly every direction from High Point, especially to the south, can be found small textile mills, each situated on the edge of a stream. Clustered about each mill is a small village. These are mainly old mills built in the days of water power. While some of these mills have been abandoned in the course of time, others have been taken over, repaired by various companies, and put back in operation. Typical of the surrounding rural mill villages are Jamestown, Central Falls, Cedar Falls, Worthville, Ramseur, Randleman, Kernersville, Erlanger, Franklinville, and Gibsonville (Figure 184).

While High Point is dominated by larger cities like Winston-Salem and Greensboro, it in turn serves as a trade center and source of employment for smaller cities. Furniture manufacturing predominates with hosiery gaining in importance. Subsidiary are firms engaged in manufacturing supplies for the furniture industry. Cotton textiles are also present, but of minor importance.

[1] The field work and preliminary analysis of this study were done by Ruth Crowell Leafer under the author's supervision, in connection with a study by the National Resources Planning Board.

[294]

FIGURE 184. THE HIGH POINT AREA

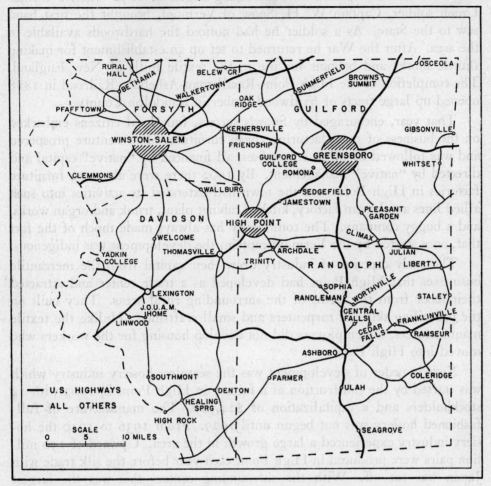

Source: See Figure 179, p. 281.

DEVELOPMENT OF THE FURNITURE INDUSTRY

In the decades after 1880 the furniture manufacturing industry was undergoing changes in its processes, its markets, its materials, and its location. In this period North Carolina turned to the making of furniture as an early step in industrialization. The industrialization of the rural community that pioneered in furniture is typical to a large extent of the movement in the Catawba Valley.

In the 1870's High Point was a small trade center for a rural area. Incorporated with 250 inhabitants in 1859 at the junction of the projected North Carolina Railroad with the intersection of two stage lines—the Great Northern and the Southern States—it boasted one factory making wagon stocks and spokes. Woodworking began in 1872 when a former Union soldier, Captain W. H. Snow of Vermont, brought the first band saw to the State. As a soldier he had noticed the hardwoods available in the area. After the War he returned to set up an establishment for making shuttle blocks and bobbins for use in the textile mills of New England. The completion of the High Point-Randleman-Asheboro Railroad in 1888 opened up large tracts of hardwood timber in Randolph County.

That year, encouraged by Snow's success, four local citizens embarked on the business of manufacturing cheap furniture. The venture prospered and was followed by other enterprises, all financed by "native" capital and directed by "native" management. By 1902 there were about 14 furniture factories in High Point and the town had extended its activities into such allied lines as a broom factory, kitchen cabinet plant, trunk and organ works, and a buggy company. The community has always made much of the fact that, once started by the Vermont captain, the development was indigenous.

The early captains of industry drew their capital from the mercantile businesses that High Point had developed as a trade center and attracted their labor from the farms of the surrounding rural areas. They built on the prevailing skills of carpenters and small craftsmen. Unlike the textile manufacturers, the employers did not develop housing for the workers who moved into High Point.

Next in order of development was the seamless hosiery industry which was started by the construction of a factory in High Point in 1903 with 14 stockholders and a capitalization of $24,500. The manufacture of full-fashioned hosiery was not begun until 1929. From 1936 to 1940 the hosiery industry experienced a large growth in the area. Upward of 150 million pairs were produced in High Point each year before the silk trade with Japan was cut off. With the surrounding centers this was the largest hosiery-producing area in the South, exceeded in the Nation only by the Philadelphia-Reading area. Approximately one-sixth of the 600 hosiery plants in the United States were located within a 75 mile radius of High Point.

In 1921 the Southern Furniture Exposition Building was erected at High Point to serve as the market for the Southern Furniture Manufacturers. It contains 275,000 square feet of exposition space. From 2,000 to 3,000 buyers attend the market during the July and January shows. By 1929 North Carolina had risen to the fifth-ranking State in the production of household furniture, and the High Point Market was outranked only by the National Market at Chicago, the New York, and the Grand Rapids Markets.

Thomasville, seven miles to the west, grew as a satellite of the development in furniture at High Point. With only one-third the population of High Point, but with larger plants using more efficient methods, it outstripped High Point in furniture production in the last decade. Two cotton textile mills with mill villages and seamless hosiery complete the town's industrial pattern. Unlike that of High Point, Thomasville's furniture industry has a larger pay roll and is more important than either hosiery or textiles.

FACTORS IN THE RISE OF THE FURNITURE INDUSTRY

As an industry in flux, furniture has been influenced by many trends. Before the beginnings of High Point, possibly by 1870, the trend was well under way in this country toward improvement in machinery, reduction in costs, the substitution of quantity production for custom-made goods, and the consequent widening of markets with the increased purchasing power of rising middle classes. With the greater availability of liquid capital, the factory system and quantity production began to dominate the industry. In spite of the fact that furniture manufacturing is not wholly adaptable to straight-line production methods, the small custom shop and the old cabinet maker were pushed further and further into the background. The output of the industry increased as costs decreased and the quality was held to improve. Furniture thus was an expanding industry at the time High Point entered the picture; and the growing markets were located in the West and South. Moreover the tendency of furniture manufacturing to resist straight-line production methods and to center on rising new markets has enabled it to resist the general trend toward concentration.

Compared with these trends toward new processes and new markets, the primary resources in the immediate High Point area do not loom so large. The chief factors were raw materials, labor supply, and transportation. Less important to the furniture industry appears to have been the new source of hydroelectric power. No furniture plants were electrified in 1900 and they have been the slowest of all major local manufacturing establishments to make use of electricity. As late as 1925 only 55.4 percent of the plants were using electricity alone or combined with other power. Only 37.6 percent were using electric power alone. Steam power was cheapest in the early days, mainly because great quantities of scrap lumber were burned in the boilers to generate steam power. However, as timber became more expensive its by-products were more closely utilized.

In its early relation to the railroad, High Point simply repeated the history of many cities. The projection of an early railroad determined the city's location; the completion of a local road served to open up sources of raw materials; and the incorporation of the old North Carolina Railroad in the Southern Railway System gave access to markets to the North and West as well as to the growing southern market. With the South's recovery after the Civil War, levels of living rose and railroad nets spread. It is not surprising, therefore, that High Point, as the furniture center farthest South, came to tap these markets.

What should be explained, however, is the appearance of High Point furniture in the national market. Here the explanation lies in the action of southern carriers in establishing low freight rates to important eastern markets. With its dependence on staple crops, the South imported much in the way of fabricated goods and farm supplies, hay and grain from western and northeastern territory. Since much of the South's export staples, cotton, tobacco, etc., went overseas, many empty cars were hauled back by the carriers. To remedy this situation the railroads offered low rates to the High Point manufacturers within the rate territory of the southern carriers, West and North to the Ohio River. When these rates were lowered sufficiently to compensate for the high rates incidental to transportation outside southern territory, High Point manufacturers were able to lay down furniture beyond the Ohio in competition with the Michigan industry. This advantage continued to nurture the High Point industry after the rate structure was consolidated under the supervision of the Interstate Commerce Commission. The present rates are the original subnormal rates subjected to the general increases and reductions that have prevailed since that period.[2]

The availability of raw materials has changed greatly within the brief period of High Point's development. In the beginning the available lumber supply easily seemed the most favorable of all local factors. The timber supply immediately around High Point was abundant. The original hardwood supply within access of High Point extending through the Appalachians has been estimated by the United States Forestry Service at more than 325 billion board feet of lumber. Today not more than 60 billion board feet remain and most of this has been culled. About 12 percent of the stand is spruce, hemlock, and pine; about 35 percent is oak of various species; and about 25 percent, chestnut. The chestnut blight, moreover, has greatly depleted this timber. The Forestry Service estimated that

[2] ". . . The long-continued policy of the southern carriers has been to maintain on articles manufactured in the South rates which would enable southern manufacturers to reach the large consuming markets in the North. . . . Those carriers say that when the furniture industry of the South was in its infancy they established, in line with that policy, rates below normal to important consuming markets in eastern territory . . . The present rates are said to be the original subnormal rates subjected to the general increases and reduction, except for certain minor modifications . . ." U. S. Interstate Commerce Commission, Furniture from southern points to trunk line and New England territories . . . Decided July 1, 1925 (100 I. C. C. Reports 127-152).

within 15 years the Appalachians will cease to be an important source of high grade hardwood and that within 20 years the virgin timber will have practically disappeared.

The depletion of hardwood has led to higher costs of raw materials, substitution of new woods such as gum, and better utilization of by-products. Higher costs of wood undoubtedly have served to effect changes in styles. Developments in upholstering have been accompanied by the increased use of hardwood veneers, glued on low-grade woods. For finishing and for specialty goods the factories of High Point have drawn mahogany from Africa and South America, cane and rattan from Singapore and the Philippines, burlap from India, hardware and the finer fabrics from New England, and plate glass from the Pittsburgh district. Increasingly they have been forced to draw upon the hardwoods from the Mississippi Valley. This depletion of its major raw materials is a serious threat to the stability of the industry. The immediate accessibility of raw materials appears to have been a primary cause of the location of the industry at High Point. As this resource becomes less accessible, what will increased costs mean to the competitive position of High Point? Statistics show that the city has not regained the level of output held before the depression, even when allowances are made for the decline in the price of furniture since 1929.

Beginning with low-priced and relatively unskilled labor, the area never developed the pattern of the old style craftsman and cabinet maker of highest artistry. In the early period the city trained its workers on low-grade furniture for a cheap market, and by the time its quality had improved, quantity production had largely replaced the tradition of the old cabinet maker. In early years at High Point tables and chairs, for example, were manufactured by separate companies; and the merchants who had to buy furniture separately, tried to match them in order to give the customer a matched suite. Gradually the product was improved, methods of production were changed, and improved styles and better designs were featured. Southern furniture production, however, has been largely of the cheaper and medium priced bedroom and dining room suites. Furniture manufactured in High Point is now classified as 15 percent fine grades, 70 percent medium grades and 15 percent cheap grades. North Carolina and Virginia combined produce about one-third of all bedroom furniture and slightly less than one-third of all dining room furniture produced in the Nation. North Carolina still leads in wooden bedroom furniture.

Most of the laborers in furniture manufacturing are semi-skilled and unskilled workers, because of the introduction of automatic machinery, departmentalization and the division of labor within departments, and the use of straight-line production methods. Last to yield has been the work of the upholsterers, but even here the skill that was once demanded has largely given way to subdivision into tasks that can be done by semi-skilled workers. Quantity production, however, must be counted in terms of hundreds rather than thousands, and "goods still require from 30 to 120 days to build." In addition a number of highly skilled tasks remain in the industry, especially in the construction of samples, the setting and operating of certain machines and in special finishing jobs. Wages vary greatly and are not always in close relation to skills. Furniture workers were largely unorganized in 1940, and High Point was no exception.

SPATIAL AND STRUCTURAL ASPECTS OF THE INDUSTRIAL PATTERN

More than is commonly realized, industrialization is responsible for changing the structural and spatial relationships of communities. The problem of a moderately sized city in a pattern of diffused industrialization can be stated in terms of the areas it dominates and the centers which dominate it. This, in turn, is reflected in the internal structure of the city itself.

High Point is a two-industry town. Furniture and hosiery offer the main sources of employment. A division of labor exists between the sexes, with men working almost entirely in furniture and about an equal number of men and women working in hosiery. With industrial workers dependent mainly on two industries subject to seasonal fluctuations with consequent lay-offs, High Point suffers from the lack of a more varied type of industrialization. Particularly needed are more skilled industries to balance the relative low-wage, semi-skilled seamless hosiery and cotton yarn plants.

In its wider aspects there is apparent the dominance of the new industrial community over the agricultural hinterland out of which it grew. On the other hand, the city itself is overshadowed by large centers. In its internal aspects there is the growth and differentiation of the city's own physical structure in its residential, commercial, and industrial districts.

The commercial, wholesale and retail areas of the city are underdeveloped. High Point's trading area extends to about a fifteen mile radius to the south of the city and only about seven miles in other directions. Winston-Salem and Greensboro give severe competition to both its retail and wholesale stores. In per capita retail trade, High Point ranks among the lowest for cities of its size in the State.

In the early days, people built their homes along the railroads, and the residential and industrial areas are now intermixed as a result of the early unplanned years of growth. A zoning commission was set up and has been operating since 1928. Most of the damage, however, was done long before 1928 and a great deal of it cannot be repaired.

Cotton mill workers live in two mill villages consisting of cottages of three to five rooms. In 1941 these houses rented at the rate of 25 cents per room per week. All the houses were old with one spigot of cold running water, no hot water, no bathtubs, and only a few kitchen sinks. Toilets were of the water closet type, some situated in an outdoor building. Water was free and electricity was 4 cents a kilowatt-hour. Furniture and hosiery workers lived within the general area of working-men's homes. For their houses, they paid from $12 to $20 a month rent. Because of their cheaper rents, cotton mill employees have lower living costs than similarly paid workers in furniture and hosiery.

High Point's relation to the surrounding areas furnishes a complex situation in which industry and agriculture play important parts. To be considered are the farmers who look to High Point for a market for their produce, and the industrial workers who live in the towns and countryside. Approximately 3,000 of the 10,132 wage earners reported for High Point live outside the city. A count from the city directory showed that they come from addresses on five rural routes and 28 cities and towns within a radius of 40 miles.

There is a complex interchange of labor between High Point and Winston-Salem, Greensboro, Thomasville, Lexington, Asheboro, and all of the smaller communities and rural areas contiguous. In the main, this movement takes place among the four predominating industries; cotton textiles, hosiery, furniture, and tobacco manufactures. Lacking interchange among the variety of industries that would be found in a metropolitan area, workers resort to greater geographic mobility supplemented by shifts between industry and agriculture. Decentralization of this type, lacking the interurban transport characteristic of more densely settled areas, was especially vulnerable to the rationing of gasoline and tires which followed the outbreak of World War II.

There is no large scale or highly mechanized farming in the area. Tobacco, the main crop, is marketed in Winston-Salem and is thus of little value to High Point. Dairying has made gains in the past fifteen years and the keeping of live-stock has also increased. High Point is a good market for both of these products. The farm problem and its adjustment to fit in with nearby city markets is much the same here as in other parts of the South. A needed development advantageous to both farmers and city dwellers is large-scale truck farming. The cultivation of fruits and berries has been suggested as a good interchange between the rural regions and High Point and as a basis for a canning industry in the city. Farmers still cling to the old way of growing a cash crop of tobacco and cotton on depleted soil instead of branching out into general truck farming.

On the other hand, members of farm families frequently seek and obtain part-time employment in the local industries. It is not uncommon, for instance, to find farmers' wives working in the hosiery mills or farm youths employed in the furniture industry during the peak winter months.

The past ten years have been marked by the tendency of city workers to move out to the rural areas. Land sales are booming in areas around High Point, usually centering around a country school. It has been found, however, that the workers who have moved to these areas do little farming beyond keeping a cow and chickens. From the standpoint of planning, this recent move of city workers to the country would suggest the possible development of suburban residential areas with low-cost housing and well-integrated small communities offering not only water, lights, and sewage disposal facilities but educational and social advantages.

CHAPTER 20

THE EFFECTS OF INDUSTRIALIZATION

EQUALLY important as a discussion of the factors contributing to the rise of industry in the Southern Piedmont is an appraisal of the effects of industrialization on the area. The following section discusses the extent to which industry is decentralized, the effects of industrialization on population and on agriculture, and the emergence of part-time farming.

TO WHAT EXTENT IS INDUSTRY DECENTRALIZED?

Since the degree of industrial concentration is a relative matter, the status of the Southeastern Piedmont may be shown by comparison with New England, one of the oldest industrial areas. In this regional comparison the textile industry may serve as a common denominator. The comparison is made before the war economy had increased the concentrations in munitions and heavy industry. In 1940, as Figure 185 indicates, there were 68 counties in the United States each with 100,000 or more cotton textile spindles. These counties are located mainly in the New England States and the Southeast. Examination of the two regions indicates that in the New England States the textile industry is highly concentrated in metropolitan areas and in the Southeast is widely dispersed. Only 13 of the 57 main cotton-spindle counties in the Southeast employed as many as 10,000 manufacturing wage earners in 1929. Thus, the textile industry in this region is comparatively scattered. To a greater extent than in New England, the industrial prominence of a county is determined by the presence of textiles and allied industries.

The shift in cotton textiles is evidently a trend toward the decentralization of a contracting industry. The peak year for cotton spindles in place was 1925 with 37.9 millions (Figure 186). By 1940 this figure had declined to 24¾ millions (Figure 185) although active spindle hours had increased with the introduction of double and triple shifts. A comparison between the two regions for this period shows that the main New England

[303]

FIGURE 185. COUNTIES HAVING 100,000 OR MORE TEXTILE SPINDLES, UNITED STATES, 1939-40

FIGURE 186. COUNTIES HAVING 100,000 OR MORE TEXTILE SPINDLES, UNITED STATES, 1925

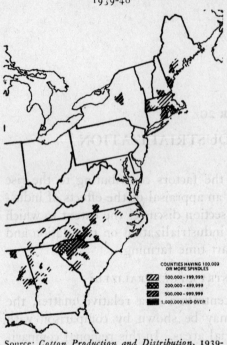

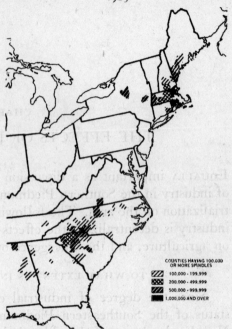

Source: *Cotton Production and Distribution*, 1939-1940, United States Department of Commerce.

Source: *Cotton Production and Distribution*, 1925, United States Department of Commerce.

counties lost 12,636,126 spindles, a decrease of 68.4 percent in 15 years while the main southern counties gained only 630,944 spindles, a 4.9 percent increase. Each of the 21 New England counties showed an absolute decline in the number of cotton spindles while 21 of the South's 57 counties showed a decline. Active spindles in all New England counties declined from 15.9 to 5.3 millions; in all counties of the cotton growing States they increased from 17.3 to 17.6 millions.

The degree of concentration can be shown further by the number and proportion of industrial wage earners as well as the density of the population. The accompanying Figures 187 and 188 show 36 Piedmont counties with less than 5,000 wage earners while the New England industrial areas had only 4 such counties in 1930.[1] Fourteen southern counties and nine New England counties had from 5,000 to 10,000 wage earners each. The Piedmont had 10 counties[2] with from 10,000 to 40,000 wage earners and

[1] In considering differences in the number of wage earners between the two areas, 16 counties have been added to Figures 188 and 189. Thirteen were added to the New England cotton-spindle counties making a total of 34 to show further the concentrated nature of the area surrounding the spindle counties. Three counties were added in the southern region bringing the total to 61 to include the entire Catawba Valley Power province. These were Alexander, Burke, and Davie which are in the Valley and did not have 100,000 cotton spindles either in 1925 or 1940.

[2] Mecklenburg had only 9,299 industrial wage earners, but was included in the census classification as an important industrial county because of the population of Charlotte. Including this county would make 11 southern counties industrially important.

FIGURE 187. NUMBER OF WAGE EARNERS IN MAJOR TEXTILE AREAS, UNITED STATES, 1940

FIGURE 188. PERCENTAGE OF INDUSTRIAL WAGE EARNERS IN THE TOTAL GAINFULLY EMPLOYED MAJOR TEXTILE AREAS, UNITED STATES, 1940

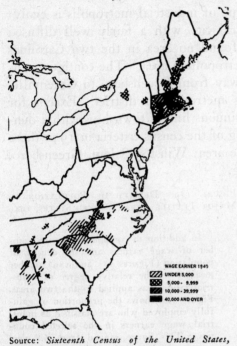

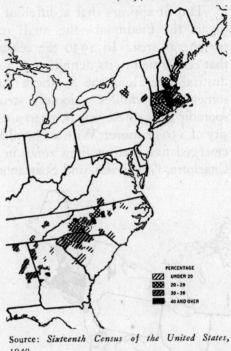

Source: *Sixteenth Census of the United States, 1940.*

Source: *Sixteenth Census of the United States, 1940.*

New England had 11 counties. The South had no major industrial area (40,000 or more wage earners), while New England had 10 counties included as parts of major industrial areas. While 61.8 percent of New England's counties were classed as industrially important (10,000 or more manufacturing wage earners), only 18 percent of the South's counties were so listed.

The density of population by counties in 1940 (Figure 189) indicates the concentration in the area. Fifteen, or 44 percent, of the counties in New England had a density exceeding 300 people per square mile. Four had a density of above 1,000 people, one non-textile county surpassing all with a density of 15,695.4. Only 5 southern counties of the total 61 had a density of over 300. Instead, 37 of the southern counties had a density of less than 100 persons. This compares with 8 New England counties, or 23.5 percent, having densities of less than 100.

In its trend toward industrialization, the area had developed a population pattern with a density much lower than that of other industrial areas. The more populated areas including the cities mentioned, have a density lower than that of the textile sections of New England. The lack of overcrowding is directly reflected in differences in housing. In southern areas single family dwellings with yard space predominate, whereas congested flats and tenements are common in the more mature economic areas of New England.

Thus it appears that a different type of industrial metropolis is evolving in the Piedmont—the small central city with a fairly well diffused peripheral area. In 1930 the census found no area in the two Carolinas that conformed to its definition of a metropolitan area.[3] The contiguous industrial area along the Southern Railway from Greensboro to Greenville, somewhat resembles a loosely strung metropolitan district. Except for sporadic gaps, there was in 1940 a continuous line of townships with a density of 150 or more. With a liberalizing of the census criteria in 1940 there emerged five metropolitan zones in the area: Winston-Salem, Greensboro, Charlotte, Greenville, and Spartanburg.

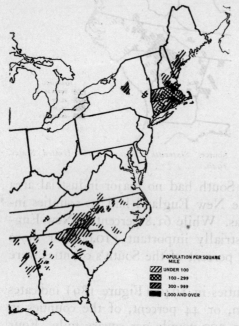

FIGURE 189. DENSITY OF POPULATION IN MAJOR TEXTILE AREAS, UNITED STATES, 1940

POPULATION PER SQUARE MILE
UNDER 100
100 - 299
300 - 999
1,000 AND OVER

In addition to comparisons in the number of wage earners and the density of population (Figures 187 and 189) another measure of the relative degree of industrialization was applied to the two areas. Figure 188 shows the proportion of gainfully employed who are classified as industrial wage earners in the selected counties. This figure ranged from 6.8 percent in the least industrial county to 61.9 percent in a highly industrialized county. In northern areas large industrial counties with over 40 percent wage earners predominate, but a definite pattern does not emerge for the two areas. This may be due to the effect that industrial concentrations have in increasing the numbers employed in trade, transportation, distribution, and the services. In a basically agrarian economy the proportions employed in such services appear unduly small.

Source: *Sixteenth Census of the United States, 1940.*

DISTRIBUTION OF INDUSTRY BY SIZE OF COMMUNITY

Further light can be thrown on the status of decentralization by studying the location of industries by size of city. Within the 17 counties in the North Carolina Piedmont are some 88 cities, towns, and villages. While all of these places offer some employment in trade and service occupations,

---

[3] The 1930 criteria for delimiting metropolitan areas were: (1) a central city of 50,000 inhabitants, (2) contiguous minor civil divisions which have a density over 150 per square mile bringing the aggregated metropolitan population to 100,000 or more. None of the Carolina cities conformed to this definition in 1930.

75 have textile plants, 29 have furniture factories, 20 metal and machine works, 18 stone, clay, and glass works, and 16 have chemical plants. Table 84 indicates the distribution by size of community. The transportation equipment, chemical, and metal industries are to a great degree concentrated in the larger cities, whereas textiles show a tendency to locate in small communities. The scatter of the several types of manufacturing plants throughout the North Carolina Piedmont is indicated in Figures 190 and 191.

TABLE 84. PERCENT AND NUMBER OF MANUFACTURING ESTABLISHMENTS BY SIZE OF CITY AND TYPE OF MANUFACTURE, NORTH CAROLINA CATAWBA VALLEY, 1938

Type of Industry	Number of Plants by Size of City						
	Unincorporated	Under 2,500	2,500-10,000	10,000-25,000	25,000 and over	Total by type of mfg.	Percent of all types of mfg.
Textiles	26	87	108	146	104	471	43.8
Furniture	6	10	25	39	66	146	13.6
Lumber	5	13	17	22	27	84	7.8
Chemicals	1	3	4	7	31	46	4.3
Leather	0	1	7	4	3	15	1.4
Metals	0	3	9	32	61	105	9.8
Paper	0	2	3	1	6	12	1.1
Stone, clay, glass	1	5	4	12	16	38	3.5
Transportation equipment	0	1	0	1	5	7	0.6
Miscellaneous	1	15	30	39	62	147	13.7
Tobacco	0	0	0	0	5	5	0.4
Totals by size of city	40	140	207	303	386	1,076	100.0
Percent by size of city	3.7	13.0	19.2	29.2	35.9	100.0	

Source: North Carolina Department of Conservation and Development, *North Carolina Handbook of Industry* (Raleigh, N. C., 1940).

TABLE 85. NUMBER OF TEXTILE ESTABLISHMENTS BY SIZE OF CITY AND TYPE OF TEXTILE MANUFACTURED, NORTH CAROLINA CATAWBA VALLEY, 1938

Type of textiles manufactured	Unincorporated	Under 2,500	2,500-10,000	10,000-25,000	25,000 and over	Total number by type of textile	Percent of all types of textile
Cotton yarns	14	37	51	43	11	156	33.1
Cotton fabrics	5	4	9	17	5	40	8.5
Hosiery	2	27	26	49	31	135	28.7
Silk, rayon	1	5	6	8	9	27	5.9
Dyeing, finishing, etc.	0	2	6	8	9	25	5.4
Miscellaneous	4	6	9	8	22	49	10.4
Apparel	0	6	1	13	15	35	7.4
Woolens, worsted	0	2	0	0	2	4	0.8
Totals by size of city	26	87	108	146	104	471	....
Percent by size of city	5.5	18.5	22.9	31.0	22.1	100.0	100.0

Source: See Table 84.

Table 85 indicates the distribution of different types of textile plants with respect to size of city in the Catawba Valley area. Thus plants making wearing apparel (80 percent), silk and rayon (62.9 percent), and dyeing and finishing (68 percent) are concentrated in cities of 10,000 and over, while cotton yarns (64 percent) and to a less extent cotton fabrics (48 percent) are found in towns of less than 10,000. Figure 191 shows the scatter of plants making various textile products in the Valley area.

FIGURE 190. THE DISTRIBUTION OF NON-TEXTILE MANUFACTURING ESTAB-
LISHMENTS IN THE CATAWBA VALLEY POWER PROVINCE,
NORTH CAROLINA, 1938

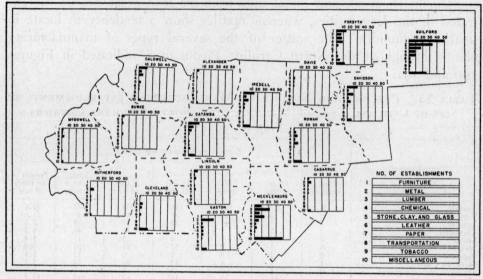

Source: See Table 84.

FIGURE 191. THE DISTRIBUTION OF TEXTILE MANUFACTURING ESTABLISH-
MENTS IN THE CATAWBA VALLEY POWER PROVINCE, NORTH CAROLINA, 1938

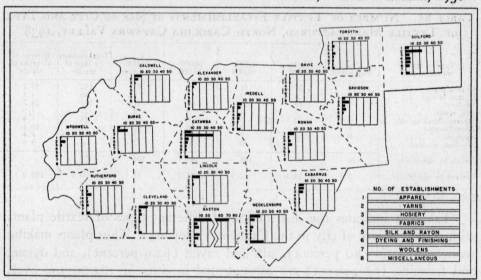

Source: See Tables 84 and 85.

INDUSTRIALIZATION AND POPULATION TRENDS IN THE VALLEY

We have seen that the rural South has the highest birth rate in the United States, that agriculture has been none too prosperous, and that along with the high rate of increase of the farm population has gone a great deal of rural-urban migration. What has been the effect of industrialization on population trends in the Catawba Valley? Has the population become concentrated in cities or has it remained largely rural? To what extent has industrialization enabled the Valley to maintain its natural increase and draw population from regions of less development? Has the increase of farm population in the area been at all comparable to that of the urban population? What effect has the depression had on migration and population increase? These questions suggest some of the possible effects of industrialization on population trends in the area.

The twenty-four counties of the Catawba power province had in 1930 over a million and a third people, of whom 37.5 percent were classified as urban. Of the rural population, 43 percent were nonfarm. These are higher proportions than were found in the combined total for North and South Carolina.

In the Catawba Valley, population has grown more rapidly than in most sections of the South. The total population almost doubled from 1900 to 1930 and the urban population multiplied nearly five times. The greatest growth occurred during the booming 1920's.

With no greater industrial opportunities elsewhere, population continued to increase during the depression period but at a lesser rate. By 1940, total population had grown to 1,575,990, an increase for the decade of 14.4 percent. This was greater than the rate of increase of the Carolinas as a whole. The rural population increased to 975,587 and urban population to 600,403. While many sections in the Southeast have barely held their own in rural population, the twenty-four Catawba counties showed a 45 percent increase from 1900 to 1930. As nearly as can be estimated this growth represents only a slight increase in the farm population, a 33 percent increase in village dwellers, and a similar increase in other rural non-farm people. In 1930, 63 percent of the population was still rural.

The large proportion of rural non-farm people in the area is a direct result of the scattering of industry, especially lumber and textiles, in smaller villages throughout the area. In the Valley, 5.3 percent of the people live in the rural towns of under 2,500, 6.6 percent in towns 2,500 to 10,000, 9.6 percent in cities 10,000 to 25,000, and 21.9 percent in cities of 25,000 and over. The remaining 56.6 percent of the population live in unincorporated areas, many around the larger centers.

The region has a high birth rate and a low death rate, the former ranging around 25 per 1,000 and the latter around 11 in the 1920's. This provides a rate of natural increase of about 14 per 1,000, or nearly one and one-half percent a year. The rural rate of natural increase is much higher, for deaths are slightly below and births above the average. T. J. Woofter, Jr., applied the rate of natural increase to the Valley population for the period of 1900 to 1930 in order to determine the amount of migration into the area. He estimated that the Valley retained the equivalent of its total natural increase during the period and received a migration amounting to 20 percent of the 1930 population. Since many of the Valley's population moved elsewhere during the period, the large migration to the area is evident. Similar procedures applied for the years 1930 to 1940 indicated that out of a population increase of 14.4 percent, only 2 percent gain was due to immigration.

About one-fifth of the Valley's population is colored. The Negro has not participated in the industrial development to the extent that might have been expected. Of all the population elements, rural and urban, white and colored, only the rural Negro has remained stationary. There is some evidence that here, as elsewhere in the Cotton Belt, white farmers replaced Negroes with the advent of the boll weevil. From 1910 to 1930 the number of urban Negroes practically doubled in the area, but the proportion of Negroes in the total population declined from 27 to 21.4 percent in the twenty-year period.

In analyzing the growth of industrial centers in the South, Woofter[4] has shown that the white population increases at a much faster rate than the Negro population. The failure of the Negro to participate in the gains of the Piedmont is due to their exclusion from many types of industry. Under prevailing conditions, the Negro can hardly expect to constitute more than a minimum proportion of the manufacturing population.

INDUSTRIALIZATION AND THE OCCUPATIONAL DISTRIBUTION

The industrialization of the Valley naturally has affected the whole distribution of occupations. The proportion in agriculture has fallen and that in manufacturing has risen. In the two Carolinas 46.2 percent of those gainfully employed in 1930 were in agriculture as compared with only 32.1 percent in the Valley area. On the other hand, the Valley had 36.6 percent in manufacturing and mechanical occupations as compared with only 23.6 percent in the States. Thus with only 18.6 percent of the agricultural workers in the Carolinas, the Valley region had 41.5 percent of the two States' total in manufacturing and mechanical occupations. In ad-

[4] T. J. Woofter, Jr., *Negro Migration* (New York: Hillman, 1920), pp. 169-170. See also his *Negro Problems in Cities* (Garden City, New York: Doubleday, Doran, 1928).

dition, the proportions in trade, public and professional services were higher in the Valley area (15.6 percent as compared with less than 14 percent). With negligible proportions of those engaged in manufacturing of glazed and stone products, the Valley had a third of all those in the two States employed in building and construction, a third of those in food products, 52 percent of those in furniture, and well over 60 percent of those employed in cotton mills, silk mills, and clothing manufactures.[5]

Yet the full effect of industrialization throughout the range of occupations has not been felt in the Piedmont. The Southeast has 12.5 wage earners for one salaried person in industry in 1937 in comparison with a ratio of 7 to 1 for the United States as a whole. Only 0.5 percent of the workers in the South's cotton textile industry can be regarded as technically skilled personnel. For the Nation the growth of industrialization, with the increased importance of engineering, has meant the development of a whole army of auxiliary technical forces. And since industrialization has meant the sale of more goods, there has developed also a great army of commercial, service, and clerical employees. In this way technical development has accentuated the growth of white collar classes, lawyers, clerks, salesmen, and technical men, engaged in processes that range all the way from blueprinting to cost accounting.[6] This group shifted from the immediate functions of physical production to duties of administration, distribution, technical supervision, and public relations is still largely undeveloped in the area. Such services tend to be concentrated in sales offices, technical and financial headquarters outside the area. The region has millhands, but too often for the area's own good, the technical and clerical talent either remains undeveloped or is drawn out of the region.

THE EFFECT OF INDUSTRIALIZATION ON AGRICULTURE IN THE AREA

What changes in agriculture have been brought about by the industrialization of the Catawba Valley? Agriculture has its own career, and it would be a mistake to look to industry as the main source of change. Changes in the Valley's pattern of farming have been traced in two selected areas: the Upper and the Lower Valley. The Upper contains the less industrialized zones in which agriculture approaches more closely the type of subsistence farming practiced in the highlands. The Lower Valley is not only more industrialized but also more adapted to staple agriculture, especially cotton.

While the Valley has been expanding in population, industry, and wealth, its agriculture has been contracting. There were 2,522 less farms

---

[5] Harriet L. Herring in A Survey of the Catawba Valley, I (unpublished manuscript, Institute for Research in Social Science, University of North Carolina, 1935), pp. 113-115.

[6] See Emil Lederer, "Technology," Encyclopaedia of the Social Sciences, 14, p. 559.

in the area in 1930 than in 1910, the area's high water mark in agriculture. In marked contrast stands North Carolina, where the number of farms increased each decade from 1900 to 1930. In the Upper Valley the average size of farm declined from 97 acres in 1900 to 54 acres in 1930 and in the Lower Valley from 84 acres to 64 acres. In the Lower Valley, a large percentage of the land area was in farms and a large share of the latter in crops.

The tendency toward smaller farms has been general in the Southeast and represents two trends: (1) abandonment of rough pasture and woodlands in farms, and (2) to a smaller degree, a decrease in the amount of cropland and plowable pasture.

The abandonment of range land and marginal acres fitted in with the general trend from the growing of livestock under open range conditions to more intensive cultivation of staple crops after the introduction of commercial fertilizer. Soil erosion has also been a factor in the loss of farm acreage. The Upper Valley, however, has changed less than the Lower Valley. In keeping with its mountain character it has only 32 percent of its farm land in crops as compared with 49 percent in the Lower Valley.

Along with contraction of acreage the Valley has experienced steady improvements in the per acre yields of the main crops—corn, cotton, wheat, and oats. Use of the better land, increased fertilization, and more intensive cultivation have contributed to this trend. The 1935 Census indicates that per acre yields have continued to increase under the crop reduction program.

From the previous discussion it is evident that the influence of industrialization on agriculture includes the stimulus of the growth of population, particularly in cities. Before the depression the farm population had not increased above the 1910 level, and along with industrialization has gone the release of waste and submarginal land in farms. As the country built up, conditions of the open range gave way. Farms have grown smaller, but by increasing expenditures for equipment and fertilizer are able to produce larger yields per acre. Commercial farming continued to grow in both areas until the advent of crop control forced a reduction in staples. This trend toward staples was due partly to the spread of the boll weevil which during the 1920's pushed cotton production north into the Piedmont, an area largely unaffected by the insect. While the number of livestock has decreased, value per animal has increased with the introduction of purebred stock. In 1930 there were 3 dairy cattle, 1 beef cattle, 23 swine, 37 chickens, and 2 work stock per 100 acres of farm land in the Valley. While there are evidences of truck farming, or diversification and dairying in the area, statistics are not available to show increases over a long period. The new agricultural program here as elsewhere has operated to increase feed and forage crops at the expense of staples. The 1935 Census accordingly shows the greatest degree of diversified farming yet developed in the Valley.

This pattern of agriculture can be partly attributed to industrial development. Abandonment of range land, more intensive cultivation, the introduction of purebred stock, and growth of dairying are all related to the development of new urban markets. In part-time farming we have another change brought about by industry.

PART-TIME FARMING IN A DEPRESSION YEAR

As industrialization increased, the country developed that dual occupation known as part-time farming. As factories were built throughout the area, farmers and farmers' sons went into industrial employment while maintaining their farm residence, and industrial workers have moved out of mill villages to farmsteads. The map of part-time farmers in the Southeast from the Census of 1930 shows their proximity to cities and industrial centers as well as to such open-country enterprises as lumbering and the production of naval stores.[7]

While it is evident that families better their condition by making the transition from agriculture to industry in the Southeast, there is some doubt as to whether any net gain in income is achieved by industrial workers from residence in the open country. No investigation has been made in the Piedmont, but a suggestive study of a newly industrialized rural area in Mississippi contrasts the levels of income in industrial, farm, and part-time farm families. In all these families the wives worked either in industry or in agriculture. Industrially employed families averaged the highest annual income, $1,010 a year (Table 86). Where both husband and wife were employed full-time in industry, little difference was found between residence in a mill village or in the open country. Lower incomes, averaging $822 a year, were found in families in which the husband farmed full-time and the wife worked in industry. The income of this group exceeded that of families in which the husband was a part-time farmer and the wife gave assistance in farm work. Here the total income averaged $721. The income of the full-time farmer's family of which no member worked in industry was the lowest of all—$524 a year. As long as industrial employment maintains an income advantage of nearly 2 to 1 over agriculture, industry will experience no difficulty in drawing workers from the farms. Farm residence, however, will continue to offer advantages to industrial workers.

[7] See R. H. Allen and Others, *Part-Time Farming in the Southeast*, W. P. A. Research Monograph, IX (Washington, D. C.: U. S. Government Printing Office, 1937), p. xxi.

TABLE 86. COMPARATIVE INCOMES OF INDUSTRIAL AND FARM FAMILIES,*
1935-1936

Type of family by industrial status	Average income per member	Size of family	Average annual income by type
Husband and wife industrially employed with open country residence...	$259	3.9	$1,010
Husband and wife industrially employed with mill village residence.....	246	4.1	1,009
Husband full time farmer, wife worked in industry..................	265	3.1	822
Husband part-time farmer, wife farm assistant......................	157	4.6	721
Husband full time farmer, wife farm assistant.......................	119	4.4	524

*Random samples picked within ten-mile radius of three garment factories in which industrially employed wives worked. Based on 40-49 schedules for each type. These were normal families; each husband and wife kept house during year. Wives were farm reared and in 17-34 year age group. No families receiving pensions or work relief. Employment defined as 150 days' work or more and census definition of part-time farmer used. Income included net incomes from farms, value of occupancy of homes, the value of inventory change in livestock and crops stored for sale.
Source: Dorothy Dickins, "Some Contrasts in Levels of Living in Industrial, Farm and Part-Time Farm Families in Rural Mississippi," *Social Forces*, 18 (December, 1939), 247-255.

No statistics are available to trace the movement toward part-time farming before 1930, but it is known that farmers have long engaged in such outside employment as road building and construction. On the basis of the census definition, 14.3 percent of the farmers enumerated in the Valley in 1930 were reported as part-time ranging from 19.1 to 5.1 percent in various counties.

PART-TIME FARMERS IN INDUSTRY

A Civil Works Administration study of part-time farming in the area revealed that, in 1933, 1,563 families averaged 5.5 persons per family and furnished a total of 2,188 nonagricultural workers.[8] These were distributed as follows: 74.3 percent were in manufacturing and mining; 8.1 percent were in trade; 6.8 percent in transportation and commerce; with lesser proportions in domestic, professional, and public service. The total number of secondary census occupations was found to be 189. They ranged from gold digging and dog training through industry to preaching. Classified according to the census groupings they show 575 workers in furniture and allied industries, 224 in cotton mills, 174 in saw mills, 172 in knitting silk and woolen mills, 159 in the building industry, with smaller numbers scattered throughout other industries. Of those reporting distance to work, nearly one-third traveled less than 5 miles and roughly one-half from 5 to 10 miles.

The nonfarm income of these families was affected by three major factors: the number of workers per family, the amount of time worked, and

[8] The schedules on which this analysis is based were secured by enumerators employed by the Civil Works Administration for the Division of Subsistence Homesteads, Department of Interior. Usable schedules for some 1,563 part-time farmers living in 33 townships were taken in 15 selected townships in three counties of the Upper Valley and the three counties of the Power Province. Since census definition was not followed in securing these schedules, this survey is not comparable with studies based on the census.

the occupational level. The effect of the depression was evident in lay-offs and low annual wages. The workers spent an average of 170 days at nonagricultural occupations and almost three-fifths (57.6 percent) had less than 200 days' work. The 1,091 families with only one worker had a median of only 136 days' employment in nonagricultural occupations.

PART-TIME FARMERS IN AGRICULTURE

Part-time farmers secure their living from two sources. In the above sample, the farm yielded them an average gross income of $357.03. This figure included the value of all products consumed by the family as well as those sold. The expenses of farm operations other than the unpaid family labor averaged $82.53, per farm, leaving a net farm income of $274.50.

If the low industrial incomes of this group during the depression were due to low wages and short working period, to what were their low farm incomes due? Comparison with farmers in three counties of the Upper Valley as reported in the 1930 Census indicates that part-time farmers operate on a small scale. Without attempting to make allowance for changes from 1930 to 1933, Table 87 indicates that the average part-time farm was about one-third (35.3 percent) as large, slightly over one-half as valuable, and produced less than one-half the gross value of products of the average general farm. In proportion to size and value of farms the gross incomes of part-time farmers are higher than the actual figures would indicate.

TABLE 87.   COMPARISON OF AVERAGE FARM VALUES IN THE UPPER VALLEY, 1930-1933

Farm value	All farms 1930	Part-time farms 1933	Ratio of part-time to all farms	Farm value	All farms 1930	Part-time farms 1933	Ratio of part-time to all farms
Average gross value of products............	$792	$360	*Percent* 45.5	Average value of land per acre.............	$ 25.82	$ 30.34	*Percent* 117.6
Average size of farm (acres)...............	75.1	26.9	35.3	Average value of farm home.........	$718.88	$709.01	98.9
Average value of farm...............	$2,842.44	$1,639.99	58.0	Average value of farm buildings......	$280.92	$114.79	40.8

Source: Rupert B. Vance in A Survey of the Catawba Valley, I (unpublished manuscript, Institute for Research in Social Science, University of North Carolina, 1935); Census of Agriculture, 1930.

To what extent does the part-time farmer produce his living on the farm? The average family consumed food worth $422.72, 56.5 percent of which was furnished from the farm. Since food furnished was valued at farm prices this figure underestimated the contribution of the farm. A mark-up of some 20 percent, depending on grades would give a food budget of $470.40 with over 60 percent furnished from the farm. Computed on the basis of prevailing farm prices, the value of food consumed amounted to seven cents per person per meal.

Housing accounted for 11.4 percent of living expenses. The 1,167 families who owned their homes were assigned an annual rent based on 10 percent of the reported value of the dwelling. On this basis owners were credited with an average annual rent of $82.08, ten percent of the value of the house. Renters paid an average annual rent of $56.45. It was found that 80 percent of rents were furnished by owned farm homes, constituting 9.2 percent of total expenses of all the families for housing.

Fuel, valued at $26.92 per family was furnished by the farm and made up 2.5 percent of the cost of living. Other living expenses which included clothing, furnishings purchased, medical, educational, and cultural needs as well as the cost of operating automobiles amounted to $148.30 per family, or 22.4 percent of expenses. These needs were purchased.

The income of the families living on this basis averaged $663.10. Of this total, 46.7 percent was furnished from the farm. As pointed out previously, many of the farms were small, two-fifths being 9 acres or less in size. On the small farm the cow, chickens, and garden plot furnished the core of the part-time farmer's live-at-home program. Proceeds from the sale of farm products amounted to only one-fifth of the total net farm income.

While saving in food was the principal economy that farm residence affords workers, cheap housing also proved an important factor. This advantage, however, is offset by the fact that farm houses were equipped with fewer conveniences. While urban conveniences were largely lacking, the type of house was no worse than those in surrounding rural neighborhoods. Most of the part-time farmers studied owned the farmstead on which they lived. Full owners made up three-fifths of the group to which may be added the 14.2 percent who rented additional land. Owners, as might be expected, had larger net farm incomes, averaging $293 as compared with $205 for tenants. The prospects for improved standards among part-time farmers rose with industrial revival and higher wages. Our analysis shows that few part-time farmers depended on the sale of agricultural products for much of their income. The gains of farm residence thus consisted of lowered costs of food and shelter.

SUMMARY

The industrialization of rural areas such as the Southern Piedmont appears to be proceeding slowly. The question is often asked: What will it mean to the Nation and the region? A study of the Catawba River Basin, the first river valley to be electrified in the Southeast, suggests some possibilities. Instead of being concentrated in great cities, much of the industrial population of the Carolina Piedmont lives in small cities, towns, and even in the open countryside. Less necessary in these days of municipal and Federal housing projects, the paternalistic mill village with its company housing is a passing phenomenon. Agriculture has changed as the rise of industries and cities opened new markets for food, fruit, dairy and truck products. Along with this went the development of part-time farming. Farmers came to supplement their incomes by working in nearby industries, and industrial workers moved out to farm homes where they could keep a cow, chickens, and a garden. Without developing any great cities, this area increased its proportion of industry, gained in wealth and population, and improved its type of agriculture. As workers gained more skill and as investments and the size of plants grew larger, efficiency and productivity increased. With Federal standards and increased unionization it seems likely that the wage level will approach more closely that of the Nation, although it is possible that the resulting increased costs may slow down the rate of industrialization.

Most people now realize that the South's population cannot continue to work in agriculture to the extent it once did when 60 percent of our cotton and much of our tobacco were sold abroad. Yet industrialization has both its gains and losses; and not all the changes have meant social advantages. With the country's agricultural needs already well supplied, the South's insistent cry for a higher standard of living can be answered only by an expanding industrial production in which its workers take part. This need will be emphasized all the more when the emergency comes to an end and the war program tapers off.

CHAPTER 21

POPULATION AND UNEMPLOYMENT

IT MAY be of some significance that both unemployment and the South have been nominated as United States' "Economic Problem Number One." In the current discussion of regional economics the problem of unemployment has not been directly related to the difficulties of the Southeast. The present chapter therefore compares the changing pattern of unemployment from 1930 through the depression to World War II in the Nation and the region. The neglect to study unemployment apparently stands in sharp contrast to the emphasis on population trends as a factor in the region's economic conditions. It is reasonable to suppose, however, that in the Southeast as in the Nation reciprocal relations may have existed between population increases and increased unemployment. T. J. Woofter's calculation of replacements in the labor force cited in Chapter 10 furnished presumptive evidence that natural increase in the rural farm population aged 18 to 64 years would lead to greater unemployment unless we had an expanding economy. Conversely, prolonged unemployment itself is likely to have adverse effects on population increase. Presumably such effects may be related to the fact that the whole population comes to be supported by a smaller proportion of the total group engaged as a working force. Moreover, changes in the age and sex ratios of both employed and unemployed workers may be expected to affect population increases and thus in turn affect population policy. In a large sense our policy in relation to unemployment and reemployment might in time come to be regarded as part of a national population policy.

In this connection it should be of value to trace the pattern of employment and population composition in the Southeast as they changed during the depression. For this purpose we can compare the regular Census of Unemployment taken in 1930, the Enumerative Check Census taken in connection with the Special Census of Unemployment in 1937, and the 1940 Census.[1]

[1] The Enumerative Check Census of the 1937 Special Unemployment Census applies age and sex distribution to the pattern of the employed, the unemployed, and those unavailable for gainful employment

THE EFFECTIVE LABOR FORCE AND THE NATURAL DEPENDENTS, 1937

The Special Census indicates that in 1937 the Nation and the region presented a pattern of employment somewhat similar (Table 88). In both areas out of every 10 men, approximately one was unable to work, and 9 were employable. Of these 9 only 6 or 7 could get jobs while 2 or 3 were left unemployed or worked on W. P. A. and other projects. Of every 10 women, 7 remained at home while 3 sought jobs—2 of whom were successful. For the total population, 4 remained at home, 6 sought jobs, but only 4 could find them. Regional-national differences were not important. The Southeast with less total unemployment than the Nation, 10.4 to 11.8 percent, had a slightly higher proportion that was not seeking work, 42.8 to 41.5 percent. The region and the Nation had the same proportion listed as fully employed, namely, 38.8 percent. Significant categories in this analysis are based on the concept of availability for employment for gain or profit. Those available constituted the labor force made up of two classes: the employed and the unemployed. The third class consists of those unavailable for gainful employment. This economic classification

TABLE 88. ESTIMATED POPULATION 15 TO 74 YEARS OF AGE BY FUNCTIONAL CLASS AND BY SEX WITH PERCENTAGE DISTRIBUTION, UNITED STATES AND SOUTHEAST, 1937 (IN THOUSANDS)

Functional class	UNITED STATES						SOUTHEAST					
	All		Male		Female		All		Male		Female	
	Number	Percent	Number	Percent	Number	Percent	Number	Percent	Number	Percent	Number	Percent
TOTAL POPULATION (15-74)	93,063	100.0	46,704	100.0	46,359	100.0	19,145	100.0	9,495	100.0	9,650	100.0
Employed or available for employment	54,474	58.5	39,978	85.6	14,496	31.3	10,948	57.2	8,058	84.9	2,890	30.0
Total unemployed	8,928	9.6	5,761	12.3	3,167	6.8	1,622	8.5	963	10.2	659	6.8
Emergency workers	2,055	2.2	1,657	3.5	398	0.9	370	1.9	287	3.0	83	0.9
Partly unemployed	5,550	6.0	4,058	8.7	1,492	3.2	1,126	5.9	788	8.3	338	3.5
Part-time workers	1,190	1.3	688	1.5	502	1.1	266	1.4	180	1.9	86	0.9
Fully employed	36,079	38.8	27,399	58.7	8,680	18.7	7,422	38.8	5,764	60.7	1,658	17.2
Ill or voluntarily idle	672	0.7	415	0.9	257	0.6	142	0.7	76	0.8	66	0.7
Not available for employment	38,589	41.5	6,726	14.4	31,863	68.7	8,197	42.8	1,437	15.1	6,760	70.0

Note: "Employed" workers consist of several groups: the partly unemployed, part-time workers, "ill and voluntarily idle," and fully employed. A distinction in this classification is that the partly unemployed are looking for more work while part-time workers do not need more work. Unemployed are the totally unemployed and the emergency workers (W.P.A., P.W.A., C.C.C., and others). Together these classes make up the total labor force. Those not available for work comprise all outside the labor market, that is, all not actively seeking gainful employment. Among these are old persons, young persons pursuing studies, and housewives whose unpaid services are confined to the home or to helping in their husbands' businesses. Contrary to the practice of the 1930 Census, so called "unpaid family workers" were included by the 1937 Census among those unavailable for work.

Source: *United States Census of Partial Employment, Unemployment, and Occupations, 1937*, I, Table 20; IV, Tables 6, 43, 54, 55, 56.

among the adult population, aged 15-74. Reduction of these three censuses to a comparable basis makes it possible to trace the developing pattern of employment among these three functional classes from April 1, 1930 to April 1, 1940. Since the Enumerative Check Census gives percentages in these functional classes only by census divisions, we have recomputed them for the Southeast. See John D. Biggers, *Census of Partial Employment, Unemployment and Occupations*, IV. Calvert L. Dedrick and Morris H. Hansen, *The Enumerative Check Census* (Washington, D. C.: U. S. Government Printing Office, 1938).

cannot rightly be understood apart from considerations of age and sex distribution which determine the natural dependents.[2]

The level of income attained in any region depends, among other things, on the amount of employment available. In depression it is realized that a larger fraction of the labor force is wasted, leaving a smaller part of the population to support the whole group. Table 89 provides estimates designed to show what proportion of the labor force was "wasted" in 1937. Part-time employed and partly unemployed are computed at half-time and the ill and voluntarily idle are counted with the unemployed. Emergency workers although returned with the unemployed are not here regarded as "wasted" manpower. This procedure gives an estimate that between a fifth and a fourth (22.5 percent) of the region's labor force was wasted in 1937. This is slightly less than the wastage in the Nation, 23.8 percent.

TABLE 89. PERCENT OF TOTAL MANPOWER AVAILABLE FOR EMPLOYMENT BY FUNCTIONAL CLASS WITH PERCENT WASTAGE OF MANPOWER, UNITED STATES AND SOUTHEAST, 1937

Functional class	UNITED STATES		SOUTHEAST	
	Percent manpower	Percent wastage	Percent manpower	Percent wastage
Total available for employment........	100.0	23.8	100.0	22.5
Totally unemployed................	16.4	16.4	14.8	14.8
Emergency workers...............	3.8	....	3.4	....
Partly unemployed................	10.2	5.1	10.3	5.2
Part-time workers................	2.2	1.1	2.4	1.2
Fully employed...................	66.2	....	67.8	....
Ill or voluntarily idle..............	1.2	1.2	1.3	1.3

Source: See Table 88.

We are also interested in determining what proportion of the group "supports" the total population. This can be estimated by including in our analysis (1) the natural dependents, those too young and too old to work, and (2) those who are not seeking work, those unavailable for gainful employment. Table 90 shows that in the Southeast 31 percent of the total population are under 15 or over 75 and thus largely dependent, 8.9 percent are "wasted" manpower, and 29.5 percent are unavailable. Thus in 1937 the Southeast's population of 27,739,000 was supported by 8,488,000 equivalent full-time workers comprising only 30.6 percent of the population. This is in contrast to the Nation where with 10 percent of their manpower "wasted," 32 percent of the population supported the total group. The difference is accounted for by the Nation's smaller proportion of natural dependents, 28.2 percent as compared with 31 percent for the Southeast.

[2] See chapters 4 and 5 where this topic is discussed in detail.

TABLE 90. DISTRIBUTION OF POPULATION BY EFFECTIVE MANPOWER, UNITED
STATES AND SOUTHEAST, 1937 (ESTIMATE IN THOUSANDS)

Population group	UNITED STATES		SOUTHEAST	
	Number	Percent	Number	Percent
Total population....................	129,533*	100.0	27,739*	100.0
Workers (full time)..................	41,504	32.0	8,488	30.6
Dependent...........................	88,029	68.0	19,251	69.4
Wasted..........................	12,970	10.0	2,460	8.9
Not available:				
15-74 years....................	38,589	29.8	8,197	29.5
Under 15 and over 75..........	36,470	28.2	8,594	31.0

*Corrected estimates of the United States Census Bureau for 1937, estimates for the United States as of November 1, for the
Southeast as of July 1.
A similar computation for white females of the Southeast shows that 12.4 percent of white females are working full time, while
87.6 percent are dependent.
Source: See Table 88.

Traditionally the problem of the support of the total population by the
working force has been met in the family. It was the family group which
supported the unemployed and those unavailable for employment along
with its natural dependents. Increasingly, economic insecurity has shifted
the burden of support of the unemployed and the aged from the private to
the public sphere. Once unemployment becomes affected with a public
interest, society comes to watch with concern its maturing youth who, simply
by growing up, may make the transition from natural dependents, a family
responsibility, to unemployed youth, a social responsibility. Important also
in this connection are the large numbers classified as unavailable for employment. Almost 7,000,000 men and 32,000,000 women, 41.5 percent
of the Nation's population 15-74, were in this category in 1937 (Table 88).
In the Southeast the unavailable amounted to 8,197,000 of which 6,760,000
were women. For any number of them to seek work and fail to find it adds
to our mounting figures of unemployed. In any society committed to the
relief of unemployment this indicates that, unless they find work, the problem of their support has shifted from the private to the public sphere.

PRIMARY AND SECONDARY UNEMPLOYMENT, 1930-1937

With these considerations in mind, we shall attempt to trace in the
Southeast the change in numbers of workers by the three functional classes,
the employed, the unemployed, and those unavailable for employment.
Any increase in unemployment from one period to another may be traced to
(1) increases in the population of employable ages, (2) lost jobs, or (3)
increased proportions of job seekers. Those who lose jobs may be regarded
as the primary unemployed, while the increased proportions entering the
labor market may be called the secondary unemployed.

In order to separate the population factor (1) from the social-economic factors (2 and 3) we have reduced the two censuses to a comparable basis and computed the differences due only to population change for each functional class. Thus to ascertain changes in the number of unemployed due to change in age-sex group composition, we computed the 1930 age specific unemployment rates for each five-year age group, male and female 15-74, and applied these rates to the 1937 population distribution. The summation of these figures gives us the amount of unemployment we should expect with the 1930 employment pattern held constant.[3]

The results of this analysis for the three functional classes are shown in Table 91 and Figure 192. The first two rows show the adjusted num-

TABLE 91. COMPARISON OF NUMBER OF WORKERS BY SEX AND FUNCTIONAL CLASS, SOUTHEAST, 1930 AND 1937 (ALL NUMBERS IN THOUSANDS)

Item	Total population aged 15-74		Employed or available for employment						Unavailable for employment	
			Total		Totally unemployed		Employed (fully or partly)			
	1 (equals 2+5)		2 (equals 3+4)		3		4		5	
	Number	Per cent	Number	Per cent	Number	Per cent	Number	Per cent	Number	Per cent
A. All										
1. Number in 1937	19,145	100.0	10,944	57.2	1,988	10.4	8,956	46.8	8,201	42.8
2. Number in 1930	16,307	100.0	8,493	52.1	253	1.6	8,240	50.5	7,814	47.9
3. Exp. number in 1937*	19,145	100.0	10,017		296		9,721		9,128	
4. Total difference (1 − 2)	2,838		2,451		1,735		716		387	
5. (a) Difference due to increase of population (3 − 2)	2,838		1,524		43		1,481		1,314	
6. (b) Difference due to change of social-economic conditions (1 − 3)	0		927		1,692		−765		−927	
B. Male										
1. Number in 1937	9,495	100.0	8,077	85.1	1,269	13.4	6,808	71.7	1,418	14.9
2. Number in 1930	8,088	100.0	6,662	82.4	196	2.4	6,466	79.9	1,426	17.6
3. Exp. number in 1937*	9,495		7,884		230		7,654		1,611	
4. Total difference (1 − 2)	1,407		1,415		1,073		342		− 8	
5. (a) Difference due to increase of poulation (3 −2)	1,407		1,222		34		1,188		185	
6. (b) Difference due to change in social-economic conditions (1 − 3)	0		193		1,039		−846		−193	
C. Female										
1. Number in 1937	9,650	100.0	2,867	29.7	719	7.5	2,148	22.2	6,783	70.3
2. Number in 1930	8,219	100.0	1,831	22.3	57	0.7	1,774	21.6	6,388	77.7
3. Exp. number in 1937*	9,650		2,133		66		2,067		7,517	
4. Total difference (1 − 2)	1,431		1,036		662		374		395	
5. (a) Difference due to increase of population (3 − 2)	1,431		302		9		293		1,129	
6. (b) Difference due to change in social-economic conditions (1 − 3)	0		734		653		81		−734	

*Conditions as of 1930.

Note: Number of workers in 1937 and 1930 adjusted for comparable definitions; employed workers include those defined in 1937 as fully employed, partly unemployed, part-time workers, and ill or voluntarily idle; unemployed include totally unemployed and emergency workers in 1937, and unemployed of class A in 1930. Due to the adjustments for comparable definitions there is a difference between figures for 1937 given here and in Table 88.

Source: *Fifteenth Census of the United States, 1930, Population*, V, Chap. 4, Tables 15 and 16; Vol. IV, Tables 11 and 23. *United States Census of Unemployment*, 1937, I, Table 20; Vol. IV, Tables 43, 54-56, Table 49, p. 111. *United States Census of Unemployment, 1930*, I, Table 18.

[3] The method involves the same principle used in computing the standardized death rate

FIGURE 192. DIFFERENCE IN NUMBER OF WORKERS BY FUNCTIONAL CLASSES
DUE TO CHANGE IN POPULATION AND SOCIAL ECONOMIC CONDITIONS,
SOUTHEAST, 1930 TO 1937

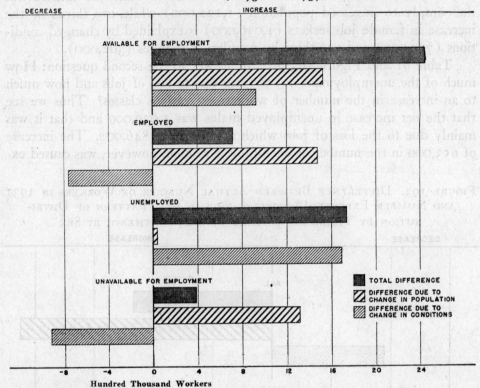

Source: See Table 91.

ber of workers in 1930 and 1937. The actual difference between the two sets of figures (third row) is due to the two factors: (1) change in number and composition of the population and (2) change in social-economic conditions. In order to separate the effects of these two factors we have computed the total difference due to change in population. Thus (column 3) the number of unemployed "expected" in 1937 was 296,000. Since the total number of unemployed in the Southeast in 1930 was 253,000 (see second horizontal line), the increase due only to change in population is shown to be 43,000. The actual increase in unemployed persons, however, was 1,735,000—representing the combined effect of population and social-economic changes. The net difference in unemployment which can be attributed to change in social-economic conditions alone is this figure minus the 43,000 population increase or 1,692,000.

On the other hand (see Figure 192) the total surplus of workers "available for employment" (category 2) of both sexes, or 2,451,000, was created both by the effect of changed population (1,524,000)[4] and changed conditions (927,000). Analyzing this change in "total workers available" by sex we see that most of the increase in male job seekers was due simply to increased population (1,222,000) while two-thirds of the increase in female job seekers (1,036,000) is explained by changed conditions (734,000) and one-third by population changes (302,000).

Table 91 and Figure 193 give an answer to the second question: How much of the unemployment in 1937 was due to loss of jobs and how much to an increase in the number of workers by various classes? Thus we see that the net increase in unemployed males was 1,039,000 and that it was mainly due to the loss of jobs which amounted to 846,000. The increase of 653,000 in the number of unemployed women, however, was caused ex-

FIGURE 193. DIFFERENCE BETWEEN ACTUAL NUMBER OF WORKERS IN 1937 AND NUMBER EXPECTED ACCORDING TO THE 1930 PATTERN OF DISTRIBUTION BY THREE FUNCTIONAL CLASSES, SOUTHEAST, BY SEX

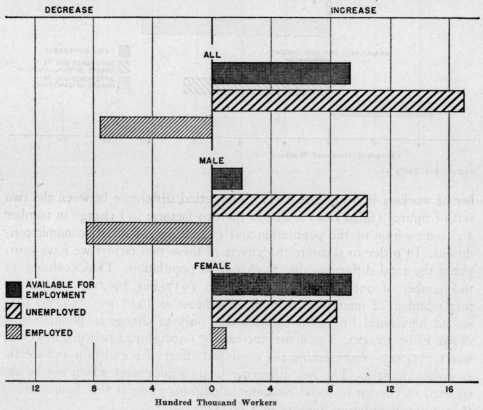

Source: See Table 91; also Rupert B. Vance and Nadia Danilevsky, "Population and the Pattern of Unemployment in the Southeast," *Southern Economic Journal*, VIII (October, 1940), 187-203.

[4] Of this 2,451,000 increased population, it would appear that (category 4) 716,000 got jobs.

TABLE 92. COMPARISON OF NUMBER OF WORKERS BY SEX AND FUNCTIONAL CLASS, UNITED STATES, 1930 AND 1937 (IN THOUSANDS)

Item	Total population aged 15-17 1 (equals 2+5)		Employed or available for employment							
			Total 2 (equals 3+4)		Totally unemployed 3		Employed (fully or partly) 4		Unavailable for employment 5	
	Number	Percent	Number	Percent	Number	Percent	Number	Percent	Number	Percent
A—ALL										
Number in 1937.........	93,063	100.0	54,503	58.6	11,012	11.9	43,491	46.7	38,560	41.4
Number in 1930.........	84,805	100.0	46,821	55.2	2,426	2.9	44,395	52.3	37,984	44.8
Actual difference.........	8,258		7,682		8,586		− 904		576	
Exp. number in 1937*.....	93,063		50,872		2,641		48,231		42,191	
Surplus over 1930 due to increase in pop. 15-74....	8,258		4,051		215		3,836		4,207	
Net difference............	*0*		*3,631*		*8,371*		*−4,740*		*−3,631*	
B—MALE										
Number in 1937.........	46,704	100.0	40,115	85.9	7,555	16.2	32,560	69.7	6,589	14.1
Number in 1930.........	42,965	100.0	36,615	85.2	2,057	4.8	34,558	80.4	6,350	14.8
Actual difference.........	3,739		3,500		5,498		−1,998		239	
Exp. number in 1937*.....	46,704		39,717		2,241		37,476		6,987	
Surplus over 1930.........	3,739		3,102		184		2,918		637	
Net difference............	*0*		*398*		*5,314*		*−4,916*		*− 398*	
C—FEMALE										
Number in 1937.........	46,359	100.0	14,388	31.0	3,457	7.4	10,931	23.6	31,971	69.0
Number in 1930.........	41,840	100.0	10,206	24.4	369	0.9	9,837	23.5	31,634	75.6
Actual difference.........	4,519		4,182		3,088		1,094		337	
Exp. number in 1937*.....	46,359		11,155		400		10,755		35,204	
Surplus over 1930.........	4,519		949		31		918		3,570	
Net difference............	*0*		*3,233*		*3,057*		*176*		*−3,233*	

*Conditions as of 1930.

Note: Number of workers in 1937 and 1930 adjusted for differences in definitions; employed workers include those defined in 1937 as fully employed, partly employed, part-time workers, and ill or voluntarily idle; unemployed include totally unemployed and emergency workers in 1937, and unemployed of class A in 1930, adjusted for comparable definitions; "expected" number of workers in 1937 computed by adjusting 1930 workers for changes in population by age-groups and sex from April, 1930, to November, 1937. Due to the adjustments for comparable definitions, there are certain discrepancies between the figures for 1937 and 1930.

Source: *United States Census of Partial Employment, Unemployment, and Occupations,* 1937, IV, Chap. VIII, Table 49, p. 111; p. 112, Table 69, p. 134. *Fifteenth Census of the United States,* 1930, Population, V, Chap. 6, Table 9; *Unemployment Census,* 1930, I, Tables 1 and 6.

clusively by the great increase in job seekers among women (734,000), for the number of jobs for women actually increased by 81,000. Obviously then the employment status of the total population reflected the combined effects of both factors. Thus the increase of 1,692,000 unemployed in the Southeast is explained by a loss of 765,000 jobs and by an increase of 927,000 job seekers—734,000 of whom were women.

In the Nation (Table 92) an increase of 8,371,000 in the unemployed was explained by a loss of 4,740,000 jobs and an increase of 3,631,000 job seekers, 3,233,000 of whom were women. Evidently while the depression served to increase reported unemployment it operated for each sex in an entirely different fashion. Increased male unemployment sprang chiefly from lost jobs; female unemployment from an increase in the proportion of job seekers. It is inaccurate, however, to deny that the increase of un-employed women was due to the loss of jobs. It was due to the loss of jobs by men—not by women. Loss of jobs by primary workers with its lower-ing of the levels of family living sent streams of secondary workers, com-posed largely of women, into the labor market. From our study of the effective labor force, we should expect unemployment to have this dual effect on our society. As unemployment decreases the size of the effective labor force supporting the total population, additional numbers must em-bark upon the search for work. Since most men are already employed or seeking employment this task falls on women.

THE POPULATION PYRAMID AND THE PATTERN OF UNEMPLOYMENT

Secondary workers were also drawn from the region's reservoir of ma-turing youth. The movement is made clear when the changing pattern of employment is studied in connection with the population pyramid. From 1930 to 1937 the proportion of "available" workers increased most sharply in the younger ages 15 to 30. Thus Table 93 indicates that in ages 15-19 the proportion of males working and seeking work increased from 34.5 to 48.7 percent; among females from 15.8 to 24.6 percent. After age 30 the employment pattern of the sexes showed a decided differentiation. The proportion of males in the labor market became stable at this age and showed slight decline thereafter. Females, however, continued to flow into the labor market until age 60. The effect of old age security measures may be seen in the decline of workers available after 65. For males 65-69 the decline was from 82.4 to 75.3 percent. Regional trends followed national trends in this respect.

Figure 194, which presents the population pyramid in terms of the

TABLE 93.   AVAILABLE WORKERS AS PERCENTAGES OF TOTAL POPULATION IN EACH AGE GROUP, UNITED STATES AND SOUTHEAST, 1930 AND 1937*

Age	UNITED STATES				SOUTHEAST			
	MALE		FEMALE		MALE		FEMALE	
	1930	1937	1930	1937	1930	1937	1930	1937
15 - 19	37.2	43.1	24.2	30.2	34.5	48.7	15.8	24.6
20 - 24	85.4	90.3	41.0	53.6	82.2	89.1	29.3	43.3
25 - 29	95.7	97.1	30.2	42.1	94.1	96.6	26.1	39.5
30 - 34	97.0	97.9	23.8	34.4	96.1	96.7	23.3	33.4
35 - 39	97.4	97.6	22.5	31.1	96.5	96.4	23.8	31.4
40 - 44	97.4	96.8	21.3	28.0	97.1	95.8	22.9	29.4
45 - 49	97.0	96.3	20.4	25.0	97.0	95.6	22.5	25.3
50 - 54	95.6	95.1	19.2	22.5	96.2	94.4	21.3	22.6
55 - 59	92.8	91.9	17.0	18.8	94.4	92.0	18.5	19.8
60 - 64	86.6	84.7	14.4	15.5	90.2	85.9	17.6	17.2
65 - 69	75.4	67.8	11.2	10.5	82.4	75.3	14.3	12.4
70 - 74	57.1	45.2	7.5	5.6	68.3	48.6	10.1	5.7

*Adjusted to a comparable definition.   "Available workers" include both job-holders and job-seekers.
Source: See Tables 91 and 92.

FIGURE 194. THE PERCENTAGE EMPLOYED, UNEMPLOYED AND UNAVAILABLE WITHIN EACH 5-YEAR AGE GROUP, 15-74, SOUTHEAST BY SEX, 1937

Source: See sources for Tables 91-93.

three functional classes in the Southeast—1937, indicates that the conflicting claims of "unemployed" and "unavailable for employment" are especially apparent in the younger ages and among females. As women attain the age of marriage and mature homemaking, their proportions in the labor market declined. Only among women in the age group 20-24 were more than two-fifths (43.3 percent) in the labor market. It is noted that by far the sex's highest rate of unemployment (11.6 percent) was found among women of younger ages, 15-24. Table 93 which also gives the pyramid for the total United States indicates that the Nation had a larger proportion of its women in the labor market than the Southeast.

REGIONAL-NATIONAL COMPARISONS

The 1937 Census makes it possible to compare rates of employment on farms and in rural nonfarm and urban areas. It is generally realized that the movement of families from the farm to the urban environment serves to increase the proportions of those seeking gainful employment. The 1937 census technicality whereby unpaid family labor on the farm was classified among those "unavailable for gainful employment" is partly responsible for this condition. Such unpaid labor contributes to the store of goods and services and, by increasing the family income, no doubt receives added payment in kind instead of in wages.

The large proportion of the South's labor force engaged in agriculture makes for significant regional-national differences here. In both the Nation and the region the proportions in the labor market increase as we move from rural farm to village (rural nonfarm) to urban areas. Roughly speaking only half of the rural farm population age 15-74 had or sought jobs, as compared with some 55 percent of rural nonfarm and over 60 percent of urban population. Significantly enough when the Nation is compared with the region it is found that the Southeast had a greater percentage of full and partial unemployment on the farms, 15 percent as compared to 11.2 percent for the Nation; a smaller proportion of total unemployment in rural nonfarm areas, 11.4 to 13 percent and an almost equal ratio in cities, 12.4 to 12.6 percent. With due consideration of the difficulty involved in the concept "unemployed farmer," the region's higher ratio of farm unemployment indicated the difficulties facing agriculture in the Southeast in 1937.

The pattern of racial employment showed important differences as between the Southeast and the Nation. In both areas more Negroes than whites were forced to seek jobs and more were unemployed. In the Nation, however, Negroes show a much higher rate of unemployment than in the Southeast. For Negro males this difference amounted to 22.5 percent unemployed in the Nation as compared with only 14.1 percent in the Southeast; for females the ratio was 16.1 to 10.2 percent unemployed in favor of the region. Comparably Negroes in the Nation furnished a higher ratio of emergency workers, 5.8 percent for males in the Nation as compared with 2.7 percent in the region.

Unemployment was undoubtedly a serious problem in the region, but it is possible to conclude from this study that the position of the Southeast as "Economic Problem Number One" did not arise from greater unemployment than that existing in the Nation. Throughout the depression period under study unemployment was lower in the Southeast, a fact which held true for Negroes as well as whites. On the surface it would seem that less manpower was "wasted" in the Southeast, but that the total population was supported by a smaller proportion gainfully employed as a working force. The load of dependents was 2.7 per worker in the Southeast as compared with 2.3 in the Nation. This is in accordance with both the region's greater proportion of children and its smaller proportion "available" for gainful employment. When analyzed this last trend can be traced to the large group of rural farm women and youth who serve as "unpaid family workers on the home farm."

The situation would indicate that compared with the Nation the South suffers from low productivity and accompanying low wages rather than from greater unemployment. Actually the South's devotion to a low level agriculture must serve to give the region a greater amount of concealed unemployment. This low level may account for the larger proportions who become job seekers as soon as the breadwinner of the family loses work. Thus from 1930 to 1937, allowing for population growth, the loss of 100 jobs gave the Nation 176 unemployed, but for the region it meant 221 unemployed. In one economic sector, moreover, the Southeast failed to hold its favorable employment ratio. By 1937 the emerging agricultural problem had served to give the region a higher rate of farm unemployment than was found in the Nation. This conclusion fits in with other studies which show that undoubtedly the problem of unemployed rural youth and of displaced tenants has attained serious proportions in the region.

The prewar picture of unemployment in the Southeast in 1937 (10.4 percent) made the return of 1930 conditions (with only 1.6 percent unemployment) seem a desirable goal. To reproduce the 1930 employment pattern in the Southeast with allowance for increase in the population would have required drastic changes. Our figures show that we would first have to induce 927,000 persons to relinquish jobs or the search for jobs and return to the ranks of those unavailable for employment. Then we would have to provide 846,000 new jobs for men and take away 81,000 jobs from women workers. Such an arbitrary shifting of workers could scarcely be expected to function in a democratic country. Another way, accordingly, would be to accept the increase in the number of those available for employment, that is, this new group of 927,000 seeking or holding jobs. Here in order to return to the low ratio of unemployment in 1930, we would have to provide 653,000 additional jobs for women and 1,039,000 jobs for men.

FULL EMPLOYMENT, 1940 AND AFTER

The solution for unemployment when it arrived in World War II was the provision of even more jobs in a war economy that drew additional women and youth out of the ranks of the unavailables. A major criticism of the 1937 Census was that many unavailables, women and youths, claimed to be seeking jobs when they really were not in the labor force. This it was felt added a fictitious bias to the reported unemployment. The 1940 Census figures showed a decrease in unemployment and an increase in the proportion of those who were not seeking employment (Table 94). Thus national unemployment declined in the period 1937-1940 from 16.2 to 11.3 percent for males and from 7.4 to 2.9 percent for females. At the same time males not seeking gainful employment increased from 14 to 20 percent, females from 69 to 74 percent. Similar trends were shown in the Southeast where reported unemployment was reduced to even lower levels

TABLE 94. COMPARISON OF NUMBER OF WORKERS BY SEX AND EMPLOYMENT STATUS, UNITED STATES AND SOUTHEAST, 1930, 1937, AND 1940

Area, sex, and year	Total population (15-74)		In labor force		Unemployed		Employed		Unavailable	
	Number	Percent	Number	Percent	Number	Percent	Number	Percent	Number	Percent
UNITED STATES	*(thousands)*		*(thousands)*		*(thousands)*		*(thousands)*		*(thousands)*	
All										
1930	84,805	100.0	46,821	55.2	2,426	2.9	44,395	52.3	37,984	44.8
1937	93,063	100.0	54,503	58.6	11,012	11.9	43,491	46.7	38,560	41.4
1940	95,947	100.0	50,839	53.0	6,856	7.1	43,983	45.8	45,108	47.0
Male										
1930	42,965	100.0	36,615	85.2	2,057	4.8	34,558	80.4	6,350	14.8
1937	46,704	100.0	40,115	85.9	7,555	16.2	32,560	69.7	6,589	14.1
1940	48,164	100.0	38,524	80.0	5,454	11.3	33,070	68.7	9,640	20.0
Female										
1930	41,840	100.0	10,206	24.4	369	0.9	9,837	23.5	31,634	75.6
1937	46,359	100.0	14,388	31.0	3,457	7.4	10,931	23.6	31,971	69.0
1940	47,783	100.0	12,315	25.8	1,402	2.9	10,913	22.8	35,468	74.2
SOUTHEAST										
All										
1930	16,307	100.0	8,493	52.1	253	1.6	8,240	50.5	7,814	47.9
1937	18,724	100.0	10,708	57.2	1,945	10.4	8,763	46.8	8,016	42.8
1940	19,198	100.0	9,848	51.3	1,111	5.8	8,737	45.5	9,350	48.7
Male										
1930	8,088	100.0	6,662	82.4	196	2.4	6,466	79.9	1,426	17.6
1937	9,287	100.0	7,904	85.1	1,245	13.4	6,659	71.7	1,383	14.9
1940	9,491	100.0	7,509	79.1	845	8.9	6,664	70.2	1,982	20.9
Female										
1930	8,219	100.0	1,831	22.3	57	0.7	1,774	21.6	6,388	77.7
1937	9,437	100.0	2,804	29.7	700	7.4	2,104	22.3	6,633	70.3
1940	9,707	100.0	2,339	24.1	266	2.7	2,073	21.4	7,368	75.9

Note: The following adjustments were necessary for comparable definition: in 1930, unpaid family workers were subtracted from all "gainful workers," and from employed workers and added to the "unavailable"; in 1937, "new workers" were subtracted from all workers "available for work" and from unemployed and added to the "unavailable"; also a small correction was necessary to include in the "labor force" persons available for work but not actively seeking jobs; in 1940, unpaid family workers were subtracted from employed, "new workers" subtracted from unemployed, and both categories subtracted from persons in labor force and added to those "unavailable"; all groups in labor force in 1940 include 14-year old children (excluding unpaid family workers) and persons over 75 years of age who are in the labor force. These two groups could not be subtracted from the total labor force because of lack of data at present; their numbers, however, should be negligible.

Source: *Sixteenth Census of the United States, 1940*, Preliminary Release, P-5, No. 9; *Fifteenth Census of the United States, 1930*, Population, V, Chap. 4, Tables 15-16; Vol. IV, Tables 11 and 23; Vol. V, Chap. 6, Table 9; *United States Census of Partial Employment, Unemployment, and Occupations, 1937*, I, Table 20; Vol. IV, Tables 43, 54-56; Vol, IV, Chap. VIII, Table 49, pp. 111-112; Table 69, p. 134; *Unemployment Census, 1930*, I, Tables 1, 6.

and the proportion of unavailables was similarly increased. In short the 1940 figures, except for those still unemployed, suggested a return to conditions of 1930.

This trend is to be explained in several ways. Greater numbers of youth were in school, 68 percent of those aged 16 and 17 as compared with 57.3 percent in 1930. Increased college enrollments indicated that this was true for all ages up to 20. Greater numbers of the aged were drawing old age insurance and assistance in 1940 and thus were unavailable. With returning prosperity, housewives had left the labor force and returned to domestic duties. This analysis suggests the source of the additional labor force needed in the war effort. Misleading answers, which in 1937 increased reported unemployment, served in the emergency of war to indicate the sex and age groups from which we drew additional workers, married women without children and older youth.

First, however, should come the unemployed. The greatest amount of unutilized labor power in 1940 was found in the Northeast where 3 million were reported unemployed (Table 95). Secondary concentrations of unemployed were reported from the Middle States and the Southeast with 2¼ and 1.4 millions respectively. The greatest proportions of unemployment were found in the Northeast and the Northwest where 17.7 and 17.3 percent of the total labor force were without work during the week before the census. The Southeast had the smallest proportion, 13.5 percent. By States unemployment ranged from 11.1 percent in Maryland to 23.9 percent in New Mexico (Figure 195). Agricultural States and the Southeast showed the smallest proportions of unemployment, Western Plains States and the Northeast the largest proportions. This figure suggests that war employment involved the problem of migration of manpower from certain stagnant economic areas to more active areas.

TABLE 95. NUMBER UNEMPLOYED AS PERCENTAGE OF ALL GAINFUL WORKERS 14 YEARS AND OLDER, UNITED STATES AND THE SIX MAJOR REGIONS, 1940

Area	Gainful workers	Un-employed	Unemployed as percent of gainful workers	Area	Gainful workers	Un-employed	Unemployed as percent of gainful workers
UNITED STATES	52,789,499	8,471,788	16.0	Middle States	14,391,736	2,259,194	15.7
				Northwest	2,765,651	479,024	17.3
Northeast	16,936,501	3,003,335	17.7	Far West	4,166,289	653,509	15.7
Southeast	10,567,628	1,427,569	13.5	Dist. of Columbia	344,033	42,117	12.2
Southwest	3,617,661	607,040	16.8				

Note: Unemployed are those seeking work (both new and experienced workers) and emergency workers on the pay rolls of Federal agencies.
Source: *Sixteenth Census of the United States, 1940*, Series P-10, No. 9, Tables 1, 6.

Table 96, which includes only those with work experience, will give an idea of the type and skills of unutilized labor reported in 1940. The largest proportions unemployed were unskilled laborers, 31.3 percent, but the largest single group in the Nation consisted of over 1¾ million semi-skilled workers, 14.1 percent of the Nation's total. In the Southeast, unskilled laborers made up the largest single group, over 300,000 unemployed. Skilled workers showed over 15 percent unemployment. The table also serves to show the difficulty involved in using the concept of unemployment in relation to farmers, unpaid family labor, and even proprietors and managers.

Next in our search for a war-time labor force came those classified as not available for employment. As the demands of expanding war economy were met, more unavailables were transferred to the labor force than ever before. World War II thus surpassed its predecessor in putting women into industry. In the aftermath, however, we bid fair to return to the conditions depicted in 1937 when unemployment due to lost job was augmented by increases due to transfer of the unavailables to the category of job seekers. To avoid a return to such a condition would require perfect

FIGURE 195. PERCENTAGE OF TOTAL LABOR FORCE UNEMPLOYED,
UNITED STATES, 1940

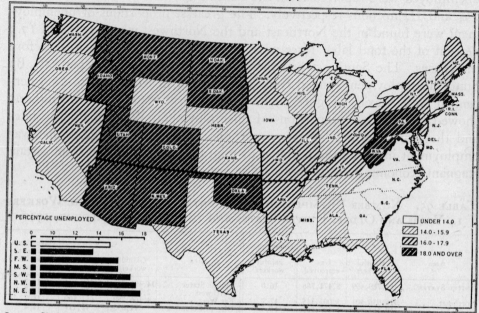

Source: *Sixteenth Census of the United States, 1940*, Series P-10, No. 9, Tables 1, 6.

TABLE 96. NUMBER OF UNEMPLOYED 14 YEARS OLD AND OVER WITH PER-
CENTAGE UNEMPLOYED* OF ALL GAINFUL WORKERS BY SOCIAL-ECONOMIC
CLASSES, UNITED STATES AND SOUTHEAST, 1940

Social-economic classes	UNITED STATES		SOUTHEAST	
	Number unemployed	Percent of all gainful workers	Number unemployed	Percent of all gainful workers
ALL	6,856,075	13.2	1,110,654	10.6
FARM	650,680	7.3	166,053	4.8
Farmers and managers	62,872	1.2	22,810	1.1
Farm laborers	587,808	15.9	143,243	9.7
Wage workers	552,616	22.2	128,999	15.3
Unpaid family	35,192	2.9	14,244	2.2
NONFARM	6,205,395	14.4	944,601	13.5
Professional	223,366	6.2	22,691	4.4
Proprietors, etc.	147,140	3.7	18,145	3.1
Clerks and kindred	923,589	10.8	96,603	9.3
Skilled workers	1,035,209	16.2	130,905	15.2
Semi-skilled workers	1,796,050	14.1	251,705	12.4
Unskilled workers	2,080,041	26.1	424,552	21.7
Domestic servants	380,237	15.1	112,086	14.2
Laborers	1,699,804	31.3	312,466	26.7

*Includes only those with work experience.
Source: *Sixteenth Census of the United States, 1940*, Population Preliminary Release, Series P-11.

synchronization of demobilized soldiers and sailors fitting into jobs left by
demobilized women workers returning to the home. In this connection we
may summarize the bearing of our analysis on long-run issues likely to
develop in the postwar period.

SOCIAL IMPLICATIONS

The preceding analysis has shown the tendency of mounting loss of jobs in depression to increase disproportionately the numbers accounted as unemployed. When primary workers, the family breadwinners, are displaced, secondary workers composed largely of women and youth enter the labor market in search of employment. Thus if the numbers displaced from jobs be counted as unity, the resulting increase in the number of unemployed will be a figure much greater than unity.

Our Table 91, Figure 192, show that a loss of 765,000 jobs in 1937 due to a change in social-economic conditions was accompanied by an increase of 1,692,000 among the unemployed of both sexes. This is equivalent to the statement that when a hundred jobs are lost in the population of the Southeast, 1930-1937, we may expect to find thereby not 100 but 221 unemployed. The same comparison for the United States gave a much smaller ratio. Here every 100 jobs lost meant 176 unemployed.

To some these figures may suggest that unemployment will always decline at an accelerating ratio whenever employment again picks up. As employment mounts, so the theory runs, the number seeking employment will decline at a greater than one to one ratio. This will be true if (1) primary workers are reemployed; and (2) if the body of secondary workers, composed largely of women, relinquish jobs or the search for jobs as primary workers are reemployed. To test this hypothesis it might be suggested that national policy in the next depression should be first directed to the reemployment of the 100 males who lose jobs. By the time this is done, it may be predicted that most of the 176 unemployed recently added to the labor market will be retired. After the war such a policy would be devoted to reemploying demobilized soldiers on the assumption that a high ratio of employed women would then become unavailable for the labor market.

Such a view, some sociologists may point out, discounts the effect of changes of habits and attitudes on women wage earners. The effect of declining births and increasing life expectancy has been to enlarge the labor market at both ends of the life span. Women as a result of experiencing both depression and war employment may no longer feel called upon to choose between jobs and marriage, but they may increasingly come to prefer pay envelopes to the child care that once went with marriage. Confronted with these imponderables we might find that reemployment of primary workers will not decrease so-called secondary unemployment as fast as the loss of jobs increased it during the depression. This leaves us with the disquieting thought that the numbers in the labor market are bound to increase, giving us a large reservoir of secondary unemployment.

Some believe that this phenomenon, characteristic of the shift to urban environment, is increased by every emergency that calls women into the labor market.

These considerations impinge on public policy in the debatable question of rationing jobs by primary and secondary workers per family. Already applied to work relief during the depression, to public employment in some States, and occasionally to private employment, this is a policy which traditional American individualism has hitherto largely avoided. It would be very repugnant to our traditional views, for example, to provide in the law that joint employment of husband and wife should not be encouraged as long as families existed in which both husband and wife were unemployed and seeking work. Certainly in regard to qualifications for jobs this policy would run into the greatest difficulties.

Some may be inclined to point out that attitudes developed in an expanding economy when more of our population was rural can hardly be maintained in an economy where most of the population is urban. Here it may be claimed that the persistence of individualistic attitudes will make necessary more collective action, that is, public relief. Others may contend that an equitable application in private industry of the distinction between primary and secondary unemployed would the more quickly reduce unemployment and thus the need for public relief. There are those, no doubt, who would claim that such a policy should make for a more even distribution of incomes and might stimulate rising marriage and birth rates.

It should be realized by all that the effect of large-scale postwar unemployment would make the struggle for jobs as much of a social and political issue as the question of relief itself. At this point, however, we are easily reminded that to make rabbit pie, one first catches the rabbit. Jobs for the postwar unemployed are not yet in sight. If apart from war, there should become apparent in our technology a longtime trend away from jobs in heavy industry for males to service jobs for women, reemployment of primary workers will become a hopeless issue, giving way to jobs for the secondary unemployed. As the skills of many primary unemployed become obsolescent, another question would arise. Under such conditions is it likely that men will follow the pattern set by women workers and gradually become "unavailable for gainful employment"? Certainly the depressing effect of such trends on marriage and the birth rates would again be of the greatest importance to population policy.

PART IV
CULTURAL ADEQUACY OF THE PEOPLE

CHAPTER 22

HEALTH AND VITALITY OF THE PEOPLE

HIGH AMONG the traits determining the cultural adequacy of any people must be listed their vitality. This remains true in spite of the fact that we are not quite agreed on the meaning to be attributed to the term, vitality. In popular speech it suggests persistence of the spark of life—an inherent tendency to live and survive in the face of all the ills that life is heir to. It is well recognized that the force of an inherent vitality can be measured only in terms of performance in an actual environment. It is this performance in terms of the environment that we call health. The spark of life grows by the fuel it feeds upon. Every favorable contribution of the environment strengthens, just as every unfavorable incidence weakens, the inherent vitality of a people. The years man lives, as Edgar Sydenstricker pointed out, are determined not only by his innate capacity to survive but by the influences of this complex environment.

The battle for life and survival accordingly can best be thought of in terms of an offense and a defense. If the harmful elements of environment comprise the offense, the inherent force of vitality musters the defense, bolstered at every point by the forces of medical care and technique which must be regarded as part of our complex social environment. Under ideal environmental conditions the battle would be decided only when the force of inherent vitality crumbles at the end of the life span. We can measure the outcome of this conflict only in terms of performance, as in death rates, morbidity rates, and length of life. In the record of performance, biology and environment are so intermingled that no separate accounting is undertaken, or in fact seems possible.

Our treatment of the vitality of the southern people is also a discussion of the healthfulness of the southern environment. Health hazards peculiar to the South are related to the geography of disease as affected by climate and rainfall. Undoubtedly the physiological strain of the low cooling power of the regions of warm humid summers does affect health but it is impossible to show any differentials in the death rates on this score. More apparent is the effect of the climate on the growth of insect and parasite life that gives the area a higher incidence of malaria, hookworm, etc. Contrary to popular belief, however, when allowances are made for age and race distribution, the death rates in the Southeast are no higher than those in the Nation.

Of equal importance is the question of the adequacy of medical services, public and private. Analysis of the health problems of a people is thus seen as one of the most difficult as well as one of the most important of our tasks. It is complicated by varying factors of race composition, of income level, of the regional distribution of a population, and its age and sex composition, each factor having its ultimate bearing on health and vitality.

In the United States to a large extent we have been compelled to render our judgments on the state of the people's health not from the figures of illness but from figures on death. This can be done only by relating rates of death to at least two conditions: (1) the age and sex make-up of the people, and (2) the cause of death. Thus death, which can be regarded as a biologically normal phenomenon at the end of the life span, must in the absence of morbidity statistics be related to the age curve of the population if it is to be accepted as a valuable index. Implicit in this procedure is the idea of the average incidence of death on a standard population under a given environmental complex. Over a period of time the changing incidence of death on a population gives a measure of the improvement in health conditions attendant upon improvement in environment and progress in medical knowledge and practice. To relate this to cause of death and thus to type of illness we need to determine standard ratios of the incidence and length of morbidity to death from each cause. Such figures if obtained, however, would last but a few years before the progress of medical services rendered them obsolete. Surgeon General Thomas Parran well stated the situation when he said that the sickness and death rates of previous years are inadequate yardsticks for the present and are useless as goals for the future. To think otherwise is to regard medical science and public health as static rather than dynamic forces.

REGIONAL VARIATIONS IN CAUSE OF DEATH

In a country as large as ours notable variations in mortality and morbidity are to be expected from section to section. Variations equally large, it is known, can be found among groups in the same locality. State differences in mortality in 1929-1931 showed important ranges. Standardized death rates for the white population varied from 7.6 in South Dakota to 15.6 in New Mexico. Both highest and lowest rates were found in the West-

FIGURE 196. THE STANDARDIZED DEATH RATES* FROM ALL CAUSES, WHITE POPULATION, UNITED STATES, 1929-1931

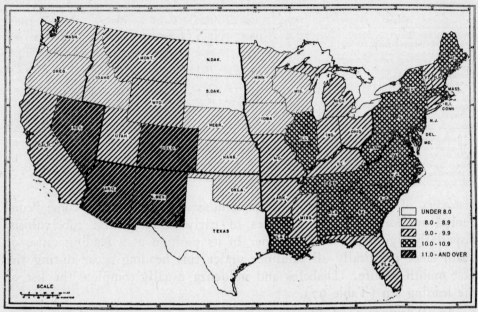

	UNDER 8.0
	8.0 - 8.9
	9.0 - 9.9
	10.0 - 10.9
	11.0 - AND OVER

* Note: Death rates are standardized on the basis of the standard million of England and Wales, 1910. Source: Louis I. Dublin and Alfred J. Lotka, *The Length of Life* (New York: Ronald Press, 1936).

ern States. With few exceptions the whole Atlantic seaboard showed rates slightly above the average, 10 to 10.9 per 1,000 population (Figure 196).

Translated into terms of the length of life, these differences would indicate that the average inhabitants of the best State may expect to live 15 years longer than the inhabitants of the worst State. If we can accept this difference as indicative of the state of public health, we might say that the worst States now lag 35 years behind the achievements of the best States in this respect. In Massachusetts it required some 35 years to accomplish a gain of 15 years in total life expectancy.

Regional differences in life expectancy are accompanied by regional variations in cause of death. The total incidence of ten principal diseases and conditions account for some three-fourths of all the deaths in the United States. Table 97 shows that within the last 40 years tuberculosis and pneumonia have given way to degenerative diseases as the leading causes of death. Fluctuating slightly from year to year, they are uniformly led by heart diseases which now account for almost one-fourth of the Nation's deaths. Its toll is almost twice that of cancer, the second most fatal disease. Next in the Nation come nephritis, cerebral hemorrhage, accidental violence, and pneumonia which ranked almost equally until the

TABLE 97. DEATH RATES PER 100,000 POPULATION IN REGISTRATION AREA BY LEADING CAUSES, 1900-1940

Cause	1900	1910	1920	1930	1938	1939	1940
Diseases of the Heart*	132.1	158.8	159.1	205.9	217.8	213.7	221.2
Cancer and other malignant tumors	63.0	76.2	83.2	97.4	115.1	117.5	120.3
Nephritis	89.0	99.1	89.2	90.9	77.5	82.8	81.5
Cerebral hemorrhage and softening**	71.5	75.7	81.7	81.1	76.5	78.0	80.5
Accidents	79.0	84.4	71.3	80.8	72.4	71.0	73.6
Pneumonia	180.5	147.8	137.0	83.4	67.8	59.3	55.0
Congenital malformations and diseases of early childhood	91.8	88.1	84.7	61.1	48.7	48.5	49.2
Tuberculosis***	181.7	136.0	97.0	63.5	44.7	43.2	42.2
Diabetes	9.7	14.9	16.0	19.0	23.9	25.5	26.6
Influenza	22.9	14.4	70.9	19.5	12.7	16.4	15.3

*Excludes diseases of coronary arteries.
**Excludes cerebral embolism and thrombosis and paralysis of unspecified origin.
***Of the respiratory system only.
Source: *Statistical Abstract of the United States, 1941*, Table 91; Bureau of the Census, *Vital Statistics—Special Reports*, 15, No. 6 (December 8, 1940).

discovery of chemico-therapy for pneumonia. Next in order come "congenital malformation and diseases of early infancy" and tuberculosis. Especially significant is the former in its position as a leading cause of death since practically all fatalities under this heading occur during the first month of life. Diabetes and influenza usually complete the list of the leading ten (Table 97).

In all regions heart diseases rank as chief of the agents of death, but in 1940 it showed variations from 18.6 percent of deaths in the Southwest to 32.3 percent in the Northeast (Figure 197). The high rank of cancer seems due to its great prevalence in the Northeast, Middle States, and Far West (Table 98). As the rates indicate, in the Southeast cancer ranks fourth for whites and eighth for Negroes (Table 99). The death rate from cancer in the Carolinas is one-third that in Massachusetts (Figure 198). Inadequate diagnosis may be a factor. It is strange that pneumonia as a cause of death ranks highest not in the colder northern States but in the southern and western areas. Poorer housing and less adequate heating undoubtedly offset the effects of the milder climate. In Colorado, Utah, Texas, Oklahoma, Arkansas, Alabama, Tennessee, and Kentucky, pneumonia, until recently, has ranked second only to heart diseases as cause of death. Less important as a cause of death, influenza tends to follow the same pattern.

Nephritis takes its highest rank among the Southeastern States where it ranks as a second cause of death among whites and third among Negroes (Figure 199). In both the Rocky Mountain areas and the grain growing States of the plains it seldom rises above fifth place. Accidental violence, chiefly auto fatalities, one would expect to find most prominent in the crowded urban East. Actually they are most important in the West and Far West where they seldom fall below third or fourth place. In the

FIGURE 197. PERCENTAGE OF DEATHS, BY TEN MAJOR CAUSES, UNITED STATES AND SIX REGIONS, 1938

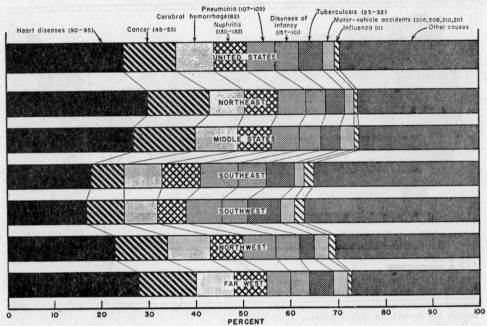

Source: Bureau of the Census, *Vital Statistics—Special Reports*, Vol. 14; State Summaries, Vol 16; Mortality Summaries by Specific Cause of Death.

TABLE 98. DEATH RATES PER 100,000 POPULATION FROM IMPORTANT CAUSES OF DEATH, UNITED STATES AND THE SIX MAJOR REGIONS, 1940

Cause of death	United States	Northeast	Southeast	Southwest	Middle States	Northwest	Far West
Heart diseases (90-95)...............	292.5	362.1	202.5	179.4	310.6	246.3	346.9
Cancer and other malignant tumors (44-55)........................	120.3	146.5	72.4	79.1	134.3	111.7	144.8
Cerebral hemorrhage, etc. (83).........	90.9	87.7	91.3	71.3	99.4	88.1	93.8
Nephritis (130-132)..................	81.5	81.5	94.1	63.4	80.5	69.2	74.2
Pneumonia (107-109)..................	55.0	51.6	64.1	59.3	53.2	46.6	48.8
Congenital malformations and diseases of early infancy (157-161)...........	49.2	43.9	59.3	59.2	45.4	51.6	41.7
Tuberculosis (13-22).................	45.9	44.2	56.0	63.1	37.2	27.5	50.5
Diabetes (61)........................	26.6	36.4	14.7	13.9	29.5	23.0	25.1
Motor vehicle accidents (170)..........	26.2	20.3	25.9	27.6	28.5	27.0	40.8
Influenza (33).......................	15.3	6.8	29.4	25.5	12.2	15.0	11.2

Note: Deaths registered by place of occurrence and related to enumerated population April 1, 1940.
Source: Bureau of the Census, *Vital Statistics—Special Reports*, 15, No. 7; Vol. 16, No. 30.

Southeast this cause is fifth for white and sixth for colored. The South, however, has fewer motor cars, one to 6 inhabitants as compared with 2.6 in the Far West. When the fatalities are related to vehicle miles six Southeastern States rank among those having highest mortality.

In the Southwest, cerebral hemorrhage falls below its usual rank, sinking to seventh place in Arizona and ninth in New Mexico. Tuberculosis rises above its rank mainly for resort States like Arizona and New Mexico,

FIGURE 198. DEATHS FROM CANCER AND OTHER MALIGNANT TUMORS
PER 100,000 POPULATION, UNITED STATES, 1940

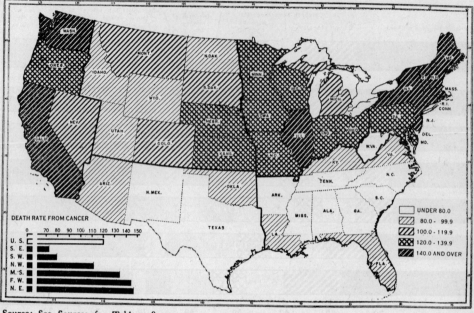

Source: See Sources for Tables 98-100.

although for unknown reasons it appears especially high in Tennessee, Nevada, and Kentucky (Figure 200). Among Negroes in all areas it has
dropped from the highest causes of death to third place. Figures 201 and
202 suggest that certain focal areas of infection exist in the Southeast for
both races. Diabetes appears among the ten leading causes of death only
in the prosperous States of the Northeast, Middle States, and Far West.
In the Southeast it is less prominent and among Negroes it falls to fifteenth place. Suicide (Figure 203) ranks among the first ten in the far
Western States like Nevada, Washington, and California while homicide
(Figure 204) is important enough to be found among the first ten in several Southeastern States. Among Negroes suicide is one of the least important, homicide one of the more important causes of death. In the Southwest, diarrhea and enteritis among children under two have been important
enough to reach the first ten causes of death; in the Southeast they stand
eleventh. In the Southeast, syphilis has been included among the first ten
causes. For the colored population of the Southeast, syphilis ranks ninth;
for the whites it is sixteenth. Malaria, once prominent in the Southeast,
has receded to twenty-third place (Table 99).

Many reasons can be assigned for these regional differences in deaths
by cause. Age differences, racial make-up of the population, the occupa-

FIGURE 199. DEATHS FROM IMPORTANT CAUSES WITH RATES PER 100,000
POPULATION BY RACE, SOUTHEAST, 1930

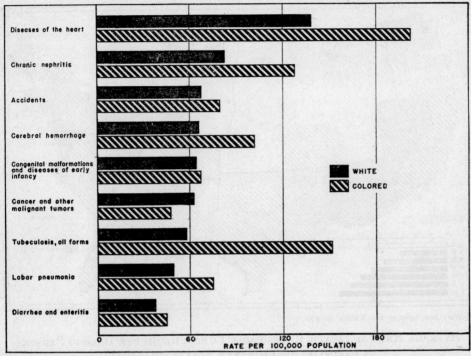

Source: Bureau of the Census, *Vital Statistics—Special Reports, 1930*, State Summaries, Mortality by
Specific Cause of Death.

tional distribution with its varying hazards, climate, varying social and economic conditions resulting in different levels of living all meet differences
in the quality and availability of health and medical services both public
and private. This last factor may show in faulty diagnosis of the primary
cause of death especially among the poorer income groups.

In the main it can be said that the degenerative diseases of age have
higher rates in the regions with higher levels of living and show an increase from 1930 to 1940 (Table 100). This is true in both the Nation
and the region for heart disease, malignant tumors, cerebral hemorrhage,
etc. Preventable diseases of youth and middle age, like tuberculosis, influenza, and diseases of infancy are highest in regions of low living standards.
They show a marked decline in death rates from 1930 to 1940. Both of
these changes are in line with changes in age composition but the decline in
deaths from the preventable diseases has represented additional important
gains in medicine, hygiene, and sanitation. However, the Southeast still has
too many deaths from tuberculosis and diseases of early infancy. Similarly
the excess death rates from degenerative diseases in the Far West and

FIGURE 200. DEATHS FROM TUBERCULOSIS (ALL FORMS) PER 100,000
POPULATION, UNITED STATES, 1940

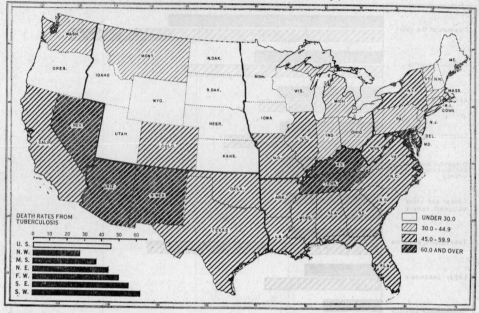

Source: See Sources for Tables 98-100.

AVERAGE ANNUAL DEATH RATES FROM TUBERCULOSIS PER 100,000 PERSONS
IN COUNTIES OF THIRTEEN STATES, 1929-1933

FIGURE 201. WHITE DEATHS   FIGURE 202. COLORED DEATHS

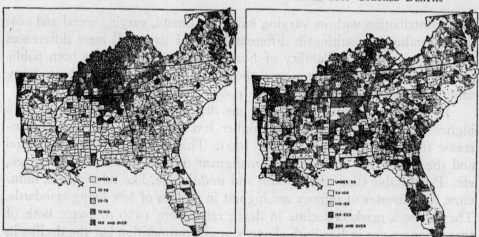

Source: Lumsden and Dower, *Some Features of Tuberculosis Mortality in the United States*, U. S.
Public Health Service.

Northeast are in line with the more mature age composition of these areas.
There is, however, one preventable cause of death which does not fol-
low the general regional pattern—deaths from motor vehicle accidents.
The Far West, a region with a mature age composition and high standards

TABLE 99. IMPORTANT CAUSES OF DEATH RANKED BY INCIDENCE AMONG WHITE AND NEGRO POPULATION, UNITED STATES, SOUTHEAST, AND SOUTHWEST, 1940

Cause of death	Total population			White population			Negro population		
	U.S. Rank	S.E. Rank	S.W. Rank	U.S. Rank	S.E. Rank	S.W. Rank	U.S. Rank	S.E. Rank	S.W. Rank
Diseases of the heart..............	1	1	1	1	1	1	1	1	1
Cancer and other malignant tumors..	2	4	2	2	4	2	6	8	7
Cerebral hemorrhage, thrombosis, softening, etc..................	3	3	4	3	2	4	4	3	3
Nephritis......................	4	2	5	4	3	6	2	2	2
Accidents and other undefined violence....................	5	5	3	5	5	3	7	6	6
Pneumonia.....................	6	6	8	6	7	8	5	5	5
Congenital malformations and diseases of early infancy.........	7	7	7	7	6	5	8	7	8
Tuberculosis (all forms)............	8	8	6	8	8	7	3	4	4
Diabetes mellitus................	9	13	13	9	10	12	13	15	15
Influenza......................	10	9	10	11	9	10	11	10	10
Syphilis.......................	11	10	12	12	16	15	9	9	9
Suicide........................	12	16	14	10	12	13	24	25	25
Diarrhea and enteritis.............	13	11	9	14	11	9	12	12	13
Appendicitis....................	14	17	15	13	14	14	17	18	16
Hernia and intestinal obstruction....	15	18	20	16	17	19	16	16	18
Cirrhosis of the liver.............	16	22	21	15	20	20	22	23	24
Senility.......................	17	14	11	18	13	11	15	13	12
Ulcer of stomach or duodenum......	18	20	22	17	21	21	20	21	23
All puerperal causes..............	19	15	17	19	15	18	14	14	14
Homicide......................	20	12	18	21	19	22	10	11	11
Communicable diseases of childhood .	21	19	16	20	18	16	18	17	19
Bronchitis.....................	22	25	25	22	24	24	27	26	26
Exophthalmic goiter..............	23	28	27	23	28	27	28	28	27
Alcoholism.....................	24	27	28	24	26	28	26	27	28
Dysentary......................	25	24	19	25	23	17	23	22	20
Pellagra.......................	26	21	23	26	22	23	19	19	17
Typhoid and paratyphoid..........	27	26	24	27	27	25	25	24	21
Malaria.......................	28	23	26	28	25	26	21	20	22

Note: Diseases of the blood vessels—arteriosclerosis, etc.—omitted because figures by race and regions not available. In the United States such diseases actually rank tenth and are more prevalent than influenza.

Source: Bureau of the Census, *Vital Statistics—Special Reports*, 14 (1940), State Summaries; Vol. 15, Nos. 6, 21; Vol. 16, mortality summaries by specific causes of death.

TABLE 100. DEATH RATES PER 100,000 POPULATION FOR SELECTED CAUSES OF DEATH, UNITED STATES AND SOUTHEAST, 1930 AND 1940

Cause of death	UNITED STATES		SOUTHEAST	
	1930	1940	1930	1940
Heart diseases (90-95)...................	213.6	292.5	158.4	202.5
Cancer and other malignant tumors (45-53)........	97.3	120.3	57.3	72.4
Tuberculosis (all forms) (23-32)................	71.5	45.9	86.6	56.0
Congenital malformations and diseases of early infancy (157-161)...	61.0	49.2	65.1	59.3
Motor vehicle accidents (206, 208, 210, 211)........	26.7	26.2	21.2	25.9
Influenza (11)........................	19.5	15.3	32.1	29.4

Note: Numbers beside causes of death are those of the 1929 International List of causes of death.

Population estimates for the U.S.: 1930 (revised mid-year estimate of the death registration area)—118,472. Population estimates for the Southeast: 1930—25,651,000. Enumerated population, April 1, 1940.

Source: Bureau of the Census, *U. S. Mortality Statistics, 1930*, Table 8; Bureau of the Census, *Vital Statistics—Special Reports*, 9, No. 30; Vol. 15, No. 7; *Statistical Abstract of the United States, 1937*, Tables 11 and 74.

of living, exceeds by far all other regions. A similar region, the Northeast, has the lowest rate per 100,000. The Southeast which falls in an intermediate range showed a considerable increase in deaths from automobile accidents.

FIGURE 203. DEATHS FROM SUICIDE PER 100,000 POPULATION, UNITED STATES, 1940

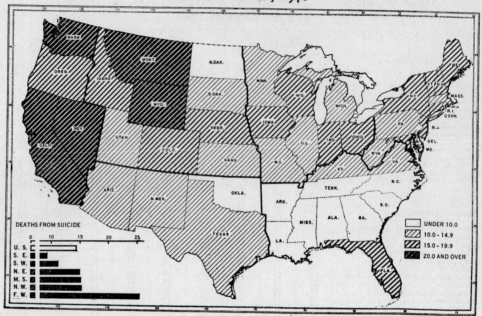

Source: See Table 99.

FIGURE 204. NUMBER OF DEATHS FROM HOMICIDE PER 100,000 POPULATION, UNITED STATES, 1940

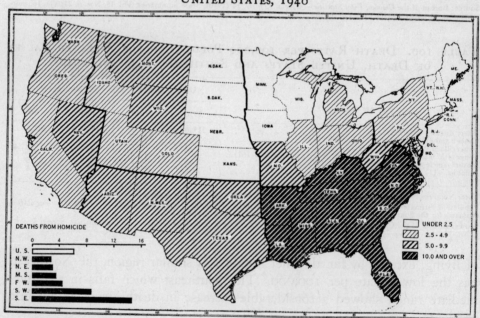

Source: See Table 99.

HEALTH IN RURAL AND URBAN AREAS

Cutting across State and regional differences in mortality are the differentials that are found to exist among ethnic, residence, and income groups after age and sex are standardized. Negroes have higher death rates than whites, low income groups have higher rates than higher income groups, and urban dwellers have higher rates than rural dwellers. Only the superior performance of rural dwellers goes against the common tendency of higher income groups to exhibit better health. Not only are mortality rates definitely higher in urban areas but the standardized death rate increases regularly with the size of the city.[1] This tendency, as we shall see later, has been reversed in infant mortality. The problem of medicine and public health in the urban environment has been stated by Theobald Smith in the following words: "Civilization from the medical aspect may be defined as the maintenance of any increasingly dense population with a falling death rate in spite of free intercourse. . . . Without the constant application of medical and preventive safeguards the human race could not sustain itself."[2]

The evidence now indicates, according to Harold F. Dorn,[3] that the unequal distribution of the benefits of modern sanitation and medicine is operating to alter the relative healthfulness of city and country residence when measured by mortality rates. Between 1900 and 1930 the death rate from typhoid decreased about 90 percent in urban areas but only 75 percent in rural areas. At the present time this disease takes relatively more than twice as many lives in rural areas as in cities. Infant mortality decreased 44 percent in urban areas and 34 percent in rural areas from 1915 to 1934. An infant is now more likely to die before completing the first year of life if born to parents living in rural areas, although this varies widely throughout the country. However, mortality from the diseases of adult life is still appreciably lower among rural than among urban residents.

In 30 years the increase in expectation of life at birth has been about 60 percent greater among persons living in urban communities than among those living in rural areas. At all ages, except 10 to 20 among females, mortality has decreased more rapidly in the urban than in the rural population. The greater occupational risks of urban males, however, are revealed by the advantage of rural over urban males in expectation of life. Around 1930 to 1940, white infants born and reared in the country can

[1] This appears true even when deaths are registered by place of residence instead of place of occurrence, as has been customary until recently.

[2] Theobold Smith, "The Decline of Infectious Disease in Its Relation to Modern Medicine, *Journal of Preventive Medicine*, Vol. II, No. 5 (September, 1928).

[3] Harold F. Dorn, "Health in Rural and Urban Areas," *Public Health Reports*, 53 (Washington, D. C. U. S. Government Printing Office, July 15, 1938), 1181-1195.

expect to live about 5 years longer than white infants in the city if they are boys and about 4 years longer if they are girls. In spite of the more rapid decline in mortality in urban communities since 1900, rural males subject to the mortality conditions of 1900-1902 had a greater life expectancy at all ages over 1 than did urban males thirty years later. In other words, the remarkable gains in the preservation of life during the past generation have merely advanced the urban population to the level of life expectancy attained by the rural population at the beginning of the century. Case rates of nonfatal illness also show that lowest rates occur among people living in the open country and in the large cities of over 100,000 population. The distribution of mental illness also favors the rural areas. In New York, a State where facilities are most adequate, the rate of first admissions is about 66 percent higher for urban than for rural residents.[4]

In every way in which ill health is measured, rural residents in the United States still possess definite health advantages over urban dwellers. Only in communicable diseases and those causing infant deaths have the health facilities and services afforded urban people served to give them equality with natural advantages of rural dwellers—space, air, sunshine, and the freedom from the dense contacts of urban masses. Increased public health for our rural people, however, would undoubtedly find its recompense in further lowering their illness and death rate.

DEATHS BY OCCUPATIONS

Among other things the health record of rural areas is due to the fact that agriculture is the least hazardous of all occupations. In the occupations that men follow it can hardly be said that death is not a respecter of persons. The incidence of mortality upon the occupations inversely parallels the degree to which they are held in social esteem. Alba M. Edward's social-economic classes[5] show an increasing death rate as we move down the scale from the professional class to the unskilled workers. The one exception to this generalization is found among agricultural workers, who have the lowest death rate of all occupations. Jessamine S. Whitney's study gives the following standardized death rates per 1,000 males by occupation in selected states:[6] agricultural workers, 6.21; professional men, 7.00; proprietors, managers, and officials, 7.38; clerical, 7.40; skilled, 8.12; semiskilled workers, 9.86; and unskilled workers, 13.10. It should be noted that within these broad classifications certain groups have higher death rates. Thus the standardized death rate for wholesale and retail dealers

[4] *Ibid.*

[5] See discussion in chapter 11.

[6] Jessamine S. Whitney, *Death Rates by Occupation* (New York: National Tuberculosis Association, 1934), p. 17. The States are Alabama, Connecticut, Illinois, Massachusetts, Minnesota, New Jersey, New York, Ohio, and Wisconsin.

is 8.17; for the semi-skilled in manufacturing, 10.03; for servants, 11.76. Highest of all is the rate of 17.26 among the unskilled in factories and in construction work.

While little research has yet been done on deaths by occupations in the Southeast, studies from other countries and areas suggest that these rates have general application. Their meaning for the region is evident. In terms of occupational environment the South's low death rate is due largely to the predominance of agriculture. The effect of further industrialization will be to increase the death rate. For crude death rates this long-run effect will be reenforced both by the accompanying movement to cities and by the aging of the population. To the extent that untrained portions of the population tend to be confined to the lower skilled occupations, mortality will increase for Negroes and poorer white workers as they move out of agriculture. This will further accent the need for public health and safety programs in the region, a trend that should be offset somewhat by the fact that per capita costs for adequate public health work is lower for the more densely settled urban populations. At that, it remains doubtful that the best public health program devised can reduce industrial death rates to the level maintained among the agricultural populations. Basic to any such hope would be improvements in the income, housing, and educational level of the less skilled wage earner, as well as improvements in working conditions to reduce occupational hazards.

NEGRO HEALTH

The Negro still suffers from a greater incidence of illness and death than his white neighbor, but the old pessimism about the inability of the race to survive has given way to the new concern about his environment. The Negro's appalling mortality in the Reconstruction Period, approaching 40 per 1,000, had been cut to 14 in 1932. Standardized for age the death rate in 14 southern States, 1931-1933, was 15.2 for Negroes and 8.9 for whites. In the previous decade, however, Negro health conditions have not improved as much as might have been expected. From 1922 to 1932 deaths from all causes for all ages declined only 2.5 percent among Negroes as compared with 7.7 percent among whites.

Back of these blanket figures are varying rates of mortality for the Negro, north and south, rural and urban.[7] The Negro's highest death rate in 1930 was found in the urban South, 21.8; his lowest in the rural South, 13.1 (Table 101). In the North this standardized death rate is higher in rural than in urban areas by 18.2 to 17.1. Higher urban mortality is especially evident among Negroes of working ages.

[7] See Mary Gover, *Mortality Among Southern Negroes*, Public Health Bulletin 235 (Washington, D. C. U. S. Government Printing Office, 1937).

TABLE 101. ANNUAL RATE OF MORTALITY FROM ALL CAUSES AT SPECIFIC AGES AMONG COLORED AND WHITE IN URBAN AND RURAL AREAS OF FOURTEEN SOUTHERN* AND NINE NORTHERN** STATES, 1931-1933

Death rate per 1,000 persons†

Section and color	All Ages		0 to 4	5 to 9	10 to 14	15 to 19	20 to 24	25 to 34	35 to 44	45 to 54	55 to 64	65 and over
	Age corrected	Crude										
Southern urban:												
Colored.........	21.78	20.40	34.65	2.91	3.75	8.49	11.43	14.05	20.63	35.45	62.44	91.10
White..........	11.77	12.43	18.63	2.48	2.14	3.21	3.85	4.72	7.52	14.24	30.35	90.33
Southern rural:												
Colored.........	13.11	12.17	20.07	1.64	1.83	4.32	7.34	9.28	12.04	17.92	30.55	74.14
White..........	7.96	8.25	13.19	1.28	1.04	1.82	2.88	3.58	4.91	8.06	18.14	67.74
Northern urban:												
Colored........	17.14	15.30	24.96	2.85	3.05	6.14	7.36	9.22	14.94	27.12	50.02	91.05
White..........	9.96	10.73	14.22	1.97	1.48	2.06	2.64	3.38	6.06	13.00	28.34	82.07
Northern rural:												
Colored........	18.16	18.79	23.22	2.24	2.80	7.48	10.22	12.61	18.51	26.63	44.89	98.49
White..........	8.41	10.99	12.44	1.32	1.11	1.96	2.97	3.49	5.07	9.23	19.80	74.67

Ratio of Colored to White rate

Southern:												
Urban..........	1.85	1.64	1.86	1.17	1.75	2.64	2.97	2.98	2.74	2.49	2.06	1.01
Rural..........	1.65	1.48	1.52	1.28	1.76	2.37	2.55	2.59	2.45	2.22	1.68	1.09
Northern:												
Urban..........	1.72	1.43	1.76	1.45	2.06	2.98	2.79	2.73	2.47	2.09	1.76	1.11
Rural..........	2.16	1.71	1.87	1.70	2.52	3.82	3.44	3.61	3.65	2.89	2.27	1.32

Ratio of Urban to Rural rate

Southern:												
Colored.........	1.66	1.68	1.73	1.77	2.05	1.97	1.56	1.51	1.71	1.98	2.04	1.23
White..........	1.48	1.51	1.41	1.94	2.06	1.76	1.34	1.32	1.53	1.77	1.67	1.33
Northern:												
Colored........	.94	.81	1.07	1.27	1.09	.82	.72	.73	.81	1.02	1.11	.92
White..........	1.18	.98	1.14	1.49	1.33	1.05	.89	.97	1.20	1.41	1.43	1.10

*Includes the Southeast plus Maryland, the District of Columbia, and Oklahoma.
**States: Illinois, Indiana, Michigan, Missouri, New Jersey, New York, Ohio, Pennsylvania, and West Virginia.
†The age distribution of the population is as of 1930.
Source: Mary Gover, *Mortality Among Southern Negroes Since 1920*, Table 5, p. 15.

It is at the productive ages 15-45 that the largest relative differences are found between white and Negro mortality. In this period respiratory tuberculosis and heart disease account for 30 to 40 percent of the total excess of colored over white mortality in the South. Among the causes of death which show a higher ratio of Negro to white races syphilis is outstanding (Table 102). Against this must be placed the fact that syphilis is more likely to be recorded as a cause of death among Negroes. Among the causes of death which show relatively low rates among Negroes are cancer, angina pectoris, and certain infectious diseases of childhood. By age, Mary Gover points out, the peak of excess colored mortality comes at 10 to 14 for respiratory tuberculosis, at 20 to 24 for the infectious and nervous diseases and pneumonia; at 25 to 34 for cancer, diseases of the heart and arteries, and at 35 to 44 for digestive diseases and diseases of the kidneys[8] (Table 101).

[8] *Ibid.*

TABLE 102. IMPORTANT CAUSES OF DEATH RANKED BY RATIO OF NEGRO RATES OF DEATH TO WHITE RATES, UNITED STATES AND SOUTHEAST, 1940

Causes of death	United States		Southeast	
	Ratio of rates	Rank	Ratio of rates	Rank
ALL CAUSES..	1.3		1.5	
1. Homicide..	11.1	1	5.6	2
2. Malaria..	9.5	2	3.5	3
3. Pellagra..	6.0	3	2.2	7.5
4. Syphilis..	5.6	4	6.5	1
5. Typhoid and paratyphoid........................	3.7	5	2.3	6
6. Tuberculosis....................................	3.4	6	2.7	4
7. All puerperal causes............................	3.0	7	2.5	5
8. Dysentery......................................	2.6	8	1.5	15
9. Influenza......................................	2.5	9.5	1.7	10.5
10. Senility..	2.5	9.5	2.2	7.5
11. Diarrhea and enteritis..........................	2.2	11	1.7	10.5
12. Communicable diseases of childhood*............	2.1	12	1.5	15
13. Pneumonia.....................................	1.8	13	1.7	10.5
14. Nephritis......................................	1.7	14	1.7	10.5
15. Congenital malformation and diseases of early infancy......	1.4	15.5	1.2	18
16. Alcoholism.....................................	1.4	15.5	1.2	18
17. Cerebral hemorrhage, etc.......................	1.3	17.5	1.5	15
18. Hernia and intestinal obstruction...............	1.3	17.5	1.6	13
19. Appendicitis...................................	1.1	19	1.2	18
20. Accidents and undefined violence................	1.0	20	1.1	21
21. Ulcer of stomach or duodenum..................	0.9	21.5	1.1	21
22. Heart diseases.................................	0.9	21.5	1.1	21
23. Diabetes mellitus...............................	0.7	23.5	0.9	24.5
24. Bronchitis.....................................	0.7	23.5	0.8	26.5
25. Goiter...	0.6	26	1.0	23
26. Cirrhosis of the liver...........................	0.6	26	0.9	24.5
27. Cancer..	0.6	26	0.8	26.5
28. Suicide..	0.3	28	0.2	28

*Measles, scarlet fever, whooping cough, and diphtheria.
Source: Bureau of the Census, *Vital Statistics—Special Reports*, 16, mortality summaries by specific causes of death.

The problem of Negro health, serious as it is in its economic and social aspects, is nothing of a medical mystery. Excess Negro mortality is made of the elements that cause excess deaths everywhere. It is related to occupational factors found in rough, heavy work, to poor housing, heating, and sanitation, to inadequate nutrition and poor medical care, and to that ignorance which condemns a people to both, when they might secure better. Only two factors might be offered as at all peculiar to Negroes rather than the poor in any group. One is the greater incidence of venereal disease, which has been attributed to a less repressive attitude toward sex in the Negro's culture. Another, a greater concentration of respiratory tuberculosis among adolescents, has been attributed both to occupational stress, poor housing, and less probably to certain physiological characteristics of the race. Table 102 shows eight diseases from which the Negro has a death rate over twice as high as that of the whites in the Southeast.

Many of the environmental conditions characteristic of Negro life operate to condition their higher infant and maternal mortality. Of the more than 250,000 Negro infants born alive each year in the United States about 22,000 die.[9] In northern States the infant mortality rate in 1933-1935 was

[9] See Elizabeth C. Tandy, *Infant and Maternal Mortality Among Negroes*, Children's Bureau Publication 243 (Washington, D. C.: U. S. Government Printing Office, 1937).

83.6 for Negroes as compared with 49.8 for whites. In the South it was 86.1 for Negroes and 53 for whites. Two-thirds of the Negro births occurred in the rural South. Midwives attend more than half of all Negro births but in the rural South about three-fourths of the births were delivered by midwives. North and South, rural and urban, it is found that the lowest Negro infant mortality rates prevail in the rural South, 80.2; the highest in the urban South, 109.3. Next highest comes the rural North, 100.9, and the next to the lowest in the urban North, 81.0. In every State, urban and rural rates show much less variation among whites than among Negroes.

More than half of the Negro infant mortality occurs in the first month of life. Neo-natal deaths were 44.8 per 1000 live births for Negro as compared with 31.7 for white infants. While the recent rate of decline in infant deaths has been as great among Negroes as whites, the mortality rate for Negro infants 1933-1935 was at the stage attained by the white group in 1915. The stillbirth rate is more than twice as high among Negroes, 72 to 32 for whites. The rate may be higher, for it is thought that Negro stillbirths are subject to less adequate reporting. Maternal mortality is also greater, being 96.1 per 10,000 live births in 1933-1935 as compared with 54.6 for whites. The principal causes of maternal death are the same as among the white group and are largely preventable.

The downward trends in deaths of Negro infants and mothers, says Elizabeth Tandy, reflect the gradual changes in public health and social conditions and indicate the adaptation of the Negro to his environment and to the increasing healthfulness of his community.[10] The case of the Negro accents the rural-urban differential in health. The development of maternal and child health programs in rural areas, however, is still in the pioneer stage in this country. These figures indicate the great need and can be matched by wholehearted acceptance by the Negroes of health facilities wherever they are made available.

[10] *Ibid.* Recent improvements in infant mortality among Negroes are discussed in Chapter 24.

CHAPTER 23

HEALTH AMONG THE ELDERS

The great triumphs of public health have been won in combating infectious disease and in saving the lives of the young. Wherever shown to be favorable, the position of the Southeast in mortality is due to its comparatively young population and its predominantly rural environment. A youthful and a rural population still offers the most fertile field for improvement in public health but it is also valuable to speculate as to what will be the health problems of the Southeast as its population matures.

LENGTH OF LIFE

Saving our population from infant mortality means that they will live long enough to die from the diseases of post-maturity. Improvement in health and vitality is shown by the extent to which man has increased the average length of life. Not until 1930 were life tables prepared covering the whole United States. Table 103, however, gives the trend of mortality

Table 103. Selected Values from Life Tables for White Males and Females, United States, 1900-1940

Time period	At birth		Age 20		Age 45		Age 70	
	Male	Female	Male	Female	Male	Female	Male	Female
Mortality rate per 1,000 persons alive at beginning of year of age:								
1900-1902*......................	133.5	110.6	5.9	5.5	12.6	10.6	58.9	53.7
1919-1921**.....................	80.3	63.9	4.3	4.3	9.3	8.1	54.6	50.2
1929-1931.......................	62.3	49.6	3.2	2.8	9.3	7.0	58.0	48.7
1930-1939.......................	57.0	45.0	2.7	2.2	8.6	6.3	56.3	45.8
1940............................	45.4	35.3	2.1	1.4	7.7	5.3	56.1	43.9
Average future lifetime:								
1900-1902*......................	48.2	51.1	42.2	43.8	24.2	25.5	9.0	9.6
1919-1921**.....................	56.3	58.5	45.6	46.5	26.0	27.0	9.5	9.9
1929-1931.......................	59.1	62.7	46.0	48.5	25.3	27.4	10.0	10.0
1930-1939.......................	60.6	64.5	46.8	49.7	25.5	28.0	9.3	10.2
1940............................	62.9	67.3	47.6	51.2	25.7	28.7	9.3	10.3

*For the original registration States.
**For the death registration States of 1920.
Source: *United States Life Tables, 1930-1939 (Preliminary)*, prepared by Elbertie Foudray and Thomas N. E. Greville under the general supervision of Morris H. Hansen, Acting Assistant Chief Statistician, Division of Statistical Research, Bureau of the Census, July 21, 1941. 1940 tables from Metropolitan Life Insurance Company, *Statistical Bulletin* (New York: December, 1941), p. 8.

and average future lifetime for the white population of registered areas from 1900-02 to 1940. In that period the life expectancy of white males at birth has increased from 48.2 to 62.9 years. White females, who live longer, had their average future lifetime increased from 51.1 to 67.3 years. The great increases were in life expectancy at birth but at age twenty the increase was considerable, some 5.5 years for males, 7.4 years for females. At age 45, increases were slight; and at age 70, hardly perceptible. These comparisons would indicate in the language of the census "that there has been no increase in the extreme limits of life, but that many persons who would have died in infancy or in early and middle life are now completing a normal life span." This is made clear by reference to the age specific rates of Table 103, for infant mortality has declined over 60 percent and mortality at age 45 by 50 percent.

Variations among States in 1930 amounted to over 20 percent, or about fifteen years in average length of life.[1] Our calculations show that little difference now exists in life expectancy between the Nation and the Southeast. In 1940 life expectancy at birth in the Nation was 67.3 years for white females and 62.94 for white males (Table 104). In the Southeast,

TABLE 104. EXPECTATION OF LIFE AND MORTALITY RATE PER 1,000, AT SPECIFIED AGES, BY COLOR AND SEX, GENERAL POPULATION, UNITED STATES, 1940

| Age | EXPECTATION OF LIFE | | | | | MORTALITY RATE PER 1,000 | | | | |
| | Total persons | White | | Colored | | Total persons | White | | Colored | |
		Males	Females	Males	Females		Males	Females	Males	Females
0	63.77	62.94	67.31	53.04	56.01	43.50	45.45	35.31	70.43	54.87
1	65.65	64.91	68.76	56.02	58.23	4.93	4.69	4.07	9.43	7.55
2	64.97	64.22	68.04	55.55	57.67	2.55	2.51	2.14	4.43	3.58
3	64.14	63.38	67.18	54.79	56.88	1.73	1.75	1.51	2.53	2.30
4	63.25	62.49	66.28	53.93	56.01	1.43	1.47	1.20	2.08	2.05
5	62.34	61.58	65.36	53.04	55.12	1.23	1.30	1.02	1.79	1.71
10	57.64	56.91	60.63	48.41	50.44	.84	.94	.67	1.24	.99
15	52.91	52.20	55.84	43.80	45.83	1.36	1.37	.96	2.74	3.04
20	48.34	47.61	51.15	39.58	41.72	2.14	2.06	1.44	5.37	5.32
25	43.88	43.12	46.54	35.76	37.87	2.62	2.43	1.81	7.28	6.38
30	39.46	38.64	41.98	32.09	34.10	3.07	2.79	2.20	8.64	7.52
35	35.09	34.20	37.46	28.49	30.40	3.87	3.58	2.79	10.28	8.96
40	30.81	29.85	33.01	25.01	26.84	5.26	5.08	3.73	13.33	12.19
45	26.68	25.69	28.67	21.78	23.58	7.47	7.67	5.28	18.02	16.00
50	22.75	21.77	24.48	18.91	20.60	10.92	11.66	7.67	25.71	22.43
55	19.09	18.15	20.50	16.50	18.10	15.89	17.64	11.38	33.15	30.04
60	15.69	14.86	16.75	14.22	15.83	22.48	25.67	17.12	36.85	33.33
65	12.56	11.88	13.30	11.88	13.46	33.28	37.61	27.20	47.41	40.38
70	9.80	9.26	10.27	9.83	11.30	50.47	56.11	43.89	61.42	52.37
75	7.42	7.02	7.68	7.91	9.38	76.15	84.60	68.59	78.02	67.86
80	5.44	5.20	5.50	6.08	7.67	117.40	127.73	110.66	110.73	84.34

Source: Computed in the Statistical Bureau of the Metropolitan Life Insurance Company on the basis of preliminary census data of population which are not likely to be changed much in the final reports. This table varies slightly from the United States Life Tables, 1939-1941, since published in *Vital Statistics—Special Reports* Vol. 19, No. 4 (January 11, 1944).

[1] "While this variation may be real, it may also be the result of inadequate reporting of vital statistics and inaccuracies in population data. This is particularly true among southern States, where we have had considerable difficulty in securing complete registration of births and infant deaths and in accurately enumerating the age of the Negro population."—Letter from C. L. Dedrick, Chief Statistician, Bureau of the Census, February 1, 1939.

TABLE 105. ABRIDGED LIFE TABLE FOR THE POPULATION BY COLOR AND SEX, SOUTHEAST, 1939-1941

Age x	White				Colored			
	Male		Female		Male		Female	
	Survivors at age x l_x	Life expectation e_x^o	Survivors at age x l_x	Life expectation e_x^o	Survivors at age x l_x	Life expectation e_x^o	Survivors at age x l_x	Life expectation e_x^o
0.......	100,000	61.68	100,000	66.80	100,000	51.62	100,000	55.02
1.......	94,160	64.48	95,410	69.00	90,684	55.90	92,691	58.33
5.......	92,864	61.36	94,290	65.80	88,839	53.03	91,061	55.35
10.......	92,313	56.72	93,848	61.10	88,162	48.42	90,480	50.69
15.......	91,816	52.01	93,502	56.32	87,416	43.81	89,836	46.04
20.......	90,961	47.47	92,887	51.67	85,847	39.56	88,038	41.92
25.......	89,678	43.12	92,027	47.13	83,102	35.78	85,536	38.07
30.......	88,316	38.74	91,042	42.61	79,803	32.15	82,611	34.33
35.......	86,757	34.39	89,829	38.15	75,919	28.67	79,053	30.76
40.......	84,774	30.13	88,336	33.75	71,592	25.24	75,088	27.25
45.......	82,043	25.94	86,439	29.44	66,044	22.15	69,833	24.10
50.......	78,270	22.18	83,974	25.22	59,396	19.34	63,837	21.12
55.......	73,244	18.52	80,571	21.18	51,240	17.01	55,930	18.74
60.......	66,211	15.21	75,841	17.33	43,110	14.75	47,352	16.69
65.......	57,322	12.17	69,034	13.78	35,171	12.52	39,486	14.52
70.......	46,246	9.46	59,359	10.60	27,404	10.36	32,177	12.25
75.......	33,290	7.16	45,832	7.96	19,975	8.29	24,712	10.20
80.......	19,727	5.39	29,645	5.93	12,711	6.63	17,530	8.37
85.......	8,970	4.02	14,901	4.41	6,784	5.33	11,220	6.71
90.......	2,792	3.02	5,305	3.29	2,955	4.29	5,945	5.55
95.......	541	2.38	1,191	2.52	973	3.60	2,667	4.58
100.......	91	1.77	196	1.82	269	2.85	1,061	3.20
105.......	9	....	22	....	57	....	250	....

Source: Calculated from: *Sixteenth Census of the United States, 1940*, Population, Second and Fourth Series, State bulletins. *Vital Statistics of the United States*, I, 1939 and 1940; Bureau of the Census, *Vital Statistics—Special Reports*, 18, State bulletins. Calculated by Nadia Danilevsky.

FIGURE 205. NUMBER OF SURVIVORS OUT OF 100,000 BORN ALIVE, BY RACE AND SEX, UNITED STATES, 1939-1941

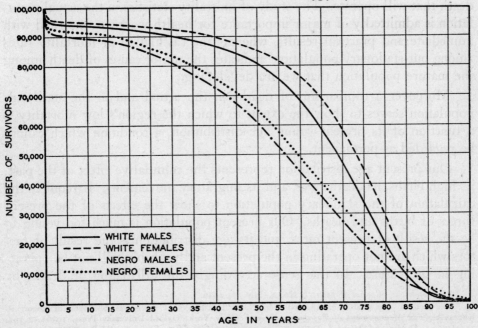

Source: United States Life Tables, *Vital Statistics—Special Reports*, Vol. 19, No. 4 (Jan. 11, 1944).

average future lifetime, 1939-1941 (Table 105), was 66.80 and 61.68 years for white females and males respectively. This slight differential decreases with advancing age, giving the southern white population, after age 25, a life expectancy equal to that of the Nation.

Life expectation for the total population of the region, however, has always been much lower, averaging approximately 57 years in 1930. This lower figure is explained by the high mortality of the colored population. For them, life expectancy at birth in 1930 was 49.33 for females, 47.25 for males. These values were but little lower than those for the Nation, 49.51 and 47.55.[2] In the 1940 tables the corresponding figures for non-white females and males was 56.01 and 53.04 in the Nation; 55.02 and 51.62 in the Southeast. Figure 205 presents for both sexes the number of survivors at different ages for white and colored populations in the Nation. The Southeast repeats the same pattern.

CAUSE OF DEATH IN A MATURE POPULATION

Projection of present population trends is hardly necessary to convince us that we will soon need fewer baby carriages and more hospitals. While the stationary population may be regarded as another "statistical fiction," calculation of deaths by cause on this basis is significant because of the present trend of the population toward the new age distribution. As we approach the life table population, we should realize the changed causes of death that will operate. The study of mortality statistics in the actual population is admittedly of major importance for health workers concerned with immediate and practical results, whereas the calculation of mortality rates among our stationary population[3] indicates the major causes of death among the mature population that we are developing.

Moreover a comparison of deaths in the actual and in the stationary population serves to show the extent to which the region's low mortality is a function of its present young age distribution, a condition which cannot be regarded as permanent.

Our present age distribution represents the cumulative effect of the past, its high births, its death rates, and its migratory movements. It requires the calculation of the stationary population to show the effects of the present forces of births and deaths. Our present population is much too young to be the result of present rates, and its age distribution is the result of factors which are not operating in the present and probably will not be operating in the future. In this sense accordingly the calculation of deaths by

[2] *Vital Statistics—Special Reports*, I, No. 2, July 27, 1936.
[3] The method here used is an adaptation by Nadia Danilevsky of procedures developed in Robert R. Kuczynski, *The Measurement of Population Growth* (New York: Oxford University Press, 1936), p 194, and Louis I. Dublin and Alfred J. Lotka in *The Length of Life* (New York: Ronald Press, 1936), p. 104.

TABLE 106. DISTRIBUTION OF DEATHS FROM ALL CAUSES BY 5-YEAR AGE
GROUPS AMONG THE ACTUAL AND STATIONARY POPULATION, WITH
CUMULATIVE NUMBER OF DEATHS AT THE END OF EACH
PERIOD, SOUTHEAST, 1930

Age period	Number of Deaths		Age	Cumulative Number of Deaths	
	Actual population	Stationary population		Actual population	Stationary population
0- 4..............	57,419	40,791	5................	57,419	40,791
5- 9..............	5,653	3,757	10................	63,072	44,548
10-14..............	4,802	3,299	15................	67,874	47,847
15-19..............	10,052	6,993	20................	77,926	54,840
20-24..............	13,453	10,459	25................	91,379	65,299
25-29..............	12,349	12,754	30................	103,728	78,053
30-34..............	11,859	13,153	35................	115,587	91,206
35-39..............	13,789	14,142	40................	129,376	105,348
40-44..............	14,154	16,934	45................	143,530	122,282
45-49..............	16,292	19,244	50................	159,822	141,526
50-54..............	18,840	23,439	55................	178,662	164,965
55-59..............	18,116	29,403	60................	196,778	194,368
60-64..............	19,253	35,491	65................	216,031	229,859
65-69..............	19,290	43,762	70................	235,321	273,621
70-74..............	20,905	50,086	75................	256,226	323,707
75-79..............	17,775	50,029	80................	274,001	373,736
80-84..............	13,371	40,653	85................	287,372	414,389
85-89..............	7,515	24,273	90................	294,887	438,662
90-94..............	3,214	8,011	95................	298,101	446,673
95 and over......	1,568	2,600	ALL............	299,669	449,273

Source: U. S. Mortality Statistics, 1930, Table 4; 1929, 1931. Fifteenth Census of the United States, 1930, Population, II ,Chap .
10, Tables 24 and 27. Birth, Stillbirth, and Infant Mortality Statistics, 1929, 1930, 1931, Tables 1 and 4.

cause among the stationary population gives us a closer approximation to
reality than such a figure for the actual population. Our calculations (Table 106) show that in a stationary population equal in size to the actual
population of the Southeast in 1930, the number of deaths would be 449,-
273 instead of the actual 299,669 (Figure 206), and thus the stationary
death rate as of 1930 would be 17.52 instead of the crude rate of 11.68.

This is a portent of the future and its meaning may be shown by an
example. If we should imagine an ideal, stationary population with a constant number of births from year to year where everybody lives to be 100
and deaths occurred only at this age, the death rate would be 10 per 1,000
population, only little less than the actual rate of 11.68 in the region. Indeed we can calculate that a death rate of 11.68 would be attained if everybody lived until 86 with no deaths before this age. It is evident that the
Southeast is still very far from this goal and that therefore the ageing of
the population will bring about an increasing total death rate in the future
even though age specific rates remain at the same level.

The crude median age of death of our regional population, however,
was only 47 in 1930 while for the stationary population it was 64 (Table
107). This difference is due to the fact that the excess in the younger ages
of the actual population unduly weights the number of deaths of the young
and therefore gives a very misleading crude median age at death for all
causes. If instead of computing the median age at death, we had computed

FIGURE 206. THE CUMULATIVE NUMBER OF DEATHS FROM ALL CAUSES BY
FIVE-YEAR AGE GROUPS AMONG THE ACTUAL AND THE STATIONARY
POPULATION OF THE SOUTHEAST, 1930

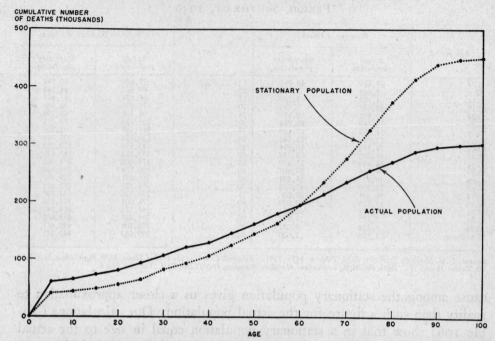

Sources: Table 106. *United States Mortality Statistics, 1930*, Table 8; All Sources necessary to compute stationary population of the Southeast. Method adopted from Louis I. Dublin and Alfred J. Lotka, *Length of Life* (New York, 1936), p. 104; Robert R. Kuczynski, *Measurement of Population Growth* (New York, 1936).

the arithmetic mean, we would have for the actual population a value several years less than 47, since the irregularities of the distribution shift the mean in the direction of younger ages. But the mean age at death, or the mean after lifetime is by definition the life expectation at birth. Should we then conclude that the life expectation of the regional population is below 47 years? Not at all; we already know that life expectation at birth for the total population in the Southeast in 1930 was about 57. We could have secured the same result if, instead of computing the median age at death in the stationary population, we had computed the arithmetic mean. There is thus a great difference between the average age at death in the actual and stationary population and it is the utilization of the latter statistical fiction that gives us the true life expectation of our present population.

Our comparison of death rates in the actual population for the United States and Southeast by 28 major causes (Table 102) shows that preventable diseases of the younger ages, puerperal causes, and malaria and pellagra, branded as diseases of poverty and ignorance, rank much higher in

TABLE 107. INCIDENCE OF DEATH FROM SPECIFIED CAUSES AMONG THE ACTUAL
AND STATIONARY POPULATION, WITH PERCENTAGE OF TOTAL NUMBER
OF DEATHS, DEATH RATE PER 100,000 POPULATION, AND
MEDIAN AGE AT DEATH, SOUTHEAST, 1930

Cause of death	ACTUAL POPULATION				STATIONARY POPULATION			
	Number deaths	Percent of total	Death rate per 100,000	Median age at death	Number deaths	Percent of total	Death rate per 100,000	Median age at death
ALL CAUSES..............	299,669	100.0	1,168.3	47	449,273	100.0	1,751.5	64
1. Heart diseases..........	40,630	13.6	158.4	64	79,275	17.6	309.1	70
2. Chronic nephritis.......	24,523	8.2	95.6	65	49,406	11.0	192.6	71
3. Tuberculosis...........	22,226	7.4	86.6	33	26,379	5.9	102.8	42
4. Cerebral hemorrhage....	19,743	6.6	77.0	64	39,402	8.8	153.6	70
5. Accidents..............	18,319	6.1	71.4	32	23,227	5.2	90.6	51
6. Lobar pneumonia.......	14,783	4.9	57.6	55	24,566	5.5	95.8	66
7. Cancer................	14,705	4.9	57.3	60	26,954	6.0	105.1	66
8. Bronchopneumonia.....	7,751	2.6	30.2	5	9,596	2.1	37.4	60
9. Communicable diseases of childhood........	5,115	1.7	19.9	1	3,738	0.8	14.6	Under 5
10. Homicide..............	4,375	1.4	17.1	31	4,713	1.0	18.4	35
11. Diseases of blood vessels.	4,010	1.3	15.6	70	8,800	2.0	34.3	75
12. Suicide...............	2,427	0.8	9.5	43	3,237	0.7	12.6	51

Note: Total stationary population is assumed equal to 25,651 thousand, the actual mid-year population in 1930.
Source: *U. S. Mortality Statistics, 1930*, Tables 5, 7, 8; *Statistical Abstract of the United States, 1937*, Table 11; *Fifteenth Census of the United States, 1930*, Population, II, Chap. 10, Tables 24 and 27; *Birth, Stillbirth, and Infant Mortality Statistics, 1929, 1930, 1931*, Tables 1 and 4; P. K. Whelpton, "The Completeness of Birth Registrations in the United States," *Journal of the American Statistical Association*, 29 (June, 1934).

the Southeast than in the Nation as a whole. On the other hand, most diseases of the older ages—heart, cancer, diabetes, etc.—show higher rates in the Nation. When colored death rates by cause for 1930 were ranked by their ratio to those for the white population, they ranged in the Southeast from ratios of 8.9 to 1 for syphilis; 4 to 1 for typhoid, and 3.3 to 1 for pellagra to 0.8 for cancer and 0.2 for suicide. For only six causes out of twenty-four in the Nation and for only four causes in the Southeast were the rates lower among the colored than among the white population. Wherever causes of death are closely connected with low standards of living and lack of education, as we have seen, the colored ratio is especially high.

The comparison of deaths in the actual and stationary population serves to show that, given present medical practices and living conditions, we may expect in the future higher death rates. At the same time, however, we will have a more favorable median age of death from all causes (64 as against 47) and from each disease in particular (Table 108). Nevertheless the number of deaths from most diseases will greatly increase. Table 106 and Figure 206 indicate that from less than 300,000 in the actual population of the South in 1930 the cumulative number of deaths will mount to almost 450,000 in the stationary population.

Significant contrasts are found in the age concentration of deaths from specified causes. Figure 207 indicates that the median age of deaths from all causes will rise from 47 to 64 with the two-thirds range shifting from the span 28 to 61 years to the span 29 to 80 years. In heart disease the

TABLE 108. IMPORTANT CAUSES OF DEATH RANKED BY MEDIAN AGE AT DEATH, UNITED STATES (TOTAL POPULATION) AND SOUTHEAST (ACTUAL POPULATION BY COLOR AND TOTAL STATIONARY POPULATION), 1930

Cause of Death	UNITED STATES Total actual population		SOUTHEAST Total actual population		White population		Colored population		Stationary population	
	Age	Rank	Age	Rank	Age	Rank	Age	Rank	Age	Rank
1. Diseases of blood vessels.........	70	1	70	1	73	1	62	1	75	1
2. Cerebral hemorrhage.............	69	2	64	3½	68	3½	57	3	69	3½
3. Chronic nephritis................	67	3½	65	2	69	2	58	2	70	2
4. Heart diseases..................	67	3½	64	3½	68	3½	55	4	69	3½
5. Diabetes mellitus................	64	5								
6. Cancer and other malignant tumors	63	6	60	5	63	5	52	5	66	5½
7. Cirrhosis of the liver............	60	7								
ALL CAUSES......................	56		47		53		40		64	
8. Hernia and intestinal obstruction..	54	8								
9. Lobar pneumonia...............	49	9	55	6	62	6	47	6	66	5½
10. Influenza......................	48	10								
11. Suicide.......................	47	11½	43	7	44	7	39	7	51	8½
12. Pellagra......................	47	11½								
13. Syphilis......................	41	13								
14. Accidents and undefined violence..	40	14	32	9	34	10	28	10	51	8½
15. Tuberculosis (all forms)..........	35	15	33	8	41	8	29	9	42	10
16. Homicide......................	33	16	31	10	35	9	30	8	35	11
17. Appendicitis...................	32	17								
18. Malaria.......................	29	18½								
19. All puerperal causes.............	29	18½								
20. Typhoid and paratyphoid........	23	20								
21. Bronchopneumonia.............	10	21	5	11	6	11	4	11	60	7
22. Communicable diseases of childhood.................	2	22	1	12	2	12	1	12	Under 5	12
23. Diarrhea and enteritis (all ages)...	Under 1	23								
24. Congenital malformations and diseases of early infancy........	First week	24								

Note: Median age at death computed for 24 diseases among the total population of the Nation, but only for 12 diseases among the population of the Southeast; therefore, rankings for the Southeast are not comparable to those for the Nation and are only valid for comparison of various population groups in the Southeast. Lobar pneumonia is below "All Causes" by median age at death for the United States, but is above for the Southeast, for all population groups given here.
Source: See Table 107

median shifts from 64 to 69 years of age and the two-thirds range from 45-78 to 53-80 years. The median age of deaths from tuberculosis rises from 33 to 42 with a shift in the two-thirds span from 20-56 to 24-67 years. Broncho-pneumonia is most interesting. With a wide two-thirds range, a slight shift from spans of 1-70 to 2-79 means a shift from 5 to 60 years in the median age of death (Table 108).

When the mortality of the actual and stationary population is contrasted in Table 107 it is found that heart disease as a cause of death would double its claim from 40,000 to 80,000 deaths. Other causes of death would also show great increases, thus: chronic nephritis increases from 25,000 to 50,000, cerebral hemorrhage from 20,000 to 39,000, cancer from less than 15,000 to almost 27,000. While tuberculosis would show slight change, the diseases of childhood are the only ones to show an actual decrease. Table 107 shows the contrast in the cumulative trend in age specific death rates from nephritis and lobar pneumonia as against deaths from the communicable diseases of childhood. Such trends are

FIGURE 207. THE MEDIAN AGE AT DEATH WITH RANGE FROM SPECIFIED
CAUSES, ACTUAL AND STATIONARY POPULATION, SOUTHEAST, 1930

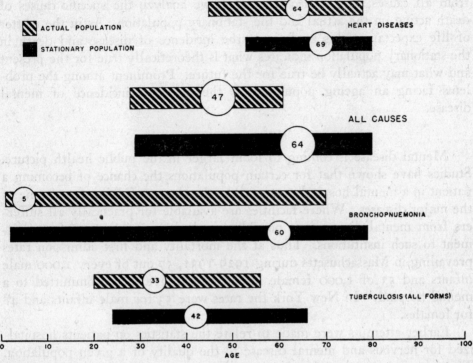

Source: See Table 107. 66 2/3 percent range centered about the median.

inevitable results of the aging process for, as Table 106 indicates, deaths among those from 60 to 70 will rise from 38 thousand to 79 thousand.

These trends can be minimized somewhat by improvements in the level of living and in the education of the people of the Southeast provided these changes are accompanied by an advance both in the science of medicine and the distribution of medical care. This will mean moreover that the efforts of scientists and physicians, successfully directed to the field of bacteriological diseases of youth, should also be concentrated on those diseases of the aging which depend for prevention and cure upon the development of such sciences as nutrition, biochemistry, and endocrinology. Even here, however, the best attack on the disease of the aged is an adequate health and nutrition program for the period of childhood and youth.

We may conclude that only by studying the distribution of deaths in the stationary population can we gain a correct idea of their occurrence both in time and number without the distorting effects of recent high fertility on age composition. The vital statistics of our actual population give us an unduly optimistic idea as to the small number of deaths and an unduly pessimistic idea as to the young age at which death occurs. True for death from all causes, this is also true when we analyze the specific causes of death acting on the actual and the stationary population. As in the matter of life expectancy, this analysis of the incidence of disease and death in the stationary population indicates what is theoretically true for the present and what may actually be true for the future. Prominent among the problems facing an ageing population is the increased incidence of mental disease.

MENTAL DISEASE

Mental disease is coming to loom larger in the public health picture. Studies have shown that for certain populations the chance of becoming a patient in a mental hospital is as great as the chance of dying from some of the major diseases. Where facilities are available for practically all sufferers from mental disease it is possible to calculate the chances of commitment to such institutions. Thus at the mortality and first admission rates prevailing in Massachusetts during 1929-1931, 57 out of every 1,000 male infants and 53 of 1,000 female infants would live to be committed to a mental hospital.[4] In New York the rates were 53 for male infants and 48 for females.

Earlier attempts were made to relate the statistics on patients hospitalized for nervous and mental disease to the quality of a given population. This approach has largely given way to the more objective approach of mental hygiene. The incidence of mental disease is seen as a function of environment in conjunction with the organism, and environment is considered in its social as well as in its public health aspect. Thus rates of commitment, it is found, are usually much lower in the rural than in the urban environment. In addition, the number of patients admitted to hospitals bears a direct relation to the provision of adequate facilities. The average duration of cases of mental disease from onset until death or dismissal is so great that few States have been able to provide anything like optimum hospital facilities. Figures on mental disease accordingly do not often mean what they say, nor say what they mean, to the man on the street.

Rates per thousand population in 1940 (Table 109) show that the Southeast and the Southwest have a lower proportion of patients in hospitals for mental disease than other regions. This condition may reflect the simpler conditions of a rural environment or it may be due simply to the lack of hospital facilities in the South. We would expect the Northeast and Far West to have the best facilities, and we find that they have the

[4] Harold F. Dorn, "The Incidence and Future Expectancy of Mental Disease," *Public Health Reports* 2001 (Washington, D. C.: U. S. Government Printing Office, November 11, 1938).

highest rates. When we relate the number of first admissions in 1940 to the total number of patients on hospital books, we find however, that the Southeast leads all the other regions, except the Far West, with 21.9 percent first admissions (Table 109). Again this is not necessarily indicative of a new trend in the increase of cases, but may represent the region's improvement in the provision of hospital facilities.

Hoping to cast some light on the geographical distribution of patients by types of mental disorder we have tried to analyze the percentage distribution of patients by type of disease within each region (Table 109). Numerically the five most important types of mental disturbances were selected: manic-depressive psychosis, schizophrenia, diseases caused by syphilis, diseases due to degeneration of tissues connected with senescence of the organism and, finally, those caused by alcoholism. These five groups comprise about 70 percent of all cases under care in hospitals for mental disease.

TABLE 109. PATIENTS IN HOSPITALS FOR MENTAL DISEASE, UNITED STATES AND THE SIX MAJOR REGIONS, 1940

Type of Disease	United States	North-east	South-east	South-west	Middle States	North-west	Far West	District of Columbia
All patients on books at end of year.........	532,999	209,634	81,415	25,198	142,214	23,773	44,144	6,621
Rate per 1,000 population*.................	4.0	5.2	2.9	2.6	4.0	3.2	4.5	
First admissions, number...................	105,989	38,158	17,855	5,087	29,244	3,973	10,641	1,031
Percent of all patients...................	19.9	18.2	21.9	20.2	20.6	16.7	24.1	
Cerebral arterio-sclerosis and senile psychosis—number...................	21,026	8,978	2,395	767	5,732	800	2,129	225
Cerebral arterio-sclerosis and senile psychosis, percent of all admissions......	19.8	23.5	13.4	15.1	19.6	20.1	20.0	
Schizophrenia, number of admissions......	20,457	7,889	2,810	1,206	5,467	798	1,931	356
Schizophrenia, percent of all admissions....	19.3	20.7	15.7	23.7	18.7	20.1	18.1	
Alcoholism (with or without psychosis)— number.............................	11,987	3,288	2,511	366	3,297	284	2,188	53
Alcoholism, percent of all admissions......	11.3	8.6	14.1	7.2	11.3	7.1	20.6	
Manic-depressive, number of admissions...	10,433	3,442	2,520	540	2,377	429	1,091	34
Manic-depressive, percent of all admissions.	9.8	9.0	14.1	10.6	8.1	10.8	10.3	
G.P. and other forms of syphilis of the C.N.S.,**—number...................	8,431	2,597	1,509	553	2,659	257	735	121
G.P. and other forms of syphilis of the C.N.S.,** percent of all admissions......	8.0	6.8	8.5	10.9	9.1	6.5	6.9	

*Number of patients related to enumerated population April 1, 1940.
**General Paresis and other forms of Syphilis of the Central Nervous System.
Source: Bureau of the Census, Vital Statistics—Special Reports, 15, No. 22.

Comparing manic-depressive and schizophrenic patients by regions, we find that the proportion of schizophrenic cases are roughly twice as high as those of manic-depressive cases in all regions except the Southeast. In the Southeast the number of patients of each type is about equal, being 14.1 and 15.7 percent of all cases respectively. This should be indicative of some actual difference since the Southwest, which is not superior to the Southeast with regard to hospital facilities, shows the same predominance of schizophrenic over manic-depressive patients as other regions.

What, then, should cause an excess of manic-depressive cases and a comparative shortage of schizophrenia in the Southeast? To characterize very roughly the two types of mental disease, we may say that the manic-depressive psychosis generally occurs when a person, usually of the extrovert type, is not adapted and cannot properly adjust to meet various strains, overstimulation, worries, etc., of a strenuous life. Schizophrenia is more apt to find its victims among persons of the introvert type who feel isolated, not because of geographic solitude, but because of a failure to be assimilated or to achieve the desired recognition from their fellow men. For instance, it is known that Negroes, while living in the South where they are surrounded by their own folk and live in customary, even though unfavorable conditions are apt to suffer much less from schizophrenia than when they migrate to the cities of the North. These characterizations of the disease would indicate that the Southeast as a homogeneous region with well established if somewhat rigid folkways, presents an environment unfavorable to the occurrence of schizophrenia. At the same time this rigidity together with other handicaps of existence may put an undue strain on some overexcitable individuals, and thus create a favorable ground for manic-depressive psychosis.

None of the remaining regional differences takes us so far afield in doubtful theory. The high percentage of patients suffering from general paresis in the Southwest is due to the high incidence of syphilis especially among Mexicans coupled with insufficient facilities for an early diagnosis and treatment of the disease in this region. The number of cases attributed to cerebral arteriosclerosis and to senile psychosis reflects the age distribution of regions. Here we would expect the Southeast to have the smallest proportions.

Finally, the percentages of mental diseases caused by alcoholism follow to a certain extent the regional distribution of deaths from alcoholism (Figure 208). The Far West ranked first in both rates in 1940, and the Southwest ranked among the lowest. The Southeast ranked third in deaths from alcoholism but second in percentages of psychosis due to alcoholism.

It is felt that variations in certain rates in the Southeast can be traced to racial differences both in the incidence of mental disease among Negroes and in facilities for their hospitalization. The greater incidence of syphilis and thus of paresis among this group is generally known. None of the data however justifies the assumption of constitutional inferiority among Negroes nor do they prove conclusively that Negroes have been subject to social and economic discrimination sufficient to affect rates of mental disease.[5]

[5] See Benjamin Malzberg, "Mental Disease Among American Negroes" in Otto Klineburg's *Characteristics of the American Negro* (New York, 1944), pp. 371-99, for a discussion of this problem based on New York figures.

FIGURE 208. THE NUMBER OF DEATHS FROM ALCOHOLISM PER 100,000
POPULATION, UNITED STATES, 1940

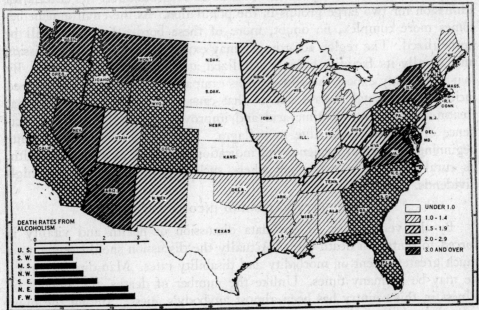

Source: United States Bureau of the Census, *Vital Statistics—Special Reports, 1940*, Vol. 15, No. 7.

In his study of mental patients in Georgia hospitals J. E. Greene[6] found that Negroes had higher hospitalization rates, notably high death rates, and low discharge rates. Georgia Negroes in spite of inadequate facilities are hospitalized at earlier ages, die at earlier ages and after a shorter period of hospital residence than do whites. Negroes compare favorably, however, in their high percentage of those discharged as "recovered" or "improved" and in low percentage readmitted.

Partly because of increased facilities for its treatment, it is commonly believed that mental disease has shown an alarming increase in recent years. Certainly the figures on hospitalization show that the number admitted increased more than 40 percent from 1926 to 1936. This trend can be checked against conditions in States with adequate facilities. Studies of first admissions in Massachusetts, New York, and Illinois, States where facilities were first made fairly adequate, show no such increases. From 1920 to 1930 the number of first admissions per 100,000 population decreased for women under 70 and for men under 45 or 50. In Massachusetts decreases also occurred among older men.[7] In the Southeast, on the contrary, increases in first admissions may be expected as the States expand

[6] "Analysis of Racial Differences within Seven Clinical Categories of White and Negro Mental Patients in the Georgia State Hospital, 1923-32," *Social Forces*, 17 (December, 1938), 201-211.

[7] Harold F. Dorn, *op. cit.*, p. 14.

their overtaxed facilities. The less exacting demands of the rural environment and the less exacting demands made on Negroes affect the criteria for admission for two large groups in the population. As the environment becomes more complex, no doubt, more of these border line cases will be hospitalized. The region accordingly may expect a rising rate of admission until finally its facilities become stabilized at a fairly adequate level. By that time many expect the anti-syphilis campaign will be felt in a lowered incidence of mental disease due to that cause. We may expect also that treatment including nicotinic acid and improved diet will lower the incidence of mental disease due to pellagra. The Southeast has made some beginnings in mental hygiene, and indications are that, as in public health, its rural areas offer a frontier where such a program would pay high dividends.

MORBIDITY RATES AND INCOME LEVELS

By the very nature of our data discussion of health and vitality is forced to center on death rates. Actually the discussion should center to a much greater extent on morbidity and disability rates. Man dies but once; he may be ill many times. Unlike the number of deaths, the amount of illness in this country has been almost anybody's guess. Among the most extensive and best planned of recent researches along this line was the National Health Survey of more than 2,300,000 urban people, undertaken by the United States Bureau of Public Health in cooperation with the W.P.A. during the winter of 1935-1936. If we can apply the result of this survey to the whole country with due regard for age, sex, and residence, we can estimate that there are six million people who are unable to work, go to school, or pursue their usual activities because of disease or injury. For all ages this amounted to 4.5 percent of the total population. The acute respiratory diseases, chiefly influenza and common colds, lead all forms of illness with 47 cases per 1,000 persons, followed by chronic diseases with 46 cases. Next in order come infections, accidents, diseases and infections of the puerperal state, digestive ailments, and other causes. The rate of loss or permanent gross impairment of members was found to be 19.6 per 1,000 persons.[8]

The Southeast has proved especially vulnerable to diseases that rank low in death-dealing power but high in drain on energy. Among these are malaria, hookworm, and pellagra.[9] While public health will finally have to face the problem of the chronic diseases of age, it will continue to find its greatest triumphs in preventing disabling morbidity among the young and the mature. Here its task centers among those having the lowest in-

[8] *The Amount of Disabling Illness in the Country as a Whole,* National Health Survey Bulletin 1 (Washington, D. C.: U. S. Government Printing Office, 1938).
[9] See Rupert B. Vance, *Human Geography of the South,* chaps. XV, XVI.

comes, were it for no other reason than the fact that the higher income classes are already provided with better medical services.

Actually we are aware of the extent to which those with low incomes are subject to the greater incidence of morbidity. No specific data on the Southeast are at hand but the fact of low income in the region makes the national figures especially significant. The National Health Survey showed that total disability per person per year ranged from 17.4 days for relief cases, and 10.9 days for those with incomes under $1,000 to 6.5 for those with incomes of $3,000 and over.[10] This difference was highest in the age group 25-64 years because it is found that occupational hazards fall heaviest on those in the unskilled and low wage trades.

The diseases and impairments were classified in broad groups and related to differential incidence on low income and relief families and those with good incomes. Thus relief families had 8.75 times as much disability for tuberculosis as families with $5,000 or more income per year. From highest to lowest the ratios between the poor and the well-to-do were: tuberculosis, 8.75; orthopedic impairment, 4.2; rheumatism, 3.69; digestive diseases, 3.4; nervous diseases, 2.87; degenerative diseases, 2.68; other diseases, 2.61; accidents, 2.21; respiratory diseases, 1.89; and infectious diseases, 1.24. Public health with its greatest triumphs in the field of infectious diseases has here given the greatest degree of equality of protection to the poor.

No adjustment of these ratios to prevailing distribution of income in the Southeast would be possible without taking into account the differential between urban and rural environment. Indications from comparative mortality suggest that a low given income will account for or accompany a higher degree of health in rural than in urban areas. How far this would go in equalizing morbidity rates no one can presume to say in our present lack of knowledge.

[10] *Disability from Specific Causes in Relation to Economic Status*, National Health Survey Bulletin 9 (Washington D. C.: U. S. Government Printing Office, 1938).

CHAPTER 24

THE TASK OF PUBLIC HEALTH

WHAT ARE the prospects of further improvement in the health and vitality of our people? No one knows, but the opinion is expressed by Louis I. Dublin that we may reasonably look forward to the time when life expectancy will reach 70 years. The attainment of this goal depends not only on continued scientific advance but perhaps even more on a better distribution and utilization of medical and health services, public and private. The low level of death and disease attained by our upper economic classes indicates what can be accomplished by the services already developed. It is safe to assume that most of the class, regional, racial, and occupational lags that we have discussed will have to be overcome for the population to attain a life expectancy beyond seventy years. The Southeast owes its present health advantages, such as they are, to its young population and its rural environment. As the region gradually loses these characteristics, the disadvantages due to the low health status of its Negro population and its low income groups will become more important unless they are offset by an increased use of all health services.

MEDICAL SERVICES AND THE FUTURE OF HEALTH

We have presented differences in death rates as representative of the vitality of the people, but it is equally reasonable to assume that they represent differences in the distribution and quality of all medical and health resources. We come now to ask how the Southeast compares with the Nation in its use of medical services, hospital and public health facilities. Medical service is a purchasable commodity; and the level of medical science no less than the distribution of doctors and hospitals depends to a large extent on the economic level of the community.

In 1940 the Southeast (Figure 209) had the lowest proportion of doctors in the Nation, one physician to every 1,101 persons as compared with one for 751 in the Nation, one for 610 in the Northeast, and one for 626 persons in the Far West. The number of possible patients for every doctor

FIGURE 209. NUMBER OF INHABITANTS PER PHYSICIAN, UNITED STATES, 1940

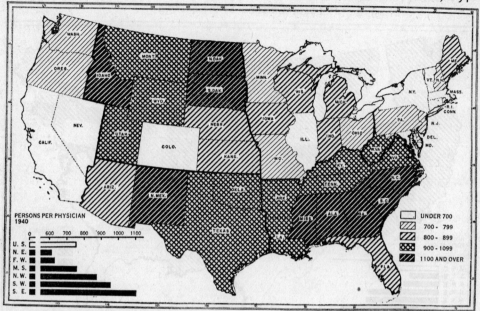

Source: *American Medical Directory, 1940*, p. 8; *Statistical Abstract of the United States, 1941*, Table 6.

ranged from 492 in New York to 1,459 in Mississippi. In 15 States, mainly in the South and West, the people had less than half the numerical chance of getting a doctor if they needed one than in New York. Thirty-two States fell below the national average of a practicing physician for every 751 persons. Southern States belong in the worst group with only Florida having as much as one physician for every 834 potential patients.

The distribution of hospitals reflects the level as well as the amount of medical care available to the population. Adequate diagnosis and treatment is often dependent upon facilities that can be provided only in hospitals. Again the Southeast lags behind the Nation. The United States had in 1939 9.7 medical care beds for every 1,000 population. The States (Figure 210) ranged from 15.3 beds per 1,000 people in Massachusetts to 4.4 in Mississippi. Twenty-five States fall below the national average of 9.7 beds per 1,000 people. Virginia with 8.6 beds per 1,000, Louisiana with 7.8, Florida with 7.1, and Kentucky with 6.6 are the only States in the Region able to climb above the rate of 6.1 common to the Southeast.

We need in this connection a measure of the extent to which people call upon physicians in case of need. While no one figure will serve to measure either the disposition or the economic ability to secure medical services, we have selected the percentage of births attended by physicians. Again the Southeast (Figure 211) secures the least medical care. In 1940 physicians

FIGURE 210. MEDICAL CARE BEDS PER 1,000 ENUMERATED POPULATION, 1940, UNITED STATES, 1939

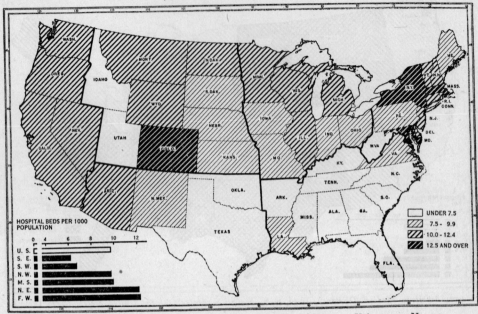

Source: United States Bureau of the Census, *Vital Statistics—Special Reports*, Volume 13, No. 12.

attended 90.8 percent of all live births recorded in the United States. This figure ranged from 99.3 percent in the Far West to only 71.3 percent in the Southeast. The States range from all births attended by physicians in Iowa and Nebraska to half, 50.2 percent, in Mississippi. In the rural areas of the Southeast and the Southwest, white, as well as Negro and Mexican births, are often attended by midwives. So widespread is the practice that the midwives are trained by the States in conferences and short courses and thus recognized as a semi-official part of the medical force.

Attempts have been made to relate delivery by midwives to the higher maternal mortality of certain areas. Local studies of counties in which midwives have large practice often show higher rates of maternal deaths in case of delivery by physicians. A selective factor operates here, however, for midwives tend to call in physicians on cases of prolonged and dangerous labor. In such cases both the birth and the maternal death would be reported as attended by a physician. Less difficult cases are reported by midwives.

In the record of the States a comparison of Figures 211 and 212 shows that the care of physicians is closely associated with low rates of maternal deaths. In 1940 deaths of mothers from all puerperal causes (Figure 212) ranged from 67.8 per 10,000 live births in South Carolina to 17.2 in North

FIGURE 211. THE PERCENTAGE OF LIVE BIRTHS ATTENDED BY
PHYSICIANS, 1940

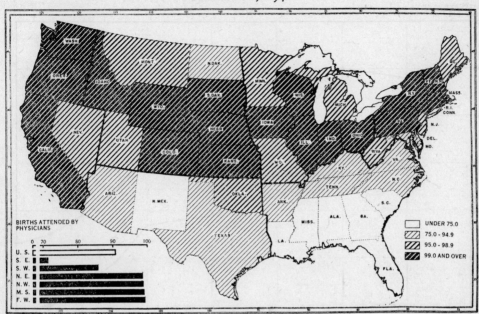

Source: United States Bureau of the Census, *Vital Statistics—Special Reports*, Vol. 14, State Summaries,
1940.

FIGURE 212. NUMBER OF MATERNAL DEATHS FROM ALL PUERPERAL CAUSES
PER 1,000 LIVE BIRTHS, UNITED STATES, 1940

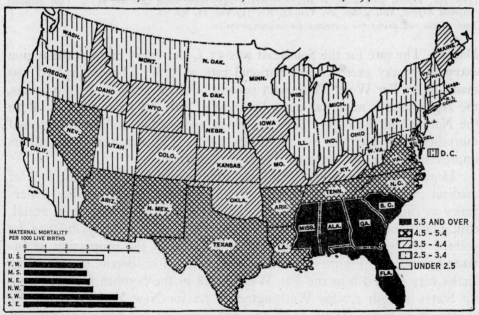

Source: United States Bureau of the Census, *Vital Statistics—Special Reports*, Volume 16, No. 52.

FIGURE 213. MATERNAL MORTALITY RATES PER 10,000 LIVE BIRTHS, UNITED STATES AND SOUTHEAST, 1927-1940

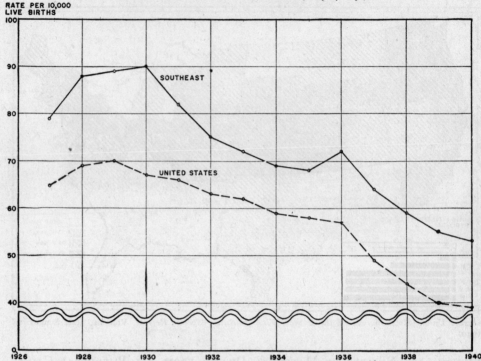

Source: *United States Mortality Statistics,* 1927-1936; *Birth, Stillbirth and Infant Mortality Statistics,* 1927-1936; Reports State Board of Health, Georgia, 1927-1928, South Carolina, 1927. *Vital Statistics —Special Reports,* Vol. 9, No. 26; Vol. 15, No. 33; Vol. 16, No. 52.
Note: Births and deaths not corrected for underregistration.

Dakota. The rate for the Southeast was 53.4, and every State in the region except Kentucky exceeded the national rate of 37.6. The best record was made by the Far West. With 99.3 percent of births attended by physicians, the region had a maternal mortality rate of only 28.3 per 10,000. Both the Nation and the region have shown an appreciable decline in maternal mortality from 1927 to 1940 (Figure 213). The Southeast with all its improvement has not bettered its relative position.

High maternal mortality indicates other conditions besides the lack of medical care. The absence of a physician at such a crucial medical emergency as childbirth may be taken as an index of various economic, racial, educational, and community disabilities. The relation may further be pointed out by referring to regional differences in the proportion of infants born dead. Figure 214 shows that rates of stillbirths per 100 live births vary from 1.9 in the Far West to 3.8 in the Southeast. The range for States is from 1.7 for Washington to 5.2 for New York, with all the Southeastern States except Tennessee and Arkansas exceeding the national rate of 3.1. The rate of stillbirths, it will be observed, is related to the

FIGURE 214. THE NUMBER OF STILLBIRTHS PER 100 LIVE BIRTHS, UNITED STATES, 1940

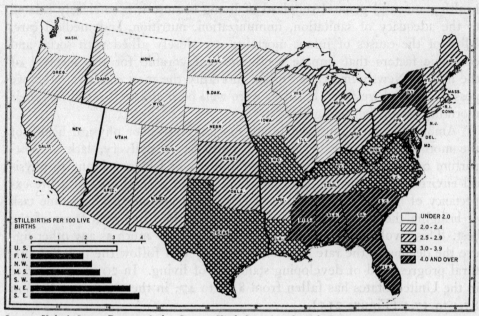

Source: United States Bureau of the Census, *Vital Statistics—Special Reports*, Volume 14, State Summaries, 1940.

rate of maternal mortality. It is safe to assume that absence of a physician's service at childbirth indicates the absence of prenatal care except such as is furnished by public health agencies. The greater occurrence of stillbirths in the Southeast may thus indicate a loss of life due to lack of medical services over and above that expected because of differences in environment. We have another difference that may be attributed to economic conditions.

INFANT MORTALITY—INDEX OF THE SOCIAL CONDITIONS FACING MEDICAL SERVICES IN THE SOUTHEAST

For two reasons infant mortality ranks as especially important in the general health picture of the Nation and the region. In the first place, infant mortality is still the focal point at which the forces of death can be attacked to the greatest advantage. Here death and disease yield more easily to the attack of education and medicine. Here the victory means more for it adds decades rather than years to the span of useful life. Moreover, areas with the highest infant deaths are the ones that have not yet approached the irreducible core of infant mortality. It is in these areas that public health officials find that their well-planned efforts yield greater returns at less cost.

Its second importance is found in the fact that the infant mortality rate serves as an index of the general cultural level. It reflects the community's health status and general standard of living because it is so closely related to the adequacy of sanitation, immunization, nutrition, and medical care. Most of the causes of infant mortality are closely allied with social and economic factors that impose conditions unfavorable for the survival of the infant. Newsholme calls "infant mortality the most sensitive index we possess of social welfare. If babies were well born and well cared for, their mortality would be negligible."[1]

Among the chief causes of infant mortality are poor physical health of the mother, inadequate or unskilled assistance at delivery, lack of post-partum care of the infant, and the multiplicity of factors relating to physical environment, nutrition, and infection. If the general goal of a life expectancy of 70 years is to be reached, we must assume the long-time task of bringing the worst areas of infant mortality into line with those of the best. This involves more than medical progress. As much as any other figure the decline in the rate of infant mortality will follow the trend of cultural progress and of developing standards of living. In 20 years this rate in the United States has fallen from 85.8 to 47; in the region it fell from 87.4 to 57.4 (Figure 215).

FIGURE 215. THE TREND OF INFANT MORTALITY,* EXPANDING REGISTRATION AREA, UNITED STATES AND SOUTHEAST, 1920-1940

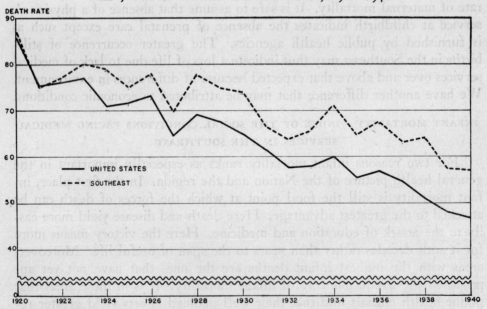

* Births and deaths not corrected for underregistration.
Source: Bureau of the Census, *Vital Statistics—Special Reports*, Volume 15, No. 11 and No. 14.

[1] Newsholme quoted in *Vital Statistics—Special Reports*, 15, No. 38.

Variations in infant mortality among nations sufficiently advanced to
report vital statistics are still very great. The record of infant mortality the
world over ranged in 1936 from 31 deaths under one per 1,000 live births
in New Zealand to 252 in Chile, a figure more than eight times as large.[2]
In the same year the United States had an infant death rate of 57. The
regional variations in infant mortality in this country are greater than
differences in the standardized death rate. By 1940 there were in the
United States 47 deaths under one for every 1,000 live births, and the
rates by states (Figure 216) ranged from 32.9 in Oregon to 99.6 in New
Mexico. The extent of these variations may be indicated by pointing out
that they are greater than those between the Netherlands and Italy in
1936. In our country the best record was shown by the Far West, with a
rate of 38.2, and the Middle States with a rate of 39.2. The worst records
were found in the Southwest with a rate of 67.5 and the Southeast with a
rate of 57.4. No State in the Southeast except Arkansas with an infant
death rate of 45.7 has a record as good as the Nation's. The high rates of
the Southwest are due to the excessive infant mortality among the Mexican
population of the region.

In order to determine whether the bad record of the South is due to its
Negro population we must look at the figures for the white population.

FIGURE 216. INFANT DEATH RATES PER 1,000 LIVE BIRTHS,
UNITED STATES, 1940

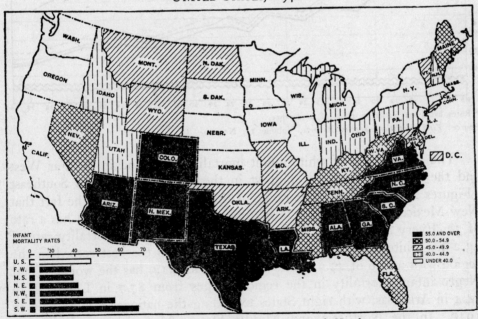

Source: Bureau of the Census, *Vital Statistics—Special Reports*, Vol. 16, No. 6.

[2] *Population Index*, 6 (July, 1940), p. 232.

In addition, infant mortality varies so greatly by rural and urban residence that an adequate racial and regional presentation will have to make use of these breakdowns. In the period from 1915 to 1940 white infant mortality in the registration area fell from 99 to 43; a decline of 57 percent. Negro infant mortality in the same period fell 60 percent from 181 to 73, a figure that is still more than two-thirds in excess of the white infant mortality rate (Figure 217).

FIGURE 217. THE TREND OF INFANT MORTALITY, WHITE AND NEGRO, URBAN AND RURAL,* REGISTRATION AREA, UNITED STATES, 1915-1940

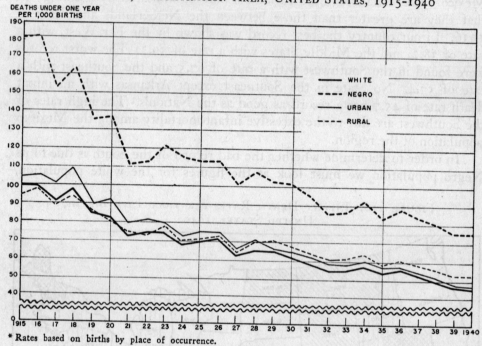

DEATHS UNDER ONE YEAR PER 1,000 BIRTHS

* Rates based on births by place of occurrence.

Source: *Vital Statistics—Special Reports,* Volume 15, No. 30.

The lowest rates of white infant mortality are found in the Far West and the Middle States, the highest in the Southwest and the Southeast (Figures 218 and 219). The range of the States is shown by the fact that New Mexico's rate of 95.9 is three times that of Oregon, which has a rate of 32. Every State in the Southeast exceeds the Nation's mortality rate of 43.2 for white infants, except Arkansas which has the best record in the region with a rate of 42.9, while Alabama with 51.9 has the worst. Total Negro infant mortality in the region ranges from 87.7 in Louisiana to 54.4 in Arkansas, with eight States exceeding the national rate of 72.9 in 1940. In the Northeast and Middle States, Massachusetts, Delaware,

Maryland, West Virginia, and Missouri exceed the national rate. Western States often show higher rates but the number of Negro births is so small as to make the rates inconclusive.

Racial differences evident in infant mortality figures indicate the great importance of social and environmental conditions. The accompanying Table 110 shows the five leading causes of infant deaths by race. These causes accounted for about 72 percent of all infant deaths during 1940. It is evident that about half of our infant mortality can be attributed to conditions related to the birth of the baby while the other half is due to acquired causes and conditions. Premature birth is the most important single cause of infant mortality. Whites, Negroes, and other races show approximately the same infant death rates of around 23 per 1,000 from conditions connected with birth. Death rates from so-called "acquired causes" range from 20.4 for whites and 49.7 for Negroes to 70.5 for other races.

TABLE 110. INFANT MORTALITY RATES FOR FIVE LEADING CAUSES OF DEATH, BY RACE, UNITED STATES, 1940

Causes of death	Mortality rates (Deaths under 1 year per 1,000 live births)			
	Total population	White	Negro	Other races
ALL CAUSES............................	47.0	43.2	72.9	91.0
Premature birth.....................	13.7	13.2	17.4	14.0
Congenital malformation.............	4.7	5.0	2.1	3.2
Injury at birth......................	4.4	4.6	3.7	3.3
Causes connected with birth.............	22.8	22.8	23.2	20.5
Influenza and pneumonia.............	7.4	6.5	13.6	22.5
Diarrhea and enteritis...............	3.5	3.1	5.5	11.7
All other causes....................	13.3	10.8	30.6	36.3
Causes closely connected with environment.	24.2	20.4	49.7	70.5

Note: Number of births and deaths not corrected for underregistration.
Source: Bureau of the Census, *Vital Statistics—Special Reports*, 15, No. 38.

The early infant deaths have been defined as death under one month of age and are reported in the vital statistics as neo-natal mortality. Under present conditions this figure is sometimes accepted as representing the irreducible core of infant mortality. This assumption, however, is not borne out by recent trends. From 1915 to 1935 the rate of neo-natal mortality fell 27 percent in the registration areas, dropping from 44.4 to 32.4. Post neo-natal mortality in the same period fell from 55.6 to 23.6, a decline of 57.6 percent. By 1940, neo-natal mortality was 28.8 and infant mortality for the other eleven months of existence had fallen to 18.3. Evidence from regional and racial variations indicate that both types of infant mortality are subject to further reductions.

As we should expect from our study of the racial figures, regional variations are not so great in the field of neo-natal mortality. The range by

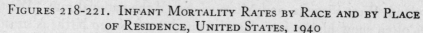

FIGURES 218-221. INFANT MORTALITY RATES BY RACE AND BY PLACE
OF RESIDENCE, UNITED STATES, 1940

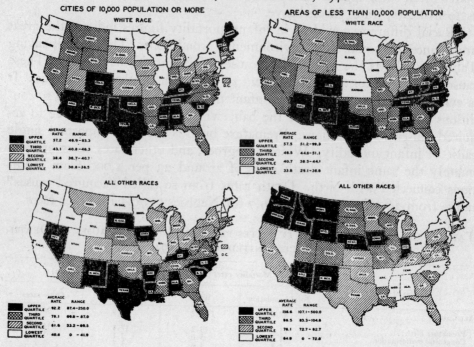

Source: See Figure 217.

States in 1940 ran from Oregon with the lowest rate of 23.1 to New Mexico with a rate of 41.6. Only Arkansas in the Southeast fell below the national rate. The Southwest with its Indian and Mexican populations possessed the highest rate, while Maine, West Virginia, and Vermont in the Northeast exceeded the national rate.

Rural-urban residence also influences the rate of infant mortality. Early conditions were bad in cities, but changes from 1915 to 1940 have reversed the relative positions of infant mortality in urban and rural territory of the registration area. This is explained by the fact that urban infant mortality declined from 103 to 44, a decrease of 57.3 percent, while the rural rate was falling from 94 to 51, a decrease of only 45.7 percent. In line with this trend, infant mortality is now lower in urban than in rural areas for the Nation. Recent development in reporting deaths by place of residence rather than occurrence emphasizes this trend more clearly.

In 1940, 39 white infant deaths per 1,000 live births occurred in the Nation's cities of 10,000 or more as compared with 46.7 deaths in areas of less than 10,000 population. Figures 218 to 221 serve to show the contrast between these two areas by race. By States the white urban rate ranged from 30.8 in Oregon to 83.3 in New Mexico. White rural rates show a higher range, rising from a rate of 31.3 in Connecticut to one of 99.3 in New Mexico. The distinctive characteristic of the Southeast is the high rate of infant mortality in its cities as contrasted with the rate in the cities of the Northeast and Far West. For the colored races in the Southeast rural infant mortality still falls below urban (Figures 220 and 221). For white infants in the region, rural mortality exceeds urban 50.5 to 44.5. In both areas the Nation makes a decidedly better showing than the Southwest.

Among the colored population infant mortality is higher in rural than urban areas by 75 to 71.6 for the Nation. Infant death rates for colored in the urban Southeast are very high, ranging from 73.8 in Tennessee to 100.9 in Kentucky. Northern cities show much better records for the Negro, few States having rates higher than 65. In their rural areas, practically all southern States show lower infant death rates. This contrast with white infant mortality shows the lag in health service for the Negro. For the Nation as a whole, figures indicate that the larger the city, the lower the rate of infant deaths.

PUBLIC HEALTH EXPENDITURES

Public health within certain limits has long been regarded as a purchasable commodity. Infant mortality rates have proved especially susceptible to reduction by well planned public health programs. Expenditures for health purposes have greatly increased in recent years reaching $1.90 per capita in 1940 for the country as a whole.[3] Public health expenditures ranged from $0.76 per person in Tennessee to $4.26 in Nevada (Figure 222). The highest expenditures were found in the Far West and in the Northeast where only West Virginia fell as low as $1.99. States of the Southeast spent least on public health. Six of these spent less than $1.00 per capita. Louisiana with $2.43 per capita was the only State in the region to exceed the national average.

It is obvious that the public health achievements of many of our areas are to be explained by the work done in municipal and county units. Figure 223 shows the distribution of county health units throughout the Nation in 1941. The map shows that the South is undertaking the task of dealing with its health problem on a county-wide basis—the plan best suited to rural areas. The extent of the health budgets and services offered

[3] Only recently have we been able to estimate the amount of money spent on public health activities by all the official agencies of the States. The 1940 study showed that some 35 separate categories of activities in State governments had public health significance. Of the amount spent, over 81 percent came from State revenues, almost 4 percent from local sources, 6.7 percent from Federal sources and 8 percent from other sources. See Joseph W. Mountin and Evelyn Flook "Distribution of Health Service in the Structure of State Government." *Public Health Reports*, Reprint 2306 (Washington, D. C.: U. S. Government Printing Office, 1943), p. 4; Table I, pp. 9-13; Table 3, p. 21.

FIGURE 222. ANNUAL PER CAPITA EXPENDITURES BY ALL OFFICIAL STATE AGENCIES FOR HEALTH ACTIVITIES, UNITED STATES, APPROXIMATE 1940 DATA

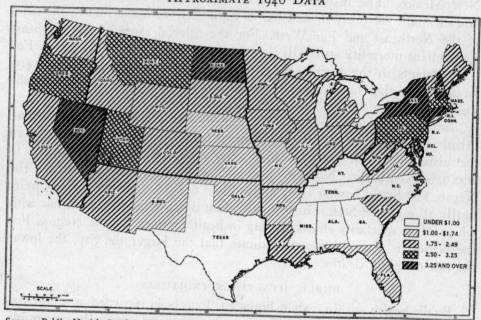

Source: Public Health Service: Joseph W. Mountin and Evelyn Flook, "Distribution of Health Services in the Structure of State Governments," *United States Public Health Bulletin*, No. 184 (1941), Table 3, p. 21.

in our great metropolitan centers like Chicago and New York would also help explain how they hold infant mortality below the figures of the Southeast.

HEALTH AND MANPOWER

The extremes of the life span, infancy and old age, are its vulnerable periods. For life's closing phases, however, there is no surcease from death —only postponement. It is to the vigorous ages then that we must look for the test of our health services. The relation of our health programs to industrial manpower and military manpower is made clearer by reports of the medical examinations of young men of draft age, 20-34. Since World War I, death rates among this group have declined nearly 30 percent. An analysis of Selective Service examinations up to March 1941 did not indicate a similar improvement in the physical condition of young men. About 43 percent had been declared unfit for general military service as compared with about 30 percent rejections in 1917-1918.[4] While draft boards and army physicians rejected 43 percent for full military duty, only 28 per-

[4] George St. Perrott, "Physical Status of Young Men, 1918-1941," *Milbank Memorial Fund Quarterly*, XIX (October, 1941), 337-344.

FIGURE 223. COUNTIES WITH THE SERVICE OF A FULL-TIME PUBLIC HEALTH
OFFICE, UNITED STATES, JUNE 30, 1941

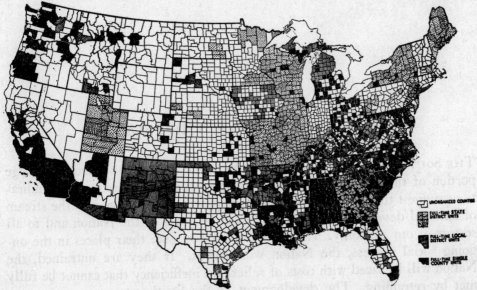

Source: United States Public Health Service: F. W. Kratz, "The Present Status of Full-Time Local
Health Organization," *Public Health Reports,* Vol. 57, No. 6 (Feb. 6, 1942), pp. 195-96.

cent were considered unfit for any service. The remaining 15 percent were
classed as fit for limited service, indicating that many had defects which
could be remedied.

One striking difference in the type of defects sufficient to cause rejection was found. Rejections because of defective teeth were four times as
high in 1940-1941 as in 1917-1918. Since army standards have not
changed since World War I, these findings suggest lack of dental care
for children and adolescents throughout the depression. Rejections for
respiratory diseases (largely tuberculosis) were only a little lower. Since
deaths from tuberculosis have been cut in half during that period, we conclude that better diagnosis prevails in present examinations.

In the main, however, important causes of rejection today are the same
as those in the draft of World War I. It is thus too early to say that the
health of young men has improved or deteriorated since 1918.[5] The examinations of 1917-1918 provided materials for medical research for
twenty years. When our own period comes to be studied in detail, we will
be able to determine whether the southern population had experienced
differentials in health beyond those discussed in the preceding chapters.

[5] *Ibid.* p. 343.

CHAPTER 25

THE EDUCATION OF THE PEOPLE

THE SOUTHEAST is likely to continue for some time as the source of a large portion of the population renewals of this country. Moreover, all indications suggest that more of the South's population will move into the stream of national development by migration to all parts of the Nation and to all sectors of our economy. If they are trained to take their places in the ongoing social process, the Nation will benefit. If they are untrained, the Nation will be faced with costs of relief and inefficiency that cannot be fully met by retraining. The development of the Southeast, so necessary to a balanced economy for our Nation, can best be furthered by an increase in the skills and aptitudes of the region's population. What are the prospects that the Southeast can perform the needed task of training its oncoming population for the demands of the future? The region's educational status and its capacity for educational and cultural development comprise an important part of the Nation's population problem both now and for the future.

In presenting this analysis we have to depend largely on measures of formal education in terms of the standards offered by the schools. Our use of these statistics does not mean that we are committed to the type of education now provided, nor does our use of figures on grades attained commit us to the approval of the classifications now used by educational authorities. It will be understood that this treatment omits detailed consideration (1) of the curriculum, (2) of teaching methods, and (3) of school administration. We make use of the statistics of formal education simply as the best available measures by which we can approximate the cultural and educational status of the people.

EDUCATIONAL STATUS OF THE PEOPLE

As our culture has grown more complex the type of education has changed, and an evergrowing portion of the population has been subjected

[380]

to longer periods of formal training. The transition from a frontier and agrarian society to a highly technical civilization has not only made this transition inevitable but has given the Nation the surplus wealth, public and private, with which to implement the change. Furthermore, increased urbanization has tended to make mass education possible by providing sufficient density of population to insure local tax support and to allow for the assembly of children in optimum numbers for instruction. For these reasons, if for no others, our city schools have long been able to offer a more adequate program than any but the most advanced rural schools.

Regional variations in educational attainments are still very great within the United States. With the completion of the 1940 Census we are able for the first time to determine the number of school years completed by the adult population by State and regional areas. Table 111 indicates that exactly half of our population aged 25 and over have had no more than 8.4 years of school and half have had more. Women have done better than men, city dwellers than farm people, and whites than Negroes. White men in cities attained the highest median years in school, 9.9; Negro men on farms the lowest, 3.7 years. Women have gone farthest on farms and in cities where white women have attained a median of 9.9 years as compared with 9.4 for white males. In the country farm boys drop out of school before girls, but in the cities a greater number of men go on to university and professional training. Rural nonfarm people stand between urban dwellers and farm people in this respect.

TABLE 111. MEDIAN NUMBER OF SCHOOL YEARS COMPLETED BY PERSONS 25 YEARS OLD AND OVER CLASSIFIED ACCORDING TO SEX, RACE, AND RESIDENCE, UNITED STATES, 1940

Class by residence	All races			Native white			Negro		
	All	Male	Female	All	Male	Female	All	Male	Female
ALL CLASSES.............	8.4	8.3	8.5	8.8	8.6	9.0	5.7	5.3	6.1
Urban...................	8.7	8.6	8.8	9.6	9.4	9.9	6.8	6.5	7.0
Rural-nonfarm..........	8.4	8.2	8.5	8.6	8.5	8.8	5.0	4.6	5.5
Rural—farm.............	7.7	7.6	7.9	8.0	7.8	8.2	4.1	3.7	4.7

Source: *Sixteenth Census of the United States, 1940*, Population, preliminary release Series P-10, No. 8.

Figure 224 indicates that the people of the Southeast are the poorest educated in the country, having attained a median of 7.4 school years completed. The best educated people live in the Far West where exactly half the adults have spent over 9.7 years in school. The States range from Louisiana with a median of 6.6 years of schooling to Utah with 10.2 years.

Table 112 is designed to show the educational ranking of the States in terms of race, nativity, and urban, rural nonfarm and rural farm residence. Best educated were urban native whites of the western States; least educated were the farm Negroes of the Southeast. Here the range was from 11.5 median years of schooling in Utah to 2.8 in Louisiana. Among native whites in practically every State the urban population had received more schooling than the rural nonfarm, and the rural nonfarm population in turn more than the rural farm. The spread between urban and rural nonfarm was usually greater than the spread between the rural nonfarm and the rural farm population. In the Northeast differences between native whites in cities and on farms rarely exceeded one year of school; in the Southeast it usually amounted to three. These differences may depend to some extent on the migration of better educated youth to the cities. While the foreign-born were less well educated than the native whites, they showed less differences because of rural-urban residence.

In the Southeast the figures showed that Floridians had the highest educational attainment, 8.3 median years of schooling. Mississippi has carried furthest the education of her native whites whether living in city, rural farm, or rural nonfarm areas, while Kentucky has done the most to educate the Negroes in all three areas. The poorest showing in the Nation was made by Louisiana in all classifications, ranging from 4.5 years for all rural farm to 7.9 years of school for urban population.

FIGURE 224. THE MEDIAN NUMBER OF SCHOOL YEARS COMPLETED BY PERSONS 25 YEARS OF AGE AND OVER, UNITED STATES, 1940

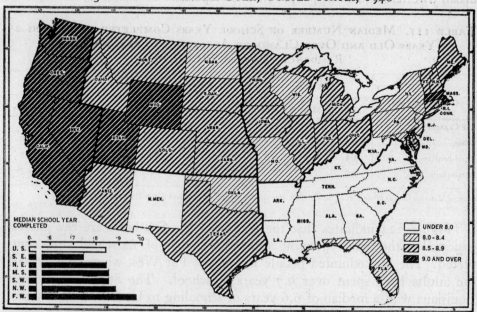

Source: *Sixteenth Census of the United States, 1940*, Series P-10, No. 8.

TABLE 112. MEDIAN YEARS OF SCHOOL COMPLETED FOR PERSONS 25 YEARS OLD AND OVER, BY RACE-NATIVITY, URBAN AND RURAL, UNITED STATES, 1940

(Median not shown where base is less than 100)

Division and State	URBAN				RURAL—NONFARM				RURAL—FARM			
	All classes	Native White	Foreign-born White	Negro	All classes	Native White	Foreign-born White	Negro	All classes	Native White	Foreign-born White	Negro
UNITED STATES......	8.7	9.6	7.4	6.8	8.4	8.6	7.3	5.0	7.7	8.0	7.2	4.1
Northeast:												
Maine............	9.1	10.2	7.4	8.2	9.0	9.5	7.8	7.6	8.7	8.8	7.7	...
New Hampshire...	8.6	9.3	7.3	8.1	8.9	9.2	7.7	...	8.7	8.9	7.6	...
Vermont..........	9.5	10.3	7.8	8.1	8.8	9.0	7.9	...	8.5	8.6	7.7	...
Massachusetts.....	9.0	10.7	7.4	8.2	9.3	10.4	7.5	6.9	8.6	9.8	6.5	2.2
Rhode Island......	8.3	8.8	6.8	7.6	8.3	8.6	7.0	7.4	8.2	8.6	6.3	...
Connecticut......	8.4	9.0	7.0	7.5	8.7	9.6	7.4	7.9	8.3	8.8	7.0	7.7
New York........	8.4	9.1	7.4	7.8	8.7	8.9	7.7	7.2	8.3	8.4	7.3	7.0
New Jersey.......	8.4	8.9	7.1	7.2	8.4	8.7	7.5	6.7	7.9	8.3	7.1	5.9
Pennsylvania......	8.4	8.8	6.1	7.1	8.1	8.3	5.2	6.6	8.0	8.1	5.7	6.5
Delaware.........	8.7	9.6	6.5	6.6	8.6	8.9	7.9	5.6	7.7	8.0	7.3	5.1
Maryland.........	8.0	8.5	6.4	6.1	8.2	8.5	8.0	5.6	7.4	7.7	7.6	4.7
Dist. of Columbia .	10.3	12.1	8.3	7.6	...	...	...	...	...	...	...	...
West Virginia.....	8.7	8.9	6.9	7.4	7.6	7.7	5.1	6.1	7.3	7.3	5.2	5.7
Southeast:												
Virginia..........	8.7	10.0	8.3	5.9	7.6	8.3	8.7	4.8	6.6	7.3	7.7	4.1
North Carolina....	8.6	10.3	10.5	5.8	7.6	8.2	11.7	5.0	6.6	7.2	8.8	4.4
South Carolina....	8.7	11.3	8.9	4.8	6.9	8.2	10.3	3.8	5.5	7.7	9.7	3.5
Georgia..........	8.1	10.0	8.8	5.1	7.5	8.6	10.1	4.0	6.0	7.2	9.2	3.5
Florida..........	8.9	11.0	8.2	5.8	7.9	8.7	8.6	4.3	7.1	7.8	8.1	3.8
Kentucky.........	8.4	8.6	7.8	6.7	7.7	7.8	7.8	5.9	7.2	7.2	7.7	5.2
Tennessee........	8.4	9.4	8.4	6.2	7.8	8.0	8.9	5.4	7.0	7.3	7.2	4.9
Alabama.........	8.3	10.3	8.3	5.6	7.3	8.2	8.0	4.5	6.1	7.1	7.6	3.7
Mississippi.......	8.7	11.7	8.4	5.8	8.0	9.9	8.5	5.0	6.2	8.1	5.4	4.3
Arkansas.........	8.9	10.4	8.4	6.3	7.8	8.3	7.8	5.3	6.9	7.4	6.8	4.6
Louisiana.........	7.9	9.1	7.3	5.2	6.5	8.1	6.1	3.5	4.5	6.3	2.7	2.8
Southwest:												
Oklahoma........	9.9	10.4	8.3	7.6	8.2	8.3	7.2	6.3	7.7	7.7	7.1	6.0
Texas............	9.5	10.6	4.8	6.8	8.7	9.3	2.9	5.7	7.5	8.0	2.4	5.3
New Mexico......	9.3	9.9	6.4	7.4	7.5	7.8	3.8	7.1	6.7	7.2	3.2	6.2
Arizona..........	9.6	10.9	6.5	7.6	8.6	9.2	4.8	7.3	7.2	8.5	3.9	6.6
Middle States:												
Ohio.............	8.7	9.4	6.9	7.4	8.5	8.6	6.9	6.9	8.2	8.3	6.8	7.2
Indiana..........	8.7	8.9	7.1	7.6	8.5	8.5	7.6	7.3	8.2	8.2	7.2	7.5
Illinois..........	8.6	9.2	7.5	7.7	8.3	8.4	7.2	6.6	8.1	8.2	7.6	6.5
Michigan.........	8.8	9.8	7.6	7.6	8.6	8.8	7.5	7.0	8.1	8.3	6.5	7.4
Wisconsin........	8.6	8.9	7.3	7.6	8.4	8.5	7.4	7.5	7.9	8.0	7.1	7.1
Minnesota........	8.9	10.0	7.7	8.4	8.4	8.7	7.4	7.8	8.0	8.1	7.3	...
Iowa.............	9.6	10.0	7.8	8.0	8.7	8.8	7.7	7.1	8.4	8.4	7.8	7.7
Missouri..........	8.6	8.8	7.5	7.4	8.3	8.3	7.7	6.5	7.9	7.9	7.4	4.9
Northwest:												
North Dakota.....	9.8	11.0	7.8	...	8.4	8.8	7.5	...	7.9	8.1	7.3	...
South Dakota.....	10.0	10.6	7.9	8.6	8.6	8.8	7.6	...	8.1	8.2	7.6	...
Nebraska.........	9.9	10.8	7.7	8.0	8.8	8.9	7.6	7.5	8.3	8.4	7.5	7.7
Kansas...........	9.3	9.8	7.3	8.0	8.7	8.8	7.2	7.5	8.4	8.4	7.5	7.7
Montana.........	9.6	10.7	7.8	8.0	8.7	9.1	7.7	...	8.3	8.5	7.7	...
Idaho............	10.5	10.8	8.2	7.5	8.9	9.0	7.9	7.0	8.6	8.7	7.8	7.4
Wyoming.........	10.3	10.9	7.6	7.9	9.3	10.0	7.4	7.5	8.6	8.7	7.5	...
Colorado.........	9.9	10.5	7.6	8.5	8.7	8.9	7.0	7.5	8.3	8.5	7.2	7.7
Utah.............	10.8	11.5	8.0	8.4	9.7	10.1	7.6	...	9.0	9.4	7.5	...
Far West:												
Nevada...........	10.5	11.3	7.9	7.6	9.5	10.5	7.5	8.2	8.4	9.0	7.4	...
Washington.......	10.1	11.0	8.2	8.2	8.9	9.4	8.0	7.9	8.4	8.6	7.8	7.6
Oregon..........	10.2	10.8	8.2	8.4	8.9	9.1	8.1	8.0	8.5	8.6	7.9	...
California.........	10.5	11.4	8.0	8.5	8.9	9.6	7.5	7.3	8.3	8.8	6.9	6.8

Source: Adapted from Henry J. Shryock, Jr., "1940 Census Data on Number of Years of School Completed," *The Milbank Memorial Fund Quarterly*, XX (October, 1942), 378-379.

The 1940 Census asked no questions about illiteracy but reported approximately 2,800,000 people 25 years old and over who had not completed a single year in school. Almost 851,000 of these were in the Southeast, giving the region an equivalent illiteracy rate of 6.2 percent as compared with 3.7 percent for the Nation. Functional illiteracy is defined in terms of inability to read and understand directions. On this basis both industry and the armed services in World War II discriminated against those with less than five years of schooling. In the Southeast 26.7 percent of those aged 25 and over had completed less than five years of school. In the Northwest only 7.1 percent. The Nation had 13.5 percent in this category (Figure 225). The States ranged from Iowa with only 4.1 percent "functional illiterates," according to this definition, to Louisiana with 35.7 percent. Figure 226 compares the region and the Nation for the whole educational range. At the other end of the scale the Nation had almost three and a half million college graduates, 4.7 percent of its adults over 25 as compared with 3.5 percent in the Southeast. Figure 227, which presents in cumulative percentage the data of Figure 226, contrasts the trends of educational progress. In the Nation three-fourths (74.8 percent) had completed 7 to 8 years of school; in the Southeast hardly more than one-half (55.4 percent). Almost one-fourth, 24.5 percent, of the Nation's adults, but only 18.2 percent of the region's adult population, had completed four years of high school.

It is not difficult to show that the educational status of the American

FIGURE 225. PERCENTAGE OF PERSONS 25 YEARS OLD AND OVER COMPLETING LESS THAN FIVE YEARS OF SCHOOL, UNITED STATES, 1940

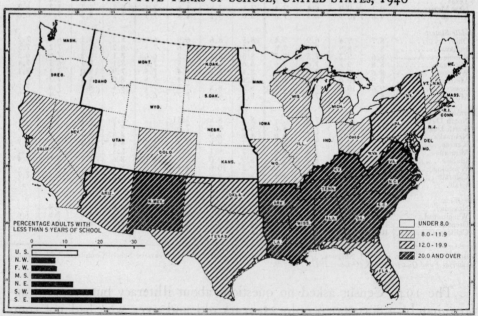

Source: *Sixteenth Census of the United States, 1940,* Preliminary Release, Series P-10, No. 8.

FIGURE 226. PERCENTAGE DISTRIBUTION OF POPULATION TWENTY-FIVE YEARS
OLD AND OVER BY GRADE OF SCHOOL COMPLETED,
UNITED STATES AND SOUTHEAST, 1940

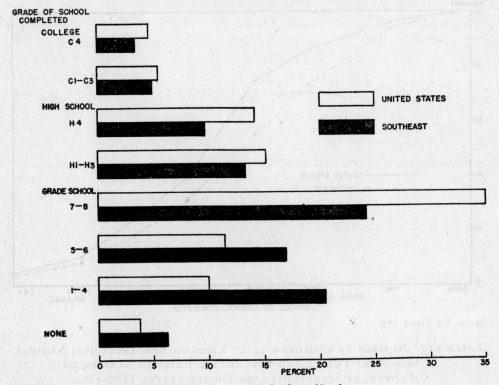

Source: *Sixteenth Census of the United States, 1940, Series P-10, No. 6.*

people has improved with each generation. To estimate the educational
status of the current school generation we can make use of enrollment figures. Census figures (Figure 227) indicated that only 39.7 percent of our
adult population have had any high school training—a figure that should
be compared with 62.5 percent of those aged 14-17 enrolled in high schools
in 1935-36 (Table 113). According to the census enumeration only 10.2
of our adults 25 and over have had any college training. In 1937-38, 14.4
percent of the population aged 19-22 years of age were enrolled in higher
institutions of learning. Figure 227 showed that 96.3 percent of the 1940
adult population had had some degree of elementary school up to the fifth
grade. If this figure is compared with the estimate that only 91.7 percent
of the children aged 5-17 were enrolled in public and private schools in
1935-36 (Table 114), it should be pointed out that many five year olds
do not attend kindergarten and that many pupils drop out of school before 17.

FIGURE 227. PERCENTAGE OF PERSONS TWENTY-FIVE YEARS OLD AND OVER
WHO HAD AT LEAST COMPLETED INDICATED GRADES,
UNITED STATES AND SOUTHEAST, 1940

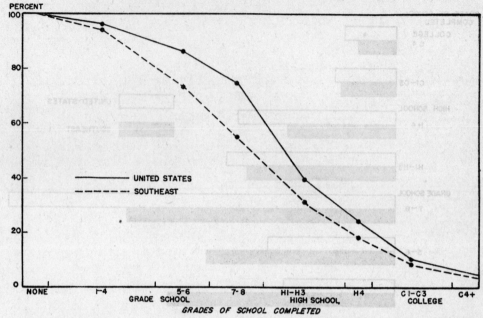

Source: See Figure 226.

TABLE 113. NUMBER OF CHILDREN 14-17 YEARS OF AGE, INCLUSIVE, NUMBER
OF SECONDARY PUPILS, AND PERCENTAGE RATIO TO NUMBER OF
CHILDREN, BY SELECTED YEARS, UNITED STATES, 1889-1890
TO 1935-1936 (ALL FIGURES IN THOUSANDS)

Year	Number of children 14-17 years of age*	Secondary grade enrollments**	Percentage ratio to number of children	Year	Number of children 14-17 years of age*	Secondary grade enrollments**	Percentage ratio to number of children
1890	5,355	203	3.7	1926	8,533	3,757	44.0
1900	6,134	519	8.5	1928	8,894	3,911	44.0
1910	7,215	915	12.7				
1920	7,773	2,200	28.3	1930	9,341	4,399	47.1
				1932	9,547	5,140	53.8
1922	7,988	2,873	36.0	1934	9,442	5,669	60.0
1924	8,238	3,390	41.2	1936	9,565	5,975	62.5

*Data for 1890 obtained from *Fifteenth Census of the United States, 1930*, Population, II, 593. Data for other years obtained from "Population Trends and Their Educational Implications," Research Bulletin of the National Education Association, XVI, No. 1 (January 1938), pp. 51-52. See also footnotes given on p. 50. Note especially that estimates for the years 1930 to 1935 are based on estimated births and for 1936 are based on the assumption of medium fertility and mortality and no immigration.
**Biennial Survey of Education, 1934-1936, II, Chap. II, pp. 55-57, Tables 1 and 2.
Source: Advisory Committee on Education, *Education in the Forty-Eight States* (Washington, D. C., 1939), p. 28.

It is evident that several factors enter into the composition of any index
of elementary education. States lacking kindergarten systems rank low
while States with a large proportion of retarded 17-year olds in schools
may rank the higher because of that negative condition. The Nation in
1935-36, it is estimated, had 91.7 percent of its children aged 5-17 enrolled

TABLE 114. ENROLLMENTS IN PUBLIC, PRIVATE, AND PAROCHIAL ELEMENTARY
AND SECONDARY SCHOOLS AS PERCENTAGE OF ESTIMATED NUMBER OF
CHILDREN 5-17 YEARS OF AGE, INCLUSIVE, UNITED STATES,
1935-1936*

State	Total enrollments	Number of children	Ratio of enrollments to number of children (percent)	Public schools		Private and parochial schools	
				Enrollments	Ratio to number of children (percent)	Enrollments	Ratio to number of children (percent)
UNITED STATES**	29,005,873	31,618,000	91.7	26,367,098	83.4	2,638,775	8.3
Massachusetts	946,060	900,000	105.1	773,239	85.9	172,821	19.2
Nevada	19,978	19,000	105.1	19,720	103.8	258	1.4
California	1,209,559	1,152,000	105.0	1,140,427	99.0	69,132	6.0
Washington	354,249	352,000	100.6	335,750	95.4	18,499	5.3
New Hampshire	109,914	110,000	99.9	78,441	71.3	31,473	28.6
Florida	302,700	393,500	99.8	385,763	98.0	6,937	1.8
Connecticut	384,318	390,000	98.5	320,888	82.3	63,430	16.3
Maine	196,233	199,800	98.2	166,507	83.3	29,726	14.9
Mississippi	615,710	628,000	98.0	608,036	96.8	7,674	1.2
New York	2,681,301	2,750,000	97.5	2,288,042	83.2	393,259	14.3
Oregon	201,152	207,000	97.2	188,361	91.0	12,791	16.0
Wyoming	58,321	60,000	97.2	56,384	94.0	1,937	3.2
Idaho	124,286	128,000	97.1	121,045	94.6	3,241	2.5
New Jersey	934,245	965,000	96.8	809,078	83.8	125,167	13.0
Colorado	252,813	265,000	95.4	239,747	90.5	13,066	4.9
Iowa	588,118	618,000	95.2	538,003	87.1	50,115	8.1
Nebraska	334,205	354,000	94.4	307,975	87.0	26,230	7.4
Indiana	752,417	798,000	94.3	691,444	86.0	60,973	7.6
Minnesota	612,559	650,000	94.2	549,129	84.5	63,430	9.8
Delaware	53,827	57,300	93.9	46,100	80.5	7,727	13.5
Oklahoma	666,614	710,000	93.9	658,049	92.7	8,565	1.2
Rhode Island	153,948	164,000	93.9	121,555	74.1	32,393	19.8
Kansas	443,145	473,000	93.7	414,275	87.6	28,870	6.1
Wisconsin	692,398	740,000	93.6	577,343	78.0	115,055	15.5
Pennsylvania	2,306,871	2,500,000	92.3	2,006,097	80.2	300,774	12.0
Missouri	787,901	860,300	91.6	711,256	82.7	76,645	8.9
Ohio	1,467,469	1,619,000	90.6	1,289,337	79.6	178,132	11.0
Vermont	79,562	88,000	90.4	68,060	77.3	11,502	13.1
Michigan	1,103,387	1,225,000	90.1	963,527	78.7	139,860	11.4
Illinois	1,580,864	1,756,000	90.0	1,327,269	75.6	253,595	14.4
Utah	142,229	160,000	88.9	140,863	88.0	1,366	0.9
Kentucky	669,807	764,100	87.7	628,101	82.2	41,706	5.5
Montana	121,835	139,000	87.7	113,762	81.8	8,073	5.8
Tennessee	664,646	764,000	87.0	653,211	85.5	11,435	1.5
Georgia	757,637	875,000	86.6	748,537	85.5	9,100	1.0
Maryland	352,260	412,000	85.5	298,157	72.4	54,103	13.1
South Dakota	163,695	193,000	84.8	153,163	79.4	10,532	5.4
Texas	1,412,963	1,672,000	84.5	1,364,627	81.6	48,336	2.9
Louisiana	526,254	625,000	84.2	465,594	74.5	60,660	9.7
West Virginia	458,305	546,000	83.9	449,732	82.4	8,573	1.6
North Carolina	895,727	1,069,000	83.8	888,775	83.1	6,952	0.7
Arkansas	467,601	560,000	83.5	460,869	82.3	6,732	1.2
Arizona	104,271	125,000	83.4	99,796	79.8	4,475	3.6
Virginia	604,168	724,000	83.4	592,038	81.8	12,130	1.7
Alabama	690,728	835,000	82.7	677,062	81.1	13,666	1.6
North Dakota	165,119	202,000	81.7	155,035	76.8	10,084	5.0
South Carolina	483,227	594,000	81.4	477,915	80.5	5,312	0.9
New Mexico	106,531	131,000	81.3	99,207	75.8	7,324	5.6

*U. S. Office of Education Bulletin, 1937, No. 2 (Advance Pages) Biennial Survey of Education in the United States, 1934-1936
(Washington: U. S. Government Printing Office, 1938), II, Chap. II, pp. 59, 61-62, 123-124. Population data as of July 1, 1936.
**The United States figure includes data for the District of Columbia.
Source: Advisory Committee on Education, *Education in the Forty-Eight States* (Washington, D. C., 1939), p. 15.

in all schools. The figures ranged from practically complete enrollment in
Massachusetts to 81.3 percent enrollment in New Mexico (Table 114).
The Southeast and the Southwest lagged in proportions enrolled. Figure
228 thus gives a fair indication of the prospective educational status of the
population.

FIGURE 228. PERCENTAGE OF ESTIMATED POPULATION 5-17 YEARS OF AGE
ENROLLED IN ALL PUBLIC, PRIVATE, AND PAROCHIAL SCHOOLS,
UNITED STATES, 1935-1936

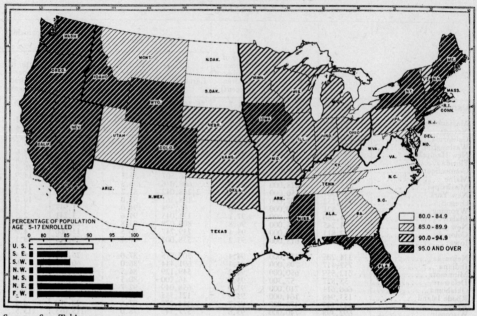

Source: See Table 114.

The increased importance of advanced training makes the proportion
enrolled in high school a valuable index of educational status. Beginning
at 3.7 percent enrolled in 1890, the curve of high school enrollment has
shown tremendous increase, the greatest coming in the decade 1910-1920,
when it rose from 12.7 to 28.3 percent, more than doubling. Because of the
difficulty involved in estimating age groups by States during mid-census
years, figures are secured giving the proportion of total public school enrollment that are found in the secondary grades. Depending on age composition and the public attitude toward extended training, it is reasonable
to assume that, where high school opportunities are readily accessible, approximately 30 percent of total public school enrollment may be found in
secondary schools. In 1938 this condition was attained in six States—Oregon, Washington, New York, Wisconsin, Massachusetts, and Utah. The
average for all pupils was 24 percent (Figure 229) and in 23 States more
than 25 percent of the pupils were found in the four highest grades. States
with large rural and Negro populations had the lowest high school enrollments. States of the Southeast were among the lowest, only North Carolina reaching as high as 20.5 percent. The Far West led with 29.4 percent of all public school pupils enrolled in high school; the Southeast
lagged with 16.2 percent.

FIGURE 229. ENROLLMENT IN HIGH SCHOOLS AS PERCENTAGE OF TOTAL EN-
ROLLMENT IN PUBLIC ELEMENTARY AND SECONDARY SCHOOLS,
UNITED STATES, 1938

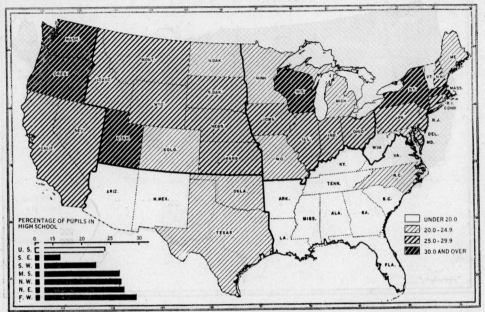

Source: U. S. Office of Education, *Statistics of State School Systems, 1937-1938*, Bulletin No. 2, 1940,
Chapter II, Figure 2, p. 16.

Out of every 1,000 pupils who entered the first year of high school in
1930-31 only 491 were graduated four years later. While to some this
trend may denote the high standards of the secondary schools, to others it
indicates low standard of communities which lack adequate schools and
fail either to motivate or to enable their young people to continue in high
school. In 1935-36 the enrollment in the last year of the Nation's high
schools was 54 percent of that in the first year. The figure ranged from
74.5 percent in Utah to 41.6 percent in Alabama (Figure 230). Again the
States of the West showed the best record and those of the Southeast the
poorest.

There are two bases it would seem to the community's ability to hold
its young in high school: one is to be found in the economic status of the
community, the other in the curriculum offered and the teaching methods
employed. Low economic status means both the inability of the community to provide good schools and the inability of the individual pupils to
attend beyond minimum requirements. Communities of low economic
status thus tend to perpetuate themselves—a fact that will be shown later
in the analysis of rural areas in the Southeast. The other basis rests on
educational policy and results from the failure to adjust the high school

FIGURE 230. PERCENTAGE RATIO OF FOURTH YEAR TO FIRST YEAR HIGH SCHOOL
ENROLLMENT, UNITED STATES, 1935-1936

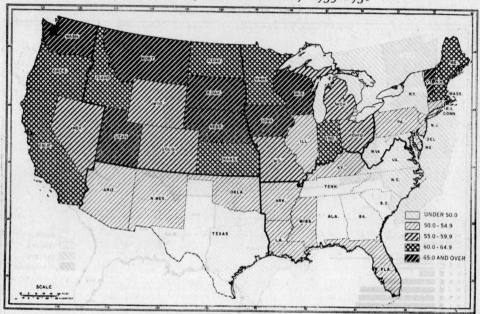

Source: *Education in the Forty-Eight States*, Advisory Committee on Education (Washington, D. C.,
1939), p. 30.

curriculum to the needs, interests, and capacities of the youthful population it is to serve, as well as the failure to adopt newer practices based upon
scientific findings as to how people learn.

The task of education obviously is only begun with the enrollment of
the population of school age. Certain questions may serve to indicate how
well the school performs its task. Do pupils attend school regularly? For
how long a term does the school function? How well are teachers trained?
How well are the schools supported? The answers to these and related
questions will serve to make clear the relative position of the Southeast.

For the Nation in 1938 the average daily attendance was 85.8 percent
of the total enrollment in public schools. In this respect the States ranged
from 92.6 percent in Michigan to 76.9 percent in Arkansas (Figure 231).
The Southwest had the worst record with 79.6 percent, the Middle States
the best with 89.5 percent. Attendance in the Southeast was only 81.2 percent of enrollment, and only in Kentucky and North Carolina did it exceed
the national average.

The average number of days attended by each pupil enrolled reflects
the length of school terms and is affected by weather, health, and transportation conditions. In 1938 the average number of days attended by pupils
enrolled in the Nation's public schools was 149.3, approximately 7.46

FIGURE 231. AVERAGE DAILY ATTENDANCE AS PERCENTAGE OF TOTAL PUBLIC
SCHOOL ENROLLMENT, UNITED STATES, 1938

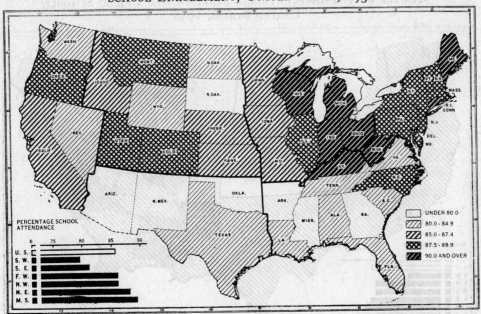

Source: *Statistics of State School Systems, 1937-1938*, Bulletin, 1940, No. 2, Figure 2, p. 18.

FIGURE 232. AVERAGE NUMBER OF DAYS ATTENDED BY PUPILS ENROLLED
IN PUBLIC SCHOOLS, UNITED STATES, 1938

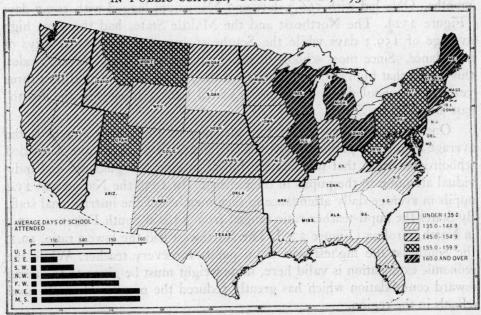

Source: *Statistics of State School Systems, 1937-1938*, Bulletin, 1940, No. 2, Table 8, p. 84; Table 11,
p. 84; and Table 13, p. 90.

FIGURE 233. AVERAGE NUMBER OF PUPILS IN DAILY ATTENDANCE FOR EACH
MEMBER OF THE INSTRUCTIONAL STAFF IN ALL PUBLIC SCHOOLS,
UNITED STATES, 1938

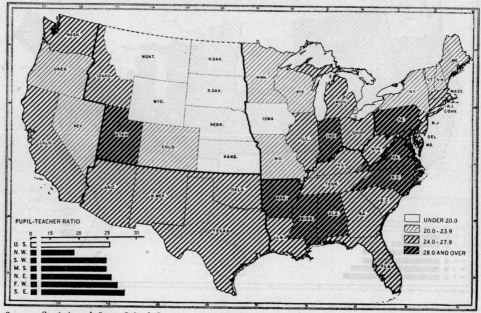

Source: *Statistics of State School Systems, 1937-1938,* Bulletin No. 2, 1940, Table 8, p. 26; Table 12,
p. 88; Table 17, p. 98.

months. Ohio led with 166.3 days and Mississippi lagged with 109.7 days
(Figure 232). The Northeast and the Middle States had the same high
average of 159.3 days while the Southeast averaged only 131.2 days of
attendance. Since most schools in the Southeast have only eleven grades,
this means that high school graduates of the region have spent almost three
years (468 school days) less time in school than graduates in the Northeast and Middle States.

One important measure of the adequacy of the school system is the
average number of pupils to each teacher, the pupil-teacher ratio. Crowded
schoolrooms mean that teachers are forced to give less guidance and individual attention to the pupils in their charge. In 1938 the Nation had 25.4
pupils in average daily attendance to each member of the instructional staff.
By States the pupil-teacher ratio ranged from 13.4 in South Dakota to 32.5
in North Carolina (Figure 233). The Northwest had the lowest ratio, 19.2,
the Southeast the highest with 27.9 pupils for every teacher. While the
economic explanation is valid here, some weight must be given to the trend
toward consolidation which has greatly reduced the number of small rural
schools in the region.

FIGURE 234. PERCENTAGE OF ELEMENTARY SCHOOL TEACHERS WITH THREE OR
MORE YEARS OF COLLEGE TRAINING, UNITED STATES, 1930-1931

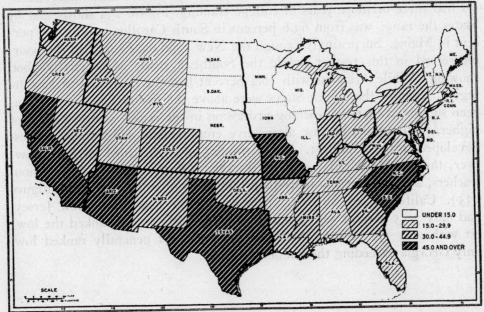

Source: *Education in the Forty-Eight States*, Advisory Committee on Education, Washington, D. C.,
1939, p. 91.

FIGURE 235. PERCENTAGE OF HIGH SCHOOL TEACHERS WITH MORE THAN
FOUR YEARS OF COLLEGE TRAINING, UNITED STATES, 1930-1931

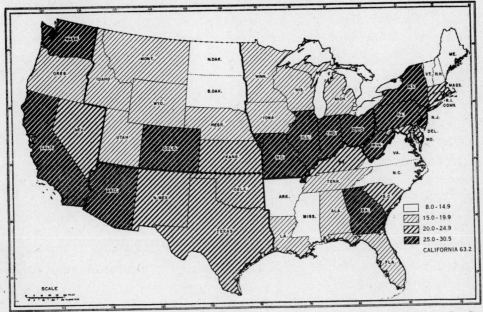

Source: *Education in the Forty-Eight States*, Advisory Committee on Education, Washington, D. C.,
1939, p. 92.

Of equal importance is the training of teachers in our elementary and high schools. In 1930-31, 27.5 percent of the Nation's elementary teachers had three or more years of college training. Figure 234 shows that by States the range was from 63.6 percent in South Carolina to only 4.6 percent in Maine. Surprisingly enough the New England States had the poorest record in this respect, while the Southeast made an especially good showing. While Arkansas with 16.4 percent had the poorest record in the region, seven of the eleven States were above the national average. It has been suggested that the teaching profession in the region secures people of higher qualifications because alternative employments for women are less developed in the Southeast. In the training of high school teachers, however, the Southeast did not show so well. Of the Nation's high school teachers, 25.3 percent had more than four years of college training (Figure 235). California led with 63.2 percent, but the next State, New Jersey, had only 30.5 percent with graduate training. Mississippi ranked the lowest with only 8.7 percent. States of the Southeast generally ranked low, only Georgia exceeding the national average.

CHAPTER 26

EDUCATION AND CULTURAL ADEQUACY

In STUDYING our cultural progress we should like to have some indication of how well our institutions are functioning in the process of developing human adequacy. How well are we now fulfilling the task of public education in the Southeast? We need a measure, based on present performance, of how far students may be expected to go in the public schools, and of how well the schools are functioning in holding their students.

HOW FAR CAN OUR POPULATION EXPECT TO GO IN SCHOOL?

It is possible so to manipulate our available data as to determine how far in school, on the basis of present performance, our current school generation may be expected to go. In its broad outline this is a method of calculating grade expectancy and is comparable to the method used by life insurance people in computing the life expectation of a population on the basis of its present performance in births and deaths. It is not our purpose to discuss in detail the methods here worked out except to say that while the grade at which students drop out of school may be compared to deaths at specific ages, the progression from grade to grade cannot be compared to survival rates simply because of the numbers of retarded students who are repeating grades. Nobody in a life table repeats a year of life, no matter how misspent. Accordingly the icy perfection of actuarial science will not apply here, for our advancement rates from grade to grade are only roughly comparable to the survival rates of the life table.

Nor can we depend on accepting total numbers in the first grade as equivalent to births in the life table. Statistics of the Office of Education unfortunately give us total numbers in grade one, not the original contingent entering the first grade during any specified year. The first grade is more than twice as full as it should be for our purpose, and the drop from first to second grade represents not school mortality so much as the effect of retardation and repetition of the grade. With these warnings by the

[395]

way we shall discuss the results of measuring the average school life and the grade expectation of our school population.

We have discussed census returns on the number of years spent by adults in school. Our present problem, however, is to estimate the number of years that will be spent in school and the grade that will be attained by a group of children entering the first grade and going through school at present school advancement and mortality rates. Table 115 and Figure 236 present the estimated enrollment in each grade in 1935 and the advancement rates from one grade to another in the spring of 1936. The advancement rate from first to second grade was found by taking the ratio of children in the second grade in 1936 to those who were in the first grade in 1935, and so on. Thus an enrollment of 786,807 white pupils in the first grade throughout the Southeastern States in 1935 gave an enrollment of 522,282 pupils in the second grade in 1936 and an advancement rate of 66 percent (Table 115). This procedure is followed for each grade. The absence of an eighth grade in many schools explains the low advancement rate from the seventh to eighth grade as well as the fact that for both races the advancement rate from the eighth grade to the first year of high school exceeds 140 percent. Interpolation of the figures between the seventh grade and first year high school gives much more reasonable advancement rates, 70 percent for Negro and 89 percent for white pupils (Figure 236).

On the basis of 1935-36 enrollment figures (Table 115) we estimate

TABLE 115. ESTIMATE OF PUBLIC SCHOOL ENROLLMENT BY RACE, SOUTHEAST, UNDER ASSUMPTION OF YEARLY ADVANCEMENT RATES AS OF 1935-1936

Grade	All schools		White schools		Negro schools	
	Enrollment	Advancement rate	Enrollment	Advancement rate	Enrollment	Advancement rate
1st............	1,452,585	55.37	786,807	66.38	665,778	42.36
2nd............	804,286	94.41	522,282	97.03	282,004	89.56
3rd............	759,333	94.51	506,770	97.09	252,563	89.34
4th............	717,663	88.51	492,023	91.76	225,640	81.42
5th............	635,196	89.61	451,480	93.89	183,716	79.08
6th............	569,178	84.59	423,895	87.90	145,283	74.95
7th............	481,494	48.77	372,604	52.13	108,890	37.28
8th............	234,832	151.82	194,238	153.46	40,594	143.99
I............	356,535	80.81	298,083	82.49	58,452	71.04
II............	287,413	78.68	245,889	79.40	41,524	74.41
III............	226,134	84.15	195,236	85.39	30,898	76.32
IV............	190,293	.....	166,712	.....	23,581	.....
TOTAL.......	6,714,942	.....	4,656,019	.....	2,058,923	.....
	Estimated number all pupils admitted to first grade: 1,007,172		Estimated number white pupils admitted to first grade: 607,217		Estimated number Negro pupils admitted to first grade: 399,955	
	Average school-life expectation: 6.67 years		Average school-life expectation: 7.67 years		Average school-life expectation: 5.15 years	
	Average grade expectation: 5.55 grades		Average grade expectation: 6.72 grades		Average grade expectation: 3.86 grades	

Source: Office of Education, *Statistics of State School Systems, 1935-1936*, Bulletin No. 2, 1937, and Bulletin No. 2, 1935; *Statistics of the Education of Negroes*, Bulletin No. 13, 1938.

FIGURE 236. ESTIMATE OF PUBLIC SCHOOL ENROLLMENT UNDER ASSUMPTION
OF YEARLY ADVANCEMENT RATES AND OF OPTIMUM ADVANCEMENT
RATES AS OF 1935-1936, SOUTHEAST, BY RACE

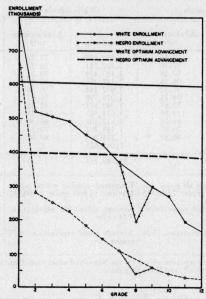

Source: See Tables 115 and 118.

that white children entering school in 1935 in the Southeast will remain in
school an average of 7.67 years; Negro children, 5.15 years.[1] The average
school-life expectation of white children the country over is much higher,
9.24 years (Table 116). As Table 116 indicates, advancement rates are
also higher. Following the methods developed in this connection, we estimate an average grade expectation in the Southeast of 6.72 grades for
white pupils and 3.86 grades for Negro pupils (Figure 237). This means
that the average child in the Southeast can expect on the basis of conditions
in 1935-36 to reach only 5.6 grades as compared with the 7.7 grades
attained by the average child in the United States.[2] (See Tables 115 and
116.) For all the 18 States maintaining separate schools for Negroes we
estimate expectancies only slightly higher than those in the Southeast,
5.43 school years and 4.18 grades (Table 116). Undoubtedly this figure
would be raised if we could include Negro pupils in *all* schools.

[1] See Rupert B. Vance and Nadia Danilevsky, "School Life Expectation and Marriage Expectation: An
Attempt to Apply the Technique of Life Table Construction to Other Fields of Sociology," *Proceedings
of Conference on Analyses and Interpretation of Social and Economic Data* (N. C. State College, Raleigh,
N. C., 1941), pp. 72-78 for discussion of method.

[2] It will be noted that these figures are lower than the median grades attained by those aged 25 and
over as reported by the 1940 Census. Our data end with the public schools while the census medians include college plus private schools. In addition, many feel that the census returns may have been over-
optimistic.

TABLE 116. ESTIMATE OF PUBLIC SCHOOL ENROLLMENT BY RACE, UNITED
STATES, UNDER ASSUMPTION OF YEARLY ADVANCEMENT RATES
AS OF 1935-1936

Grade	All schools		White schools		Negro schools*	
	Enrollment	Advancement rate	Enrollment	Advancement rate	Enrollment	Advancement rate
1st............	3,623,589	70.58	2,858,556	77.74	765,033	43.83
2nd............	2,557,589	97.30	2,222,241	98.25	335,348	90.98
3rd............	2,488,534	97.28	2,183,434	98.21	305,100	90.64
4th............	2,420,846	95.94	2,144,303	97.57	276,543	83.32
5th............	2,322,560	95.32	2,092,144	96.86	230,416	81.36
6th............	2,213,864	94.71	2,026,398	96.22	187,466	78.35
7th............	2,096,751	79.65	1,949,871	82.82	146,880	37.54
8th............	1,670,062	113.85	1,614,923	112.21	55,139	161.88
I.............	1,901,366	84.70	1,812,107	85.30	89,259	72.48
II.............	1,610,457	79.07	1,545,762	79.24	64,695	75.00
III.............	1,273,388	86,59	1,224,867	87.00	48,521	76.26
IV.............	1,102,627	.....	1,065,625	.....	37,002	.....
TOTAL.......	25,281,633	.....	22,740,231	.....	2,541,402	.....

Estimated number all pupils admitted to first grade: 2,928,913	Estimated number white pupils admitted to first grade: 2,460,937	Estimated number Negro pupils admitted to first grade: 467,976
Average school-life expectation: 8.63 years	Average school-life expectation: 9.24 years	Average school-life expectation: 5.43 years
Average grade expectation: 7.74 grades	Average grade expectation: 8.28 grades	Average grade expectation: 4.18 grades

*Negro schools of 18 States maintaining separate schools for the Negro and white races (Southeast, Delaware, District of Columbia, Missouri, Oklahoma, Texas, Maryland, and West Virginia).
Source: See Table 115.

FIGURE 237. SCHOOL LIFE AND GRADE EXPECTATION FOR WHITE AND NEGRO
PUPILS ENTERING PUBLIC SCHOOLS UNDER THE ACTUAL AND OPTIMUM
ADVANCEMENT RATES AS OF 1936, SOUTHEAST

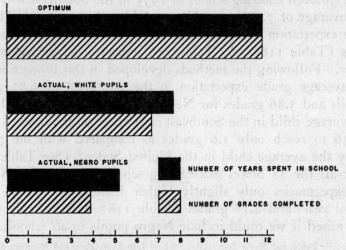

Source: See Tables 115 and 118.

The first year of school life is the most hazardous, suggesting a comparison with the effects of infant mortality on the life table. The great hazard here, however, is retardation rather than school mortality. The situation is indicated when we contrast actual grade enrollment in the

Southeast in 1929-30 with the 1930 Census figures on school attendance by ages (Table 117). The actual enrollment here includes the public and private schools in the region. Theoretically complete enrollment is based on the optimum assumption that all children 6-17 are enrolled in school, each in the grade corresponding to his age.

TABLE 117. POPULATION AND SCHOOL ATTENDANCE BY SINGLE YEARS FROM 6 TO 17 YEARS INCLUSIVE, AND ENROLLMENT IN PUBLIC AND PRIVATE SCHOOLS COMBINED, BY GRADES, SOUTHEAST, 1929-1931

Age	Population	School attendance		Grade	School enrollment	
		Number	Percent of Population		Number	Percent of population
6 years..........	638,904	319,373	50.0	1st	1,588,972	248.7
7 "	614,661	496,084	80.7	2nd	832,237	135.4
8 "	648,554	572,679	88.3	3rd	772,915	119.2
9 "	609,400	555,817	91.2	4th	711,221	116.7
10 "	626,225	585,921	93.6	5th	598,794	95.6
11 "	544,672	513,626	94.3	6th	514,403	94.4
12 "	593,317	553,131	93.2	7th	415,133	70.0
13 "	545,971	501,544	91.9	8th	207,522	38.0
14 "	577,132	494,363	85.7	I	275,899	47.8
15 "	547,147	412,345	75.4	II	207,779	38.0
16 "	579,738	341,098	58.8	III	155,555	26.8
17 "	556,131	235,997	42.4	IV	120,304	21.6
TOTAL.......	9,221,126	5,581,978	60.5		6,400,734	69.4

Note: Enrollment in public schools for 1929-1930; in private schools—for high school, the same year, for the grades of elementary school enrollment as of 1930-1931 (enrollment by grades for elementary private schools could not be obtained for 1929-1930). School attendance as given here is not the "average daily attendance" computed in the School Reports of the Office of Education, but is the term used by the Bureau of the Census for school enrollment, i.e. "the school-attendance tabulation is based on the replies to the enumerator's inquiry as to whether the person had attended school or college of any kind since September 1, 1930." (See Introduction to Vol. III, Population, Census of 1930).
Source: *Fifteenth Census of the United States, 1930*, Population, II, Chap. 12, Table 21; Office of Education, *Statistics of State School Systems*, Bulletin No. 20, 1931; *Enrollment in Private Schools*, Bulletin, No. 2, 1933.

Enrollment in the first grade is thus shown to be 249 percent of the six-year-old population (Table 117). The cumulative effect of retardation extends through the fourth grade where actual enrollment is 116.7 percent of theoretically complete enrollment. Until the incidence of retardation is lessened, the decline in births will show less effect on first grade enrollment than is generally expected. The reciprocal effect of retardation is further augmented by school mortality in the upper grades. From grade five to the fourth year in the high school the ratio of actual to theoretically complete enrollment progressively falls from 95.6 to 21.6 percent (Figure 238).

When the school attendance returns of the census are checked with the size of the school population in the Southeast, it is found that only 50 percent of the six-year olds, 81 percent of the seven-year olds, and 88 percent of the eight-year olds were actually attending school in 1930 (Table 117, Figure 239). These figures furnish additional evidence of the extent to which the large enrollments in the lower grades result from retardation. The highest proportion of attendance is reached by the eleven-year olds, 94.3 percent. Here also actual enrollment is 94.4 percent of theoretically

FIGURE 238. COMPLETE ENROLLMENT BY GRADES CONTRASTED WITH THE
ACTUAL ENROLLMENT, SOUTHEAST, 1929-1931

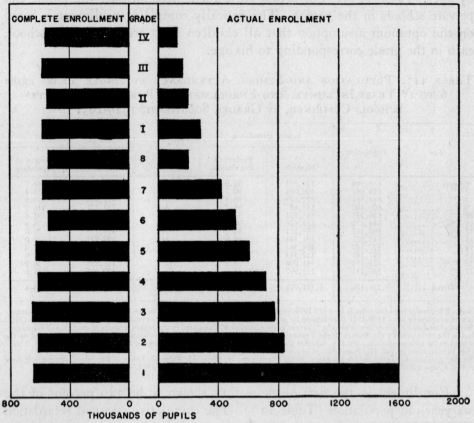

Source: See Table 117.

complete enrollment (Table 117). For the Negroes actual enrollment exceeds the enrollment that would prevail under optimum entrance and advancement rates until beyond the fourth grade; for the whites, until beyond the fifth grade.

That a potential high school population of 556,000 in 1930 yielded only 120,000 enrollment in the last year of our high schools may offer consolation to those who feel that too many in our population are attempting to go on to higher education and professional and white-collar jobs. In the Southeast, it hardly seems that this point has yet been reached.

No one, however, can find consolation in that bottleneck of our educational system, the first grade. Here total enrollment exceeds theoretically complete enrollment by 149 percent. The Southeast may be a region of white sixth graders and colored third graders, but for those who clear the hurdle of the first grade it becomes a region of white eight and a half grad-

FIGURE 239. POPULATION OF SCHOOL AGE AND SCHOOL ATTENDANCE,
CHILDREN, AGE 6-13, SOUTHEAST, 1929-1930

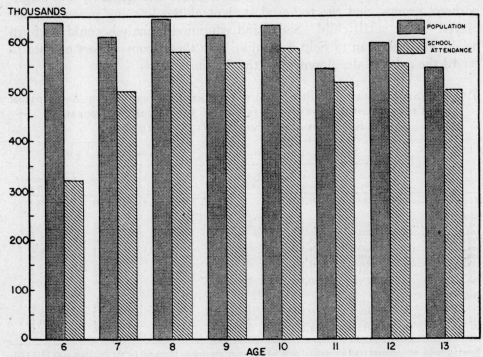

Source: See Table 117.

ers and colored fifth graders. The transition from the first to the second grade is thus shown to be the most vulnerable link in our educational system. The youth problem of the future is brewing here. From grade one through grade four the actual enrollment in our schools exceeds the equivalent age groups in the population. To what is this situation due? In setting our school entrance age at six, have we ignored all the facts of individual differences and placed on the shoulders of some children greater burdens than they can bear? Have we overemphasized certain technical aspects of our approach to the child? Do we place too much emphasis on the ability to read, or do we, because of large classes and inadequate personnel, fail to teach the minimum amount of reading skills required?

Here it seems is the chance for research that should mean much to our future cultural development. It has taken compulsory education to bring these conditions to our notice, and it will require extended social analysis to explain them. To what extent are they to be assigned to the incidence of hereditary deficiencies on the part of certain elements in our population, to the effect of social and cultural isolation on certain groups, or to defects in the school system especially in the first grades? Undoubtedly all these factors are present; and thus need exists for cooperation between the student of individual differences and abilities, the student of community and neighborhood groups, and the technical student of the learning process as displayed in the small child. Social and educational analysis could perform no greater task than to help determine how these many factors operate to retard the cultural development of the Southeast.

TABLE 118. ESTIMATE OF PUBLIC SCHOOL ENROLLMENT UNDER ASSUMPTION OF YEARLY ADVANCEMENT RATES AND OF OPTIMUM ADVANCEMENT RATES, BY RACE, SOUTHEAST, 1935-1936

Grade	Enrollment in white schools			Enrollment in Negro schools		
	Actual rates	Optimum rates	Percentage difference	Actual rates	Optimum rates	Percentage difference
TOTAL...........	4,656,019	7,223,594	55.1	2,058,923	4,735,389	130.0
Elementary:						
1st...............	786,807	607,217	−22.8	665,778	399,955	−39.9
2nd..............▼.......	522,282	606,185	16.1	282,004	399,075	41.5
3rd..............	506,770	605,154	19.4	252,563	398,197	57.7
4th..............	492,023	604,125	22.8	225,640	397,321	76.1
5th..............	451,480	603,098	33.6	183,716	396,447	115.8
6th..............	423,895	602,314	42.1	145,283	395,495	172.2
7th..............	372,604	601,531	61.4	108,890	394,546	262.3
8th..............	194,238	600,749	209.3	40,594	393,599	869.6
High School:						
I year.........	298,083	599,968	101.3	58,452	392,654	571.8
II year.........	245,889	599,188	143.7	41,524	391,712	843.3
III year.........	195,236	597,750	206.2	30,898	389,362	1160.2
IV year.........	166,712	596,315	257.7	23,581	387,026	1541.3

Note: Optimum advancement rates are survival rates for stationary populations computed for the Southeast as of 1919-1931. Estimated number of white pupils admitted to white schools in 1935 was 607,217; admitted to Negro schools, 399,955.
Source: Office of Education, *Statistics of State School Systems*, Bulletin No. 2, 1935 and 1937; *Statistics of Negro Education*, Bulletin No. 13, 1938; all sources necessary for the computation of life tables.

These figures on actual conditions lead us to inquire as to what we might expect under the assumption of optimum or ideal conditions. Optimum conditions would assume school facilities ample to provide for all pupils and an adjustment of school programs to pupils' capacities and interests so adequate that none would drop out or be retarded in his progression from grade to grade. Thus, optimum advancement rates assume no child's dropping out of school for reasons other than death, and no repetition of grades during the whole school-life span. Table 118 and Figure 240 give the comparison of results obtained. If we assume 607,217 white children entering school in both cases, we obtain a total enrollment of 4,656,019 pupils under actual conditions and 7,223,594 pupils under "optimum" conditions, or an increase of 55.1 percent. A similar computation shows an increase of 130 percent in the enrollment of Negro students under optimum conditions.

The grade expectation for white and Negro pupils has been presented in Figure 237. The upper bars show the optimum advancement rates and grade expectation for both races. Since survival rates for whites and Ne-

FIGURE 240. ENROLLMENT BY GRADES IN PUBLIC SCHOOLS ON THE BASIS OF
ACTUAL ADVANCEMENT RATES AS OF 1936 AND OPTIMUM
ADVANCEMENT, SOUTHEAST, BY RACE

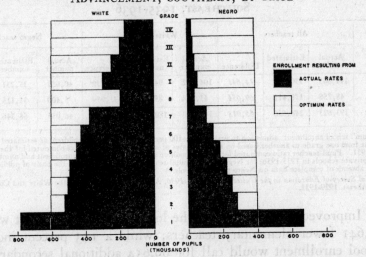

Source: See Table 118.

groes do not differ much during the period 6 to 17 years of age, the results
obtained for the school life expectation of each race were so close (11.9 for
white children as against 11.8 for Negroes) that one bar showing the optimum grade expectation of 11.8 for both races is sufficient. The remaining
bars indicate the actual expectation for white and Negro children on the
basis of advancement rates in 1936.

Many inadequacies found in our schools, in communities, and among
pupils and their families furnish reasons why this optimum is not attained.
Thus communities are not financially able to provide full school facilities;
many families suffer handicaps of isolation and inadequate economic resources that keep children out of school; school curricula are not adjusted
to pupils' interests and capacities. In planning for long-time cultural development, only one of these handicaps should be regarded as definitely
prohibitive. That is the incapacity of those children who are so mentally
retarded as to be incapable of carrying through the school program. Even
here feebleminded children, whatever their true proportion in the school
population may be, are capable of profiting from especially designed programs for backward children.

No one knows what an optimum educational program would demand
of the people. It is worth while, however, to estimate the number of additional teachers we would need under the assumption of optimum enrollment in the region. On the basis of pupil-teacher ratios in 1936 the Southeast (Table 119) would need 55,013 additional teachers, an increase of 28

TABLE 119. ACTUAL NUMBER OF TEACHERS IN PUBLIC AND PRIVATE SCHOOLS
AND ESTIMATED NUMBER UNDER ASSUMPTION OF ACTUAL PUPIL-
TEACHER RATIO AND OPTIMUM SCHOOL ENROLLMENT,
SOUTHEAST, 1935-1936

School grades	All teachers			White teachers			Negro teachers		
	Actual number	Estimated number	Difference	Actual number	Estimated number	Difference	Actual number	Estimated number	Difference
ELEMENTARY ...	144,865	130,224	−14,641	104,232	94,993	−9,239	40,633	35,231	−5,402
SECONDARY.....	48,758	118,412	69,654	43,358	85,297	41,939	5,400	33,115	27,715
TOTAL.........	193,623	248,636	55,013	147,590	180,290	32,700	46,033	68,346	22,313

Note: "Optimum" school enrollment: admission to first grade—100 percent of six-year old children, as estimated in 1935; rates of advancement from one grade to another based on survival rates of stationary population, as computed for the Southeast by race for 1929-1931. Pupil-teacher ratio computed for white schools on the basis of combined enrollment and number of teachers in public and private schools in 1935-1936; for Negro schools pupil-teacher ratio computed on the basis of public schools only because of the absence of complete data on Negro private schools.
Source: *Biennial Survey of Education in the United States, 1934-1936;* Abridged Life Tables for the White and Colored Population of the Southeast, 1929-1931.

percent. Improved advancement in the lower grades means that we would need 14,641 fewer elementary teachers; while a 143 percent increase in high school enrollment would call for 69,654 additional secondary teachers. In the lower grades white schools would lose 9,239 elementary teachers; Negro schools, 5,402 teachers. In the secondary grades, white high schools would require 41,939 new teachers; Negro schools, 27,715 new teachers.

These figures represent the direction of our population trends and our cultural development. Fewer children entering the early grades, fewer children suffering the handicaps of retardation will be met by the increasing trend toward secondary education for all the people. This trend which has developed slowly but surely is already being felt in the teacher training program of the region. In time to come it may involve the retraining of elementary school personnel for high school teaching.

CHAPTER 27

CLOSING THE GAP IN SOUTHERN EDUCATION

WE ARE hardly in position to estimate what the Southeast can do in the future until we see what it has done in the past. The present low educational status of the Southeast may be discouraging, but it is not the result of lagging behind the rest of the country in recent years. It comes, in fact, at the close of a period in which the region has made the most rapid educational progress. The region started from the lowest position, and since 1870 has made heroic efforts to close the gap in its public education program, efforts that now have a history extending backward for almost seventy years.

SCHOOL ENROLLMENT AND SCHOOL POPULATION

There are, no doubt, several ways in which we might estimate the measure of success which has attended these efforts. One such method is shown in Figure 241 (Tables 120 and 121), where the increases in school enrollment from 1870 to 1938 are set against the background of the region's increase in population aged 5-17. For the Southeast the task of closing the gap between the population ready for school and the population enrolled has been an arduous one, but the slant of the upward lines indicates that it has been accomplished to a greater extent than could have been expected in 1870. The campaign for universal education in the three decades from 1870 to 1900 produced the most rapid acceleration in the upward trend. While the school population (5-17) of the Southeast grew from 3.35 to 6.19 millions, public school enrollment climbed from 1.1 million to 3.9 million (Tables 120 and 121). Nevertheless, the proportion of the region's population in school, 63.1 percent, was only slightly higher in 1900 than the Nation's in 1870. Rapid gains continued until 1938 when the region's public and private schools contained 6.7 million pupils out of a possible 7.7 million—a ratio of 87.5 percent as compared with 93.1 percent for the Nation (Table 123).

TABLE 120. ESTIMATES OF SCHOOL POPULATION BY RACE, UNITED STATES AND SOUTHEAST, 1870-1938

Year and school population	UNITED STATES			SOUTHEAST		
	All	White	Negro	All	White	Negro
Population (5-17 inclusive):						
1870	12,055,443	10,528,271	1,527,172	3,349,782	2,034,413	1,315,369
1880	15,065,767	12,956,717	2,109,050	4,270,119	2,447,787	1,822,332
1890	18,543,201	16,032,354	2,510,847	5,357,495	3,182,457	2,175,038
1900	21,404,322	18,699,180	2,705,142	6,186,525	3,849,470	2,337,055
1910	24,239,948	21,308,829	2,931,119	6,655,714	4,207,341	2,448,373
1920	27,728,788	24,829,542	2,899,246	7,196,088	4,725,464	2,470,624
1930	31,571,322	28,668,665	2,902,657	7,714,093	5,280,512	2,433,581
1932	32,031,549	29,127,849	2,903,700	7,776,200	5,346,500	2,429,700
1934	32,392,749	29,488,649	2,904,100	7,825,000	5,398,600	2,426,400
1936	31,618,000	28,672,000	2,946,000	7,831,600	5,379,100	2,452,500
1938	30,789,000	27,800,700	2,988,300	7,660,726	5,182,126	2,478,600
Population (5-13 inclusive):						
1870	8,757,952	....	....	2,451,793	....	....
1880	11,124,402	....	....	3,258,806	....	....
1890	13,188,548	11,369,670	1,818,878	3,875,019	2,298,509	1,576,510
1900	15,287,527	13,335,616	1,951,911	4,282,101	2,591,636	1,690,465
1910	17,019,650	14,902,413	2,117,237	4,638,215	2,884,496	1,753,719
1920	19,992,947	17,919,881	2,073,066	5,199,567	3,426,578	1,773,049
1930	22,230,101	20,197,085	2,033,016	5,416,123	3,713,618	1,702,505
1932	22,553,414	20,519,662	2,033,752	5,459,380	3,758,590	1,700,790
1934	22,744,049	20,710,017	2,034,032	5,493,696	3,795,216	1,698,480
1936	22,259,000	20,195,680	2,063,320	5,498,300	3,781,500	1,716,800
1938	21,676,000	19,599,500	2,076,500	5,377,826	3,643,026	1,734,800
Population (14-17 inclusive):						
1870	3,297,491	....	....	897,989	....	....
1880	3,941,365	....	....	1,011,313	....	....
1890	5,354,653	4,662,684	691,969	1,482,476	883,948	598,528
1900	6,116,795	5,363,564	753,231	1,904,424	1,257,834	646,590
1910	7,220,298	6,406,416	813,882	2,017,499	1,322,845	694,654
1920	7,735,841	6,909,661	826,180	1,996,521	1,298,886	697,575
1930	9,341,221	8,471,580	869,641	2,297,970	1,566,894	731,076
1932	9,478,135	8,608,187	869,948	2,316,820	1,587,910	728,910
1934	9,648,700	8,778,632	870,068	2,331,304	1,603,384	727,920
1936	9,359,000	8,476,320	882,680	2,333,300	1,597,600	735,700
1938	9,113,000	8,201,200	911,800	2,282,900	1,539,100	743,800

Note: Figures for the Negro population include all colored prior to 1900 in accordance with the Bureau of Education Reports. The Negro population of the United States given here includes only 17 States prior to 1900 and 18 States (with addition of Oklahoma) thereafter; the remaining Negro population enrolled in unsegregated schools is included with the white.

Population estimates for the whole group (5-17) is given for all years in Statistics of State School Systems; estimates for the subgroups (5-13 and 14-17) were not given for all years; in some cases, they were estimated by applying percentages computed on the basis of the nearest available Census enumeration.

Source: *Reports of the Commissioner of Education*, 1871 (Report, 1871); 1879-1880 (Reports, 1880-1881); 1889-1890 (Report, 1890, I and II); 1899-1900 (Report, 1900, I and II); 1909-1910 (Report, 1911, II)—U. S. Department of the Interior, Office of Education, Statistics of State School Systems. *Biennial Survey of Education*, 1919-1920 (Bulletin No. 9, 1922); 1929-1930 (Bulletin No. 20, 1931); 1931-1932 (Bulletin No. 2, 1933); 1933-1934 (Bulletin No. 2, 1935); 1935-1936 (Bulletin No. 2, 1937)—U. S. Department of the Interior, Office of Education, Statistics of State School Systems. *Biennial Survey of Education*, 1937-1938 (Bulletin No. 2, 1940, Chap. 2)—Federal Security Agency, U. S. Office of Education, Statistics of State School Systems. Also *Statistical Abstracts of the United States* (1901-1940), chapters on Education. For special sources on Negro education: *Reports of the Commissioner on Education*, 1889-1900 (Report, 1890, II, p. 2063); 1899-1900 (Report, 1900, II, p. 2501); 1910 (Report, 1910, II, p. 1262); 1913-1916 (Biennial Bulletin 1916, No. 39—report of T. J. Jones, 2v.); and *Biennial Survey of Education*, 1919-1920 (Bulletin No. 29, 1922); 1925-1926 (Bulletin No. 19, 1928); also *Statistics of the Education of Negroes*, 1935-1936 (Bulletin No. 13, 1938)—U. S. Department of the Interior, Office of Education, Statistics of State School Systems.

Figure 242 (Tables 120 to 122) makes possible a comparison of the region's trend by races. Great as have been the gains in white enrollment, the graph shows rapid gains in Negro education after 1890 from the low point at which it started in 1870. In 1870 barely 260,000 out of 1,315,369 Negro children, aged 5-17, were in school, a proportion of less than 20 percent. In 68 years this grew to 1,963,501 out of 2,478,600, a ratio of 79.2 percent as compared with 87.8 percent for white school enrollment in the Southeast. While school population and enrollment began to drop off in 1938, the percentage of all children in school has continued its upward trend in the region through 1940. Behind the figures presented

Table 121. Pupils Enrolled in Public Schools Classified by Elementary and High Schools and by Race, United States and Southeast, 1871-1938

Year and type of school	United States			Southeast		
	All	White	Negro	All	White	Negro
Elementary and High:						
1871	7,561,582	7,251,582	310,000	1,080,057	820,057	260,000
1880	9,867,395	9,082,686	784,709	2,035,243	1,367,243	668,000
1890	12,722,631	11,425,672	1,296,959	3,166,538	2,091,538	1,075,000
1900	15,503,110	13,943,040	1,560,070	3,903,894	2,610,894	1,293,000
1910	17,813,852	16,064,999	1,748,853	4,536,770	3,078,467	1,458,303
1920	21,578,316	19,474,601	2,103,715	5,565,607	3,871,703	1,693,904
1930	25,678,015	23,395,437	2,282,578	6,284,269	4,402,521	1,881,748
1932	26,275,441	23,922,121	2,353,320	6,404,184	4,471,029	1,933,155
1934	26,434,193	24,004,095	2,430,098	6,555,564	4,552,434	2,003,130
1936	26,367,098	23,928,117	2,438,981	6,585,901	4,596,989	1,988,912
1938	25,975,108	23,563,141	2,411,967	6,512,153	4,548,652	1,963,501
Elementary: (including Kindergarten)						
1890	12,519,668	11,224,831	1,294,837	3,156,177	2,081,614	1,074,563
1900	14,983,859	13,429,021	1,554,838	3,863,028	2,572,867	1,290,161
1910	16,898,791	15,157,577	1,741,214	4,450,576	2,996,005	1,454,571
1920	19,721,161	17,634,584	2,086,577	5,362,363	3,675,155	1,687,218
1930	21,278,593	19,108,601	2,169,992	5,564,884	3,754,969	1,809,915
1932	21,135,420	18,918,081	2,217,339	5,588,035	3,744,125	1,843,910
1934	20,765,037	18,498,124	2,266,913	5,652,353	3,759,896	1,892,457
1936	20,392,561	18,142,516	2,250,045	5,607,776	3,748,153	1,859,623
1938	19,748,174	17,544,091	2,204,083	5,459,956	3,639,057	1,820,899
High School:						
1890	202,963	200,841	2,122	10,361	9,918	443
1900	519,251	514,019	5,232	40,866	38,027	2,839
1910	915,061	907,422	7,639	86,194	82,462	3,732
1920	1,857,155	1,840,017	17,138	203,244	196,548	6,696
1930	4,399,422	4,286,836	112,586	719,385	647,552	71,833
1932	5,140,021	5,004,040	135,981	816,149	726,904	89,245
1934	5,669,156	5,505,971	163,185	903,211	792,538	110,673
1936	5,974,537	5,785,601	188,936	978,125	848,836	129,289
1938	6,226,934	6,019,050	207,884	1,052,197	909,595	142,602

Note: Public High Schools are those specifically reported as such by the Bureau of Education and therefore do not include professional, vocational or preparatory schools, and 7th and 8th grades of Junior High Schools; figures for Elementary Schools include the latter. Thus, elementary schools include grades 1-8 (or 1 to 7), while High Schools include grades 9 to 12 (or 8 to 11 in States with 7-grade elementary schools). Negro enrollment prior to 1930 includes all colored. Negro enrollment given here for the United States includes 18 States only (minus Oklahoma prior to 1900) where schools are segrated by race; the remaining Negro enrollment is included with the white. Definition of high school as adopted here and in the latest reports of the Bureau of Education could not be traced in 1870 or 1880. Figures for 1870 and 1880 partly estimated.
Source: See Table 120.

in these ascending lines must lie much of the dramatic history, told and untold, of the region's valiant struggles and able leaders.

Division of these trends into elementary and high school enrollment, Figure 243 and Table 121, brings out significant contrasts. From 1890 until 1930 enrollment in the elementary schools is shown to be increasing; after 1930 it declines in the United States, and after 1934, in the Southeast. For both areas it is clear that the great gains have been in the high schools, and that these gains have continued at an accelerated pace into the more recent decades. In 1890 the total public high school enrollment in the Southeast was only 10,361. The greatest increase came in the period 1920 to 1930 when high school enrollment rose from 203,244 to 719,385. By 1938 it exceeded 1,052,000. In 1890 3.8 percent of the Nation's youth, aged 14-17 were enrolled in public high schools as compared with 1.1 percent of the whites and 0.1 of the colored youth in the Southeast (Table 122). By 1900, 3.9 percent in the region and 10.3 percent in the Nation were en-

TABLE 122. RATIO OF ENROLLMENT IN PUBLIC SCHOOLS TO SCHOOL
POPULATION, UNITED STATES AND SOUTHEAST, 1871-1938

Year and type of school	UNITED STATES			SOUTHEAST		
	All	White	Negro	All	White	Negro
Ratio of enrollment in elementary and high schools to population 5-17 years inclusive:						
1871	62.7	68.9	20.3	32.2	40.3	19.8
1880	65.5	70.1	37.2	47.7	55.9	36.7
1890	68.6	71.3	51.6	59.1	65.7	49.4
1900	72.4	74.6	57.7	63.1	67.8	55.3
1910	73.5	75.4	59.7	68.2	73.2	59.6
1920	77.8	78.4	72.6	77.3	81.9	68.6
1930	81.3	81.6	78.6	81.5	83.4	77.3
1932	82.0	82.1	81.0	82.4	83.6	79.6
1934	81.6	79.9	83.7	83.7	84.3	82.6
1936	83.4	83.5	82.8	84.1	85.5	81.1
1938	84.4	84.8	80.7	85.0	87.8	79.2
Ratio of enrollment in elementary schools to population 5-13 years inclusive:						
1890	94.9	98.7	71.2	81.4	90.6	68.2
1900	98.0	100.7	79.6	90.2	99.3	76.3
1910	99.3	101.7	82.2	96.0	103.9	82.9
1920	98.6	98.4	100.6	103.1	107.2	95.2
1930	95.7	94.6	106.7	102.8	101.1	106.3
1932	93.7	92.2	109.1	102.4	99.6	108.4
1934	91.3	89.3	111.5	103.0	99.1	111.4
1936	91.6	89.8	109.0	102.0	99.1	108.3
1938	91.1	89.5	106.1	101.5	99.9	105.0
Ratio of enrollment in high schools to population 14 to 17 years inclusive:						
1890	3.8	4.3	0.3	0.7	1.1	0.1
1900	8.5	9.6	0.7	2.1	3.0	0.4
1910	12.7	14.2	0.9	4.3	6.2	0.5
1920	24.0	26.6	2.1	10.2	15.1	1.0
1930	47.1	50.6	12.9	31.3	41.3	9.8
1932	54.2	58.1	15.6	35.2	45.8	12.2
1934	58.8	62.7	18.8	38.7	49.4	15.2
1936	63.8	68.3	21.4	41.9	53.1	17.6
1938	68.3	73.4	22.8	46.1	59.1	19.2

Note: Ratio expressed as percentage of corresponding population group. Whenever the percentage exceeds 100 there is evidence that the population enrolled in elementary grades is not limited to the group 5-13 years of age. This fact is true for other periods also, but when percentages are below 100 we cannot prove it on the basis of data given here.
Source: See Table 120.

rolled in both public and private high schools (Table 123). By 1920 this had grown to 13.4 and 26.8 percent; by 1930 to 31.3 and 50.8 percent, respectively.

Throughout the Nation this trend represents more than an increase in the provisions made for educating the people; it represents something of the social revolution to be found in the cultural leveling of classes. For whatever it is worth, high school education is more and more becoming the social heritage of all Americans. Of the Nation's population 14-17 in 1938, 73.2 percent were enrolled in high schools, public and private; of the region's, only 48.2 percent (Table 123). Only 19.2 percent of the Negro youth 14-17 in the Southeast were enrolled in public high schools as compared with 59.1 percent of the whites (Table 122).

Recent enrollment trends are especially worthy of study in relation to population trends. The factors influencing enrollment may be balanced somewhat as follows: We may expect increased enrollment in our schools (1) if we have a larger proportion of six-year-old children entering the first grade, (2) if we increase the numbers enrolled in public kindergartens,

FIGURE 241. POPULATION 5-17 YEARS INCLUSIVE AND ENROLLMENT IN ALL
PUBLIC SCHOOLS, UNITED STATES AND SOUTHEAST, 1870-1938

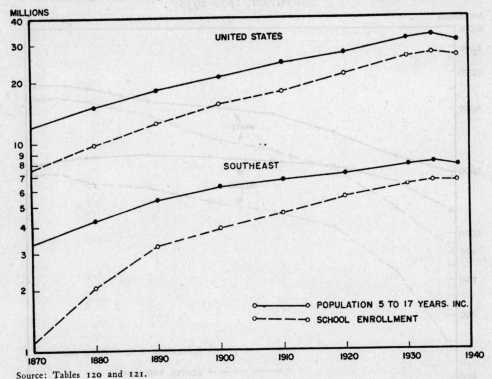

Source: Tables 120 and 121.

and (3) if we have less "dropping out of" school in the upper grades. We may, however, expect decreased enrollments (1) from the decrease in the number of births, (2) if fewer grades are repeated, and (3) if fewer over-age children are admitted to the first grade. Significant contrasts are evident in the recent trends of elementary and high school enrollments.

Since 1930 the elementary enrollment has been declining in the United States (Figure 244). From 1930 to 1932 the elementary schools lost 143,173 pupils, from 1936 to 1938 the loss was 644,387, or 3.2 percent. Elementary enrollment steadily increased in the Southeast until it began a decline in 1934-1936 that reached 2.6 percent from 1936 to 1938. Declining births and improvement in the progress from grade to grade have now reached the point where it appears they will continue to counteract the trend toward increased enrollment in the early grades. This trend also prevails in the Southeast where the elementary enrollment of the Negro school population is still far from complete.

In contrast high school enrollment in both the Nation and the region has shown continued increases. The peak of these increases, however, was

FIGURE 242. THE TREND IN THE POPULATION OF SCHOOL AGE, 5-17, AND
PUPILS ENROLLED IN ALL PUBLIC SCHOOLS, BY RACE,
SOUTHEAST, 1870-1938

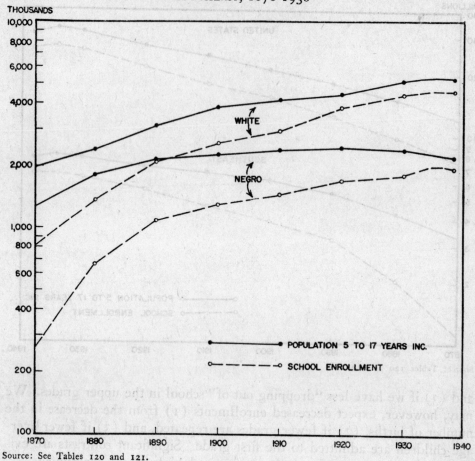

Source: See Tables 120 and 121.

passed in 1930-1932, when 740,599 new students enrolled in the public high schools of the Nation, giving an increase of 16.8 percent (Figure 244). In the same period enrollment in the Southeast showed an increase of 96,764 equal to 13.5 percent. Since then, the rates of increase have declined to 4.2 percent in the Nation and to 7.6 percent in the region, for the period 1936-1938.

The major factor influencing the decline in elementary school enrollment is the fall in the birth rate. To show how this operates we have attempted to relate the indices of fertility and school enrollment for the ten-year period, 1927-1936. By allowing a seven-year lag to births, the close relation that fertility bears to total enrollment in the first grade can be shown graphically for the Nation and the region as in Figures 245 and 246.

TABLE 123. PUPILS ENROLLED IN PRIVATE SCHOOLS AND PUPILS ENROLLED IN PRIVATE AND PUBLIC SCHOOLS COMBINED, WITH RATIO OF ENROLLMENT TO SCHOOL POPULATION, UNITED STATES AND SOUTHEAST, 1900-1938

Year and type of school	UNITED STATES			SOUTHEAST		
	Private	Private and Public		Private	Private and Public	
	Number	Number	Ratio*	Number	Number	Ratio*
Elementary and High:						
1900	1,351,722	16,854,832	78.7	166,646	4,070,540	65.8
1910	1,558,437	19,372,289	79.9	215,065	4,751,835	71.4
1920	1,699,481	23,277,797	84.0	190,963	5,756,570	80.0
1930	2,576,157	28,254,172	89.4	156,070	6,440,339	83.5
1932	2,723,666	28,999,107	90.5	178,187	6,582,371	84.7
1934	2,691,033	29,125,226	89.9	177,866	6,733,430	86.1
1936	2,638,775	29,005,873	91.7	181,304	6,767,205	86.4
1938	2,687,483	28,662,591	93.1	190,693	6,702,846	87.5
Elementary:						
1900	1,240,925	16,224,784	106.1	134,102	3,997,130	93.3
1910	1,441,037	18,339,828	107.8	168,038	4,618,614	99.6
1920	1,485,561	21,206,722	106.1	125,649	5,488,012	105.6
1930	2,234,999	23,513,592	105.8	117,795	5,682,679	104.9
1932	2,320,251	23,455,671	104.0	132,718	5,720,753	105.2
1934	2,330,941	23,095,978	101.5	138,291	5,790,644	105.4
1936	2,251,466	22,644,027	101.7	138,132	5,745,908	104.5
1938	2,240,650	21,988,824	101.4	143,239	5,603,195	104.2
High School:						
1900	110,797	630,048	10.3	32,544	73,410	3.9
1910	117,400	1,032,461	14.3	47,027	133,221	6.6
1920	213,920	2,071,075	26.8	65,314	268,558	13.4
1930	341,158	4,740,580	50.8	38,275	757,660	31.3
1932	403,415	5,543,436	58.5	45,469	861,618	37.2
1934	360,092	6,029,248	62.5	39,575	942,786	41.7
1936	387,309	6,361,846	68.0	43,172	1,021,297	43.8
1938	446,833	6,673,767	73.2	47,454	1,099,651	48.2

*For total enrollment, ratio to all school population (5-17 years inclusive); for elementary, ratio to enumerated or estimated population 5 to 13 years inclusive; for High School, ratio to enumerated or estimated population 14 to 17 years inclusive.
Note: Private pupils given here include pupils enrolled in private and parochial schools as estimated by the Office of Education; private high schools do not include private commercial, professional, and vocational schools.
Source: See Table 120.

Births show greater year-to-year fluctuations than first-year enrollments, largely because of the stabilizing effect of retardation on the total numbers in the first grade. National indices show a downward trend for the high points reached around 1928. In the Nation the decline in births after 1921 initiated a decline in enrollment that began in 1928 and continued without a break in spite of some rise in the number of births in 1924. From 1928 to 1936 first grade enrollments fell from an index value of 106 to 90 (Figure 245). In the Southeast, fluctuating births that finally broke downward after 1921 and 1924 are accompanied by an enrollment trend that declined much more slowly after 1928. In catching up with its task of enrolling the school population, the Southeast exhibits an interesting phenomena. Using the base period 1927-1936 as 100 for enrollment and the decade 1920-1929 as base period for births, it is found that the enrollment index holds up better than the birth index by 1934. Thus while from the high point of 1921 to 1929 the regional fertility index fell from 112 to 88, the enrollment index in the period 1928-1936 fell from 106 to only 92 (Figure 246). On the favorable side, this trend may be due to better enforcement of compulsory school attendance laws, and perhaps bet-

FIGURE 243. PUPILS ENROLLED IN PUBLIC ELEMENTARY AND HIGH SCHOOLS,
UNITED STATES AND SOUTHEAST, 1890-1938

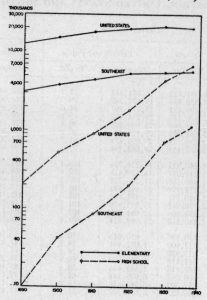

Source: Table 121.

FIGURE 244. THE PERCENTAGE CHANGE IN ELEMENTARY AND HIGH SCHOOL
ENROLLMENT, UNITED STATES AND SOUTHEAST BY
2-YEAR PERIODS, 1928-1938

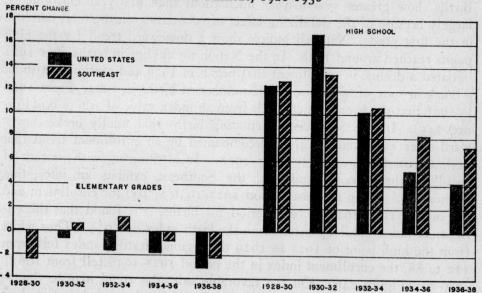

Source: United States Office of Education, *Statistics of State School Systems, Bulletins No. 5* (1930),
No. 20 (1931), and *No. 2* (1933, 1935, 1937 and 1940).

FIGURE 245. INDICES OF NUMBER OF PUPILS ENROLLED IN FIRST GRADE
(1927-1936) AND NUMBER OF CHILDREN BORN (1920-1929),
UNITED STATES

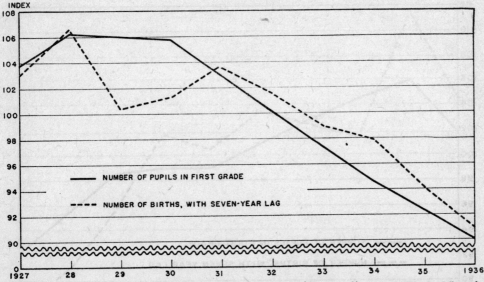

Source: "Population Prospects and Public Schools," *School Life* (May, 1938), p. 305; U. S. Office of Education, *Statistics of State School Systems, 1935-1936* (1937), Bulletin No. 2; *Statistics of the Education of Negroes, 1935-1936* (1938), Bulletin No. 13; *U. S. Birth, Stillbirth and Infant Mortality Statistics, 1920-1929.*

ter roads and transportation facilities. On the unfavorable side it represents the retardation in the first grade, previously shown.

We will do well not to claim too much for these enrollment figures. Enrollment in school has never been synonymous with the achievement of an education. Nevertheless for the Southeast, as for any area, getting the children in school was the necessary first step. Their retention in school and their grade advancement furnish the two other prerequisites for normal educational progress.

SEVENTY YEARS OF EDUCATIONAL PROGRESS

Over a range of 70 years educational conditions have steadily improved in the Southeast, cutting down the gap between the region and the Nation. Table 124 shows that, in the ratio of average daily attendance to enrollment, the region began with a better record than the Nation, 68.6 to 60.1. By 1890 they were even at 64.1 percent and then the Nation drew ahead, closing in 1938 with 85.8 percent to 81.2 percent for the region. In this measure the white Southeast has reached the point held by the Nation in 1930, while the Negro schools have barely passed the Nation's 1920 record.

In 1871 the school term averaged only 77 days in the Southeast as compared with 132 days in the Nation (Table 125). The terms were in-

FIGURE 246. INDICES OF NUMBER OF PUPILS ENROLLED IN FIRST GRADE (1927-1936) AND NUMBER OF CHILDREN BORN (1920-1929), SOUTHEAST*

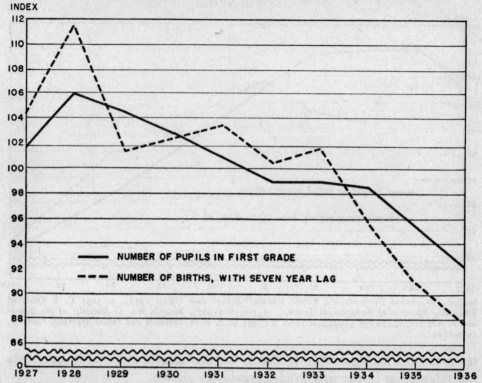

INDEX

NUMBER OF PUPILS IN FIRST GRADE
NUMBER OF BIRTHS, WITH SEVEN YEAR LAG

* A seven year lag was allowed because births are reported for the calendar year while the school year begins in the autumn of the preceding calendar year. For computing the indices, we assume the mean of the series of each decade as 100.0 and use this as a basis for other years.
Source: See Figure 250, p. 421.

creased, reaching 96 and 144 days respectively in 1900, 151 and 173 days in 1930, and 164 and 174 days in 1938, when the region came within 94 percent of the national average. The white schools had an average term of 166 days in the Southeast as compared with 154 days for the Negro schools.

In pupil-teacher ratio, the Nation led the Southeast 38 to 44 in 1871 (Table 124). Under the stress of compulsory education, the ratio rose to 49 in the Southeast in 1900 as compared with 37 in the Nation. Both areas saw the ratios gradually improved until they stood in 1938 at 28 for the Nation and 33 for the Southeast. For the region's Negro schools the ratio was 41, a point passed by the region's white schools in 1910.

Educational expenditures have increased at a greater rate than other educational indices. Not all of this increase should be attributed to a rising price level; part should be attributed to an increase in the quality of edu-

TABLE 124. NUMBER OF PUPILS IN AVERAGE DAILY ATTENDANCE, RATIO OF
ATTENDANCE TO ENROLLMENT, NUMBER OF TEACHERS AND PUPIL-
TEACHER RATIO, ELEMENTARY AND HIGH SCHOOLS,
UNITED STATES AND SOUTHEAST, 1871-1938

Item	1871	1880	1890	1900	1910	1920
Number pupils in average daily attendance						
United States: All........	4,545,317	6,144,145	8,153,635	10,632,772	12,827,307	16,150,035
White......	....	....	7,339,925	9,651,746	11,721,678	14,734,001
Negro......	....	....	813,710	981,026	1,105,629	1,416,034
Southeast: All........	741,011	1,332,107	2,030,507	2,510,877	2,929,733	3,798,869
White......	....	....	1,346,007	1,693,877	2,009,956	2,622,442
Negro......	....	....	684,500	817,000	919,777	1,176,427
Ratio of attendance to enrollment						
United States: All........	60.1	62.3	64.1	68.6	72.0	74.8
White......	....	....	64.2	69.2	73.0	75.6
Negro......	....	....	62.7	62.9	63.5	67.3
Southeast: All........	68.6	65.4	64.1	64.3	64.6	68.3
White......	....	....	64.4	64.9	65.3	69.1
Negro......	....	....	63.7	63.2	63.1	66.5
Number of teachers*						
United States: All........	200,515	286,593	363,922	423,062	523,210	679,533
White......	....	....	339,850	395,749	490,413	640,887
Negro......	....	....	24,072	27,313	32,797	38,646
Southeast: All........	24,530	45,611	67,573	80,441	100,723	134,478
White......	....	....	47,886	58,736	75,196	104,131
Negro......	....	....	19,687	21,705	25,527	30,347
Pupil-teacher ratio**						
United States: All........	38	34	35	37	34	32
White......	..	..	34	35	33	30
Negro......	..	..	54	57	53	54
Southeast: All........	44	45	47	49	45	41
White......	..	..	44	44	41	37
Negro......	..	..	55	59	57	56

Item	1930	1932	1934	1936	1938
Number pupils in average daily attendance					
United States: All............	21,264,886	22,245,344	22,458,190	22,298,767	22,298,200
White............	19,593,073	20,442,498	20,564,195	20,413,077	20,408,404
Negro............	1,671,813	1,802,846	1,893,995	1,885,690	1,889,796
Southeast: All............	4,784,215	5,063,511	5,184,315	5,248,954	5,288,468
White............	3,414,021	3,585,911	3,632,011	3,709,343	3,751,573
Negro............	1,370,194	1,477,600	1,552,304	1,539,611	1,536,395
Ratio of attendance to enrollment					
United States: All...........	82.8	84.7	85.0	84.6	85.8
White...........	83.7	85.5	85.7	85.3	86.6
Negro...........	73.2	76.6	77.9	77.3	78.4
Southeast: All...........	76.1	79.1	79.1	79.7	81.2
White...........	77.5	80.2	79.8	80.7	82.5
Negro...........	72.8	76.4	77.5	77.4	78.3
Number of teachers*					
United States: All...........	880,365	892,945	869,316	893,347	918,715
White...........	828,910	838,703	814,116	834,390	856,986
Negro...........	51,455	54,242	55,200	58,957	61,729
Southeast: All...........	174,366	178,270	173,454	186,300	197,246
White...........	133,366	135,630	129,964	140,267	148,811
Negro...........	41,000	42,640	43,490	46,033	48,435
Pupil-teacher ratio**					
United States: All...........	29	29	30	30	28
White...........	28	28	29	29	27
Negro...........	44	43	44	40	39
Southeast: All...........	36	36	38	35	33
White...........	33	33	35	33	31
Negro...........	46	45	46	43	41

*Teachers including principals and supervisors but excluding superintendents and other officials.
**Pupil-teacher ratio as computed here is the ratio of pupils enrolled to all teachers including principals and supervisors.
Note: Data for 1871 and 1880 partly estimated for the Southeast. Educational Statistics are given for 1871 and not for 1870, because since 1870-1871 the school year begins from September 1, and not from January 1, as it did formerly, and therefore statistics for 1870 are incomplete. Estimates for 1870 are only given for the Nation as a whole.
Source: See Table 120.

cational services. During this period, the number of school buildings has increased 97 percent in the Nation and 115 percent in the Southeast (Table 125). From 1890 to 1938, the value of school property per building increased from $1,526 to $31,018 in the Nation and from $343 to $13,531 in the region, a national increase of twenty fold as against a regional increase of thirty-nine fold (Table 126). This increase in value indicates the gradual trend toward abandonment of the one-room schoolhouse. From 1920 to 1938 the Nation saw its proportion of one-room school buildings decline from 70 to 53 percent, the region from 65 to 43 percent (Table 125). In 1880 the Nation had school property valued at $21 per pupil enrolled, the Southeast at only $3. By 1938 this had increased to $274 for the nation and $110 for the region. Although since 1880 the region's original per pupil property values had been multiplied by 36.6 as compared with 13 for the Nation, they were still only 40.1 percent of the national average per school child.

From 1871 to 1938 the Nation increased its total expenditures for education thirty-fivefold, rising from $63,397,000 to $2,233,110,000 (Table 126). Expenditures in the Southeast were increased more than sixtyfold, rising from $4,112,000 to $259,863,000. Expenditures per pupil enrolled in the region were half the Nation's average in 1871, $4 to $8. Both figures have been multiplied about tenfold, but the region has a lower ratio in 1938, $40 to $86, than in 1871 (Figure 247). In the region more of the increased expenditures have been devoted to enrolling the unenrolled children of school age.

From 1880 to 1938 the Nation increased its total salaries paid to public school teachers from $55,943,000 to $1,262,392,000, a twenty-two fold

TABLE 125. STATISTICS OF EDUCATION, UNITED STATES AND SOUTHEAST, 1871-1938

Item	1871	1880	1890	1900	1910	1920	1930	1932	1934	1936	1938
Number of schoolhouses:											
United States	116,312	178,122	224,526	248,279	265,474	271,319	247,289	245,941	241,428	238,867	229,394
Southeast	24,593	....	55,902	64,268	64,946	68,829	57,733	56,339	54,863	55,321	52,765
One-room schoolhouses:											
United States	......	......	......	......	......	189,227	148,712	143,445	138,542	132,813	121,178
Southeast	......	......	......	......	......	44,562	30,615	29,120	27,543	25,831	22,501
One-room schoolhouses as percent of total:											
United States	......	......	......	......	......	70	60	58	57	56	53
Southeast	......	......	......	......	......	65	53	52	50	47	43
Average length of school term:											
United States											
All	132	130	135	144	158	162	173	171	172	173	174
Negro						120	132	135	142	146	153
Southeast											
All	77	75	86	96	123	133	151	154	153	158	164
White						140	164	160	160	167	166
Negro						115	132	124	138	143	154

Note: Average length of school-term is the mean length for the United States and for the Southeast, the median value for the 11 Southeastern States.
Source: See Table 120.

TABLE 126. FINANCIAL STATISTICS OF EDUCATION, UNITED STATES AND
SOUTHEAST, 1871-1938

Item	1871	1880	1890	1900	1910	1920	1930	1932	1934	1936	1938
Total expenditure ($1,000):											
United States	63,397	78,095	140,507	214,965	426,250	1,036,151	2,316,790	2,174,651	1,720,105	1,968,898	2,233,110
Southeast	4,112	6,076	11,876	15,677	38,706	99,777	234,052	213,600	178,531	217,523	259,863
Expenditure per pupil enrolled (dollars per capita):											
United States	8	8	11	14	24	48	90	83	65	75	86
Southeast	4	3	4	4	9	18	37	33	27	33	40
Total salaries to teachers* ($1,000):											
United States	37,833	55,943	91,836	137,688	253,915	613,405	1,250,118	1,265,303	1,066,651	1,146,164	1,262,392
Southeast		4,856	9,707	13,129	27,739	64,253	143,603	136,512	114,727	129,548	152,750
Average salary per teacher* (dollars per capita):											
United States	189	195	252	325	485	871	1,420	1,417	1,227	1,283	1,374
Southeast		106	144	163	275	478	824	766	661	695	774
Total value of school property ($1,000):											
United States	130,383	209,572	342,532	550,069	1,091,008	2,409,719	6,211,327	6,581,540	6,624,771	6,731,325	7,115,377
Southeast		7,021	16,789	24,716	79,742	219,320	646,376	671,166	631,692	667,526	713,979
Value per pupil enrolled (dollars per capita):											
United States	17	21	27	35	61	112	242	250	251	255	274
Southeast		3	5	6	18	39	103	105	96	101	110
Value per schoolhouse (dollars per capita):											
United States	1,121	1,177	1,526	2,216	4,110	8,881	25,118	26,761	27,440	28,180	31,018
Southeast			343	385	1,228	3,186	11,196	11,913	11,514	12,066	13,531

*Teachers including supervisors and principals, but excluding superintendents and other State or county administrative officials.
Note: Data for 1871 and 1880 for the Southeast are based on incomplete reports and were partly estimated. All figures refer to public schools only, elementary and high schools combined.
Source: See Table 120.

increase. In the Southeast such expenditures rose from $4,856,000 to $152,750,000, a thirty-onefold increase. In 1880 the average annual salaries of teachers were ridiculously low, $106 for a 75 day term in the Southeast and $195 for a 130 day term in the Nation, with the regional average salary only 54.3 percent of the national salary. By 1938 these averages had grown to $774 and $1,374, but the ratio of the Southeast to the Nation was 50.4 percent, no proportionate gain (Figure 248). In terms of comparative educational advance, it has required hard running for the Southeast to stand still. To catch up with national standards may demand a greater burst of speed than the region can muster.

In summary how does the Southeast, after seventy years of striving for educational progress, compare with other regions? Table 127 and Figure 249 are presented to show the extent to which the six regions varied from the national average in six measures of educational progress in 1938. The Far West and the Northeast share educational leadership, exceeding the national average by anywhere from 20 to 75 percent. More than any other region the Middle States fall around the national average. The Southeast is shown to lag in every particular, followed by the Southwest in four measures. The three rural regions—Northwest, Southeast, and Southwest— share negative deviations on economic indices. Least consistent is the Northwest, which deviates positively from the national average in four measures, negatively in two others.

FIGURE 247. TOTAL ANNUAL EXPENDITURES PER PUPIL ENROLLED IN PUBLIC
SCHOOLS, UNITED STATES AND SOUTHEAST, 1871-1940

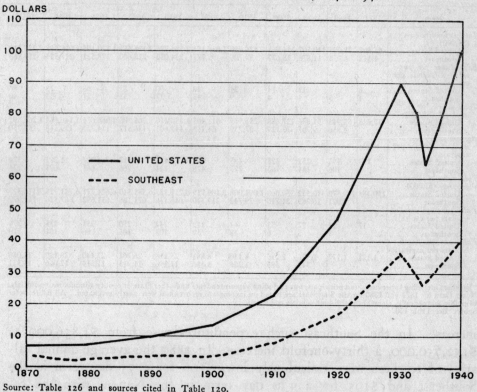

Source: Table 126 and sources cited in Table 120.

FIGURE 248. AVERAGE SALARY PER TEACHER, UNITED STATES
AND SOUTHEAST, 1871-1940

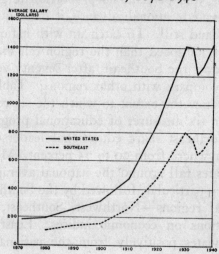

Source: Table 126.

TABLE 127. REGIONAL DIFFERENTIALS IN EDUCATIONAL STATISTICS
(PERCENTAGE DEVIATIONS FROM UNITED STATES VALUES),
1937-1938

Educational statistics	Percentage deviations from United States values					
	Northeast	Southeast	Southwest	Middle States	Northwest	Far West
Cost of education per pupil enrolled....	+37.5	−54.2	−26.4	+ 9.7	− 4.2	+45.8
Average annual salary of teachers*....	+37.0	−43.7	−24.0	+ 0.4	−30.9	+45.2
Average value of school property per pupil............................	+39.4	−59.9	−35.0	+20.1	+ 1.1	+25.2
Enrollment in high school as percentage of total enrollment............	+13.8	−32.5	− 7.1	+10.4	+11.7	+22.5
Number of teachers per 1,000 pupils**.	− 1.0	− 8.9	+ 2.3	+ 2.3	+32.8	− 4.6
College enrollment as percentage of population 19-22 years, inclusive...	+ 0.6	−34.4	− 6.5	+ 6.5	+15.2	+76.8

*Includes supervisors and principals but excludes superintendents.
**Ratio of number of teachers employed excluding principals and supervisors per 1,000 pupils in average daily attendance.
Source: Federal Security Agency, U. S. Office of Education, *Statistics of State School Systems*, 1937-1938, Bulletin No. 2, 1940; *Statistics of Higher Education* (press release June, 1940).

FIGURE 249. REGIONAL VARIATIONS, POSITIVE AND NEGATIVE, FROM
NATIONAL AVERAGES IN EDUCATION, 1937-1938

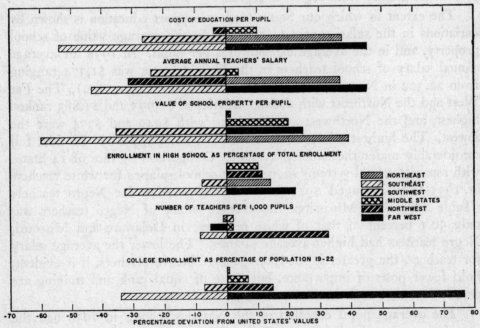

Source: Table 127.

CHAPTER 28

THE ECONOMICS OF EDUCATION

WITHIN LIMITS the education of all the people, like public health, must be regarded as a purchasable commodity. It competes in the public mind with the necessity of supporting other social services and is limited in extent by the economic resources and interests of the people. In spite of the almost unanimous devotion of the American people to education, its support varies greatly from region to region.

The extent to which our States tend to support education is shown by variations in the salaries paid to teachers, in the average value of school property, and in the average expenditures per pupil. In 1938 the average annual salary of school teachers in the United States was $1,374 ranging from $2,322 in New York to $479 in Mississippi (Figure 250). The Far West and the Northeast with average salaries of $1,995 and $1,883 ranked highest, and the Northwest and Southeast with $949 and $774 were the lowest. The highest salary in the Southeast, $1,003, paid in Florida, fell considerably under the national average. Comparison by race of 14 States with separate school systems showed that school salaries for white teachers in 1935-1936 averaged $947 as compared to $646 for Negro teachers (Table 128). In Mississippi the average salary of Negro teachers was only 30.1 percent of that of white teachers; in Delaware and Missouri, Negro teachers had higher average salaries. The lower the average salary for teachers, the greater is the discrepancy. Negro teachers, it is evident, hold fewer posts of importance, but those of equal rank and training are on a lower salary scale in the Southeast.

The average pupil enrolled in the Nation's schools in 1938 had the use of property valued at $274. Depending on where he lived, this varied from $81 in Tennessee to $470 in New York (Figure 251). Values in the Northeast, $382, were more than three times as great as those in the Southeast, $110. Florida, again the best State in the Southeast, attained an average property value of only $210 per pupil enrolled. A comparison in 10

FIGURE 250. AVERAGE ANNUAL SALARY PER TEACHER, PUBLIC SCHOOLS, UNITED STATES, 1938

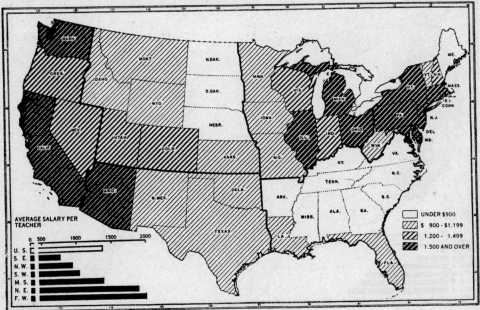

Source: *Statistics of State School Systems, 1937-1938*. Bulletin, 1940, No. 2, Table 17, p. 98; Table 32, p. 120.

TABLE 128. AVERAGE SALARY OF TEACHERS, PRINCIPALS, AND SUPERVISORS, BY RACE, FOURTEEN STATES, 1935-1936

State	White	Negro	Ratio of average salary of Negro to white teachers (percent)	State	White	Negro	Ratio of average salary of Negro to white teachers (percent)
All States reporting .	$ 947	$ 646	68.2	Arkansas..........	$ 550	$ 316	57.4
Missouri...........	1,031	1,332	129.2	Florida............	1,030	493	47.8
Delaware...........	1,538	1,664	108.1	Louisiana..........	931	403	43.3
Oklahoma..........	926	821	88.7	Alabama..........	709	328	42.6
Maryland..........	1,515	1,187	78.3	Georgia...........	709	282	39.8
North Carolina.....	811	543	68.9	South Carolina.....	825	302	36.6
Texas.............	991	604	60.9	Mississippi........	788	247	30.1
Virginia...........	901	520	57.6				

Note: The average salary in each case was weighted by the corresponding number of positions.
Source: Advisory Committee on Education, *Education in the Forty-Eight States* (1939), p. 100.

Southern States by race in 1936 showed the average value of school buildings, sites, and equipment to be only $36 per Negro pupil as compared with $183 for white pupils, a ratio of approximately one-fifth (Table 129). In Maryland the per capita value of school property for Negro pupils was a little over half that for white pupils; in Mississippi, only 7.3 percent. Equipment for Negro schools was even more meager.

A better index is the amount spent on education. The average cost of education per pupil enrolled in public schools, which includes all current

FIGURE 251. Average Value of School Property per Pupil Enrolled in Public Schools, United States, 1938

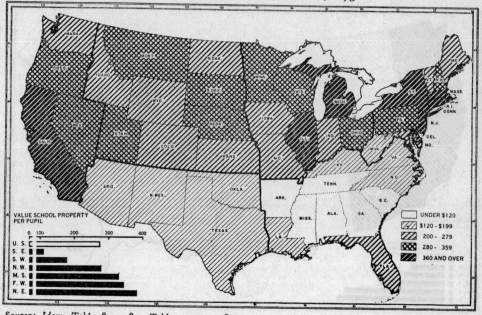

Source: *Idem*, Table 8, p. 83; Table 24, p. 108.

TABLE 129. Value of School Property per Pupil Enrolled, by Race, Ten States, 1935-1936

State	Value of sites, buildings and equipment		Ratio of Negro to white value per pupil (percent)	State	Value of sites, buildings and equipment		Ratio of Negro to white value per pupil (percent)
	Per white pupil	Per Negro pupil			Per white pupil	Per Negro pupil	
All States reporting ..	$183	$ 36	19.7	Georgia............	$103	$ 22	21.3
				Florida.............	248	49	19.8
Maryland............	273	151	55.3	Alabama...........	111	20	18.1
Virginia.............	146	44	30.1	South Carolina......	145	24	16.5
North Carolina......	158	46	29.7	Mississippi.........	147	11	7.3
Arkansas...........	103	24	23.3				
Texas..............	282	63	22.3				

Source: Advisory Committee on Education, *Education in the Forty-Eight States* (Washington, D. C., 1939), p. 116. Enrollment and value of school property for all pupils taken from *Biennial Survey of Education, 1935-1936*, pp. 103, 81; and for Negro pupils only from David T. Blose and Ambrose Caliver, *Statistics of the Education of Negroes, 1933-1934* and *1935-1936*, Office of Education, Bulletin No. 13, Table 28.

expenses exclusive of interest and capital outlay, was $72 in 1938, ranging from $22 in Mississippi to $130 in New York (Figure 252). The Far West spent $105, more than three times the $33 expended per pupil in the Southeast. Both the Northwest with $69, and the Southwest with $53, fell below the national average. Only Florida in the Southeast spent as much as $49. Expenditures in 1936 per Negro child 5-17 in the Southeast were 15.4 percent of the national average, for the average white child in the Southeast, they were 59.6 percent (Table 130). Table 130 shows how

FIGURE 252. ANNUAL COST OF EDUCATION PER PUPIL ENROLLED IN
PUBLIC SCHOOLS, UNITED STATES, 1938

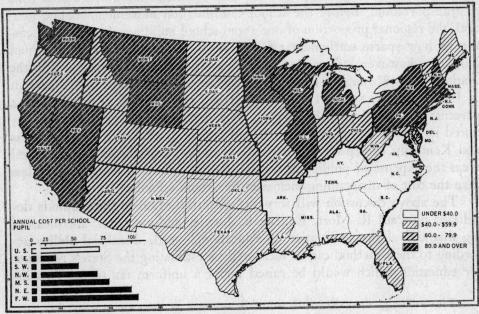

Source: *Idem*, Table 8, p. 84; Table 34, p. 124.

TABLE 130. COMPARISON OF AVERAGE EXPENDITURE ON EDUCATION, BY RACE,
UNITED STATES AND SOUTHEAST, 1935-1936

Item of expenditure	United States all (percent)	Ratio of Southeast Value to National Total			Item of expenditure	United States all (percent)	Ratio of Southeast Value to National Total		
		All (percent)	White (percent)	Negro (percent)			All (percent)	White (percent)	Negro (percent)
Average salary per teacher*...........	100.0	54.2	62.0	30.4	Average value of school property per child 5-17 years of age.	100.0	39.9	53.5	10.8
Average current expenditure per child 5-17 years of age.....	100.0	44.2	59.6	15.4	Average value per school building........	100.0	42.8	64.8	9.0

*Includes principals and supervisors.
Source: United States Office of Education, *Statistics of State School Systems, 1935-1936*, Bulletin No. 2, 1937; *Statistics of the Education of Negroes, 1935-1936*, Bulletin No. 13, 1938.

the Southeast, white and colored, ranked in per unit measures in comparison with the Nation in 1938. Average expenditures and values for white schools usually amounted to 60 percent of the Nation's average; for Negro schools they rarely exceeded 15 percent.

These comparisons, it will be realized, are hardly adequate to indicate the differences in the level of education the country over. It costs more for teachers to live in New York than in Mississippi, and thus it can be assumed that teachers' salaries and per pupil expenditures can be somewhat larger without providing better instruction. Conversely, the small classes found in sparsely settled rural areas are more expensive, and, if overcome by consolidation of rural schools, the improvement necessitates added costs of transportation. Before the school-consolidation movement became general, the regional proportion of one-room school buildings served as a measure of how sparse settlement affected rural education. One-room school buildings, however, still made up 52.8 percent of all such structures in the Nation in 1938, ranging from 88 percent in South Dakota to 7.2 percent in Utah (Figure 253). The Far West had the smallest proportion, 26.4 percent; the Northwest the largest, 71.7 percent. The Southeast had reduced its proportion of one-room school houses to 42.6 with only Arkansas and Kentucky exceeding the national average. Consolidation gives rural areas the expense of public bus transportation—which in many cases is less than the cost of maintaining inefficient one-room schools.

The above discussion will serve as an introduction to the methods developed by Paul R. Mort, Eugene R. Lawler and associates[1] for measuring financial ability in relation to educational need. Financial ability according to their method can be measured by estimating the State's revenues for education which would be raised under a uniform tax plan. This in-

FIGURE 253. ONE-ROOM SCHOOL BUILDINGS AS PERCENTAGE OF ALL SCHOOL BUILDINGS, UNITED STATES, 1938

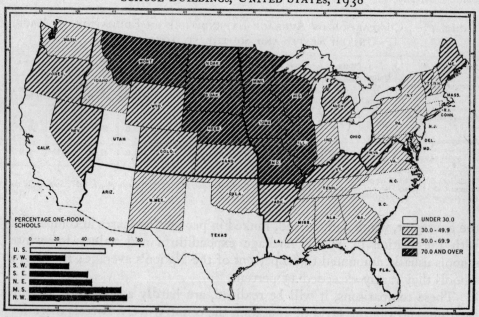

Source: *Idem*, Figure 10, p. 50; Table 23, p. 106.

[1] *Federal Support for Education* (New York: Columbia University Press, 1936); *Principles and Methods of Distributing Federal Aid for Education* (Washington, D. C.: U. S. Government Printing Office, 1939).

volves the knowledge not only of total income but of the distribution of income among groups. In order to determine the units of educational need they applied correction factors by States to all children of school age, 5-17. In sparsely settled rural areas a graduated correction factor not to exceed 1.70 was applied to allow for the high cost of small classes or the transportation expenses attendant upon consolidation of rural schools. In larger communities with higher costs of living a correction factor was applied, ranging from 1.00 in communities of 2,500 to 10,000 to 1.30 in communities of 500,000 and over. The results are called units of educational need instead of children of school age.

Figure 254 uses this method to present indices of the difficulty each State faces in educating its children of school age. The index of educational need results from applying the correction factors to the population residence breakdown and is thus the ratio of the computed number of units of educational need to the number of children, 5-17. As Figure 254 indicates, the index of educational need ranged from 1.51 in the Northwest to 1.24 in the Northeast. By States the range is from 1.62 for North Dakota to 1.19 for New Jersey. Twenty States, all rural, exceed the national average in the general measure of the difficulty of educating children 5-17, four

FIGURE 254. INDEX OF EDUCATIONAL NEED, UNITED STATES, 1930

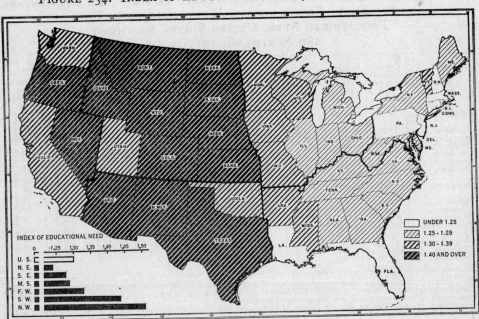

Source: Mort and Lawler, *Principles and Methods of Distributing Federal Aid to Education*, 1939, pp. 68-69.

fall on the average, and 24 fall below it. It is notable that none of the Southeastern States exceed the national index of 1.30. Unlike the Plains States of the West, rural population in the Southeast in the main has sufficient density of settlement to admit a cost of education below the national average.

Table 131 (columns 2 and 3) shows that in 1935-1936 the United States had over 41.6 million such units concentrated mainly in the Northeast, with 27.8 percent of the Nation's total, and the Middle States, with 26 percent. The Southeast came next with 24 percent, and the Far West was last with only 5.7 percent. When actual educational expenditures are reduced to these terms (Table 131, column 1, and Figure 255), it is found that the United States spends an average of $39.79 per unit of educational need as compared with $65.06 in the Far West and $18.03 in the Southeast. As might be expected, the three rural regions fall below the national average, and the three urban regions rise above it. Figures 256 and 257 compare these expenditures in relation to the needs of States within the two contrasting regions, the Southeast and the Northeast. They should be compared with the chart of the regions, Figure 255. The dotted guide lines represent a minimum expenditure of $48 per unit necessary to secure a defensible foundation program.[2]

TABLE 131. DISTRIBUTION OF CURRENT EXPENDITURE FOR PUBLIC ELEMENTARY AND SECONDARY EDUCATION PER WEIGHTED CENSUS UNIT OF EDUCATIONAL NEED, UNITED STATES, SOUTHEAST, AND NORTHEAST, 1935-1936

Area	Current expenditure per unit (Dollars)	Number weighted units (Thousands)	Percentage distribution of units	Cumulative percentage	Area	Current expenditure per unit (Dollars)	Number weighted units (Thousands)	Percentage distribution of units	Cumulative percentage
UNITED STATES..	39.79	41,639	100.0	100.0	Virginia.........	20.38	933	9.3	87.6
					Louisiana........	21.77	751	7.5	95.1
Southeast......	18.03	9,983	24.0	24.0	Florida..........	33.53	493	4.9	100.0
Southwest.....	24.65	3,797	9.1	33.1					
Middle States..	42.46	10,809	26.0	66.3	NORTHEAST......	56.40	11,559	100.0	100.0
Northwest......	35.96	3,001	7.2	40.3					
Northeast......	56.40	11,559	27.8	94.1	Maine..........	32.65	251	2.2	2.2
Far West......	65.06	2,373	5.7	99.8	Vermont........	33.58	116	1.0	3.2
					West Virginia....	33.68	678	5.8	9.0
SOUTHEAST......	18.03	9,983	100.0	100.0	Maryland........	36.08	527	4.5	13.5
					New Hampshire..	42.30	137	1.2	14.7
Arkansas.......	12.16	728	7.3	7.3	Pennsylvania....	44.70	3,119	27.0	41.7
Alabama.......	14.55	1,064	10.7	18.0	Rhode Island....	48.75	204	1.8	43.5
Mississippi.....	15.48	810	8.1	26.1	Connecticut.....	50.92	494	4.3	47.8
South Carolina .	15.71	750	7.5	33.6	Delaware........	54.02	74	0.6	48.4
Georgia........	15.82	1,136	11.4	45.0	Massachusetts...	61.59	1,165	10.1	58.5
North Carolina.	17.53	1,348	13.5	58.5	New Jersey......	62.33	1,188	10.3	68.8
Tennessee......	18.72	984	9.9	68.4	New York........	74.28	3,606	31.2	100.0
Kentucky......	19.66	986	9.9	78.3					

Note: Current expenditure on education excludes interest and capital outlay. Weighted units of educational need are computed by multiplying the number of children 5-17 years of age in each locality by a correction factor allowing for variations in need depending on the cost of living or the sparsity of population.
Source: Mort and Lawler, *Principles and Methods of Distributing Federal Aid for Education* (1939), p. 68, Table 15 and p. 12, Table 1.

[2] Mort and Lawler, *Principles and Methods of Distributing Federal Aid for Education* (Washington, D. C.: U. S. Government Printing Office, 1939), p. 20.

AVERAGE CURRENT EXPENDITURES FOR PUBLIC EDUCATION PER UNIT OF
EDUCATIONAL NEED, 1935-1936

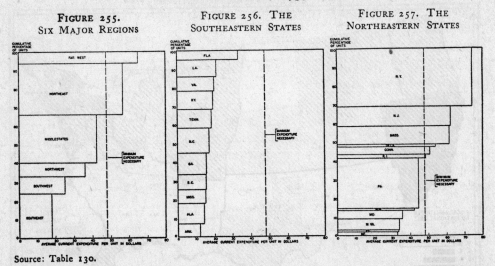

FIGURE 255.
SIX MAJOR REGIONS

FIGURE 256. THE
SOUTHEASTERN STATES

FIGURE 257. THE
NORTHEASTERN STATES

Source: Table 130.

The weakness of the Southeast is found in the lack of financial ability
to support education. Comparison of the financial strength of States is
made by the application of a uniform tax plan consisting of six separate
taxes. Under conditions as of 1935-1936, this tax is estimated to yield
almost 2.7 billion dollars. For the Nation this would give $65 per unit
of educational need, ranging from $26 in the Southeast to $105 in the
Northeast (Figure 258). The range of the States is from an estimated
yield of $15 per unit in Mississippi to $188 in Delaware.

Ability to support education at an adequate level may be regarded as a
result of the relation between the units of need in each area and the amount
of taxable wealth and income. The task of relating educational need to
financial ability to support education is attempted in Table 132 where the
41.6 million units of educational need in the Nation are related to the
$2,692,728,000 that would be raised by the uniform tax plan. The North-
east has 27.8 percent of the national educational needs and 45.2 percent
of its financial ability to support education, a ratio of .61. The Southeast at
the other extreme has 24 percent of the needs to 9.8 percent of capacity,
a ratio of 2.45. Figure 259 indicates that by States this ratio goes from the
extreme of Mississippi, where need is 4.24 times financial ability, to Delaware, where need is only one-third of ability. In all the Southeastern
States except Virginia and Florida, need exceeds ability by more than two
to one.

How do States of differing needs and financial ability compare in the
efforts they put forth to support education? To some extent this may be

FIGURE 258. FINANCIAL ABILITY OF STATES TO SUPPORT EDUCATION PER UNIT
OF EDUCATIONAL NEED, UNITED STATES, 1935-1936

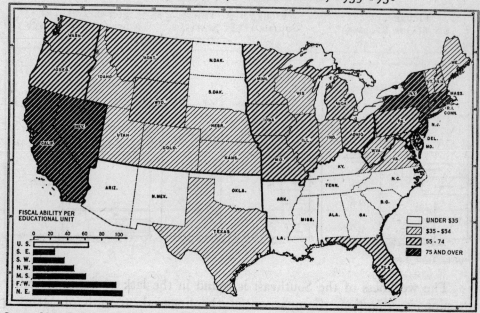

Source: Mort, Lawler and Associates, *op. cit.*, Table 10, p. 50; Table 15, p. 68.

TABLE 132. RATIO OF THE PERCENTAGE OF EDUCATIONAL NEED TO THE
PERCENTAGE OF FINANCIAL ABILITY, UNITED STATES AND
THE SIX MAJOR REGIONS, 1935-1936

Area	Educational need		Financial ability		Ratio of percent need to percent ability
	Thousands of units	Percentage distribution	Thousands of dollars	Percentage distribution	
	(1)	(2)	(3)	(4)	(5) = (2) ÷ (4)
UNITED STATES.............	41,639	100.00	2,692,728	100.00	1.00
Northeast..................	11,559	27.77	1,217,706	45.22	0.61
Southeast..................	9,983	23.96	263,490	9.78	2.45
Southwest.................	3,797	9.12	138,664	5.15	1.77
Middle States..............	10,809	25.97	670,969	24.92	1.04
Northwest.................	3,001	7.20	143,563	5.33	1.35
Far West..................	2,373	5.70	231,505	8.60	0.66
District of Columbia........	117	0.28	26,831	1.00	0.28

Note: Financial ability measured by the estimated yield of a uniform tax plan applied to the various States and including 6 separate taxes (progressive personal income tax, real estate tax, business income tax, stock transfer tax, severance tax, and corporation organization tax). Educational need expressed in "weighted census units" which represent the number of children 5-17 years of age in 1935 in each community multiplied by a correction factor which takes care of the variations in educational need in connection with the costs of living or density of population in the community.
Source: Mort and Lawler, *op. cit.*, p. 68, Table 15, and p. 50, Table 10.

measured by the degree to which citizens will limit other public services in order to pay for public education. Figure 260 ranks the States according to the proportion of tax collections that are spent on public education. Wealthy States with the best records spend the smallest proportion of their taxes on education while the States of the Far West and Southeast, often

FIGURE 259. THE RATIO OF EDUCATIONAL NEED TO FINANCIAL ABILITY,
UNITED STATES, 1935-1936

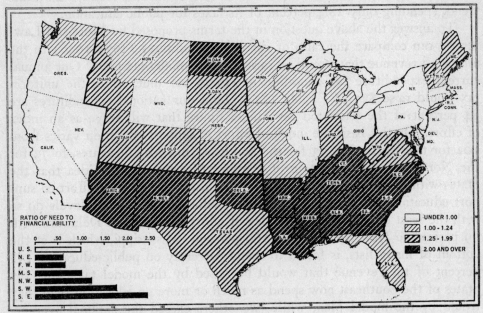

Source: Mort, Lawler and Associates, *op. cit.*, Table 18, p. 88.

FIGURE 260. RANK OF STATES ACCORDING TO PERCENTAGE OF TAX COLLEC-
TIONS SPENT FOR PUBLIC SCHOOLS, UNITED STATES, 1938

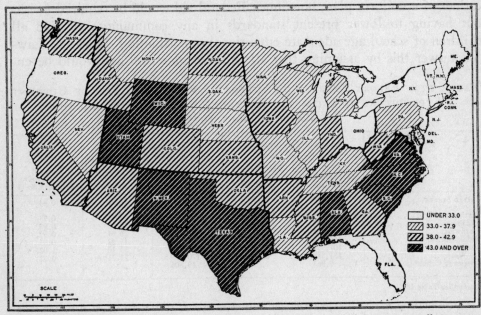

Source: National Education Association: "School Costs and State Expenditures." *Research Bulletin,* 1941.

with the poorest records, spend 43 percent or more of their tax dollars. Florida, which makes the best record in the Southeast, follows the same trend, spending only 28.4 percent of its taxes for public education.

To answer the above question in the terms proposed by Mort and Lawler we can compare the ratio of current expenditures (1935-1936) to the estimated revenue that would be raised by the model tax plan.[8] Our annual current expenditure for education is $39.79 per unit, while the uniform tax would raise $47.53 (Table 133). Thus our national expenditures are 84 percent of the estimated revenue, a figure that will serve as an index of effort. On this basis the index of effort to support education varies from 102 for the Northwest, 93 for the Southeast and Middle States, to 73 for the Northeast. An inspection of Figure 261 bears out the idea that the States with the poorest educational record exert the greatest effort to support education, while those who support education at highest levels do so with the least effort. Thus the index of effort ranged from Delaware with 39 percent to New Mexico with 160 percent. Mississippi, which is at the bottom of many lists, is found to spend currently on public education 138 percent of the revenue that would be raised by the model tax plan. Six States of the Southeast now spend as much or more on education than they would by the model plan, while two others exceed the national average. Nevertheless all these States fall below the Nation's average in expenditures for education and in other measurements of educational standards.

If every State used all of its tax resources according to the best indications of a uniform plan, how much Federal aid would be required (without having to lower present standards in any community) to give all children of school age adequate educational opportunities? Mort and Lawler answer this by assuming that all children of school age would be en-

TABLE 133. EFFORT EXERTED TO SUPPORT EDUCATION (RATIO OF CURRENT EXPENDITURE TO ESTIMATED REVENUE) UNITED STATES AND THE SIX MAJOR REGIONS, 1935-1936

Area	Actual current expenditure		Estimated revenue		Ratio of expenditure to revenue (Effort)
	Total (Thousands of dollars)	Per weighted census unit (Dollars)	Total (Thousands of dollars)	Per weighted census unit (Dollars)	
UNITED STATES..............	1,656,799	39.79	1,979,156	47.53	0.84
Northeast...................	651,976	56.40	894,928	77.42	0.73
Southeast..................	179,945	18.03	193,670	19.40	0.93
Southwest.................	93,605	24.65	101,928	26.84	0.92
Middle States.............	459,012	42.46	493,149	45.62	0.93
Northwest.................	107,914	35.96	105,516	35.16	1.02
Far West..................	154,386	65.06	170,159	71.71	0.91
District of Columbia........	9,961	.....	19,806	.....	....

Source: See Table 131.

[8] Here estimated revenue is computed on the basis of an average effort equal for all states and therefore is only 73 percent of financial ability which assumes maximum effort.

FIGURE 261. EFFORT EXERTED TO SUPPORT EDUCATION: RATIO OF EXPENDITURES TO ESTIMATED REVENUES UNDER UNIFORM TAX SYSTEM, UNITED STATES, 1935-1936

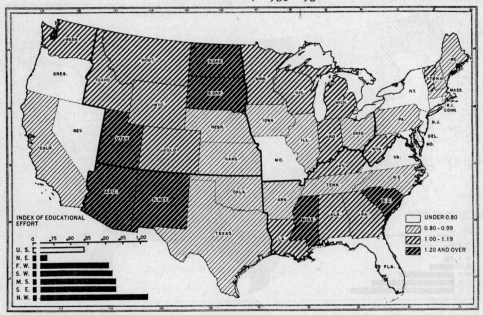

Source: Mort and Lawler, *op. cit.*, Ch. III, p. 20.

TABLE 134. FEDERAL AID NECESSARY TO ENABLE ALL STATES TO PROVIDE ADEQUATE SUPPORT TO EDUCATION, UNITED STATES AND THE SIX MAJOR REGIONS, 1935-1936

Area	Total amount (Thousands of dollars)	Per weighted census unit (Dollars)	Actual expenditure per unit (Dollars)	Area	Total amount (Thousands of dollars)	Per weighted census unit (Dollars)	Actual expenditure per unit (Dollars)
UNITED STATES...	575,665	13.83	39.79	Southwest.......	91,911	24.21	24.65
				Middle States....	85,211	7.88	42.46
Northeast........	35,900	3.11	56.40	Northwest.......	50,939	16.97	35.96
Southeast........	306,186	30.67	18.03	Far West........	5,518	2.33	65.06

Note: Total amount of Federal aid as given here is the amount computed according to plan I (distribution in proportion to financial need in order to secure a "defensible foundation program" with a minimum of $48 annual current expenditure per unit in all communities without placing additional handicaps on local initiative); weighted census units of educational need computed by multiplying the number of children 5-17 years of age in each locality by the index of educational need; third column gives the actual current expenditure per weighted census unit.
Source: Mort and Lawler, *op. cit.*, p. 20, Table 3 and p. 68, Table 15. *Biennial Survey of Education;* Office of Education, *Statistics of State School Systems, 1935-1936,* Bulletin No. 2, 1937, Tables 3 and 26.

rolled and that a minimum of $48 would be spent on each pupil allowing for the corrections for rural and urban conditions. To carry out such a program as of 1935-1936 would cost $575,665,000 in Federal aid (Table 134). Over half the sum, $306,186,000 in fact, would go to the Southeast, where Federal aid of over $30 per educational unit is needed. For the Nation the average sum needed per unit would be $13.83, as compared with only $3.11 in the Northeast and $2.33 in the Far West. As Figure 262

FIGURE 262. FEDERAL AID PER EDUCATIONAL UNIT NECESSARY TO ENABLE
ALL STATES TO PROVIDE ADEQUATE SUPPORT TO EDUCATION,
UNITED STATES, 1935-1936

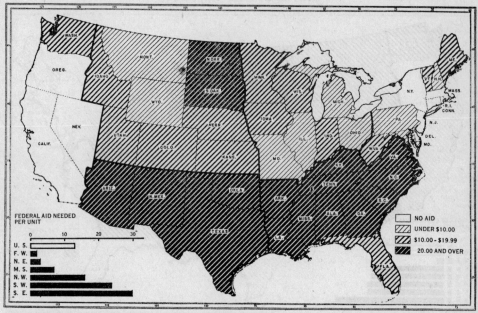

Source: Mort, Lawler and Associates, *op. cit.*, Table 20, p. 20.

shows, the nine ablest States would need no Federal aid to carry out this
program. After taxing themselves to capacity under the uniform plan, 16
States would still need $20 or more per unit of educational need. Missis-
sippi would need $37.78. The least need in the Southeast is found in Flor-
ida, amounting to $10.33 per unit. It has been suggested that the first use
to which such sums should be put in the South is to bring the Negro schools
up to adequate standards.

THE BASIS OF SUPPORT FOR EDUCATION

As public education has grown in this country from little to big business, it has found its traditional origin something of an economic handicap
in carrying out its professed aims. The task of education was originally
assumed by the local district which undertook the burden of tax support.
One of the great aims of education has been to equalize the cultural and
economic opportunities offered to our oncoming citizens. Here, however,
the local areas have of necessity been forced to perpetuate their own economic inequalities in the education of their children. Coming later into
the field, the Southeast found wide variations in the fiscal ability of local
districts. Thus the region has led in the movement to seek a wider basis
of tax support in the county and in the State.

TABLE 135. PERCENTAGES OF SCHOOL INCOME FROM STATE, COUNTY, AND LOCAL SOURCES, UNITED STATES, 1935-1936

State	Source			State	Source		
	Local	State	County		Local	State	County
UNITED STATES.........	63.5	29.4	7.1	North Dakota.........	64.0	24.3	11.7
				Arkansas..............	63.4	34.9	1.7
SOUTHEAST.............	28.3	45.3	26.3	New York.............	62.8	37.2	....
				Ohio.................	61.4	37.4	1.2
Nebraska..............	99.0	1.0	....	Idaho.................	59.6	6.7	33.7
South Dakota..........	97.5	2.5	....	Utah.................	56.3	43.7	....
Iowa.................	96.6	1.1	2.3	Michigan.............	55.2	44.5	0.3
Rhode Island..........	94.2	5.8	....	California............	50.6	48.2	1.2
New Hampshire........	92.4	7.6	....	Nevada...............	49.6	16.5	33.9
Connecticut...........	91.3	8.7	....	Maryland.............	46.0	23.6	30.4
Illinois..............	90.0	10.0	....	South Carolina........	45.4	49.8	4.8
Massachusetts.........	89.3	10.7	....	Washington...........	41.2	48.0	10.8
Kansas...............	84.8	0.3	14.9	Mississippi...........	39.4	41.8	18.8
Vermont..............	82.1	17.9	....	Texas................	35.6	54.3	10.1
Pennsylvania..........	78.8	21.2	....	Kentucky.............	34.9	40.0	25.1
New Jersey............	78.7	2.0	19.3	Florida...............	30.6	50.2	19.2
Montana.............	74.9	2.5	22.6	Virginia..............	29.6	32.7	37.7
Colorado.............	74.0	....	26.0	New Mexico...........	24.4	51.7	23.9
Indiana..............	73.5	26.5	....	Arizona..............	23.3	74.4	2.3
Wisconsin............	73.3	16.2	10.5	Tennessee............	20.0	23.6	56.4
Missouri.............	71.9	23.0	5.1	North Carolina.......	13.8	86.2	....
Maine...............	69.5	30.5	....	Louisiana.............	13.3	47.8	38.9
Oregon..............	69.5	....	30.5	Alabama..............	11.9	49.5	38.6
Oklahoma.............	69.8	30.2	....	Georgia..............	9.3	42.6	48.1
Minnesota............	66.6	29.2	4.2	Delaware.............	7.7	92.3	....
Wyoming.............	66.4	7.6	26.0	West Virginia.........	0.0	50.8	49.2

Source: Office of Education, *Statistics of State School Systems, 1937*, Bulletin No. 2, Figure 5 and Table 7 (Washington, D. C.: U. S. Government Printing Office).

The way each State meets this problem is largely a matter of historical development, and good plans can be found that have many variations in the degree of local, county, and State support of education.

The support of public education should be studied from both the point of view of (1) the level of government and (2) the type of tax. Thus it is estimated that for all the States in 1935-1936 the local school district furnished 63.5 percent of all school support; the State, 29.4 percent; and the county, 7.1 percent. Table 135 and Figure 263 show that the degree of support offered schools by the local district ranged from 99 percent in Nebraska to none in West Virginia. Similarly the proportion of school income furnished by the State government ranged from 92.3 percent in Delaware and 86.2 percent in North Carolina to none in Colorado and Oregon. Much less of the support of schools is undertaken by the county as a fiscal unit but here the variation ran from 56.4 percent in Tennessee to none in 16 States. In the Southeast, the State has assumed about 45 percent; the county, 26 percent; and the local district, 28 percent of tax support. Thus it is evident the Southeast has gone further than the Nation in transferring the tax burden from the local school district.

The type of tax employed bears a close relation to the unit of government shouldering the main support of education. Thus the main resource of both local and county units is still the general property tax—a tax largely on land, a form of property that has not been very productive of

FIGURE 263. THE PERCENTAGE OF PUBLIC SCHOOL INCOME DERIVED FROM STATE, COUNTY, AND LOCAL SOURCES, UNITED STATES, 1935-1936

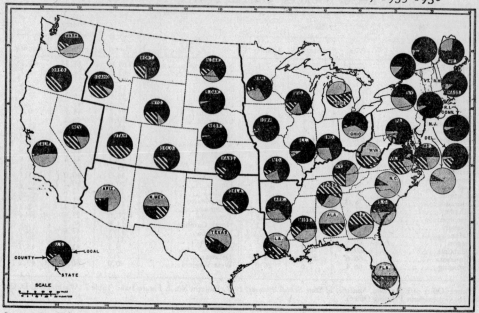

Source: See Table 135.

FIGURE 264. PERCENTAGE OF APPROPRIATIONS FOR PUBLIC SCHOOLS DERIVED FROM THE GENERAL PROPERTY TAX, UNITED STATES, 1935-1936

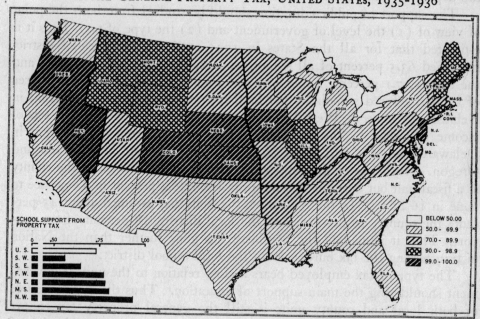

Source: See Table 136.

income between the two World Wars. In 1935-1936 this tax furnished 73.2 percent of the support of education, ranging from 100 percent in the five States of New Jersey, Colorado, Kansas, Nevada, and Oregon to 15.1 percent in North Carolina and 8.1 percent in Delaware (Table 136 and Figure 264). Business and miscellaneous taxes, largely corporation taxes, produce 8.7 percent of total support, ranging from 29.6 percent in South Carolina to nothing in six States.

TABLE 136. PERCENTAGE DISTRIBUTION OF STATE AND LOCAL TAXES APPROPRIATED FOR PUBLIC ELEMENTARY AND SECONDARY SCHOOLS, BY TYPE OF TAX, UNITED STATES, 1935-1936*

State	Property	General sales	Selected sales	Highway	Business and miscellaneous	Personal	State	Property	General sales	Selected sales	Highway	Business and miscellaneous	Personal
ALL STATES	73.2	7.0	4.4	2.2	8.7	4.5	Missouri	78.8	4.9	4.6	....	7.8	3.9
							Pennsylvania	78.9	(†)	6.7	....	10.7	3.7
SOUTHEAST	63.5	7.5	9.8	4.1	12.6	2.5	Minnesota	79.6	....	.7	....	14.4	5.3
							Tennessee	80.9	1.5	12.6	....	3.5	1.5
Delaware	8.1	....	1.9	....	69.7	22.2	Vermont	81.1	....	2.4	....	9.4	7.1
North Carolina	15.1	31.4	1.9	....	44.2	7.4	Wisconsin	84.2	....	2.2	....	9.2	4.4
							Indiana	85.6	4.3	7.7	....	2.1	.3
New Mexico	50.3	38.7	6.5	....	3.7	.8	Maryland	86.7	....	3.9	....	6.6	2.8
West Virginia	50.6	34.0	1.0	....	12.9	1.5	South Dakota	89.3	10.5	....	....	....	.2
California	51.8	29.6	4.4	....	8.8	5.4	Massachusetts	89.3	....	.1	....	.9	9.7
Arizona	52.5	22.4	10.8	....	10.0	4.3	Utah	89.7	5.0	....	....	2.8	2.5
South Carolina	56.0	....	10.5	....	29.6	3.9							
Florida	57.6	.6	4.6	26.8	5.2	5.2	Illinois	90.0	10.0	....	....	....	....
Washington	57.8	19.2	6.2	....	13.7	3.1	Connecticut	92.4	....	1.7	....	4.9	1.0
Michigan	58.1	14.8	3.5	....	21.1	2.5	Idaho	93.2	3.2	2.9	....	.7	....
Texas	58.5	....	20.1	15.9	5.1	.4	New Hampshire	94.4	....	2.6	....	2.4	.6
Ohio	62.7	18.4	5.6	8.6	4.6	.1	Wyoming	94.4	2.4	1.0	....	2.1	.1
Oklahoma	62.6	7.8	20.8	....	6.0	2.8	Rhode Island	95.3	....	.5	....	3.4	.8
New York	63.1	(†)	2.6	4.3	15.7	14.3	Montana	97.4	....	.7	....	1.0	.9
Mississippi	65.8	16.0	7.6	....	8.8	1.8	Maine	98.3	....	....	....	1.7	....
Louisiana	67.9	....	24.5	4.2	2.2	1.2							
Alabama	68.2	10.6	12.3	....	8.3	.6	Iowa	99.0	.2	.2	....	.5	.1
Georgia	69.0	(†)	3.7	14.0	11.2	2.1	Nebraska	99.7	....	.2	....	.1	(†)
							New Jersey	100.0	(†)	(†)	....	(†)	(†)
Kentucky	70.7	10.1	13.2	....	5.3	.7	Colorado	100.0	....	....	....	....	....
Virginia	70.8	....	6.6	....	19.8	2.8	Kansas	100.0	....	....	....	....	....
North Dakota	75.6	17.1	....	....	7.3	....	Nevada	100.0	....	....	....	....	....
Arkansas	76.7	12.5	10.7	....	.1	....	Oregon	100.0	....	....	....	....	....

*"Selected sales" include all commodity taxes except "general sales." "Personal" taxes include income, inheritance, and gift taxes. "Business and miscellaneous" taxes include the business taxes and the "all other nonproperty" taxes.
†Less than 0.05 percent.
Source: Clarence Heer, *Federal Aid and the Tax Problem* (Washington, D. C.: U. S. Government Printing Office, 1939), p. 41; Appendix D for sources of data and method of estimation; Table 8 for taxes included.

About 11.4 percent is raised through taxes on consumption. The general sales tax accounts for 7 percent, and the range is from New Mexico, where this tax contributed 38.7 percent of the support of education to 20 States which have no general sales tax. Special sales or luxury taxes are used by more States but contribute only 4.4 percent to the support of education in all the States. The range is from 24.5 percent of educational support in Louisiana to ten States making no use of such taxes.

Personal income and inheritance taxes, so important in the Federal budget, contribute approximately 4.5 percent to education in the States as a whole. Here the range is from 22.2 percent in Delaware to none in nine States. Highway taxes are used to support education in only six States, the largest use being in Florida, where they support 26.8 percent of the burden. In many States, some in the Southeast, the highway fund is well supported by gasoline and other taxes, while the educational budget is often in arrears. This has given rise to political struggles to "divert" part of the highway fund to the further use of State equalization funds in the support of public education. Unsuccessful as they have proved, these efforts bid fair to continue in States that are hard pressed to meet the educational budget.

CHAPTER 29

FROM THE GRASS ROOTS TO THE COLLEGE

THE PREDOMINANCE of the local district and the county unit in the support
of education gives play to valuable qualities of local self-government and
individual initiative, but it makes the variations in educational opportunity
within States much greater than we have indicated in discussing their comparative ranking. A great gulf still remains in the Southeast between the
educational opportunities offered in the urban and rural environments.
School facilities in the larger cities of the region usually rank well with
those throughout the Nation. It is the rural school districts with their lack
of standards and weak financial basis that lag woefully behind. In addition to their lower incomes and greater numbers of children per 1,000
adults, rural areas encounter all the difficulties inherent in low densities of
population, inadequate transportation to school centers, and cultural tra-
ditions too immature to give adequate support to education.

EDUCATION IN LOCAL AREAS OF THE RURAL SOUTHEAST

In a study of school services in an Arkansas county within the shadow
of the State University, J. L. Charlton[1] has analyzed these conditions. The
115 open-country school districts in the county contained 80 percent of the
farm population, but enrolled in high school only 11 percent of those of
high school age. The 14 districts which contained villages or towns with
4-year high schools enrolled more than 60 percent of their high school
population. These two groups contain basically the same type of people,
for the urban dwellers in the main have moved into town in the last generation. From this one fact their children are to profit greatly, at a ratio
of six to one, in access to education and its related cultural and material
rewards.

The central districts with their superior economic resources had fewer
children for whom to provide schools, and over a ten-year period received

[1] *School Services in Rural Communities in Washington County*, Bulletin No. 398 (Fayetteville, Arkansas: Arkansas Agricultural Experiment Station, 1940).

[437]

for support of schools nearly twice as much revenue per enumerate as did the open-country districts. Moreover, about 80 percent of the population of these districts was concentrated in the towns in which the high schools were located. Rural schools were deficient in length of term, in training of teachers, in buildings and equipment. Moderately well-off farmers in these rural districts often had to send their children to central districts and to pay tuition, even though they had paid the required tax for support of their own inadequate local schools. Poorer farmers were forced to see their children go without adequate education. One district was found from which no student had attended a 4-year high school in the preceding ten years. High school enrollments were found to vary with distance from the school and to change with changes in bus routes and transportation rather than with changes in wealth and income. The amount of taxable wealth to support education on the local district basis ranged from less than $300 per school enumerates in poor districts to over $1,200 in towns.

In a study of ten rural school districts in upland South Carolina, Henry L. Fulmer[2] showed how the education of the child is restricted by the limitation of the small school district. The management of these schools was in the hands of elected trustees who selected teachers, disbursed funds, and influenced the teaching program. In all the elementary schools, one or more teachers were related to trustees, and in most of the districts a change of trustees in a school election meant a change of teachers. In some districts trustees appointed teachers without advice or knowledge of school principals. The teachers were usually products of the local community and local schools and had had a median of 1.8 years of college training. There was little professional educational leadership and 24 of the 36 teachers did not belong to a teachers' association or group.

There was a high percentage of retardation; 48 percent of all the pupils had repeated one or more grades. By standard tests the scores of seventh grade pupils were found to be three to four years lower than those of the grade pupils in a nearby urban school. Eleventh grade pupils scored lower than urban eighth graders. These youth were not receiving the benefits of library services, recreational activities, and health education. No aids to teaching were used beyond the required State texts and routine class periods.

While the schools were routine and uninspiring, the study points out that some responsibility can be placed on the fact that the pupils are insufficiently and improperly nourished. Many farms did not produce enough meats, vegetables, fruits, and milk to feed the family. Three-fourths of the tenant families stated that they did not produce enough but-

[2] *An Analytical Study of a Rural School Area*, Bulletin No. 320 (Clemson, South Carolina: South Carolina Agricultural Experiment Station, 1939).

ter and milk for home needs, and 23 percent of these families had neither cows, hogs, nor home gardens. Medical examination by the county health department indicated that 90 percent of the pupils suffered from major health defects. Tax analysis showed that back of each school child there was only $297 worth of taxable property. From these meager resources there was allowed for school purposes the annual sum of $4.54 per pupil.

Such are the pictures of education in the countryside that are presented by realistic studies of the way the local district functions in the South's poorer agricultural areas. Deficiencies in rural education ranged all the way from inadequate tax support to a cultural tradition inadequate to uphold the education that the available income might purchase. Part of that inadequate tradition may rest in the devotion to the outmoded small district with its partisan politics, its inadequate local support, and its lack of professional standards. The deficiencies of this type of education penalize dwellers in the countryside both in their adjustment to the rural environment and in their competitive struggle with those who dwell in urban centers

HIGHER EDUCATION IN ITS REGIONAL ASPECTS

The capstone of our educational system is found in the college and university. If our people are to be prepared for leadership, if States are to overcome their handicaps and if local areas are to go forward in cultural development, they must make use of the aid offered by higher education. How do our regions stand in their devotion to college and university training?

It is one thing to measure the degree to which opportunities for higher education are made available to a people and are utilized by them. It is quite another thing to interpret the meaning of these facts. Although many of our best universities are privately endowed institutions supported by philanthropy, some idea of regional contrasts in higher education can be secured by studying the amount of public funds devoted to its support. In 1932 this figure amounted to $1.97 per adult in the United States and ranged from $5.47 in North Dakota to $0.90 in Massachusetts (Figure 265). Western and southern States rank among those spending the most public funds per capita for the support of higher education; New England States, Illinois, Pennsylvania, and New York spend the least. It is in higher education that private institutions are of the greatest importance in this country. The most notable of these universities, located in the rich and early settled eastern States have been regarded as national institutions, partly because the funds which established them come from the exploitation of national resources in national markets. To some extent, as our figures suggest, these endowed institutions of higher learning have saved eastern

FIGURE 265. THE AMOUNT OF PUBLIC FUNDS, STATE, COUNTY AND CITY, DEVOTED TO PUBLICLY SUPPORTED HIGHER EDUCATION PER INHABITANT 21 AND OVER, UNITED STATES, 1932

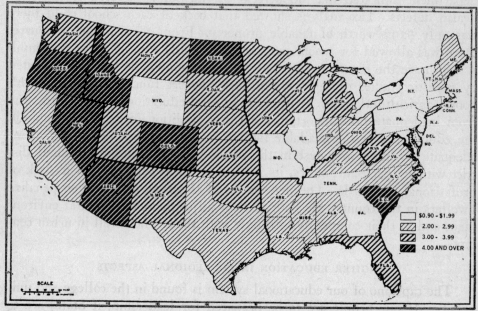

Source: *Education in the Forty-Eight States* (Washington, D. C., 1939), p. 171.

States the necessity of developing expensive State university systems. Coming later to the development of higher education, the States of the West and South were not able to escape this necessity.

A good idea of the proportions who go on to higher education can be secured by relating college and university enrollments by States to the population of college age, 19-22 (Figure 266). This measures the facilities for higher education in each State, but takes no account of the number of southern students who attend college outside their region or the many who come into the region for their education. Thus the index is not an adequate measure of proportions going on to higher education in each State; to some degree it measures the extent to which some States may depend on others to carry on the task of education for them.

No one can presume to say what proportion of the Nation's youth should attend college. For the United States in 1937-1938, it appeared that college enrollment was approximately 14.4 percent of youth of both sexes aged 19 to 22 (Figure 266). The greatest devotion to higher education existed in the Far West, where one-fourth of the youth of college age were enrolled. The least was found in the Southeast where 9.4 percent were enrolled. The Southwest is the next lowest with 13.4 percent enrolled. Utah shows the highest enrollment, 27.6 percent; Mississippi,

FIGURE 266. STUDENT ENROLLMENT IN INSTITUTIONS OF HIGHER LEARNING PER 100 POPULATION AGED 19-22, UNITED STATES, 1937-1938

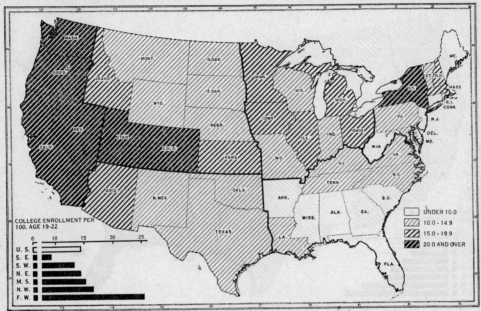

Source: For student enrollments see Table 137; for population data, Table 138.

New Jersey, Arkansas, and Delaware the lowest, ranging from 6.9 to 5.6 percent. We can, no doubt, be safe in assuming that a higher proportion of the youth of New Jersey and Delaware secure college education elsewhere than those of Mississippi and Arkansas.

Until recently women have been somewhat restricted in their opportunities for higher education. It is of interest to note that women do not yet make up half of the total student enrollment in our colleges, summer schools to the contrary notwithstanding. In the period 1937-1938 women students comprised 40.5 percent of total college enrollment in the Nation (Figure 267). Again we recognize a condition, although we can not presume to say what our standards should be. It is most significant to note that the backward and chivalrous South has the highest ratio of women in college, 45.9 percent for the Southeast and 44 percent for the Southwest. The enlightened Northeast with its long history of higher education has the lowest ratio, 38.3 percent. In Tennessee, as Figure 267 shows, almost half of all college students are women, 49.7 percent; in New Hampshire only one-fourth, 25.8 percent. The Southeast also has the highest proportion of women on its college faculties, 35.5 percent; the Northeast, the lowest, 24.6 percent (Table 137). In this respect the South and West would appear to partake more of the modern temper.

FIGURE 267. PERCENTAGE OF WOMEN STUDENTS IN TOTAL ENROLLMENT,
INSTITUTIONS OF HIGHER LEARNING, UNITED STATES, 1937-1938

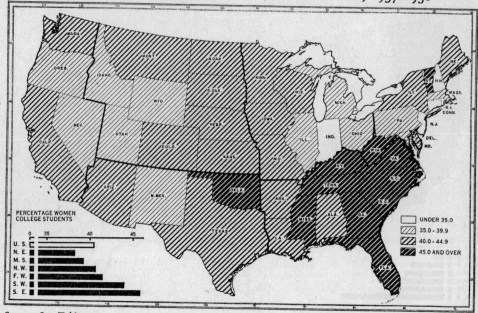

Source: See Table 137.

TABLE 137. STATISTICS OF HIGHER EDUCATION, UNITED STATES AND THE
SIX MAJOR REGIONS, 1937-1938

Educational statistics	United States	North-east	South-east	South-west	Middle States	North-west	Far West	D.C. and U.S. Service Schools
Number Institutions......	1,690	401	369	136	475	140	145	24
Faculty:								
All............	123,677	40,160	21,507	7,766	32,047	8,264	11,741	2,192
Men...........	87,990	30,267	13,863	5,095	22,765	5,676	8,532	1,792
Women.........	35,687	9,893	7,644	2,671	9,282	2,588	3,209	400
Percent women..........	28.9	24.6	35.5	34.4	29.0	31.3	27.3	
College enrollment:								
All.............	1,350,905	407,872	202,552	103,498	379,438	93,732	138,412	25,401
Men...........	803,893	251,742	109,592	57,947	230,299	55,545	81,006	17,762
Women.........	547,012	156,130	92,960	45,551	149,139	38,187	57,406	7,639
Percent women.........	40.5	38.3	45.9	44.0	39.3	40.7	41.5	
Degrees conferred:								
Bachelors........	169,943	51,466	26,341	14,018	44,946	10,891	14,163	3,118
Masters.........	21,628	8,863	1,787	1,263	6,456	1,319	1,449	491
Doctors.........	2,932	1,323	157	44	1,020	58	244	86

Note: U. S. Service Schools include U. S. Military Academy, U. S. Naval Academy, and U. S. Coast Guard Academy. Faculty given as full-time equivalent units. Number of students comprises resident college enrollment, September to June. Degrees conferred do not include honorary degrees.
Source: Office of Education, *Statistics of Higher Education, 1937-1938*, press release of June, 1940.

The Negro still remains largely outside the sphere of influence of higher education, and his status affects, as it rightly should, the standing of the Southeast in this field. Only 9.4 percent of the region's youth aged 19-22 can be found enrolled in the region's colleges. Almost 12.2 percent of the white youth of the Southeast are so enrolled, ranging from 17 percent in Louisiana to 7 percent in Arkansas (Table 138). In spite of recent advances, it is evident that few Negroes reach the college level in the South. Of the Negroes aged 19-22 in the region, only 3.7 percent are enrolled in the Negro colleges in the Southeast (Table 138). In 1936-1937 Mississippi had only 971 Negroes in college as compared with 4,839 in North Carolina. Table 139 gives the number of institutions, teachers, and students for States which have separate colleges for Negroes. Within the Southeast the proportion of Negro youth enrolled in college varies from 1 percent in Mississippi to 7 percent in Kentucky. It is found that the border States with the smaller proportions of Negro population make a better showing than States with larger numbers. It is realized that the wealthier if not the abler Negro students attend northern and eastern universities, but no figures are available that will allot enrollment by race to State of residence or nativity.

TABLE 138. COMPARISON OF NEGRO AND WHITE COLLEGE
ENROLLMENT, SOUTHEAST, 1937

Area	WHITE		NEGRO		Area	WHITE		NEGRO	
	Student enrollment (number)	Ratio to population 19-22 (percent)	Student enrollment (number)	Ratio to population 19-22 (percent)		Student enrollment (number)	Ratio to population 19-22 (percent)	Student enrollment (number)	Ratio to population 19-22 (percent)
SOUTHEAST.......	176,411	12.17	26,141	3.74	Kentucky......	18,814	10.46	1,183	6.97
					Tennessee......	20,856	11.76	2,722	6.33
Virginia..........	19,779	13.75	3,376	6.46	Alabama.......	15,104	10.67	2,713	3.25
North Carolina...	23,891	12.80	4,839	5.61	Mississippi.....	10,946	13.12	971	1.07
South Carolina...	12,034	14.91	1,933	2.64	Arkansas.......	8,075	7.13	1,488	3.46
Georgia..........	18,482	11.80	2,333	2.26	Louisiana......	18,744	16.97	3,069	4.51
Florida..........	9,686	12.72	1,514	3.83					

Note: Total student enrollment (both races) is given for the academic year 1937-1938, while Negro enrollment in institutions of higher education is for 1936-1937. Strictly comparable data were not available. White and Negro population estimated as of 1937 for the ages 19 to 22 inclusive; enrollment for white students obtained by subtracting Negro enrollment from total. Source: Monroe N. Work (ed.), *Negro Year Book, 1937-1938* (Alabama: Tuskegee Institute), pp. 197-205; Office of Education, *Statistics of Higher Education, 1937-1938*, press release of June, 1940; *Fifteenth Census of the United States, 1930*, II, Chap. 10, Tables 27 and 28; John D. Biggers, *Census of Partial Employment, Unemployment and Occupations, 1937*, IV (Washington, D. C.: U. S. Government Printing Office), p. 134.

The Northeast and Middle States together have over one-half of the institutions, faculties, and students devoted to higher education in this country (Table 140). With 58.3 percent of the college enrollment in 1937-1938, they conferred 58.4 percent of the bachelor's degrees, 71 percent of the master's, and 80 percent of the doctor's degrees. The Southeast had more small institutions, a fair ratio of faculty to students, and of bachelor degrees to students. Figure 268, which shows the percentage ratio of first degree graduates, 1933-1934, to freshmen 1931-1932, suggests the degree of continuity in higher education. In the Nation the college seniors made up 44.3 percent of the entire freshmen for the given years, the figure ranging from 81.8 percent in Rhode Island to 25.1 percent in Utah. The Students in eastern States showed the highest tendency to finish college; those in the West and South the lowest.

TABLE 139. EDUCATIONAL STATISTICS OF NEGRO HIGHER EDUCATION, UNITED STATES, 1936-1937

Area	Number institutions	Number teachers	Number students enrolled	Area	Number institutions	Number teachers	Number students enrolled
Southeast............	100	2,595	26,141	Other States.........	33	1,097	11,254
Virginia..........	8	288	3,376	Oklahoma........	2	61	738
North Carolina....	13	293	4,839	Texas............	13	278	4,296
South Carolina.....	14	308	1,933	Maryland........	4	88	736
Georgia...........	13	335	2,333	Delaware.........	1	19	83
Florida...........	5	192	1,514	West Virginia.....	3	105	931
Kentucky.........	4	78	1,183	Missouri.........	2	42	688
Alabama..........	7	293	2,713	Kansas...........	2	31	160
Mississippi.......	14	225	971	Pennsylvania.....	3	51	468
Arkansas..........	7	140	1,488	Ohio.............	1	74	680
Louisiana.........	6	173	3,069				
Tennessee........	9	270	2,722	Total.........	133	3,692	37,395

Note: These statistics include government and private universities and colleges for Negroes; a large number of them, in addition to college students enumerated here, also offer some courses for high school, elementary, and other students. Hence, the 3,692 teachers enumerated here are not employed exclusively as college professors.
Source: Monroe N. Work (ed.), *Negro Year Book, 1937-1938.*

TABLE 140. PERCENTAGE DISTRIBUTION OF STATISTICS OF HIGHER EDUCATION, UNITED STATES AND THE SIX MAJOR REGIONS, 1937-1938

Educational statistics	United States	North-east	South-east	South-west	Middle States	North-west	Far West	D.C. and Military Academies
Institutions................	100.0	23.7	21.8	8.0	28.1	8.3	8.6	1.5
Faculty (both sexes)........	100.0	32.5	17.4	6.3	25.9	6.7	9.5	1.7
Students (both sexes).......	100.0	30.2	15.0	7.7	28.1	6.9	10.2	1.9
Degrees conferred:								
Bachelors..............	100.0	31.2	16.0	8.5	27.2	6.6	8.6	1.9
Masters...............	100.0	41.0	8.2	5.8	29.9	6.1	6.7	2.3
Doctors...............	100.0	45.1	5.4	1.5	34.8	2.0	8.3	2.9
Population, 19-22 years of age...................	100.0	30.0	22.9	8.2	26.4	6.0	6.1	0.4

Note: See Table 137 for definitions.
Source: See Table 137; for population data, see Table 138.

Lacking the institutions of graduate standing, the Southeast did not give a proportionate number of master's and doctor's degrees. Nevertheless the figures are encouraging for they show quantitatively the extent to which higher education has increased in the area. With 21.8 percent of the institutions, the region had 17.4 percent of the faculty and 15 percent of the Nation's students (Table 140). To them it awarded 16 percent of the bachelor's degrees, 8.2 percent of the master's, and 5.4 percent of the doctor's degrees. It is in their graduate training that the great endowed institutions of the East approach nearest the status of national universities, serving all regions. Until the quality of the region's instruction and training can be further improved, this, no doubt, represents a fair ratio. But this, it should be stated, represents a fair ratio, not of those southerners who should secure graduate instruction, but of the share which can now be provided in the region. The same cannot be said of higher education for the Negro. Here because of a long existing lag, improvements in quantity and quality must be made, step by step, as rapidly as facilities and support can be provided.

FIGURE 268. PERCENTAGE RATIO OF FIRST DEGREE GRADUATES, 1933-1934
TO FRESHMEN, 1931-1932, UNITED STATES

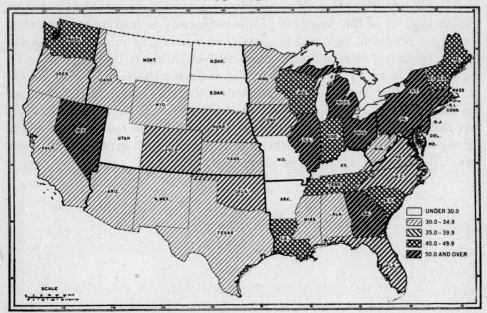

Source: *Education in the Forty-Eight States*, 1939, p. 164.

CONCLUSION

In summary, the relation of education to cultural adequacy and national survival is not difficult to show. The function of education has often been given legal definition in our courts. One well-phrased statement reads: "Free schooling furnished by the State is not so much a right granted to pupils as a duty imposed upon them for the public good. . . . While most people regard the public schools as a means of great personal advantage to the pupils, the fact is too often overlooked that they are the governmental means of protecting the State against the consequences of an ignorant and incompetent citizenship."[3] In our modern day the direct consequences are threefold: military, economic, and political. Citizens with less than five years of schooling are now limited in their participation in the defense of their country. Ignorant citizens are more likely to become public charges and thus increase the Nation's relief bill. Citizens ill-informed and prejudiced become the prey of demagogues and thus tend to break down the equitable functioning of government so necessary for the preservation of the free ballot in a democracy.

[3] Fogg vs. Board of Education of Littleton, 76 N. H. 299.

Free public education for all children is one social value to which our country is committed. It is therefore a commentary on our sense of realism in this country that these three simple arguments have never appealed to the intelligence of the American people sufficiently to lead them to develop a national program, designed to support an educational minimum irrespective of residence, race, and economic status of children. In World War II we suffered from a lack of manpower in the armed forces and from a lack of skilled labor that could be attributed directly to regional and class variations in the educational level the country over. Nations that neglect the essentials of national survival should not talk too much in terms of their ideals of democracy when, as our preceding chapters show, they have allowed these ideals to go unrealized.

CHAPTER 30

LEADERSHIP AND CULTURAL DEVELOPMENT

MORE THAN anything else the future cultural and economic development of the Southeast will depend on leadership. Leadership is a thing of quality and therefore difficult of definition and discussion. Quality is demanded, but for the achievement of cultural maturity any society needs men of ability and talent, however defined, in quantity. Democracy depends on the talent of the many as well as the distinction of the few. Where large numbers are concerned some measure of statistical analysis is possible.

The preceding discussion of higher education offers one approach to the study of leadership. The region's proportion of youth in college offers some indication of those who may be expected to go on to achieve distinction in professional and technical fields. Of these groups some will qualify as leaders, others as the auxiliary force necessary to implement leadership in technical, economic and cultural development.

The present chapter attempts to approach the baffling question of the adequacy of leadership from several points of view. The leadership of the regions as that of the Nation stems from tradition. The South has an older tradition of distinguished leadership and its past may well be examined in order to compare its ability to produce men of distinction with that of other regions. For the recent past and the present we can compare the region's production of men of talent with that of the Nation. We can also use the region's representation in the professions as an index of its ability to support specialists and men of proficiency. In addition the discussion in the preceding chapter of the proportion of the population securing higher education offers an index to the amount of leadership to be expected in the future.

THE REGIONAL DISTRIBUTION OF MEN OF DISTINCTION

Has the South had in the past its share of men of distinction? There is hardly any way of answering this question except by the method of comparison. The question then becomes how do the southern States compare with the rest of the Nation in the production of great men? A second question arises in connection with regional differences in the fields in which these men won distinction, and a third has to do with the migration of notables to different regions.

The completion in the period 1927-1934 of the *Dictionary of American Biography* with its 13,633 biographies of non-living notables, selected by specialists on the basis of well established criteria of prominence and achievement, affords us an opportunity to study the geography of distinction in the United States.[1] For the dividing period we take the Civil War and separate the notables into two groups—those dying before and those dying after January 1, 1866. The historical limit means that we shall be confined largely to the consideration of three regions—Northeast, Southeast, and Middle States.

There are 13, 633 notables listed in the *Dictionary*. Of these, 78.4 percent or 10,684 are native white and thus can be related to a necessary population base in our calculations. This consideration plus regional variations in ethnic composition dictated the necessity of excluding the foreign-born, Negro, and Indian groups from our calculations. It is noteworthy, however, that about 16.5 percent of those listed in the *Dictionary* are foreign-born; 4.5 percent, Negroes; and 0.6 percent, Indians. By making some adjustments in the time factor these figures can be related to base populations. The foreign born and Indians are well represented; Negroes and women are underrepresented. Thus in 1890 foreign-born whites composed 15 percent of the total population and 16.5 of the notables. The average Negro population between 1790 and 1860 was 16.8 percent of the total for the same period but Negroes made up only 4.5 percent of the notables. Indians in 1880 were 0.3 percent of the population and their notables made up 0.6 percent of the total. American-born women, it may be pointed out, comprise only 4.7 percent of all native white notables. Obviously, mothers and wives who shared in the struggles and had a large part in accounting for the "fame" of notable men are, by the very nature of things, omitted from separate listings.

BIRTH RATES OF NOTABLES

For all regions the decade 1800-1810 was the highest point in the birth of great men (Figure 269). The Northeast ranks highest in the production of notables, reaching in this period a high "birth rate" of 22.2 per million native white population; the Southeast is next with 16.6, the Mid-

[1] Cf. Dumas Malone, "The Geography of American Achievement," *Atlantic Monthly*, 154 (December, 1934), 669-679. This first analysis by the editor of the *Dictionary* has the great advantage of being written against the background criteria on which the selections were based.

dle States with 16.0.[2] All successively fall until the decade 1850-1860 shows the Northeast with 5.4, the Middle States with 2.8, and the Southeast with 2.6 notables born per million population. Outstanding among the States is Massachusetts which reaches a birth rate of notables of 40.4 per million during two decades, while South Carolina and Virginia have rates of 17.8 and 16.0 respectively in their best decades. Ohio leads the Middle States. All other regions, as we shall see, because of later settlement have had to develop more of their great men out of imported articles.

The results give support to the oft expressed view that leadership is on the decline and great men are becoming fewer. Both in the Nation and its regions distinction, it seems, is passing from the leaders to the masses. The numerical chances of becoming famous are greater during the founding of a small nation than in maintaining the country after it becomes more populous. Stated more precisely, the chances of achieving distinction as measured by the criteria of the *Dictionary* are diminishing. In the decades from 1790 to 1820 the national "birth rate" of notables was above 19 per million,

FIGURE 269. BIRTH RATES OF NOTABLES PER 1,000,000 NATIVE WHITE POPU-
LATION, UNITED STATES AND THREE REGIONS WITH
MASSACHUSETTS, 1790-1860

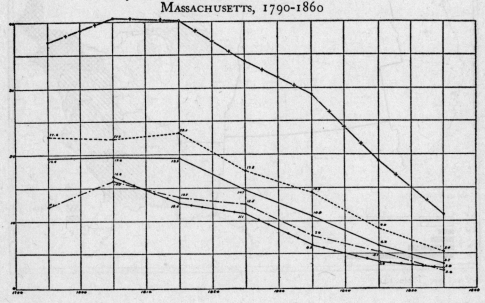

Source: See Table 141.

[2] For a discussion of methods used, see Rupert B. Vance and Nadia Danilevsky, "The Geography of Distinction: The Nation and Its Regions, 1790-1927." *Social Forces*, XVIII (December, 1939), 168-172.

from 1820 to 1860, it progressively fell by decades from 14.7 to 10.8 to 6.3 to 3.7 (Figure 269).

Over the whole period, 1790-1860, the Nation's average was 9.9 notables per million population. The Northeast led with a rate of 13.6 followed by the Southeast with 6.9 and the Middle States with 4.8. Figure 270, which shows the distribution by States, indicates that the District of Columbia led with a birth rate of 31.4. As the Mecca of the great and near great the District drew temporary residents from all regions. They gave birth in Washington to notable children who with justice can hardly be assigned to any region.

Massachusetts, Connecticut, and Rhode Island had the next highest rates followed by New York and the rest of New England. South Carolina rather than Virginia led the Southeast, with Alabama and Florida bringing up the rear. Late comers to the brotherhood of States showed the lowest birth rate of notables according to the criteria of the *Dictionary*.

FIGURE 270. AVERAGE BIRTH RATES OF NOTABLES PER MILLION NATIVE WHITE POPULATION, UNITED STATES, 1790-1860

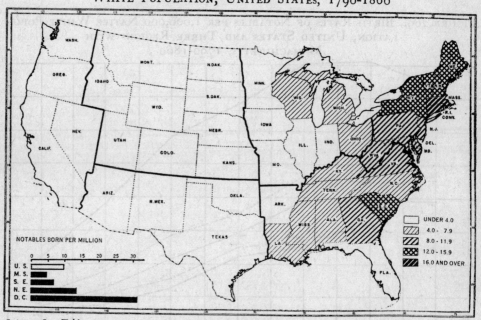

Source: See Table 141.

FIELDS OF LEADERSHIP

It is the general feeling that while the Old South led in military and political leadership it lagged in literature, education, and science. Our study enables us to test these distinctions among the various fields of leadership. The callings in which leaders most often rise to distinction differed greatly both by periods and by regions. Basic to this analysis was the grouping of all careers listed in the *Dictionary* into three main headings with many subdivisions (Table 141). These are: (1) Political Culture, including those prominent in government and politics, law, and war; (2) General Culture, including those prominent as leaders in religion and philanthropy, education, literature, medicine, art, science, and in social movements; and (3) Technology and Economic Production, including leaders in engineering, invention, finance and commerce, industry, agriculture, crafts, transport and communication. Last comes a small group called (4) Others and composed of explorers, outlaws, famous athletes, etc. The classification of notable men according to the functions performed in the culture differs greatly from the task of setting up an occupational distribution. Table 141 shows how characterizations given by the *Dictionary* were translated into this scheme. Notables listed as distinguished in several fields were distributed fractionally as, for example, George Washington was listed as one-half statesman and one-half general.

Before the Civil War the avenues leading to fame were somewhat different as may be seen from Figure 271. Leadership in our early period centered in statecraft, law, and war. After 1865 Political Culture shows

TABLE 141. FUNCTIONAL CLASSIFICATION OF NOTABLES BY CALLINGS

I

POLITICAL CULTURE

Government: statesman, president, senator, governor, diplomat, legislator, mayor.
Politician: political leader, party leader.
Army: soldier, general, Indian fighter, spy.
Navy: naval officer, privateersman.

II

GENERAL CULTURE

Religion and Philanthropy: clergyman, theologian, bishop, missionary, apostle of peace, philanthropist, religious worker, humanitarian, masonic ritualist, reformer, settlement worker, relief worker.
Education: educator, teacher, professor, lecturer, orator, librarian, philosopher.
Literature: author, writer, poet, playwright, almanac maker, publicist, newspaperman, journalist, critic, editor, lexicographer.
Medicine: physician, surgeon, hygienist, epidemiologist, ophthalmologist, dentist, veterinary.
Art: artist, sculptor, architect, musician, dancer, singer, engraver.
Science: astronomer, geographer, chemist, naturalist, anatomist, hydrographer, geologist, metallurgist, mathematician, statistician, ethnographer, philologist, scholar, economist, sociologist.
Leaders of Movements: labor leaders, labor agitators, Revolutionary leaders: Revolutionary heroine, Revolutionary patriots, signers of Declaration of Independence, women suffragists, loyalist, patriot, unionist, Mother of Confederacy, secessionist, and abolitionist.

III

TECHNOLOGY AND ECONOMIC PRODUCTION

Engineer: civil, mechanical engineer.
Inventor.
Commerce: merchant, trader, slave trader, fur trader, chandler, bookseller, business man.
Finance: banker, financier, insurance man.
Industry: manufacturer, ice king, meat packer, mechanic, lithographer.
Agriculture: planter, farmer, pomologist, horse-breeder, cattle man, agriculturist.
Crafts: carpenter, cabinet maker, silversmith, glass blower, printer, glazer.
Transport and Communications: Transport: R. R. builder, R. R. director, shipbuilder; Communication: organizer of telephone and telegraph systems.
Aviation: aviator, pioneer in aviation.

IV

OTHERS

Explorers: traveler, explorer, pioneer, scout, colonial ranger, frontiersman, trapper.
Adventurer: bad man, desperado, burglar.
Athletics and Sports: tennis player, coach, horse racer, baseball player.

Source: Adapted from Dumas Malone (ed.), *Dictionary of American Biography*, New York, 1939, by Rupert B. Vance, "The Geography of Distinction: The Nation and Its Regions 1790-1927," *Social Forces*, XVIII (December, 1939), 173.

the greatest decline, falling from 43.5 to 28.1 percent of the total. Preeminence passed in the second period to General Culture which increased its share of the total number of notables from 41 to 53.7 percent. All items in all fields of General Culture increased except religion and leaders of movements. Technology and production increased its share of the famous from 13 to 16.6 percent, but in spite of our economic achievements, industry and the crafts seem underrepresented, in the *Dictionary*. The difficulty of achieving note in these fields may indicate that here achievement is as much a matter of group cooperation as of exceptional leadership.

Regional contrasts are notable and in the main are what might be expected. The Northeast in the first period shows the greatest concentration of its leadership in General Culture, 45.7 percent compared with 25.8 percent for the Southeast (Figure 272). Religion leads all fields of distinction in the Northeast region embracing 357 notables, 16.4 percent of all its great in the first period. Southern born notables were concentrated in Political Culture where 63 percent of all its leaders were developed as compared with only 37.6 percent for the Northeast. In law the variation in favor of the Southeast was not so great, 15.2 compared with 13.8 percent; but in government the Southeast's lead was 29 to 11 percent. In war the same region led 18.8 to 12.8 percent. In technology and production the distribution favored the Northeast, 15 to 6.2 percent.

In spite of the decline in political development during the second period, the Southeast had 50.5 of its leaders in this field as compared with only 21.8 percent for the Northeast and 29.4 percent for the Middle States (Figure 273). No region had so large a proportion of its notables in any

FIGURE 271. THE PERCENTAGE DISTRIBUTION OF AMERICAN LEADERS BY PHASE OF CULTURE IN WHICH THEY WON FAME IN TWO PERIODS

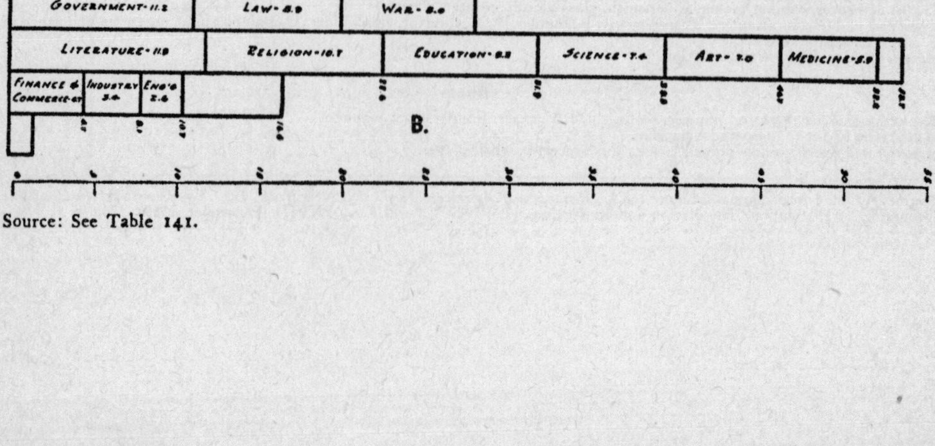

Source: See Table 141.

calling as the South had in these three: government, 21.7 percent; war 15.3 percent; and law, 13.5 percent. In General Culture the Northeast in this period had 58 percent of its native-born leaders; the Southeast only 37.3. By now the Middle States had 53 percent of their native-born in this field. The proportion of religious leaders declined still further, being outstripped by literature in every region. In the Northeast, in fact, 674 writers, 12.3 percent of the total, composed the largest single brace of notables in the region. Scientists reached as high as 8 and 9 percent of all notables in the Northeast and Middle States but remained at only 4 percent in the Southeast. In this period educators and artists also loomed larger in all regions.

Economic culture also claimed a greater share of the famous, 17.5 percent in the Northeast, 15 percent in the Middle States. Here again the South lagged with only 10 percent. Five and four-tenths percent of the Northeast's distinguished were in commerce and finance as compared with only 2.5 percent for the Southeast. The Northeast produced 279 noted inventors and engineers as compared with only 37 for the Southeast. Yet in spite of its agrarian culture the South had only 2.5 percent of its notables listed as outstanding in agriculture.

FIGURE 272. THE OCCUPATIONAL DISTRIBUTION OF AMERICAN LEADERS BY REGIONS BEFORE 1866

FIGURE 273. THE OCCUPATIONAL DISTRIBUTION OF AMERICAN LEADERS BY REGIONS AFTER 1866

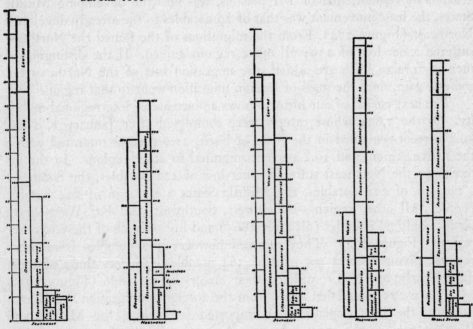

Source: See Table 141.

The Old South produced fewer leaders according to its population than other areas. If we should take into account the Negro population and their inability to rise to positions of distinction in this period the region's discrepancy would be much greater. In addition these leaders were concentrated in political culture where as much as any group they aided in establishing the early Nation. When the region lost political preeminence after the Civil War it lacked a tradition of leadership in education, science, economics, and the technical arts adequate to hasten its economic and cultural development.

The transition to the second period showed that, while in the Southeast the proportion of leaders was increasing in general economic culture, the region had already fallen behind the newly developed Middle States except in the fields of government, law, and military leadership (Figure 273).

THE MIGRATION OF NOTABLES

There remains the question as to how well migration of notables served to distribute leadership over the Nation. Despite the great mobility of our population, Figure 274 shows that the great majority of our notables lived out their lifetime and attained distinction in the State in which they were born. Of 2,880 native whites who completed notable careers before 1866, 63.5 percent remained in their native States, 23.5 percent migrated within the region of birth and only 13 percent migrated to another region. The greatest movement, that of 171 persons, was into the developing Middle States, the least movement was that of 26 notables to the already developed Northeast (Figure 274). From the migrations of the famed the Northeast suffered a net loss of 239; all other regions gained. If the distinguished men of foreign birth are added, the migration loss of the Northeast becomes a gain, since the mass of foreign migration went to that region.

The next period of our history shows an increase of interregional mobility. Of the 7,634 whose careers were completed after January 1, 1866, 59.2 percent remained in the State of birth, 21.6 percent migrated within the native region, and 19.2 percent migrated to other regions. In the interchange the Northeast suffered a net loss of 422 notables, the Southeast a net loss of 228 notables, the Middle States a net gain of 244 notable people. All other regions—Northwest, Southwest, and Far West—gave birth to only 70 notables (all after 1865) and lost only 28 of these to other regions (Figure 274). They received however 392 notables from other regions, giving them a net gain of 364 notables. Seventy-three of these moved early, and had completed their careers before 1866 (Figure 275).

Figure 275 shows that apart from the foreign immigration the Northeast was the least dependent on imported leadership; the Middle and Western regions the most. As may be expected, the Southeast took a

FIGURE 274. MOBILITY OF AMERICAN LEAD-
ERS BORN WITHIN THREE REGIONS BY
PERIODS

FIGURE 275. SOURCE BY REGION OF BIRTH OF
AMERICAN LEADERS RESIDENT IN THREE RE-
GIONS BEFORE AND AFTER 1865

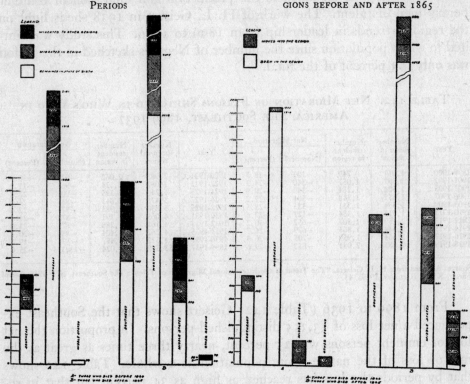

Source: See Table 141.

smaller proportion of its leadership from other regions in the second
period. In the post-war period the Southeast had 132 leaders, including
some carpetbaggers, who were born in the Northeast.

In both periods the Northeast exported the most talent, some 1,024
souls including many ministers and teachers; the Southeast came next with
468, including many leaders in statecraft, law, and war. Both the greatest
total movement and the greatest net migration of notables have been to
the Middle States, 733 and 415 respectively. One of the handicaps of the
Southeast was its failure to secure a proportional share of the distinguished
men of foreign birth. To determine to what environment should go the
credit for developing migrating talent—to the State of birth or to the State
of achievement—is beyond the scope of our analysis.

RECENT TRENDS IN THE BIRTH AND MIGRATION OF MEN OF TALENT, 1897-1936[3]

No biographical dictionary can presume to assay the worth of men now

[3] Adapted from H. L. Geisert, "The Trend of the Interregional Migration of Talent: The Southeast.
1899-1936," *Social Forces*, XVIII (October, 1939), 41-47. See also his The Balance of Interstate Migration in the Southeast, 1870-1930, with Special Reference to the Migration of Eminent Persons (unpublished
doctoral dissertation, University of North Carolina, 1938), p. 125.

living, but it has been customary for studies to rely on the listings in *Who's Who in America* as an index to the production and migration of contemporary men of talent. The work of H. L. Geisert in 1938 sheds light on the region's trends in leadership from 1899 to 1936. This study was limited to white population since the number of Negroes sketched in the period was only 0.3 percent of the total.

TABLE 142. NET MIGRATION OF PERSONS SKETCHED IN WHO'S WHO IN AMERICA, THE SOUTHEAST, 1899-1937

Year	Number born in region	Number resident in region	Net Migration		Year	Number born in region	Number resident in region	Net Migration	
			(Number)	(Percent)				(Number)	(Percent)
1899-1900....	1,051	749	−302	−28.7	1920-1921..	2,983	2,062	−921	−30.9
1901-1902....	1,397	1,057	−340	−24.3	1922-1923..	3,087	2,124	−963	−31.2
1903-1905....	1,624	1,284	−340	−20.9	1924-1925..	3,246	2,345	−901	−27.8
1906-1907....	1,852	1,348	−504	−27.2	1926-1927..	3,478	2,643	−835	−24.0
1908-1909....	1,834	1,311	−523	−28.5	1928-1929..	3,856	2,983	−873	−22.6
1910-1911....	1,911	1,384	−527	−27.6	1930-1931..	4,065	3,193	−872	−21.5
1912-1913....	2,159	1,507	−652	−30.2	1932-1933..	4,161	3,288	−873	−21.0
1914-1915....	2,544	1,865	−679	−26.7	1934-1935..	4,262	3,404	−858	−20.1
1916-1917....	2,664	1,959	−705	−26.5	1936-1937..	4,322	3,487	−835	−19.3
1918-1919....	2,883	2,031	−852	−29.6	1899-1937..	53,379	40,024	−13,355	−25.0

Source: Adapted from H. L. Geisert, "The Trend of the Interregional Migration of Talent: The Southeast, 1899-1936, *Social Forces*, XVIII (October, 1939), 43.

From 1899 to 1936 (Table 142) Geisert shows that the Southeast experienced a net loss of 13,355 distinguished persons. In proportion the net loss of eminent persons was 25 percent, nearly three times as great as the rate of loss of the native white population as a whole. Table 142 shows that by periods the loss has reached as high as 31 percent but that in recent years it has fallen below 20 percent of the region's resident notables.

At the same time that the region has been reducing its net loss of talent by migration it has been producing a proportionately larger number of notables in recent years.

The average age of those listed in *Who's Who* is around 56 years. Relating eminent persons to period of birth, Geisert found that from 1870 to 1886 the number born in the Nation increased from 20,842 to 28,038; in the Southeast, from 2,983 to 4,322.

Relating the birth of notables to the number of native white women of childbearing age we find (Figure 276) that the birth rate of notables in the Nation 1850 to 1886 rose from 22.1 to 39.4 per 10,000 native white women 20-44. In the region the rate rose from 13.5 to 30.3. Although below the Nation's rate, the Southeast's production of talent increased at a much sharper rate. Between 1870 and 1886, the Southeast showed a steady increase in the number of native-born achieving eminence, and, in addition, continued to contribute a larger and larger proportion of the total number of distinguished persons born in the United States. Between 1870 and 1886, the ratio of region's percentage of nationally eminent persons to its percentage of the women of childbearing age increased by 5.1.

Not only did the Southeast increase its yield of distinguished persons during the period, but it was able to attract a larger proportion of the eminent people living in the United States. In 1900, 25.6 percent of the native white population of the United States lived in the Southeast; by 1936, only 24 percent of this group resided in the region. In 1900, 9 percent of the eminent persons in the United States lived in the Southeast, but by 1936, 11.3 percent of this group were living in the region (Table 143). The gain in eminent residents, however, has not paralleled the increase in the production of eminent native-born. Whereas a steady increase for each decennial period was observed in the case of the regional yield of distinguished persons, a steady percentage increase in eminent residents has occurred only since 1922. Between 1902 and 1910, there was a steady decline in the percentage of the Nation's eminent persons living in the Southeast. This trend was temporarily reversed after 1912, but again a slight decline occurred after 1918. Since that time, an appreciable increase in the percentage of notable residents has been evident. In 1900, the ratio of the region's percentage of the Nation's eminent persons to its percentage of the Nation's native white population was 0.35, and by 1936, it had increased to 0.47.

FIGURE 276. BIRTH RATES OF WHO'S
WHO NOTABLES PER 10,000 NATIVE-
WHITE WOMEN OF CHILDBEARING
AGE, UNITED STATES AND SOUTHEAST,
1850-1890

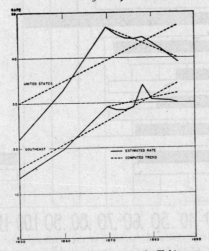

Source: H. L. Geisert op. cit., in Table 142.

An examination of the data for the individual States of the Southeast reveals widespread differences in the production of eminent persons, although the rankings of the eleven States changed but little during the 38-year period (Figure 277). At the beginning of the period, South Carolina, which ranked first at both the beginning and the end of the period, was producing proportionately four times as many notables as was Arkansas, which was in last place. However, by the close of the period, the differences between the two States, which still retained the same relative positions, was less marked. By 1936, South Carolina had produced approximately three times as many living eminent persons as Arkansas. South Carolina was the only State to have a ratio of notables in excess of its share of the national population before 1870, and during the last two biennial periods, it had a higher ratio than had been attained by any other State of the region at any time. Virginia was the only other State to have a similar ratio for more than two biennial periods and by 1936, it had displaced Florida in second position. By the end of the period, Mississippi had moved up to third place, North Carolina was in fourth position, and was followed by Florida and Georgia. Nine of the eleven States were

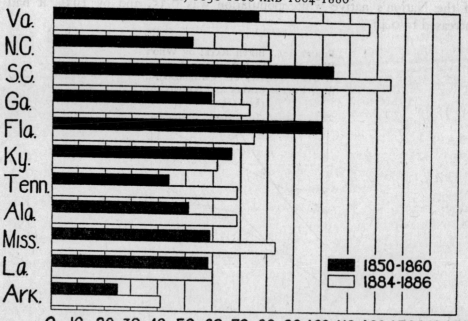

FIGURE 277. RATIOS OF EMINENT PERSONS BORN IN THE SOUTHEAST BY STATES, 1850-1860 AND 1884-1886*

* Note: This ratio is the percentage that each State has of the Nation's *Who's Who* born within its border divided by the States percentage of all native-white women of childbearing age for the period.
Source: See Tables 142, 143.

TABLE 143. RATIOS OF THE PERCENTAGE OF UNITED STATES NOTABLES LIVING
IN THE SOUTHEAST TO THE PERCENTAGE OF THE
TOTAL POPULATION, 1900-1936

Year	Native white population of the Southeast*	Native white population of the United States*	Population of the Southeast or percent of the U. S. total	Eminent persons living in Southeast†	Eminent persons living in United States†	Eminent People in the South or percent of the U. S. total	Ratio of column 7 to column 4
(1)	(2)	(3)	(4)	(5)	(6)	(7)	(8)
1900	10,504,686	41,053,417	25.6	749	8,326	9.0	.35
1902	10,909,505	42,740,449	25.5	1,057	11,137	9.5	.37
1904	11,314,324	44,427,481	25.5	1,284	14,016	9.2	.36
1906	11,719,143	46,114,513	25.4	1,348	15,770	8.5	.34
1908	12,123,962	47,801,545	25.4	1,311	15,873	8.3	.33
1910	12,528,783	49,488,575	25.3	1,384	16,997	8.1	.32
1912	12,927,482	51,275,251	25.2	1,507	18,215	8.3	.33
1914	13,326,181	53,061,927	25.1	1,865	20,790	9.0	.36
1916	13,724,880	54,848,603	25.0	1,959	21,257	9.2	.37
1918	14,123,579	56,635,279	24.9	2,031	21,351	9.5	.38
1920	14,522,279	58,421,957	24.9	2,062	23,045	8.9	.36
1922	15,020,385	60,764,888	24.7	2,124	23,809	8.9	.36
1924	15,518,491	63,107,819	24.6	2,345	24,891	9.4	.38
1926	16,016,597	65,450,750	24.5	2,643	26,394	10.0	.41
1928	16,514,703	67,793,681	24.4	2,983	28,234	10.6	.43
1930	17,012,812	70,136,614	24.3	3,193	29,148	11.0	.45
1932	17,510,918	72,479,545	24.2	3,288	30,009	11.0	.46
1934	18,009,024	74,822,476	24.1	3,404	30,510	11.2	.47
1936	18,507,130	77,165,407	24.0	3,487	30,835	11.3	.47

*Estimates based on United States Census, *Population*, 1900-1936.
†*Who's Who in America*, 1899-1936.
Source: Adapted from Geisert, *op. cit.*, p. 45.

producing proportionately more notables at the end of the period; only two states, Florida and Kentucky, registered an actual decrease in the ratio of eminent persons to women of childbearing age (Figure 277).

While changes in the productivity of the several States indicate changes in the opportunities in these States, the proportion of eminent residents is undoubtedly a better criterion of social and economic opportunities. Although there occurred a lessening of the differences between the States in the yield of eminent persons during the 38-year period, a reversal of this trend was evidenced in the case of eminent residents. At the beginning of the century, Florida, which during the entire period had a higher proportion of distinguished residents than any other State, had proportionately three times as many eminent residents as Arkansas, which was in last position. In the ensuing years, the differences between the several States became greater and, by the end of the period, Florida had a ratio nearly seven times that of Arkansas. While Florida has occupied an unique position, the trend is nevertheless evidenced by a comparison of the standings of the other States of the region. Louisiana, in second place at the beginning of the period, had approximately twice the proportionate number of eminent residents as had Arkansas. At the end of the period, Virginia, which had moved up to second position, had proportionately nearly four times as many eminent residents as Arkansas. At the end of the period, six States had attracted a larger proportionate number of distinguished residents, two States, South Carolina and Mississippi, remained unchanged,

FIGURE 278. RATIOS OF THE PERCENTAGE OF THE NATION'S EMINENT PERSONS RESIDENT IN THE SOUTHEAST BY STATES, 1900-1902, AND 1934-1936*

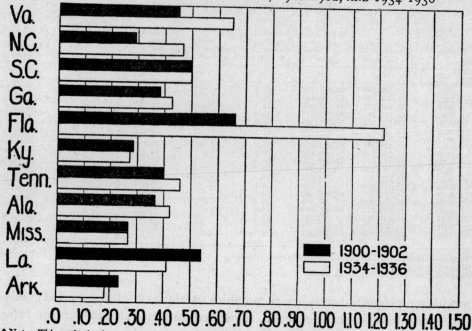

* Note: This ratio is the percentage that each State had of the Nation's *Who's Who* resident within its borders divided by the State's percentage of the total native-white population for the period.
Source: See Tables 12, 143.

and three States, Kentucky, Louisiana, and Arkansas, had relatively fewer eminent residents than at the beginning of the period (Figure 278).

Although the Southeast contained a smaller proportion of the total number of native white women of childbearing age in the United States at the end of the period, it was producing a larger proportion of the eminent people born in the United States. Between 1870 and 1886, the Southeast showed a steady increase in its proportionate yield. Since the region was able to increase its contribution to the total number of notables in the United States in the face of a heavy loss of eminent individuals by migration, it would appear that the reserve supply of undeveloped ability in the region was more than sufficient to replace any losses of developed talent. The actual increase in the yield of notables in a number of States as well as the region as a whole indicates an increase in opportunities to achieve eminence.

Geisert's study shows that not only was the Southeast able to increase its yield of distinguished persons, but it attracted a larger proportion of the eminent people in the United States. The rapid increase in the number of eminent people resident in the Southeast since 1920 would appear to indicate a diminishing of the migration of this class of people from the region. Nevertheless, the gain in notable residents has not equalled the increase in the production of distinguished persons. If the increase in eminent residents, as well as the increase in the yield of notables, is indicative of greater opportunities within the region, there may well be reason to anticipate that the trend will continue in the future, and that at some not too distant date, the Southeast may be able to offer adequate opportunities for the development of its distinguished offspring.

PROFESSIONAL PERSONS AS INDEX OF LEADERSHIP[4]

Certainly not all leaders belong to the professions any more than all professional persons qualify for leadership. More than in any other group in the occupational statistics, however, they may serve as an index of the proportion of leaders, specialists, and technically qualified persons to be found in the various regions.

Kenneth Evans in his study found that the professions ranked lowest in the Southeast. In Edwards' social economic classification (Chapter 11, Figure 94), professional persons in 1930 made up 6 percent of the gain-

FIGURE 279. THE NUMBER OF PROFESSIONAL PERSONS PER 100,000 POPULATION, UNITED STATES, 1940

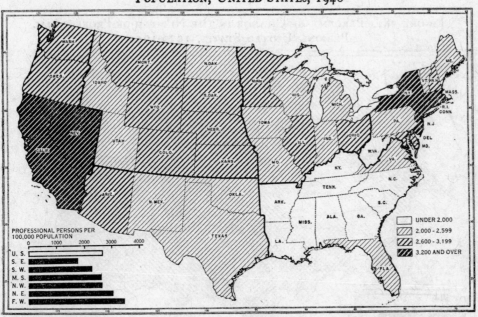

Source: *Sixteenth Census of the United States, 1940*, Series P-6, P-11, State Summaries.

[4] Adapted from Kenneth Evans, "Some Occupational Trends in the South," *Social Forces*, XVII (December, 1938), 184-190. See also his Changing Occupational Distribution in the South with Special Emphasis on the Rise of Professional Services (unpublished doctoral dissertation, University of North Carolina, 1938).

FIGURE 280. PERCENTAGE INCREASE IN NUMBER OF PROFESSIONAL PERSONS
PER 100,000 POPULATION, UNITED STATES, 1910-1930

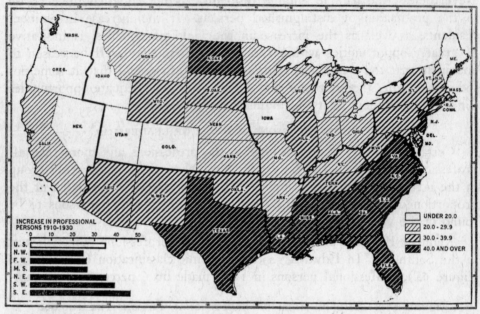

Source: See Table 144.

FIGURE 281. PERCENTAGE CHANGE IN THE NUMBER OF PROFESSIONAL
PERSONS, UNITED STATES, 1930-1940

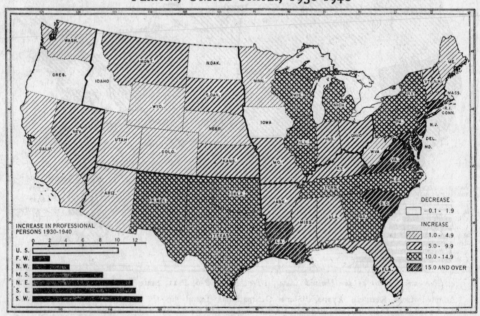

Source: Kenneth Evans, *op. cit.*; *Sixteenth Census of the United States, 1940*, Series P-6, P-11.

fully employed population of the Nation, ranging from 4.1 percent in the Southeast to 7.8 percent in the Far West.

Figure 279 ranks the States according to the number of professional persons per 100,000 population in 1940. The range was from 3,491 for the Far West to 1,756 for the Southeast. California and New York rank the highest with 3,745 and 3,673, Mississippi the lowest with 1,400. The proportionate increase in professional persons from 1910 to 1930 is shown in Figure 280. The Southeast led all regions with a gain of 46.8 percent Florida and the Carolinas led all the States with over 66 percent increase, while Nevada lagged with 4.2. Figure 281 shows that this increase continued through the depression for all but four of our States. Both southern regions outran the national rate of gain with Delaware and Louisiana leading. The Far West may be approximating the saturation point in professionals, for it gained only 2 percent.

Kenneth Evans, in his study in this field felt that the southern regions offered the greatest possibility of accelerated changes in occupational distribution in the future, both because of their present relatively low number of such workers in proportion to population and because of recent expansion in nearly all professional services. The Southeast, with 1,568 professional persons per 100,000 population in 1930, fell below the corresponding ratio for the Nation and all other regions, except the Southwest, for the earlier census period, 1910. The extent of this lag in multiplying job opportunities on new levels of employment and in making available important services in the professional field was further emphasized by the fact that the two southern regions showed the highest rates of increase for the 20-year period covered.

This composite lag for the southern regions in number of professional persons was the result of an almost uniform lag in each of the separate professional services that go to make up the total group of professional persons. A comparison of the regions and the Nation (1930) in the number per 100,000 population in certain specified professional pursuits bears out this statement (Table 144). In only two professional groups, clergymen and county agents, did the Southeast rank higher than the Nation as a whole. Its lowest proportional rank was in scientific services, chemists, and technical engineers. Extreme differences were found among the regions in the number per 100,000 population of workers engaged in performing most of these services which have come to be regarded as increasingly important to the welfare of people, both urban and rural.

The low ranks of the southern regions in relative number of professional persons emphasize the continued need for expansion of professional services in these regions, while recent increases indicate a trend in the

TABLE 144. NUMBER PER 100,000 POPULATION IN SPECIFIED PROFESSIONAL PURSUITS, 1930

Professional pursuit	United States	South-east	South-west	North-east	Middle States	North-west	Far West
Actors and showmen	61.3	27.3	49.5	80.9	49.0	36.0	162.7
Architects	17.9	7.1	11.2	26.4	16.7	7.1	30.7
Artists, sculptors, and teachers of art	46.6	12.0	20.7	69.0	48.5	18.2	93.9
Authors, editors, and reporters	52.4	23.0	36.5	66.3	46.6	47.8	111.8
Chemists, assayers, and metallurgists	38.3	13.3	21.6	57.8	40.6	22.9	44.0
Clergymen	121.2	135.6	136.8	107.8	118.8	141.1	111.6
College presidents and professors	50.4	43.0	49.6	47.4	51.7	70.8	61.4
Dentists	57.8	29.3	33.5	66.3	66.4	60.0	94.1
Designers, draftsmen, and inventors	83.7	16.5	25.0	136.3	101.5	20.7	91.8
Lawyers, judges, and justices	130.7	88.0	121.1	152.1	126.4	117.6	171.6
Musicians and teachers of music	134.5	60.4	96.5	167.0	134.3	118.9	263.8
Osteopaths	5.0	1.7	3.6	3.9	6.6	9.1	11.2
Photographers	32.2	13.3	24.4	36.2	34.1	30.7	71.4
Physicians and surgeons	125.2	95.1	108.0	138.0	130.0	113.6	159.6
Teachers	865.5	720.1	889.9	851.6	878.4	1,240.4	958.7
Teachers (athletics and dancing)	15.2	7.5	10.7	18.8	14.5	12.4	31.5
Teachers (school)	850.3	712.6	879.2	832.7	863.9	1,228.0	927.2
Technical engineers	184.3	81.5	127.1	242.7	185.3	124.7	332.5
Civil engineers and surveyors	83.1	50.1	75.5	95.8	75.0	68.6	173.7
Electrical engineers	47.1	17.1	24.0	72.5	46.4	26.4	68.2
Mechanical engineers	44.3	11.4	17.5	63.6	56.5	15.1	60.0
Mining engineers	9.7	2.9	10.1	10.8	7.4	14.6	30.6
Trained nurses	239.6	129.6	137.1	313.1	235.8	213.6	372.4
Veterinary surgeons	9.7	5.7	7.4	6.2	14.6	20.4	10.3
County agents, home demonstrators, etc.	4.5	6.8	7.0	2.2	3.9	7.6	6.2
Librarians	24.1	8.3	11.0	28.9	27.8	21.6	46.9
Social and welfare workers	25.4	12.8	11.6	34.9	27.0	13.8	36.7
Chiropractors	9.7	3.5	12.4	6.9	10.8	17.2	27.2
Healers	14.4	4.2	9.9	15.8	14.3	11.3	45.5
Religious workers	25.5	13.8	20.1	32.3	24.1	28.6	38.2

Source: Adapted from Kenneth Evans, "Some Occupational Trends in the South," *Social Forces*, 17 (December, 1938), p. 189.

TABLE 145. NEGRO PROFESSIONAL WORKERS PER 1,000 NEGRO POPULATION, UNITED STATES AND THE SIX MAJOR REGIONS, 1930

Area	Total Negro population	Negro professional worker		Area	Total Negro population	Negro professional worker	
		Number	Rate per 1,000			Number	Rate per 1,000
UNITED STATES	11,891,143	115,765	9.74	Middle States	1,181,115	14,466	12.25
				Northwest	97,229	1,593	16.38
Northeast	1,570,859	18,918	12.04	Far West	90,638	1,720	18.98
Southeast	7,778,473	63,823	8.20	District of Columbia	132,068	2,784	21.08
Southwest	1,040,761	12,461	11.97				

Note: Classification of "professional workers" as used by Alba M. Edwards of the Bureau of the Census.
Source: Adapted from Kenneth Evans, Changing Occupational Distribution in the South with Special Emphasis on the Rise of Professional Services (unpublished doctoral dissertation, University of North Carolina, 1938), Table XLVI.

direction of "catching up" with the rest of the Nation. There is nothing inherent, however, in this trend to guarantee its automatic continuation to the point of desirable balance within the region or among the regions in the Nation. Underlying the high percentage of increase in relative number of professional persons in the southern regions is, of course, the extremely low point from which the trend starts. And there is, in addition, the fact that at the end of the period in 1940, there still existed wide differentials between the South and the Nation in occupational distribution and in the availibility of all needed professional services.

Table 145 shows that the Negroes in the Southeast had the lowest proportion of professional workers of any region, 8.2 per 1,000 Negroes as compared with 19 in the Far West. Figures 96 and 97 in Chapter 11 also indicate under-representation of Negroes in these ranks. In spite of the lower numbers of Negroes in professional services and of their greater difficulty in rising into jobs on upper social-economic levels, the elimination of Negroes does not change the ranking of the southern regions in comparison with the Nation and with other regions. The achieving of occupational balance includes, but is obviously a more complex task than that of insuring equal cultural participation for the Negro population of the South, as difficult as that may be.

The obverse of the Southeast's lack of leadership is the fact that population increase in the region, in large measure, means the banking up of population in occupational levels where job opportunities are relatively limited. The war brought new dynamics into this static situation, and thus renewed the challenge that occupational redistribution offers both to the Nation and the region.

Several conclusions emerge from the study. Defined in terms of fame, leadership appears to diminish as we draw near the present. This may be the familiar optical illusion of the greatness of the distant founding fathers. But when measured in mass terms of simple talent and professional competence, leadership appears to be increasing both in the Nation and the region. The Southeast never equaled New England in leadership and it had a greater rate of decline as the fateful decade of 1860 approached. In talent and professional competence the Southeast still lags behind the Nation but its rate of gain shows not only the need but the possibility of closing the gap.

Evans' analysis showed that the problem of leadership and that of occupational mobility are closely related. The Southeast needs leadership if it is to achieve a more normal occupational distribution for its people. As the redistribution levels up the occupational hierarchy some few from the ranks of professions and specialists will develop that special talent, once characteristic of the South, which carries on to leadership for the economic and cultural development of whole masses of the people.

PART V

SOCIAL POLICY AND REGIONAL-NATIONAL PLANNING

CHAPTER 31

THE FORMULATION OF REGIONAL-NATIONAL POPULATION POLICY

THROUGHOUT PRECEDING chapters we have noted the relation of the conditions discussed to public policy. The discussion has raised questions that affect the future development of our national policy in the fields of agriculture and land utilization, in industrial location, unemployment and income distribution, in public health, public education, and social security. In the main, it can be said that the basic problems treated in this volume bear on two large fields in which national policy has not yet been formulated. These are the areas of (1) population policy and (2) the policy of regional-national development. It is our contention that sufficient factual materials are being developed in these fields to justify initial analysis of the issues involved in the determination of national policy.

SOCIAL RESEARCH AND POLICY FORMULATION

In a democracy the determination of policy is regarded as a rational process involving the adjustment of various group interests to the general welfare in terms of national goals to be sought. Basic to the process are the (1) social values held by members of a given society, (2) the indication of new goals to be sought, and (3) the readjustment of policy and procedures toward the new goals. The first indication that new goals should be sought is often given by research which demonstrates the conditions of maladjustment which have developed under previous social policies.

If the conditions disclosed by research prevent the realization of values held by the society or if they impinge on policies already adopted, they threaten national and group interests sufficiently to lead to the consideration of new policies. On this basis we can say that social research itself is affected with a public interest and bears a function in policy making.

When the issues are stated in this fashion it is doubtful whether any large group in our society would care to challenge the importance of social science in the formulation of public policy. There are, however, many considerations which operate to make the relation more complicated than the above statement suggests. Many of those who are devoted to the values of research doubt the competence of social scientists to write what we may call the prescriptions for public policy. This attitude, which is held by many sociologists and economists, does not involve doubt of the scientific value of social facts as facts. It is related, among other things, to the danger of bias involved in the selection of social facts. Since there exists in every society the danger of confusing individual, class, and group interests with the national interests, there is the tendency on the part of the public to confuse the function of the impartial scientist with that of the biased advocate. It is this confusion which some careful researchers seek to avoid by confining their work to a bare statement of facts without pointing out implications and interpretation. A second element closely related to bias is the fact that no specialist can hope to know or fully appreciate the bearing of other specialisms on his conclusions. Thus, for example, it would be possible for a majority of the experts in social work to advocate a policy which the majority of economists would oppose. A third reason for caution is the gap that exists between public policy and public administration. Thus many desirable goals are likely to go unrealized in public policy because of difficulties in administration.

Accordingly whatever competence the social sciences may attain, it is generally agreed that the determination of public policy does not fall within their scope. There are many reasons for this conclusion beside the fact that the world has never been ruled by the philosopher-kings that Plato visualized in his *Republic*. These reasons can be summarized by saying that the social studies aspire to be sciences while the determination of public policy must remain an art. As an art it involves the compromise of conflicting claims of rival parties and groups in the interest of the total welfare. Basic to the scientific viewpoint is the feeling that facts are objective entities and thus cannot be ruled out of existence by political compromises. By participation in the conflict over policy making, economists and sociologists have feared to lose the objectivity and freedom from bias essential to science.

Unlike a work of art which may be regarded as an entity—a good in itself—the literature of information raises the question: to what end? This is especially true of social and economic research whose findings are related to a national and cultural context. Such research may have two possible implications: (1) It may be designed to arrive at general natural laws or hypotheses similar to those prevailing in the natural sciences. In this respect neither sociology nor economics has yet been able to complete a rounded picture of the universe in which it operates. (2) On the other hand, research may serve as the basis for the development of public policy in a given field. This is not the whole purpose of social research as conducted in our colleges and universities, but its importance may be suggested by the statement that if public policy is not based on information it will obviously be based on misinformation or none at all.

It is, of course, logical to contend, as some do, that national policy is normally based on prejudice and emotion and that facts count only as they serve to reenforce tradition. The mistake involved in this reasoning may be clarified by saying that while social values, including the national interest and legal and constitutional commitments, undoubtedly operate to determine the policies that will be based upon a given set of facts, social facts themselves serve to determine not only what is feasible but often what is desirable. Social policy accordingly may be regarded as the conclusion of a logical syllogism whose major premise is the social values held by the group and whose minor premise is the social facts in so far as they can be developed by research.

Obviously, the social values of any society exert a determining force. The same set of facts, if they existed in Russia and the United States, could lead to opposite policies simply because of the different sets of values on which the two governments are predicated. What remains to be pointed out, however, is that over long periods of time the complex of social values themselves are subject to rational redirection on the basis of new conditions, new facts, or even of old facts newly discovered.

Thus there exists a certain validity behind the demand that an analysis of maladjustments in society be accompanied by a discussion of the issues involved in the reformulation of policy. It is the seriousness of the situation that gives to research its initial relevance; and it is only by the nature and profundity of the changes recommended that the reader can judge the seriousness of the condition discussed. Then there is the question of relative competence. Admitting that the politician is competent to estimate the force of public opinion behind the demands of various groups, he may make use of this knowledge only to solve the question of how best to win the next election. Knowledge of the facts must go over into the determination of public policy and here the results of research are the nearest to competence.

Thus in spite of his modesty the social scientist who uncovers and analyzes social facts will be asked: What do you recommend? As an honest man who values his own integrity, as a citizen who admits a public duty, and as an expert in whose training society has made an investment, the social scientist after admitting his reservations of ignorance and bias must indicate his choices of policy for whatever they may be worth. Nor should he be overwhelmed by this assumption of high responsibility, for he may rest assured that even his facts will be discounted by practical men of affairs as impossible theory while his cautious recommendations will be regarded as partisan statements by every faction whose interests they oppose. But if his facts are facts and still disregarded, he may take what consolation he can to himself in the knowledge that they also will count in the long run to come.

PUBLIC POLICY AND SOCIAL PLANNING

The implementation of social policy is found in the process we have come to call social planning. What is the nature of planning in a democracy characterized as is our society by a liberal capitalistic economy? In the first place, as John Dewey once pointed out, the ideal to be sought, is not a *planned society* but a continuously *planning society*. There is as far as we know no permanent solutions to economic and social problems. Society exists as a continual process of adjustment and readjustment of its multiple groups and individuals. Unless society is continually adjusting and readjusting its elements fall so far out of balance that integration and equilibrium are not achieved. Lags and injustices arise and disequilibrium and disorganization ensue.

Throughout history the methods of meeting these maladjustments have been sporadic reforms, revolutions, civil wars, and international war. William Graham Sumner once defined revolution as a liquidation of the accumulated maladjustments in the mores. Revolutions sometimes destroy the mould of society and then break down at the point where they attempt to carry over to the new economic and political order. To some extent social planning can be regarded as a new movement that has arisen in modern society as a result of the failure of older attempts at social change. It is not Utopian, it is not revolutionary; in some respects it is not even reformist. Its aim is to prevent the need for these violent changes before they occur. Its goal is not a definitely planned society, fixed once and for all, but a continually planning and replanning society. The process itself is dynamic, for the goal is not static organization but one continually adjusting and changing as new goals are set and old ones achieved.

Democracies like other societies must face the danger of crises and wars but in the more normal course of events it can be said that social planning had its beginnings in need of governments to plan their budgets ahead. Social and economic planning as is often said depends on prediction and control. These measures are involved in the process of balancing appropriations and expenditures. In addition, the budget itself comes to be regarded not as an accountant's statement but as incorporating long run plans and measures of control. In adopting these measures government is simply following the best procedures of business where corporations have found it necessary to plan policy in advance of current operations.

Scientific knowledge is needed to determine the direction in which society is likely to move, and control measures are required to effect needed adjustments. Adjustment and security may be regarded as the keynotes of society's planning just as they are the goals of free individual initiative and self-development. Social security as governmental policy may fail if it attempts to provide social insurance for inefficient economic alignments. Adjustment is more dynamic, for it represents not only the efforts that individuals and groups make to remedy their own undesirable situations but includes the additional incentives and pressures that society may use to hasten these desirable changes. The processes of seeking more education and migrating to areas of greater economic opportunity represent individual adjustments that also operate in the interests of greater economic security of the total society. By aiding in such adjustments liberal governments can develop the control measures adequate to social planning in a democracy.

Once assured that processes of continued adjustment are facilitated, government may then make the attempt to underwrite certain minimum guarantees against those dangers of unemployment and old age for which the individual in our society is unable to prove adequate adjustment. No social security program, however, can hope to succeed in a dynamic world if it cancels out the push toward adjustment. The assurance of continuing adjustment and readjustment among the various sections of a national economy is prerequisite to the success of any system of social security. No government, however rich, can afford to underwrite the social insurance for a system held rigid by economic barriers and monopolies. Later we shall see that these two concepts of adjustment and security have operated in the development of population policy.

REGIONAL-NATIONAL POPULATION POLICY

The formulation and articulation of population policy presents additional difficulties. The adjustment of regional to national needs, the theme of this chapter is only one factor involved in the equation. While the answer must be sought in terms of population replacements such a policy must meet three basic criteria. It must make for national survival, it must serve the goal of economic stability, and it must be democratic.

The United States as Thompson and Whelpton[1] point out, had a practical and effective population policy dating almost from the beginning of white settlement. That the policy met the first two criteria seems to be indicated by our history. The tendency of land grants, settlement

[1] Warren S. Thompson and P. K. Whelpton, *Population Trends in the United States* (New York: McGraw-Hill Book Company, 1933), chap. XI.

policies, easy immigration, homestead laws, and the slave trade, itself, were all calculated to increase population numbers. It was by this means the various communities expected to increase the safety of life, the value of property, and raise the standard of group living. The first major reversal in our national policy was signalized by restriction of foreign immigration—a task which was accomplished by the quota legislation of June 3, 1921, after debate lasting over five decades.

The same policy that encouraged unrestricted immigration also looked with favor upon the rearing of large families. This attitude was given official sanction in the Federal legislation of 1873 in the so-called "Comstock Laws" which made use of the Federal power over customs, the mails, and interstate commerce to suppress the circulation of contraceptive information and devices as "obscene literature and articles of immoral use." Between the nonenforcement of restrictive laws and the breaking of them by individuals in the sanctity of the family, the influence of anti-contraceptive legislation in maintaining the birth rate steadily dwindled until the invalidation of the law by judicial decision in the New York Superior Court in 1936 (United States vs. Dr. Hannah Stone). Nevertheless this policy undoubtedly served to increase class differentials in the birth rate—an effect not foreseen by its proponents.

As it has developed the effective policy in this country is now (1) one of restriction by the government of population increase from without by the control of immigration, and (2) restriction by individuals of increase from within by family limitation. Throughout our history we have with the aid of immigration obtained sufficient births by reliance on spontaneous and unregulated fertility to populate a continent. We are now approaching the position where we will have to plan a population policy.

We cannot hope to accommodate a continually increasing population but in our present state of knowledge it would seem safe to accept as a goal the stabilization of our numbers around the level we should reach in 1960-1980, some 150 to 160 millions.[2] At such a figure manpower will be adequate for national defense without subjecting us to the Malthusian pressure of population upon land and natural resources. To hold our numbers stationary even at 160 millions will not give us the economic dynamic we once experienced by virtue of a continually increasing population, but it will save us from the economic collapse to be feared if population began a downward spiral.

It is accordingly not the goal of a stable population but the means of its attainment that must pass the tests of both democracy and economics. Under the assumptions of democracy there are two sets of values to be considered: individual and collective. Individual values derive from the doc-

[2] Warren S. Thompson, *Population Problems* (New York: McGraw-Hill Book Company, 1942), p. 438.

trines of individual liberty so cherished in our democratic tradition. In their bearing on population they include the right to marry or refrain from marriage, free of state coercion, and the right to have few or no children free from pressure of state power. It is here that the democracies part company with the totalitarian governments which have not hesitated in this field to employ the coercive power of the state.

In so far as our population policy is based on democratic assumptions they have been stated in terms of individual freedom which is taken to mean the individual's freedom from State interference. Except in the few States where the Catholic Church is strong this has also meant the freedom of organized private agencies to agitate for birth control and for private philanthropy to organize and finance clinics for contraceptive services. Freedom from governmental restrictions, however, is not freedom from ignorance or poverty. Even where freedom to limit family size is not restricted by law, it may be distinctly circumscribed by social conditions. The failure of contraception among those most needing it does not result from repressive measures on the part of the government, but it is doubtful if these conditions will be greatly changed short of positive State measures. This is true in spite of the fact that privately organized birth control agencies have received freedom for educational propaganda and clinical practice.

The extent to which this freedom represents a distinct departure in policy—a departure so distinct that it would not be tolerated in either totalitarian or Catholic countries—is shown by their program. The national organization, the Planned Parenthood Federation of America as the successor to the old American League for Birth Control has set up its three major objectives in the fields of education, medical services, and research. The Federation's educational program is devoted to calling the attention of leaders in medicine and the public to the medical, social, and economic importance of child-spacing programs. In the field of medicine its goal is to have planned parenthood accepted as a normal part of maternal and child health programs, whether under the auspices of hospitals, public health clinics, or in the office of the private practitioner. The research program is devoted both to the development of simpler, more effective, and less expensive techniques of conception control and of measures leading to the reduction of sterility among those married couples who wish children and are unable to have them.[3]

These conditions have brought us to the verge of a new development in a regional population policy for the South. As in the Nation, this policy finds its basis in economic needs. The unbalanced man-land ratios of the Southeast force the necessity of further adjustment on the population in its

[3] Richard N. Pierson, M. D., "Planned Parenthood in a War Year," *Human Fertility*, VII (March, 1943), 1-4.

search for security. These adjustments include forced migration, low wages, and the necessity for increased industrialization. In addition it is realized that as more attention is paid to child care and maternal health deaths decrease, standards rise, and the birth rate falls. An important factor in this advance among upper and middle class families has been the freedom of the family physician to prescribe contraception in private practice.

The public health service has been generally accepted as one means of bringing medical advances to the general population. What could be more logical than for the States of the region to pioneer in making birth control an official part of the public health service? This new policy was signalized when in 1937 the North Carolina State Board adopted as an optional part of the county health program a contraceptive service for mothers too poor to afford family physicians. South Carolina and Alabama have since developed state programs endorsed by the State medical societies and administered by the State boards of health. In 1942 four additional State medical societies—those of Florida, Tennessee, Virginia, and West Virginia—passed resolutions recommending the provision of child-spacing information by private and public health physicians. A survey in 1939 showed that the Southeast had 136 of the 166 public health contraceptive services then established in the United States. The development of these services in our analysis is to be regarded as the beginnings of a regional population policy in the area of highest fertility.

The effect that this development is likely to have on fertility in rural areas is shown by an experiment in a coal mining county of West Virginia.[4] In Logan County in 1936-1938 contraceptive services were made available to over 1300 rural nonfarm women, 32 percent of those aged 15-44 in the county. This group controlled over 50 percent of the county's fertility. The uncontrolled chances of conception, it appeared, were no higher in the Appalachians than elsewhere, but the region's higher birth rates were influenced by an age of marriage two years younger than the national average. About a third of the Negroes and a half of the whites had sought to limit family size before they contacted the service, but their average efficiency of 50 percent had meant a reduction of only 10 to 15 percent in the chance of conception. After admission to the service, the birth rate among this group fell 41 percent—a decline that would have reduced the county's birth rate by 20 percent, if extended to all rural nonfarm women. After two years, however, only 36 percent of the women were still using the prescribed methods.

The experiment shows the effectiveness of even imperfect methods. The greater part of the gain in protection was due to increased precautions,

[4] Gilbert Wheeler Beebe, *Contraception and Fertility in the Southern Appalachians* (Baltimore: The Williams and Wilkins Company, 1942), especially chaps. III and V.

contraceptive exposure increasing 70 to 80 percent as compared with only 20 to 30 percent gain in contraceptive efficiency. Among other things the experiment indicated that family limitation alone is not a method by which the region can achieve social and economic parity with the Nation. Such service it showed should be medical in nature, but the need went far beyond the protection of a few women against medically contra-indicated pregnancy. The policy it was concluded, should be social and economic as well as therapeutic; and the analysis showed that costs can be reduced 50 percent by integration with public health services already in existence. Similar experiments with both urban and rural Negroes show that they are willing and able to make use of such services to improve their health and social conditions.

There may be little disposition to deny that the implementation of this policy fits in with our assumptions of democracy and will help to meet the economic needs of the South. No one is likely to contend, however, that by itself this departure meets the criteria of a national population policy. The plain fact is that we cannot hope to hold numbers stable after 1980 unless we can reverse the trend of our national and class fertility. That we now have population replacements in the United States is due to the fact that the groups ignorant of contraception and isolated from the strain of keeping up with urban and middle class standards still have families large enough to make up the deficit. All attempts based on persuasion and education to increase fertility in the middle classes and those best able to provide for children have so far met admitted failure. The two-child family is becoming the accepted ideal of the middle class.

No society, even under the most favorable mortality conditions, can maintain itself without a significant proportion of large families. At present demographic rates it will require an average of approximately three children per fertile family to maintain our population. This makes allowance for those women who do not marry, those who either die or become widowed or divorced before the end of their reproductive life, for those who prove sterile or childless, and for the children who die before maturity. Many distributions of family size will yield a self-replacing population, but all of these require that about 40 percent of the married women bear four or more children. Differential fertility, it must be realized, is simply evidence of the lag with which family limitation has percolated downward through the social strata. As the process is completed the birth rate in the Nation may fall below replacements, not likely to rise again.

"At present," Frank Notestein points out, "as a Nation we are obtaining just enough large families to maintain a stationary population only because freedom to limit fertility is withheld from large populations in our most poverty stricken areas."[5] When this freedom is brought to these populations the birth rate will fall below the replacements, unless we can develop a population policy that either takes account of the present values of society or develops new values based on family affection, national survival, and economic security. Such a policy, if it is to be conceived in terms of democracy will not place on the least fortunate the burden of doing the most to maintain population.

In the meantime, as he points out, "there are many couples who want children and could have them if they had proper medical attention, or if parenthood entailed less severe economic penalties. This situation points clearly to the need for a much greater emphasis on the positive aspects of the freedom of parenthood by both the birth control and the eugenics movement. Freedom of parenthood which means the freedom to limit but not to express fertility is at best a negative freedom. Both kinds are essential to a democratic society that intends to maintain its culture and stock through the voluntary acceptance of the obligations of parenthood."[6]

Any policy for population is accordingly part and parcel of our larger policy, economic and political. Certainly there can be no better touchstone for our total national policy than this question: Is it conducive to the conservation and development of our total human resources? A final emphasis accordingly is placed on expanding economic opportunity so that by adding to our total wealth, our maturing population may expect to secure the means necessary to physical and cultural growth. In this task regional planning for the South will loom large.

[5] Frank Notestein, "Some Implications of Current Demographic Trends," *Journal of Heredity*, XXX (March, 1939), 125-126.
[6] *Ibid.*

CHAPTER 32

WANTED: THE NATION'S FUTURE FOR THE SOUTH

THE ATTAINMENT of a population stabilized at adequate numbers is not to be regarded as a worthy goal if it is to be done at the cost of the poverty and ignorance of those who do the most to maintain replacements. If these handicaps are visited upon the children of the more fertile classes and regions, the quality of oncoming population will suffer further deterioration. Nevertheless, in view of our need for replacements, the restriction of numbers by itself seems at best a negative policy. Granting that children under present trends may become fewer, positive policy would indicate the conservation and development of human resources wherever found. This study of the South suggests that this goal can best be attained by regional-national planning.

More than anything else the future of the Southeast depends upon the development of resources and capacities that are as yet largely unrealized. The region has natural resources and human resources. These forms of wealth are primary, but for their development they depend upon the building up of technological resources, institutional resources, and capital resources. The creation of these secondary forms of wealth, as Howard W. Odum has pointed out, are matters of organization, skill, and previous experience.[1] This is both an economic and a cultural task in which the Nation is as vitally concerned as the region itself.

THE FUTURE WE WANT

In making plans for our future development it is essential to decide in what direction the Nation and the region are going. Better still, we should agree as to the place we want to go. Three questions are involved in this decision: (1) What do we want? (2) What do we have? and (3) What must we do to get from what we have to what we want?

[1] Howard W. Odum, *Southern Regions of the United States* (Chapel Hill: University of North Carolina Press, 1936), pp. 337-339.

Stated in these terms the question of what the South wants admits of a very definite answer. The South wants to share the Nation's future. It is not the existence of regional inequalities that disturbs the South so much. It is their persistence over the generations. Is this to continue into the indefinite future, America's dream of equality of opportunity to the contrary? In the chances of war things are likely to get worse before they get better. The South is committed to the prosecution of the war and, while it cannot contribute its proportionate share of money to the war effort, it is contributing its proportion of manpower. The South is characteristically optimistic about the war; it is not so optimistic about its place in the nation's future. The new regionalism is an indication of this trend, and if one had to phrase its implications it would be in seven words: Wanted: The Nation's future for the South.

It is a basic contention of the present study that national policy toward regional development assumes similar goals. The national interest in regional development accordingly is related to such desirable goals as increased economic well-being, equalized cultural and educational opportunities, and effective national defense. Only on this basis can the Federal power expect to secure the tax resources which support and the manpower which defends our national survival.[2]

In its simplest form the relation of the regions to the Nation is the relation of the parts to the whole—the old problem of securing unity out of diversity expressed in our motto—"E pluribus unum." In organization and political administration we have the forty-eight States and their Federal union but, in the problems of public policy involved in fields like interstate migration, conservation, agriculture, social security, etc., we can think of areas possessing certain geographic, economic, and social characteristics in common. Thus, for example, we simplify both the problems of research in land utilization and those of administering agricultural programs by thinking in broad terms of types of farming regions, covering many States. So logical is this development that practically all Federal agencies intrusted with the administration of programs have found it advisable to set up regional areas based on such criteria.[3]

In the Tennessee Valley Authority the Southeast has the outstanding development in regional-national planning so far projected in the United States. The presence in the region of this national project serves to indicate the importance of regional development in the whole national policy. In defense, in power production, in navigation and flood control and in

[2] National Resources Planning Board, *Regional Planning, Part XI—The Southeast* (Washington, D. C.: U. S. Government Printing Office, 1942), pp. 8-11.
[3] National Resources Planning Board, *Regional Factors in National Planning and Development* (Washington, D. C.: U. S. Government Printing Office, 1935).

economic well-being, national progress and security in a country as large and diverse as ours is dependent on the integrated development of broad regional areas.

We cannot discuss planning without considering whether improvement in the state of technology and the industrial arts would not raise the standard of living in the Southeast and thus for the Nation. A former director of the T.V.A. once imagined that Daniel Boone might have sat down with an Indian hunter of the Tennessee Valley and told him: "There is ten times as much wealth in the valley as you are getting out of it." Today with electrification and modern agricultural and industrial methods the T.V.A. is in the position of saying to the people in the Valley: "There is ten times as much potential wealth in this region as we are realizing."

The Southeast is only one among many regions that make up our national domain. While it is recognized that our regional areas are more likely to develop along complementary than identical lines, the goal of the process involves a fair degree of equalization and integration in the total progress of the Nation. Economic security and cultural opportunity are common goals for all the areas of the Nation. Only as regional needs, resources, and capacities are balanced against each other through full and free discussion can we arrive at an integrated national policy.

National policy as reflected in the social legislation enacted by Congress in recent years has gone far to implement these values. If one were to summarize in popular language the intent of this legislation from 1932 to 1942 it might well read as follows: "It is now generally recognized by the national governments of democratic countries that it is the function of organized society to make possible the best and fullest use of the *productive* resources of the Nation so that every able-bodied man may be afforded a continuing opportunity to earn, through his *productive* labor, a decent living, and to enjoy this living within the institutions of freedom established and guaranteed by the Nation, thereby promoting the defense of the Nation, the general welfare, and his own well-being."[4] Nor can it be said that our system of government and our way of life is functioning properly until every able-bodied man is, in fact and not just in theory, afforded this continuing opportunity.

These goals are obviously so desirable that the national interest in regional development need only be stated to be recognized. The problem accordingly becomes one of working out adequate and efficient means to their accomplishment. Here we enter the field of public policy where it is desirable to state regional goals and to evaluate the means of reaching them in terms of national programs.

Programs looking toward these ends may be initiated at the Federal

[4] I am indebted to Wilhelm Anderson for this statement of the issues.

level and adjusted for regional variations in economic and social conditions. Conversely they may be developed out of regional needs initiated at State and local government levels and yet demand Federal power and administration for their implementation. The important thing is that the Federal structure of our government as it has evolved is designed to aid regional progress through programs involving Federal-State relations.

NATIONAL POLICY AND REGIONAL DEVELOPMENT

The importance of these issues for future policy is indicated by the extent to which regional divergencies still prevent the attainment of social values to which we are committed. Education here serves as an example. In terms of social values we have long been agreed on the basic principle of the maintenance of equality of opportunity among our people wherever found. Devotion to the value of education, some have claimed, is almost a fetish among our people. Certainly it is seen as the chief means for the equalization of opportunity as well as the government's means of protecting itself from the consequences of an ignorant and incompetent citizenry. Nevertheless all studies of the subject show how much we lack of equalizing educational expenditures. In spite of well-developed patterns of Federal grants-in-aid, the relations between our Federal and local governments were such that during the period of change that characterized the New Deal no major advances were made. That we have yet to achieve equality of educational opportunity indicates that regional-national policies are still to be formulated if we hope to reach the goal set by social values.

Another indication of the trend is the growing impatience with the term "sectionalism" as applied to regional aspirations. Liberal publicists in the Nation and the region are willing to argue the merits of regional plans and proposals, but less and less do the regions deserve to have any of their worthy ambitions dismissed under the old term "sectionalism." Sectionalism must be recognized as a possible danger in any country as large and diverse as our own. It is not always realized, however, that one of the legitimate aims of national-regional planning is to aid in providing the conditions that make the development of sectionalism unlikely. Economic diversities and inequalities may offer the basis for sectional consciousness and sectional movements. Where the economic interests of certain areas are sufficiently divergent from those of the Nation and other major areas, we may expect conflict centers to develop. A diversified economy equally balanced among the extractive, manufacturing, service, and financial interests is accepted as primarily essential to a modern nation. Lack of such balance may so penalize a region that it fails to share in national prosperity. National strength and unity follow when all regions have an appreciable stake in enterprises that lead to national prosperity.

Regionalism, it is true, should be regarded as a form of local patriotism, but like good local self-government it is in alliance with rather than in opposition to national interests. Regionalism thus represents a movement toward national strength. Instead of the old fighting pattern of sectionalism which in the end became a divisive movement, the regionalist would substitute a program of regional-national integration in which the Nation would gain much of its power from the balance and accommodation of regional variations.

A GOAL FOR THE FUTURE

In discussing the future we want for the Southeast, it should be possible to state a common goal so that we can see the subsidiary issues simply as means to an end upon which we are agreed. If our experiences with depression and war have meant anything, Howard W. Odum has pointed out, they have increased our determination "to conserve, develop, and make more useful those two great sources of the good society, . . . our natural wealth and our human wealth."[5]

If our desires did not exceed their realization, there would be little hope for progress in the area. We may begin with the future we want and then attempt to realize the distance between what is actual and what is potential and attainable, not tomorrow but in the reasonable future of a generation or so hence.

Actually, we shall not know how to appraise the resources we have unless we know what we want to do with them. We must know, as Erich W. Zimmermann[6] pointed out, what kind of society we want to develop in this region before we can realize what kind of resources we possess. Natural resources are simply those aspects of the physical environment which men use to satisfy individual and social needs. Without man's control and direction, resources lie inert and unused. What people want and need thus determine not only what use they will make of inert nature; they determine what portions of their physical environment they will develop and what they will leave untouched.

If we were to make an all-inclusive statement of the regional goal that best fits with the long-time goal of national planning, it might well be a higher level of living for the great mass of the South's population.[7] Unemployment, inadequate income, underconsumption, and inefficient use of natural and human resources are seen as the constituents of a low standard in a nation as richly endowed as America. "A modern nation," it has been

---

[5] "New Sources of Vitality for the People," *Journal of the American Dietetic Association*, 14 (June-July, 1938), 417.

[6] "Resources of the South," *South Atlantic Quarterly*, 32 (July, 1933), 213-226.

[7] See the writer's statement in National Resources Planning Board, *Regional Planning, Part XI—The Southeast*, pp. 42-43.

pointed out, "can not avoid balancing its total production-consumption budget. This can be done at a low level with a great deal of unemployment, inefficiency, and suffering; or it can be done at a high level with full employment, high efficiency, and a better life for all."[8]

For the total population, higher standards of living are required not only to save human resources from the deterioration due to malnutrition, poor housing and the inadequate satisfaction of cultural needs, but to insure the level of activity necessary to keep the economic mechanism functioning. In the long run it must be realized that the Nation can balance its budget and carry its fiscal burden only by stabilizing the national income at a high level—possibly in the case of the United States at approximately one hundred billion dollars annually. The attainment of such an income level would serve two functions. It would (1) greatly reduce the necessity for emergency expenditures and (2) raise the tax base. It would thus conserve our human resources by balancing consumption at a high level with the production necessary to assure full employment. In postwar planning the achievement of this goal seems the only thing likely to prevent the recurrence of a great depression.

The Southeast is a strategic area in this approach for its population, suffering from real and concealed unemployment, low productivity, and low income, has a per capita consumption of the goods and services produced by our industrial economy that is lower than any region in the Nation. Thus the region's need to balance production and consumption at high levels fits in with desirable national goals.

The hopes and aspirations which any people hold for their region as a part of the Nation and the world are seen as the necessary major premise of any regional plan. The regional survey which furnishes the inventory of resources and capacities is the minor premise of the syllogism whose conclusion is the regional plan of development.[9] In this analysis, then, population policy is closely integrated with the future of our physical resources and with the economic organization and governmental plans necessary to their fullest utilization and development.

THE FUTURE OF PHYSICAL RESOURCES

We may begin accordingly with some account of what we should expect from our national wealth. It is something of a paradox to say that in the Southeast we need a fuller utilization of physical resources for the benefit of the present generation balanced with fuller conservation for the benefit of future generations.

[8] National Resources Planning Board, *After Defense What?* (Washington, D. C.: U. S. Government Printing Office, 1942).

[9] For details see National Resources Planning Board, *Regional Planning, Part XI—The Southeast.* Also John V. Van Sickle, *Planning for the South, an Inquiry into the Economics of Regionalism* (Nashville, Tennessee: Vanderbilt University Press, 1943).

It is a fuller, not a lesser, use of our physical resources that we must strive for in the Southeast simply because of our need to achieve a higher standard of living. It must be emphasized moreover that not full use but abuse is the enemy of conservation. Conservation is not to be defined as abstinence for the sake of posterity, but rather as living on a replaceable flow of goods instead of on stored-up capital. Thus stated the distinction is between the cropping and the mining of resources.

It is fortunate that in its large scale dependence on organic resources the agrarian Southeast is capable of developing what we may call a flow economy rather than a store economy. The annual increase of flocks and herds and the growth of crops, like the flow of water power, comes as an increment from the hands of nature without greatly diminishing its capital store. Sound conservation practices may help to give higher yields for the present and yet conserve nature's capital endowment for the future. Mineral resources, however, must be regarded as a store, for a mine once rifled is not replaceable. The flow economy of organic life is also violated when resources of virgin forests, fisheries, and even soils are cleared out at one fell swoop.

Although it must be realized that these two concepts tend to shade into each other, the idea of utilizing a flow of energies and resources instead of rifling a store is valuable in distinguishing between the tendencies of a short-run and a long-run economy. Water power is accepted as a perfect example of the use of a flow of energy, but if a water power reservoir is allowed to silt up it becomes an example of the store economy, for it loses each year a part of its original capital of stored-up energy. The sign of a mine, it is said, is a hole in the ground, and the depletion of minerals is usually regarded as a good example of the store economy. With the rise of the junk man and the utilization of scrap, however, we are developing a continuous flow of resources in the field of metals to supplement the depletion of ores. While this process cannot extend to the conservation of coal and oil, the transition to the use of water power makes possible a greater use of energy in the long-run economy.

Plans for future development in the Southeast will thus attempt to provide for greater utilization and conservation by building up the resource base and thus increasing the flow of energy and resources. Restoration of soil fertility and further extension of soil conservation practices are necessary to provide a continuous flow of agricultural production; further extension of scientific forestry in private and public holdings is necessary to provide for the continuous production of timber resources. Those who plan for wildlife conservation realize that the stock of game will never again be large enough to admit of its use as an essential food resource. Here the problem is one of building up natural wealth to the point where the annual increase of game may be used for the recreation of hunters and fishermen. Scientific forestry, on the contrary, is not reduced to the assumption that we can have lumber only by depleting all the resources of virgin timber. Continuous operation of forest resources and multiple use appear entirely feasible. The South's greatest problem in the field of conservation of resources is that of soil erosion—a loss that if left unchecked will threaten the whole basis of the flow economy.

Finally we are led to a consideration of the relation of physical resources to human resources in terms of the long-run implications of a flow economy. Since our man-land ratio is unbalanced on the side of too many men and too little good land, one corrective is to increase the quantity of good land. Land here must be understood in a very broad sense as practically synonymous with "nature." Hence capital investment in such things as soil conservation, terracing, increased fertility, better farm buildings, improved oyster beds, better orchards, disease-resistant species of crops, and purebred livestock is building up the land part of the ratio quite as much as capital investment in a drainage project, a coal mine or a hosiery mill. When capital is poured into the land side of the ratio it makes the man side relatively scarcer and hence more valuable.[10]

PUBLIC POLICY AND HUMAN RESOURCES IN INDUSTRY

It is the persistence of regional inequalities over the generations that implements the demands for regional-national planning. In this country we have over a large area the closest approximation to the assumptions underlying free individual initiative, namely: free trade, free mobility of the people, free education, and no legal restrictions on the movements of goods, capital, and people. If the assumptions underlying laissez-faire really worked, the people might have moved out of the South if conditions were hopeless. Industries might have moved in and developed the region as its resources proved valuable. While these processes of adjustment have taken place, they must be aided by regional-national planning.

Regional variations in resources, productivity, wages, and income are so great within the Nation and the region that we should not only expect but encourage the continued flow of both capital and labor. Here the development of national policy has come in the integration of the Federal and State employment services in what amounts to a program of guided migration. Spontaneous population movements will continue but they need no longer be based on false information or no information. In addition, the F.S.A. and the W.P.A. have cooperated in experiments in subsidizing the migration of farm workers from overcrowded areas to areas of greater opportunity.

[10] I am indebted here to a statement by Albert S. Keister in National Resources Planning Board, *Regional Planning, Part XI—The Southeast.*

The crowding is the greatest and incomes are the lowest at the base of the occupational pyramid. Unless those near the bottom can climb to higher levels of skill and capacity, increased migration will simply serve to share the poverty with other regions with no benefit to the general welfare. Programs for developing the skills of oncoming youth have been developed in the N.Y.A., in apprenticeship training, and in the upgrading procedures adopted in war industries. As new techniques are tested and applied we may expect raw recruits to increase their worth to prospective employers and to society at the same time. Obviously higher skills are needed not only in the industrial discipline, but in agriculture and forestry as well.

It was in the quests for higher levels of income and higher standards of living, that the Southeast turned originally to industrial development.[11] Regional variations in wages still exist throughout the United States, but the Southeast especially has come to be known as the region of the differential wage. There were many reasons, no doubt, for low wages in the Southeast, but presumably they derived from (1) inadequate capital equipment, (2) large population increases, (3) the pressure of labor seeking escape from an over-crowded agriculture, and the (4) population's lack of training in the industrial discipline.

In terms of balancing needed consumption with potential production, this tends to establish the balance at a low level, the lowest in the Nation. The Southeast may not soon be able to change these conditions, but it can make up its mind whether under normal conditions low wages should be regarded as a permanent resource of the region.

This new attitude toward human resources is also made necessary by the fact that in our industrial life national policy has underwritten certain guarantees of social security that are threatened by the population pressure in the Southeast. In our effort to conserve human resources and maintain standards, the national policy has set up certain levels below which the Federal power cannot and does not allow the States to fall. The Fair Labor Standards Act thus sets up minimum wages and maximum hours of work to which industries must conform, if their products are to move in interstate commerce. Programs of social security and unemployment compensation, together with Federal aid to public highways, to vocational and agricultural education, all set up minimum standards below which States must not fall.

Three corollaries as to future industrial development in the Southeast seem to follow from the assumptions behind the Fair Labor Standards Act. First, while standards affect only minimum wages they will in time come

---

[11] See author's statement in National Resources Planning Board, *Regional Planning, Part XI—The Southeast*, pp. 45-46; also "Human Resources and Public Policy: An Essay toward Regional-National Planning," *Social Forces*, XXII (October, 1943), 23-25.

to be felt throughout the whole level of wages and skills. Secondly, if southern industry and labor are to gain access to national markets, they must in the long run be equal in efficiency and productivity to any in the Nation. Third, southern firms on the margin of bankruptcy cannot long be saved from the consequences of mismanagement by recourse to the payment of substandard wages. When such firms fail, their laborers and their share of production will be taken over by more efficient firms in the region, if they can make the grade; outside, if they cannot. Higher standards, it is now generally recognized, offer industry its one hope of disposing of its product in mass markets once the war boom has passed. It is doubtful if the Southeast or any other region can present legitimate claims to stand in the way of the development of a national minimum wage.

There remains the problem of those who may face unemployment even at a high level of economic activity. In our national policy, the problems of those who grow too old to work, those who are temporarily unemployed, and those who for various reasons are unemployable are met in the program for social security. In this situation, as in the Fair Labor Standards Act, we can no longer depend upon the assumptions prevalent in classical economics as to the beneficent effect of unregulated supply and demand on unprotected units of labor. By action of the State, the political citizen is now an economic citizen with certain minimum rights of economic security underwritten by the State.

In the enactment of laws providing for unemployment compensation, old-age insurance, and the provision of relief and made work for the unemployed, we have abandoned laissez-faire economics in a return to an older conception of social policy.[12] The wealth of the Nation is pledged to a collective underwriting of the economic welfare of citizens at certain minimum standards. This, it must be realized, makes national-regional planning imperative in the economic sphere. Postwar unemployment is now accepted as a risk to our total national security, pledged as it is to this new program. To support insurance against unemployment on the part of the few requires a high level of employment among the many. To support old-age retirement funds for the increasing numbers of the aged will require a continuing high level of national income. These conditions are worth reviewing for they emphasize the stake that our national policy has assumed in underwriting high levels of employment, productivity, and total national income. With its solvency at stake in carrying out its guarantees of security to its citizens, the Nation cannot proceed on the assumptions of the older economic order. It is no longer enough for the Nation to

[12] For the author's view that security represents a return to the values of earlier community life, see his "Security and Adjustment: The Return to the Larger Community," *Social Forces*, XXII (May, 1944), 363-370.

hope for continued employment and high national income; it must seek to plan for the achievement of these conditions.

The Southeast offers an especial problem in this field because two of its major groups, agricultural and domestic laborers, remain outside the guaranties of unemployment and old-age insurance. More than in any other region these two groups predominate in the economic life of the Southeast. The result was that in 1937 when the Nation had 70 percent of its employed workers covered by old-age insurance, the Southeast had hardly half, indicating the predominance of agriculture in the region. Thus the Southeast had half of its employed women in covered occupations as compared to three-fourths in the Nation—but less than half of its men workers were found in covered occupations as compared with 70 percent for the Nation (Table 146). The region with lower incomes is thus left with larger numbers to be provided for by the various forms of public relief which depend largely on the fiscal capacity of the States. For the region to reach and maintain a high level of income and security for its future workers a way must be found to extend to these groups the benefits of our social security program.

TABLE 146. EMPLOYEES AGED 15-64 COVERED BY OLD-AGE INSURANCE AS PERCENTAGE OF ALL WORKERS AVAILABLE FOR EMPLOYMENT AND ALL WORKERS EMPLOYED 15-64, UNITED STATES AND SOUTHEAST, 1937
(Workers in Thousands)

Area and Sex	Number Workers 15-64		Workers 15-64 Covered by Insurance		
	All available	Employed	Number	Percent of all available	Percent of employed
UNITED STATES					
ALL...............	52,630	41,994	30,024	57.0	71.5
Male...............	38,363	31,247	21,801	56.8	69.8
Female............	14,267	10,747	8,223	57.6	76.5
SOUTHEAST					
ALL...............	10,511	8,573	4,238	40.3	49.4
Male...............	7,670	6,465	3,150	41.1	48.7
Female............	2,841	2,108	1,088	38.3	51.6

Note: Workers available for employment include totally unemployed, emergency workers, partly unemployed, fully employed, part-time workers, and ill or voluntarily idle. Employed workers include 4 categories (all mentioned above less first two groups). Number of workers covered by old-age insurance includes some persons who reached the age of 15 or 65 during 1937; the latter had to be included because they could not be separated by sex for the Southeast. However, the number added to those strictly 15-64 years of age in 1937 is too small to be of any importance for this estimate.

Source: Bureau of Old-Age Insurance, Analysis Division, "Old-Age Insurance" Social Security Bulletin, Vol. 2, (March 1939), Table 11, p. 77. U. S. Census of Partial Employment, Unemployment, and Occupations, Vol. IV (See our Tables 88, p. 319, and 93, p. 326.

None of this discussion should imply that the Southeast will not continue its movement toward industrialization. It may suggest, however, that the means will differ somewhat from those once advocated. Artificial inducements to increased industrialization through municipal subsidies in the form of free factory sites, tax exemption, and outright subsidy have not proved their worth in the region. They are not needed in the war program and it is doubtful if they long continue. Low wages, moreover, will come to count less than increased productivity. A certain normal growth of industrialization continued throughout the depression, was accelerated under defense, and is no doubt to be expected in the future. The Southeast can reasonably expect to continue to process its raw materials in meeting the rising demands of its own regional markets. In certain products, it has shown its ability to manufacture for the Nation, and, with further equalization of class freight rates, where these are shown to be discriminatory, it should have the chance to expand these markets.

It may not lead us too far astray to suggest that in time we may develop a national policy in regard to the regional location of industry.[18] This question will be raised by the disposal of government-financed plants. Whether they are to be abandoned or transferred to private enterprise for the production of peacetime needs will depend largely on variations in the regional pattern of industry. The TVA, for example, has already affected the location of industry in several fields. In addition, increased facilities for financing regional industry and small business may be indicated. This is likely to be needed in the post-war period, for small business, unable to secure war contracts, has been hard hit by priorities and actual shortages of necessary materials.

The moot question of the South's industrialization, it appears, has created more controversy than any other phase of regional development. Here again we need a realization on the part of the Nation and the Southeast that high standards of living, increased income and higher wages are necessary to balance our production-consumption budget at a higher level. Economic advance of the South is essential to further national progress. This will include greater technical capacity and higher levels of economic organization and resource use both in agriculture and outside. Further industrialization of the South in processing its raw materials and in utilizing its human resources is likely to continue and should be accompanied by a gradual rise in the purchasing power of labor through enforcement of Federal standards of minimum wages and maximum hours in all basic interstate industries.

Much controversy can be avoided in the future development of the South by the realization that the region has to make no drastic choices on the all-or-none basis. We do not have to choose all-out-migration, all-out-industrialization, nor even all-out-diversification to the exclusion of staple crops. The principle to be served is one of balance. While we seek to improve agriculture, we shall also seek to make the best use of industry

[18] See National Resources Planning Board, *Industrial Location and National Resources* (Washington, D. C.: U. S. Government Printing Office, 1943).

and of migration opportunities. The goal to be sought and the touchstone of development is higher utilization of resources and higher standards and levels of living for our total population, regional and national. It is these trends that the war effort has accelerated and it is these gains that postwar reconstruction should seek to conserve.

At the end of America's first great War for Independence over 165 years ago, the statesmanship of the colonial South helped give the Nation the conception of unity and liberty for which today it is again fighting in theatres of war abroad. The facts at hand make it clear that there is abundant opportunity after the war for cultural and economic statesmanship in the South to set an example for the Nation in securing and maintaining in this region "an ever-increasing release of the power of human nature in the service of a freedom which is cooperative and a cooperation which is voluntary."[14]

[14] John Dewey, *Freedom and Culture* (New York, 1939), p. 176.

BIBLIOGRAPHIC NOTES*

PRIMARY SOURCES

United States Department of Commerce
Bureau of the Census
Sixteenth Census of the United States, 1940, Government Printing Office, Washington, D. C.
Reports on Population
Volume I. Number of Inhabitants by States. Total Population for States, Counties, and Minor Civil Division; for Urban and Rural Areas; for Incorporated Places; for Metropolitan Districts and for Census Tracts.
Volume II. Characteristics of the Population: Sex, Age, Race, Nativity, Citizenship, Country of Birth, School Attendance, Education, Employment Status, Class of Worker, Main Occupational Group, and Industry Group.
Volume III. The Labor Force: Occupation, Industry, Employment, and Income by States.
Volume IV. Population Characteristics by Age, Marital Status, Relationship, Education, and Citizenship by States.
Reports on Housing
Volume I. Data for Small Areas by States; Block Statistics for Cities.
Volume II. General Characteristics of Housing by States.
Volume III. Characteristics by Monthly Rental or Value by States.
Volume IV. Mortgages and Owner-occupied Nonfarm Homes by States.
Reports on Agriculture
Volume I. Statistics by Counties for Farm, Acreages and Values with Related Information for Farms and Farm Operators. Livestock and Livestock Products; and Crops.
Volume II. Statistics by Counties for Value of Farm Products; Farms Classified by Major Source of Income and Total Value of Products.

---

* Since the volume is provided with bibliographic footnotes to main sources cited, the bibliography is limited to primary sources and selected secondary materials useful in the present approach to population study.

Volumes I and II also include the United States Summary by States
First Series: Number of Farms, Uses of Land, Values, Principal Classes
of Livestock and Livestock Products and Specified Crops Harvested.
Second Series: Farm Mortgages, Taxes, Labor, Expenditures and Mis-
cellaneous Farm Information.
Volume III. General Report: Statistics by Subjects for the United States
and by States. Includes Farms, and Farm Property; Color, Tenure,
and Race of Farm Operators; Farm Mortgages; Work Off Farms,
Age and Years on Farms; Cooperatives, Labor, Expenditures, Machin-
ery, Facilities. Also includes Third Series Summary: Value of Farm
Products, Farms Classified by Major Sources of Income and by Total
Value of Products.

Reports on Manufactures
Volume I. General Report—Statistics by Subjects.
Volume II. Reports by Industries, Groups 1 to 20.
Volume III. Reports by States—Statistics for Industrial Areas Counties
and Cities.
Biennial Census of Manufacturers, 1921—
Issued every odd year since 1921.
Reports for years preceding Decennial Census 1919, 1929, 1939 are
published in Decennial Census.
No reports issued for 1941 and 1943.

Vital Statistics—Special Reports
Numbers 1—Current
Odd-numbered volumes include a variety of reports, special studies,
analytical articles, and official instructions and definitions, pertain-
ing to natality and mortality data and related subjects.
Numbers 2—Current
Even-numbered reports consist of State summaries giving in identical
form comparable vital statistics for each State.

Official Compendia.
Statistical Abstracts of the United States. Annual from 1930—Current.
Abstract of the Fifteenth Census of the United States, Washingon, D. C.,
1933.
Vital Statistics Rates in the United States, 1900-1940, Washington, D. C.,
1943.

SELECTED SECONDARY SOURCES

Valuable contributions to population literature both in books and in scientific journals will be found listed by author, subject, and country or region in
the quarterly bibliography, *Population Index* (1935-) published by the School
of Public Affairs, Princeton University and the Population Association of
America, Princeton, New Jersey. There is no journal in the United States
devoted to population but detailed analyses are often published in the *Milbank
Memorial Fund Quarterly, Journal of the American Statistical Association;*

the *Journal of Human Biology,* the *Journal of Human Fertility,* in special issues of *The Annals* of the American Academy of Political and Social Science, and especially in the sociological periodicals, *American Journal of Sociology, American Sociological Review,* and *Social Forces.* More marginal materials will be found in periodicals in the field of geography, public health, etc. *Public Health Reports* often contain valuable materials for population students as does the *Statistical Bulletin* issued by the Metropolitan Life Insurance Company, New York.

The best single volume for placing American trends against the background of world demography is *World Population: Past Growth and Present Trends* by A. M. Carr-Saunders (Oxford: Clarendon Press, 1936). The standard account of population history and status in this country is the valuable Social Trends monograph, *Population Trends in the United States* by Warren S. Thompson and P. K. Whelpton (New York: McGraw-Hill, 1933). It may be supplemented by two texts in the field, Warren S. Thompson, *Population Problems* (Third Edition, New York: McGraw-Hill, 1942), Paul H. Landis, *Population Problems: A Cultural Interpretation* (New York: American Book Company, 1943).

The treatment of declining births and the social implications of differential fertility which reached a high point in *Dynamics of Population* by Frank Lorimer and Frederick Osborn (New York: Macmillan Company, 1934) was carried further on a regional basis in one of the most enlightened of government reports, *The Problems of a Changing Population* (Washington, D. C.: National Resources Committee, 1938). It should be supplemented by Raymond Pearl's most important contribution, *The Natural History of Population* (London: Humphrey Milford, 1939), a first-hand study of family limitation. The best study of internal migration and the major contribution of economics to population analysis in this country is still found in the report of the Study of Population Redistribution, *Migration and Economic Opportunity* (Philadelphia: University of Pennsylvania Press, 1936) by Carter Goodrich and staff. It can be supplemented by two research memoranda: Warren S. Thompson, *Internal Migration in the Depression* (1937), and Rupert B. Vance, *Population Redistribution Within the United States* (1938), both publications of the Social Science Research Council, New York City. Among the work of rural sociologists in population that of T. Lynn Smith, *The Sociology of Rural Life* (New York: Harper and Brothers, 1940) is notable both for its knowledge of southern conditions and its analysis of the location and settlement factors. The one adequate study of rural population in the depression is still T. J. Woofter and Ellen Winston, *Seven Lean Years* (Chapel Hill: University of North Carolina Press, 1939), a somber if objective record.

The regional approach to the analysis of the cultural adequacy of a people stems from Howard W. Odum's *Southern Regions of the United States* (Chapel Hill: University of North Carolina Press, 1936). This monumental work may be supplemented by Rupert B. Vance, *Human Factors in Cotton*

Culture (Chapel Hill: University of North Carolina Press, 1929), a descriptive study of the cotton culture complex before agricultural control, and Rupert B. Vance, *Human Geography of the South: A Study in Regional Resources and Cultural Adequacy* (Chapel Hill: University of North Carolina Press, 1932). Erich W. Zimmermann, *World Resources and Industries* (New York: Harper and Brothers, 1933), a functional analysis of the availability of resources in agriculture and industry, should be read in connection with Chapter 1 and Part V.

The most valuable account of the development of population policy in any country is that written by Alva Myrdal, *Nation and Family: The Swedish Experiment in Democratic Family and Population Policy* (New York: Harper and Brothers, 1941). It may be supplemented from the more theoretical side by Gunnar Myrdal, *Population: A Problem for Democracy* (Cambridge: Harvard University Press, 1940). The one American volume on this subject, Frank Lorimer, Ellen Winston, and Louise K. Kiser, *Foundations of American Population Policy* (New York: Harper and Brothers, 1940), devotes one chapter to policy analysis.

Those interested in methods used here and elsewhere in population analysis may well begin with Margaret Jarman Hagood, *Statistics for Sociologists* (New York: Reynal and Hitchcock, 1941) Part V, "Selected Techniques for Population Data," and thence proceed to the methods developed by R. R. Kuczynski in his *Measurement of Population Growth* (New York: Oxford University Press, 1936). Reference may be had to standard volumes on vital statistics by Arthur Newsholme, George C. Whipple, and Raymond Pearl, and to appendices on method in Lorimer and Osborn, *op. cit.* and D. V. Glass, *Population Policies and Movements* (Oxford: Clarendon Press, 1940), pp. 400-415. Alfred J. Lotka has been the principal contributor to theory and methods dealing with the stable population. In addition to its value in methodology, Louis I. Dublin and Alfred J. Lotka, *The Length of Life: A Study of the Life Table* (New York: Ronald Press, 1936) is the standard work on life expectancy. For a valuable short method it may be supplemented by Lowell J. Reed and Margaret Merrill, "A Short Method for Constructing an Abridged Life Table," *The American Journal of Hygiene*, XXX (September, 1939) 33-62, also reprinted in *Vital Statistics—Special Reports* 9, No. 54. The various methods involved in calculating internal migration from United States data are explained in C. Warren Thornthwaite, *Internal Migration in the United States* (Philadelphia: University of Pennsylvania Press, 1934), also republished as Appendix A in Carter Goodrich (*op. cit.*, pp. 675-699), and C. Horace Hamilton, *Rural-Urban Migration in North Carolina, 1920-1930* (Raleigh, North Carolina: State College, 1934), Bulletin 295.

A future course for population research together with discussion of methods involved has been charted by P. K. Whelpton in *Needed Population Research* (Lancaster, Pennsylvania: The Science Press Printing Co., 1938). Questions of regional planning are further discussed by John V. Van Sickle in *Planning for the South: An Inquiry into the Economics of Regionalism* (Nashville, Tennessee: Vanderbilt University Press, 1943).

GENERAL INDEX TO TEXT*

* References to regional status and characteristics will be found under topics rather than under the regional category. Roslyn Ribner assisted in the preparation of the index.

[493]